A History of the British Isles

A History of the British Isles

Prehistory to the Present

Kenneth L. Campbell

Bloomsbury Academic
An imprint of Bloomsbury Publishing Plc

B L O O M S B U R Y
LONDON · OXFORD · NEW YORK · NEW DELHI · SYDNEY

Bloomsbury Academic

An imprint of Bloomsbury Publishing Plc

50 Bedford Square	1385 Broadway
London	New York
WC1B 3DP	NY 10018
UK	USA

www.bloomsbury.com

BLOOMSBURY and the Diana logo are trademarks of Bloomsbury Publishing Plc

First published 2017

British Library Cataloguing-in-Publication Data
A catalogue record for this book is available from the British Library.

ISBN: HB: 978-1-4742-1667-8
PB: 978-1-4742-1668-5
ePDF: 978-1-4742-1670-8
ePub: 978-1-4742-1669-2

Library of Congress Cataloging-in-Publication Data
A catalog record for this book is available from the Library of Congress.

Cover design by Adriana Brioso
Cover images: © (top) Shomos Uddin/Getty Images; (bottom) Kav Dadfar/Getty Images

Typeset by Deanta Global Publishing Services, Chennai, India
Printed and bound in Great Britain

CONTENTS

LIST OF ILLUSTRATIONS

ACKNOWLEDGEMENTS

First and foremost, I offer my appreciation to Emma Goode for suggesting this project to me and for her unwavering support, patience, and belief in this book. I also owe a great deal of thanks to Emily Drewe, Frances Arnold, Beatriz Lopez, Ian Buck, Dan Herron, Deepika Davey, and Grishma Fredric, and the rest of the editorial and production staff at Bloomsbury and Deanta who have worked so hard to help this book towards completion. The comments on the initial proposal by a number of anonymous reviewers from both Britain and the United States helped me to conceptualize better the organization, themes, and subject matter of the text, while two reviewers who read the entire manuscript offered many invaluable suggestions and corrections. Roger McCormack also read the entire manuscript, which is much better for his comments, suggestions, and corrections. Jennifer Giannone and Matt O'Brien read chapters and passed along much helpful advice. Of course, any errors of omission or commission that remain are entirely my own responsibility.

In addition, I need to acknowledge the support of Monmouth University for a summer sabbatical to work on the text and for supporting me in myriad ways as I worked on it. This especially goes for my colleagues in the Department of History and Anthropology, particularly my chair, Dr Richard Veit. Thanks as well to my English daughter-in-law, Rebecca Keen, for sharing many insights and enjoyable conversations on English history, literature, and popular culture, as well as to Caleb for bringing Becky into our family. My wife, Millie, has been as supportive as ever; she has not only been respectful of the time needed to write this book but protective of that time.

I am grateful for the opportunity to publically thank the people of the British Isles who have treated me so kindly and made all of my visits and stays there over the years so thoroughly enjoyable. I can finally thank John Morrill, Bill Speck, and Jim Sharpe for spending time with me some years ago and sharing their thoughts on their own work and on British history in general; I will never forget their kindness and generosity.

Introduction

It is impossible to teach or learn everything about the past: it is therefore necessary to select from the vast stock of what might be studied about the past. Making such a selection tends to affirm the importance of what is included, even though what is excluded is not necessarily of lesser importance.

National Curriculum History Working Group: Final Report, 1990

Why a new history of the British Isles? In the summer of 1994, I sat down with Professor John Morrill in his office at Cambridge University for a fascinating conversation on the current state of British history at that time. I came away from that conversation convinced that the model of teaching and writing about political, social, and cultural history independently without integration needed to be abandoned for an approach that combined the three types of historical inquiry. Dr Morrill cited Norman Jones's *The Birth of the Elizabethan Age: England in the 1560s* (1993) as an example of a recent text that had done just that. Jones not only did not ignore the life of Queen Elizabeth I or her impact upon her subjects, but he also considered the ways in which the views of the lower orders and the larger political culture in which she operated affected royal policy and the destiny of the nation. In the past twenty years, myriad works integrating political, social, cultural, religious, and intellectual history have appeared in print, including a series of decade-by-decade studies of sixteenth- and seventeenth-century England published by Blackwell. Other examples include Lisa Jardine's *Reading Shakespeare Historically* (1996), Garry Wills's *Witches and Jesuits* (1995), and James Shapiro's *The Year of Lear: Shakespeare in 1606* (2015), which show the necessity of placing the works of Shakespeare within their historical and social context. The slew of works available that adopt a similar approach has helped inform my own historical position on the events that comprise the history of the British Isles.

In 1995, Dale Hoak edited a book called *Tudor Political Culture*, which he noted was the first book-length study of the subject. Hoak offers a solid definition of political culture when he writes:

The difference between politics and political culture is essentially the difference between political action and the codes of conduct, formal and informal, governing those actions. A history of the former treats the players of the game, a history of the latter, what the players presume the nature and limits of their game to be.[1]

Hoak's work includes chapters by various authors on such subjects as 'the symbols, rituals and mentalities of popular political culture and the relevant intersections of literature and the arts'.[2] While unremitting reading is necessary for even a modicum of knowledge, it is my pleasure to share here some of the insights that I have gained from my reading and study of the political culture and history of the British Isles.

Fashionable in the recent historiography of the British Isles is a de-emphasis on English perspectives. In 1995 Steven Ellis and Sarah Barber wrote:

> There is clearly a need for a history of the British Isles which examines the relations between the different peoples of the archipelago and the process of state formation which created the two modern states there.[3]

Of course, it is hard to ignore the large impact that England has had on the British Isles. England has been given preponderant attention, but the Scottish, Irish, and Welsh experience vis-à-vis England deserves our attention as well. Ellis and Barber's co-edited book covered the early modern period from 1485 to 1725, one that the editors considered crucial in the process of state development that led to a UK comprising Britain and Ireland. A similar project for the preceding period was undertaken by Michael Brown in his 2013 book, *Disunited Kingdoms: Peoples and Politics in the British Isles: 1280–1460*. Brown saw in this earlier period a process of state development that redefined the relationship between the constituent parts of the British Isles (England, Ireland, Scotland, and Wales) in fundamentally important ways. Though many of the early works on political culture focused on the sixteenth century, the impetus for expanding the study of English history to incorporate the rest of the British Isles largely originated in the work of seventeenth-century historians.

A primary goal of this text is to successfully integrate the histories of England, Ireland, Scotland, and Wales in a unified manner, which will fuse seemingly disparate histories. More importantly, it will make the fractious histories of the four countries making up the British Isles comprehensible, a laborious task that historians have heretofore only grasped at. Though the British Isles will be examined as a whole, the roles that each region has played in that history will be proportionally emphasized. Here, I can only appeal to Lewis Mumford's defence of his own work as written by someone who refused 'to recognize the no-trespass signs that smaller minds erected around their chosen fields of specialization'. The focus on political culture and the integration of social, political, and cultural history, I believe, will make it easier to integrate the British Isles as a whole into a single narrative. Some of the most important developments in the history of the British Isles, such as the coming of Christianity, the Reformation, the civil wars of the seventeenth century, the Enlightenment, the Industrial Revolution, and the two World Wars of the twentieth century, just to name a few, affected each region of the Isles in epoch-changing ways.

This text will also include an examination of how individuals responded to milieu-changing (or shattering) developments – repudiating the Great Man approach – and the ways in which they were reflected in the culture of the period. As religious, social, political, economic, and cultural change obviously interpenetrate, interweaving these phenomena is eminently plausible. This work argues that politics should be viewed as an extension of a particular culture, as well as an influence upon it, rather than a disembodied factor in a nation's life. As the aforementioned Dale Hoak indicates, the whole concept of political culture assumes a larger ideological and cultural framework which prescribes the power of an individual.

This brings me to another major premise of my book and an important aspect of my approach to history: the constant dialogue between the past and the present. As William Faulkner famously wrote, 'The past is never dead. It's not even past.' Again, each period of history cannot be understood without reference to the continuing influence of the past upon it. It is perhaps a commonplace among British historians that the Wars of the Roses of the fifteenth century form an important part of the backdrop to an understanding of the Tudor period. But I think the same approach can be applied equally fruitfully when writing about other periods of British history. British popular culture and society, for example, was changing in the 1960s, but how many people at that time were still influenced by memories of the Great Depression and the Second World War, particularly among the generation that was still in power at that time? The spectre of history is a constant, sometimes oppressive, presence. Why has the First World War remained such an important topic for novelists and film-makers in the late twentieth and early twenty-first century? Irish history abounds with examples in which past events, such as the rebellions of 1641, 1798, and 1916, influence later developments down to the present, not to mention the Famine of the 1840s or the annual Protestant commemorations of William of Orange's seventeenth-century military victories in Northern Ireland. The Scottish political theorist Tom Nairn has written of the plight of the contemporary monarchy that 'Prince William and Catherine Middleton can't help falling into a trap formed of the hysteria of counter-decline and a wilful failure to quit a darkening stage'.[4] Yet the English political analyst Anthony Sampson, while recognizing that in fact parliamentary sovereignty had long ago eclipsed the political clout of the monarchy, as recently as in 2004 affirmed that 'the overriding advantage of a monarchy is the continuity it provides, as the embodiment of a nation'.[5]

A focus on Britishness and the history of Great Britain as a separate entity constitutes a popular historiographical topic, a trend which has taken shape through such works as Keith Robbins's *Great Britain: Identities, Institutions and the Idea of Britishness* (1998) and Linda Colley's *Britons: Forging the Nation 1707–1837* (1992). Colley stresses Protestantism as a major unifying factor among England, Scotland, and Wales. The Reformation predated the 1707 Act of Union that marks the beginning of her study, but antagonism with Catholic France during the eighteenth century helped to bind cohesive Protestants in the British Isles. The Act of Union elicited Scottish support in the course of the eighteenth century, but its immediate passage was controversial among Scots who believed that their leaders had been bribed to accept unity with England. Similarly, the Jacobite rebellions of the eighteenth century against English rule and the later Highland Clearances complicate the matter of a single British identity even for the eighteenth century. Significantly, Colley does not include Northern Ireland in her definition of 'Britishness', even though it, along with the rest of Ireland, became united with Great Britain in 1801 and her study concludes in 1837. The Reformation represented a historical dividing line that helped to make Ireland unique in relation to England. This difference in religion fostered ethno-religious conflicts, strife only recently resolved. But the leadership role that Irish Protestants took in the Irish Rebellion of 1798 and in the nationalistic nineteenth-century organization, Young Ireland, argues against a 'British' identity for Northern Ireland and for Protestantism as a unifying political force across the Isles.

Interestingly, there have been no general histories that focus on the UK as a unit of study as there have been its constituent parts, Great Britain, or the British Isles as a whole. Some books, such as Brian Harrison's *Seeking a Role: The United Kingdom, 1951–1970* (2009), have done so for specific periods. Perhaps this is because, despite being a nation-state, the UK has not represented a useful unit of study. Hugh Kearney called it a 'multi-ethnic conglomerate whose shifting patterns of historical development resemble those of states such as Spain or the Habsburg Monarchy'.[6] This lacuna speaks to problems of identity, some of which will be addressed in this text, as well as why even the Republic of Ireland cannot be excluded from a general study of the UK.

As for the question of identity, the political geography of the British Isles has been in an almost constant state of flux from the prehistoric period to the present. Their political geography chiefly demonstrates the lack of a fixed political or cultural identity unifying the British Isles throughout their storied and fractious history. There has not always been 'an England' and if one goes back far enough in geologic time, the contemporary British Isles did not always exist. Linda Colley is a widely respected historian and her book on *Britons* is highly acclaimed and extremely influential, but when she wrote that British identity had become solidified 'ever since' the period that ended in 1837, she failed to anticipate the ways people within Great Britain would wrestle with the question of identity in the twenty years since the publication of her book. Raphael Samuel contested the point of a fixed 'British' identity even for the nineteenth century:

> It is a curious fact that the third quarter of the nineteenth century saw the nationalities of Britain drawing farther apart, both from each other and from Westminster, or at any rate launching out on paths which can retrospectively be seen to point in the direction of a clearer identity or greater independence.[7]

Samuel recognized that the existence of a single 'British' identity is laden with problems and, for that matter, if there was this chimeric identity it was defined in different ways, by different people, in different locations. Like the Irish, a Welsh desire for a distinct identity burgeoned in the nineteenth century.

These historical debates have marked contemporary politics. Tony Blair attempted to inject new life into the notion of 'Britishness' during his time as prime minister from 1997 to 2007. Yet, as will be discussed later in the text, Blair was also a proponent of the devolution of power to Wales, Scotland, and Northern Ireland – a move Blair implemented to ensure harmony among these regions and between them and England. If so, his plan is not working. As early as 1999, the English journalist Andrew Solomon observed in the *New York Times Magazine* that 'it is possible to think, to talk about the abolition of Britain without the risk of hyperbole'.[8] The fact that England, Scotland, Wales, and Northern Ireland all participate as separate teams in the Football World Cup and other international sports tournaments speaks volumes about the extent to which they have resisted a single, common British identity.

Another set of issues is raised by the question of the British Empire, which is included as part of this book (it could hardly be ignored). As British people travelled around the globe settling and establishing their presence in colonies, one could argue that the whole concept of Britishness was forced upon a non-British world. There are many fine histories of the British Empire; this book will mainly examine the Empire vis-à-vis its impact on the British Isles. Gender, ethnicity, and race obviously play central roles in the modern world. Nor are these topics unrelated to the general themes of this text related to political culture and identity. Immigrants from the lands comprising the British Empire, like India and Pakistan, arrived in Britain and adopted the nationality of their new country and attempted to assimilate. Britishness itself is now an identity that embraces people of varied cultural, ethnic, religious, and national backgrounds. More importantly, it is seen by proponents of Britishness as the one identity capable of holding a diverse population together. Ireland has also faced enormous immigration of late, shifting the way Irish identity is construed.

But to the extent that identities are self-constructed (the postmodern project), does it even make sense to talk in terms of alternatives such as English/British? John Ormond proposed the notion of interlocking identities in his 1988 book *Divided Kingdom*, suggesting that 'it is possible to feel simultaneously Scottish, British, and European; Ulster and British; or Welsh and European'.[9] In the almost thirty years since Ormond wrote, people in Scotland, England, Wales, and Northern Ireland have begun to question their 'Britishness', just as others have challenged whether they want the UK to remain a part of the European Union, resulting in the vote on 23 June 2016 for the UK to leave Europe, the so-called Brexit. The 2014 defeat of a Scottish referendum on independence has only increased the popularity of the Scottish National Party, not diminished it. Ormond suggested that the English were the only members of the UK who did not have an identity outside of being British, or what he called 'Anglo-British'. Yet books such as Robert Tombs's *The English and their History* (2014) suggest that defences of particular cultural and political traditions may increase, the latter, of course, coming at the expense of a unified British identity, something the Brexit vote is only likely to accelerate.

The principle of selection is always a concern with any text. Contemporary scholarship based on postmodernism and feminist theory and class analysis would deny the very concept of a 'collective history' for the peoples of the British Isles and challenge any attempt at narrative as impossible and the mere pretence of objectivity as a phallocentric, capitalist construction.[10] It is proper for intellectuals to engage in such debates, but incumbent upon the historian not to be paralysed by them. Nairn asserts that 'there is a long-range transmission of community from one age into another, through a myriad of idioms and altering channels, which is too little understood'.[11]

This text does contain a narrative of sorts, but it is intended neither as a celebration of the history of the British Isles nor as a condemnation of it – the history of the British Isles is, and remains, far too nuanced and complex for a moralistic approach to have any weight. Both within and outside of the academy, debates have raged in Britain and Ireland about what kind of history should be taught, whether it should celebrate the achievements, struggles, and sacrifices of the British or Irish, whether it should involve a rather more critical look at each nation's history, or whether it should essentially ignore such issues and focus on the lives of everyday people. This book is focused on considering each period of the history of the British Isles in individual chapters, while offering an analysis based on an in-depth reading of primary and secondary sources; readers are left to make their own judgements and where I do have specific points to make readers should only accept them if they seem plausible or convincing. Traditional storylines will be included, but will be combined with the integration of the most recent scholarship on each topic.

The opening ceremony at the London Olympics in 2012 attempted to present a visual demonstration of a shared history that celebrated Britain and attempted to remind its own citizens and the world of the importance of the British past. As visually oriented as contemporary society has become, we need to go deeper than meanings that can be conveyed through photos, films, museum displays, and ceremonies to more fully come to grips with the meaning of the past, not for its sake, but for ours. I hope that readers encountering this subject for the first time will find it helpful and interesting and that those familiar with the general outline of the history of the British Isles will find much to surprise them or at least get them to think about familiar topics in new ways. It is my desire not only that readers outside the British Isles understand the Isles' history and its salience, but also that readers within England, Scotland, Wales, and Ireland gain a greater appreciation of their own culture and history, as well as those of the other regions with which they share a small – but extremely fascinating and historically significant – part of the world.

FIGURE 1 *Stonehenge.*
Daren Leonard/EyeEm/Getty.

1

Prologue to history:

The prehistory of the British Isles

The events of human lives, both the mundane or everyday and the important or unusual, encompass both past experience and portents for the future. Time and looking back is bound up in carrying forward the process of life and culture. While as archaeologists we normally see time in terms of chronologies, as something to be used to study the past, we should perhaps examine in more detail the lived experience of time.

GABRIEL CONNEY, *Landscapes of Neolithic Ireland* (2000)

The British Isles are a product of the geological history of the earth, once covered in ice and connected to the European continent. However, archaeological evidence places the earliest permanent settlements of human beings in Britain and Ireland about 10,000 years before the Common Era, even earlier in southern Britain. This does not include traces left by people who had previously visited the islands or lived there before the last Ice Age. In fact, in 2010 flint tools were discovered at a beach in Norfolk along the coast of East Anglia with a provenance indicating inhabitancy 800,000 years ago. The oldest evidence for human presence in Wales are some Neanderthal teeth discovered in a Pontnewydd cave that date to about 230,000 years ago. But most accounts of the prehistory of the British Isles begin with the return of permanent settlement to the island after the last Ice Age.

Among these, the earliest settlements in Wales have been dated to about 10,000 years ago, while Scotland's are a thousand years later. Scholars now think that Ireland was inhabited as early as 9000 BCE and England between 10000 and 9000 BCE. The longest continuous settlement in the UK currently appears to have been Amesbury in Wiltshire, occupied since about 8820 BCE. Because of a dearth of archaeological evidence, however, we know very little about the people who inhabited the British Isles until the Mesolithic period, or Middle Stone Age, which dates from around 7000 BCE.

Contrary to the way in which Britain and Ireland have tended to see themselves historically, DNA evidence has proven to geneticists that the people of the British Isles are very closely related and that their genetic make-up has actually changed very little over time, despite the later immigration of Romans, Germanic tribes, and Scandinavians, among others. The medical geneticist Stephen Oppenheimer has postulated that the ancestors of people from all parts of the British Isles originally began migrating from Spain about 16,000 years ago. It has been proposed that they returned to Spain or southern Europe when the glaciers expanded to once again make the British Isles uninhabitable but that it was their descendants who returned to the British Isles 10,000–12,000 years ago. Genetically, at least, the English, Welsh, Scottish, and Irish are not separate peoples, contradicting past notions of Anglo-Saxon supremacy.

These early inhabitants of the islands were traditional hunters and gatherers. Settled agriculture did not become ubiquitous until about 4000 BCE. In Ireland, people mainly hunted deer and wild pigs, but along the coast there is evidence that they used harpoons and nets to spear or catch fish, seals, and porpoises. Because the sea provided additional resources for the hunter and gatherers of the Mesolithic period, it is not surprising that many of their settlements were along the coasts, including, for example, the Mesolithic site on St Brides Bay in Pembrokeshire in Wales. Excavations at sites like Mount Sandel in modern-day County Derry in Northern Ireland indicate that during the Mesolithic period people resided in circular huts with a stone hearth in the centre. Piles of garbage known as kitchen middens contain bones, shells, and stone tools that provide most of the evidence for the existence of these sites.

The dates for the Mesolithic Age vary from place to place, but the period lasted in the British Isles until about 4500 BCE. One of the most important Mesolithic sites in Scotland is that of Kinloch on the island of Rum in the Inner Hebrides, which contains evidence of toolmaking in the form of tens of thousands of stone flakes and is one of a series of Mesolithic sites in the region dating from around 6600 BCE. In the mid-1980s Caroline Wickham-Jones discovered over 100,000 artefacts on the island pointing to a settlement that survived for a millennium. At Mount Sandel, wooden and stone tools have been found, along with thousands of microliths (miniscule blades used to fashion their tools and weapons).

The Neolithic period which followed lasted in the British Isles from about 4500 to 2500 BCE. The cause of the transition from the Mesolithic to the Neolithic is hotly contested. Julian Thomas, for example, has argued that the hunters and gatherers of Britain would not have 'domesticated plants and animals, developed the skills of potting, started to make leaf-shaped projectile points, or begun to build long barrows, chambered cairns, and ditched enclosures independently without contact with Neolithic groups in Atlantic Europe'.[1] Thomas proposed a contrast between the Neolithic cultures of the European continent and the Mesolithic cultures of the British Isles. But this claim does not seem entirely consistent with DNA evidence. The evidence fails to indicate a massive influx of new people into the region. Furthermore, the tools found at agricultural settlements include javelins and arrows, demonstrating how settled agriculture complemented rather than replaced hunting and gathering – a find, moreover, consistent with current scholarship on the transition from the Mesolithic to the Neolithic in other locations as well. Of course, this does not rule out continued contact with the Continent, especially given the number of coastal settlements and the utilization of boats by Mesolithic people. In fact, Barry Cunliffe has argued that the English Channel and the North Sea should not be viewed as geographical barriers separating Britain from the European continent but rather as a convenient passageway connecting them.[2] Cunliffe argues for the continuous historical existence of what he calls 'an Atlantic system' and a 'North Sea system' connecting Britain to Europe.

The idea of a gradual transition also makes more sense than a rapid adoption of new ways introduced from an exogenous force, although these explanations are not mutually exclusive. In fact, Thomas does not suggest a one-time flood of immigrants from the Continent, but rather a back-and-forth process between Britain and the Continent that occurred over a long period of time. Overlapping use of different styles of pottery, rather than the linear chronological progression proposed by the prominent early-twentieth-century Australian-born archaeologist V. Gordon Childe, also suggests that different settlements evolved according to individual patterns and not as part of a single, unified historical process. It is probably best, then, to think of the transition to settled agriculture as a process rather than an event, and one that occurred over centuries, if not millennia.

There is no doubt, however, that the landscape of the British Isles in 3000 BCE looked very different than it did 1,000 years earlier. Settled agriculture meant that people congregated in larger groups in more permanent residences, changing the nature of social relationships and allowing for the development of a new cultural milieu associated with fertility rites, for example. A growing population contributed to the spread of agriculture. There is no doubt a marked mutuality in this progress, in which each development reinforced the other. A warming climate played an important role as well in both the increase of population and the conditions that allowed for agriculture to flourish. The cultivation of livestock and the introduction of dairy products such as milk and cheese into people's diet helped to sustain a healthier and larger population. Forests were cleared, fields planted, and village settlements were constructed, with the characteristic round houses erected in the most fertile areas of the islands. Fields were laid out in rectangular patterns, demarcated from one another by ditches, fences, and stone walls. At this point the concept of land ownership, less important in a traditional hunting and gathering society, became entrenched. This did not necessarily mean individual ownership, however, as is evidenced by the clan systems that evolved in Ireland and the Scottish Highlands. Southeastern England was more fertile than the mountainous north and west, though some smaller areas were found suitable for farming; the same is true of Scotland, while prehistoric farmers in Ireland worked around the bogs, rocks, and mountains to clear the forests in exactly those spots where crops such as oats, wheat, and barley could grow.

One of the richest Neolithic sites in Ireland is at Lough Gur in County Limerick. Pollen samples taken from the site indicate how Ireland's early farmers cleared forests to take advantage of the most fertile soil on the island, making it an important location in the transition to settled agriculture. The early residents at Lough Gur practised the domestication of livestock, including cattle, goats, and sheep. They made some of their own tools, but there is also evidence of materials from other regions that indicate the beginnings of trade as well. Ongoing work by Seamas

Caulfield, Gretta Byrne, Noel Dunne, and Graeme Warren since the 1960s at Belderg
Beg, Behy, Glenulra, and Céide Fields along the northern coast of County Mayo
has also provided invaluable insights into the life of Neolithic Ireland. These sites,
along with Carrownaglogh, also in County Mayo, provide a sense of the layout of
the field systems used by Neolithic farmers, which include clearly delineated lines
found under the soil to indicate where walls had once stood to divide small plots
of land. Evidence suggests that these fields were under cultivation until around
2500 BCE, about the time that the Neolithic period gave way to the Bronze Age.
Chris Stevens, Dorian Fuller, and Martin Carver have argued that by about 3300
BCE arable farming in the British Isles had largely given way to a pastoral economy,
with settled agriculture only becoming common again about 1500 BCE in the middle
of the Bronze Age.[3] They attribute the decline of arable farming to climate change
and population decrease, three developments that have frequently gone together
historically. Their conclusions are supported by evidence for the regeneration of
woodlands in some areas of Ireland towards the end of the Neolithic period. In
addition, dental evidence suggests that late Neolithic people ate fewer grains than
did their earlier or later counterparts. Finally, we have the reappearance in the
archaeological record of granaries, querns, and other finds associated with extensive
field cultivation dating from about 1500 BCE.[4]

Both Behy and Glenulra contained court cairns (tombs) that had been submerged
in the peat, but whose stones were clearly visible after excavation. Burial cairns
were not unusual for the Neolithic period and numerous ones have now been
found throughout Northern Ireland and the rest of the British Isles. In Scotland the
burial cairns in Caithness, which date from the fourth millennium BCE, represent a
significant grouping of passage-graves, while there is also a sizeable burial cairn at
Wideford Hill in Orkney that dates from around 3000 BCE. More than 3,000 burial
mounds and cairns have been found in Cornwall in southwestern England as well.
The complete absence of written records and the relative paucity of archaeological
evidence make the finds that we do have from the prehistoric periods all the more
interesting and important, especially when they are as spectacular as the monument
at Stonehenge on Salisbury Plain in southern Britain or the passage-grave at
Newgrange in Northern Ireland. The construction of elaborate stone circles that
potentially demonstrate a sophisticated understanding of observational astronomy,
of which Stonehenge is the most popular, provide aperçus into Neolithic people
that go beyond merely knowing something about their material life. In the fourth
millennium BCE, either life had become easier for people so that they could afford
to invest such time and resources in building these elaborate monuments to the dead,
or their religious sensibilities had shifted enough to make this a priority equal to that
of their material or physical well-being.

The widespread existence of these circles and their sudden appearance in about
3300 BCE suggest the possibility of a significant shift in religious beliefs occurring
around that time that may have been associated with the transition from extensive
cultivation of arable land to more of a pastoral economy. Stonehenge, the largest and
most grandiose of these circles, is famous for its large standing dolerite 'bluestones'
imported from Wales, which were actually erected in the third building phase at the
site about 2300 BCE. This date is consistent with recent evidence of the abstraction
of similarly sized stones from Carn Menyn in the Preseli Hills of Pembrokeshire,

Wales, towards the end of the third millennium BCE. (Prehistoric people had been extracting stones from this site since Mesolithic times going at least as far back as 6000 BCE.[5]) This is the strongest evidence yet beyond the type of stones used at Stonehenge that the rocks used there were actually quarried in Wales and transported the 173 miles from Carn Menyn to Stonehenge.

The larger stones occupy the centre of the circle and are surrounded by smaller bluestones ringed by even smaller sarsen stones that are native to the region of Salisbury Plain. We are still learning about Stonehenge; for example, an exceptionally dry summer in 2013 happened to reveal previously obscured patchmarks at the site. These patchmarks point to gaps in the site where stones should have been placed to conform to the design of the rest of the site, demonstrating that Stonehenge actually represents an unfinished work. The patchmarks also revealed that there was more to learn about Stonehenge and inspired further noninvasive investigations of the site. The most recent discoveries based on such advanced technology as aerial laser scanning and radar that penetrates below ground have revealed a much larger planned setting for the Stonehenge site.

As Kate Ravilious recently reported in *Archaeology*, the new information that has come to light 'has revealed seventeen new monuments and thousands of as-yet-uninterpreted archaeological features, including small shrines, burial mounds, and massive pits, across nearly five square miles of the Salisbury Plain'.[6] In fact, two miles north of Stonehenge two large pits line up with Stonehenge astronomically, as does the two-mile-long mound known as the 'Cursus', which preceded Stonehenge by about 400 years. Stonehenge, therefore, was apparently built in alignment with pre-existing human-made features of the landscape rather than the other way around. The contemporaneous site most similar to Stonehenge, interestingly, is located in North Wales. The latter site is considered the original location of the larger stones imported to Stonehenge. However, standing stones from the late Neolithic period also include those at Callanish on the island of Lewis in the Outer Hebrides and the famous Ring of Brodgar on Orkney, as well as dozens of smaller stone circles scattered throughout the British Isles; Lough Gur includes a ring of thirteen stones, the largest stone circle in Ireland. These seem to represent ritual burial sites similar to those found at Llandegai in Gwynedd, Wales, and Duggleby Howe in Yorkshire.

In addition to the stone rings found throughout the British Isles, passage-graves such as those found at Newgrange in County Meath, Ireland, and Avebury in southern England speak of the connections that Neolithic people saw between burial, the afterlife, and the cosmos. The alignment of the opening to the passage-grave at Newgrange to receive the first light of the morning during the Winter Solstice, and the days surrounding it, is consistent with recent theories on the positioning of the doorways in the roundhouses from Iron Age Britain. During the Winter Solstice, the sun illuminates the entire chamber through a small aperture for about 15 minutes. Like Stonehenge, Newgrange is part of a much larger ceremonial landscape in Northern Ireland that includes the additional passage-graves at Dowth and Knowth. Newgrange is located in the centre of the other two, in the middle of the area known as the Bend of the Boyne. These are only three of several dozen burial mounds and stone circles that also dot the region.

Avebury actually predates Stonehenge and has acquired a designation as one of the premier ancient historical sites in Britain. Like Stonehenge, Avebury is part of a larger ritualistic landscape that predated it by at least a thousand years, although Avebury did not remain in use for as long as Stonehenge did. It also shared Stonehenge's function as a ceremonial site where Neolithic people came together, probably to invoke the aid of the spirits whom they worshipped and to reaffirm their connections with related tribes who shared the same religious beliefs. Avebury's outer ring, which at one time comprised 100 stones, makes up a circle larger than any found elsewhere in Britain. But, as large as Avebury is (1,150 feet or 350 metres in diameter), those who used the site reached it by traversing West Kennet Avenue, a nearby prehistoric site covering a little over 1.3 miles (2 kilometres) that was itself lined with standing stones.

What exactly these sites meant to the people who built them or visited them remains uncertain, but they most likely served, like all ceremonial landmarks, to commemorate the unifying beliefs and values of the society. Sites like Newgrange and Stonehenge are obviously multivalent, subject to the prejudices of the historian or archaeologist who is writing about them, which can preclude an objective uncertainty of what the sites meant to contemporaries. Like Stonehenge, Newgrange was not built and forgotten, but part of a living society that must have viewed it with the same combination of awe and reverence as attached to the pyramids of Egypt or monuments like the Lincoln Memorial in Washington DC.

Newgrange contains over 200,000 tonnes of stone, covered with earth to form a mound on top of a hill that is visible from the surrounding countryside. Constructed around the same time as the first phase of Stonehenge, c. 3200 BCE, Newgrange belonged to a society that had already cleared the area of forests and introduced settled agriculture and livestock to the region. Even if some of these fertile areas were subsequently abandoned, the forests did not completely grow back as humans began to transform the appearance of the land, which they continued to do through the construction of passage-graves and burial mounds. The small entrance to the grave at Newgrange leads through a narrow passage to a large central chamber with a high roof that creates the illusion of a vast open space within the earth. This burial chamber becomes illuminated not only during the Winter Solstice but by sunlight for the rest of the year when the sun is positioned overhead the entranceway. The chamber remains completely dark otherwise, leading to theories that it could have been intended to simulate in death the recreation of the womb prior to birth. The sudden appearance of light could have paralleled the moment when light enters the womb as new life emerges from it. But the elaborate design also seems to have included acoustic considerations, either for the benefit of the departed or for ceremonies that were performed in the chamber by the living. Martin Borosan speculates that Newgrange must have been 'designed to house and facilitate what must be the most extraordinary lighting effect in the history of theatre ... using the structure's acoustic properties to create a spectacular fusion of sound and light just at the sunrise'.[7]

The most well-known Neolithic settlement in Scotland, and perhaps all of Britain other than Stonehenge, is the wonderfully preserved village of Skara Brae, which was first excavated by V. Gordon Childe, beginning in the 1920s. Skara Brae, on the Bay of Skaill, was occupied from approximately 3200 to 2600 BCE, closely paralleling the times at which Stonehenge and Newgrange were in use. The finds at Skara Brae have provided a sense of the lifestyle of its Neolithic inhabitants, whose human remains indicate that they reached a height of about 5' 3". The village consisted of a number of underground housing units connected by a network of passages. For a long time, Skara Brae stood out for its singularity, but the discovery of additional sites in the past forty years, including Barnhouse, Stonehall and Crossiecrown, Pool, and Stowe Bay, have provided a holistic picture and proven that Skara Brae was not 'unique', although not all of these other sites contained the same types of underground dwellings that were exemplified at Skara Brae.[8] The reasons for the abandonment of Skara Brae are still a matter for speculation, but seem not to have included a sudden catastrophe, as Childe had originally speculated, with climate change providing one logical explanation for a gradual abandonment of the community.

The discovery of numerous arrowheads and human remains that indicate wounds consistent with violence indicates that the Neolithic period was not an altogether peaceful time. But the Bronze Age that followed and lasted until about 700 BCE saw the emergence of a martial society. Fraser Hunter has argued that 'bronze daggers are more likely to have been used for warfare than hunting, while experimental work shows that the halberd (a dagger-like blade mounted transversely on a shaft), long considered a ceremonial weapon, would have possessed deadly effectiveness in battle'.[9] Additionally, in 2002 the human remains of an individual given the name of the 'Amesbury Archer' were discovered about 3 miles from Stonehenge. The Amesbury Archer had died in the early Bronze Age around 2500 BCE before the last phase of construction at Stonehenge was completed. Since earlier burials at Stonehenge most likely involved cremation, this is the earliest full body human burial discovered in the vicinity. His nickname derives from the weapons carefully placed around his body in his grave. But Hunter did not find a preponderance of

FIGURE 2 *Skara Brae – entrance to a dwelling at the Neolithic settlement, Orkney Islands, Scotland.*
Hmproudlove/E+/Getty.

individuals who died from battlefield wounds among the human remains that survive from Bronze Age Scotland and actually sees a reduction in the number of weapons in the Iron Age after about 200 BCE.

One of the most surprising things about the Archer, given the proximity of his burial to Stonehenge, is the fact that he was born in a foreign country. Individual burials date from about this time and the presence of other everyday objects such as drinking beakers found in contemporaneous graves indicate a definite belief in the afterlife; the Amesbury site also contained the earliest set of gold ornaments found in Britain.[10] The Amesbury Archer is complemented and often linked with the discovery of seven individuals buried about the same time, also near Stonehenge, collectively known as the Boscombe Bowmen, consisting of three male adults, one teenager, and three children; scientific analysis has placed their origins as either in Wales or the Lake District of northern England, leading to speculation that the men, at least, may have helped transport the last massive bluestones to Stonehenge from Wales.

Among the more fascinating archaeological discoveries from prehistoric Britain are those human remains that have collectively become known as 'bog bodies'. These individual remains, such as the body known as 'Lindow Man', found in 1984 in a peat bog in Cheshire, have been especially well preserved because of conditions associated with bogs that permit the bodies to dry out before they can decay. Bodies may also be preserved under certain other conditions, such as the lack of exposure to air or exposure to certain chemicals that deny life to the microbes that eat away at the flesh. Almost 2,000 such bodies have been found throughout Northern Europe.

The distinction of the oldest bog body found so far belongs to 'Cashel Man', who lived about 2000 BCE and was discovered in Cashel Bog in Ireland. One theory regarding those bodies that have been found is that they were either criminals or deposed rulers who had been executed and unceremoniously dumped in a bog, the result of wounds discerned in some of the finds. Lindow Man is a prime example of this; the English criminal pathologist Iain West studied the remains and concluded that this man had been a victim of ritualistic violence that included having his throat slit, his neck broken, and his head bashed in, though the historian Ronald Hutton regards West's conclusion as tentative and not as a confirmation of the practice of human sacrifice, as some have suggested.[11] Cashel man also suffered from severe physical injuries, including a broken arm, a broken back, and multiple axe wounds. The youthful nature of a number of the recovered bog bodies may also suggest that they died of wounds that might have been ritualistic in nature.

If the wounds on these individuals indicate some kind of official human sacrifice associated with the rites of kingship, the date of Cashel Man pushes back the time frame of such practices from the Iron Age to the early Bronze Age.[12] But other bodies have been found that seem to represent more traditional burials, along with remains of other artefacts such as pottery and weapons. These bodies have been so well preserved that we even know what they ate before they died, in the case of Lindow Man, barley, oats, seeds, and meat. But his stomach also contained traces of mistletoe pollen, which may have acted as a sedative or had some religious significance.[13] Such finds do not prove conclusively the theory associating the bog bodies with ritualistic execution or sacrifice, but they do provide important physical evidence of our prehistoric ancestors.

In another fascinating recent discovery, tests conducted in 2011 on four mummified bodies found at South Uist in the Outer Hebrides revealed that they were made up of composite body parts, including one comprising parts of at least three different people with a male skull and a female pelvis. The leading expert on later British prehistory, Mike Parker Pearson has speculated that the remains were related to ancestor worship, were not buried immediately, and that 'the mixing up of different people's body parts seems to be a deliberate act' because they might have continued to play an active role in community ritual.[14]

Socially, village compounds of round houses became much more common in the Bronze Age. The Bronze Age also saw the first systematic mining activity in the British Isles, particularly of tin, while the economy began to expand in other ways as well, namely with trade in cloth and leather goods, pottery, and metal products. Gold from the Wicklow Hills in Ireland and tin from Cornwall were in use by the end of the third millennium BCE. Copper mining was taking place in southern Ireland and North Wales by about 1600 BCE.

As noted above, the Bronze Age lasted until about 700 BCE, at which time it gave way to the Iron Age. These chronological distinctions may seem artificial, but they are rooted in evidence of material and cultural changes that appear in the archaeological evidence. It should be understood, however, as Peter Rowley-Conwy has pointed out, that the 'three-age' system of Stone Age, Bronze Age, and Iron Age is a historical construct that originated in the nineteenth century that serves as a helpful analytical tool but should not be presumed to be, in his words, 'objectively *correct*'. Rowley-Conwy continues, 'It is impossible for us to "un-think" our unthinking understanding of it, but we must try at least to become aware that we operate entirely within that understanding, and realize that there was a time when the Three-Age System was new and contentious; when it was just one of a number of competing ways of discussing the early human past.'[15]

During the early Iron Age that immediately preceded the coming of the Romans, the native inhabitants of the British Isles adopted a culture that derives its name from a village on Lake Neuchâtel in Switzerland known as La Tène, where the first material remains of this culture were discovered in the nineteenth century. The La Tène phase of Celtic culture had been preceded by a period known as Hallstatt, which lasted from about 800 until about 500 BCE and was characterized by the introduction of iron metallurgy for both weapons and quotidian objects and the appearance in Ireland, Britain, and the European continent of the Gündlingen sword, which, though made of bronze, were longer than Bronze Age swords. The Hallstatt and La Tène cultures are primarily distinguished from one another by their artistic designs and styles of pottery. The patterns on La Tène pottery and other material objects, including weapons, armour, jewellery, tools, and other household objects, tended to feature circles, curves, and spiral designs, along with certain common representations of birds and other animals. Other common motifs include 'disembodied heads with almond-shaped eyes and fierce mustaches, long and fanciful horse heads, and willowy statues of women'.[16]

The presence of both Hallstatt and La Tène culture in the British Isles further confirms Barry Cunliffe's emphasis on the extent to which their inhabitants shared a common culture with the European continent. La Tène spread to both southern and northern Britain, as well as Ireland, while also flourishing in the areas now known as France, Germany, Switzerland, and the Czech Republic. The peoples who shared this culture also seem to have had a homogeneous social structure, political culture, and religious beliefs, while speaking dialects of the same Celtic language. The notion of the Celts as a separate people who settled in Ireland has given way to a view of them as common ancestors for the inhabitants of the British Isles as a whole, insofar as the Celts can even be regarded as a single people. The name itself derives from the Greeks and Romans, who distinguished them as a broad group of European inhabitants unrelated to themselves. Some would deny the existence of either a Celtic people or single Celtic culture, but the word has become most useful, in fact, in describing the culture and a grouping of common languages with the designation 'Celtic'. These originated on the European continent and one variant spread to Ireland; as J. P. Mallory puts it, 'The Irish language was not "native" to Ireland, but evolved from a Celtic predecessor that was carried into the island long after its initial settlement.'[17]

La Tène culture probably circulated among different peoples in the British Isles and back and forth between Britain and the Continent rather than in one direction from one place to the other. Local artisans likely embellished or augmented original designs acquired through trade, which then could be exchanged to further influence artisans in other sites, or even the original sites from which the style came. This explanation could account for variations within a broadly unified cultural tradition. In addition to a revolution in metalworking, the Iron Age seems to have featured a significant shift in religious beliefs as well, perhaps involving the practice of ritual human sacrifice; without direct written testimony, this must remain a tentative conclusion and somewhat controversial.

What is known as the prehistoric period lasted longer in Ireland, Wales, and the Scottish Highlands than it did in England and southern Scotland because the former remained unconquered by the Romans, who give us the first written records of British history. But Roman accounts can be misleading. As this chapter hopefully has demonstrated, the Romans did not encounter a culturally barren society or undeveloped landscape. On the contrary, thousands of years of human life in the British Isles had not only left their mark on the island but had seen the development of human societies capable of great achievements and the sustenance of life that was undoubtedly full of meaning and purpose for those people who lived in each of the earlier times that preceded the coming of Roman Britain. The process by which Britain became part of the Roman Empire did not occur without resistance or without some amalgamation occurring between two distinct cultures.

FIGURE 3 *Hadrian's Wall.*
Neal Witty/EyeEm/Getty.

2

Roman Britain:

From Bath to the Antonine Wall

*It is debatable whether the conquest of Britain was wise in any case.
Once it had become an objective, it would certainly have been
better to carry it through in its entirety and completely subjugate
both the main island and Ireland.*

THEODOR MOMMSEN, *A History of Rome under the Emperors*
(translated by CLARE KROJZL) 1883

*'We British are used to woman commanders in war,' she cried. 'I am
descended from mighty men. But now I am not fighting as an ordinary
person for my kingdom and wealth. I am fighting as an ordinary person for
my lost freedom, my bruised body, and my outraged daughters.'*

Speech by BOUDICCA, as recorded by the Roman historian, Tacitus,
Annals of Imperial Rome (translated by MICHAEL GRANT)

Conquest and colonization

When the Romans, led by Julius Caesar, first arrived in Britain in 55 BCE, they had
no idea of the size or the extent of the land or even if it was completely surrounded
by water, but within a century the Romans would establish a presence on the island
that would make them the hegemon in England for over three and a half centuries.

In many ways it made sense for the Romans to expand into Britain, because
the people who lived there were closely connected to the Celtic tribes that Caesar
had conquered in the Roman province of Gaul on the other side of what is now
known as the English Channel. In fact, Caesar used the assistance that the Gauls had
received from a British tribe called the Belgae as the justification for his invasion.

Caesar brought with him 10,000 soldiers to conquer Britain and subordinate it to the Roman Empire. The ninth-century British historian Nennius reported that Caesar 'sailed with some sixty vessels to the mouth of the Thames, where they suffered shipwreck whilst he fought against Dolobellus, (the proconsul of the British king, who was called Belinus, and who was the son of Minocannus who governed all the islands of the Tyrrhene Sea), and thus Julius Caesar returned home without victory, having had his soldiers Slain, and his ships shattered'.[1]

For all of Caesar's greatness and victories elsewhere, he unexpectedly had difficulty subordinating Britain to the empire. He quickly returned to Gaul and left it to later emperors to conquer Britain, beginning with the re-invasion of the island launched by Claudius in 44 CE. According to the Roman historian, Cassius Dio, Claudius undertook the invasion of Britain based on a request from a native ruler named Bericus, whose subjects had risen against him and driven him from the island. This time the Romans meant business; Claudius arrived with a force four times the size of Caesar's.

Native resistance to the Romans arose almost immediately, beginning with a revolt led by Caratacus, the son of a prominent British king named Cunobelinus, better known as Cymbeline, the title character of one of Shakespeare's plays. Cunobelinus had died prior to the Roman invasion, leaving his kingdom to Caratacus and his brother, Togodumnus, but excluding a third brother, Amminius. Amminius sought the assistance of the Romans in regaining his lands. The Romans pursued the followers of Caratacus to Anglesey, where they had taken refuge, and annihilated them. Caratacus was captured and sent to Rome, while the Romans seized the territory they desired in the southern lowlands.

The rebellion of Caratacus was quickly followed by the revolt of the Iceni in the year 47. At first, like Amminius, the Iceni were receptive to becoming clients of the Romans, but they rebelled when the Romans treated them contemptuously, for example, by trying to make the Iceni docile by disarming them. The Romans quickly crushed the revolt, but they also alienated a potential ally and helped to ensure that the conquest of Britain would be more violent and prolonged than it needed to be. The Romans further angered British tribes by recalling loans that the recipients had interpreted as gifts. The most famous revolt against the Romans in Britain occurred in 60 CE and was led by the warrior-queen of the Iceni, Boudicca. Boudicca revolted when the Romans attempted to seize her land after the death of her husband, Prasutagus. Roman brutality towards the Iceni also helped to provoke the rebellion and, of course, helped exacerbate matters considerably. In the ensuing struggle, according to Tacitus, the Romans lost perhaps 400 lives, compared to an estimated 80,000 British deaths.

The Roman conquest of Britain was a prolonged and sanguinary affair that took more than thirty years to consummate. Claudius, the man given most of the credit for the successful invasion of Britain, spent a total of only sixteen days there himself. The man, in fact, mostly responsible for the establishment of Roman authority in Britain was actually the Roman governor Julius Agricola, who expanded and augmented Roman power to the north and west after firmly establishing control in the south and east. Agricola sent exploratory expeditions as far north as the Orkneys, which proved to the Romans that Britain lacked a land bridge to the Continent. As Agricola's forces moved to expand the territory controlled by the Romans, according to Tacitus, 'at no time was Britain more agitated, nor its fate more critical: veterans were butchered, Roman colonies burned, armies cut off from their base; one day men fought for their lives and on the next day for triumph'.[2] Tacitus reported an estimated death toll among Romans and natives in this power struggle of 70,000, the majority of them British casualties. Of the British, Tacitus reported that they 'did not take or sell prisoners, or practice other war-time exchanges' and 'could not wait to cut throats, hang, burn, and crucify – as though avenging, in advance, the retribution that was on its way'.[3]

Once Agricola had firmly established Roman rule over much of Britain, he turned his attention to providing order and transforming the British people under his rule into law-abiding, tax-paying subjects who would be left in peace as long as they acquiesced to Roman authority. Border areas in the north and west were placed under more direct military rule, while an effort was made to establish a modus vivendi between soldiers and settlers in areas more firmly under Roman control. He built forts and stationed legions at strategic locations, such as Manchester, Chester, York, and Newcastle. The Romans divided the province into administrative districts called *civitates*. The first capital of Roman Britain, built largely by forced labour among a local tribe called the Trinovantes, was called Camulodunum (modern Colchester), before it shifted to Londinium. London was simply too conveniently located for easy access via the Thames for more effective communication with the Continent and, thus, with Rome. Archaeological excavations in London have revealed the exact area circumscribed by the wall of the Roman city, as well as a number of public buildings, including baths and a third-century temple dedicated to the Persian god, Mithras, who was particularly popular among soldiers. But Tacitus reported that London was not originally a Roman settlement, but rather a popular gathering place for merchants even prior to the arrival of the Romans.

Economy and society of Roman Britain

It took a long time for the native inhabitants of Roman Britain to become fully reconciled to Roman rule. Life did not immediately change for the majority of the populace, who preserved many of their local traditions and customs. The Romans, for their part, also attempted to retain their customs and brought their own practices with them; however, in time, both natives and colonists could not help but influence one another. The Romans would always remain a minority in Britain and the Roman soldiers who served there could not help but intermingle with the native population, with whom they ended up trading at markets, socializing at the baths, and intermarrying.

At the top of Roman society were the wealthy landowners who lived in villas and had their land worked by farmers tied to the land known as *coloni*. They tended to build these villas on lands with the best soil, such as can be found in much of southern England, often involving fields that had been cultivated in the Iron Age. Quita Mould offers a good description of the villas, which were characterized by 'highly decorated tessellated floors and painted plaster walls that graced the reception rooms of wealthier households', compared to 'the majority of homes [which] had very plain interiors and people walked on floors of opus signinum, timber boards of simply beaten earth'.[4] The original villas were quite crude and basic structures, but they were improved upon, as John Wacher in his *Portrait of Roman Britain* makes clear:

> By the second century villas were becoming larger and more elaborate; a few possessed mosaics and bath wings, while the basic architectural form was changing. In many cases they now had wings projecting from the ends of the main ranges of rooms.[5]

The villas also featured raised hearths, though in most homes people still cooked over a fire in the middle of their hut. Material finds associated with Roman villas in Britain include metal locks and keys and all sorts of pottery, as well as wood and glass containers and amphoras for wine or oil. But the owners of these villas did not control the entire landscape, which remained dotted with small villages inhabited by peasant farmers. Some farms simply continued in operation, with local inhabitants expected to surrender a heavy portion of their harvest estimated at between 50 and 60 per cent to their new Roman overlords.

Recent evidence has suggested the existence of extensive wine-making at Wollaston in Northamptonshire and related sites in the middle Nene Valley dating from the second and third centuries.[6] Textiles, primarily wool and flax were also manufactured in Britain; most textile manufacturing was done in the home, primarily by women or household slaves. Hemp was cultivated in Roman Britain for use in ropes and sails. Local dyes in use included 'woad for blue, bedstraw and (imported) madder for red, lichens for purple, and weld for yellow'. J. P. Wild has identified a few features of clothing manufacture that might have derived from foreign influence, but on the whole believes it was done largely in a manner similar to that practised during the Iron Age.[7]

Despite domestic manufacturing, not all goods utilized in Roman Britain were produced in Britain. The Romano-British population also wore garments made of imported fabrics like silk. Grave artefacts indicate the importation of other foreign objects into Roman Britain from as far away as southeastern Europe and southern Russia, including those belonging to an unidentified male dubbed the 'Gloucester Goth'.[8] This find is consistent with others from Roman Britain that suggest that Roman soldiers were frequently stationed elsewhere before being dispatched to Britain. Local production of iron weapons became an expedient adopted to help save on the expenses derived from importing all the weapons necessary for the Roman army in Britain.

The construction of bathhouses, one of the primary trademarks of Roman civilization, has long been viewed as one of the main features of the Romanization of Britain. But Adam Rogers has recently argued that in Roman Britain 'urban development was the result of a unique sequence of events and motives incorporating the ideas and actions of local peoples, landscapes, histories, myths and external inputs and influences',[9] a process that is particularly evident in the town of Bath, known to the Romans as Aquae Sulis.

Aquae Sulis: Bath as a window on Roman Britain

Aquae Sulis reflects the extent of the fusion of Roman and native British culture and society. In pre-Roman times, people approached the hot spring at this location to worship the Celtic goddess Sulis; the Latin name of the town means the 'waters of Sulis'. The Romans conflated Sulis with Minerva, the Roman patron goddess of the springs; the head of her statue is on display at the Roman Bath museum, as is a stone gorgon's head that resembles Neptune, another symbol frequently associated with Minerva. These are both done in a classical style, but the symbolism of those statues is more representative of an emerging Romano-British culture rather than a volte face, in which the British wholly adopted Roman culture while neglecting indigenous tradition; the resemblance of the gorgon's head to the sun, for example, may symbolize the heat of the sacred springs.

Although the Romans built baths elsewhere in England and made them a hallmark of Roman civilization throughout their empire, no baths approached the size and monumental nature of those at Aquae Sulis. There the baths' size and beauty are all the more impressive, given that Bath was not one of the administrative centres of Roman Britain and had no political significance attached to it. The main bath, or the Great Bath, is still well preserved with its surrounding colonnades, but it was flanked by two other pools that were distinguished by their varying temperatures. In the architecture, too, native craftsmanship and motifs accompany the large columns and classical design of the buildings. The reliance upon local materials for the construction of the site conforms to a practice used at other locations of Roman construction throughout Britain. Bath, like the Roman towns of Cirencester, Lincoln, and Wroxeter, was constructed of stones derived from local quarries, though in the case of Bath the Romans also used tombstones from the graves of local inhabitants in the construction of the town walls. Coal was used to heat the altar dedicated to Minerva/Sulis, as it was also used to heat the Roman villas in the region.

FIGURE 4 *Great Bath of the Roman baths complex, Bath, England.*
Olaf Protze/LightRocket/Getty.

Roman soldiers patronized the baths here and elsewhere, which would have been only one of the frequent occasions on which they intermingled with the local civilian population. As stated above, Romans would have socialized with the native people at the baths, and many would have met their wives here, despite the fact that soldiers had been discouraged from intermarrying. (The Roman army, in fact, encouraged soldiers to have sex with one another to avoid contracting diseases from the local populace and perhaps as a way of encouraging an esprit de corps.) To the Romans, the baths were not a luxury reserved for the well-off, but rather regarded as a quotidian necessity, an important part of preserving Roman custom and ritual throughout the empire. In addition, they provided a convenient meeting place to converse with friends about matters both grave and frivolous. Artefacts found at the baths in Caerleon indicate crafts such as embroidery, weaving, and mending were practised there, activities that did not preclude, and often fostered, social interaction.[10] Such artefacts provide further evidence that women and children used the baths, along with British men and Roman soldiers.

The Roman Baths museum contains coins, tombstones, and a stone head of a woman that dates from the first century, all of which open us into everyday life in Roman Britain. The museum also has a number of artefacts such as would have been found in a typical Roman home at the time when the Romans inhabited Bath. Lead tablets have been found at Bath (along with wooden tablets found at Vindolanda, one of 'the largest samples of Roman handwriting found in Britain'[11]) which stressed the extent to which writing played a role in quotidian life, as they cover quite a catholic range of subjects. Coupled with these writings are the numerous stone inscriptions that can be found at the site and throughout Roman Britain. These stone inscriptions are all the more valuable because of the complete absence of books from this epoch. As much as for any civilization from the Ancient Near East, discovering information about Roman Britain is wholly dependent upon archaeological finds such as these tablets and inscriptions. The authors of the lead tablets from Bath are apocryphal and may have been written by Romans or Britons; the fact that scholars cannot tell the difference again accentuates the integration of the two cultures. Also of great interest are the penates, small bronze statuettes representing guardian gods kept in Roman homes to oversee all domestic matters – the well-being of the household, their sleep, chores, and particularly meals. These domestic gods, or lares, would have stood in a lararium, the family's shrine which sometimes took the form of a model classical temple. Every home kept a shrine or altar where an act of reverence took place every day.

Everyday life in Roman Britain

Although the initial conquest of Britain was quite violent, in the second and third centuries Britain became one of the most peaceful provinces in the entire empire. Romans generally preferred to live in towns, a significant number of which existed in Roman Britain, which may be surprising given its location on the far outskirts of the Roman Empire. The towns stood in marked contrast to the rural villas, but also complemented them as part of a blending of rural and urban life. Local farmers provided food and goods for the towns, whose merchants dealt with the owners of the villas and the officials in charge of provisioning the army. One of the most significant results of the use of aerial photography in the study of the ancient British landscape has been the discovery of the land division into numerous small family farms in addition to the large estates surrounding or encompassing local villages. The size and number of large estates, however, seems to have increased by the fourth century. Still, the economy depended on an influx of money from Rome, which could only be justified by the needs of defence; this might have led the governors of the province to exaggerate the threat of raids along the border, which Hadrian's Wall had been built to protect. Ronald Hutton has estimated that a civilian population of between 50,000 and 200,000 existed primarily to serve a military contingent of 10,000–20,000 Roman troops stationed in the northern area of the frontier.[12] In fact, some of the villages in this region would primarily have served as lodges for soldiers and officials travelling to and from the frontier.

The people of Roman Britain shared a similar diet with their Iron Age predecessors, but with some differences. The Iron Age population of Britain ate more pork and beef than after the Roman conquest as a supplement to sheep as their primary source of meat. In Roman times, people seem to have learnt to prepare their food somewhat differently thanks to the introduction by the Romans of something called a mortarium, defined as 'a robust, open form of bowl or basin, with a prominent rim and spout'.[13] The intermixture of plants, animal fats, and dairy products in the moratoria, however, raised questions about whether the resulting products might have been for dietary or cosmetic purposes. Of course, they perfectly well could have been used for both; we know that the Romans did use moratoria to blend oils, sauces, and to mix foods with seasonings, herbs, and spices, but the use of animal fats in particular suggests that their use went beyond the simple processing of grain.[14] Assuming that they were also used for cosmetics or face creams, this could certainly indicate that greater care for one's personal appearance may have been one significant impact on everyday life of the Romanization of Britain. There is also evidence that the native inhabitants paid more attention to their personal hygiene, including the discovery of a number of Romano-British toiletry sets, including such items as nail files, nail cleaners, and tweezers.[15]

Rural inhabitants may not have shared all of the material benefits of Roman civilization as those enjoyed by residents of the towns, but this does not mean that their lives were completely unaffected or unadulterated. Roman law and custom, for example, generally accorded less respect to women's roles within society than did Celtic tradition; therefore, Romanization probably impacted native British women negatively. The continued prestige enjoyed by women in Irish law and society in the early medieval period in what Lisa Bitel has called a 'land of women' that did not come under Roman authority contrasts starkly with the change in the status of women that appears to have occurred in Roman Britain.[16] Yet such influences, if they did occur, were part of a long process of acculturation and not as readily apparent as the more tangible impact of the introduction of Roman material goods into British towns and villages. Romano-British pottery and jewellery manufactured in the towns and even Roman coins from the fourth century have shown up at a number of rural sites.

As regards the diffusion of culture to Roman Britain, most towns at least had an amphitheatre for public performances, and a few, including Canterbury, Verulamium, and Colchester had actual theatres. It is doubtful whether the rural population would have attended the performances that occurred there, however. Still, one could make a case that Britain had become as Roman as any other province in the empire outside of Rome itself, with its population enjoying the benefits of peace. Of course, like residents of other provinces, the farmers and townspeople of Roman Britain had to render unto Caesar and were affected when the economy of Rome began to stagnate in the third century. But the Romans had built an infrastructure of towns, roads, bridges, and walls that would remain in place for use by local inhabitants even after the end of Roman authority in the early fifth century.

Religion in Roman Britain

The Romans no more imposed their religious beliefs wholesale on the British people who came under their rule than they did any other aspect of their civilization. As the famous eighteenth-century historian Edward Gibbon so eloquently put it in *The Decline and Fall of the Roman Empire*, 'The various modes of worship which prevailed in the Roman world, were thought by the people to be equally true, by the philosopher as equally false, and by the magistrate, as equally useful.' In fact, most representations of deities did not conform to the classical style of the image of Minerva at Aquae Sulis or the head of the Deified Claudius at Colchester. But religion did play an important role in Roman Britain; temples of one kind or another are found almost everywhere that a Roman settlement existed. It also took a multiplicity of forms, from the worship of native pagan gods, to the introduction of the Roman gods and Near Eastern mystery cults, including Mithraism and Christianity, and frequently involved a blending of Roman and Celtic deities, such as the conflating of Sulis and Minerva at Bath. In fact, Romans tended to worship at many of the same sacred sites revered by the natives of the island during the Iron Age. Celtic religion tended to focus more on nature worship without such an ordered pantheon of anthropomorphized gods as were revered by the Romans. The sixth-century British monk, Gildas, who wrote one of the first histories of Britain, spoke of his pagan predecessors worshipping hills, mountains, and rivers. But, as a Christian, Gildas refused to say much more about 'the devilish monstrosities of my land, numerous almost as those that plagued Egypt, some of which we can see today, stark as ever, inside or outside deserted city walls: outlines still ugly, faces still grim'.[17] We do have some statements from Julius Caesar on the Druids; scholars, however, have tended to discount his association of the Druids with witchcraft and human sacrifice as pretexts for his military conquests and the advance of Roman civilization at their expense, so he might not be of much value either.[18]

We, therefore, have to rely largely on archaeological evidence for our knowledge of Romano-British religious beliefs and practices before the coming of Christianity. Dogs appear surprisingly frequently in art and in the form of small figurines found at religious shrines and wells, perhaps foretelling the affection that modern British people frequently lavish on their canine pets. Peter and Ann Woodward suggest that connections with hunting and its associated Roman goddess, Diana, provide the likely context for dogs serving as religious icons.[19] Likewise, the presence of chicken remains at several Roman temples might be connected to the symbol of the cockerel, associated with the Roman god Mercury.[20] Then, as now, black birds, such as crows and ravens symbolized death and had strong associations with prophecy and the supernatural.[21]

Tradition says that Christianity first arrived in Britain at Glastonbury, which legend has it was founded by Joseph of Arimathea in the first century. While this is possible, given Glastonbury's location in southern England, evidence does not exist for a strong Christian presence in Britain until the later stages of Roman rule in the fourth century, with the exception of stories of Christian martyrs in Britain during the third century when the emperor Diocletian increased the persecution of Christians. Gildas says that before this 'Christ's precepts were received by the inhabitants without enthusiasm; but they remained, more or less pure' until that time.[22]

Christians, of course, had less sympathy for the pagan gods of the Celts than did other Romans, who generally remained religiously tolerant as long as their imperial subjects gave their political obedience to the empire. (As we have seen, the identity of the Celts themselves remains problematic, but it is common at this time to refer to Celtic religion as a legacy from the prehistoric period that survived the coming of the Romans. The historical designation of Wales, Ireland, and Scotland as a 'Celtic fringe' is an arbitrary distinction separating the pre-Roman population of the British Isles based on those lands that never came under Roman control). In fact, the Romans often simply appropriated Celtic gods or goddesses and merged them with their own deities, as with Sulis and Minerva. But Ben Croxford has challenged the interpretation that the iconoclastic destruction of pagan images is evidence of a Christian presence, noting that fragmentation of images can be done for positive as well as negative reasons in order to make separate religious use of the fragments, an argument supported by the disproportionate number of heads that survive intact among such broken images.[23] Nonetheless, the conversion of Emperor Constantine to Christianity in the early fourth century certainly created opportunities for Christians to openly practice their faith and missionaries to spread it within the empire, including Britain. It is significant that when Constantine summoned a church council at Arles in 314, only one year after the legalization of Christianity, it was attended by three bishops from British dioceses and two additional representatives of the Christian church in Britain.

For most of the period of Roman rule, Celtic religions, apart for Druidism, which the Romans sought to eradicate because it was believed to foster human sacrifice, survived in a modus vivendi or in combination with these other faiths. Although Christianity triumphed in the end, there is actually more evidence for Mithraism prior to the fourth century, with temples found as far west as Caernarfon and Caerleon in Wales and as far north as Hadrian's Wall at the frontier of the northernmost boundary of the Roman Empire.

The frontiers of Roman Britain

The Romans could not make up their minds on where exactly the boundaries of Roman Britain should lie. They established fully thriving towns such as Carlisle, founded in 80 CE, and Corbridge, founded in 86 CE, in the northern frontier zone, before pushing those boundaries farther to the north into what is now Scotland. In fact, Agricola may have had ambitions to conquer the entire island, before he was ordered to retreat from Scotland, according to Tacitus, after the Battle of Mons Graupius in 84 CE. This battle apparently made it clear that the empire could not afford the troops that would have been necessary to conquer Scotland, and Agricola withdrew to a line that approximated where Roman soldiers would construct a wall during the reign of Emperor Hadrian forty years later.

For most of the time between 127 and 410 CE, Hadrian's Wall, stretching the 73 miles between Wallsend on the river Tyne and Bowness on the Solway Firth, represented the northernmost boundary of Roman Britain. Built during the reign of its namesake, the emperor Hadrian (r. 117–38), its construction followed a period of expansion into Scotland under the emperor Trajan. Trajan followed an expansionist policy elsewhere as well, sending Roman troops farther into Romania (Dacia to the Romans) and southwest Asia, and Hadrian may have simply thought that his predecessor had spread the empire too thin. Hadrian seemed to be obsessed with defining the boundaries of the empire, which he attempted to demarcate in Germany as well. But the British wall was probably built to protect the settlements that Hadrian wished to sponsor on the frontiers as he consolidated the boundaries of the empire as much as to mark those boundaries or defend the rest of the province.

The Romans constructed the wall entirely out of material found in the region, primarily sandstone and timber. Civil settlements grew up around the wall and roads were built connecting it to the areas to the south. Along the wall, gates called milecastles existed at regular intervals to regulate traffic across the border, which the wall was not meant to prevent anyone from crossing. Each milecastle had two observation towers that looked over the ramparts and the vast expanse of countryside visible on both sides of the wall, making it unlikely that any sizeable enemy force could approach any portion of the wall unnoticed. A massive ditch in front of the wall made it even more formidable.

There is also an inscription dating from 130 CE dedicated to Hadrian in the monumental arch leading to the forum in the frontier town of Wroxeter (Viroconium Cornoviorum in Latin) near the Welsh border. Wroxeter has proven to be a particularly valuable archaeological site because the city was never rebuilt after the Romans and a plethora of coins (over 6,000) and other artefacts have been unearthed there, including a silver mirror estimated to date from the early third century that rivals those found anywhere else in the Roman Empire. The graffiti present on many of the tiles and pots discovered at Wroxter suggest that a largely literate population lived here at the far reaches of the empire. Wroxeter was first occupied by the Romans in 48 CE as a base from which to invade northern Wales, but remained a prominent defensive outpost and grew to become the fourth largest city in the province. Aerial photography has confirmed the existence of active farms in the area surrounding Wroxeter that would have made the urban community there sustainable.

Hadrian sought to make the frontier areas amenable to those soldiers stationed there, which could have had something to do with both the construction of the wall and the town of Wroxeter. This practice seems to have continued under Hadrian's successors, including Pius Antoninus (r. 138–61), under whom the Romans already pushed the boundary of Roman Britain farther north and began construction of a new wall. At least ten Roman bathhouses have been found at forts along the Antonine Wall, including one on Golden Hill in Duntocher, Scotland excavated by Lawrence Kepple, who attributes their smaller size when compared to those at Hadrian's Wall to the smaller garrisons stationed there.[24] Mike McCarthy has excavated Carlisle and found a significant building programme that began in the middle Antonine period and included the construction of new roads, public buildings, and waterworks.[25] These sites, especially Wroxeter, became places where legionnaires could settle with their families, and did not merely serve as temporary military outposts. Hadrian clearly prided himself not only on augmenting and controlling the borders but on bringing the benefits of Roman civilization to the far corners of the empire.

The Antonine Wall spanned the narrowest part of Scotland from the Firth of Forth to the north bank of the River Clyde west of Glasgow, a length of about 37 miles (60 kilometres). The Antonine Wall served much the same purpose as Hadrian's Wall, as both a defensive outpost and as a way of regulating traffic in and out of the empire. What prompted this expansion northward so soon after such an elaborate building project as Hadrian's Wall is still a matter of conjecture, but the Romans may have found the need to consolidate the territory in between the two walls under Roman rule as a further defensive measure and decided that building a second wall was the best way to do this.

Just because the Romans never conquered Ireland or parts of Scotland and Wales does not mean that the people who lived in these places were unaware of them. Roman pottery has been found as far north as the Orkneys. The Romans tended to portray all of their enemies as barbarians, leaving us with a biased and distorted view of both the Scots and the Picts. The Picts were no more primitive than the Iron Age inhabitants of southern Britain before they had come under Roman rule and had just as many contacts with the European continent. The Picts were formidable warriors, but they also pursued such pacific pursuits as farming, fishing, and craftsmanship, probably utilizing silver and other materials gained from raids on Roman Britain.

For the most part Roman Britain in the century after the construction of Hadrian's Wall was a fairly peaceful, stable, and secure province, its boundaries well established and protected. Roman Britain came increasingly under attack in the third and fourth centuries, including raids in the north on both sides of Hadrian's Wall. Beginning around the middle of the third century, the Romans began to construct a succession of forts along the southern and eastern coasts as a line of defence against raids by Saxon pirates. Forts on the western shores were meant to keep Irish raiders out of Britain. After raids intensified, culminating in a multipronged invasion by Picts and Scots in 367, the Romans began to withdraw from Hadrian's Wall as part of a general retrenchment, leading to the abandonment of Britain as a viable province when Rome itself was attacked by the Visigoths in 410. In 367, not only did army defences prove inadequate, but it is likely that members of the army actually abetted the enemy. The eighth-century Christian historian Bede describes the ensuing consequences of the decline of the Roman military presence in Britain:

On the departure of the Romans, the Picts and Scots, learning that they did not mean to return, were quick to return themselves, and becoming bolder than ever, occupied all the northern and outer part of the island up to the wall, as if it belonged to them. Here a dispirited British garrison stationed on the fortifications pined in terror night and day, while from beyond the wall the enemy constantly harassed them with hooked weapons, dragging the cowardly defenders down from their wall, and dashing them to the ground. At length the Britons abandoned their cities and wall and fled in disorder, pursued by their foes. The slaughter was more ghastly than ever before, and the wretched citizens were torn by wild beasts.[26]

Holistically, however, the frontiers, on all sides of Roman Britain, seem to have been well defended for the centuries prior to 367, and their failure to hold towards the end of Roman rule had more to do with developments in the western half of the empire as a whole than with any general inadequacy.

The end of Roman Britain

When Constantine III attempted an imperial coup in 407 from his position as head of the army in Britain, he contributed to the demise of Roman rule there at a time when the Romans needed all available troops to help defend their position in Gaul and Italy. It used to be suggested that buried hoards such as the famous Mildenhall Treasure indicated that members of the Roman elite quickly hid their most valuable possessions upon being recalled to Rome following the sack of the city by the Visigoths; however, Robin Fleming has suggested that these buried treasures resulted more from the turbulence of the political situation in Roman Britain itself.[27]

The presence of such hoards is indicative of how little the Roman upper classes had to fear from possible invasions during the period known as the Pax Romana. The Roman Empire provided the security that allowed a class of large landholders to exist and flourish in the first place. When Rome no longer offered protection against Saxon raiders, the people of Britain withdrew their allegiance, rebelling against the rule of Constantine in 409, the year before the Visigoths' sack of Rome. At this point, local aristocrats had as much to fear from people within the province as from those coming from the outside.

The native British, according to Zosimus, 'were obliged to throw off Roman rule and live independently, no longer subject to Roman laws. The Britons therefore took up arms and ... freed their cities from the barbarians threatening them.'[28] John Moreland has argued that challenges to authority were symbolized by a new burial tradition that emerged in the mid-fourth century – that of males buried with belt-fittings and a crossbow-brooch, both appropriated symbols of Roman authority.[29] After 409, the people had even less reason to respect imperial authority as trading networks broke down, almost no new currency flowed into the province, and taxes went uncollected. There appears to have been an almost total collapse of provincial authority and, within a very short time, Roman Britain passed into history with the people who lived there left to shift for themselves to forge an entirely new political culture out of its ruins. Britain, however, had not so much been abandoned by the Romans as the British had found it necessary to assert their own independence from the Roman Empire at a time when it could no longer offer its benefits or protection.

Survivals and legacy

Scholars have attempted to find evidence to suggest that Roman Britain survived the early-fifth-century military crisis; James Campbell, for example, has pointed to the existence of 'about 140 memorial inscriptions ... from between the fifth century and the eighth from Wales, about forty from the southwest of Britain, and a handful from the southern part of modern Scotland'.[30] Alan Lane has recently challenged an interpretation that life and urban development continued at Wroxeter for another century or two after the sack of Rome in 410.[31] But not a single Roman villa seems to have thrived much longer than the collapse of provincial authority around that time. Yet Roman Britain had seen the introduction of a literate culture, the subdivision of much of Britain into administrative districts, the establishment of a concept of legitimate political authority, the distribution of coins which continued to circulate even after the flow of new ones stopped, and the construction of buildings that did not disappear overnight and roads that lasted far longer. Farming continued in many of the same areas as practised under the Romans, even if the overall agricultural economy became more pastoral.

Martin Henig, in a 2002 review of Neil Faulkner's book on the subject, wrote that 'far from rejecting Romanitas, the Britons of the last days fought manfully, and in large part successfully, to preserve their classical legacy, and even to introduce it into Ireland and parts of Scotland where Rome's political writ had never run'. He cites the accomplished Latin of Gildas and St Patrick as examples of that classical legacy.[32] This contradicts the position of Michael Jones, who argued in 1996 that the British could not have fought too hard to preserve the Romanization of Britain if millions readily accepted the authority of the Anglo-Saxon kings who came to the island with followers numbering in the mere tens of thousands.[33] Jones cited Gildas in support of his theory that the native British had very little use for Roman values, a position he found entirely consistent with 'a substantially negative attitude towards the Roman past' in native British literary sources.[34]

A few years later Jane Webster added to a growing attack on the whole concept of 'Romanization' by suggesting that the native British had been 'creolized' instead. By this, Webster meant the 'merging of two languages into a single dialect [denoting] the processes of multicultural adjustment (including artistic and religious change) [similar to that] through which African-American and African-Caribbean societies were created in the New World'.[35] In the past twenty years, Rome has drawn more frequent comparisons to modern empires in a view that argues that the Romans exploited Britain for its natural resources without much regard for the benefits that it brought to the indigenous inhabitants of the island. Hugh Kearney compared the villas of Roman Britain to 'the hacienda of colonial Mexico or the "big houses" of eighteenth-century Ireland'.[36] Webster's view, however, is more consistent with the interpretation offered in this chapter of a Romano-British culture that represented a blending of native and Roman elements in such areas as art and religion. It was this culture – neither fully Roman nor entirely British – that the Angles and Saxons encountered when they migrated to Britain in the fifth and sixth centuries.

FIGURE 5 *Cemetery with Celtic cross, Glendalough, Ireland.*
Taken by Richard Radford/Moment/Getty.

3

Anglo-Saxon England and the Celtic lands in the early Middle Ages

As we must all expect to leave
our life on this earth, we must earn some renown,
if we can, before death; daring is the thing
for a fighting man to be remembered by.
BEOWULF (translated by MICHAEL ALEXANDER)

St Patrick and early Irish Christianity

The fall of Roman Britain left an enormous legacy even in the parts of the British Isles that never came under the Roman occupation, primarily in the form of the spread of the Christian religion. Roman Christians took an interest in Ireland even before the mission of a young Romano-British aristocrat-turned-missionary named Patrick arrived there in the 430s. Ireland already had a bishop, a certain Palladius, whose mission clearly formed part of a wider initiative on the part of the Roman Church to spread the Christian faith to pagan lands.

Patrick arrived in Ireland as a captive slave, a victim of raids on the west coast of Britain conducted by Irish pirates who took advantage of the weakened state in which the Romans had left the island when they withdrew their official presence in 410. He endured six years of slavery, in which he was mainly forced to tend livestock, before, inspired by a dream about a ship prepared to take him to freedom, he managed a daring escape that could have meant death had he been caught. However, he had undergone some kind of spiritual conversion experience that led him to put his trust in God and convinced him that he needed to return to Ireland to preach the Gospel. What made Patrick's conversion so remarkable was the solitary nature of it; like Paul on the road to Damascus, whatever Patrick experienced did not derive from any immediate human influence, though his previous exposure to Christianity could certainly have helped to pave the way for his sudden conversion in ways that are impossible to trace historically. Patrick was also smart enough to realize, however, that he needed training before he could begin his career as a missionary. The ship on which Patrick left Ireland landed in Gaul. At that time, a relatively close connection existed between Ireland and Gaul, where Patrick may have studied before returning to the land of his captivity, with a visit to reunite with his family in Britain in between. Patrick's own claims for his lack of education may have simply served as an example of his humility and are somewhat belied by his own writings, namely his *Confessions* and the *Letter to Coroticus*.

The challenge that Patrick and any Christian missionaries faced in Ireland was its lack of political unity, divided as it was into dozens of rival petty kingdoms each with its own individual ruler. Patrick did not ignore the rulers and their courts; one account has him baptizing seven kings in a single day. However, he seems to have taken his message more directly to the people than was actually common at this time; there are stories of Patrick baptizing 12,000 people in the province of Connaught alone. One of the reasons why Christianity triumphed in Ireland, as elsewhere in Northern Europe, was the ways in which it merged with rather than completely replaced native pagan traditions. Celtic spirituality predated the arrival of Christianity and helped to prepare the way for the acceptance of the invisible power and mystery of the Christian God and the heroic death and resurrection of Jesus. These beliefs were reinforced by the miraculous powers attributed to missionaries such as Patrick, of whom the ninth-century historian Nennius wrote that he 'gave sight to the blind, cleansed the lepers, gave hearing to the deaf, cast out devils, raised nine from the dead, redeemed many captives of both sexes at his own charge, and set them free in the name of the Holy Trinity'.[2]

Patrick, by all accounts, had a long and illustrious career in Ireland, gaining numerous converts and raising the general profile of the Christian faith there. According to the *Annals of Ulster*, Patrick founded 365 churches, ordained 3,000 priests, converted 12,000 people, and saved the lives of forty dying individuals through the power of his prayerful intercession on their behalf.[3] Patrick did not depart from the Roman form of church organization – Ireland retained its bishops, which included Patrick – but from the beginning Irish Christianity began to take on its own distinct identity nonetheless. Here the lack of Roman occupation and influence had an important impact on Irish history. The relative absence of Roman influence may have made the inhabitants of the island more receptive to the new religion at the same time that they may have felt unencumbered by traditions already established in the Roman Church. For example, almost from the beginning monasticism would play a heightened role in Irish Christianity than in Britain or on the European continent, even though monasteries existed throughout the Christian world. Irish monasteries became even more popular and widespread after Patrick's death. Abbots of monasteries began to exercise independent authority, provoking a certain amount of jealousy among the native Gaelic chieftains, particularly those who had not yet converted to Christianity from their polytheistic pagan beliefs.

Irish monasticism also looked more favourably on women residents than the patriarchal Benedictine monasteries that were so prevalent on the European continent. In contrast to the Benedictines, not only did Irish monasteries accept cohabitation among married members of their communities, but female abbesses could preside over mixed-sex monasteries and wield as much – and sometimes more – authority than male abbots. However, as Lisa Bitel has shown, Irish women did not totally escape the taint of sin associated with them by virtue of their sex that was inherent in medieval Christian attitudes to a large degree. Yet she also finds this association balanced by the association of sex with love in Irish romance literature and coupling traditions that occurred beyond the influence of Irish law and church authorities. In fact, the prevalence of laws and concerns about adultery and cohabitation seem to speak to the frequency with which these practices occurred; fortunately, in Ireland the influence of women within the church and society in general helped to temper the demands of society with the inevitable complications of human relationships between real men and women.[4]

Another prominent characteristic of Irish Christianity was its dynamic and aggressive expansionism in the form of intense missionary activity within and outside of Ireland. Columba (521–97) arrived at the island of Iona off the northwestern coast of Britain in 563, which became a base for his missionary activity in the lands of the Picts that would eventually become known as Scotland. Columba was engaging in a practice that came to be referred to as 'White Martyrdom', in which Irish missionaries left their homeland for the hard life of a missionary abroad since they did not face persecution at home. Columba founded a number of additional monasteries, including Durrow and Kells in Ireland, but Iona became the spiritual site most associated with his life and missionary activity. Columba's biographer, Adomnán recorded many miracles performed by the saint that enhanced his status and reputation within the Celtic church. He was even said to have stopped the Loch Ness Monster from terrorizing the local population near Inverness!

Columbanus (c. 543–615) ranks with Patrick and Columba as one of the great missionaries and representatives of Irish Christianity in the early medieval period. Possessing a powerful and charismatic personality, he not only influenced the conversion of countless individuals but attracted the support and interest of the Frankish monarchy and nobility during his missions on the European continent. In his popular study of early Irish Christianity, *How the Irish Saved Civilization* (1995), Thomas Cahill argued that the Irish, by preserving the learning of the ancient world brought to the island by Greek monks fleeing the political chaos that accompanied the fall of the Roman Empire in the West, had placed themselves in a position to transmit that learning at a later date back to the Continent from which it had originated. Columbanus did play an important role in the establishment of monasteries in Europe, but he would have looked at Cahill's formulation quite differently. To Patrick, Columba, and Columbanus, it was not the Irish who had saved civilization but rather Christianity that had saved the Irish; the desire of Columba and Columbanus to proselytize in foreign lands followed as the natural outcome of that conviction.

One of the most visible differences that separated Irish Christians from their Roman counterparts involved the date on which they celebrated Easter. Columbanus wrote a series of letters to Pope Gregory the Great defending the Irish method for calculating the date, but he was unlikely to change the minds of either the pope or the adherents of the Roman practice whom he encountered in the Frankish kingdom. Representatives of the Irish church agreed to abide by the Roman date at the Synod of Whitby in 664; the Welsh, by contrast, did not get around to addressing the difference in their calculation of Easter from that of the Roman Church until a bishop of Bangor named Elvod attempted to impose the Roman date in 755, and even then the other Welsh bishops resisted. South Wales finally adopted the Roman date in

777, but as late as 809 the bishops of Llandaff and Menevia were still resisting the change in date because of their refusal to recognize the authority of the archbishop of Gwynedd. The main religious significance of this controversy had to do with the belief in the sanctity of holy days, which needed to be observed correctly in order to honour God properly; if Christians were celebrating the holiest day of the church year on different dates, some of them obviously had it wrong and would have been seen as offending God in the process.

Angles, Saxons, and Jutes: Migrations and invasions

Meanwhile, in these centuries, Britain witnessed the arrival of numerous foreigners who would completely transform its political landscape. The eighth-century historian Bede (c. 673–735) says that 'these newcomers were from the three most formidable races of Germany, the Saxons, Angles, and Jutes'.[5]

The Saxon invasion of Britain did not take place in one fell swoop. In fact, Saxons already living in Britain at the time of the departure of the Romans in 410 participated in the defence of the island and its native inhabitants. Nor did any kind of massive migration take place that displaced the native inhabitants, sending them scurrying to the remote northern and western regions of the island. The most well-known leader from the earliest period of post-Roman Britain, the legendary King Arthur, is known only from later sources such as the Irish *Annals of Ulster* and Nennius's *History of the Britons*, which both refer to a commander of Romano-British troops named Artorius who defeated an invading force near the end of the fifth century at a place called Mons Badicus. Archaeologists have proposed a sizeable hill fort in South Cadbury in southwestern England as the location of Arthur's mythical kingdom of Camelot, which became so central to the cultural legacy of this period from the medieval period to modern times. The site, first excavated in the 1960s, clearly indicates the presence of a strong ruler in this region from around the date when Arthur is believed to have lived. The hall, which measures 63 × 34 feet, might have even been large enough to fit a round table.

The mythical King Arthur remains far more important than his actual historical counterpart, but if the fort did belong to the historical Arthur, he ruled at an important transitional time between the fall of the Western Empire and the establishment of the Anglo-Saxon kingdoms. We can surmise that the Saxons largely migrated on boats that sailed up the Thames River to spread out from London into the kingdoms associated with their name, Essex (the land of the East Saxons), Sussex (South Saxons), and Wessex (West Saxons). Meanwhile, the people collectively known as the Angles probably entered through the estuaries of several rivers that flow into the Wash, a bay in eastern England, where the kingdom of East Anglia emerged, or the Humber River farther north where they established the kingdom of Northumbria. These kingdoms, which also included Kent, where a group called the Jutes (who gave their name to the Danish peninsula of Jutland), settled, and the kingdom of Mercia in the Midlands soon lost whatever degree of ethnic identity they possessed when they arrived, which was probably very little. These so-called Angles, Saxons, and Jutes likely brought Franks, Frisians, and members of other groups with them before they settled down to merge with and intermarry among the native population, which was by then Romano-British.

The newer residents of Britain did not, then, simply replace the native population, nor did they drastically alter agricultural patterns or engage in a massive land clearing, as historians had once thought. The image of a violent, chaotic, and turbulent dark age following the abandonment of Britain by the Romans comes largely from our earliest written account of the period, the work of Gildas, the sixth-century British monk, who may have had reason to exaggerate the barbarity of the Saxons because of his disdain for their polytheistic and pantheistic pagan religion and his own longing for Roman culture.

Interestingly, the area of occupation by the Anglo-Saxons more or less coincided with the previous Roman occupation, leaving those areas left outside the Roman zone – Pictland, Wales, Cornwall, and Ireland – to continue to develop independently in accordance with their own political and religious traditions. We know little of the Picts in this period, mainly because of the scarcity of inscriptions in their native language, with the few that do exist consisting almost exclusively of the names of persons or places. Ireland remained a politically divided island, but one recently inspired by Christianity to expand its influence to Pictland and beyond. Some new independent kingdoms emerged in Wales with the disappearance of Roman authority, including the Welsh kingdom of Gwynedd, first mentioned in the memorial stone of a man named Cantiorix that dates from the beginning of the sixth century, while Cornwall, whose native language was actually closer to that spoken in Ireland than the one that emerged among the Welsh, continued to constitute a separate political region.

The invasions and migrations of the post-Roman period did have some important effects on the lands where the newcomers did settle, however. For example, they brought with them their pagan beliefs and certainly influenced the decline of Christianity in what is now England before the mission of Augustine to Kent at the end of the sixth century and the successful efforts of the Irish missionaries in Northumbria. In addition, warfare among the rulers of the various kingdoms fostered the displacement of previous kings or local authorities, while the violence, in turn, reaffirmed the martial values of early medieval society. The inability of any single kingdom to achieve dominance in this period also had long-term repercussions that both inhibited political consolidation for centuries and made the region more susceptible to outside attacks at a later date.

The Sutton Hoo burial ship and other archaeological finds from the early Middle Ages

We can understand more about the new society that emerged in the early medieval period by turning to a brief examination of some of the surviving archaeological evidence from that time. Because the Anglo-Saxons built mainly in wood, archaeology for this period has not yielded as many physical remains as Roman Britain did, but several spectacular finds have greatly altered our view of a period once thought of as the 'dark ages'. The presence of what archaeologists call 'dark earth' provides evidence of rebuilding and continuous occupation of the same sites; London, for example, experienced continued occupation throughout this period, the evidence hidden for centuries under successive layers of building and development. The values of the warrior culture celebrated in poems such as 'Beowulf' and 'The Battle of Brunanburgh' come to life in the finds of weapons, helmets, and shields, but these finds must not blind us to the peaceful continuation of daily life throughout the British Isles for much of the early medieval period.

Major archaeological evidence, especially in Ireland and on the perimeter of the new Anglo-Saxon kingdoms, comes from hill forts and ring forts, some of which date from earlier periods but which underwent reoccupation after the collapse of Rome. At least five generations occupied one such fort at Cadbury Congresbury in Somerset after the mid-fifth century.[6] The use of the same objects across several generations could indicate an impoverishment of the material culture of the period or simply an economical pragmatism based on the continued functionality of the pottery and glass objects. Other sites from Wales at about the same time, such as Dinas Powys in Glamorgan, indicate a wider variety of everyday objects comparable to those found at Cadbury Congresbury.

As for the Anglo-Saxon kingdoms themselves, the most spectacular discovery has been the burial ship of an East Anglian king found at a location called Sutton Hoo in the 1930s. Actually, since the site contains no evidence of the actual physical remains of the deceased, it is thought to be a cenotaph that commemorates the death of a king whose body was unavailable for interment with the ship. Nonetheless, the ship burial contains an abundance of wealth and material goods, both valuable and everyday objects. They range from a ceremonial whetstone to a harp, which provides evidence of the kind of oral literary tradition that gave rise to epic poems such as *Beowulf*. The whetstone speaks to the strong associations between the manufacture of tools and weapons and power in early societies. The site also contained an axe-hammer, recently reinterpreted as intended for use in animal sacrifice by the king, further illustrating the priestly function of pagan kingship.[7] In addition, the ship contained Frankish coins and gold and silver objects which came from as far away as southwest Asia. The source of this king's wealth could provide further evidence of the continued prosperity of post-Roman Britain since it may very well have derived from local sources rather than overseas plunder.

More recently, Terry Herbert's 2009 discovery with his metal detector of the Staffordshire hoard has led to yet another reassessment of what we thought we knew about early medieval Britain. This site contained over 4,000 individual items that, like those found at Sutton Hoo, date from the mid-seventh century. The hoard probably represents the victory spoils of the king of Mercia. It is possible, though, that he did not deposit all of the items at a single time: 'Reopening a small pit, he could have heaped his trophies, gold and silver fittings stripped from enemy weapons, on top of hundreds of other fragments deposited during previous visits over many years.'[8] Mercia was in the process of becoming the dominant power among the seven kingdoms known as the heptarchy at that time. This find provides both confirmation and partial explanation of that fact, given the wealth that the king of Mercia obviously possessed. Since we might imagine that most wealth from this period disappeared long ago, this find must represent only a tiny fraction of the riches that circulated at the time. The hoard also reveals the accoutrements of a military culture, as judged by the gold and silver sword hilts and fittings, as well as the tiny fragments of a complete helmet, very few of which have survived from this period. One such helmet reconstructed from Sutton Hoo had a Swedish provenance, though the style seems to be influenced by the Romans, who themselves imitated helmets worn by Sassanian soldiers from Iran. The vast wealth and beautifully ornamented objects of the Staffordshire hoard confirm the impression given by the Sutton Hoo ship burial of the rule by truly wealthy and powerful warrior-kings starting to dominate the island.

Offa's Dyke presents an example of a massive construction project comparable to Hadrian's Wall in its attempt to provide a boundary that would separate one part of Britain from another, in this case Wales from Mercia and, eventually, England. Offa ruled from 757 to 769, a period in which he undoubtedly made Mercia the most powerful kingdom in Britain and must have established a strong centralized government to oversee a project of such magnitude. There is evidence of Offa's international prestige based on his connections with Charlemagne, but if Offa's Dyke, which stretches for almost 150 miles (about twice the length of Hadrian's Wall) were all that remained it would form a strong enough basis for those conclusions.

As for Pictland, the Dupplin Cross, as well as partial fragments from Birsay and Albemarle, provides indications of the use of a military formation called a 'shield-wall'. This constituted a defensive formation of tightly packed warriors who could hold a line and use their shields to protect themselves from incoming arrows at the same time. Yet other finds, including arrowheads, indicate the use of archers and cavalry in addition to infantry in the armies of the Picts. The Pictish victory over a Northumbrian army at Nechtanesmere, depicted on the cross slab found in the Aberlemno churchyard, indicates that the Picts still posed a formidable threat around the end of the seventh century. Even as late as 966, a native army from Moray in the northeast won a great battle at Kinloss that ended with the decapitation of the defeated Scots, as depicted on the Sueno Stone that was carved in the aftermath of the victory.[9] By that time, however, most native Picts had become amalgamated with the Irish Scots, with the recorded unification of Scotland under Kenneth I in 843 perhaps serving as the key date in that transition.

In addition to these major finds, evidence from everyday life such as dental analysis has confirmed, for example, that burial sites identified as 'Anglo-Saxon' in fact contain the remains of native Britons. In addition, native Britons certainly made use of Anglo-Saxon objects once the newcomers settled on the island, further complicating the ethnic identity of grave sites from this period. Furthermore, recent archaeological excavations at sites such as Mucking, Essex, Yarnton, Oxfordshire, Catholme, Staffordshire, and Bloodmoor Hill, Suffolk have begun to provide a better picture of rural settlements during the Anglo-Saxon period.[10] These have generally confirmed the revised picture of the period as one of continuity and prosperity that belies the traditional interpretation of this period as 'the dark ages'. Even the estates of Roman villas appear to have continued in use by the same families who simply adapted themselves to a less pretentious way of living more in keeping with the changing social and political realities of the period than as a result of an absolute economic decline, though a relative decline certainly cannot be ruled out.[11]

Finally, the craftsmanship behind such ornamental objects as rings, buckles, and brooches has long elicited admiration from Anglo-Saxon specialists and belied the image of the period as backward. The ninth-century silver pendant cross found at Gravesend provides one good example. Croziers, and chalices, also illustrate the rich material culture associated with churches and monasteries during the early medieval period. They belong to the broader story of the conversion of pagans to Christianity achieved by the missionaries that came from Rome to the southeast corner of Britain and the Celtic missionaries from Ireland that approached from the northwest.

Christian missions to Britain

Our main source for the Christianization of Britain comes from the writings of Bede (c. 671–735), a Northumbrian monk whose *Ecclesiastical History of the English People* contains a fair amount of bias in favour of the Roman Church to which he belonged. Bede gives much of the credit to Pope Gregory the Great, who sent the missionary Augustine in the year 597 to convert the English people, supposedly because he had witnessed some handsome Angles at a slave market in Rome. Bede tells us that Gregory decided that this race of 'angels' deserved to be converted to the Christian faith, though not, apparently, to be rescued from slavery. In response to Augustine's query regarding the difficulty of attracting native priests because of the ideal of clerical celibacy, Gregory responded that it would be better to relax the rule on celibacy and allow for married priests than to exclude qualified men from the priesthood, a proto-Anglican solution to the problem. Gregory also encouraged Augustine to remain flexible with regard to local customs 'for things should not be loved for the sake of places, but places for the sake of good things'. Bede followed his inclusion of the correspondence between Gregory and Augustine with this simple description of the reintroduction of Roman Christianity to southern England:

> Augustine proceeded with the king's help to repair a church which he was informed had been built long ago by Roman Christians. ... He also built a monastery a short distance to the east of the city, where at his suggestion King Ethelbert erected from the foundations a church dedicated to the blessed Apostles Peter and Paul enriching it with many gifts.[12]

It might be mentioned, however, that the king of Kent, Ethelbert (c. 560–616), had already married a Christian Frankish princess, Ethelberga, who, instead of Augustine, perhaps deserves the credit for reintroducing Roman Christianity to southern England.

Bede also includes mention of numerous miracles performed by the saints and missionaries of the early church in England. In the early Middle Ages, people generally converted because they became convinced of the power and truth of the new faith – because it provided practical advantages in this world (though this did not necessarily exclude personal edification or communion with God). Miracles played an important role in demonstrating that power and truth and promising access to the kind of magic that might assist with healing illness, growing crops, or even attaining victory in battle. Furthermore, life was precarious and death not just an eventual certainty but a common occurrence. No religion claimed to offer such certainty in regard to the unknown realm of the afterlife as Christianity did, King Edwin of Northumbria reminded his council in 627 shortly after his own conversion. In a famous speech recorded by Bede, an adviser of Edwin compared a human lifespan to the flight of a sparrow who enters a barn and remains safe and warm while inside without knowing what awaits it when it flies out the window opposite from that through which it entered.

Roman missionaries not only had to convert the kings in order to make significant headway with the people, but they also had to accommodate themselves to the king's political authority, in exchange for which they received legal protection. Ethelbert promulgated a law code in which the very first law called for the protection of church property. The laws of Wihtred of Kent from 695 called for fines of fifty shillings for anyone violating church property and exempted the church from royal taxation. Wihtred's laws also reinforced some of the moral concerns of the Church by prohibiting 'illicit unions'; though the prescribed penalty involved separation from the fellowship of the church rather than any actual punishment by the state, this would have been worse than death for some people. In fact, the laws specifically state that those separated from the church would not forfeit their property; still, it remains significant that the king was promulgating royal laws that addressed the concerns of the church, including a law that 'if a husband sacrifice to devils without his wife's knowledge, he is to forfeit all his property'.[13]

Meanwhile, Celtic missionaries from Ireland made substantial headway through the establishment of missions at important centres such as Dál Riata in Scotland. Even Bede gives credit to Columba for the conversion of the northern Picts to Christianity around the year 565, though he says that an earlier missionary named St Ninian had prepared the ground for him through the conversion of many people in southern Pictland prior to Columba's arrival. Even so, Bede acknowledges Columba's holiness and success as a missionary, writing that he converted a powerful Pictish king named Bride and his people through preaching and example, from whom in return he received the island of Iona to establish his religious settlement.

Then, in the early seventh century, Celtic missionaries succeeded in converting the royal family of Bernicia in Northumbria. Celtic Christianity made great headway in the north and its traditions left a lasting mark there. This influence can be seen through the pre-eminence of English monasteries such as Lindisfarne and even Bede's monastery at Jarrow, where Celtic spirituality, love of learning, and artistic traditions merged with Roman discipline. Colin Symes has seen this influence as well in the resemblance of the stone crosses of Northumbria to those in Celtic lands, the emphasis on a greater personal relationship with Christ, and the practice of worship in the vernacular.[14]

However, those Roman missionaries and authorities who competed with Celtic and native British Christianity adopted a tough stance against native British Christians who did not follow Rome; the seventh-century archbishop of Canterbury Theodore of Tarsus had regarded non-Roman Christians as heretics. His discouragement of the use of British Latin contributed to its disappearance in Wales by the end of the seventh century. At the Synod of Whitby of 664, King Oswy of Northumbria and representatives of the Roman Church persuaded a delegation of Celtic Christians to accept the authority of the pope and the Roman date for celebrating Easter. If Bede overestimated the historical inevitability of these developments, he can be forgiven as a monk likely to see the hand of God behind them.

In short, the church served as an important unifying factor long before any thought of political unification among the kingdoms of the heptarchy. The Christianization of the British Isles had been a gradual process, achieved over several centuries, rather than decades. Still, by the eighth century, the British Isles shared a common religious culture, despite the division of the islands into so many rival kingdoms. This was why Bede's introduction of the conception of not only an English church but also an English people stands out as such an important moment in the history of the British Isles.

Viking invasions

It took another 150 years, however, for England to begin the process of political unification. The major impetus in that direction came from the outside invasions of foreigners from the north who collectively became known as the Vikings. *The Anglo-Saxon Chronicle* lists as the main event for the year 787 an attack by the Northmen on the southern coast of England. This turned out to be the first of many around the British Isles, including a devastating raid upon the monastery at Lindisfarne in 793. Bede's monastery at Jarrow suffered a shattering attack the following year. Reports of the frequency of Viking raids on sites around the coasts of the British Isles in the first half of the ninth century are hard to ignore and must have terrified the population, especially given the propensity of the invaders to take those whom they did not kill into captivity to sell as slaves.

The word 'Viking' appears in the *Oxford English Dictionary* for the first time in 1807 and was still virtually unknown when Queen Victoria ascended the throne thirty years later.[15] Janet Nelson has argued that interest in 'the Vikings' reveals 'more about quests for identity on the part of those that devised them than about ninth-century Scandinavians'.[16] One problem of historical interpretation is a false dichotomy of Scandinavian Vikings versus the Irish or the British. Irish and British kings constantly attacked one another, raided each other's territories, and even sacked and destroyed churches. The Vikings hardly constituted any kind of unified force either; wars among Scandinavian kings occurred as frequently as those in the British Isles. Furthermore, native British or Irish rulers sometimes aligned themselves with the Vikings against their enemies, as the Cornish did against Ecgbryht of Wessex in 838. The scant sources make it difficult to recover the truth behind the myth and tell a coherent story about it. There is no question, however, that invasions from the north from the eighth to the tenth centuries provided a disruption in the continuity of life in the British Isles in a way that never occurred in the earlier period of Germanic migrations.

What was different about the Viking invasions of the ninth century that contributed to a disruption in the continuity of the history of the Isles? First, the Viking invasions brought about a clash between a pagan and a Christian ethos in a way that the Anglo-Saxon invasions had not. Secondly, evidence from Scandinavia tells a different story than that gleaned from the *Anglo-Saxon Chronicle* and other sources from the

British Isles. Scandinavians who fought or settled in Britain and Ireland maintained contact with people from their homeland, again, in a way that did not seem to happen when the Angles, Saxons, and Jutes migrated across the North Sea. Some warriors who fought in Britain or Ireland fought in Saxony or other locations on the European continent as well, with locations in Denmark or Sweden continuing to serve as their home base, even as late as the tenth and eleventh centuries. Thirdly, the natives of the British Isles fought back external invasions providing an incentive for greater levels of unity and cooperation among previously competing states. The *Anglo-Saxon Chronicle* records a great victory by an ealdorman named Wulfheard at Southampton over thirty-seven ship's companies in 840. The Danes, however, won a battle against Wulfheard's successor, Aelthelhun at Portland a year later. In 848 a combined Irish army from Munster and Leinster defeated an invading force at a place in Leinster called Sciath Nechtain. What was probably the largest invading fleet landed in East Anglia in 865, marking an escalation of the hostilities that helped prepare the way for the further unification of the Anglo-Saxon kingdoms under the next king of Wessex, Alfred the Great (r. 871–99).

This invasion fleet of 865 contained a sizeable enough force to allow the Vikings to establish a permanent position in England, at least in the north. Earlier fleets, such

FIGURE 6 *Statue of Alfred the Great, Winchester, England.*
Richard Fairless/Moment Open/Getty.

as the one that Wulfheard turned back in 840 or the twenty-five ship's companies that the Saxons fought at Carhampton in 836, had been relatively small. The 865 invasion started a trend towards larger armadas containing between 120 and 250 ships.[17] The Vikings established themselves at York in 867; an invading army reached Mercia the following year. At this point Aethelred, the king of Wessex, came to the assistance of Burgred of Mercia, further solidifying the alliance between the former rival kingdoms.

The relative absence of actual references to the Vikings in the ninth-century version of the *Anglo-Saxon Chronicle* suggests that perhaps their actual threat to Wessex itself may have been exaggerated. Churches seem to have remained largely intact throughout the south during Alfred's reign. Monasteries, too, suffered more from disrepair than destruction, a fact that Alfred's Welsh biographer Asser blamed on the native inhabitants.[18] Originating in Wessex, the authors of the *Anglo-Saxon Chronicle* may have overemphasized the significance of Alfred's military victories when the Vikings appeared perfectly content at this point to accept payment to settle elsewhere. The Danes had much more military success outside of Wessex and may have been content enough with their conquests that their raids on Wessex may have simply aimed at ensuring its nonintervention elsewhere. Alfred, however, displayed personal qualities of leadership that other kings of the period seemed to lack and still emerged as the only native king to successfully withstand the Vikings, even if he did need to buy them off. His victory at Edington in 878 not only preserved the independence of Wessex but also led to an agreement with the Danish King Guthram that included the Viking's conversion to Christianity.

The Anglo-Saxon poem *Beowulf*, which represents our best source for the amalgamation of pagan Scandinavian and Christian values, tells us that the Vikings thought it an honour to die in battle. The hero who did so would then reunite with his forefathers in Valhalla, their version of the afterlife. The poem celebrates the martial values that were instilled from birth in a warrior society. The Angles and Saxons continued to share these values long after they had nominally converted to the Christian faith, which must at times have led to conflicted beliefs. The similarities between the Anglo-Saxon and Scandinavian cultures not only helps to cast the Viking invasions in an entirely different light, but also helps to explain the ease with which those Scandinavians who did settle in the British Isles, like their Roman and Germanic predecessors, quickly assimilated into the native population.

Viking settlements

The establishment of Viking settlements overlapped chronologically with military invasions; settlements began as early as the mid-ninth century, while Scandinavian invasions of the British Isles continued to occur deep into the eleventh century. The earliest settlements began as winter encampments known as *longphorts*, which were not permanent residences, but these soon gave way to Viking towns and cities. Even then, these settlements remained part of the larger Scandinavian world with deep connections to their homelands. Furthermore, settlements could always serve more than one purpose; warriors, merchants, and craftsmen lived side by side so that a village intended as a temporary camp could quickly become a centre of trade and manufacturing as well as a military base. Mary Valante writes of Viking towns in this period that they 'regularized and controlled international trade in Ireland, making the Irish dependent on them for certain materials, especially silver. But it is equally clear that the Scandinavians were just as dependent on the Irish. ... The Vikings raided and traded within the peripheral areas around each town in order to acquire a wide variety of goods and raw materials for trade, including slaves and wheat.'[19] Archaeologists are still uncovering new evidence about these settlements and the mutual trading arrangements that they reflect, though some scholars still warn against underestimating the destructive impact of the Vikings and the psychological trauma that they caused.

The Viking settlement at Woodstown in Ireland provides a particularly good example of one such multipurpose site. Archaeological evidence from the site, including a plethora of iron nails, reveals its purpose as a centre for manufacturing or repairing damaged ships. Recent archaeological digs at Skaill in Orkney have turned up 'quantities of iron metalworking debris and iron nails and rivets, bone pins and combs, whetstones, amber and glass beads, steatite bowls and a Hiberno-Norse ringed pin in almost mint condition'.[20] An archaeological dig in the 1970s on Coppergate in York (Jorvik) uncovered mostly articles of peaceful, everyday life, not of war. The residents of Jorvik engaged in leather making, iron working, jewellery making, and the manufacture of combs from antlers and other everyday items, such as shoes and clothing. The Vikings had their recreational pursuits as well, as evidenced in the game pieces and ice skates (made from bones) also found at the site.

The earliest Viking settlements in the Isles possibly occurred along the Atlantic coast of Scotland by about 800, though these settlements were not numerous at such an early date and some scholars remain unconvinced by extant sources. Evidence from combs made of reindeer bones and antlers indicates Scandinavian contacts here in the ninth century.[21] As the founding of Dublin about 840 indicates, Ireland came next, where the Vikings also founded the towns of Limerick, Waterford, and Annagassan, as well as building their own fort to replace a previous one at Cork. They established settlements in England and Wales in the ninth century as well – fewer in Wales, which did not possess as much arable land as England and had fewer rivers that provided access to the interior. The *Anglo-Saxon Chronicle* reports that Alfred took a force into Mercia to battle an invasion force and ended up 'sharing' some of the land with them. But settlement was an ongoing process; radiocarbon dating on recent finds from the island of Orkney indicates a date of settlement in the eleventh or twelfth century. Although prolonged, the process of settlement had a cumulative effect, especially in England where the 1087 *Domesday Book* records over 300 names with a suffix of 'by', indicating their Scandinavian origins.[22] Scotland also contains many place-names of Scandinavian origin; whereas Danish influence predominated in England, linguistic evidence from Scotland reveals a greater extent of Norwegian settlement. Scandinavian place-names in Ireland outside of the main Viking towns indicate a greater degree or rural settlement, especially along the east coast, than previously thought.[23]

Settlements, of course, did not mean that wars ceased or that all contact remained peaceful; Irish chronicles continued to refer to the Vikings as 'foreigners'. In 998

Brian, the son of Cennédigh better known as BrianBorú, won an important victory for the Irish over the 'foreigners of Dublin'. Yet in 1000, the residents of Dublin gave hostages to Brian to secure the city, which relied upon goods and supplies from natives in the surrounding countryside. There are all kinds of problems with viewing Viking invasions and Viking settlements as belonging to separate periods, especially because the chronology of both could vary so much from place to place. Rivalries between Norwegians and Danes factored into these different chronologies, not to mention those raiding parties that acted outside the auspices of any established political authorities. Still, this long period of contact between Scandinavia and the British Isles helped to facilitate the movement of people from one region to the other, though most of the flow occurred in the direction of Britain and Ireland. As much as the Vikings are known for raids and plunder, through their settlements they brought wealth and trade back into the economy in ways that definitely benefited the local population. Probably the greatest impact that the British Isles had on the Viking settlers would be their conversion to Christianity, which helped ensure the continuing influence of the church and the monastic ideal for the remainder of the medieval period and, unfortunately, the eradication of whatever sources would tell us more about the pagan beliefs and practices that preceded this change.

The church and the monastic ideal

The mission of George, bishop of Ostia, to the Mercians during the reign of Pope Hadrian I (772–95) illustrates the ongoing efforts of the Roman Church to expand its influence in the eighth century. The monastic ideal best embodied in the foundations of St Columba, held special appeal for Irish Christians, but the Latin form of Benedictine monasticism quickly caught on in the Anglo-Saxon kingdoms and contributed heavily to the cultural revival known as the Northumbrian Renaissance of the seventh and eighth centuries. Michael Drout has referred to this period as 'the Golden Age of Anglo-Saxon monasticism'.[24] Through its monasteries, England joined Ireland in the preservation and furtherance of an artistic and literary culture, despite the lack of political unity.

This movement, which started in the age of Bede, culminated in the intellectual reputation of Alcuin of York, who went on to establish a palace school for the great Frankish king Charlemagne in 781. Monastic education flourished elsewhere in the Isles as well, as revealed, for example, by recent archaeological evidence of a monastic school at Inchmarnock in Scotland, where inscribed slates demonstrate lessons using both Latin and ogham writing.[25] In ninth-century Wales, the term 'metibion lleyn', which T. M. Charles-Edwards has translated as 'sons of literature', was a common description of members of a Christian community below the level of abbot or bishop.[26] An older contemporary of Bede, St Aldhelm (c. 639–709), a noted scholar and author of an important treatise on the monastic ideal, De Virginitate, hailed from the monastery of Malmesbury in Wessex. Aldhelm studied at Canterbury with the Greek scholar, Theodore of Tarsus, before spending thirty years as abbot of Malmesbury and ending his life as bishop of Sherborne. Aldhelm's De Virginitate and Bede's Ecclesiastical History of the English People are only two examples of original prose works composed by monks during this period, including a number of other treatises by Bede that ranged from saints' lives and biblical commentaries to scientific treatises. In the early twentieth century, the Benedictine scholar Francis Aidan Gasquet discovered in the monastery of St Gall in Switzerland a biography of Gregory the Great written at Whitby in 713. Monks produced not only the gorgeous illuminated manuscripts such as the famous Book of Kells and Lindisfarne Gospels, but also poetry of great power and suggestiveness that reveals something about the nature of their religious beliefs. For example, the cross appears as an image of triumph rather than suffering and even takes on anthropomorphic qualities in the following:

> Yet lying there   for a long time
> I gazed in sorrow   at the Savior's tree,
> until I heard   this highest rood
> begin in speech   to speak these words:
>
> 'It was many years ago   – I yet remember –
> that I was hewn down   in a corner of the holt
> torn away from my roots ...'[27]

Monasteries suffered a decline as a result of the devastation of the Viking raids that began at Lindisfarne in 793. An attack on Bede's former monastery at Jarrow quickly followed the raid on Lindisfarne. The monastery founded by Columba at Iona suffered from a Viking raid in 806 that killed sixty-eight residents of the community. Vikings burnt the monastery on Inishmurray Island off the west coast of Ireland in 807. Thus began a period in which monastic communities needed to remove to remote locations if they were to survive at all, leading to a concomitant decline in monastic culture throughout the British Isles.

Early signs of a cultural and religious revival occurred during the reign of Alfred the Great, who patronized learning and scholarship, as well as churches and monasteries. Alfred's reign prepared the way for a new era in the history of the English church. He sponsored an ambitious programme to have important Latin works translated into English. Alfred is personally credited with translating several works, including Gregory the Great's *Pastoral Care* and Boethius's *Consolation of Philosophy*. The installation of a relative of his biographer Asser as archbishop of St David's in Wales indicates Alfred's close association with the Welsh church. However, St David's was only one of two archbishoprics extant in Wales at this time (the other being the see of Gwynedd), and Alfred's influence only went so far. The laws of Hwyel the Good (c. 880–950), issued in 928, for example, call for the right of each king to determine the claims of the church to its land upon his ascension to the throne.

During the reign of Edgar (959–75), a new reform movement began under the leadership of Dunstan, archbishop of Canterbury, Aethelwold, bishop of Winchester, and Oswald, bishop of Worcester and, after 972, archbishop of York. These men modelled their ideas for monastic renewal on that which had begun at the French abbey of Cluny earlier in the ninth century. The Cluniac reform movement developed in response to the perceived laxity that had emerged among increasingly wealthy monasteries. The movement also reflected a reaction against lay influence over the church, the abbey of Cluny owing allegiance solely to the pope at a time when most abbots also served as lay vassals to a king or lord who, at times, might even be at odds with the pope or the church hierarchy. William, Duke of Aquitaine, had founded the abbey in 909 but provided for its spiritual autonomy at the same time. The monastic revival in Britain, which included a major boom in monastic construction overseen by Aethelwold, culminated in a 973 document emanating from Winchester called *An Agreement on the Way of Life for the Monks and Nuns of the English Nation*, which demonstrates the strong influence that continental practice had on the English reformers.

The monastic revival of the tenth century led to a new renascence of cultural activity as well, building upon the literary achievements and translations of Alfred's reign. As one might expect, religious works such as sermons and devotional tracts featured prominently among the compositions that survive from this period. But the main purpose of the reformers was to change the habits (pun intended) of monks and nuns. In the early stages of British monasticism, the sixth-century monk Gildas had written his rules on penance, laying down strict guidelines for the behaviour of monks and the consequences of any moral lapses. For example, Gildas stipulated that

> a presbyter or deacon committing natural fornication or sodomy who has previously taken the monastic vow shall do penance for three years. He shall seek pardon every hour and keep a special fast once every week except during the fifty days following the Passion. ... He shall have his bed meagerly supplied with hay. ... He shall at all times deplore his guilt from his inmost heart. Above all, let him show the readiest obedience. After a year and a half he may receive the eucharist and come for the kiss of peace and sing the psalms with his brethren, lest his soul perish utterly from lacking so long a time the celestial medicine.

Yet, Gildas had wanted to punish not only sins, but the mere intentions to commit sins such as sodomy: 'If a monk (merely) intends to commit (such) a sin [natural fornication or sodomy] he shall do penance for a year and a half. The abbot has authority, however, to modify this if his obedience is pleasing to God and the abbot.' Such information must have depended on confession and the trust that individual monks had in their abbots to not impose too harsh a penance for such a confession, but abbots must also have depended on the desire of individual monks to overcome such impulses and willingly submit to a penance imposed upon them that would help them to atone for their sin and get right with God. This was the spirit that the ninth-century reformers had in mind in their efforts to revive the original spirit of the monastic ideal.

The late Anglo-Saxon period: War and changing political realities

The monastic revival could not have occurred without the aegis of kings like Alfred and Edgar, who ruled during relatively stable periods compared to those which preceded and followed them. It is easy in a survey text (or course) to gloss over the violent, turbulent, and uncertain nature of Anglo-Saxon politics in the tenth century, giving a false sense of the extent to which the kings of Wessex had gained control of the kingdom and could now be confidently listed in any succession chart for the history of the monarchy. Wessex's authority was not guaranteed just because it was the one kingdom that remained relatively intact after the first century of Viking invasions. A similar distortion occurs in Irish history, where Brian Ború is portrayed as a high king of Ireland to create something of a nationalist legend analogous to the myth surrounding Alfred the Great in England. Ireland remained a fractious society divided among numerous petty kings exercising direct if informal control over separate rural areas. In tenth-century Wales, Hwyel the Good achieved a degree of political unity that had not previously existed, passing his kingdom along to his son, Owain ap Hywel in 950; but this unity did not last either, as Gwynedd reasserted its independence during Owain's reign.

One of the ways in which these kings, beginning with Alfred, sought to curb disorder in their own kingdom was to pass laws that reaffirmed the importance of lordship, designating authority to their most powerful supporters. Law codes of the period also imposed fines intended to limit the extent of blood feuds, which remained part of the culture. For example, the early-seventh-century laws of Ethelbert of Kent stated:

> If anyone kills a man, he is to pay as an ordinary wergild 100 shillings.
>
> If the slayer departs from the land, his kinsmen are to pay half the wergild [man-price].
>
> If a freeman lies with the wife of a freeman, he is to atone with his wergild, and to obtain another wife with his own money, and bring her to the other's house.[28]

Family rivalries extended to the level of kings themselves, with weaker kings always susceptible to challenges from relatives, rivals, or, barring domestic drama, foreign invaders. For example, Aethelstan (r. 924–39) had to fight off a challenge from Aethelwald, the son of his father's second wife, and only succeeded to the throne upon the death of his younger stepbrother.

Aethelstan, building on the achievements of his father, Edward the Elder and his aunt, Aelthelfleda, exercised authority over much more of England than had Alfred. He added control over Northumbria to that over the rest of the previous kingdoms of the heptarchy. Still, Aethelstan remained wary of his own nobles who were capable of, at any moment, throwing their support to a rival, while simultaneously being on guard against foreign invasion. He came to prefer residing in Mercia instead of Wessex. He brought an alliance together to repulse a joint invasion by the British kings of the Scots and Strathclyde and the Norse king of Ireland at the Battle of Brunanburgh, the title of an important poem that provides key insights into the changing political realities of the tenth century while reaffirming the importance of war for shaping those realities. The poem indicates the importance of the growing alliance between Mercia and Wessex and, like an Anglo-Saxon *Iliad*, celebrates an important military victory while reflecting an emotional sense of the cost and tragedy of war in the lives of the young men killed as a result. Aethelstan brought about a greater degree of unity than had existed under Alfred, but had the Battle of Brunanburgh (and possibly any number of additional battles for which no poems have survived) turned out differently, this would not have been the case.

Meanwhile, Aethelstan's successors, Edmund I (939–46) and Eadred (946–55) continued to fend off Viking raids, while guarding against internal threats; Edmund was assassinated by an exiled thief named Leofa. Prior to his death, he had seen much of the Danelaw, which his predecessors had largely conquered, fall into the hands of an invading force from Dublin led by Olaf Guthfrithsson. The *Anglo-Saxon Chronicle* records that Edmund regained these lands in 944, after which he conquered a land identified as 'Cumberland', which he ceded to Malcolm, the king of the Scots, in exchange for a military alliance. This did not prevent Olaf Sihtricson, a cousin of Olaf Guthfrithson, from renewing his attacks on the Danelaw during the reign of Eadred. The *Chronicle* reports that Eadred also launched a brutal attack on Northumberland when the people there threw their allegiance to a rival king, Eric. They eventually made their peace with Eadred, but not before they had slaughtered one of the king's garrisons.

Wales also continued to experience both internal and external conflicts in the third quarter of the tenth century after the death of Hywel, both in the south and over Gwynedd in the north. Gwynedd suffered separate invasions in 961, 962, and 967, the last by an English army under Aelfthere, the ealdorman of Mercia. Internal divisions in Ireland over the title of high-kingship dominated the tenth century, alongside the continuation of the Viking threat.

The role of war as the locomotive of the history of the kingdoms of the British Isles continued as a result of a new wave of Viking invasions from Denmark that plagued England during the reign of Aethelred the Unready (968–1016) (actually, 'Aethelred Unraed', an ironic sobriquet that literally meant 'noble council, no council', but the more apt modern nickname has stuck). Marginal annotation in the *Anglo-Saxon Chronicle* from this period refers to invasions as an almost daily event.[29] Attacks on Anglesey in 971 and 972 resulted in a renewal of tribute payments to the Danes, a major theme in English history over the next several decades. The English did sometimes fight back; a contemporary poem on the Battle of Maldon, fought between the East Saxons and the Danes in Essex in 991, pays tribute to the valiant but unsuccessful efforts of the Saxons to defeat the invading army. The poem recounts the appearance of a Viking messenger on the shores of the kingdom demanding tribute in exchange for protection. In a Churchillian response,

> Brythtnoth raised his shield, waving his slender spear; angry and resolute, he answered: ... Viking messenger, go back and give your people news of hatred and defiance – for here with his troops stands a dauntless earl who intends to defend this country, Ethelred's realm, the people and land of my lord.[30]

A series of attacks on Wessex around Christmastime in 1006 caused such widespread destruction that the *Anglo-Saxon Chronicle* says that every shire in Wessex became afflicted with the burning and pillaging by the Vikings, the chronicler reporting that people wondered how they would ever get rid of them. The answer came the next year; the cost was 30,000 pounds.

The state of warfare that ensued between the English and the Danes culminated with the death of Aethelred's son, Edmund Ironsides, in battle in 1016 and the accession of the Danish king, Cnut, to the English throne that same year.

This may have been a blessing. Cnut's peaceful reign contributed to England's economic prosperity. He preserved order and maintained Anglo-Saxon institutions and traditions while putting an end to the fighting. He even married Aethelred's widow, Emma of Normandy, in 1017, the year following Aethelred's death. The sources do not portray Emma as marrying Cnut from a position of weakness, as she was safely ensconced in Normandy at the time of the marriage negotiations, in which she is credited with securing a promise that only her future sons would inherit the kingdom, ruling out Harold, Cnut's son by a previous marriage. Emma is also reputed to have played a role of power and influence during Cnut's reign and may have acted as regent when he was away from England.

Cnut had won the English throne by conquest, but he intended to keep it by adapting himself to Anglo-Saxon ways and traditions. Recognizing the superior wealth of the kingdom that he had conquered, Cnut made England the centre of his empire and resided there for most of the time. Already a Christian, Cnut proved loyal to the English church and the papacy as well. The English clergy supported him, seduced by rewards of land and money. But Cnut's dynasty did not long survive his death in 1035. His two young sons succeeded him peacefully, but by 1042 both had died without heirs, the throne reverting back to the West Saxon heir, Edward, the son of Emma and Aethelred.

The nobility expected Edward to provide continuity and hoped that he would affirm the past political and religious traditions of the country. But Edward had spent his formative years in Normandy, making some Norman influence inevitable. Gradually, as native bishops and archbishops died off, Edward began replacing them with Normans. Edward retained the Saxon nobility, but surrounded himself with Normans at court and employed them in his household. This soon began to alienate some of the native earls, particularly Edward's brother-in-law and the strongest among them, Godwin of Wessex. An issue regarding the succession may have led to a rebellion directed against the king in 1051. According to the *Anglo-Saxon Chronicle* it had resulted from 'the foreigners' turning Edward against the native earls after a dispute in Dover that had resulted in the deaths of almost forty men. Godwin and Edward were soon reconciled, but the events of 1051–2 had created a level of distrust between Saxons and Normans that would persist throughout the reign.

In the medieval period, hereditary descent constituted only a part – and a relatively small part at that – of the criteria used to determine legitimate kingship; who would rule England at any given time was an open question influenced by a combination of hereditary right, the approval of the leading men of the kingdom, the military power of the claimant to the throne, the wishes of the previous king, and the approval of the church. Ever since the reign of Alfred, earls and other members of the nobility served at the pleasure of the king and collected taxes for him. Anglo-Saxon political culture thus already resembled that of the Frankish kingdom that has come to be designated by the modern term of 'feudalism'. Possession of the land, on which all power and wealth were based during this period, ultimately derived from the authority of the king, who expected political and military service from those who held it. Since the church held land, it too could be considered as falling under royal control, its bishops and abbots vassals of the king as much as representatives of the church. The role of the king's council, the Anglo-Saxon 'witan', was to advise and serve the interests of the king, not to act as an independent body.

Upon Edward's death in 1066, Harold Hardrada, the king of Norway, sought to follow in Cnut's footsteps and restore England to Scandinavian hegemony. A second claimant to the throne, Godwin's son, Harold of Wessex, was the most powerful man in England and had the support of the Witan and, he claimed, the blessing of the deceased king Edward. The victor, however, would be Duke William of Normandy, who would bring a new dynasty – and a new era – to the British Isles when he invaded England in 1066.

FIGURE 7 *Historical re-enactors recreate the Battle of Hastings, 14 October 2012.*
Oli Scarff/Getty Images News.

4

Conquest, colonization, and culture:

The High Middle Ages from 1066 to 1348

Normans and English, incited by different motives,
have written of king William: the former have praised him to
excess; extolling to the utmost both his good and his bad actions:
while the latter, out of national hatred, have laden their
conqueror with undeserved reproach.
WILLIAM OF MALMESBURY, *Chronicle of England,* c. 1125

The Norman Conquest of England

After the death of Edward the Confessor in 1066, Harold of Wessex was in the best position of the three claimants to the throne. Unlike William of Normandy and the Norwegian king, Harold Hardrada, he was already present in England. Furthermore, a group of leading nobles quickly crowned him king. Harold was an exemplar of the tradition of West Saxon rule in England. Despite being betrayed by his brother Tostig who aligned himself with Harold Hardrada, Harold of Wessex defeated their combined forces at the Battle of Stamford Bridge on 25 September 1066. If he had defeated William, history might remember him, along with Alfred the Great, as one of the great kings of English history.

Instead, William put an end to Harold's brief reign on 14 October 1066 at the Battle of Hastings. Upon hearing of Edward's death, William began putting together an army of infantry, cavalry, and archers that drew soldiers from nearby Brittany, Flanders, and other parts of France as well as his native Normandy. William was as determined to punish Harold – whom he regarded as flouting a personal oath sworn on his 1064 visit to Normandy – as he was to assert his own claim to the English throne. While Harold was occupied with the Norwegian invasion of northern

England, William prepared his fleet and his army to sail for the southern coast of England once the winds shifted in a favourable direction. They did so in time for William to land at Pevensey Bay near the coastal town of Hastings, located at the entrance to the Straits of Dover.

After the Battle of Stamford Bridge, Harold marched his weary army south and had barely begun to establish a fortified position at Senlac Hill near Hastings when William's army attacked. According to the *Anglo-Saxon Chronicle*, not all of Harold's army had arrived by the time the battle started. Some of Harold's earls rode on horseback, but he mainly depended on his infantry and the tactic of forming a 'shield wall' strong enough to repulse their attackers. At Hastings, the Norman cavalry only broke through the Anglo-Saxon shield wall after Harold's death on the battlefield left his army devoid of a leader. According to one tradition, Harold's wife or consort, Edith the Fair, identified the body and persuaded William to allow her to have it buried at Waltham Abbey. Despite this account, more than a century later Gerald of Wales reported a curious legend that King Harold survived the Battle of Hastings and escaped to Chester, where he lived for a long time as an anchorite hermit below the church of St John's, the remnant of a hope and desire for a surviving Saxon king in the dark days following the Norman Conquest.

The early phase of Norman rule in England was accompanied by William annexing the land he had conquered and transferring ownership to his leading barons under terms typical of the system known as feudalism, reinforced by William's claims of continuity based on his assumption of the throne by hereditary right. William may have intended to rule according to Anglo-Saxon traditions, but the consequences of his reign justify his actions as a 'conquest' of England, as he placed the sceptred Isle under wholly foreign rule, failing to retain any English statesmen. The establishment of Norman rule throughout England took the outward form of a castle-building programme, especially in the North at York, Durham, and Newcastle-upon-Tyne. It took the Normans longer to subdue the North than southern England, even though William took extreme measures to do so in 1069–70, sending small bands of troops throughout Yorkshire to devastate the local population. After the murder of Robert de Comines, whom William had sent to control the North, William pursued a scorched earth policy dubbed the 'harrowing of the north', resulting in the establishment of Norman lordships whose charge was to maintain and augment control and protect the kingdom from Scottish, Danish, or Norwegian invasion. David Douglas remarks in his biography of the Conqueror, 'So terrible was the visitation that its results were still apparent twenty years later.'[1]

Then, in 1071, William turned south to put down a rebellion whose leaders, Hereward and the Earl of Morcar, took refuge in Ely. Hereward's opposition to Norman rule became immortalized in *The Deeds of Hereward*, written in the following century during the heyday of the Norman aegis, when it was perhaps safe to allow acknowledgement of a worthy enemy. Guerrilla warfare by Anglo-Saxons against their Norman overlords continued throughout William's reign, despite the harsh repression of these early resistance movements in the years immediately following the conquest. In 1072, William sent an emissary named Ralph to Durham to secure the allegiance of its inhabitants. The chronicler Simeon of Durham reports that Ralph experienced an inexplicable weakness in his back that prevented him from getting out of bed to collect the tribute that William was demanding from the people, an affliction that miraculously disappeared as soon as he had left the diocese. Nonetheless, by 1073 William had secured rule over vast areas of Britain, including some territory in Wales.

In 1068, William had managed to acquire an oath of allegiance from Malcolm III, the king of Scotland. However, Malcolm was married to Margaret, the sister of Edgar the Atheling, the nephew of Edward the Confessor. Therefore, Malcolm's children were heirs of the previous ruling English dynasty, the House of Wessex. As a result, Malcolm might have felt a modicum of allegiance to the traditional Anglo-Saxon nobility. He also greatly resented the encroachment of Norman armies into his territory and began making retaliatory raids into northern England, according to William of Malmesbury, in the hopes of exacerbating the English king's anxiety. To make matters worse for William, the Danes launched another invasion of English territory in 1085. Henry of Huntingdon says that the threat from Denmark was serious enough to compel William to bring over numerous soldiers to England from the Continent. In 1093, William's son, William II, known to history as William Rufus, accused Malcolm of swearing a false oath and sent a force against him led by Robert Mowbray, the Earl of Northumberland. Malcolm met his death in the ensuing Battle of Alnwick, but two years later, Mowbray himself participated in a revolt against William II. William remained sensitive to the ability of the opponents of Norman rule to find refuge in Scotland when necessary. Thusly, the Scots and the people of northern England continued to cause problems for William the Conqueror and his successors.

In only two decades, William the Conqueror dramatically transformed the political culture of England and so firmly consolidated and augmented Norman rule there that the power of future kings could only be challenged by Anglo-Normans who were beneficiaries of the conquest or who had a connection with the Norman royal family. William had ordered a nationwide survey of his new kingdom that resulted in the famous Domesday Book of 1086; the process of counting and recording the resources and possessions of England and its subjects strongly buttressed the centralized power of the monarchy. William also stipulated that all military service owed to any of his English vassals needed to take place in the armies of the king, another example of the augmentation of centralized power. Finally, William extended his authority over the English church as well, speaking to his recognition of the overt opposition many native churchmen felt over the dispossession of the land of the Anglo-Saxon nobility. Still, for the next 100 years, his successors concentrated on consolidating their power in England prior to the expansion of Anglo-Norman rule over Ireland.

The Anglo-Norman Conquest of Ireland

In eleventh- and twelfth-century Ireland, local Irish kings contended for power, with different kingdoms frequently gaining and losing power vis-à-vis other fiefdoms throughout this epoch. The combination of the decentralization of power and the possibility of exploiting local rivalries made Ireland a target for invasion should any foreign king prove bumptious enough to undertake the task. However, William I and his successors were too preoccupied with establishing their control over England and defending their border with Scotland to concern themselves with Ireland. Insofar as

William and his dynasty showed any expansionist proclivities, Wales would take
first priority over Ireland based on its geographical proximity. Once Anglo-Norman
barons, the feudal hierarchy ensconced by William I, gained a foothold in Wales,
however, it was natural that they would soon develop propinquity with Ireland.
During the twelfth century, Anglo-Norman barons gained a greater amount of
autonomy during the tumultuous reign of Stephen (r. 1135–54), who required their
support in his civil war against Matilda, the daughter of King Henry I (r. 1100–35)
(see below). This series of events delayed the Norman Conquest of Ireland for a full
century after the Conquest of England. This could occur only once an English king
felt secure enough in power and had sufficient military prowess to consummate
an invasion. Even then it came about not as a result of a premeditated plan, but in
response to indigenous Irish elements.

In 1170, after a conflict broke out in Ireland between Dermot Mac Murrough of
Leinster and Tiernán O'Rourke of Breifne, the English king Henry II (r. 1154–89)
launched an invasion of Ireland. The ostensible purpose of the invasion was to bring
Dermot back to his confiscated lands. The dispute between Dermot and Tiernán was
subsumed under a larger struggle for political control of Ireland between the northern
king, Murtough MacLochlainn of Ailech, and the king of Connaught, Rory O'Connor.
Mac Murrough had aligned himself with MacLochlainn, while O'Rourke counted
himself among the supporters of O'Connor. O'Rourke also had a personal vendetta
based on the fact that Dermot had kidnapped his wife and would be satisfied with
nothing less than Dermot's total downfall. Dermot originally sought the assistance
of allies from the Norman lords in Wales, but the aforementioned provision dating
to the reign of William the Conqueror that vassals of the English king could only
provide military service in royal armies helped to ensure Henry's involvement.

Henry was anxious to check the unbridled power of his Welsh vassals and had
already sent royal constables to oversee their castles in an effort to trammel their
autonomy. Like William's invasion of England in 1066, Henry's military foray into
Ireland carried with it the imprimatur of the papacy. To strengthen this Rome–
London axis, Henry had purportedly been given the right to rule Ireland and reform
its church in a document known as *Laudabiliter*. This document, in turn, was based
on the theoretical right of the papacy to bestow territorial possessions on worldly
rulers based on a forged document of the eighth century known as the Donation of
Constantine.

Henry, who had not accompanied the initial invasion fleet, arrived himself in
Ireland near Waterford on 17 October 1171. The *Annals of Ulster* record that Henry,
accompanied by a fleet of 240 ships, 'came to land at Port-lairgi and received the
pledges of Munster. He came after that to Ath-cliath and received the pledges of
Leinster and of the Men of Meath and of the Ui-Briuin and Airgialla and Ulidia'.
The Irish church, surprisingly, was not hostile to the cause of the English king.
Furthermore, Henry's personal presence in Ireland after 1171 inspired respect from
lesser Irish kings who thought Henry might prove capable of inculcating order on
the island. Even those who did fight back were not unified enough to put up a strong
enough resistance to the invasion. As in England, some residual resistance followed
the initial success of the invasion, but by 1175, when Henry asserted his feudal
rights over Ireland at the Council of Gloucester, his position in Ireland was firmly
established.

The Norman Conquest of Ireland had analogous consequences to William the Conqueror's invasion of England, at least in the area of Ireland under Anglo-Norman control. As in England, the Normans brought over their own ruling class, who received land grants from the king. Henry essentially adopted an attitude towards the Anglo-Norman barons in Ireland similar to those whom he supported in England and Wales, as well as those who had become vassals of the Scottish kings in the twelfth century. As in England, royal vassals could practice subinfeudation, the practice of dividing one's lands held as fiefs from the king among vassals of their own, but these lesser vassals were still not permitted to fight in private armies but only in the armies of the king. A Welsh earl named Richard FitzGilbert de Clare, better known as 'Strongbow' was among the vassals of Henry who accompanied the invasion of Ireland. Strongbow married the daughter of Dermot Mac Murrough and inherited his kingdom upon the death of his father-in-law. It was Strongbow's marriage and concerns about his possible stake to the kingship in Ireland which facilitated Henry's decision to personally take charge of Ireland. Henry's invasion of Ireland represented an important turning point in the relationship between Ireland and England, but English monarchs did not always exercise their claims over the island and it would take until the late seventeenth century for the entire island to come under English control.

Kingship and medieval political culture in Scotland and Wales

The Norman Conquest had profound implications for both Scotland and Wales as well, the latter of which William I invaded in 1081. During the reign of Constantine in the early tenth century, the precedent had been established for the coronation of the Scottish king at Scone, on a chunk of red sandstone that became known as the 'Stone of Scone'. A century of royal nonentities followed, however, until strong kingship finally began to emerge from the Scots during the reign of Malcolm II (r. 1005–34). Malcolm, according to the Scottish chronicler, John of Fordun, began his reign by obtaining the consent of the leading chieftains of the kingdom as a condition for accepting the throne; they not only approved his accession but subordinated the hereditary succession to his line. By this time, the practice of rival chieftains raiding and plundering one another's territories had made some kind of centralized authority desirable. According to James Fraser, such raids emanated primarily out of private feuds and tribal vendettas, as opposed to the result of standard political or economic motives for expansion. Thus, it was going to take a strong centralized authority to inhibit these deeply ingrained premodern practices.[2]

Malcolm II bestowed the borderland known as Cumbria in northwest England upon his grandson Duncan without the consent of the Anglo-Saxon king Aethelred. However, this area was still vulnerable to attack by the Danes and prone to internal disorder, leading Malcolm to bring 'down great part of [his] army with woeful slaughter'. In 1039, in the brief interregnum between the death of King Cnut and the accession of Edward the Confessor, Malcolm's grandson, the Scottish king Duncan attempted to invade England but suffered a humiliating defeat at Durham.

The usurper Macbeth had hoped to succeed to the throne when Malcolm II died, but was himself killed in battle in 1057.

With the death of Malcolm III in 1093 (which even the anti-Norman chronicler Simeon of Durham regarded as a blessing because of the havoc the Scottish king wreaked in northern England), Scottish kings began to concentrate on consolidating their hold on their own territory and enhancing their power in Scotland. Malcolm's successors, particularly Edgar (r. 1097–1107) and Alexander I (r. 1107–24) began to develop a system of defence which relied on knights resident in the royal household under the charge of a constable appointed by the king. David, prince of the Cumbrians and the younger brother of Alexander, augmented his clientele to include vassals from England and Flanders. In 1124, David became king and introduced a series of Norman reforms in Scotland, including a greater reliance on written records, the construction of castles for defence, and the granting of special privileges to Scottish boroughs. Border conflict between England and Scotland continued, with one notable episode occurring in 1174 when a group of English nobles took it upon themselves to organize a force at Newcastle-upon-Tyne to put a stop to Scottish raids into English territory. Their success against King William I of Scotland inspired a poem that appeared in the *Chronicle* of Pierre de Langtoft:

> King Henry is glad of the deeds of the men of the North;
> He has so well rewarded them with rich gifts,
> That all the others throughout his kingdom
> Are come to the King to be at his will.[3]

The English chronicler William of Newburgh remarked upon the Scottish soldiers' refusal to leave the battlefield upon William's capture. These soldiers were even joined by those who had not been present but came as fast as they could to share the fate of their defeated hero.

In the Magna Carta of 1215 (see below), King John of England agreed to respect the rights and liberties of the new Scottish king, Alexander II (r. 1214–49), and to return his sister and other hostages to him. This was a sign that the border wars between England and Scotland were finally starting to wind down. Alexander began to concentrate on extending his rule over the Scottish Highlands instead of below the Anglo-Scottish border. As part of his efforts to expand northward, Alexander II challenged Norwegian control over the Hebrides and the Isle of Man, which were both added to the Scottish kingdom under his successor, Alexander III. In 1266, King Magnus VI of Norway agreed to the Treaty of Perth, ceding his remaining claims to Scottish territory, which now fell entirely under the jurisdiction of the Scottish king, making him a worthy rival to the king of England. One advantage that the kings of Scotland had over the kings of England in this period was that their power was not diffused and they had less to deal with from refractory subjects.

In contrast to Scotland, Wales had yet to emerge as a separate independent kingdom by the time of the Norman invasion. After the Norman Conquest, Wales was roughly divided into three types of territory: those under direct Norman rule; those areas where the Normans ruled indirectly and received tribute from Welsh princes; and the Welsh principalities that remained independent kingdoms. The three main independent Welsh kingdoms were the northwestern kingdom of Gwynedd,

Powys in the east, and the southern kingdom of Deheubarth. After the Norman Conquest, in general, the Anglo-Normans controlled the south, while Welsh princes continued to rule in the north. But the Earl of Chester on the border of northern Wales was given a modicum of latitude to augment Anglo-Norman authority over Wales as much as possible.

In Wales, the Norman Conquest coincided with the life of Gruffudd ap Cynan, who would have a great influence on Welsh history and the relationship between England and Wales. Gruffudd ap Cynan sought to take Gwynedd back from the princes of neighbouring kingdoms who had gained control there. The close connections between Ireland and Wales are accentuated by an examination of Gruffudd ap Cynan's early life, which he spent in Ireland. He was not the only one vying for control of Gwynedd, however, as the Norman earls of Chester and Shrewsbury made inroads in the region in 1098.

In his efforts to regain Gwynedd, Gruffudd ap Cynan received the support of Gruffudd ap Rhys, prince of Deheubarth. Gruffudd ap Rhys was forced to flee to Ireland from the Anglo-Norman de Montgomery brothers, who launched their own revolt against the recently crowned Henry I (r. 1100–35) in 1101. Henry stymied their revolt and launched his own attack on Wales. Henry's invasion caused enormous devastation and many casualties. Gruffudd ap Rhys returned from Ireland and made another attempt to establish a strong native-ruled principality in Wales in Deheubarth. For a time, having made peace with Henry I, he succeeded in suppressing the challenges of rival princes, but he rebelled against Norman rule the year after Henry died in 1136. His rebellion was short-lived, however, due to his own death a year later.

The attempt to establish English hegemony over Wales did not always come in the form of armed warfare; in 1188, Gerald of Wales tells us, Baldwin, the archbishop of Canterbury, travelled to Wales to meet with Rhys ap Gruffudd and other leading members of the Welsh nobility. The Welsh were extremely anxious to prevent Baldwin from visiting the see of St David's, lest it lose its independent status and become subordinated to Canterbury. Ten years later, however, an English invasion resulted in the slaughter of 3,700 Welsh soldiers, while, according to the contemporary English chronicler Roger of Wendover, the English suffered only one casualty that resulted from friendly bow-fire.[4] Then in 1211 King John led an English army into Wales in which he 'penetrated in great force into the interior of that country as far as Snowdon, destroying all the places he came to; he subdued all the princes and nobles without opposition, and received twenty-eight hostages for their submission for the future'.[5]

A new Welsh hero had emerged in Gwynedd around this time to stake his claim to a large portion of Wales in the figure of Llywelyn ap Iorwerth or Llywelyn the Great (c. 1172–1240). In 1221,

> Llewellyn king of Wales, with a large army, laid siege to a castle called Buet (Builth); Reginald de Brause, whose town it was, earnestly besought assistance from the king that by his means the siege might be raised, as he was not able to effect this by his own means. The King, therefore, as he ought not to desert his nobles, marched thither with a large army, and raised the siege, the Welsh, as was their custom, taking to flight. The king then marched towards Montgomery with his army, ordering all the property of the Welsh which they met with, and their cattle, to be collected for the support of his followers who were with him.[6]

Llywelyn the Great continued to intermittently fight the English and, although he eventually reached a truce with Henry III, by 1267 his grandson, Llywelyn ap Gruffudd was strong enough to gain recognition as Prince of Wales from the Welsh princes, except from Maredudd ap Rhys. In the Treaty of Montgomery of 1267, Henry III acknowledged his authority in exchange for an annual tribute of £12,000. His status within Wales made Llywelyn exceedingly dangerous from the perspective of the next English king Edward I (r. 1273–1307), who had him declared a rebel in 1276.

In August 1277, Edward invaded Gwynedd with an army of 15,000 infantry, 9,000 of whom were Welsh, and 800 knights. Edward secured Llywelyn's allegiance in the Treaty of Aberconwy, but no other Welsh princes signed the agreement. The remaining princes would find themselves conquered within seven years, leaving the English in control of Wales for the first time in history.

By 1284, the number of kings and the definition of kingship had both 'narrowed decisively' (in the words of Robin Frame).[7] Wales remained politically fractious, not fully absorbed into the English kingdom, but not politically united under a single Welsh king either. Between the kings of England and Scotland, two rulers had essentially established their authority over the British Isles. These areas were also subordinated to the influence of a feudal political culture emanating from England. For instance, it became increasingly common for rulers with any claim to authority throughout the British Isles to have men willing to take up arms under the insignia of their ruler, to support a system which resembled the network of lord–vassal relationships characteristic of feudalism rather than the more traditional system of alliances based on kinship, marriage connections, and reciprocal gift giving that characterized the early medieval period. It is to a closer examination of the English political culture that prevailed in the twelfth and thirteenth centuries that we now turn.

English political culture, 1100–1273

In England, the Norman Conquest had not clarified the issue of monarchical legitimacy, but only served to muddy the concept further because William's own alleged 'right' to the throne was predicated upon the competing claims of hereditary right and foreign conquest, which had seemingly overridden the tradition of election and coronation which ensconced Harold on the throne. If anything, William's invasion had established the principle that might makes right and opened the door for future challenges to any ruler too weak to defend his claim militarily. The allegiance that vassals owed to their lords rested not only, or even primarily, on the sense of honour involved in the oath of homage and fealty which they took, but also on the respect that they had for their lord or king in a political network that relied so heavily on interpersonal relationships. William I exacerbated the succession issue further by bequeathing his Norman duchy to his oldest son, Robert, and the English throne to his younger son, William Rufus, thus dividing his land between them and weakening the position of both.

Henry I's reign (1100–35) saw the granting of town charters as a further means of enhancing royal authority within his kingdom. Another change implemented by Henry was the practice of sending itinerant justices throughout his kingdom to hear civil and criminal cases to expand royal justice. The Normans retained the Anglo-Saxon administrative districts of 'hundreds', which presented those accused of the most serious crimes for trial when the judges arrived on their circuit. Lesser cases were heard in the monthly hundred court sessions that were held throughout the year. Each case would be heard by twelve freeholders, or freemen, the origin of our modern jury system. The north remained a matter of special concern for Henry, though Judith Green describes his policy there as 'reactive' rather than proactive.[8] In other words, Henry responded in the north when he needed to put down open rebellion, but was mainly content to maintain the status quo there because of his ambitions in France, where he sought to combine once again the titles of King of England and Duke of Normandy that William the Conqueror had sundered and given to his sons William Rufus and Robert.

Henry I also landed himself in the middle of an altar-throne kerfuffle known as the investiture controversy. This controversy was the product of a reform movement burgeoning in Rome that began in the mid-eleventh century and aimed at ending church abuses such as simony (the buying and selling of church offices) and nepotism. Other aims of the movement included enforcing clerical celibacy and reducing if not wholly eliminating the ability of secular rulers to appoint clerical officials to positions within the church, a widespread practice known as lay investiture. When one of the reformers, a monk named Hildebrand, was elected to the papacy as Pope Gregory VII in 1073 he made a strenuous effort to prevent the German emperor, Henry IV, from practising lay investiture, but Henry refused to stop the practice and ended up invading Rome and chasing Gregory to Naples, where he died in 1085. The papacy could not afford to cede complete control over church appointments to secular rulers, as was implied by Henry's stance and victory, so Pope Urban II launched a new initiative in 1095 designed to restore the primacy and prestige of the sullied papacy. He called for a crusade and exhorted Christians from across Europe to join in an effort to liberate the Holy Land from the Muslim Turks.

Urban had just appointed the highly respected Anselm, an Italian cleric serving as abbot of Bec in Normandy, as archbishop of Canterbury, who was soon driven into exile by William Rufus, who refused to accept the appointment. Henry I and Anselm negotiated the Concordat of London, a compromise agreement essentially recognizing the right of the church to appoint its own officials, while giving the king the right to approve or veto those appointments.

Henry I had made a good start towards establishing a centralized monarchy and extending royal authority in England, but he died without a male heir and those efforts became temporarily derailed. Henry's daughter, Matilda, claimed her right to the English throne, but most of the English nobility supported Stephen of Blois, the grandson of William the Conqueror. They did so largely because they viewed Stephen as the statesman best able to maintain peace in the kingdom, though this did not stop them from appealing to baser motives by trying to gain lands or power in exchange for their support. New castles proliferated throughout England, built by nobles wishing to protect themselves from the forces of whichever claimant they failed to support, producing a general feeling of anarchy and civil war.

King David I of Scotland also took advantage of the problems of the English king by aligning himself with Matilda while seeking to expand his territorial claims along the border between the two countries. David had some success before his defeat at the 1138 Battle of Standard, a decisive victory for Stephen in the civil war.

In 1139, Matilda joined with her half-brother, Robert, Earl of Gloucester, in an invasion set upon dethroning Stephen and placing Matilda on the throne as her father's only legitimate heir. Matilda remained in England for nine years, during which she attracted enough support to keep pressure on Stephen but not enough to unseat him from the throne. Relations between Stephen and Matilda finally began to improve when Matilda agreed to relinquish her claim to the throne in exchange for Stephen's recognition of her son's right to succeed him.

Whenever monarchy is at its weakest, there appears the need to re-emphasize the values associated with a strong, legendary figure in the hopes that a new king will emulate their example and return the country to a golden age. It was during the reign of Stephen that Geoffrey of Monmouth, a Welsh clergyman, wrote his influential *History of the Kings of Britain*, a work which became the main source for the beliefs and stories associated with the mythic King Arthur. Matilda's son, Henry II (r. 1154–89), proved to be just such a figure. He dominated not only the British Isles during his tenure as king of England, but was a seminal force in French and European politics. Whatever harm Stephen's reign had done to the long-term prospects of the English monarchy, Henry II quickly undid through his strong and adroit leadership.

In addition to the power adhering to himself from being king of England, Henry also inherited the French county of Anjou and the duchy of Normandy, before gaining control over the duchy of Aquitaine in southern France by virtue of his marriage to his first wife, Eleanor, while staking his claim to Ireland after the invasion of 1170. Eleanor of Aquitaine (c. 1122–1204) had divorced her first husband, King Louis VII of France in 1152 after fifteen years of marriage, so her remarriage to Henry in 1154 was quite a coup for the new king of England. In fact, Henry sought to employ the military might of his English kingdom towards creating an English-led European empire. To this end, he sought to re-establish the principle that all military service must be performed in the armies of the king by issuing his baronial charters (*cartae baronum*) in 1166. These charters required his barons to inform him of the number of knights under them who owed military service, as well as the amount of service they owed. Fifteen years later, Henry completely reorganized his military administration in the Assize of Arms (1181), which made rank and wealth the criteria for determining the amount of military equipment each of his subjects was expected to possess. Henry also centralized the entire process of military recruitment from his highest ranking barons to the average freeman.

Furthermore, Henry laid the foundations of a royal bureaucracy, a policy reflected in the *Dialogue of the Exchequer*, written by his treasurer Richard Fitznigel between 1177 and 1179. Henry also continued the practice of his grandfather of sending itinerant justices throughout England to hear cases, after which they would consult each other in an effort to centralize Henry's legal administration on the basis of what would become the English Common Law. Henry's chief justiciar, Ranulf de Glanvill (1112–90), wrote a *Treatise of the Laws and Customs of England* that seems to have circulated widely based on the number of manuscript copies that have survived.

But Henry's attempt to extend his control over the English church and to subject English clerics to royal, instead of ecclesiastical justice, provoked the opposition of his archbishop of Canterbury and close personal friend, Thomas Becket. The Concordat of London had recognized the state as having control of the bodies of Christians and the church authority over people's souls. Becket affirmed the

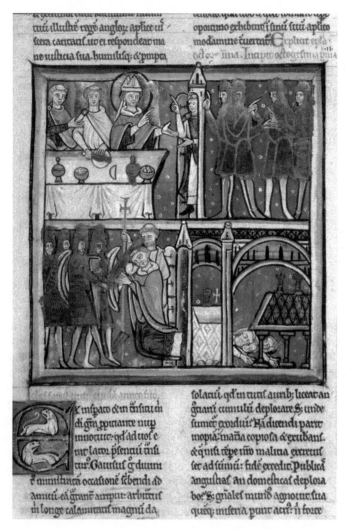

FIGURE 8 *Earliest known manuscript illustration of conflict between Henry II and Thomas Becket.*
Print Collector/Hulton Archive/Getty.

primacy of the church in both spiritual and secular matters.[9] Becket also claimed the right to appoint clerics to positions within the English church without royal interference, thus reviving the most contentious issue of the investiture controversy. Furthermore, Becket's excommunication of William of Eynsford, a tenant-in-chief of the king, flouted another previous agreement requiring royal consent for such an action, another indication that the Becket controversy involved substantive matters, as opposed to the simple issue of whether the state or the church had the right to try members of the clergy who had committed crimes against the state, which is generally seen as the main locus of conflict between Henry and Becket. Becket's challenge to Henry's authority resulted in his murder by four of Henry's knights in Canterbury Cathedral on 29 December 1170.

Henry emerged from the Becket controversy chastened but still strong. For the rest of his reign, with the nobility cowed and the church generally solicitous of Henry's support after his demonstration of penance after Becket's murder, the main threat to his rule came from his rebellious sons, who were exploited by Henry's estranged wife Eleanor, whom Henry kept imprisoned for the last fifteen years of his reign.

The reaction of the nobility to the growing power of the monarchy under Henry II came quickly during the reign of Henry's sons Richard I (r. 1189–99) and John (r. 1199–1216). In 1190, Richard embarked on the Third, or King's Crusade, and left his chancellor William Longchamp in charge of the kingdom. In Richard's absence, Longchamp faced opposition from the barons in England over his attempt to extend his power by taking control of as many castles as he could.[10] Despite John having been named Lord of Ireland by Henry II and Richard spending most of his reign outside of his English kingdom, Richard had no wish to cede royal control and even attempted to extend his authority over Ireland at John's expense. Furthermore, in 1198, Richard's justiciar, William Fitz-Peter, led an army into Wales to lift a siege against the Norman William de Brause by a Welsh king named Wenuwen.

In 1185 John had made the first visit to Ireland by a member of the royal family since Henry II's expedition of 1171. John returned to Ireland in 1210 to put down a disturbance among the Anglo-Norman nobility, using the opportunity to issue a decree extending English law to the areas under royal control in Ireland. But John had even greater problems with his barons at home, having forfeited most of his lands in France to Philip II, better known as Philip Augustus. John had increased his fiscal demands while reducing the amount of royal patronage to overcome his financial difficulties at home. His rebellious nobles complained about 'military services overseas, the Crown's exploitation of its feudal rights and the restrictions and savagery of the Forest Law'.[11] John may have been able to overcome these objections had he not suffered an ignominious defeat at the Battle of Bouvines at the hands of Philip Augustus in 1214 that further increased the contempt the nobility felt for John.

The struggle between the king and his Anglo-Norman barons reached an apogee when King John was presented with the Great Charter, or Magna Carta, on the field of Runnymede in 1215. The fame of Magna Carta rests primarily on the following provision:

> No free man shall be seized or imprisoned, or stripped of his rights or possessions, or outlawed or exiled, or deprived of his standing in any way, nor will we proceed with force against him, or send others to do so, except by the lawful judgment of his equals or by the law of the land.

Magna Carta speaks of John's unpopularity with the Anglo-Norman nobility of his kingdom and his own archbishop of Canterbury, Stephen Langton, whose initial appointment to the see John had opposed, but Igor Djordjevic argues that the main transformation of John into the bête noire of English history occurred only with his appearance in the Robin Hood stories of the fifteenth century.[12] Djordjevic argues that contemporaries would have seen John's struggle with Pope Innocent III and Philip II of France as far more significant than Magna Carta, which John was quick to repudiate, despite the fact that the charter he signed contained a promise not to revoke nor diminish any of the privileges granted therein. Magna Carta also guaranteed the freedom and liberties of the English church, but Pope Innocent's rejection of the charter put him on the opposite side of his previous protégé, Langton. John might have salvaged something of his reign, but he died a year later at Newark Castle in October 1216. John's reputation may have indeed been exacerbated as a result of his portrayal in the Robin Hood stories, but the chronicler Matthew Paris wrote later in the thirteenth century that 'foul as it is, Hell itself is made fouler by the presence of John'.

It should be mentioned that Matthew Paris was writing in the context of the continuing struggle between the monarchy and the nobility that plagued the reign of John's son and successor, Henry III (r. 1216–73) as well. Most notably, a group of barons led by Simon de Montfort (c. 1208–65), the Earl of Leicester and Henry III's brother-in-law, issued in 1258 a document called the Provisions of Oxford, which sought to reiterate and in some cases expand the principles contained in the Magna Carta. After Henry abrogated the Provisions in 1262, backed by King Louis IX of France to whom both sides had appealed for arbitration, the barons finally took up arms against the king in 1264. After a major victory by the rebel barons in May 1264 at the Battle of Lewes, followed by a fifteen-month period in which Simon de Montfort became the de facto ruler of England, the king's son, Prince Edward escaped from captivity and rescued the monarchy. In 1265, at the pivotal Battle of Evesham, Edward crushed the army of Simon de Montfort and followed up his victory with cruel reprisals. In the words of a contemporary account:

And then Sir Edward and his side pursued those who survived all over the fields, and everywhere killed them. Within the town, the abbey courtyard, the cemeteries and the monastery church the dead bodies lay thick and dense on the ground like animals, and, what was horrendous to see and painful to speak of, the choir of the church and the inside walls and the cross and the statues and the altars were sprayed with the blood of the wounded and dead, so that from the bodies that there were around the high altar a stream of blood ran right down into the crypts.[13]

Edward I and the conquest of Wales

After crushing baronial resistance in England at Evesham, Edward turned his attention to Wales, where the English had never completed their conquest of the territory and where they had found that they could not wholly rely upon the allegiance of the Marcher Lords appointed to represent them. Meanwhile, Llywelyn ap Gruffudd had built on the achievements of his predecessors in Gywnedd to augment his authority in the direction of asserting his rights over the land along feudal lines similar to principles employed by the English and Scottish kings. Even the terms of military service – six weeks owed in the army of the king – matched the typical stipulation in most feudal contracts. Edward summoned Llywelyn to pay homage to him in England, but when Llywelyn failed to appear, Edward immediately decided upon an invasion of North Wales.

The turning point of Edward's conquest of Wales was the attack on Llywelyn in 1277, as he was able to push Llywelyn back into Gwynedd and isolate him from the other Welsh princes. But he still had to deal with those princes, who resisted Edward's attempt to impose English law in Wales, meaning that Llywelyn had not yet been deprived of his base of support. Edward therefore assumed direct control over northern Powys and the Welsh territories of Rhos and Tegeingl in northeastern Wales. But there was still more work for Edward to do to conquer Wales, especially after some of the same Welsh princes, including Llywelyn's brother Dafydd, turned against Edward due to a perceived lack of reward for their support. Furthermore, Edward was no longer content to rule Wales by proxy through feudal lords who only owed a nominal allegiance to the king; he now sought to place Wales completely under English legal jurisdiction.

After the death of Llywelyn at the Battle of Orewin Bridge in 1282, Edward gained more extensive control in Wales than that held by any previous English king. David Carpenter describes the death of Llywelyn and its aftermath:

> On 11 December, in the valley of the Irfon near Builth, with 'the flower of his people killed', he was cornered while fleeing through the woods and run through with the body by a man at arms, Stephen of Frankton. His head was cut off and sent to Edward, who ordered it to be put up on the Tower of London, crowned with mocking ivy. It was a pathetic and tragic end to so glorious a career.[14]

But Edward's victory had cost him a fortune, which necessitated greater funds for the subsequent occupation. The war of 1282–3, which outlasted Llywelyn's death because it had primarily been precipitated by a revolt of other Welsh princes to begin with, was particularly onerous. It finally ended with the death of Dafydd in October 1283, but it was with the death of Llywelyn that 'the Welsh polity which he and his family had fostered was uprooted'.[15]

John Davies has provided a useful reminder that the conquest of Wales was anything but inevitable and that had Edward failed, its history might have turned out much differently:

> Edward I, the most powerful of the medieval kings of England, was obliged to devote the entire resources of his kingdom to the task at a time when that kingdom was united under his authority. If the Principality had survived his reign, it is difficult to believe that there would have been in England in the following century the unity or the determination to undertake its destruction. The political history of Wales from 1066 onwards may be viewed in terms of an increasing subjection to the power of the crown of England, with the victory in 1282–3 as a natural and inevitable climax; on the other hand, it would be legitimate to stress the increasing ingenuity of the leading Welsh rulers, to emphasize the potential of the embryonic state created by them, and to consider its downfall, not as an inevitable happening, but as the result of an unexpected combination of factors.[16]

Edward's success in Wales had been greatly assisted by a kind of logistical revolution where the king used the practice of purveyance to obtain supplies for the army shipped directly from the counties. Chester and Dublin became the main centres from which supplies were distributed. Private merchants supplemented those supplies obtained under the purveyance system by transporting additional goods straight to the army, but they became necessary as the government's purveyance efforts took effect with great success.[17] Edward kept his army well fed and well paid, guaranteeing his ability to keep them in the field. Edward's invasion of Wales was one of the most systematic and thoroughly organized campaigns in the history of medieval warfare that had lasting ramifications for future military tactics and strategy, relying heavily on infantry and archers, supported by axe-wielding soldiers who cut down the forests that the Welsh liked to use for cover.

Edward also demonstrated an awareness of the importance of having the backing of the church behind his expansionist policy, using the church hierarchy to get his message out to the lower clergy who would elucidate and validate his military policies to the people. David Bacharach describes the process by which he did this:

> The government used two methods to mobilize the administrative resources of the church, both of which relied heavily on the English episcopate. The first and more common method was to order the chancery to issue a royal writ to the archbishops of Canterbury and York requiring these two leading prelates of England to issue orders to all of the bishops, monasteries, and other ecclesiastical jurisdictions within their archdiocese to carry out the royal will regarding the dissemination of information, that is royal propaganda, and the organization of religious rites on behalf of soldiers in the field. The second method was to issue this same information and orders to all of the leading ecclesiastical officers of the kingdom in the form of a circular writ, thereby bypassing the archbishops.[18]

At the same time, he also began to restrict money leaving the country for Rome, starting with the Crusade tax, according to Kathryn Hurlock, because he required funds for the conquest of Wales.[19] Once he had defeated the Welsh, Edward used an extensive castle-building programme as his major means of extending and maintaining control there, much as William the Conqueror did in England following the Norman invasion. This construction programme proved enormously expensive, however, and some castles were left uncomplete at the end of Edward's reign. The occupation of Wales was costly in other ways as well, taking manpower away from the armies Edward needed to fight wars in France and, later, Scotland.

The most significant change that Edward contributed to the political culture of England was the establishment of Parliament as a permanent feature of the political landscape during his reign. Edward viewed Parliament as an aid to royal authority, not as a check upon its power. His so-called Model Parliament of 1295 only derives the name because of all of Edward's parliaments, it most closely resembled the form that Parliament eventually took. It is not at all clear that Edward ever intended this; he simply summoned the members of the political community to a particular assembly he thought best suited what he hoped to accomplish at that particular meeting. In 1295, he must have desired broader representation from within that community because he issued a writ to the sheriff of Northamptonshire – and similar ones to seventeen additional sheriffs – stating that 'we require you to cause two knights from the aforesaid county, two citizens from each city in the same county, and two burgesses from each borough ... to be elected without delay, and to cause them to come to us at the aforesaid time and place'. However, he reversed himself just two years later, asking the sheriff of Yorkshire to elect 'two of the most upright and law-abiding knights of the county; and they are to have full power for themselves and the whole county'. The main purpose for which Edward wished to consult his parliaments was to gain support – financial and political – for war in France. Edward was more forceful when it came to the church, on which he placed such financial demands as to raise considerable objections from the hierarchy, not only in England but in Rome. But he could be high-handed with the nobility as well – anyone who did not accede to his financial demands in Parliament risked accusations of treason.

By 1294, Edward had provided order and stability in the aftermath of the baronial rebellion without significantly alienating his subjects or his nobility, as John and Henry III had done. The wars that Edward had fought in Wales and France had earned him a reputation as one of the foremost warrior-kings of his age. His conquest of Wales led contemporaries to compare him to the legendary King Arthur, who was also said to have unified England and Wales under his rule. Edward embraced the comparison, travelling to Glastonbury in 1278 to observe the reburial of the alleged remains of Arthur and Guinevere and forming his own round table in Wales in 1284. In Scotland, the death of Alexander III in 1286 left Scotland with a three-year-old queen, Margaret, the Maid of Norway, as a result of the earlier deaths of Alexander's two sons and his wife, also named Margaret. The Scots managed to extract from Edward a promise to respect Scottish independence in the Treaty of Northampton in 1290; whether or not Edward was going to honour that promise remained to be seen.

The Scottish wars of independence

Edward started by meddling in Scottish politics, securing the appointment of own protégé John Balliol as acting king. Wendy Stevenson argues that the Scots had already taken a dim view of Edward's rule prior to this based on their knowledge of how oppressive Edward was towards his English subjects, something of which they wanted no part even in the form of his indirect influence through Balliol. Nonetheless, a number of Scottish nobles swore allegiance to Edward and allowed him to mediate in the succession dispute.

All indications are that Balliol intended to rule in his own right and not merely as a pawn of Edward, despite his pledge of allegiance to the English king. But Balliol had made the mistake of accepting the Scottish throne from Edward on terms that included the phrase 'saving our right and that of our heirs when we shall wish to speak thereupon'.[20] Edward first seized the opportunity to further exercise control when he agreed to hear Scottish legal cases referred to him at Westminster, contrary to Scottish tradition. Edward had agreed to respect Scottish law and customs in the Treaty of Birgham of 1290, which the Scots now accused him of flouting. It seemed that Edward intended to establish the same kind of judicial control over Scotland that he had previously applied to Wales after 1284. When he summoned Balliol himself to appear at his English court, Balliol responded by attempting to terminate the English yoke as soon as Edward was away in France.

By 1296, England was at war with Scotland. Edward, as he had done for the war in Wales, used the church to justify his war against Scotland, even accusing the Scots of having violated English churches in the North.[21] Edward's propaganda also used specific crusading language to encourage support for the Scottish wars. Edward struck the first blow at Dunbar, defeating a Scottish army and putting an end to the Scots' acceptance of Balliol as their overlord.

In 1297, Edward, having just begun his war with Scotland, went to Flanders to join Count Guy in his rebellion against their mutual enemy, King Philip IV (the Fair) of France. While Edward was in Flanders, William Wallace rose to a position of authority in Scotland, having gained the support of both the Scottish people and the ruling class. A Scottish army headed by William Wallace and Andrew Murray soundly defeated the English at the Battle of Stirling Bridge on 11 September 1297 to regain the initiative. Edward returned, however, and crushed Wallace's army on 22 July 1298 at the Battle of Falkirk in central Scotland 20 miles (32 kilometres) northeast of Glasgow. Scotland's political leadership accepted peace terms with Edward in 1304, even though Wallace attempted to keep the resistance movement going. Wallace would be captured and killed by the English in 1305, but he had established a precedent for the leadership of an independent Scottish kingdom that Robert Bruce would utilize in his own propaganda that portrayed him as following in Wallace's footsteps.[22]

In fact, it was Bruce's decision to seize the Scottish throne in 1306 that initiated the next phase in the war. The change in political leadership did not produce immediate victory; Bruce lost the next battle at Methven, but recovered to win the Battle of Loudon Hill in 1307. Edward I died in 1307, but the English mustered forces for another invasion under Edward II in 1314.

For his invasion of Scotland in 1314, Edward II put together a huge multinational army, which, according to the fourteenth-century Scottish poet John Barbour, consisted of troops from Wales, Ireland, Poitiers, Aquitaine, and Bayonne, in addition to those from England. Barbour, in hyperbolic pastiche, estimated the total English force at 100,000, with 40,000 of them on horseback, compared to Bruce's army of 30,000; Scottish historians estimate that the English outnumbered the Scottish by something like 17,000 to 8,000, but with four times the number of cavalries. The English also relied on a large number of Welsh soldiers, who could not have been too happy to fight alongside their former enemies and apparently demonstrated this through intemperate drinking. Recognizing English military superiority, Bruce had avoided a pitched battle since Loudon Hill and mainly fought using guerrilla tactics. The main advantage that the Scots had was the terrain at Bannockburn, the narrowness helped to negate England's numerical advantage while the sogginess of the ground prevented English horses from gaining a firm footing for the attack.

It is only in retrospect that the Scots achieved their independence in 1314, for the English did not acknowledge this at the time nor did the Scots believe that the English were done fighting. The two sides did not negotiate a truce until 1328. But the Scottish victory at Bannockburn had legitimized the regal authority and dynasty of Robert Bruce, who followed up Bannockburn by raiding northern England while his brother Edward launched an invasion of Ireland that came very close to succeeding. While Edward diverted the English from Scotland with his Irish invasion, Robert Bruce made the transition from war leader to king, appointing an administration that was largely clerical in nature. He granted charters to Aberdeen (1318) and Edinburgh (1328) that indicated that the new Scottish monarchy would rely on the towns as much as the nobility. He ruled through a Scottish parliament, which passed a new series of laws that provided a new legal framework for early modern Scotland. Perhaps most importantly, he further unified the country, rewarding his supporters without pursuing a harsh vengeance on those who had opposed him in the past. In the Declaration of Arbroath (1320), the Scots stated unequivocally that 'as long as but a hundred of us remain alive, never will we on any conditions be brought under English rule'. The Declaration also expressed the wish that the English would leave the Scots in peace and be content with what they had. For the most part, the English did leave the Scots in peace, at least temporarily.

Literary and cultural developments in the High Middle Ages

The High Middle Ages produced a renascence in learning, a vibrant literary culture, and an artistic and architectural transformation that constituted what historians refer to as the twelfth-century Renaissance. The church remained at the centre of most cultural changes in the High Middle Ages, from the founding of new monastic orders such as the Carthusians and the Cistercians to the growth of pedagogy arising out of the cathedral schools and the first universities. The Carthusians and the Cistercians were among half-dozen new monastic orders that sought to restore monasticism to its original ideals and to free their orders from the taint of worldly corruption that had once again become associated with the Benedictines. But whereas the monasteries had exercised almost an exclusive monopoly on education in the early medieval period, by the twelfth century urban cathedral schools had become prominent. These schools contained the origins of the first universities. The main purpose of the cathedral schools and the universities remained the preparation of young men for careers in the church; most men did not seek an education unless they intended to pursue a clerical career. Frank Barlow noted the irony that girls could more easily obtain a secular education than boys because women in religious orders were not necessarily expected to have an education.[23]

St Anselm of Bec was one of the first theologians of the High Middle Ages to systematically use logic and reason in support of the Christian faith, an attempt at synthesis that culminated in the theology of St Thomas Aquinas in the thirteenth century. Anselm's biographer Eadmer captured the theologian's intention brilliantly:

> Owning in reason as in faith a gift from God, he was assured that the legitimate researches of the one can never be in conflict with the divinely authorized convictions of the other; and made it his task, not indeed to give a rational analysis of Christian doctrine for his method was not analytical but laboriously and fearlessly to follow up the deductions of reason, as knowing that their ultimate conclusion would be in perfect harmony with revealed dogma.

The writings of John of Salisbury (1120–80) and Gerald of Wales (1146–1223) reflect concerns about changing moral and political values that had accompanied the rise of the new secular monarchy that emerged under the Angevin dynasty founded by Henry II. John's most important work, the political treatise *Policraticus*, was written around

1159 to provide ethical guidelines for princes whose power the precepts of the church seemed unable to trammel. Gerald of Wales, although he is better known for his *Journey through Wales* and *History and Topography of Ireland*, also wrote a work towards the end of the twelfth century called *De Princpis Instructione* ('On the Instruction of Princes'), in which he uses morality tales and examples to illustrate the virtues that he wishes to inculcate in a prince or king to prevent him from becoming a tyrant.

Historical chronicles represented another major form of writing during this period. The problem with medieval chroniclers, as M. T. Clanchy has pointed out, was the fact that no one knew if they were telling the truth or not; the fabricated legends in Geoffrey of Monmouth could pass as historical truth while more-or-less factual chronicles might be distrusted based on a common belief that anything written down could not be trusted.[24] Those who wrote chronicles also sometimes wrote biographies and other works. Matthew Paris, a monk and chronicler who flourished at the Benedictine monastery of St Albans from 1217 until 1259, wrote highly favourable biographies of Stephen Langton and Thomas Becket. Medieval chroniclers often combined biography with history and did not exclude the workings of God from their treatment of history. 'Nor shall my history be wanting in thy praise, Wistan,' writes William of Malmesbury, before adding,

> I will not, I say, pass thee over in silence, whom Berfert thy relation so atrociously murdered. And let posterity know, if they deem this history worthy of perusal, that there was nothing earthly more praiseworthy than your disposition; at which a deadly assassin becoming irritated, despatched you: nor was there any thing more innocent than your purity towards God, invited by which, the secret Judge deemed it fitting to honour you: for a pillar of light, sent down from heaven, piercing the sable robe of night, revealed the wickedness of the deep cavern and brought to view the crime of the murderer.[25]

This period also saw the appearance of vernacular literature, in particular epic poems such as the *Orkneyingers' Saga* which deals with the tenth-century wars involving England, Scotland, and Denmark. Welsh tales such as the *Mabinogi* were collated and preserved in the early-fourteenth-century *White Book of Rhydderch* (in Welsh, 'Llyfr Gwyn Rhydderch'). These included the stories involving the mythical figure of Rhiannon. Readers are introduced to her in a story in which Pwyll, the prince of Dyfed, despite being in love with Rhiannon, gives her away to a visitor to whom he had promised the fulfilment of any request. In Ireland, poets such as Muireadhach Ó Dálaigh, who flourished in the early thirteenth century, demonstrated an original creativity and wrote on a wide variety of subjects. Much bardic poetry from medieval Ireland took the form of encomia directed at the king or patron that the poet served, of which the following line by Muireadhach is typical:

> Many a shaft with bright slender loop has been drawn by Cathal's tapering palm: the graceful palm of Cathal the Redhanded has cast a quick battle spear.[26]

Like the universities and Gothic architecture, romance literature came to the British Isles as a French import. Aquitaine was a main source of the troubadour poetry and romance literature of the twelfth century; Henry II's marriage to Eleanor and his own territorial possessions in France provided an entrance for this material into English courtly circles. English compositions in the tradition of French romance include *The Romance of Horn*, *The Lai of Haveloc*, and *The Folie of Tristan*, which is set in Cornwall and almost certainly derives from a Cornish tradition.[27] Of course, these secular works did not replace but rather complemented spiritual and devotional reading, which would have been readily available to the courtly lady and gentleman as well.

Judith Weiss notices that few new English romances appear after about the mid-thirteenth century after a promising start in the twelfth.[28] The intellectual and literary revival of the twelfth century did not come to a screeching halt in 1250, but there was a shift in the culture as a whole in the second half of the thirteenth century. The first indication of a change in the attitude of the church occurred in 1231 when Pope Gregory IX issued a new set of regulations for the University of Paris. In the same year, not coincidentally, Gregory established the Inquisition to combat heresy in Western Europe. During the twelfth century, the church had felt secure enough as an institution that it did little to employ extensive censorship or arrogate control over the curriculum at cathedral schools and universities. In the thirteenth century, the church began to feel threatened by the spread of the dualistic heresy of Albigensianism in southern France and the rise of a group of scholars at the University of Paris known as the Latin Averroists for their adherence to the rationalistic teachings on faith by the Spanish Muslim scholar Averroes (1126–98). Just as Thomas Aquinas was developing his brilliant synthesis of faith and reason in works like his *Summa Theologica*, the church issued a condemnation in 1277 of the rationalistic teachings of Averroes and some of the principles of Aristotle that Aquinas had incorporated into his synthesis.

As the papacy began to look askance at the increasing application of reason and the ideas of Aristotle to the Christian faith, English scholars such as Robert Grosseteste (c. 1175–1253) and Roger Bacon (c. 1220–92) developed a more empirical approach to knowledge that they confined to the natural world or what we would call science, leaving the teachings of the faith to the church as a separate branch of knowledge. Grosseteste and Bacon still ran afoul of the church for their teachings and ideas, which placed too much emphasis on reason and relied too heavily on Greek and Arab learning for the increasingly reactionary late medieval church.

The break with the prevailing system of medieval theology that attempted to harmonize faith and reason began with the transitional figure of John Duns Scotus (John 'the Dunce' of Scotland) (c. 1265–1308), who rejected the synthesis proposed by Thomas Aquinas because it subjected God too much to rational analysis and thus rejected the deity's power and freedom. The Englishman William of Ockham (c. 1285–1349) took the teachings of Duns Scotus even further in the direction of the separation of faith and reason, arguing that God was totally unfathomable to the understanding of human beings, which should be channelled in other directions while worshipping and believing in God on the basis of faith alone. Ockham ran afoul of the papacy on other matters, both for his defence of the doctrine of apostolic poverty, which struck at the wealth and property of the church, and for his defence of the right of English kings to tax the clergy without papal permission:

> For ... the pope does not have any power over the temporal goods given to the English churches, unless by human authority, and as the English kings have conceded it to him.[29]

By the end of the thirteenth century, the altar-throne rivalry had resumed apace. It would play an even larger role in the coming centuries, with the relations between English rulers and the papacy undergoing enormous strains that helped to prepare the way for the break with Rome under Henry VIII in the sixteenth century.

Social developments in the High Middle Ages

Virtually every textbook that deals with medieval social history includes some variant of the quote, attributed to a ninth-century bishop, that society in the Middle Ages consisted of three classes: 'those who fought, those who prayed, and those who worked the land'. However accurate this saying might have been in the ninth century, the High Middle Ages brought new social realities that included an emerging merchant class and the growth of a market economy. Christine Eisenberg, in her excellent book *The Rise of Market Society in England, 1066–1800*, suggests that it is entirely possible that

> with the Norman Invasion in the eleventh century, a specific form of feudalism developed in England that was more encouraging of the emergence of market-supported (and therefore flexible) trade than were the comparable governance and economic structures on the European continent.[30]

Trade between England and the Continent certainly predated the conquest, which would have only opened up additional opportunities; not only trade between England and Normandy or France, but trade with Italy and Spain also increased in this period. English merchants continued to utilize their Scandinavian trading contacts in the regions surrounding the North and Baltic Seas, while the Norman Conquest strengthened preexisting contacts with France and undoubtedly brought new ones. England's centralized government, beginning with the conquest and continuing with the support offered to towns and merchants by the monarchy from Henry I onwards, greatly facilitated the growth of trade. English merchants also benefited from the lack of any internal trade barriers, the security provided by Norman officials, and a centralized system of justice sponsored by monarchs such as Henry I and Henry II who took crime very seriously. The internal chaos of the civil wars of the mid-twelfth century did not eliminate trade or lead to the decline of towns, but it did encourage them to build stronger walls as they needed to look out more for their own defence.

The steady rise in the population also had a tremendous effect on English society and contributed to the change in the direction of a more market-oriented society, which flourished alongside the traditional feudal hierarchies and institution of serfdom that still kept many peasants tied to the land. Land was still the main source of power and income, giving feudal lords tremendous advantages, but even the management of their estates and their position in society was affected by the increased importance of trade and the rise of towns. Population growth certainly had something to do with the noticeable rise in prices that seems to have occurred in the late twelfth and thirteenth centuries that had landlords seeking to increase agricultural output still further.[31] Nor was the nobility as hostile to trade as is sometimes claimed. By the thirteenth century nobles were beginning to support their own boroughs as a means of eliciting additional revenue to supplement their landed income in an inflationary age.

Geographical mobility was a surprising feature of life in the High Middle Ages, mainly owing to the growth of towns and the rise of trade, which created new opportunities for travel and relocation. In addition, the Crusades outside of Europe and the general prevalence of peace and political stability within it provided additional inducements to travel. Certainly, in England large cities benefited from the internal stability following the civil war of the mid-twelfth century and its concomitant guarantee of royal protection. The city of York, for example, was transformed in the course of the High Middle Ages from essentially a fortified centre of royal administration into a thriving urban centre that featured new constructions of both religious and secular buildings from churches and monasteries to castles and hospitals.[32] York, like other towns, also sat in the midst of a large trading network that included the surrounding countryside and smaller market towns that area merchants would have included in their rounds in addition to the larger metropolis.

While the new opportunities that were opening up for merchants and towns provided the possibility that peasants could escape the countryside and gain their freedom from a life of perpetual servitude, those peasants that remained in the countryside did not all live exactly the same kind of life as one another. Wales had more individual family farms than England, whose land had been completely reorganized by William the Conqueror. William gave large tracts of land to his leading barons, who in turn divided their land among vassals who presided over the manors where most English farming was carried on. Most serfs received tracts of land within the widely utilized open-field system of agriculture, from which they derived all benefit from their usufruct. Instead of individual farmers cultivating their own fields, villages typically used collectively owned teams of oxen to plough large open fields that contained land called the desmesne whose produce belonged to the lord of the manor, alongside those strips of land adhering to individual peasants. Since these fields needed regular periods of rest to allow for the replenishment of nutrients required to grow crops, either one-half or one-third of the land was allowed to lie fallow each year; in the later three-field system, fields were rotated for spring and autumn planting and only remained fallow every third year.

Alongside those agricultural villeins or serfs who worked the land, each village or manor employed different individuals who might be called industrial villeins, including carpenters, blacksmiths, millers, brewers, cobblers and others who performed necessary tasks or provided necessary services. Some peasants, known as cottars, had no land of their own to farm and had to get by assisting others in the fields or finding whatever work they could. Sometimes this necessitated leaving the manor, or even drifting around the countryside to find work as shepherds, or in Wales and Ireland, as miners or peat-diggers.[33]

Marriage was, of course, the norm for most men and women in medieval society, with the exception of those who entered the church, of whom celibacy was expected, if not always practised. The arranged nature of most marriages, particularly those among members of the royal family and aristocracy, helped give rise to the courtly love tradition, which held that true love was only possible outside of marriage. Such a conception perhaps helped to legitimize adulterous relationships, though these probably would have occurred anyway, since they took place among the members of every social class. The medieval church looked suspiciously upon unmarried women because its conception of social order and the difference between the sexes included the necessity of placing women in a subordinate role to men. The exception to this rule would have been widows, who could exercise some independent authority on their own, for example, by taking their husband's place as a guild member after his death. If they did remarry, in some instances they could even transfer their guild membership to their new husbands if he practised the same profession.[34] When Eileen Power, among the first generation of twentieth-century scholars to specifically focus on medieval women's history, began to look she found evidence of women's heavy participation in trade and industry. In fact, she concluded:

> There was hardly a craft in which we do not find women. They were butchers, chandlers, ironmongers, net-makers, shoe-makers, glovers, girdlers, haberdashers, purse-makers, cap-makers, skinners, bookbinders, gilders, painters, silk-weavers and embroiderers, spicers, smiths and goldsmiths among many other trades.[35]

The centuries of the High Middle Ages were remarkably free of social strife or clashes between the aristocracy and peasants. Most conflict that did arise was of a political nature and occurred among members of the ruling class. In these prosperous times, lords proved remarkably amenable to negotiations with their serfs to grant them greater freedoms or the ability to market their own produce. Lords may have resented the growth of towns and the stipulation that an escaped serf could gain his freedom in a year and a day if he remained in a town undetected, but population growth ensured that there were plenty of labourers in both town and countryside. Generally, the more economically prosperous the area, the more privileges lords were willing to grant to their serfs.

Because Jews were excluded from careers in the church or state, they turned to commerce and moneylending, providing a valuable service to medieval society at a time when Christians were prohibited by the church from charging interest, which was equated with the sin of usury. Of course, this caused resentment among Christians who became debtors to Jewish moneylenders, from whom the church itself often borrowed money. Still, the Jewish population, which seems to have been almost nonexistent in England before the Norman Conquest, did fairly well under the Anglo-Normans. William initially invited a group of Jews to relocate from Rouen to London in the aftermath of the conquest. A delegation of Jewish bankers arrived in Limerick in 1079, probably also from Rouen. The London community appears to have prospered and become well established by the 1130s.[36] But the Jewish presence expanded beyond London under the Angevins beginning with the reign of Henry II. After that, we begin to see occasional signs of trouble and dismay among Christian institutions when they fell too heavily in debt to Jewish moneylenders. In 1173, the abbot of Bury St Edmonds dismissed his cellarer because he had incurred for the abbey a debt of £60; the chronicler Jocelyn of Brakelond says that the new cellarer, a Master Dennis, was able to reduce the debt to £30 by his measures of economy.[37] Yet at the same time Jewish merchants also were recognized as a necessity in many places. Kevin Down suggests that the expansion of agriculture that followed the Anglo-Norman invasion of Ireland in 1170 would not have been possible without the influx of capital provided by Jewish merchant bankers that entered Ireland at that time.[38] During the wars of Edward I, the Jews became targets of Edward's economic caprice and malice, first suffering enormous taxes and fines, followed by imprisonment, followed by their expulsion from England altogether, the result of religious prejudice, financial greed, and the unbridled power of the king.

In 1279, Edward I's Parliament passed the Statute of Mortmain to address one of the problems that over time had affected medieval economic and social life. Over the centuries, so many laymen had bequeathed land to the church out of pious devotion or in an effort to atone for their sins that the church had become the largest landholder in England, owning perhaps as much as a third of the total. This proportion was not uniform across the country; in places with the largest monastic estates, such as Kent where the archbishop of Canterbury had extensive manorial holdings, the percentage could be even larger whereas it was likely not as high in, for example, Sussex or Surrey.[39] The Statute of Mortmain decreed that in the future no landowner could give or bequeath land to the church without the permission of his lord since it involved the permanent alienation of the lord's land, which had only been given to his vassal on a conditional basis.

Edward took several additional steps to place restrictions on his nobility, including the Statute of Westminster (1285), which stipulated the circumstances under which a lord could confiscate land from a tenant and the Statute of Quo Warranto, which asked 'by whose warrant' landowners had possession of their land. The point of the statute was to force landowners to prove that they had received their grant from the king and to coerce them to apply for a new grant if they could not do so. Finally the Statute of Quia Emptores prohibited the future practice of subinfeudation, by which lords had divided their lands to gain vassals who owed them service. For some time, English kings had accepted scutage, monetary payments in lieu of military service, so that they could hire mercenary soldiers who might prove more reliable than the independent knights whose length of military service was restricted by feudal contract. As royal power increased, so did its supporters in the towns and boroughs who now found themselves included in Edward's parliaments as important members of the realm, alongside the nobility.

The weakness of Edward II (r. 1307–27) would provide the nobility with something of a reprieve from the harsh policies of Edward I, but by then they faced other problems. The fourteenth century began with a series of falling temperatures, crop failures, and epidemics that culminated in the plague known as the Black Death of 1348. In the midst of this precarious situation, the English monarchy embarked on a renewed war with France that involved intermittent hostilities that lasted more than a century and did much to shape the political culture of the fourteenth and fifteenth centuries.

FIGURE 9 Chronicles of *Enguerrand de Monstrelet (1357–1453)*, episode of the Hundred Years War, France, fifteenth century.
Photo 12/Universal Images Group/Getty.

5

Plague, politics, and power:

The later Middle Ages from the Black Death to the Wars of the Roses

Is all our travail turned to this effect?
After the slaughter of so many peers,
So many captains, gentlemen and soldiers
That in this quarrel have been overthrown
And sold their bodies for their country's benefit,
Shall we at last conclude effeminate peace?
Have we not lost most part of all the towns –
By treason, falsehood, and by treachery –
Our great progenitors had conquered?
O, Warwick, Warwick, I foresee with grief
The utter loss of all the realm of France!

WILLIAM SHAKESPEARE, *Henry VI, Part I*, Act 5, Scene 4

The Hundred Years War and its effects on political culture

Edward III (r. 1327–77) inherited the throne after the deposition and murder of his father, Edward II (r. 1307–27). He also inherited the long-standing rivalry with France over the territorial claims of the English kings there that dated back to the twelfth and thirteenth centuries. His immediate predecessors, Edward I and Edward II, had both gone to war in France to regain lands alienated from the English Crown by their predecessors. Edward began his reign in the shadow of his French mother,

Isabella, and her lover and consort, Roger Mortimer, who had made peace with France and Scotland. In 1330 Edward III asserted himself and emancipated himself from the influence of Mortimer and his mother. He then resumed the Scottish wars, winning an important victory at the Battle of Halidon Hill in 1333 that sent the young Scottish king, David II, the oldest son of Robert Bruce, into exile in France. He then resumed the French wars in 1337, initiating what would become known as the Hundred Years War.

Not long after the beginning of the war with France, Edward was having difficulty recruiting soldiers and persuading Parliament to grant additional funds for his campaigns. Edward held a great tournament at Windsor in 1344 in an effort to promote the chivalric ideals of knightly valour and drum up support for his French campaign. Edward even announced that he was going to revive the order of King Arthur's Knights of the Round Table. Edward himself was not an avid reader of chivalric romances, but the Arthurian legend was such a significant part of the political culture that he knew enough to realize how strong an appeal such a proposal would have.

Edward's troops still ended up at a tremendous numerical disadvantage in France, but they did have the advantage of a secret weapon: the longbow, the effects of which the contemporary French chronicler Froissart vividly describes:

> The English archers then advanced one step forward, and shot their arrows with such force and quickness, that it seemed as if it snowed. When the Genoese felt these arrows, which pierced through their armor, some of them cut the strings of their crossbows, others flung them to the ground, and all turned about and retreated quite discomfited. ... The English continued shooting, and some of their arrows falling among the horsemen, drove them upon the Genoese, so that they were in such confusion, they could never rally again.[1]

The French failed to rally against the English onslaught at the 1346 Battle of Crécy, the first major triumph of the war for either side. They regrouped in time to fight another major battle at Poitiers ten years later, but the English had retained their military and tactical advantage and dealt the French another crushing defeat.

The French king John II (r. 1350–64) signed a truce, the Treaty of Bretigny, in 1360 in which he acknowledged English control over Calais and Gascony. The reign of his successor Charles IV (r. 1364–80), which was characterized more by small skirmishes and guerrilla warfare than major pitched battles, did little to change the status quo. Tragedy did strike the English, however, with the untimely death in 1376 of Edward III's oldest son, Edward, the Prince of Wales, better known to history as the Black Prince (though this does not seem to have been a name used during his own lifetime). The Prince of Wales had led the march from Gascony that precipitated the tremendous victory at Poitiers and represented for many the heroic archetype associated with late medieval kingship. When Edward III died the following year, the throne fell to his eleven-year-old grandson, who became King Richard II.

In 1381, the levying of a new poll tax precipitated a major uprising known as the Peasants' Revolt, which was also the culmination of long-standing grievances dating back to Parliament's decision to freeze wages in a Statute of Labourers following the great mortality known as the Black Death of 1348 (see below). After taking their anger out on local magistrates, merchants, and aristocrats, a mob of peasants, primarily from Kent and Essex, marched on London, where they committed more murders and mayhem under their self-proclaimed leaders, Wat Tyler and John Ball. Richard, only fourteen years old at the time, surprisingly risked his personal safety to meet the rebels, successfully negotiating a sudden end to the uprising. In doing so, he temporarily gained the respect of the nobility, particularly when he reneged on his promises to redress the peasants' grievances. Tyler and Ball were executed, order restored.

After the promising beginning marked by his bold conduct during the Peasants' Rebellion, however, Richard did much to alienate the English nobility, including pursuing a peaceful policy in a stalemate during the Hundred Years War. In the course of his reign, Richard relied increasingly on his personal household for the administration of the kingdom, keeping his own counsel, while keeping the nobility and Parliament at bay. He conferred patronage on those with whom he had a personal relationship, including grants of titles, land, and monetary rewards.

Richard's opponents openly accused him of madness and partly justified their rebellion against him on those grounds. Richard undoubtedly displayed megalomaniacal tendencies that saw him demand greater and greater displays of homage and subservience from his nobility and members of his court. He had a massive throne constructed to elevate himself further in the eyes of his people and reinforce his power and majesty.[2] He had his political opponents imprisoned, executed, or exiled, including his cousin Henry Bolingbroke, the son of John of Gaunt, who rebelled in 1399 when faced with a decade in French exile.

The overthrow of Richard II bore some resemblances to the downfall of Edward II earlier in the century, but with one significant difference. Edward II was succeeded by his son, but Richard had no direct heirs. Henry of Lancaster, the son of John of Gaunt, seized the throne by force and was crowned King Henry IV (r. 1399–1413), after which he had to defend his throne against those who questioned the legitimacy of his title. His success in doing so went a long way towards establishing his legitimacy, because strength, rather than some abstract hereditary right, is what the English valued most in their ruling monarch. By the time of his death, no one questioned the legitimacy of his son, Henry V, not least because Henry V quickly displayed all of the attributes that defined late medieval kingship.

Opposition to Henry's rule did not merely derive from his usurpation of Richard's throne, but had more to do with the nature of his own regime. The revolt of Owain Glyn Dwr in 1400 is probably the exception, since Owain seized upon the opportunity of the dethronement of Richard to declare Welsh independence. To meet this threat and others and to secure his throne generally, Henry found it necessary to raise taxes, which did nothing to endear him to his new subjects. By 1406, he faced rebellion in England as well as Wales, leading Henry to turn to Parliament for assistance, thus restoring Parliament to the position it had attained before the autocratic rule of Richard II.

By the time of his death in 1413, Henry IV had left his son, Henry V (r. 1413–22) with a pacified country and a nobility that was anxious for a resumption of the French wars. Henry V quickly obliged them; to achieve victory, however, required the support from a broader cross-section of the population, as a result of the changing nature of late medieval warfare that assigned a larger role to the infantry as knights on horseback became increasingly vulnerable to pikes and arrows and more restricted by increasingly heavier armour. Given the weakening bonds of the feudal system and the fact that most of Henry V's soldiers were not members of the nobility, the king had to find ways to instil loyalty, esprit de corps, and martial valour in the soldiers who fought for him at Agincourt in 1415. Henry's personal charisma and the powerful, almost mystical, reverence people held towards the monarch played important roles in his success. The fact that Henry celebrated mass three times on the eve of the battle could have reinforced Henry's reputation for piety, although his intention in doing so was probably more personal in nature given the risks associated with late medieval warfare – even for kings, as Richard III would discover later in the century.

Perhaps we should not make too much of the role played by the inspiration of the king in leading his soldiers into battle as a factor in its outcome. Recent archaeological discoveries indicate that the English fought on more even numerical terms at Agincourt than had previously been thought. Still, the famous speech that Shakespeare puts in the mouth of the king in his play *Henry V* does much to capture the bond between 'we band of brothers' that the entire political and military culture of fifteenth-century England was designed to cultivate:

> We few, we happy few, we band of brothers;
> For he today that sheds his blood with me
> Shall be my brother; be he ne'er so vile,
> This day shall gentle his condition;
> And gentlemen in England now abed
> Shall think themselves accursed they were not here,
> And hold their manhoods cheap whiles any speaks
> That fought with us upon Saint Crispin's day. (Act 4, Scene 3)

As for the battle itself, Henry had marched his soldiers to Agincourt with the intention of employing a strategy similar to that which accounted for the great English victories at Crécy and Poitiers. Once again, English longbowmen, stationed on the two flanks of the attacking French cavalry, proved decisive in victory. The muddy conditions of the field slowed the French men-at-arms who trailed the cavalry, making them easy targets.

In the aftermath of the battle, Henry negotiated a peace that made him heir to the French throne, which fell to his infant son, Henry VI after Henry V's sudden death in 1422. But in the next decade, Joan of Arc emerged as a symbol of French patriotism, leading Charles, the French heir to the throne, to the city of Reims for his coronation as King Charles VII (r. 1422–61). Joan was ultimately captured by the Burgundian allies of the English and turned over to them for trial and execution as a heretic, but she had revived French morale by achieving enough military success to turn the tide of the entire war. By 1453, England, having seen its longbows surpassed by French cannons as weapons of destruction, retained the port of Calais as her only possession in France.

Military defeat, combined with the deteriorating psychological condition of King Henry VI, weakened the English monarchy. The English people had poured money into the royal coffers to finance a war that ended in a humiliating defeat, and the king, whose claim to the French throne had formed the primary basis for the conflict, took the brunt of the blame. The aristocracy, however, ended the Hundred Years War with their power in England intact. Deprived of opportunities for plunder and glory in France, they valued their power and prestige on their own estates all the more highly. To that end, they hired armed retainers, leading to the continuation of a militarized political culture that survived the end of the Hundred Years War in 1453. These hired mercenaries generally received an annual salary in order to secure their loyalty and availability, as well as daily stipends for time actually served in their lord's service. This system, referred to by historians derisively as 'bastard feudalism', however, did not so much cause a political crisis in England as it arose in response to one. Its negative reputation derives from a perceived corruption of a political–military relationship based on lofty principles of honour, duty, fealty, and humble obedience to one's social superior to a relationship centred on mercenary principles of monetary gain. However, in uncertain times marked by a weak central monarchy, anyone with political ambitions or simply with lands and position at stake naturally sought to form alliances with friends, neighbours, and kin to bolster their security.

Furthermore, the concept of feudalism and its attendant emphasis on loyalty and honour was not completely abandoned, however much these principles had declined from the golden age of chivalry in the eyes of contemporaries such as Sir Thomas Malory, the author of *Le Morte d'Arthur* ('The Death of Arthur'). The reality in the late fifteenth century was that the choice for aristocrats was not between an idealized form of chivalry and a bastardized version of it, but rather between a bastardized version of it and its death altogether. Bastard feudalism would probably not have such a bad reputation were it not associated with a period dominated by a succession dispute and the civil war known as the Wars of the Roses; but before we turn our attention there, let us look at the social and religious developments that affected this earlier period, as well as the political cultures of the rest of the British Isles during the period when England was at war with France.

The Black Death and social change in the fourteenth and fifteenth centuries

In the twelfth and thirteenth centuries, the increase in population in the British Isles had led to higher agricultural prices, making it worthwhile for peasants and landlords to cultivate marginal lands and enhance the value of land. Grain prices remained high in the early decades of the fourteenth century because crop shortages balanced any stagnation of population levels. But the extremely heavy rains in 1315–1317 caused floods that rendered many lands useless and washed away seeds necessary for the planting of the next year. The year 1316 saw wheat yields of about 55 per cent of normal, which was the lowest such figure in a 140-year period beginning in 1270.[3]

The outbreak of the Hundred Years War in 1337, therefore, increased taxation just as the climate was getting colder and wetter and the economic plight of the common people growing. Citizens of Carlisle in northern England turned to the king of Scots in the hopes of relief from the economic depredations of King Edward III, whose armies had become entangled in a conflict with the French. While Edward's army was winning the Battle of Crécy, the king found himself faced with a growing rebellion that emanated from Carlisle and spread across northern England. In one instance, residents of Newcastle diverted water from wells intended for a local friary supported by the Crown.[4] Commoners throughout England that autumn

> 'assumed to themselves the royal power', boarded ships provisioned for English troops in Gascony and the north of France, confiscated corn from town merchants and sold it to their townspeople at prices they deemed just and took over municipal governments.[5]

The Black Death of 1348 made these earlier difficulties seem mild by comparison.

Some historians no longer think of the Black Death as the defining event it was once considered to be, arguing that the political and social changes it precipitated would likely have occurred anyway and that the severity of the bubonic plague outbreak of 1348 and 1349 itself was exacerbated by preexisting conditions.[6] For example, geographical mobility, once thought to have been mostly a result of the plague, is now also known to have preceded it. Even before the plague, the authority that landlords held over their serfs or tenants varied according to individual personalities and circumstances; it was not uncommon for either free or unfree tenants to change residences multiple times in the course of a lifetime. Such geographical mobility, combined with the growing distinctions between free and unfree tenants, posed a threat to social harmony in country villages prior to the advent of the plague, but did not undermine it because social cooperation was still so important to the economic success of a village. Furthermore, as the earlier difficulties of Edward III indicate, expressions of political discontent did precede the arrival of the Black Death in England by several years.

Nonetheless, it is hard to argue that a plague that swept away 40 to 50 per cent of the population (numbers that have been confirmed by recent archaeological research) was not the most significant development of the century, if not of the entire late medieval period. The plague had a tremendous psychological impact, providing a powerful reminder of the omnipresence and inevitability of death and bequeathing a burdensome emotional legacy to those who lost loved ones and survived the catastrophe. Kinship bonds remained important, while the general sense of community within medieval villages remained intact, if it did not get stronger, among the survivors of such a devastating epidemic. Support from family and neighbours took on added significance in changing economic times. Most people remained in their native villages and tried to carry on as best they could. Such geographical mobility as did exist merely brought people into an existing network of village relationships, as opposed to upsetting or overturning established communities. Habits of deference die hard and many peasants continued to perform their yearly obligations and to observe manorial customs, even if they could have avoided doing so. They also continued to attend the semiannual manorial courts that dealt with minor village offences and disputes and that still provided justice for the majority of villages throughout England.

The plague had other effects as well, which in some ways improved the circumstances of those who survived it. Rents decreased and competition for labour put both peasants and workers at an advantage vis-à-vis their landlords and employers. The English Parliament passed the Statute of Labourers in 1351 in order to redress this disadvantage for the upper classes by freezing wages at pre-plague levels. However, those peasants brought up on charges of violating the statute tended to get let off with a nominal fine ranging from about six pennies to two shillings (twenty-four pennies). Moreover, the nobility had more of a vested interest in attracting additional labour to their depleted estates, leading them to circumvent the law as much as peasants did. Increased movement of tenants provided opportunities for the renegotiation of leases, which, in these economic circumstances, led to both lower rents and less onerous labour obligations. In 1352, the carter John Boltash of Wroughton pled guilty to receiving two bushels of wheat for ten weeks' work, a substantial increase over the one bushel he previously received for ten weeks' work.[7] This rise of payment-in-kind was fairly typical of the period, judging from other similar cases brought before the courts. By 1400 most landlords had begun to transfer virtually all labour services to cash rents, leading to the almost total abolition of serfdom. The redistribution of land in Wales following the failed revolt of Owain Glyn Dwr in the early fifteenth century led to new tenant–landlord relationships and the end of serfdom there as well.

After the Black Death, peasants also began to marry without bothering to ask the lord's consent. The increased freedom accorded to peasant women to accept (or reject) marriage proposals contrasted sharply with the further restricting of the personal freedom of aristocratic women that occurred at this time. As economic challenges presented themselves to the aristocracy, the choice of a marriage partner, if anything, became even more important, with marriage becoming the sole purpose of aristocratic daughters from a male perspective.

The Peasants' Rebellion of 1381 is generally viewed as a case of rising expectations on the part of the lower classes, as opposed to the result of deteriorating economic conditions, but falling wheat prices after 1375 began an economic downturn that contributed to peasant discontent at that time. By the end of the century, however, the economy had recovered somewhat, largely as a result of the viability of wool prices as a supplement to rural income that encouraged the transfer of much land from arable to pasture. When the wool trade began to decline in the first half of the fifteenth century, the growth of a native cloth industry began to make up the difference. Wages actually increased steadily in the fifteenth century, with workers earning higher real wages in this period than at any other time until the twentieth century.[8] Increased output meant a higher standard of living as married couples began to limit family size in response to the larger demographic crisis (whether consciously or unconsciously).

The plague had, therefore, not effected radical or sweeping social changes, while some of the above changes may have occurred over a longer period of time without it. It cannot simply be neglected, however, and its effects may have been more subtle and long-lasting than historians can measure. Apropos, the peoples of the British Isles responded positively and resiliently to the demographic crisis of the fourteenth century and did not sink into a depression with irremediable effects. If some towns and villages disappeared because of a high mortality rate, others survived and thrived, continuing to serve as markets that linked town and countryside in an interlocking network that made the economy viable for centuries to come, particularly in England. Goods found consumers in a growing economy that combined cash payments with barter exchanges, even if, or more likely because, there was a decline in the total number of people overall.

After the Hundred Years War ended in 1453, there followed a period characterized by civil war and disorder in the countryside during which peasants, more vulnerable because of the weakness of a centralized government to which they could appeal, lost ground to the nobility, who became all-powerful within their local fiefdoms. Landed aristocrats spending more time at home took greater care, for example, to enforce their legal rights to keep peasants out of forests and parks, which were reserved for the rich. The lack of centralized authority seems to have led to a significant increase in crime, making it perilous for peasants even to take their goods to market. Murder rates were on the rise, including a spree that afflicted the valley of Weardale in County Durham in 1471–2.[9] The fact that Thomas Malory included a promise not to rape in the oath taken by King Arthur's knights in his 1461 Le Morte d'Arthur indicates that rape was also perceived to be more common at that time. It was not that rape by knights did not occur before; Chaucer describes one incidence of rape by a knight in 'The Wife of Bath's Tale' from The Canterbury Tales. Legal protections existed for women from sexual violence, but then, as now, accusations undoubtedly represented a small fraction of the number of crimes committed, convictions even less. Late medieval society placed a premium on virginity, so assaults on young, unmarried women tended to be taken more seriously by the judicial system and by society as a whole, in addition to being physically more verifiable.[10] Nonetheless, Parliament passed legislation aimed at preventing the kidnapping and forced marriages of widows in both 1382 and 1453 in response to a changing political culture deeply affected by the prolonged war between England and France. Of course, once married, women legally fell under the almost complete control of their husbands and had little recourse if they turned out to be physically abusive.

John Wycliffe: New ideas about the relationship between church and state

The fourteenth century brought changes in religious ideas as in so many other areas, which in turn greatly affected the political culture of the period because of how closely church and state had been linked in the political culture of the High Middle Ages. In large part, the new religious sensibilities of the period came as a response to the effects of famine, plague, and warfare that led some people to question whether or not they were living through the end times. Between 1305 and 1417 the church hierarchy seemed to distance itself from the people at a time of great spiritual need.

The 1305 transfer of the papacy from Rome to Avignon, located just outside the southern boundaries of French territory at the time, became a scandal for many Christians. For roughly the first three-quarters of the fourteenth century, the English kings viewed the Avignonese popes with suspicion because of their ties with France, especially after the beginning of the Hundred Years War in 1337. In fact, Parliament responded to the situation in 1351 by passing a Statute of Provisors that limited papal appointments to positions within the English church. Parliament followed up two years later with the Statute of Praemunire, forbidding appeals to the papal court on any matters that concerned the prerogatives of the English king. Shortly after Pope Gregory XI finally decided to return the papacy to Rome in 1377, the College of Cardinals split into French and Italian factions and elected separate popes, leading to what became known as the Great Schism. During the Great Schism, Scotland gave allegiance to the French popes in Avignon, based on Scotland's political alliance with France. The support that the English gave to the Roman popes meant to contemporaries that either Scotland or England followed an invalid pope, potentially invalidating the sacraments in one of the two kingdoms.

The main response to the religious crisis in England came from an Oxford professor named John Wycliffe, who was originally from Yorkshire. Wycliffe was personally guilty of participating in two of the common abuses for which the church of this period was criticized: pluralism, the holding of more than one clerical position, and absenteeism, or deriving income from a parish in which one did not actually reside. Wycliffe, however, was one of the first reformers to emphasize the ultimate authority of the scriptures, believing that any papal decrees or church traditions needed to be questioned if they lacked biblical support. Wycliffe did not deny the authority of the papacy to issue laws to benefit the church as long as they did not contradict the Bible. To the extent that they had biblical support, they derived their authority directly from God, not from the pope or his advisers.[11] One of Wycliffe's central ideas was that a layman in a state of grace with God possessed a greater moral authority than any member of the clergy, including the pope, who lived in a state of sin. Wycliffe expressly denied the infallibility of the pope, even on matters of doctrine, calling into question the whole justification for the pope as the head of the church.

At a time when secular monarchs were seeking increased power in their own realms, including over the church, Wycliffe provided a theoretical justification for their claims to higher authority. Wycliffe defined the role of the kingdom as 'the institution of few and just laws, in their wise and precise execution, and generally speaking in the defense of the status and rights of each and every one of its loyal subjects'.[12] In return, Wycliffe suggested, the people owed their complete allegiance to the king. It is not surprising, then, that Edward III turned to Wycliffe in the 1370s when, needing additional revenue to finance his war with France, he sought additional support for his desire to tax the clergy. In an age when many people in England regarded the French popes as having forfeited their spiritual authority, the king acquired greater latitude in mediating the position of the church within his own kingdom.

Wycliffe argued that the king had the responsibility of defending the church and the clergy, just as he did the rest of the population. Wycliffe uses the analogy between the body and the kingdom, with the king as the head or the heart, which supported all other bodily functions. In general, then, Wycliffe provided strong support for the claims of Edward III and kingship in general, though his defence of royal authority had its limits; he argued – citing Aristotle – that the king existed for the state of the law, not the other way around.

Wycliffe's teachings entered the popular realm and inspired a following among people who became known as Lollards. They also inspired the leaders of the Peasant's Rebellion of 1381, the most prominent of which was a priest named John Ball, who espoused his radical views preaching to peasants in the marketplace. Froissart quotes Ball as saying, 'My good friends, matters cannot go on well in England until all things shall be in common; when there shall be neither vassals nor lords; when the lords shall be no more masters than ourselves.'[13] Ball's preaching, however, would not have resonated with so many people had not much of the populace already become convinced that the government was wicked and that the upper classes had conspired to oppress the lower.

Thanks to the protection of powerful allies such as John of Gaunt, Wycliffe died peacefully in 1384 without ever being officially charged with heresy. He prudently retired from Oxford in 1381, however, given the tarnishing of his reputation among the upper classes because of the association of his ideas with the Peasant's Rebellion. It was mainly in response to Wycliffe's ideas and their spread among the Lollards that in 1401 Parliament passed the act concerning heresy, which prescribed the death penalty for religious heterodoxy. The act accused 'divers false and perverse people of a certain new sect' of preaching and teaching 'divers new doctrines, and wicked heretical and erroneous opinions contrary to the same faith and blessed determinations of the Holy Church'. As if this were not enough, the act stated that the Lollards 'do wickedly instruct and inform people, and as such they may excite and stir them to sedition and insurrection, and make great strife and division among the people'. The secular and religious authorities in England were aware of a radical religious movement that had taken root in Bohemia under the leadership of a Catholic priest named Jan Huss, who had also been inspired by Wycliffe's ideas. In 1415 the Council of Constance found Wycliffe guilty of heresy and, not content to let him lie in peace, had his bones exhumed and burnt. The same council burnt Jan Huss, still very much alive, at the stake.

Wycliffe anticipated the Protestant Reformation of the sixteenth century in a number of ways. For example, he challenged the Catholic doctrine of transubstantiation, according to which the bread and wine of the Eucharist became physically transformed into the body and blood of Christ during the sacrament. Furthermore, his followers, the Lollards, did not disappear despite the legislation of 1401; the familiarity of their descendants with the ideas of Wycliffe may have helped to facilitate the rapid acceptance and spread of Protestant ideas in some parts of England in the sixteenth century.

The unpopularity of the church hierarchy and the support for Wycliffe from both nobles and peasants did not mean, however, that the Catholic religion lacked support from the majority of people in the British Isles during the fourteenth and fifteenth centuries. The feast of Corpus Christi, and its accompanying procession with the elevated host of the Eucharist, first proclaimed by Pope John XXII in 1317, became one of the most popular celebrations on the church calendar for late medieval Christians. An increasing amount of devotional literature catered to the growing numbers of people who could read, especially in the second half of the fifteenth century after the invention of the printing press. These works, and popular Christianity in general, encouraged individual believers to cultivate a more personal relationship with God. The transition from public to private confession was one manifestation of this development; the increase in spiritual mysticism in which the Christian sought direct communion with God outside of the sacramental system of the church was another.

Langland, Chaucer, and the emergence of English literature

The birth of English literature predated the invention of the printing press by Johan Gutenberg in the mid-fifteenth century and had already taken on greater significance through the popular writings of William Langland and Geoffrey Chaucer. Langland, best known for his allegorical tale, *Piers Plowman*, wrote more for the common people, whereas Chaucer, who spent most of his time in aristocratic circles, wrote more for the entertainment of the upper classes.

Langland's ideas were so radical for the time that he prudently wrote his work anonymously. Langland gave voice to the concerns of the lower classes about the wealth of the church, social inequality, and political corruption. His poem concludes with the triumph of the antichrist and the allegorical figure of Conscience leaving the church to embark on a pilgrimage in search of Piers Plowman. Piers emerges as a Christ-figure, the humble peasant who like Jesus, the carpenter's son, will save the church from corruption and restore it to a state of purity. Langland's ideas resonated with the followers of John Wycliffe, who not only attacked the wealth of the church but also its doctrine by advancing the idea of the priesthood of all believers. In the minds of the peasants who rebelled in 1381, murdering the archbishop of Canterbury and other wealthy clerics in the process, the church had become an oppressive institution that had strayed far from the teachings of Christ and its true spiritual purpose. Unlike Wycliffe, Langland was primarily an advocate of moral reform rather than a critic of Catholic theology. Still, Langland, like Wycliffe, flirted with heresy, which Parliament made a capital offence in 1401.

FIGURE 10 Piers Plowman, *fourteenth century, London. British Museum.*
Photo 12/Universal Images Group/Getty.

Chaucer, whose father was a wine merchant but who became a page at the age of fourteen in the household of Edward III's daughter-in-law, entered the aristocracy through his marriage to his wife Philippa, a member of the household of Edward III's French wife, Philippa of Hainault. Chaucer's sister-in-law, Catherine Swynford, went on to marry Edward's son, John of Gaunt, the Duke of Lancaster, whose own son became King Henry IV. Freed from the obligations that business imposed on his father and grandfather, Chaucer had the leisure time necessary to pursue his writing even as he performed an impressive array of diplomatic duties. Although Chaucer spoke French, he followed a trend already begun in France and Italy of choosing to write in his native vernacular, the first major English writer since perhaps the author of *Beowulf* to do so.

Chaucer's *Canterbury Tales* resembles the format of the Italian writer Giovanni Boccaccio's *Decameron*, written about the same time; Boccaccio's novel features a group of ten people who told ten stories each to while away the time as they awaited the subsiding of the plague in Florence, while Chaucer has a rather larger group of pilgrims on their way from London to the shrine of Thomas Becket at Canterbury each agree to tell four stories, two apiece on their way to and from their destination. In both *The Canterbury Tales* and *Troilus and Criseyde*, Chaucer sets ancient stories within a contemporary context; even the descriptions of clothing and armour match those current in the fourteenth century.

In 'The Knight's Tale', Chaucer portrays the knight as a representative of moral idealism whose strength allows him to fight in the name of justice, a portrayal that it is easy to mistake for satire but that still represented an ideal to which knights could aspire in the fourteenth century.[14] The Prologue to the tale begins:

> There was a KNIGHT, a valiant man,
> who, from the time when he had first begun
> to venture out, had loved chivalry,
> truth and honor, liberality and courtesy.[15]

In *Troilus and Crisyede*, Chaucer builds on this portrayal of the ideal knight:

> So like a man of arms, so like a knight
> He seemed, so full of high courageousness,
> For he had both the body and the might
> For gallantry, as well as hardiness;
> And then to see him in his fighting dress,
> So fresh, so young, so thoroughbred, so trim,
> It was a very heaven to look at him.[16]

Chaucer in *Troilus and Criseyde* also took up the medieval theme of courtly love. Courtly love literature traditionally appealed to women more than men and Chaucer's works were no exception in this regard. Chaucer followed many of the conventions of the courtly love tradition in this poem, with romantic love in the end giving way to a higher, more spiritual love of God.

Chaucer and Langland were both laymen, but intellectual and literary culture still revolved around the church to a large degree. A monk from Bury St Edmund's named John Lydgate, for example, translated into English a French poem on 'The Dance of Death' on a visit to Paris in the 1430s. Through poems such as this one, we see the continuing cultural impact of the Black Death through a kind of pessimism that the twentieth-century Dutch historian Johan Huizinga regarded as permeating late medieval society. The poem speaks of death and pestilence as striking anyone at any moment, regardless of one's age or social status. The frequent artistic rendering of the *Danse Macabre* during the fifteenth century served as a vivid reminder for the living to view themselves as part of a larger community that included the dead as well. Other types of popular religious literature in the fifteenth century included saint's lives, fables and morality tales, devotional texts, and instruction manuals on how to live a good Christian life. In addition to his translation of 'The Dance of Death', Lydgate wrote verses to commemorate the lives of saints, one of a number of writers to do so, including Osbern Bokenham, whose *Legendys of Hooly Wummen* contained the lives of thirteen female saints. Richard III's reading included a biography of Matilda of Hackeborn, a thirteenth-century mystic. In the fifteenth century, even the clerical writers composed their works in English for lay readers, who now had the ability to internalize their religious experience outside of the church.

Popular tales and ballads also circulated, many of them centring on the mythical figure of the outlaw who eventually became known as Robin Hood:

> LYTHE and listin, gentilmen,
> That be of frebore blode;
> I shall you tel of a gode yeman,
> His name was Robyn Hode.

These tales date primarily from the second half of the fifteenth century and deal with a mythical figure, not a historical one, leaving authors of the various works in the tradition to shape them for their own purposes, often representing thinly veiled attacks on the clergy or the nobility. Although the tales of Robin Hood offer, at times, a clear satire on aristocratic values, they end up preserving these values as much as they mock them. Robin, although an outlaw, displayed exactly the kind of courtesy and manners that should have belonged to an aristocracy that had failed to live up to its own ideals. According to A. J. Pollard, this may have been a strategy for attracting the interest of aristocratic readers, while at the same time offering a critique of them by transferring their values to a common yeoman.[17] Again, we see respect for women as among the foremost characteristics of such chivalric behaviour:

> Robyn loved Oure dere Lady;
> For dout of dydly synne,
> Wolde he never do compani harme
> That any woman was in.

However, we should not place too much emphasis on their appeal to the nobility or their affirmation of the code of chivalry, since Robin Hood was definitely an outlaw who frequently challenged the established political order. However, within this broad definition, Robin Hood appears in a variety of guises in the literature, ranging from the good-hearted fellow who robs from the rich to give to the poor, to a violent criminal who lives by his own moral code. His romantic association with Maid Marion dates from the mid-sixteenth century and is absent from the fifteenth-century literature. Several Scottish writers, including Andrew of Wyntoun and Walter Bower took up the English tale and made some attempt to treat him as a real historical figure who lived during the middle decades of the thirteenth century. The stories are the product of an age that had seen political developments after the failure of the Peasants' Rebellion of 1381 generally go against the lower classes, who needed a champion who could stand for an indictment of political corruption, social inequality, and clerical greed and immorality.

Perhaps the most revealing literary text in regard to the political culture of the fifteenth century is Sir Thomas Malory's *Le Morte d'Arthur*. Malory offers a critique of the decline of the ideals of chivalry and knighthood that had accompanied England's participation in the Hundred Years War and the succession dispute that followed and precipitated the dynastic struggle known as the Wars of the Roses. The high water mark of England's participation in the Hundred Years War occurred in 1415 with King Henry V's famous victory at the Battle of Agincourt. Henry brought Normandy under English control and received recognition as the heir to the French throne in the 1420 Treaty of Troyes, but fell ill and died unexpectedly in 1422 at the age of thirty-five. Henry's youth, valour, and charisma had made him the living embodiment of the legendary King Arthur.

Henry's father had only just started a dynasty that some regarded as illegitimate, but King Arthur himself was also viewed by some as a pretender; throughout the stories refashioned by Malory, the disputed succession continually provides a cause for war.

In *Le Morte d'Arthur*, Malory's knights are courageous, honourable, impervious to pain, and always willing to take up a challenge, while refusing to press any advantage that they had over an opponent if they were not engaged in a fair fight. The novel has its fair share of romance as well, explicitly affirming the courtly love tradition as much as Chaucer had in *Troilus and Criseyde*:

> Tristram was put in the care of the king's daughter, Iseult the Fair, who was a skilled physician. ... While Tristram was recovering, he often played his harp. Iseult was enchanted and begged him to teach her to play also, and in the course of the music lessons they fell deeply in love.
>
> ... Sir Palomides the Saracen ... too fell in love with Iseult (for she was the most beautiful woman in the land) and offered her many magnificent gifts, and even to become christened if it would please her.[18]

There are other ways in which Malory's book would have resonated with readers familiar with the Hundred Years War and the ongoing Wars of the Roses; at one point, the Knights of the Round Table ask Arthur to allow them to return to Britain from France because they have been away from their wives and estates for too long. But Malory continually reminds his readers that things were not as they once were, his own age frequently contrasted to that time 'when true chivalry was well appreciated'. Malory's Camelot is set in a utopian medieval springtime, which might be contrasted with what Huizinga called 'the autumn of the Middle Ages' in which Malory lived. Yet Malory included the well-known prophecy that Arthur, 'the once and future king' might return one day to restore the golden age, a promise that his contemporaries clung to as they sought another Henry V to return England to its former glories.

Literature and culture in Scotland, Wales, and Ireland

The Arthurian legend also loomed large in Scotland, as did the code of chivalric values upon which the stories associated with it were based. To this day, the hill known as Arthur's Seat is located outside of Edinburgh; the etymology of the name is murky but the fact that so many Scots have connected it to Arthur's Camelot remains significant nonetheless. Scotland shared in the medieval obsession with relics, with those associated with Arthur and the Knights of the Round Table rivalling more explicitly Christian ones in popularity. Of course, Scotland had its real-life heroes to celebrate as well, especially Robert Bruce and William Wallace. James Barbour's epic poem 'The Bruce' did the most to enshrine the exploits of the former into Scottish historical memory. Barbour was the first major Scottish poet to write in the vernacular, which matched his nationalistic purpose in celebrating Bruce's heroic qualities.

The Kingis Quair (The King's Book), attributed to King James I (1394–1437) provides an example of the extent to which literary culture had permeated the Scottish court by the early fifteenth century. The poem, written in 1425, is the king's lament over his imprisonment. He wonders, 'Quhat have I gilt, to faille my fredome in this warld.' James, who spent eighteen years in English captivity, takes solace in Boethius's *Consolation of Philosophy*, which the author had also written in prison to avoid succumbing to despair. In James's poem, in the midst of his misery in the Tower of London, the king is inspired by the beauty of a woman whom he spies from his window. This paralleled his real-life experience of falling in love with and ultimately marrying Joan Beaufort in 1424. The poem next recounts a dream in which the king receives a visit from Venus, the goddess of love, who refers his case to Minerva, the goddess of wisdom, who reveals to James that his love is true. The poem shows the influence of Chaucer, particularly 'The Knight's Tale', and of the French classic 'The Romance of the Rose', written by Guillame de Lorris and Jean de Meun, through its courtly love themes, but the presence of Minerva shows the influence of Boethius through its emphasis on the love of wisdom. Scholars of Scottish literature recognize in the poem a classic medieval allegory in which a foolish young man learns the value of wisdom and the true meaning of love after enduring hardship.

The Welsh nationalist poet, Iolo Goch (c. 1320–98), who described Owain Glyn Dwr as 'the best of Welshman mot strong', perhaps helped to prepare the way for the Welsh to support his rebellion in 1400. However, Goch had previously written a poem in 1347 dedicated to King Edward III. He would have composed this poem shortly after the Battle of Crécy, and therefore was probably seeking to put Wales in the good graces of the victorious king by supporting his cause in France. Dafydd ap Gwilym who flourished in the mid-fourteenth century, was known for poems such as 'Morfudd fel yr Haul' (Morfudd like the Sun) and 'Merched Llanbadarn "The Girls of Llanbadarn"', which dealt with themes of love and sexual desire. These poems indicate the presence of the courtly love tradition in Wales. Cross-cultural contacts between the Welsh and the French in general seem to have been increasing during the fourteenth century. Llywelyn Bren, who led a revolt against Edward II in 1316, possessed a personal copy of *The Romance of the Rose*. Tudur Penllyn, who wrote during the second half of the fifteenth century, when Wales experienced a significant rise in poetic output, continued the courtly love genre in 'Converse Rhwyng Welshman and an Englishwoman'.

In Ireland, fourteenth-century bards continued the tradition of singing the praises of prominent kings and nobles, as can be seen in 'The Triumphs of Turlough' or 'Caithréim Thoirdealbhaigh', which combines both poetry and prose. J. A. Watt found little nationalist sentiment in the Annals or the poetry of the period, though he does cite one poem addressed to Tomás Mág Shamhradháin (d. 1343) of County Cavan that laments the lack of unity among the Irish chieftains in the face of foreign conquest.[19] Seoán Mór Ó Dubhagáin (d. 1372), the author of *Triallam timcheall na Fódla* (Let us travel around Ireland), was the most well-known and prolific poet in fourteenth-century Ireland. Translations of works in other languages also enriched Irish culture, including Ó Mathghamhna's translation of *The Travels of Marco Polo*, although he worked from a bastardized English translation rather than the original language. Another important translation was the 'Stair Ercuil agus a bás' (The history of Hercules and his death), based on the English printer William Caxton's *The recuyell of the historyes of Troye*, which dated from about 1474.[20] In addition, compilers began to preserve older Irish literature in manuscript collections such as the *Great Book of Lecan*, compiled in County Sligo by Giolla Íosa Mór Mac Fir Bhisigh about 1417. 'Lorgaireacht an tSoidhigh Naomhtha', a poem on the quest for the Holy Grail, a topic which figures largely in Malory's work and much Arthurian literature, dates from the fifteenth century. One of the most important literary patrons in Ireland in the second half of the century was Fínghin Ó Mathghamhna (d. 1496), who was based southwest of Cork.

Scottish political culture in the fourteenth and fifteenth centuries and the renewed quest for Welsh independence

In 1328, the year after the deposition of Edward II, the English government officially recognized Scottish independence, under its new king, who became King Robert I. The Scottish Declaration of Arbroath of 1320 had provided the ideological foundations for the new Scottish nation. The declaration affirmed that the Scots had lived as an independent people at peace with the English until the encroachments of Edward I in the late thirteenth century. It also recalled Edward's vile actions:

> The deeds of cruelty, massacre, violence, pillage, arson, imprisoning prelates, burning down monasteries, robbing and killing monks and nuns and yet other

outrages without number which he committed against our people, sparing neither age nor sex, religion nor rank, no-one could describe nor fully imagine unless he had seen them with his own eyes.

While the Declaration of Arbroath affirmed Robert Bruce's title to the Scottish throne, it made clear that the larger point was Scottish independence from the English. The king's title was essentially dependent on his ability to preserve that independence. The most celebrated phrase in the whole declaration states, 'It is in truth not for glory, nor riches, nor honors that we are fighting, but for freedom alone, which no honest man gives up but with life itself.'

Yet even these developments did not put an end to the English threat to Scottish autonomy. Nor were the Scots completely unified in the conflict; Edward III aligned himself with the Scottish Balliol family, promising to restore their rule over northern Scotland in exchange for their recognition of English rule in the south. The Scots had to rely on a new generation of military leaders, such as Sir Alexander Ramsay, to protect and preserve Scottish independence.

David II, the son of Robert Bruce, sought to capitalize on Edward III's absence from England in 1346 by launching an invasion of northern England within weeks after the Battle of Crécy. But English armies won a crushing victory over the Scots at the Battle of Neville's Cross, which resulted in the capture of the Scottish king. This led to the acceptance of English authority by many Scots living in the borderlands between the two countries. A group of leading Scottish churchmen appointed three bishops and the Scottish chancellor, a man named Brechin, to negotiate the release of David II from captivity. They successfully negotiated David's release in 1357, but the decade that David had spent in captivity had increased the power of the Scottish church and nobility at the expense of the Crown. England capitalized on this situation by making alliances with the Scottish nobility. However, in 1388 the Scots took advantage of a feud between the two dominant families in northern England, the Percys and the Nevilles, to launch another invasion that resulted in the Battle of Otterburn in 1388. This time the Scots came prepared with an army constituted of an estimated 40,000 infantry and 12,000 cavalry, garnering a significant victory for the Scots.

Scotland, then, took advantage of English involvement in the Hundred Years War to emerge from the late medieval period as an independent nation. Scotland emerged from the fifteenth century as a strong, unified, centralized state, despite a succession of royal children too young to assume the throne during the reigns of James I (r. 1406–37), James II (r. 1437–60), and James III (r. 1460–88). James I returned from his English captivity in 1424, but was murdered in Perth thirteen years later. James II died before the age of thirty, James III before he turned thirty-seven. For most of this period, English kings were in no position to take advantage of the problems of the Scottish Stewart dynasty, as they struggled mightily in the period of dynastic uncertainty that followed the end of the Hundred Years War.

Wales had also remained a troubled borderland, with Welsh incursions into England increasing in frequency in the later decades of the fourteenth century. Richard's rule had been an onerous and oppressive one for the Welsh, as for his other subjects; the Welsh saw his overthrow and the political uncertainty that followed as a chance to throw off the English yoke. The brewing conflict between Wales and

England came to a head with the revolt of Owain Glyn Dwr in September 1400, the year following the deposition of Richard II and his replacement by the Lancastrian Henry IV. The Lancastrian revolt of 1399 sent political ripples throughout the British Isles; the Welsh, among others, wondered what this change in dynasty might mean for them.

Owain Glyn Dwr was a prominent and skilful leader who had the knowledge and experience to guide a successful revolt. The Welsh from the beginning of the rebellion viewed Owain Glyn Dwr as the embodiment of a long-prophesied hero who would rise and galvanize his people behind the cause of Welsh independence. Inheriting the lands of Rhys ap Gruffydd from his mother and princely blood from his father, Glyn Dwr came from one of the most powerful and prominent families in Wales. Glyn Dwr succeeded, at least temporarily, in driving the English out of Wales and establishing an independent kingdom.

Although Glyn Dwr's rebellion had restored a degree of national pride in Wales, the revolt led the English to view the Welsh as a crude and barbarous people similar to their views of the native Irish at that time. Lyn Arner has seen the popular fifteenth-century literary work, *Sir Gawain and the Green Knight* as essentially English colonialist propaganda aimed at reinforcing this negative stereotype of the Welsh. *Sir Gawain and the Green Knight* was written some time during the last half of the fourteenth century when the Welsh resistance that culminated in Glyn Dwr's revolt was on the rise. Although the authorship is unknown, the dialect is considered that of northwestern England in the vicinity of the Welsh border.[21] In this interpretation, Gawain, one of King Arthur's knights, represents the civilized English in their quest to subdue the evil and barbaric Welsh.

The Statute of Drogheda and Ireland in the late Middle Ages

Meanwhile, English policy in Ireland during the fourteenth and fifteenth centuries was largely characterized by a desire to at least maintain the status quo in which England directly controlled lands in the southeast radiating outward from Dublin, while seeking to protect those settlers on the borderlands between this territory, called the Pale, and those areas still under the direct control of native Irish chiefs. The weakness and deposition of Edward II followed by Edward III's preoccupations with France created an opening for these Irish chiefs to put pressure on those lands over which the English had only a tentative hold. The native Irish could only really threaten individual territories rather than English rule as a whole, mainly because Ireland still lacked any kind of political unity in the lands not controlled by the English. Irish kings or chieftains remained more concerned with consolidating, maintaining, or expanding control in their local area, usually at the expense of other Gaelic chiefs, than with ousting the English from the island. Still, they presented enough of a threat that appeals from the Anglo-Irish nobility led Edward III to dispatch his son, Lionel, the Duke of Clarence, to Ireland in 1361 to provide assistance. The presence of Lionel in Ireland until 1366, with one hiatus in England in 1364–5, at least sent a clear message regarding Ireland's continued importance to the Crown, despite its other preoccupations. Lionel waged a series of military campaigns in Ireland, but he accomplished little more through them than the defence of his own lands.

The English government did not completely ignore Ireland during this period, but Anglo-Irish lords felt increasingly vulnerable nonetheless. The English in Ireland frequently relied on bribes commonly known as 'black rents' in order to prevent attacks and preserve peace with their Irish neighbours. Such policy was fluid rather than constant though, relationships frequently shifting between peace and war depending on the strength of rival parties. Gaelic leaders such as the O'Kellys of Ui Maine and Art MacMurrough Kavanagh (c. 1357–1416), the king of Leinster, represented significant obstacles to the extension of English authority.

An Irish Parliament that met in Dublin came into existence around the same time that the English Parliament began to meet more frequently in the early fourteenth century. In Ireland, however, the Crown at first had less incentive to include those below the rank of the nobility in these assemblies, which dealt mainly with administrative matters instead of serving as a means of gaining popular support. Still, as in England, representation in the Irish Parliament seems to have expanded during the course of the fourteenth century, with commoners and members of the lower clergy attending the assembly by the 1370s. The Irish Parliament by that time had begun to perform the tasks of hearing petitions, approving taxation, and passing legislation, the same activities practised by its English counterpart.

Although none of these duties were performed to nearly the same degree or with the same frequency as in the English Parliament, the Irish Parliament did pass some notable legislation. In particular, in 1367, the Irish Parliament passed the infamous Statutes of Kilkenny, which sought to prohibit marriage between the English and the Irish and proscribed other types of contact as well, including the sale of horses or armour to the Irish, even during times of peace. Englishmen were forbidden to speak Gaelic or to wear native dress. The Statutes also sought to clearly distinguish English from Irish lands and prohibited the Irish from occupying English lands or using them for pasture. Finally, the Statutes forbade English nobles in Ireland from making war on one another, lest they become divided in the face of the Irish threat. The Statutes of Kilkenny reflect a certain amount of anxiety and insecurity with regard to the situation in Ireland, where the Gaelic population was reviving after the onslaught of the Black Death and close proximity had bred familiarity as well as contempt. They also reveal just how much control the English government had over the Irish Parliament that the latter would pass such an unrealistic set of laws based on what the English, but obviously not the Anglo-Irish, wanted. For this very reason, the Statutes failed to achieve their main objective of preventing English settlers from adopting Irish ways and customs.

One of the reasons that Richard II went to Ireland in 1394 was to reaffirm royal authority there and to reverse the threat of Irish encroachment upon English lands. But after Richard's deposition in 1399, English settlers in Ireland had to once again rely mainly on their own defence, especially because England remained preoccupied with France and the Hundred Years War in the first half of the fifteenth century and the Wars of the Roses thereafter. In this the Anglo-Irish were largely successful; the extent of English-controlled land in Ireland remained approximately the same at the end of the Hundred Years War as it was at the beginning. But this meant no overall gains either, with the English controlling only a little more than a third of the entire island. English authorities in borderlands such as Louth realized that the best they could do was to hold on to what they had, while, after a time, the Irish recognized that the English were there to stay, making a rough modus vivendi more the objective on both sides than outright conquest.

Dynastic issues in England, Scotland, and Wales in the fifteenth century

In England, Henry VI's weakness and bouts of insanity led to a series of protests in 1449–50, one aim of which was to place Richard, the Duke of York on the English throne. In 1451, Thomas Young, an MP from Bristol, proposed in the House of Commons that Richard be designated as Henry's heir. Richard began to apply pressure on the king to recognize him as heir, basing his claim largely on the support of the people. Richard had acted prematurely, however, for Henry VI was not yet ready to give up the throne, supported by the determined assistance of his queen, Margaret, and her uncle, Edmund, the Earl of Somerset. The Parliament that met at Reading in March 1453 affirmed its support for the king and his proxy, Somerset, turning its back on Richard. The exact timing of Henry's insanity remains unclear, as he would lapse in and out of a passive state of almost total apathy, but Henry acted quickly in March 1454 to have his infant son recognized as his heir by the leading men of the kingdom, including Richard Neville, the Earl of Warwick, who became known as the 'kingmaker'.

While Henry worked with Margaret's help to secure the future of his reign and dynasty, England's final defeat in the Hundred Years War undermined his credibility as a ruler in the eyes of the people. Furthermore, Henry's maladroit rule, inviting inner revolt and foreign aggression, was seen as threatening England's peace and stability. The shadow of Henry V hung over the reign of his son. A 1455 poem celebrated the benefits of the reign of Henry V, which England now lacked:

> Above all things, he kept the law and peace
> Throughout all England, that no insurrection
> Nor any riots were not made to cease.

Some members of the nobility had also lost confidence in the king, the show of support in the Parliament of 1453 notwithstanding. In the words of Polydore Vergil (1470–1555):

> This finally, was the end of the foreign war, and likewise the renewal of civil calamity: for when the fear of an external enemy, which had kept the kingdom in good exercise, was gone from the nobility, such was the contention amongst them for glory and power, that even then the people were apparently divided into two factions, according as it became afterwards, when those two, that is to say, king Henry, who derived his pedigree from the House of Lancaster, and Richard duke of York, who conveyed himself by his mother's side from Lionel, son of Edward the Third, contended for the kingdom. By means whereof these two factions

grew shortly so great through the whole realm that, while the one sought by any manner to subdue the other, and raged in revenge upon the subdued, many men were utterly destroyed, and the whole realm brought to ruin and decay.[22]

In 1461, Edward, the son of Richard, Duke of York, accepted the crown and began his reign as King Edward IV. At first Edward sought to make peace with the former enemies of his father, while relying on the support of powerful figures such as Warwick. In 1467, Edward gave a speech before Parliament in which he announced his intention to finance his reign from his own lands and resources rather than to burden the people with additional taxes. While Warwick became suspicious that Edward might become too independent, his military successes and ability to hold power created confidence in the king among most of the nobles in the shires.

In May 1464 Edward privately married Elizabeth Woodville, a poor widow whose first husband was a Lancastrian. Although Elizabeth plainly intended to use her position as queen to advance the interests of her family, the nobility at first accepted the marriage and continued to support Edward, who remained the dominant partner in his marriage, unlike Henry VI, whose queen, Margaret, was clearly stronger than her husband. However, Edward's masculinity and royal bearing did not prevent some disaffected members of the nobility, including Warwick and members of his own family, from rising against him in 1469. Fortunately, Edward had a strong enough army and was a capable enough military leader to prevail against them. By 1471 he had re-established his authority throughout most of the kingdom. Edward increasingly relied on his brother, Richard, Duke of Gloucester, especially to govern the north, making him lord lieutenant there in 1480. Meanwhile, Lady Margaret Stanley bided her time while she prepared her son, Henry Tudor to one day inherit – or seize – the throne. She, of course, largely kept these plans to herself and openly supported the Yorkist monarchy.

On 9 April 1483, Edward IV took his last breath; two days later, the people of London heard Edward V proclaimed king; a date of 4 May was set for his coronation. The Woodvilles, in the meantime, plotted to exclude Gloucester from an important role in the new regime. In short, they wanted Richard removed from the role of Protector to which his standing as the dead king's brother seemed to entitle him. Richard, feeling the need to defend the Yorkist claim to the throne, decided he could not sit idly by and would need to become king himself. With Richard in York, the Woodvilles needed to have the young Edward crowned as soon as possible to make any action against him appear treasonous. Their plan failed; Richard seized the initiative and had himself crowned king; once he did he faced little immediate opposition. He took advantage of this situation and immediately set about to consolidate his power. The first year of Richard's reign proceeded as expected and the smooth functioning of the government left no question of Richard's right to rule or of his legitimacy.

The thorny problem of Richard III and the disappearance of his two young nephews have plagued historians and intrigued novelists and amateur historical detectives ever since the fifteenth century. On the one side are those convinced of Richard's guilt in the murder of the princes, the prevailing view since the accession of Henry VII fostered by the Tudor propagandist Sir Thomas More and reinforced by Shakespeare's villainous portrayal in his play, *Richard III*. On the other side are ardent defenders of Richard, the strongest case made for his total innocence appearing in a 1951 mystery novel, *The Daughter of Time*, by the Scottish crime writer Josephine Tey (the nom de plume of Elizabeth Macintosh). A moderate position appears in Michael K. Jones's brilliant *Bosworth 1485: The Psychology of a Battle* (2003), which argues that Richard was probably guilty of the murders but treats the need for late medieval kings to eliminate their rivals as a political necessity and not the act of an evil criminal. However, if that were the case, Richard would surely have proclaimed the deaths of his rivals to prevent an opposition rallying around them, something which he never did. If he did not want to admit to murder, he could have blamed their deaths on his cousin, the Duke of Buckingham or illness, but he also could have made sure that people knew he was now heir apparent. Furthermore, to bolster their case against him Richard's enemies fabricated earlier charges against him and claimed that he had plotted to kill the children even before the death of Edward IV, which does not seem to have been the case.

In 1484, Parliament produced a document called the *Titulus Regius*, which provides the clearest statement of the grounds for Richard's title as king. The main significance of *Titulus Regius* is its claim that the two young princes, Edward and Richard, were illegitimate because of an invalid marriage between their father, Edward IV, and their mother, Elizabeth Woodville. *Titulus Regius* also affirms Richard's desire and ability to provide good government and to rule in the best interests of the English people.

No matter what Richard claimed, however, he could not put the succession dispute behind him. He faced challenges from multiple factions, including from the exiled Henry Tudor, who now emerged as the leading Lancastrian candidate for the throne. Richard's unpopularity increased after the death of his wife, Anne Neville, in March 1485, which was followed by false rumours that Richard intended to marry his niece, Elizabeth of York. Henry, meanwhile, solicited the aid of the French king, Louis XI, who wished to see the House of York overthrown because of the military assistance that it had habitually provided to the Duke of Burgundy, his bitterest enemy. Richard fought valiantly at the Battle of Bosworth Field on 22 August 1485, while Henry Tudor remained safely behind the lines. It could not be said at the time that the Wars of the Roses had ended but Henry became king after the battle and remained on the throne until 1509. Meanwhile, Richard's body lay un-mourned and unrecovered, until a team of archaeologists discovered his remains underneath a Leicester car park in 2012.

Conclusion

The Battle of Bosworth Field traditionally marks the end of the Middle Ages in many standard works of British history. The beginning of a new dynasty did not inherently mean a change in political culture, much less in basic economic and social realities. Yet, in fact, the sixteenth century did bring about significant changes in each of these areas. While Henry Tudor and his successors cannot take full responsibility for all of these changes, the long century from 1485 to 1603 over which they ruled demonstrates as much as any period in the history of the British Isles that individuals have made a difference in that history. Henry's initial handling of the Irish situation helps to illustrate this point. An Irish army led by the Ulster chief Aodh Rua in 1487 possessed guns, which entered Irish warfare at that time and presaged a greater level of difficulty in subduing the native population. The Anglo-Irish nobility sensed a greater urgency to subdue the native Irish at the borders of their territory and petitioned the new king, Henry VII, to help them do so. By 1494, Henry was ready to turn his attention to Ireland, appointing Sir James Ormond to the important position of constable of Limerick Castle and bestowing upon him lands in Kilkenny, Meath, and Tipperary. He sent Sir Edward Poynings, an accomplished military and political leader, to Dublin to take charge of the administration there. Poynings called an Irish Parliament, which convened in Drogheda on 1 December 1494, which passed an act that became known as Poynings' Law, which stated that any law passed in England applied equally to Ireland as well. Then, in 1496 Henry VII turned around and reappointed Gerald Fitzgerald, the Earl of Kildare, as his deputy lieutenant in Ireland, despite Fitzgerald's past opposition to the king. In doing so, he converted an enemy into a faithful ally. Other decisions as shrewd as this one help to explain Henry's success in establishing the new Tudor dynasty.

FIGURE 11 *John Knox preaches reform in St Giles, Edinburgh court of Mary Stuart. Reformation wall.*
Godong/Universal Images Group/Getty.

6

Religion, warfare, and dynastic politics:

The Tudors and the Stewarts in the sixteenth century

Why do we not consider what contradictions we find in our own judgments; how many things were yesterday articles of faith, that to-day appear no other than fables?

MICHEL DE MONTAIGNE, 'That It is Folly to Measure Truth and Error by Our Own Capacity', 1580 (translated by CHARLES COTTON)

Religion and politics in the sixteenth century: The English Reformation

The Protestant Reformation of the sixteenth century affected every region in the British Isles; it just did not affect England, Scotland, Ireland, and Wales in the same way. In Ireland, for instance, the English-controlled area of the Pale – which in 1500 constituted a fairly small area along the eastern coast extending inland from Dublin to the earldom of Kildare – at first acquiesced in the religious changes introduced by Henry VIII (r. 1509–47), but Catholicism remained the dominant faith in those parts of the island not controlled by the English. In Scotland the northeast became more associated with an Episcopalian church (based on the Protestant Church of England) while the Lowlands adopted a different form of church governance called Presbyterianism.

Henry VII (r. 1485–1509) had to overcome a number of challenges in order for his son to inherit the kind of authority that would allow him to make the sweeping religious changes that removed England from the Roman Church and the authority of the papacy. First, to facilitate an end to the dynastic quarrel between the Yorkists and Lancastrians, he married Elizabeth of York, the daughter of Edward IV. Second, Henry had to walk a fine line between curbing the power of the nobility and eliciting their support, without which he could not have ruled at all. Henry needed their support, because even after 1485 he continued to face challenges from pretenders to the throne such as Lambert Simnel and Perkin Warbeck, two impostors who attracted significant support by claiming to be the Earl of Warwick and the son of Edward IV, respectively. Henry waited until 1504 to ask Parliament to outlaw private armies, which it did in the Statute of Liveries; even this merely gave Henry the opportunity to be selective in his enforcement of the prohibition. Third, Henry devised various ways to raise revenue for the royal coffers, some of them highly unpopular and of dubious morality, if not legality. He made particular use of fines, starting with the ones he levied against those who had fought against him at Bosworth Field on the grounds that they were guilty of treason. The passage of the so-called acts of resumption by Parliament allowed him to reclaim land that had been alienated from the Crown during the Wars of the Roses.

Finally, Henry VII sought to acquire legitimacy for his rule through a series of foreign marriages that he arranged for his children. Henry, whose shaky claim to the English throne came through his mother, Margaret Beaufort, had good reason to fear the stigma of illegitimacy attached to the Lancastrian regime. Henry identified himself strongly with his Lancastrian heritage, such as it was, particularly with the legendary Henry V, after whose tomb he modelled his own. Still, he sought international recognition for his rule by negotiating the marriages of his daughter Margaret to King James IV of Scotland, his daughter Mary to King Louis XII of France, and, most famously and portentously, of his son Arthur to Katherine of Aragon, the daughter of King Ferdinand and Queen Isabella of Spain. The marriage alliance with Spain had the extra advantage of bringing with it a sizeable dowry from the wealthy Spanish monarchs.

The 1501 marriage between Arthur and Katherine was a brief one; Arthur died prematurely just five months after the wedding. Katherine's chaperone, Doña Elvira Manuel, always maintained that no sexual relations took place between Arthur and his Spanish bride. King Ferdinand believed her and permitted Katherine to become engaged to Henry Tudor's second son, the future Henry VIII. It does strain credulity to think that Katherine, a devout Catholic, would have wilfully perpetuated a falsehood until her death by swearing that she entered her marriage to Henry as a virgin. Years later, when Henry sought a divorce from Katherine on the basis of a canon law that forbade marriage to a brother's widow, Katherine went so far as to indicate her willingness to submit to the pope's decision on the matter if Henry would swear that she entered their marriage bed un-intact; he never did. This issue only became important because Katherine failed to provide Henry with a male heir after eighteen years of marriage, which became either the impetus, or the excuse, depending on which viewpoint one takes, for Henry's desire to marry Anne Boleyn, the daughter of Sir Thomas Boleyn and Elizabeth Howard. The Boleyns were a minor noble house, who rose quickly to prominence once Henry married Anne, but the Howards were among the wealthiest and most powerful families in England.

From the beginning, Catholic critics of the English Reformation have seen its origins as tainted by Henry's lust for Anne, which they saw as the primary cause for the shift in Henry's religious policy. Yet Henry's break with Rome would not have been possible without the prior introduction and spread of reformed ideas from the Continent. Many of those interested in reform still wished to preserve the unity of the church, but Henry also tapped into a popular strain of anticlericalism and anti-papal feeling that went back to at least the fourteenth century. Henry, however, would have had no need to split with Rome if Pope Clement VII approved his request for a divorce. Clement, afraid of Katherine's powerful allies on the Continent, particularly her nephew, the Holy Roman Emperor Charles V, attempted to stall Henry, only providing an amorphous indication that he might give him a favourable answer at some future date. In response, Henry decided to call Parliament to request legislation designed to force the pope's hand.

By 1533, Parliament had approved a number of acts that encroached upon papal prerogatives, culminating in the Act in Restraint of Appeals that was virtually a declaration of independence from the papacy. This act forbade judicial appeals outside of the English kingdom, including on matters of religion, opening the door for Henry to achieve his divorce without approval from Rome. The Act in Restraint of Appeals, along with several dozen other pieces of legislation, including the 1533 Act of Supremacy making Henry 'supreme head' of the church in England, placed the early stages of the Reformation on solid legal ground. To the twentieth-century political historian G. R. Elton, the involvement of Parliament had saved England from taking a path towards despotic absolutism, but later developments would demonstrate that the role that Parliament was to play in the future and the extent of its power were hardly resolved in the 1530s. This future uncertainty does not negate the importance of Parliament's role, but it then still largely acted as a tool of the monarch, only developing much of an independent voice later in the century.

By 1533, Henry had also dismissed two leading Catholics, Cardinal Thomas Wolsey and Sir Thomas More, from the position of lord chancellor, turning instead to Thomas Cromwell, an ex-soldier who had risen to influence serving under Wolsey, and Thomas Cranmer, a Cambridge divine, to guide him through his divorce and carry out his plans to unite the church and the state. Anne Boleyn's own conversion to the reformed religion, however, played a key role in pushing Henry to go beyond the break with Rome. This feat was accomplished by promoting reform-minded clerics within the church who pushed it in a Protestant direction. A contemporary credited Anne personally with the promotions of several Protestant clerics, including those of Cranmer to archbishop of Canterbury and Hugh Latimer to bishop of Worcester. Anne also became associated with a reform faction at court that included Cromwell, whose own religious beliefs may have been more sincere than he is often given credit for. As soon as Anne was crowned as Henry's queen in 1533, monks at Burton-on-Trent assumed that Cromwell would not allow them to proceed with the election of a new abbot.[1] In this view, the dissolution of the monasteries, which began in 1536, becomes an outcome of the ascendancy of the reformed faith and not merely a cynical land grab on the part of Cromwell, acting on behalf of the Crown.

The distinguishing characteristic of the English Reformation before the dissolution of the monasteries was the assumption by the king of supremacy over the English church, made official in the 1533 Act of Supremacy. A deeply pious Catholic, Thomas More refused to take a required oath in support of the Act of Supremacy; when pressed at trial for his refusal to do so, he equivocated about his reasons, as Robert Bolt depicted memorably in his 1962 play, *A Man for All Seasons*. Bolt portrayed

More as a defender of individual rights against state tyranny who refused to violate his own conscience in swearing to the oath, a theme that resonated with audiences during the 1960s. Yet More, who would have denied the privilege of conscience to those whom he deemed heretics, opposed the oath chiefly because he believed that Henry had assumed power that Henry's former chancellor would have reserved for the church – and everyone, including Cromwell, knew it, a realization that led to a guilty verdict and More's execution.

A more nuanced picture of More than that provided by Bolt has emerged that takes into account his inconsistencies and the hatred he often held for those who disagreed with him, in addition to the sincerity of his beliefs and his principled opposition to the king. Similarly, the work of recent historians has shown Cromwell to be far from the heartless, scheming Machiavellian depicted in Bolt's play.[2] Far from seeking More's death, Cromwell spent hours trying to persuade him to take the oath prior to his trial, realizing that More's submission would send a powerful message to other Catholic leaders throughout England. More refused to take the oath, nonetheless, and there is no need to question the sincerity of his motives for his refusal, living as he did in an age that took matters relating to one's potential salvation or damnation extremely seriously. He did, after all, refuse to listen to pleas from his wife that he take the oath on grounds that he would not endanger his soul.

The most serious opposition that Henry faced to the religious changes introduced came from the North, where many people retained their allegiance to the old faith. There was a legitimate need for monastic reform in England at the time of the Reformation; the number of monks and nuns had declined from the heyday of medieval monasticism, leaving underpopulated institutions in control of vast tracts of land. But monasteries retained their popularity in the North, where a Lincolnshire gentleman named Richard Aske led a rebellion in 1536 that became known as the Pilgrimage of Grace. Aske took umbrage not only with the religious changes imposed from London but also with the changing nature of the Tudor state. He thought that the state had illegally expanded its power at the expense of the church and, on behalf of the rebels, demanded the preservation of the Catholic Church in England. The rebels began by restoring about sixteen monasteries of the fifty-five that had been dissolved by Cromwell at that point.[3] The rebellion attracted support from all levels of the social spectrum from the peasantry to the highest echelons of the nobility. Some of the nobles decided that it would be better to take control of the rebellion rather than have popular resentment turn on them. Thomas Howard, the Duke of Norfolk, Charles Brandon, the Duke of Suffolk and George Talbot, the Earl of Shrewsbury led Henry's armies northward to confront the rebels, who numbered between 30,000 and 40,000, but the rebellion collapsed without a battle when Aske agreed to negotiate with the king, a decision that cost him his life.

The Pilgrimage of Grace had represented a serious threat to Henry, but his Reformation had its share of popular support as well. In some instances, the people took religious matters into their own hands, such as the crowd that gathered at Lawhitton in Cornwall in 1535 to deprive their parish priest of his chalice and other papist accoutrements.[4] Cambridge, which fell strongly under the influence of Renaissance humanism and Continental Protestant thought, proved particularly sympathetic. Such Lutheran ideas as justification by faith alone and the priesthood of all believers attracted popular support among the London merchant community; even Thomas More's son-in-law, the lawyer William Roper, found the new theology appealing. People in areas such as Colchester, for whom Lollardy had held a strong attraction, also proved particularly sympathetic to reform ideas.[5] Even in a religiously traditional village such as Morebath, the clergy enforced the Henrician legislation and the people found ways of accommodating themselves to religious change.[6]

One thing should have been clear at the end of Henry's reign, however, as it has become to later historians: the English Reformation was not over nor so firmly established that it could not have been reversed, as Henry's oldest daughter, Mary, attempted to do when she became queen in 1553. Still, we should not minimize those changes that did occur under Henry, including the dissolution of the monasteries, the abolition of numerous saints' days, and the translation and availability of the Bible in English. Even Mary made no attempt to return the confiscated monastic lands to the church. Furthermore, a series of royal injunctions in 1538 had required every parish to own a Bible, condemned the veneration of relics, and instructed parishioners to regard images of saints not as icons but as memorials liable to be removed at any time. Also in 1538, Henry moved on from the traditional monastic orders to the dissolution of the houses of the Franciscan and Dominican friars. Finally, the establishment of the royal supremacy over the English church ensured that politics and religion would become even more inextricably intertwined than they had been previously. The Henrician Reformation was only the first stage of the English Reformation, which most historians now see as a process rather than an event, but it was an important stage that could not be easily undone, even by the Catholic Mary.

On the other hand, those of a traditional religious bent resented the loss of holy days, wished to continue to hear the mass in Latin, and took comfort in the old ways and rituals. As the Pilgrimage of Grace demonstrated, some people lamented the loss of monasteries that had provided a spiritual ideal (even if there was inevitably some corruption) for laypersons in the midst of an evil world to admire and emulate as much as possible. Throughout England defenders of the clergy and the Catholic religion vied with anti-clericalists as well as sincere believers in the reformed religion; such was the religious situation inherited by the young King Edward VI when he ascended the throne after Henry's death in 1547.

Although a mere boy when he succeeded to the throne, Edward, the son of Henry VIII and his third wife, Jane Seymour, demonstrated at a young age a precocious zeal for the Protestant faith and an aptitude for religious understanding. The Scottish reformer John Knox, who was admittedly biased towards the Protestant Edward, called him 'the most godly and virtuous King that hath been known to have reigned in England or elsewhere'.[7] In the first stages of reform under Edward, images, religious shrines, the Catholic mass, and pilgrimages all became proscribed. Religious processions and such traditional practices as the distribution of ashes on Ash Wednesday also became forbidden. Parishes had sermons distributed to them that stressed Protestant doctrines such as justification by faith alone. Clerical marriages became legal, with many clergymen availing themselves of the opportunity to take a wife. In 1549 Thomas Cranmer, as archbishop of Canterbury, introduced the First Book of Common Prayer, and followed that up with a revised second version a few years later that moved further in the direction of Protestantism by eliminating prayers for the dead among other remnants of Catholic practices.

If the English Reformation seems directed from above, this is only partly true at best, for each of the last four Tudor monarchs – Henry VIII, Edward VI, Mary, and Elizabeth – felt pressures from below that played an equally important role in determining the future direction of religious change. In 1537, for example, a Great Council of nobles met under royal auspices and supported greater moderation in the pace of religious change, no doubt largely in response to the Pilgrimage of Grace. Cromwell and Cranmer also had to make adjustments to the Ten Articles of the reformed faith proposed in 1536 under pressure from conservative members of the clergy. People at the local level frequently dictated the actual pace of religious change, with some areas conforming more easily and others doing so outwardly, if at all, depending on their proximity to London and the frequency of visitations from church authorities. The Tudors themselves fostered the illusion of royal control and a stable England, as compared to the preceding century. In reality, England experienced a profound level of social change that undermined that impression.

Social mobility and social change in the sixteenth century

Even as England clung to a model of society that featured a rigid dividing line between the nobility and gentry on the one hand and those of lesser status on the other, contemporary social and cultural shifts were occurring that blurred that line. One factor in changing attitudes towards class was the Protestant ethos of 'the priesthood of all believers', which challenged older notions of hierarchy. Two additional major changes that occurred in the sixteenth century went hand in hand: a rise in population and an increase in prices. The population of England and Wales increased from between 2.2 and 2.5 million in 1500 to approximately 4.1 million in 1570 and perhaps 4.8 million in 1600.[8] A massive influx of Spanish gold from the New World entered Europe and helped to drive up prices, a trend exacerbated in England by successive debasements of coinage starting under Henry VIII.

An increase in population did not necessarily mean a shift in social structure, which still retained its basic medieval features. However, in England, Scotland, and Wales a distinct class of small family farmers who owned their own property occupied a spot below the nobility and gentry and above tenant farmers and agricultural labourers, even though William Harrison grouped these yeomen with tenants and labourers under the single designation of 'countrymen' in his 1600 *Description of England*. England possessed many more of these small landowners than either Scotland or Wales. Their counterparts in the towns would have included artisans, craftsmen, shopkeepers, and those who made their living providing a variety of professional services. Writing about the same time as Harrison, Thomas Wilson did identify yeomen as a separate category from 'countrymen', but he grouped 'townsmen' together as a single category. In fact, the growing urban population of the period called forth an increasing number of professionals such as doctors and lawyers and specialized shopkeepers that constituted more of an upper middle class within the towns. Similar social changes occurred in the areas of Ireland under English control, where a rising population encouraged entrepreneurial farming among the more modest landowners and fed a growing urban population. In Gaelic Ireland, however, where population did not increase significantly and land rents remained stable, the main social division remained that which separated landowners from their landless tenants.

Outside of Gaelic Ireland, the challenges of the economic changes that occurred in the sixteenth century led to an increase in the number of dispossessed people who were forced to leave their homes or farms in search of work or some means of survival elsewhere. In England, London absorbed a large number of these people; Bucholz and Ward estimate an increase from 120,000 to 675,000 in the two centuries after 1550.[9] By the end of the sixteenth century, America had started to attract interest leading to the first settlements by people migrating from Britain, though the first permanent English colonies in North America were not established until the seventeenth century.

Unfortunately, a corresponding increase in agricultural production does not seem to have occurred to match the growth of population, meaning less food for more people and serious deprivation, if not starvation, in years of bad harvests. This situation was exacerbated by the beginnings of the 'enclosure movement', in which large landowners enclosed fields previously cultivated by tenants and cottagers in order to use them for the more commercially profitable raising of sheep for their wool; Thomas More refers to this situation in *Utopia* when he speaks of sheep that 'eat up and swallow down the very men themselves'. Rents increased now that the land was becoming profitable again, all the more so as the long leases granted during the fifteenth century began to expire. Scholars such as D. C. Coleman have, in fact, concluded that enclosure was not widespread at this time, occurring mainly on marginal lands in the English midlands; more was not justified by the price of wool which had not appreciably risen since the mid-fourteenth century and was still competitive with grain prices. Thomas More may have exaggerated then the effects of this early enclosure movement, but its beginnings were harbingers of a further shift in the direction of an agricultural society that responded more directly to markets and away from a subsistence model.

In fact, landowners, cloth manufacturers, and urban employers increasingly had their need for workers superseded by the growth in the general population. Wages stagnated around 1520 as well, as the labour shortage caused by the depopulation of the late Middle Ages came to an end. These economic circumstances led to growing tensions between classes in the countryside that contributed to both the Pilgrimage of Grace in 1536 and the Western Rising of 1549, otherwise known as the Prayer Book Rebellion because of popular opposition in southwestern England to the introduction of Thomas Cranmer's *Book of Common Prayer*, as well as other rebellions that occurred with regular frequency in Tudor times.

Without a growth in urban opportunities for employment in this period, however, the extent of poverty and unemployment would have been even worse. Adolescent girls and young women could supplement their family's income by hiring themselves out as nannies, seamstresses, domestic servants, or teachers. Of course, the main ways in which young women could help their families were through advantageous marriages at all levels of society; the marriage rate among women in the Tudor period was therefore extremely high, perhaps as much as 90 per cent. In 1601, the government took the then radical step of taking some responsibility for the poor with the passage of the Act for the Relief of the Poor, otherwise known as the Elizabethan Poor Law, although the law still made the parish responsible for the distribution of poor relief. This parish-based system remained the basis for poor relief in England and Wales until 1834.

Increases in rent only went so far to offset the rising cost of living for the upper classes, who had greater expenditures and felt social pressure to maintain certain styles of dress and living in order to retain the respect of their peers. During this period, landlords could not raise rents as much as they would have liked as a result of the limits of deeply ingrained social customs regarding tenancy and the recourse that tenants had to courts to defend their interests. For some landowners, enclosure represented a survival mechanism motivated more by the desire to keep up with inflation rather than a disregard or contempt for the poor. The transference of land in Tudor England, whether from the church to the monarchy, from the monarchy to the gentry, or within the landowning class, all did much to alter the balance of power. John Leland took note in the 1530s of the precipitous decline of the Mallett family of Yorkshire that resulted from a combination of land sales and a plethora of female descendants who had to be married off, leaving their reduced estates in the possession of a single individual. Conversely, the sale and redistribution of the monastic lands confiscated in the 1530s in particular made some landowners much wealthier and brought others into the landowning class for the first time. Yeoman farmers, and even tenants and cottagers, also stood to gain from land sales by the aristocracy or those individual members of the gentry who had to sell land to make ends meet.

To the extent that the gentry became the dominant class in the House of Commons, which gained in influence throughout this period, one might legitimately speak of their growing power and importance, even if individual members of the gentry did not share the same economic fate as one another. Still, for all the economic pressures and increased competition for power from the Crown and the gentry, the aristocracy remained the dominant social class and the main repository of military power, despite the abolition of private armies by Henry VII. They still stood at the top of a feudal hierarchy and could call men to arms, as they frequently did in the rebellions that some of them led against the monarchy in the course of the sixteenth and seventeenth centuries. Unlike other models of political power such as the urban princes who guided the Italian city-states during the fourteenth and fifteenth centuries or the later court-based aristocracies central to the absolute monarchies of the seventeenth century, the English elite remained a landed aristocracy whose power and prestige derived from their country estates.

Religion and politics in the sixteenth century: The Scottish Reformation

The Scottish Reformation differed from the English Reformation in two main respects: Scotland's official break with Rome occurred a generation later than did that of England, and took place at the instigation of leading members of the clergy and nobility and not the monarch. In the first half of the sixteenth century, the Scottish monarchy once again had to survive two regencies for young monarchs whose fathers died in battle: that of James V, whose father James IV (r. 1513–42) had died at the Battle of Flodden Field in 1513, and that of Mary, Queen of Scots, after James V died shortly after the Battle of Solway Moss in 1542. Scotland remained relatively stable during the minority of James V, as members of the clergy and the nobility stepped in to fill the void, but the country was not without its share of intrigue. Queen Margaret sought to consolidate her position as regent through marriage to Archibald Douglas, the sixth Earl of Angus, but when she discovered his unfaithfulness she sought a divorce. James seized control of the throne and assumed his personal rule in 1528. The decline of Margaret, the sister of Henry VIII, contributed to the already deteriorating relationship between England and Scotland.

The Scottish–French alliance, cemented through the marriage of James V and Mary Guise, a daughter of one of the leading Catholic families in France, worked against the prospects of a Reformation in Scotland, which James personally opposed. Cardinal David Beaton oversaw the Scottish church and pursued a close friendship with France as well. James had aligned his power with that of the upper clergy in defence of both royal authority and the church. All of this led Henry VIII to send an army northward in an attempt to deprive his enemy France of Scottish military support. The imprisonment of many leading Scottish nobles after Solway Moss, in addition to those who died in battle, left an additional power vacuum when James V died from the plague three weeks later, a void that Mary Guise and Cardinal Beaton were only too happy to fill. Mary, Queen of Scots, was just a week old at the time of her father's death.

John Knox helped to shape the way in which the Scottish Reformation would be remembered and interpreted through his own account of its history, written in the 1560s. He portrayed the Reformation in Scotland as the triumph of the true religion over the forces of darkness and worldly opposition. He attributed the early death of Edward VI and the reign of his Catholic successor, Mary Tudor, to Satan who 'intended nothing less than the light of Jesus Christ utterly to have been extinguished within the whole isle of Brittany [sic]'.[10] Knox saw the French as the enemy of the Reformation throughout Europe as well as in Scotland.

Theologically, Knox began as a Lutheran. In fact, the religious principles that he enunciated in his first public debate in 1547 could have just as easily been written by Martin Luther, the great German religious leader credited with starting the European Reformation who had just died the previous year. At that time, Knox affirmed the belief that the papacy was the antichrist, that God, not the pope or any man, was the head of the church, and the simplicity of the sacraments as practised in the New Testament. He attacked the church hierarchy, prayers for the dead, and the existence of purgatory. After nineteen months as a French galley slave, however, he was less inclined to share Luther's political conservatism and reliance on a princely magistrate to reform the church.

Upon his release by the French, Knox steadily moved towards Calvinism, especially after the time during Mary Tudor's reign (1553–8) that he spent in Calvin's Geneva, which he called 'the most perfect school of Christ that has been on earth since the days of the Apostles'. Some discontented members of the Scottish nobility began to write to Knox in 1557 urging him to return. He returned to Scotland shortly after Mary Tudor's death in 1558 and published a notorious diatribe against female rule called *The First Blast of the Trumpet against the Monstrous Regiment of Women*. In it, Knox argued that neither nature nor the Bible nor history supports the concept of a female sovereign, which he stated was a 'subversion of good order, of all equity and justice'. He went so far as to say that it made no more sense to allow a woman to rule a nation than a madman, an invalid, or a fool: 'And such be all women, compared unto man in bearing of authority. For their sight in civil regiment is but blindness; their strength, weakness; their counsel, foolishness; and judgment, frenzy, if it be rightly considered.' Knox's ideas were firmly rooted in male attitudes towards women during this period – women had no special status in society apart from their association with men, as reflected in the metaphorical Great Chain of Being. This concept postulated a hierarchy of beings with God and the angels positioned above man, who, in turn stood higher than animals, plants, and minerals, respectively. Shakespeare and other sixteenth-century writers strongly reinforced this idea in an effort to preserve a sense of order in an age of social instability and anxiety.

Knox's attitudes towards female rulers did not prevent him, however, from seeking an alliance with Elizabeth I (r. 1558–1603), the new queen of England and daughter of Henry VIII and Anne Boleyn. Elizabeth overlooked Knox's misogyny, which was probably ubiquitous at the time, and offered support to the Scottish Reformation, a first step in creating the possibility for an eventual political union between the two countries, something that Knox himself would not have opposed. Pressure from the

FIGURE 12 *Elizabeth I, Queen of England and Ireland, c.1588. Version of the Armada portrait attributed to George Gower. The last Tudor monarch, Elizabeth I (1533–1603) ruled from 1558 until 1603. National Portrait Gallery.*
Print Collector/Hulton Fine Art Collection/Getty.

lay nobility forced the regent, Mary Guise, to allow Protestant preaching as long as she could go on celebrating mass, an arrangement that would be duplicated when her daughter assumed the throne a few years later. Protestant leaders drew up the Scottish Confession of Faith in 1560, emphasizing preaching, the sacraments, and church discipline as the three pillars of the Reformed faith.

After the break with Rome, the Scottish church faced the same problem that confronted all national Protestant churches: how to provide enough ministers trained in the new faith to staff the churches throughout the country. Some parishes had to share ministers, at least temporarily, briefly replicating the practice of pluralism that reformers had criticized as an abuse of the old church. The Scottish church, however, not only managed to staff virtually every church in Scotland, but it generally did so with well-educated, university-trained clergy.

During the minority of James VI, the Scottish church eventually took on its Presbyterian form, in which officials (presbyters) selected by each congregation met in a national assembly as their church's representative to consider matters of doctrine, discipline, and practice. During the 1570s and 1580s, Protestantism spread throughout Scotland, including the Highlands, despite the lack of a translation of the Bible into Gaelic, which would not occur until 1801. When James began his majority rule, he realized the importance of maintaining the Protestant church in Scotland, even as his own wife, Anne of Denmark, converted to Catholicism in the mid-1590s.

Religion and politics in the sixteenth century: The Reformation in Ireland and Wales

The increase in royal authority that occurred when Henry VIII added the title of Supreme Head of the English church to that of king had serious implications for both Ireland and Wales. Henry took advantage of the rebellion of Thomas Fitzgerald, the ninth Earl of Kildare, popularly known as 'Silken Thomas', to further extend his direct authority over Ireland. In 1541 the Irish Parliament passed legislation making Henry the king of Ireland, and by extension giving Ireland the designation of a kingdom. As a result of this act, Irish lords were expected to swear allegiance to the king in order to keep their lands, which now became fiefs granted by the king. This measure had the effect of producing greater conformity among the Anglo-Irish nobility, but royal authority still did not extend over the entire island, whatever Henry's claims. Henry's desire to add the Irish Crown to his list of titles was directly tied to the English Reformation as Henry sought to establish his headship over the Irish church as well and end its allegiance to the papacy. The greater difficulty that he experienced getting the Irish Parliament to approve the dissolution of the monasteries in 1536–7, however, provided an early indication of Ireland's greater reluctance to abandon Catholicism.

Henry succeeded at an official level at making the Church of Ireland Protestant, encountering little resistance from the clergy in Dublin, but he could not prevent most of the Irish population from remaining Catholic. Although Henry now claimed the legal authority to impose the Protestant faith on the entire island, he lacked the resources to do so. He had already spent £40,000 to crush the Kildare Rebellion, an amount which Thomas Bartlett has estimated at forty times the annual revenue from the island.[11] The Crown did step up the process of dissolution in 1539; by the time of his death Henry had done away with every single monastery within the Pale.[12] There he softened the blow by offering pensions to the disposed monks and nuns. Furthermore, the Henrician religious settlement retained many religiously conservative elements that allowed Catholics to view his Reformation as more political than religious in nature.

Even those predisposed not to accept the religious changes were not in a position to protest in the wake of the disastrous failure of the Kildare Rebellion in 1534. The problem was not so much within the Pale as that the population outside of the Pale remained stubbornly Catholic and had even managed to preserve their monastic institutions during the dissolution period of the 1530s and 1540s. In his *View to the Present State of Ireland* (1596), the poet Edmund Spenser argued that force and violence would work much less than 'mildness and gentleness' in spreading the ideas of the Reformation in Ireland. Spenser assumed that most Irish knew little of the theological issues at stake and that they mainly hated the Protestant faith because they associated it with England. For that reason he advocated sending Irish Protestants among the people to convert them instead of English missionaries. Spenser expressed confidence that if early missionaries such as Patrick and Columba could convert the Irish from paganism to Christianity it should be relatively easy for Protestant missionaries armed with the true religion of the Gospels to convince the native Irish of the false worship and idolatry associated with popery. As it turned out, Spenser underestimated both the continuing appeal of Catholicism for large numbers of the Irish population and the intensity of religious divisions among Irish Catholics and Protestants, both native and settlers who by that time had begun arriving from across the Irish Sea.

At the time of the Reformation, the Welsh had no representatives in the English Parliament that enacted the legislation that broke with the papacy and produced a religious change in their land. It is doubtful whether they would have taken such a step on their own. The 1531 execution of Rhys ap Gruffudd, a prominent Welsh nobleman who was suspected of conspiring to seize power in Wales, showed Henry's concern with political conformity at a sensitive time when he was already contemplating his break with Rome and marriage to Anne Boleyn. The main immediate impact of the Reformation in Wales was the dissolution of the monasteries, which occurred simultaneously with the attack on English abbeys. Of the twenty-seven remaining Welsh monasteries, twenty-four met their demise in 1536–7.[13] As in England and Ireland, the confiscation of monastic lands extended royal authority at the expense of the church while simultaneously reinforcing key aspects of Protestant doctrine at the expense of what both Henry and Cromwell regarded as popish superstition.[14] The Pilgrimage of Grace had only strengthened their commitment to total dissolution whereas at first they had remained open to leaving some of the larger monasteries open. In Wales, as elsewhere, religious and political conformity went hand-in-hand; in February 1536 the English Parliament passed an act affirming a political union between England and Wales and placing English and Welsh subjects on equal terms with one another, but under English law.

The Welsh gentry by and large accepted the Reformation and accommodated themselves to it, though it took until later in the century for them to become positive advocates of the Protestant faith. As in the Scottish Highlands, Protestantism flourished in Wales despite a predominantly oral culture and a delay in getting the Bible translated into the language of the people. Part of the appeal of the Reformation for lay Christians elsewhere was the encouragement it provided for them to read the Bible for themselves, thus providing encouragement to a rise in literacy. The Welsh did not need to wait as long for their own translation, however, thanks to the commitment of Welsh reformers to the enterprise. The Reformation also had the effect of creating a stronger sense of unity between English and Welsh Catholics, who were well represented at the English College in Rome in the 1570s. Welshmen such as Owen Lewis and Morys Clynnog reinforced this notion by referring to the College as the 'Seminarium Britannicum'.[15]

The Reformations in the British Isles in European context

The Reformations that occurred in the British Isles took place from the beginning within a larger European context and every stage of religious change that took place there in the sixteenth century had serious international ramifications. Pope Clement VII hesitated to rule on Henry VIII's request for a divorce from Katherine of Aragon mainly because her nephew, the Holy Roman Emperor Charles V, happened to invade Rome in 1527 and the pope had no wish to anger him further. Wolsey pleaded with both for time to change the other's mind, but neither relented in time to prevent his downfall. When the pope asked Henry to intervene with the emperor on his behalf, appealing to Henry's title of 'Defender of the Faith', which Pope Leo X had bestowed upon him for writing a *Defense of the Seven Sacraments* in opposition to Luther in 1521, Henry shot back saying that 'if the Roman pope had fought in the cause of religion and not temporal power, I should have considered that to be my course of action'.[16] However, Henry, still hopeful that the pope would grant a divorce at that point and not yet ready to completely cut his ties with Rome, did offer to provide financial assistance should the French king, Francis I, decide to send an army.

After the break with Rome, Henry had to be constantly wary of attitudes towards England among the Catholic powers of Europe. When Henry's third wife, Jane Seymour, died in 1536, his advisers immediately saw the opportunity to further a Continental alliance, with early considerations focusing on France or the Low Countries. Henry and his councillors lived in fear that France and Spain would reach a truce, putting Protestant England at the mercy of an alliance between those two Catholic kingdoms. The French, seeking to beat the Habsburgs to an English alliance, actually proposed for Henry to marry a sister of Mary Guise and offered a younger son of King Francis I as bridegroom for Princess Mary, the daughter of Henry and Katherine of Aragon. But a truce signed between Francis and Charles V at Nice put an end to those preliminary negotiations and left Cromwell struggling to find a match for Henry that would at least help counterbalance the dangerous détente reached by the Habsburg and Valois monarchs.

This wider European context helps to explain Henry's violent shift back in the direction of Catholicism in 1539 in the form of the Six Articles, known to Protestants as 'the whip with six strings'. These articles confirmed the Catholic doctrine of transubstantiation, whereby the bread and wine became transformed during the Eucharist into the body and blood of Christ, denied that the laity needed to receive both the bread and the wine during communion, confirmed the principle of clerical celibacy, and affirmed both private masses and auricular confession, all of which ran counter to Protestant sensibility if not doctrine.

During Edward's reign, John Dudley, the Duke of Northumberland, began to shift foreign policy towards the French and away from the Habsburgs because of the close connection between the latter and the Catholic princess Mary, whose accession to the throne he would try to prevent by installing his daughter-in-law, Lady Jane Grey, as queen when Edward died in 1553. When Northumberland assumed power in 1549, the Edwardian Reformation had only gone so far to establish Protestantism in England, but it had raised the expectations of reformers throughout Europe. In a close examination of a contemporary portrait, *Edward VI and the Pope: An Allegory of the Reformation*, Margaret Aston has demonstrated the strong links Protestants made between the young Edward and the biblical king Josiah, whose war on idolatry Edward was expected to imitate.[17] Northumberland's government went so far as to establish a 'Stranger Church' in London under the leadership of the Polish reformer Jan Łaski to embrace Protestant refugees of various nationalities from the Continent. Treaty with France meant peace with Scotland, but Northumberland needed as much support as he could muster if he were to succeed at placing Lady Jane on the throne at the expense of Mary. Edward's premature death in 1553 deprived him of the time necessary to build a strong enough coalition within England to prevent Mary's accession, however.

When Mary Tudor became queen, she not only attempted to restore England to the Catholic faith but also completely reoriented English foreign policy towards an alliance with Spain and the Habsburgs. This enhanced the prospect of yet another renewal of war between England and France, since the Spanish Habsburg dynasty had renewed its struggle for European supremacy with the French Valois kings. Despite native opposition to her repugnant marriage to Philip II, Mary's hostility to France, England's long-time enemy, would have still resonated with many of her subjects, who were becoming increasingly nationalistic and xenophobic. When Mary did declare war on France in 1557, the proclamation offered as justification Northumberland's French policy and French sympathy for Wyatt's Rebellion, a popular uprising directed against Mary in 1554, as well as Mary's disappointment that the French had not grown more favourably disposed towards her in the course of her reign. The proclamation did not explain how her marriage to the French king's greatest enemy was supposed to effect that result. The war ended in disappointment for Mary and England, which surrendered Calais, its last remaining territorial possession on the European mainland.

Meanwhile, Cardinal Reginald Pole returned to England to direct Mary's religious policy at home, beginning by absolving England for its break with Rome under Henry VIII and welcoming the country back into the Catholic fold. In 1549, Mary's first Parliament repealed most of the religious legislation carried out under Edward VI, including restoring the prohibition against marriage by the clergy. In 1555, Parliament renewed laws that made heresy, independent of the political charge of treason, a crime against the state punishable by death. Mary's religious policies galvanized international Protestant opposition against her, a factor often overlooked in her decision to persecute English Protestants, about 300 of whom she burnt at the stake during her brief reign. The Marian persecutions inspired John Foxe to write his *Acts and Monuments*, better known as the 'Book of Martyrs', placing Mary's Protestant victims in a long line of heroic Christian martyrs dating to the early days of Christianity under the Roman Empire.

Eamon Duffy and revisionist historians have attempted to explain Mary's policy, if not justify it, on the basis of several considerations. First, there was the recalcitrance and extreme beliefs of those executed, which may have landed them in equal trouble with a mainstream Protestant regime. Second, the executions occurred in an historical context in which martyrdom was sought by religious minorities and persecution expected by authorities against religious nonconformists. The 300 victims of the Marian persecutions represent about a tenth of those executed by European states for religious reasons between 1525 and 1565.[18] Third, Marian authorities used the public burnings as opportunities for Catholic preaching to convert the audience back to what they regarded as the true faith or to reinforce the truth of Catholic teachings among the faithful.[19] Finally, Duffy also notes that the English Protestants who went to their deaths under Mary seem to have been mainly turned in by private individuals rather than rooted out by state authorities. Yet, these protestations notwithstanding, Mary's government still had in common with the Spanish Inquisition sanguinary persecution to enforce religious authority, a parallel accentuated by Mary's marriage to Philip II of Spain.

Those Protestants wishing to leave Britain during Mary's reign had no shortage of options in Germany and Switzerland; even the Catholic Henry II of France welcomed English refugees as a way of striking back at Mary for her marriage to his enemy, Philip. The experience of the English religious refugees in Germany and Switzerland increased their sense of belonging to an international Protestant community, for which the Frenchman John Calvin had emerged as the leading spokesperson from Geneva. The influence of Geneva was rivalled by that of the Netherlands, where Dutch Protestants in the 1560s embarked on a revolt to defend their faith and achieve their political independence from Catholic Spain.

The Elizabethan religious settlement, as Patrick Collinson has convincingly demonstrated, was largely shaped by pressures from English Protestants who wished to see the church reformed along the lines of those Calvinist churches with which they had gained experience during their exile under Mary.[20] At the beginning of the French wars of religion in 1562, Elizabeth dispatched 6,000 troops to Normandy to provide military assistance to the French Calvinist Huguenots. After 1563 entire liturgies intended to serve the same purpose substituted for those in the Book of Common Prayer.[21] In short, both Elizabeth's domestic religious policy and her foreign policy were influenced by pressure from the international Protestant community at home and abroad.

Elizabeth also had to contend, however, with the prospect of a unified Catholic front against a Protestant England after France and Spain made peace once again in the Treaty of Cateau-Cambresis in 1559. During the 1560s, Elizabeth's council constantly worried about the Catholic threat and the possibility of a Catholic succession. The beginning of the French Wars of Religion in the 1560s helped to distract France, but the Northern Rebellion of 1569 held great potential danger for

Elizabeth because it called international attention to English Catholic discontent with her religious policies. The Northern Rebellion finally got the attention of the papacy, which at this juncture had retained open diplomatic relations with Elizabeth. After her excommunication by the Pope Pius V in 1570, Elizabeth faced numerous plots against her throne and life, most designed to replace her with her Catholic cousin, Mary, Queen of Scots.

The rise and fall of Mary, Queen of Scots

In 1558, at the age of sixteen, Mary Stewart, the daughter of King James IV of Scotland and his French wife Mary Guise, married Francois, the dauphin or heir to the French throne. Fate intervened in the lives of Mary and Francois when King Henry II died as a result of an infection sustained when a lance splinter entered his head during a jousting accident in July 1559. Henry's death left Francois and Mary as king and queen of France, but fate intervened again when Francois died a year later. Meanwhile, in May 1559 the Protestant leaders in Scotland, inspired by the incendiary sermons of John Knox, had staged their revolt against the regency of Mary Guise, despite her efforts to be conciliatory towards them in hopes of preserving her position there. The French, in response, sent troops to back the regency and crush the revolt. The move backfired. In response, Elizabeth, knowing that the Catholic Guises regarded her as illegitimate because of the circumstances of her mother's marriage to Henry VIII, sent money to the Scottish 'Lords of the Congregation', the leading Protestants among the Scottish nobility.

In 1560, with Mary, Queen of Scots, still in France, the Scottish Parliament passed a series of measures that removed Scotland from the Roman Church, adopted a Confession of Faith inspired by Calvinist theology, and brought Scotland into the Protestant fold. The Catholic Mary's return to Scotland in 1561 posed a potential threat to the Scottish Reformation and, potentially, to English Protestantism as well, since, in the eyes of some Catholics, she had a stronger claim to the English throne than did Elizabeth. Not only was Mary a Catholic, but as a younger woman with a certain amount of beauty and charisma, she posed a potential threat to steal the affections of Elizabeth's subjects away from her. Although their roles would soon become completely reversed, at the time of the widow Mary's return to Scotland, it was Elizabeth who was tainted by scandal, thanks to the suspicious death of Amy Dudley, the wife of Robert Dudley, Elizabeth's frequent companion and rumoured lover. William Cecil, Elizabeth's trusted minister and adviser, recognized the danger this scandal posed to Elizabeth, especially with a rival female monarch with a claim to the English throne resident in Britain. According to the terms of Henry VIII's will, Katherine Grey would probably have had the strongest legal claim to the throne if Elizabeth had died before 1568, when Katherine passed away. Nonetheless, Mary's mother and other relatives had urged her to stake her claim to the English throne from the time of Elizabeth's accession.

Shortly after Mary returned to Scotland, James Stewart, the Earl of Moray and Mary's illegitimate half-brother, had already turned many of the leading Protestant lords against her by stoking fears that she would attempt to restore Catholicism and persecute and burn Protestants as Mary Tudor had done in England. Knox, in particular, railed against her, comparing her to Nero, and refusing to back down in a personal confrontation with the queen. Her marriage to Henry Stewart, Lord Darnley in a Catholic ceremony in July 1565 placed her even more at odds with her Protestant subjects and their leaders (even though Darnley was a professing Protestant at the time of the marriage). Moray led the rebellion against her authority; the marriage had threatened not only the Reformation but his own political ascendancy. But Mary still had support among some Protestants, most notably William Maitland of Lethington. James Hepburn, the Earl of Bothwell also came to her support to crush the rebellion, temporarily sending Moray into exile in England.

From there, events spun quickly out of control for Mary, some of her own doing. In September 1565 Mary wrote to Philip II of Spain, indicating that she and Darnley had only gone along with the religious changes in Scotland for fear that they would lose their thrones otherwise, while making it clear that she would welcome assistance from Spain in restoring the Catholic Church to her realm. In June 1566, Mary gave birth to a son, but only after the murder of David Riccio, an Italian lute player who had become a political adviser and personal confidante and whom Darnley suspected of being Mary's lover. Mary was heart-broken by the death of Riccio; she blamed his death on Darnley and looked to Bothwell and the Earl of Morton for support, despite Morton's participation in Riccio's murder. The machinations of Darnley's enemies and Mary's allies culminated with Darnley's murder at the house known as Kirk o'Field in Edinburgh. Mary quickly developed a close relationship with Bothwell, their open cavorting appearing unseemly in one so recently widowed. Mary needed a strong ally and Bothwell fit the bill, but in the end their relationship not only did not save her but contributed significantly to her ultimate downfall. The Scottish Parliament deposed Mary in 1567 and attempted to consolidate the Reformation by passing a law requiring any future monarch to take an oath swearing that he or she would defend the reformed faith.

On 14 July Elizabeth had written to her Scottish ambassador, Sir Nicholas Throckmorton, seeking to provide assurances to Mary both for her own safety and that of her son, James, whose right to rule Elizabeth promised to defend as if he might be 'our child out of our own body'. Ten days later Mary abdicated from a position of captivity in Loch Leven Castle, the Scottish Crown passing to her one-year-old son. Moray was designated as regent, a position he occupied until his assassination three years later. Mary was not done yet, however; she escaped from captivity and Archibald Campbell, fifth Earl of Argyll and one of the leading Protestant lords, put together an army of about 6,000 men to challenge Moray. Mary might have yet retained her throne, but in 1568 at Langside just south of Glasgow her forces met defeat. Mary was not interested in being captured once again and fled to England three days later. Elizabeth would have preferred Mary remain in Scotland, but she could hardly allow her potential rival the freedom to exchange her Scottish throne for an English one.

The Protestant scholar George Buchanan, who became tutor to the young king James, wrote A Dialogue Concerning the Rights of Scotland, using Calvinist resistance theory to justify Mary's deposition. But the nobility had continued to fight among themselves, keeping open the possibility of Mary's restoration. Scotland remained divided after Mary's departure, erupting into a civil war that would not subside for another six years. Moray's assassination by James Hamilton, one of Mary's supporters, in 1570 was particularly significant because of the destabilizing effect it had on Scottish politics. Moray's death had deprived Scottish Protestants of their political leader and potentially opened the door to a Catholic restoration. Moray's replacement, the Earl of Lennox was assassinated in 1571, while another faction removed the Earl of Morton as regent in 1578, executing him three years later.

Meanwhile, Elizabeth had taken care not to disparage Mary as a legitimate female sovereign; the anti-Mary campaign in England focused on her Catholicism and threat to the English throne instead of denying her legal right to rule in Scotland. Mary believed that Elizabeth owed it to her as her cousin and another ruling monarch to help restore her to her rightful throne and constantly implored her to do just that. As in so much else, Elizabeth vacillated, preferring inaction to any action that might have potential drawbacks. Admitting that her deposition was legal might encourage those who opposed Elizabeth's right to rule, but Elizabeth could not bring herself to restore her rival to the Scottish throne either and give hope to Catholics insurgents in her own realm.

In 1586 Elizabeth's spy network uncovered evidence of Mary's direct correspondence with Philip II as part of a conspiracy to assassinate Elizabeth known as the Babington Plot, which contained direct proof of Mary's approval of the plan and finally allowed the queen's ministers to convince her to sign Mary's death warrant that sealed her fate. In her last letter, written to her former brother-in-law, Henry III of France, Mary comes across as a somewhat pathetic self-pitying martyr who complains of two decades of abuse at the hands of Elizabeth. Mary asserts her readiness for death, though she protests her total innocence of any crime. She complains of not being allowed to see her chaplain for confession or last rites, strengthening her claim to die as a martyr to her faith rather than for any alleged treason on her part. In denying any such culpability, Mary remained disingenuous and self-serving to the end.

After Mary's execution, Elizabeth trod lightly in her correspondence with James, who was under some pressure from some of his subjects to avenge the death of his mother whom they had still regarded as the legitimate queen of Scotland. Although Elizabeth refused to designate a successor, James must have known even at that point that his odds were pretty good and he did not want to jeopardize his chances at inheriting the English throne after her death. Mary's death had solved the long-standing problem of a rival queen living in close proximity to Elizabeth, but it brought her conflict with Philip II of Spain to a head.

'I have the heart and stomach of a king': Queen Elizabeth I

Mary's execution drew the ire of Philip II, but the Anglo-Spanish rivalry had been brewing for quite some time. Philip finally declared war on England in 1587, but Elizabeth, if anything, was fortunate to have delayed this event as long as she did. John Hawkins had started raiding Spanish ships and territories, as well as impinging on the slave trade between Africa and America as early as the 1560s. Hawkins's cousin, Sir Francis Drake, did even more to provoke the Spanish; Drake, a fanatical Protestant, fought a private war with Spain for decades while waiting for a broader conflict to emerge. Hawkins and Drake had both the financial backing and the tacit approval for their schemes from Elizabeth herself.

Almost two decades had passed since the Northern Rebellion unsettled her reign and Pope Pius V had cut her off from the Catholic Church. In the interim, Elizabeth had cultivated an alliance with France centred on a marriage proposal from Francis, the Duke of Alençon, later the Duke of Anjou, probably the closest that Elizabeth ever came to walking down the aisle. Such an alliance could only be seen as an anti-Habsburg pact that would have placed both England and France on the side of the Protestant Dutch rebels led by William of Orange who had entered into open rebellion against Spain. Still, some members of the council, especially Francis Knollys who had served the previous Protestant regimes of both Henry VIII and Edward VI, had a hard time accepting any alliance with Catholic France for religious reasons, which might have had some influence on Elizabeth's decision not to go through with the wedding. At any rate, any chance at an alliance with France, through marriage or otherwise, ended when Catholics murdered tens of thousands of French Protestants during the St Bartholomew's Day Massacre on 23 August 1572.

A few weeks before the Massacre, Dutch rebels seized control of Flushing at the mouth of the Scheldt River, and Count Louis of Nassau had taken the Habsburg stronghold of Mons, which was located on the border between France and Flanders. Elizabeth had previously supported a volunteer army led by Sir Humphrey Gilbert to assist the Dutch rebels. The St Bartholomew's Day Massacre inaugurated an unexpected truce between Philip and Elizabeth, who recalled Gilbert from the Netherlands in November 1572. Both the English and Spanish viewed this rapprochement as a temporary arrangement forged by expediency, however, with tensions mounting steadily between them over the next decade and a half.

The first thirty years of her reign had also given Elizabeth ample time to extend her authority throughout her kingdom, ably assisted by her loyal ministers, principally William Cecil, who was with her on the day that Mary died and stood by her from the very beginning of her reign. John Guy has noted the extent to which Cecil, along with Knollys and several other prominent individuals such as Bedford, Cave, Pembroke, and Rogers, extended their authority in the provinces, where they served as Justices of the Peace, at the same time that they sat on Elizabeth's Privy Council.[22] Guy compared the sweeping restructuring of government under Elizabeth to that undertaken by Russia following the Bolshevik Revolution of 1917.[23] Seen in this light, the Northern Rebellion of 1569 might be viewed as a counter-revolutionary movement aimed to restore Mary, Queen of Scots, to her rightful throne and to insert a different aristocratic faction at the centre of Elizabeth's government to replace upstarts like Cecil. The Duke of Norfolk headed this Catholic faction and emerged as the most likely candidate to become the fourth husband of Mary, Queen of Scots, and bring his power to bear on the Scottish situation.

England had therefore split into two separate factions, between those who had supported Mary Tudor, crushed the abortive attempt to place Lady Jane Grey on the throne when Edward died, and fought for the Crown against Wyatt's Rebellion on the one hand and those who had held power under Edward, temporarily supported Lady Jane Grey, and at least some of whom had openly defied Mary by fighting against her or fleeing to the Continent on the other. Deep political schisms existed that could not be ameliorated; this was one of the reasons why Cecil penned a succession bill in 1563, the same year that Elizabeth narrowly escaped death during a bout with smallpox, to give the Privy Council authority in the event of Elizabeth's death. Elizabeth survived, however, and did her best to minimize conflicts between the two groups. For example, between 1558 and 1588, she summoned the Parliament seven times, enough to keep the parliamentary tradition alive but a small number compared to the reigns of her immediate predecessors, thus lessening the opportunities for conflict to arise at the political centre.

Elizabeth herself was especially sensitive to religious opposition; she clashed with both Parliament and her own church hierarchy over religious issues. By 1585 she had become particularly concerned about the free licence that ministers seemed to feel they had to preach just about anything:

> You suffer many ministers to preach what they list, and to minister the sacraments according to their own fancies – some one way, some another – to the breach of unity; yea, and some of them so curious in searching matters above their capacity as they preach they wot not what: that there is no hell, but a torment of conscience; nay, I have heard of there by six preachers in one diocese the which do preach six sundry ways.[24]

Elizabeth wanted 'one truth' preached throughout her kingdom and recommended that unprepared ministers simply be given homilies written in the reign of Edward VI to read before their congregations. She particularly objected to private religious meetings known as conventicles 'where every merchant must have his schoolmaster and nightly conventicles expounding Scriptures and catechizing their servants and maids, in so much that I have heard how some of their maids have not sticked to control learned preachers, and say that such a man taught otherwise in our house'.[25] She also quarrelled with MPs over the issue of free speech within Parliament, which its members started to claim as a constitutional right.

The one issue on which the queen and her Parliament did agree was the need to reduce the internal threat from English Catholics, resulting in growing legislation in the 1570s and 1580s that imposed penalties on those who did not conform to the Church of England. Increasingly, Elizabeth's government viewed outward practice of Catholicism as tantamount to treason. The execution of the English Jesuit Edmund Campion in 1581 is one of the best examples of the implementation of this view, leading to his apotheosis as a Catholic martyr and a twentieth-century hagiography by Evelyn Waugh.[26] Still, her religious policies drew complaints from the more ardent Protestants known as Puritans that the regime did not enforce the anti-Catholic legislation enough or do enough to guard against the Catholic threat to the throne.

The Elizabethan regime was thus primarily preoccupied with preserving some kind of precarious unity that would keep her secure on the throne and prevent the kinds of divisions among her subjects that would lead to civil war, such as England had experienced a hundred years earlier and France was then enduring. But Elizabeth could not forget about the threat from Spain or Philip's desire to see Mary Stewart upon the English throne. In the Netherlands, the Anglo-Spanish truce had collapsed by the 1580s and Elizabeth had resumed English support for the Dutch rebellion.

By 1585 Elizabeth's old friend, Robert Dudley, now the Earl of Leicester, embarked for the Netherlands with another 'private' army to prevent the latest attempt of the Habsburgs to impose military rule there. Philip was not inclined to excuse this interference any more than the raids of Hawkins and Drake, even if Elizabeth disavowed personal responsibility for the expedition. The execution of Mary Stewart was a breaking point and finally led Philip to declare war on England.

Nothing could have done more to unify Elizabeth's subjects behind her, especially when Spain launched a massive Armada of 130 ships transporting about 8,000 sailors with the intent of landing some 20,000 soldiers on the coast of England. The Armada left Spain in May 1588 and entered the English Channel that July. The English navy, if such it can be called, dispersed the Armada, which had anchored in the Channel, mainly by sending 'fire ships', small craft set ablaze, steering in the direction of the large Spanish vessels, which pulled up anchors and became dispersed by what was later deemed a 'Protestant wind'. The defeat of the Armada was commemorated in ways large and small and passed into legend as the highpoint of Elizabeth's reign, even though the war with Spain lasted another sixteen years and only ended after she was dead. On 8 August Elizabeth personally journeyed to Tilbury down the Thames from London, where she gave the most famous speech of her reign, telling an assembly of soldiers:

> I have always behaved myself, that under God, I have placed my chiefest strength and safeguard in the loyal hearts and goodwill of all my subjects, and therefore I am come amongst you, as you see, at this time, nor for my recreation and disport, but being resolved in the midst and heat of battle, to live or die amongst you all, to lay down for my God, and for my kingdom, and for my people, my honor, and my blood, even in the dust. I know I have the body of but a weak and feeble woman, but I have the heart and stomach of a king, and of a King of England too, and think foul scorn that Parma or Spain, or any Prince of Europe should dare to invade the borders of my realm; to which, rather than any dishonor shall grow by me, I myself will take up arms, I myself will be your general, judge and rewarder of every one of your virtues in the field. I know already of your forwardness, you have deserved rewards and crowns; and we do assure you, in the word of a Prince, they shall be duly paid you.[27]

The defeat of the Armada was among the most significant factors leading her younger contemporaries who survived into the reign of her successor to look back on Elizabeth's reign as a golden age. But the political divisions of her reign had never really gone away and resurfaced in the 1590s in the court rivalry between Sir Robert Cecil, son of William, and the charismatic adventurer, Robert Devereux, the Earl of Essex.

In the end, Elizabeth had turned her greatest weakness into her greatest strength – as a single female ruler, she could make a claim to exceptionality, remain free from male domination and control, if not from male influence, and profess total devotion to her people and her country because she did not have to divide her attention with a husband or children. Elizabeth had not completely solved all of her country's problems, but she had demonstrated that a female ruler could reign without a king and steer her country through particularly troubled times caused by religious divisiveness and the intrusion of religion into politics. By comparison with France, England had survived the turbulent divisions of the Reformation century relatively unscathed – so far.

FIGURE 13 *A group of supposed witches being beaten in front of King James I, c. 1610.*
Hulton Archive/Getty.

7

From Stewart to Stuart:

Political culture, the monarchy, and the three kingdoms, 1603–1642

This royal throne of kings, this sceptered isle,
The earth of majesty, this seat of Mars,
This other Eden, demi-paradise,
This fortress built by nature for herself
Against infection and the hand of war,
This happy breed of men, this little world,
This precious stone set in the silver sea,
Which serves it in the office of a wall,
Or as a moat defensive to a house,
Against the envy of less happier lands;
This blessed plot, this earth, this realm, this England.

WILLIAM SHAKESPEARE, *Richard II*, Act 2, Scene 1

Hail, King! For so thou art. Behold where stands
Th' usurper's cursed head. The time is free.
I see thee compassed with thy kingdom's pearl,
That speak my salutation in their minds,
Whose voices I desire aloud with mine.
Hail, King of Scotland!

WILLIAM SHAKESPEARE, *Macbeth*, Act 5, Scene 8

Shakespeare and history

William Shakespeare (1564–1616) had such a large impact on English political culture because he encapsulated and helped to define the values and ideas that permeated Elizabethan and early Jacobean society, and also because many of his plays dealt with British history. Andrew Gurr has argued for a shift in the interests of English playgoers that occurred in the 1590s in the direction of a demand for more serious plays, perhaps as a result of the fright of the Spanish Armada in 1588 and the war with Spain.[1] Shakespeare's sources of information for his history plays included critical histories such as Polydore Vergil's 1534 *History of England* and the more recent *Chronicles of England, Scotland, and Ireland* (1587) by Raphael Holinshed, but he also used sources strongly biased in favour of the Tudor dynasty such as Edmund Hall's 1548 *Union of the Families of the Two Noble and Illustre Families of Lancastre and York*.

His favouritism towards the Tudor dynasty, most obvious in *Richard III*, extended to his plays dealing with the first three Lancastrian kings, Henry IV, Henry V, and Henry VI. In dealing with Henry VI, however, Shakespeare had to face the fact that his reign coincided with France's victory over England in the Hundred Years War in 1453. This humiliating defeat had led contemporaries to compare Henry VI unfavourably with his heroic father, Henry V. In *Henry VI, Part II*, therefore, Shakespeare portrays the last Lancastrian king in a way that minimizes Henry's role in the turmoil caused by the rebellion of Richard, Duke of York.

Shakespeare's historically inspired plays convey some information about the past, but their larger purpose related to the political needs of the present, which always took precedence over factual accuracy. In *Henry V* Shakespeare completely ignores the legitimate heir to the French throne at the end of the play during the arrangement of the marriage between Henry and Catherine of Valois.[2] In *Henry VI, Part I*, the Duke of Somerset is actually an amalgamation of two individuals who bore that title; these are just a few of the ways in which Shakespeare departed from his sources in the Henry VI trilogy.

Does Shakespeare's factual inaccuracy matter? Only insofar as early modern playgoers had the sense that they were watching real events unfold on the stage before them. They would have subconsciously absorbed the representation of history unfolding on stage as true, in the same ways that films and television miniseries, such as *Elizabeth* (1998) or *The Tudors* (2007–10), however historically inaccurate, influence our view of the past far out of proportion to anything we might read on the same subject. Whether Shakespeare changed history for the purposes of the play or to reflect his own political views, therefore, hardly matters in terms of the impact that these changes had on the way that the English perceived their history. In fact, Shakespeare wrote plays on such a wide range of topics and his characters took such varied stances on religious and political matters that it is hardly worth the attempt to deduce the playwright's own private beliefs, though many have tried.

Still, Shakespeare matters to our understanding of early modern British history because of the relations and affinities between drama and contemporary political developments of concern. Shakespeare's contemporary, the iconoclastic atheist

Christopher Marlowe appeals to a post-Reformation audience in his play *Edward II*, when Edward says,

Why should a king be subject to a priest?
Proud Rome, that hatchest such imperial grooms
For these thy superstitious taper-lights,
Wherewith they antichristian churches blaze,
I'll fire thy crazed buildings, and enforce
The papal towers to kiss the lowly ground. (Act 1, Scene 4)

In Shakespeare's *Henry V*, the marriage alliance of Catherine of France and Henry V would have conjured up images of the negotiations between Elizabeth and her French suitor, the Duke of Anjou. In the play, Catherine has started to learn English in preparation for her marriage to Henry. Her lesson focuses on the naming of body parts in a way that suggests that Catherine's body was now a part of Henry's dominion, symbolizing the English conquest of French territory. This scene would have also provided a powerful reminder that, as recently as the reign of Mary Tudor, England had lost its last territorial possession in France, the port of Calais. In *Richard III*, Shakespeare made the defeat of Richard at Bosworth Field the fulfilment of a prophecy foretold by Elizabeth Woodville, the great grandmother of Elizabeth I, thus reminding his audience of the providential view of history that culminates in the heaven-sent defeat of the Armada and the glories of Elizabethan England.

Examples abound of ways in which Shakespeare's history plays reflect the history and politics of his own age. John of Gaunt's famous 'this sceptered isle' speech in *Richard II* speaks to an image of English greatness that was meant to reflect the pride shared by his late sixteenth-century audience, rather than to resurrect a historical sentiment dating from the late fourteenth century. Henry V's 'band of brothers' speech calling his soldiers to arms also would have stirred Shakespeare's audiences to think of Spain, and perhaps Ireland, rather than the actual French army that threatened Henry's troops at Agincourt. The words of the title character in *King Lear*, written in 1606, would have resonated with those who had just lived through the old age and death of a reigning monarch:

'tis our fast intent
To shake all cares and business from our age;
Conferring them on younger strengths, while
Unburden'd crawl toward death. (Act 1, Scene 1)

Shakespeare wrote *King Lear* in the immediate aftermath of the Gunpowder Plot of 1605, in which a small group of Catholic terrorists conspired to blow up Parliament and in the process assassinate King James in the hopes of preparing the way for a restoration of the Roman faith. Therefore, the tragic death of King Lear would have evoked not only memories of the recent passage of Elizabeth but also the imagined death of their current monarch, James. The play, like the Gunpowder Plot, raised, as the death of a monarch frequently did, the problems related to royal succession and called to mind how close the English had come to reverting to a stage of civil war under Elizabeth and the possibilities that still remained for political anarchy in the kingdom.[3] In *Macbeth*, as well, the assassination and overthrow of a legitimate monarch with the assistance of the three witches and evil conjurors would have spoken directly not only to a king whose father had been assassinated and who had his own life threatened by the Gunpowder Plot, but also to a king and his subjects who believed that the power and presence of witchcraft was on the rise.[4] A crisis narrowly averted when Guy Fawkes and barrels of gunpowder were discovered in the basement of Parliament immediately prior to a session at which James was scheduled to be present raised the equal possibility that, as in the play, the plot might have succeeded, giving truth to the lines:

> Confusion now hath made his masterpiece!
> Most sacrilegious Murther hath broke ope
> The Lord's anointed temple and stole thence
> The life of this building. (Act 2, Scene 3)

Shakespeare's history plays were not at variance with the purposes that nonfiction historical writing was meant to serve in early modern England. Thomas More constructed dialogue in his *History of Richard III* and shaped the narrative to suit his political aims to justify the Tudor dynasty. In his *History of the Reign of King Henry the Seventh*, Francis Bacon does the same thing when he praises the first Tudor monarch for his wisdom, justice, concern for morality, and protection of the weak, as evidenced, for example, by making the kidnapping of women a capital offence. This lesson, no doubt, was intended for King James I, to whose reign we will turn after a brief look at some of the important characteristics and developments that shaped society in early modern Britain.

Social mobility and social change in the first half of the seventeenth century

Shakespeare's plays reflect contemporary social values as well as the political culture of the period. For example, Lear's faithful and unmarried daughter Cordelia is the paragon of female submission and humble obedience to her father's wishes in comparison to her selfish sisters and their grasping husbands. Thomas Gataker, writing in 1623, called 'an evil wife, a contentious woman' the worst of all evils. Gataker acknowledged that it was just as great an evil for a woman to be saddled with an evil husband: 'For what is said of one is as true of the other, the relation between them being alike.'

One's married status or the state of one's marriage undoubtedly did much to affect the lives of early modern men and women, yet recent scholarship has focused on the ways in which women developed their own network of relationships with other females to create a world where they could assert their status independent of the men in their lives. Women, for example, expressed their admiration or sympathy, their friendship and respect, through the gifts that they gave one another.[5] The process of giving birth also remained part of an exclusively feminine sphere, with men completely excluded from the birth room and babies delivered almost exclusively by mid-wives.

But it was also within this personal feminine sphere that accusations of witchcraft largely developed, prior to the intervention of male authorities. In a society in which people readily believed in the power of witches to cause misfortunes – a child's illness or death, a business failure, chickens that stopped laying eggs or cows that stopped giving milk, fire or property damages due to storms, just to name a few examples – more influential or fortunate women easily became suspicious of less powerful women who might be tempted to take recourse in witchcraft or black magic for real or imagined slights. Poverty, old age, spinsterhood, childlessness, the death of a child or husband all might be perceived as motives of those suspected of witchcraft. In early modern British society, women knew which of their female acquaintances might have reason to hold a grudge or harbour resentment or jealousy, and, through local gossip, those who had a prior reputation for witchcraft or black magic. However, not everyone in a community always agreed on who might be considered a witch and even an individual with such a reputation might live in a community for years before facing a legal accusation of witchcraft.

When witchcraft accusations did come to the attention of male authorities, a largely feminine tradition that associated witchcraft with folklore, magic, and ancient orally transmitted wisdom (such as the ability to make potions to cure or harm) fused with the largely male tradition deriving from church authorities that associated witchcraft with diabolism, or devil worship. The English Parliament passed a new Witchcraft Act in 1604, the first significant legislation on the subject since 1563. Whereas the earlier act had focused on actual property damage and required a second offence before capital punishment would even be considered, the new act called for the death penalty for anyone who 'shall consult, covenant with, entertaine, imploy, feed or reward any evil and wicked spirit, to or for any intent of purpose'. King James himself had written a treatise on witchcraft called *Daemonologie* that stressed the diabolical nature of the phenomenon and introduced Continental ideas, such as belief in the celebration of the witches' Sabbath which was believed to invert the ceremonies of Christian worship in homage to Satan, into the British Isles. The amalgam of these two conceptions of witchcraft can be seen in the examination and trial of the Pendle witches that took place in Lancashire in 1610. The confession of one Elizabeth Sowtherns, for example, referred to her temptation by a 'Spirit or Devill in the Shape of a Boy, the one halfe of his Coate blacke, and the other browne, who bade this Examinate stay, saying to her, that if she would give him her Soule, she should have any thing she would request'. Ann Whittle testified that the Devil appeared to her in the shape of a man and asked her for a body part to suck upon; displaying uncommon modesty for a witch, she said she only consented when he said he would be satisfied with a rib.

These accusations took root in and were no doubt related to a society that was changing in the direction of increased social mobility stemming partly from the inflationary trends of the sixteenth century. Increased geographical mobility accompanied social mobility, meaning a much more constant influx of newcomers to towns and villages than used to be thought characteristic of early modern society. The historian Live Helene Willumsen estimates that the population of Edinburgh doubled from 12,000 to 24,000 from 1560 to 1640. She also estimates that during the seventeenth century, the total percentage of the population living in towns in Scotland almost doubled from 3 per cent to 5.3 per cent.[6] Many moved because they were evicted from their land or could not find enough work to earn a living. The Statute of Artificers sought to restrict the movement of homeless vagabonds without providing a remedy for their poverty, but apprentices and journeymen could accept opportunities in London or another town that might be lacking in their place of origin. The emergence of a market society in England allowed for greater freedom of movement than had the guild system, but introduced more uncertainty and insecurity into economic life as well.

It is important to note that the vast majority of the population still lived in rural areas and made their living from agriculture or related trades. In fact, agricultural productivity had assumed a new prominence with the rise in population beginning in the sixteenth century and the period is replete with agricultural manuals and guides. A number of innovations, including the introduction of turnips as a fodder crop generally associated with the eighteenth-century agricultural revolution, were introduced by the early seventeenth century. In rural settings, women worked as much as men, their contribution naturally a more vital part of family income the lower down the social scale they were. Despite an overall growth in the population, individual villages remained small, requiring all able-bodied persons, including women and children to participate in the labour necessary for a successful harvest and the marketing and manufacturing of goods and produce. In fact, women continued to play a key economic role in both town and countryside. In urban settings, wives still assisted husbands with their shops, crafts, or trades.

In the early seventeenth century, the ability to acquire land in Ireland or North America became a means for upward mobility for some individuals. Once there, however, settlers attempted to model overseas colonies on their society at home. The desire of the English and Scottish settlers in Ireland to live in isolation from the Irish speaks volumes about how they regarded the Irish as an inferior race, in addition to their desire to establish their own society rather than to build something new. In North America, unlike the French, who maintained close relationships with the Indians in their endeavours in North America, the British focused on establishing their own settlements and keeping them free of Indian influence, leading to more frequent wars and hostile encounters between the settlers and the natives.

In the early seventeenth century, upward mobility for males generally meant moving into the rather loose category of 'gentlemen', which could be accomplished through education, successful military service, or commercial prosperity. The latter, in particular, would have enabled one to purchase land and, perhaps, a coat of arms that could serve as a visible mark of distinction. Together, the aristocracy and gentry dominated politics throughout the British Isles, with Anglo-Irish landlords in Ireland more clearly distinct from the rest of the people than their counterparts in Wales, England, or Scotland. The aristocracy remained most powerful; one must be careful not to underestimate the power of the House of Lords in the English Parliament, even though most studies focus on the House of Commons, where most of the contention between king and Parliament played out in the seventeenth century. Yet neither the aristocracy nor the gentry represented a monolithic group when it came to politics; the great political conflicts of the seventeenth century derived from divisions within the landowning class of gentlemen, who did not necessarily think alike or view their political interests in similar ways. Such divisions were stronger in England at the beginning of the seventeenth century than in Wales, Ireland, or Scotland, a fact for which the Scottish king James VI seemed particularly unprepared when he inherited the English throne on the death of Elizabeth I in 1603.

The union of the crowns in James VI and I

The contemporary author Thomas Dekker, in a work largely dedicated to the suffering caused by a plague that scourged London in 1603, described James's apotheosis in the English capital:

> King James is proclaimed. Now does fresh blood leap into the cheeks of the courtier; the soldier now hangs up his armour and is glad that he shall feed upon the blessed fruits of peace; the scholar sings hymns in honour of the Muses, assuring himself now that Helicon will be kept pure, because Apollo himself drinks of it. ... They saw mirth in every man's face; the streets were plumed with gallants; tobacconists filled up whole taverns; vintners hung out spick and span new ivy-bushes (because they wanted good wine) and their old rain-beaten lattices marched under other colours.[7]

In his 'A Panegyrike Congratulatory' (1603), celebrating James's accession, the English poet and historian Samuel Daniel wrote:

> And now she is, and now in peace therefore
> Shake hands with Union, O thou mighty State,
> Now thou art all *Great-Britaine* and no more,
> No Scot, no English now, nor no debate;
> No borders but the Ocean and the shore:
> No wall of *Adrian* serves to separate
> Our mutuall love, nor our obedience,
> Being Subjects all to one imperiall Prince.[8]

The English and Welsh were both relatively open to the accession of James VI to the English throne, considering his nearly two decades of experience ruling Scotland, his Protestant upbringing, and his hereditary descent from the Tudor dynasty through King Henry VII's daughter Margaret, wife of James IV and grandmother of James VI. However, the English people did not view the union of the crowns as synonymous with the union of the two countries. James, on the other hand, harboured hopes of uniting England and Scotland into a single kingdom of 'Great Britain' to formally consolidate the union of the crowns and establish a firm foundation for peace between the two former enemies. As happy as he was to inherit the English throne, he had ambitions for his reign that provoked opposition among his new subjects almost from the very start.

The parliaments of both countries opposed the initiative from the beginning. In England hostility derived at least in part from anti-Scottish prejudice. The House of Commons produced a document that was published under the title 'Objections Against the Change of the Name or Style of England and Scotland into the Name or Style of Great Brittany'. The authors of this document regarded such a name as apt to cause confusion in foreign policy, as well as contrary to reason and 'matters of honor'. The first objection listed stated:

> That in Constituting or Ordaining of any Innovation or Change, there ought to be either urgent Necessity, or evident Utility; but that we find no Grief of our present Estate, and foresee no Advancement to a better Condition by this Change; and therefore desire it may be shewed unto us.

This reactionary view was recorded in a subsequent passage:

> We find no Precedent, at home or abroad, of Uniting or Contracting of the Names of Two several Kingdoms, or States, into One Name, where the Union hath grown by Marriage, or Blood; and that those Examples, which may be alleged, as far as we can find, are but in the Case of Conquest.[9]

James provoked further resistance in England as a result of his insistence on the divine right of kings and the sacred nature of kingship. He placed a special emphasis on the sacral nature of the king's body and told his English subjects at the beginning of his reign that his very presence had brought peace to England.[10] He held himself above Parliament and the courts and regarded both civil and ecclesiastical officials as directly dependent upon him for their positions. In addition, James ran up against the more libertarian Common Law tradition in England, which relied less on an absolutist model than did Roman law, which prevailed in James's Scottish kingdom.

James had written in his *Trew Law of Free Monarchies* in 1598 that it was every monarch's duty

> to maintaine all the lovable and good Lawes made by their predecessours: to see them put in execution, and the breakers and violaters thereof, to be punished, according to the tenour of the same: And lastly, to maintaine the whole countrey, and every state therein, in all their ancient Priviledges and Liberties.

In person, however, James insisted on those prerogatives possessed by absolute monarchs and did so in a way that alienated his English subjects who had started to think more in terms of the rights of the people and had already begun to tire of the absolutist tendencies of the Tudors. This stunning development in English political culture took James by surprise and provoked a strong reaction from him. With good reason did James respond to Puritan demands for an abolition of the episcopacy by emphatically stating, 'no bishop, no king', since his bishops constituted his main allies in his conflict with his English subjects. For example, Richard Bancroft, his archbishop of Canterbury, proved a stalwart defender of monarchical authority against the challenges of the Puritans at the Hampton Court Conference, which met in 1604. The bishop of Chichester, Lancelot Andrewes, defended the sacred authority of the king in 1610, the same year in which James's French counterpart, Henry IV, was murdered by a Catholic assassin.

Still, James had not come to England to cause a furore. He retained all fourteen of Elizabeth's Privy Councillors and kept other office holders in place. He entertained a delegation of Puritans on his way to London, receiving their 'Millenary Petition', which demanded an end to what they perceived as various abuses and remnants of Catholicism in the Church of England. James promised to look into church reform, though he was not about to replace the Church of England with Scottish Presbyterianism. His coronation speech stressed the benefits he sought to bring to the English people, only indirectly alluding to his political philosophy that supported the divine right of kings.

The problem for James at the beginning of his reign was twofold: first, many people in England regarded the religious settlement as fractious and sought further reforms in the established church, while a small minority of English Catholics still hoped for a return to Rome, and a growing Separatist movement rejected the notion of an established church and state authority over religion altogether. The Millenary Petition – which was said to contain a thousand signatures, hence the name – was only one manifestation of the pent-up demand for church reform at the time of James's English coronation; 1604 saw legislation introduced in the House of Commons to end the church abuses of pluralism and non-residency and to procure 'a learned and godly ministry'. Second, the political constitution and the prerogatives of the king and the rights of Parliament were nebulous, creating ambiguity that each side tailored to its own ends.

In response to Puritan demands for change, James convened the Hampton Court Conference in 1604, even though it ended up essentially affirming the 'via media' or middle way of the Protestant Church of England defined by Elizabeth I. James and his bishops rejected appeals to do away with the Book of Common Prayer (Puritans thought it too formulaic and ritualistic) and to revise the 39 Articles, which had defined Anglican doctrine in a moderately conservative way since 1563. The major significance of the Conference turned out to be the decision to commission a new English translation of the Bible, which was published in 1611 and became known as the King James Bible. Long thought to be a translation that favoured a set religious and political agenda, recent evidence has demonstrated that teams of translators worked on the translation in relative isolation from one another rather than as a committee. It made a major contribution to the English language and is considered one of the great literary achievements in English history. At the time, however, it did little to assuage the sensibilities of those disappointed by the scuttling of their reform agenda at the Conference. Furthermore, James found other ways to alienate Puritans, both the nonconforming Separatists and those who remained within the established church, including the publication in 1617 of a list of sports that would be allowed on Sundays, which ran counter to his opponents' Sabbatarian tendencies.

In response to the Gunpowder Plot, James composed an Oath of Allegiance to be required of all his Catholic subjects in which they would forswear the power of the pope to depose sitting monarchs. The vast majority of lay Catholics, most of whom had never supported the Gunpowder Plot in the first place, had no problem taking the Oath. As a result, the number of Catholics executed for treason steadily dwindled for the rest of the reign, with none at all occurring after 1618. His treatment of Separatists, however, belies James's reputation as a tolerant ruler. James's treatment of the English Baptists, for example, drove many of them, along with other Separatists, first to the Netherlands and then to North America aboard the Mayflower; as for those who stayed at home, James's treatment of them provoked the Baptist leader John Murton to lament 'the long and lingering imprisonments for many years in diverse counties of England, in which many have died and left behind them widows and many small children'.

Politically, James relied on the ability of Robert Cecil, made Earl of Salisbury in 1605, to steward Parliament. Salisbury's adroitness allowed James's first Parliament to sit until 1610, despite antagonisms between its members and the king. These differences were not merely theoretical; they were also financial, as became evident in the famous Bates's case of 1608, in which the English merchant, John Bates of the Levant Company, agreed to bring a test case before the courts challenging the Crown's right to impose import duties without parliamentary consent. James won that battle in the courts, but the dismal state of royal finances presented a major problem for James and represented the only practical leverage that the House of Commons held over the king. James had ended the war with Spain, begun in 1587, in 1604, partly because he sincerely desired to pursue a peaceful foreign policy and partly to save money (or at least to have it to spend on other things, such as the jewellery and gifts with which he lavished his courtiers).

Even on the matter of the law, James regarded himself as the kingdom's chief lawgiver and tended to adopt an absolutist 'rex est lex' (the king is the law) stance, which ran contrary to Parliament's insistence on its prerogatives and the hallowed tradition of English Common Law. The leading defender of the Common Law tradition was the jurist Sir Edward Coke (1552–1634), who wrote most of his legal treatises during James's reign. Coke issued a legal challenge to the prerogatives of the monarchy vis-à-vis Parliament and the entire theoretical basis of the idea of divine-right monarchy by asserting the importance of the Common Law as the basis for Parliament's place in the English constitution. Dismissed from his judicial position in 1616, Coke also championed the use of impeachment of royal officials for violations of the Common Law, which was employed against Sir Francis Bacon in his position as lord chancellor on charges of bribery in 1621.

The Commons articulated their viewpoint in a 'Form of Apology and Satisfaction' in 1604 that asserted the rights of Parliament to determine its own membership and allow its members to engage in free speech without fear of arrest or reprisals. James never officially received the document, but he certainly was aware of its existence; he also became aware of the disgruntlement in Parliament as a result of *Goodwin v. Fortescue*, in which the king tried to intervene in a disputed parliamentary election. James promised to uphold English political customs and traditions, except, however, *in cases when he might deem it necessary to do otherwise.*

Foreign policy and the Thirty Years War: The European context for James's reign

If James quarrelled with his English subjects and Parliament mainly over religious and domestic issues in the early years in his reign, his later years saw this conflict increasingly shift to the realm of foreign policy. The year 1618 marked a major turning point in James's reign, as it did for European history in general, with the outbreak of a conflict in Bohemia that would eventually engulf most of Europe and ultimately become known as the Thirty Years War. James's subjects, especially those who leaned towards Puritanism, thought it crucial that James intervene in the conflict to defend the cause of international Protestantism. As the English historian John Rushworth put it at the time, the outbreak of war in 1618 was a 'high business to the whole Christian world, and the issue of it had main dependence upon the king of England, being the mightiest prince of the Protestant profession'. Calls for English intervention became louder after 1620, when James's son-in-law, Frederick of the Palatinate, was ousted as king of Bohemia following his defeat at the Battle of White Mountain, after which imperial forces followed up this victory by depriving Frederick of his lands in the Palatinate itself.

While James addressed Parliament in order to defend his decision not to intervene, sermons from pulpits throughout England expressed concern for Frederick and Elizabeth and the future of the Protestant cause in Europe generally. Elizabeth personally appealed to her father in a letter written on 13 November 1620, asking him 'to protect the king [Frederick] and myself by sending us succor; otherwise we shall be brought to utter ruin' and 'and not to abandon the king at this hour, when he is in such great need ... for if he should perish, I will perish also with him'. James was not indifferent to the plight of his daughter and son-in-law, but he hoped to restore them to their lands through diplomatic negotiations rather than war. James asked Parliament for money, indicating that he would send an army the following year if the situation still warranted it. But King Philip III of Spain had sent an army to assist his Habsburg cousin, the Holy Roman Emperor Ferdinand, and intervention by England would have renewed the war with Spain, something James desperately wanted to prevent. The year 1621 came and went, with James's promise of armed intervention in the Palatinate unfulfilled. James continued to cling to his belief that negotiations with Spain represented his best chance to restore Frederick to power.

James recognized that England lacked the money and military capability of fighting an effective land war at that time, but this did nothing to lessen the estrangement between the king and Parliament or allay the concerns and anxieties of many of his subjects. James's pro-Spanish foreign policy culminated in his attempt to arrange the marriage of his son, Charles, to a Spanish royal bride. These negotiations, which began in 1621, called forth a strong reaction from political pamphleteers such as John Reynolds and Thomas Scott, who believed the 'Spanish match' would serve as a prelude to England's subordination to Spain and an attempt to impose Catholicism on the country. The House of Commons issued a remonstrance that denounced the king of Spain as the leader of 'a strange confederacy of the Princes of the Popish Religion, aiming mainly at the advancement of theirs, and subverting ours, and taking advantages conducing to that end, upon all occasions'.[11] Such concerns did not stop Charles, accompanied by the Duke of Buckingham, from travelling to Spain in 1623 in an attempt to seal the alliance; their failure to do so met with widespread relief and applause at home.

Concerns about the Thirty Years War in England did not end with James's reign in 1625, despite the military intervention in Germany of the Protestant king of Denmark, Christian IV, that same year. Charles I inherited fears about the growing power of Catholicism abroad, which he did little to quell. The fall of the Huguenot stronghold of New Rochelle to Cardinal Richelieu in 1628 both alarmed the English and represented an indictment of Charles I's foreign policy after the English military had ineptly attempted to intervene on behalf of the French Protestants. The defeat of the Danes in 1629 marked a low point in the fortunes of the Protestant cause in Europe. The threat to European Protestantism provoked the intervention of the Lutheran King Gustavus Adolphus of Sweden. Gustavus Adolphus emerged as a Protestant hero with whom Charles suffered by comparison; in fact, Charles's English subjects developed a deep fascination with his Swedish counterpart before Gustavus died at the Battle of Lutzen in 1632.[12]

Scotland, Ireland, and Wales under James and Charles

Here we must take a step back and ask: What had the reigns of James VI and I meant for Scotland? Despite James's inability to get his two kingdoms recognized as a single country by either the English or the Scots, his acquisition of the English throne did have tangible benefits for his northern kingdom. Scotland now had protection from a power close to home and no longer had to worry about an English invasion, while still retaining its autonomy. Having failed to alter the constitutional relationship between his English and Scottish kingdoms, James had continued to pursue separate policies in both because of their different religious and political makeup. But he did not have any more success endearing himself to his Scottish subjects than he did with the English. James continued to take an active interest in Scottish politics, but he did not even return to his native land until 1617. When he did return, he angered his Scottish subjects by hearing a service conducted according to the English prayer book and by having an organ and choir installed in his chapel at Holyrood Palace in Edinburgh, each imposition an affront to their Presbyterian sensibilities. He caused further alienation by attempting to impose a measure of ecclesiastical uniformity with the Perth Articles of 1618, though ministers and presbyters seem to have objected more to them than the rest of the Scottish people.[13] Scottish Presbyterian leaders opposed James's interference with a church that they had fought to establish and a faith that they had successfully spread throughout the Scottish Lowlands. The royal visit had begun with an auspicious series of celebrations, but it ended in disappointment on both sides; James never visited Scotland again.

Charles I attempted to reform the Scottish government almost immediately upon his accession in 1625 and he threatened to deprive those who had benefited from the sale of lands by his predecessors with his Restitution Edict (1625). A dozen years later, his attempt to impose the Anglican prayer book on Scotland brought England and Scotland into direct conflict once again, a struggle that threatened to undo Charles's monarchy altogether. John Livingstone wrote in 1638 that in September 1637, after the introduction of the new prayer book to Scotland,

> a great many petitions from several parts were presented against the Service book; these being denied by the king the number of the petitioners and their demands increased for they desired not only exemptions from the Service book but from the

five ceremonies of Perth and the High Commission Court, and these things being denied they at last also asked for freedom from episcopacy and a free parliament and General Assembly.[14]

The signing of a National Covenant followed in March 1638, in which the Scots pledged their allegiance to the Presbyterian Kirk (church) while swearing that they would resist the imposition of what they saw as a foreign form of worship that too closely resembled that of the Catholic Church. If the attempt to introduce a new prayer book into Scotland was a mistake, Charles's decision to fight the Scots over the issue was an even bigger one. But at the time Charles simply could not understand how his subjects could disobey him. He challenged the Scots militarily because he believed that in the end they would not dare to use force of arms against the army of their lawful sovereign. Furthermore, Charles believed in the rightness of his policy, one that had originated with his father and which he saw himself as carrying through in accordance with God's wishes. In addition, the king had his contemporary defenders, even for his policy in Scotland. The Royalist John Taylor, for example, wrote a poem in 1640 that reminded his readers that Charles was 'Gods [sic] lieutenant', while defending the prayer book as well. He asserted that

Ten millions of their braines can ne're devise
A book so good as that which they despise;
(The Common Prayer I meane) if they should sit
Ten thousand yeares, with all their Art and witt,
They would prove Coxcombs all, and in the end,
Leave it as 'tis, too good for them to mend.[15]

Charles, however, had so alienated both his English and his Scottish subjects that a poem was unlikely to succeed in averting an even deeper crisis, much less convince Presbyterians of the merits of the Anglican prayer book. He did not know it at the time, but Ireland was also moving towards a rebellion that would cause him just as much trouble as the Scottish crisis.

James had assumed the English throne in 1603 just as the Nine Years War in Ireland begun in Elizabeth's reign was wrapping up, a fortuitous coincidence that furthered James's desire to be a king of peace. The Nine Years War did not immediately deprive most Catholics in Ireland of their land, but the north now endured an English military presence and had lost its autonomy. Furthermore, their status on the land had become less secure and many natives in the years that followed found that they had been downgraded to tenants of English landlords. When Hugh O'Neill and about 100 other landlords fled Ireland in 1607, an event known as 'the flight of the earls', James seized their lands and opened them up for further colonization.

This aristocratic exodus deprived the native Gaelic population of their leaders. In their absence, England launched the Ulster Plantation project in 1609–10, not long after the Virginia Company established a new colony in North America. Many of the same merchants and companies invested in both. Scottish colonists were drawn more to the north of Ireland, perhaps because of geographical proximity, or, as has been suggested, because the terrain there more closely resembled that of Scotland, whereas English colonists mostly occupied the south. The Ulster Plantation was modelled on the settlement of Munster in southern Ireland, which began in 1587 and resumed in 1601 after being disrupted by the war with Spain and the Nine Years War in Ireland. North America also provided opportunities for migration from Britain in the early decades of the seventeenth century, but Ireland in some respects offered the more attractive alternative because it did not lie an ocean away. In fact, about 100,000 people migrated from Britain to Ireland prior to 1641, more than five times the number that went to North America.[16] By the end of James's reign, English and Scottish settlers had established a separate society in Ulster. They had their own schools and churches and their own local market economy. They held the best lands, relegating the native population to lands that were virtually barren.

Charles never set foot in Ireland and only began to take notice of it after 1633. For their part, the Irish remained politically quiescent as long as the English government more or less left them alone, even after the establishment of the Munster and Ulster plantations. However, in 1632, Charles appointed Thomas Wentworth as Lord Protector of Ireland, looking mainly for him to raise revenues that might accrue to the royal coffers. Wentworth inflamed an already volatile situation with his policy of 'Thorough' in which he ruthlessly exploited the Irish while imposing a rigid authority over the island. Still, as long as Wentworth remained in control, the Irish remained quiet for the time being, leading Charles to believe that his policies were a success.

By contrast with both Scotland and Ireland, Wales was perhaps the least affected by the change of dynasties because its union with England had already been consummated in 1536, though a separate Council for Wales still existed to oversee affairs there. The Welsh had also adopted the Protestant religion of the Church of England, removing one potentially important source of animosity that had remained present in Ireland. It helped, of course, that the Welsh had their own Bible and had the religious doctrines of the Reformation communicated to them in their own language, a method that the English did not offer to the Irish. Furthermore, Welsh religious culture, like that of the English, did not embrace the more dour aspects of Calvinist Protestantism associated with Scottish Presbyterianism, such as the doctrine of predestination and the strict emphasis on the totally depraved and sinful nature of human beings.

John Donne and the literary and intellectual culture of the early seventeenth century

The literary and intellectual culture of the British Isles in the early seventeenth century cannot be separated from the political and religious culture of the period. History, poetry, drama (as we have seen in our discussion on Shakespeare), and natural philosophy all reflected the concerns and anxieties of the age. Sir Walter Raleigh wrote that it was 'the end and scope of al[l] Historie, to teach by example of times past, such wisdom as may guide our desires and actions' and that 'we reade Histories to informe our understanding by the examples therein found'.[17] Raleigh, and other historical scholars of the period, looked to ancient and biblical history for many of the lessons that they wished to apply to England's current situation. Unfortunately for Raleigh, history did not provide the unequivocal answers to contemporary political issues for which he and others sought. When Raleigh looked at history, he saw both inconsistency and consistency; he saw that God did not always favour the same form of government, sometimes supporting a government that balanced the powers of governors and people and sometimes monarchy, even tyranny. The popularity of Raleigh's *History of the World* testifies to an increased reading public interested in history. George Abbot, the archbishop of Canterbury, initially censured Raleigh's work, primarily because it was alleged to have been 'too sawcie in censuring princes'. However, authorities soon changed their minds and allowed the book's publication in 1614, followed by a second printing three years later. Nine more editions followed by the end of the century and the book remained in print until the nineteenth century.

Literacy had increased in England, Scotland, and Wales, due in part to the influence of the Reformation, which had stressed the importance of reading the Bible and the importance of the priesthood of all believers. Raleigh's contemporary, Francis Bacon, thought, in fact, that there were too many grammar schools and too many people seeking education, writing to James in 1611 that there were 'more scholars bred than the state can prefer and employ'.[18]

Raleigh's book had a pessimistic tone, which it shared with many other contemporary literary works based on motifs such as death, decay, and the approaching end of the world. The plague that greeted James's ascension to the English throne could hardly have seemed an auspicious omen in an age that put great stock in such portents. Thomas Dekker, quoted earlier in conjunction with the excitement that accompanied the arrival of the new king, went on to describe the effects of the plague on the people of London in *The Wonderfull Yeare*:

> What an unmatchable torment were it for a man to be barred up every night in a vast, silent charnel-house hung, to make it more hideous, with lamps dimly and slowly burning in hollow and glimmering corners; where all the pavement should instead of green rushes be strewed with blasted rosemary, withered hyacinths, fatal cypress and ywe, thickly mingled with heaps of dead men's bones – the bare ribs of a father that begat him lying there, here the chapless hollow skull of a mother that bore him; round about him a thousand corpses, some standing bolt upright in their knotted winding-sheets, others half mouldered in rotten coffins that should suddenly yawn wide open filling his nostrils with noisome stench and his eyes with the sight of nothing but crawling worms.[19]

Poets such as John Donne (1572–1631) and his younger contemporary George Wither (1588–1667), who as young men wrote poems of love, both later turned to more serious reflections. At the age of twenty-five in 1613 Wither had written his 'Faire Virtue, Mistress of Philarete', challenging those who

> suppose
> Beauty goodness doth oppose;
> Like those fools who do despair
> To find any good and fair.

By the reign of Charles I, however, Wither had developed strong Puritan leanings and in 1628 wrote his poem, 'Britain's Rembrancer', using the outbreak of the plague that had afflicted London as an opportunity to denounce the immorality of the age and predict future calamities for England. John Donne moved to London at the age of seventeen to pursue a career in law, which had become an avenue for the rapid advancement of many young would-be gentlemen at that time. This did not stop him from writing some of the most well-known love poetry in the English language, such as the opening lines from his poem 'The Bait':

Come live with me, and be my love,
And we will some new pleasures prove
Of golden sands, and crystal brooks,
With silken lines, and silver hooks.

By the time he was nineteen, however, Donne had already become concerned enough about his soul that he considered converting to Catholicism before settling on a clerical career in the Church of England. His biographer Isaak Walton quotes him: 'I grow older, and not better; my strength diminisheth, and my load grows heavier; and yet, I would fain be or do something; but that I cannot tell what, is no wonder in this time of my sadness; for to choose is to do; but to be no part of any body, is as to be nothing: and so I am, and shall so judge myself, unless I could be so incorporated into a part of the world, as by business to contribute some sustentation to the whole.'[20]

Another source of cosmic pessimism besides the regular recurrence of the plague came from the impact that new discoveries about the world and the heavens – particularly the heliocentric view of Copernicus, the discovery of a new star in 1572 that demonstrated the mutability of the heavens, and the invention of the telescope that revealed, among other things, the imperfections on the moon – had on religious sensibilities. For example, in 1580 Francis Shakelton, an Anglican minister, had written a treatise called *A Blazying Starre*, in which he suggested that the appearance of a comet that year portended Christ's second coming. In his 1611 poem, 'An Anatomy of the World: The First Anniversary', Donne used the death of his patron's teenage daughter, one Elizabeth Drury, to comment on the theme of the frailty and decay of the whole world. The death of Elizabeth Drury seemed to confirm just how sick the world was, for

Her death hath taught us dearly that thou art
Corrupt and mortal in thy purest part. (ll. 61–2)

Donne speculates that if the world is sick there is little hope for humanity, which deceives itself about the very possibility of health.

And can there be worse sickness than to know
That we are never well, nor can be so? (ll. 93–4)

In 1616, Godfrey Goodman, a chaplain at the royal court, also focused on the idea of the corruption of humanity and the decay of the world in his treatise *The Fall of Man*.

John Speed (1552–1629) found reason for pessimism in the advances of the Turks, who had become 'such a terror to the whole world, lurking in the by-corners of Asia like runnegades and thieves'.[21] Speed, however, also found reasons for optimism in the preservation of the reformed religion in England, its delivery from popery, and its triumphs over its enemies, particularly Spain. He was not alone. Beliefs such as those enunciated by Donne and Goodman disturbed George Hakewill, a Calvinist author and clergyman, who felt compelled to respond to them in 1627 in *An Apologie of the Power and Providence of God*. Hakewill did not believe in the eternity of the world, but he did not see the decay of the world very much in evidence either. He asserted that the end of the world would come in one fell swoop, rather than as the result of decay and old age. He defended God from the charge that He had created a world that would continually fall into a further state of disrepair.

Finally, John Milton (1608–74) provides another example of a young man open to love, travel, exploring different cultures, and composing poetry on a variety of classical and secular themes who eventually turned to more serious subjects. Milton earned his bachelor's degree from Cambridge in 1628 and his master's degree there in 1632, after which his anti-clerical views led him to decline an oath that would have allowed him to enter the Anglican ministry. Instead he set himself up as a teacher who emphasized moral and classical education, though he also saw the value of practical learning that incorporated the experience of those who had practised skilled trades and professions. The author of *Paradise Lost*, while at Cambridge, wrote a series of Italian sonnets modelled on the fourteenth-century Italian humanist Petrarch that addressed the themes of love and desire, while also carrying on an emotional and possibly sexually charged correspondence in Italian, Latin, and Greek with a close male friend, Charles Diodati.[22] In 1638, he travelled extensively in Italy, a destination that provided him with a cultural and intellectual experience unavailable to him in England. The experience, however, did not alter his commitment to the Protestant faith but rather reinforced it. By the time he returned home, developments in the British Isles had moved the islands closer to the greatest crisis they would face until perhaps the Second World War. Unlike the Second World War, however, when Britain and Northern Ireland endured aerial bombings and the grim possibility of conquest by Nazi Germany, in the mid-seventeenth century the threat and crisis originated from within.

The Personal Rule of Charles I:
The political culture of the 1630s

Charles I lived in the long shadow cast by his deceased brother, Henry, who had been esteemed by many as the most perfect prince who ever lived. Henry was only eighteen when he died in 1612. Charles, six years younger, lacked the charisma and confidence of his older brother, to whom members of the court were naturally drawn independently of his position as heir to the throne. Furthermore, Henry had a special rapport with their sister Elizabeth; the shy and timid Charles grew up isolated and alone. Henry's death at a young age enshrined his memory and ensured that the new heir could never live up to the expectations of what his brother might have been. The death of his popular and outgoing brother would only have intensified Charles's sense of inadequacy, at the same time that he, as heir to the throne, would have been saddled with increased expectations coming from outside himself. Charles idolized Henry; far from rejoicing about becoming next in line to the throne, the insecure twelve-year-old prince was devastated by his brother's death. Charles was determined to carry on in the tradition of his older brother, but the popularity of his brother only underscored his own shortcomings.

Yet Van Dyck's virtuoso portraits of Charles as king depict him as a regal figure at variance with contemporary portraits of Charles's father. One of the most famous portraits of James, that by Daniel Mytens of 1621 that hangs in the National Portrait Gallery, reveals an old and weary king, slumped in his chair, his arms resting limply on the arms of his throne. By contrast, Charles was always portrayed with good posture holding his head high, his poses regal and graceful.[23] Charles attempted to rule as a Continental-style monarch, complete with a lavish and dignified court atmosphere that celebrated the king's refined tastes in art and culture. Charles sought to inject an air of serious formality, beauty, and elegance into his court that was largely absent from his father's.

His reign began inauspiciously. He immediately quarrelled with Parliament in 1626 over his request for finances to support his campaign in France. This was not entirely Charles's fault; the relationship between Parliament and the English monarchy had become increasingly contentious since the time of Elizabeth, who frequently quarrelled with it over religious subjects and issues of parliamentary free speech. After 1611, James only called Parliament three times: 1614, the year of the so-called Addled Parliament, which lasted less than two months and refused to honour James's financial requests, and again in 1621 and 1624, in which James's foreign policy and the proposed Spanish match for Charles led to open hostility from the House of Commons. But after dismissing his first Parliament, Charles did little to abet his own cause. In 1627, for example, the Five Knights' Case called attention to Charles's policy of relying on forced loans to the monarchy and the imprisonment of those who failed to comply.

The 1628 Parliament passed the Petition of Right, demanding an end to illegal imprisonment, forced quartering of troops, the imposition of martial law, and stating 'that no man hereafter be compelled to make or yield any gift, loan, benevolence, tax, or such like charge, without common consent by act of parliament'. The political ideology behind the Petition of Right drew reinforcement from Ben Jonson's play, *The New Inn*, which was performed for Parliament immediately prior to the beginning of its 1629 session.[24]

Nothing in the English political tradition prevented Charles from dismissing Parliament in 1629 and refusing to call it for eleven years, but his Personal Rule, as the period between 1629 and 1640 is known, certainly ran counter to contemporary expectations and the prevailing political culture of the time. Charles's exercise of royal prerogative conflicted with the tradition of the Common Law, while his decision to rule without Parliament violated the sense that the English people had of it as an institution that represented their interests. However, both the king and Parliament believed they had the law on their side and both sides appealed to the traditions inherent in England's 'ancient constitution'.

Religious tensions formed the backdrop to Charles's Personal Rule; the division between conformist and nonconformist ministers in James's reign carried over into that of his son, made starker by the religious reforms associated with William Laud, who became archbishop of Canterbury in 1633, and the religious ideology known as Arminianism. Based on the thought of the Dutch Protestant theologian, Jacobus Arminius (1560–1609), this ideology emphasized the freedom of the will in matters of salvation, bringing its adherents closer to Catholic theology and challenging the Calvinistic belief in predestination. Laud was not as theologically dogmatic as he is often made out to be; for example, he thought the issue of free will versus predestination to be a mystery that was too laborious to disentangle. Still, he alienated his opponents as much with his authoritarian and confrontational style as with his substance, while the visible side of his reforms smacked of Catholicism to many of his Protestant subjects.

Puritans ratcheted up the rhetoric in response to the changes adopted under Laud, which included having communion tables placed behind rails, enforcing the wearing of the white clerical gown known as a surplice at public services, and the decoration and repair of churches to restore beauty and dignity to them as houses of God. These changes ran counter to Puritan sensibilities, especially in London, which had evolved into a chaotic mishmash of overlapping parishes and competing ministers, many of whom attracted large audiences for their anti-establishment sermons and lectures. Puritans in both England and Massachusetts divided over issues centring on antinomianism, a Protestant heresy which fostered the belief that because grace is thought free to God's elect they could sin without jeopardizing their salvation.

Anti-Catholicism also played a strong role in both the hostility towards Arminianism and suspicions that Charles was too tolerant of, if not actually fostering, Catholicism in his own court. English Protestants had come to associate popery with tyranny in the course of the Reformation; it was easy for Charles's critics to see his religious and political policies as connected, linked by the Catholic tendencies towards absolutism. The fears associated with the Thirty Years War and the strength of the Counter-reformation forces in Europe at the time made Charles's leanings towards Arminian theology seem all the more subversive to English Puritans. Members of the gentry such as Oliver Cromwell (1599–1658) became appalled by developments at court, incensed at Charles's disregard for their opinions as demonstrated by his refusal to call Parliament, and fearful that their own hard-won economic gains in a period of social change might be jeopardized by arbitrary government and taxation or the king's fiscal policies. The extension of a tax known as 'ship money', previously confined to coastal towns in times of war, to the entire country during peacetime struck many as particularly egregious. The courts upheld the tax in 1637 when a merchant named John Hampden refused to pay it, but ship money became so unpopular that the government found it difficult to collect it thereafter.

The conflict with Scotland over the prayer book in Scotland proved to be the turning point of Charles's reign. The First Bishops' War hardly deserves to be called a war and ended without bloodshed. Fooled by the Scottish commander, Alexander Leslie, into thinking that the Scots had many more troops than they actually did, the Royalist forces backed down at the town of Kelso. Charles, following a pattern common throughout his rule, agreed to negotiate before changing his mind and determining to follow his original course. In this case, he agreed to refer his proposed religious changes in Scotland to a general assembly. Charles's failure to subdue the Scots diminished the rebels' respect for their foe. In turn, when an assembly rejected episcopacy and the modified prayer book and called for all Scots to subscribe to the covenant, the king became more determined to raise a larger army to crush the Scots by force. The Scots also raised a larger force, deploying part of it in the west to prevent an invasion from Ireland, part in the east near Aberdeen, and the rest in the south to defend Scotland against the king's army. The Scots bought additional weapons from the Netherlands and even looked to France for additional troops, bringing back memories of the 'auld alliance'. Reminiscent of the role that the nobility played in assuming leadership during the reign of Mary Queen of Scots, the Scottish Parliament empowered the Lords of the Articles to run the government in a direct challenge to the authority of the king. Wentworth, recalled from Ireland, encouraged the king to call Parliament in order to raise money for the war but to remain firm in his dealings with it. He had estimated that £300,000 would be necessary to raise an army large enough to defeat the Scots. Charles followed his advice, ending his Personal Rule and calling for the English Parliament to meet in April 1640 to deal with the Scottish crisis. Many members of Parliament, however, had their own agenda and were not particularly eager to help Charles force a religious settlement on Scotland that they themselves did not necessarily support for England.

The origins of the British Civil Wars

The English historian John Morrill once referred to the English Civil War as the last of the religious wars of the seventeenth century, challenging the prevailing Marxist perspective, which viewed it through the lens of class conflict, and stirring a fair share of renewed debate about the subject. The relatively recent historiographical focus on viewing the English Civil War, which began in 1642, in the context of Charles's three kingdoms of England, Scotland, and Ireland has done much to reinforce the merits of Morrill's characterization. Any general theory of causation, of course, needs to be situated firmly within the context of the events that led to war in the first place and supplemented with consideration of whether or at what point these wars could have still been avoided. For some historians, the pressure to avoid war in England between king and Parliament still existed in 1642 right up to the outbreak. For others, the Irish Rebellion of 1641 was the point of no return. Still others see the turning point as 1637 and Charles's decision to impose the prayer book on Scotland. The seventeenth-century Puritan Nehemiah Wallington thought it somewhere in between, recording that 'in April 1639 our King with his armies went against *Scotland*, and we looked for nothing but civil wars, and that the sword should be sheathed in one another's bowels'.[25] The Bishops' Wars were certainly centred on religion and drew sympathy from those opposed to the king's ecclesiastical policies in England. When Charles introduced a new set of ecclesiastical canons in 1640, he perpetuated the religious divide within his English kingdom. The canons began with an affirmation of the divine right of kings and an assertion that armed rebellion against the monarchy was a sin against God worthy of eternal damnation.

The timing could not have been worse. Charles called Parliament to meet in April 1640, hoping to gain financial support for his war against the Scots; instead, Parliament confronted him with long-standing religious and political grievances. Charles dismissed what became known as the 'Short Parliament' after only three weeks. By September, a plot to overthrow Charles had emerged, centring on the

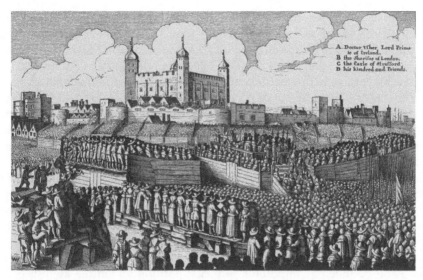

A. Doctor Usher Lord Prims
     te of Ireland.
B the Sherifes of London.
C the Earle of Strafford.
D his kindred and friends.

FIGURE 14 *Execution of Strafford, after the original by Václav Hollar. Thomas Wentworth, first Earl of Strafford, was executed on Tower Hill on 12 May 1641, following the passing of a Bill of Attainder by Parliament, which was reluctantly agreed to by Charles I.*
Culture Club/Hulton Archive/Getty.

fiercely anti-Catholic Earl of Warwick and the rebellious parliamentary leader John Pym, who met secretly in Essex at that time. When the Scots invaded England during the Second Bishops' War, however, Charles had no choice but to convene his second Parliament of the year – the last one he would ever call.

The outbreak of the Irish Rebellion in October 1641 reinforced the notion of Catholic perfidy and widened the lacuna between the king and Parliament because neither trusted the other with an army to crush the revolt. In Ulster an Irish army under Sir Phelim O'Neill captured Charlemont castle and the town of Dunganon, initiating the revolt. Within a day, the additional towns of Moneymore, Portadown, Tandragee, and Newry had fallen into the hands of the rebels. By November, violence spiralled out of control, resulting in the deaths of a number of English and Scottish Protestants. The Irish Rebellion revived fears of a Catholic plot in England and definitely made compromise more difficult.

On 1 December 1641, the House of Commons presented Charles with the Grand Remonstrance, which referred to 'the rights of parliaments' and 'the property and liberty of the subject'. Its passage actually indicated how divided the House of Commons still was politically as it squeaked through by a margin of only eleven votes. However, Charles further alienated his opponents, as well as those who might have been sitting on the fence, by ordering the arrest of his leading critics, including Pym. Even that measure did not unify Parliament, many conservative members of which remained suspicious of the radical religious agenda of their Puritan counterparts.

The dividing lines were largely drawn before the war; fundamental political issues were at stake that caused a serious rift in society throughout the British Isles and even extended to England's North American colonies. As convenient as it is to label Charles's opponents as 'Puritans' and his adherents as 'Arminians' the reality of the split between Royalists and Parliamentarians was far murkier. Individuals of one religious persuasion or another may have joined either side, depending on their political views, which in the end may have been more decisive in determining allegiance in the civil wars than religion. However, religion must not be discounted as a motivating force in that political support for Parliament and religious sympathy with Puritanism frequently coexisted in the same individuals who would have had difficulty in separating them. If forced to do so most of them would surely have said that religion was more important than politics. Furthermore, while many people did take sides, a number of people on both sides of the Atlantic hoped for peace and planned to sit out the war if one should occur.

The complications of the relationship between politics and religion can be illustrated in the use of the Anglican theologian Richard Hooker by both sides, the subject of an illuminating book by Alexander Rosenthal.[26] Defenders of the Royalist cause found consolation in the conformist and moderate theology of Hooker, which seemed to support the Arminian viewpoint more than the Calvinist one. Parliamentarians, who needed a theoretical foundation for challenging Charles since the king still occupied an important and legal position within the English political system, found Hooker useful in this regard, because he had identified Parliament as the main source of law in the kingdom and affirmed the importance of the consent of the people in the governance of the kingdom.

Once war started in 1642, both sides divided into moderates who hoped for a compromise that would quickly bring the two sides together and hardliners who wished for a total military victory that would allow them to negotiate from a position of strength. In general, in England Parliament drew its strength from the south and east and Royalists from the north and west, while in the colonies Anglican Virginians mainly sided with the Royalists and Massachusetts Puritans with Parliament. But each of the above generalizations about the origins of the wars obscures more than it clarifies, especially the last one, for the civil wars of the 1640s tore apart and divided counties, towns, villages, and even families.

FIGURE 15 *Entry of Charles II into London, reproduced from the* Koninklijke Beltenis
van Karel II, *published in 1660. Charles II returned to London on 29 May, 1660, his 30th
birthday, and took his place as king of England.*
Culture Club/Hulton Archive/Getty.

8

Civil wars, Interregnum, and Restoration:

From Edgehill to the Battle of the Boyne

The experience I have had of your worth, and the happiness I have enjoyed in your friendship are wounding considerations when I look upon this present distance between us ... that great God, which is the searcher of my heart, knows with what sad sence I goe upon this service, and with what a perfect hatred I detest this war without an Enemie. ...We are both upon the stage and must act those parts that are assigned to us in this Tragedy: Lett us do it in a way of honor, and without personal animosities, whatsoever the issue be.

Parliamentarian WILLIAM WALLER to his Royalist friend
SIR RALPH HOPTON, 16 June 1643

Civil wars: Divided societies

If King Charles I had not attracted enough political and military support during the summer and autumn of 1642, there would have been no civil war in England. No single reason explains the motives of those who, in the end, decided to stand by the king. Allowing for the multiple motives that would apply to each individual in a decision of this magnitude, some supported the king primarily to defend the established church from the influence of the Puritans and Presbyterians, some out of a sense of personal loyalty to their sovereign, some from a political belief in the sanctity and efficacy of monarchical rule, and others simply for mercenary reasons.

Those who backed Parliament also did so for a combination of political and religious motives, but here too motivations were often mutually interdependent.

Parliament went to war hoping to gain additional concessions from Charles, especially after the army plots of 1641, in which Charles had schemed to have his military forces crush the Scots once and for all. Charles had already made numerous concessions since the beginning of the Long Parliament in October 1640, but these had the – probably unintended – effect of allowing him to stall for time until the religious radicals leading the opposition alienated some of their support within Parliament by demanding the abolition of the episcopacy 'root and branch'. In February 1641 Parliament passed the Triennial Act, which stipulated that Parliament must sit for at least one 50-day session every three years. In July Parliament abolished the Court of High Commission, the supreme ecclesiastical court in England that was particularly offensive to Puritans. Perhaps most significantly, Charles permitted the impeachment, arrest, and execution that May of his loyal adviser, Thomas Wentworth, the Earl of Strafford. Although Charles did not react to Strafford's death immediately, this may have been the biggest factor in his decision to enact revenge on Parliament. But in January 1642 the king ordered the arrest of his leading parliamentary critics, but in doing so he inspired Parliament to raise its own army to defend itself.

At the beginning of the war, neither the political nor the military leaders on the parliamentary side spoke of dethroning the king. The leaders of Parliament hoped to prevent absolute monarchy and sought to limit royal control over the church so that they might carry out reforms that would undo many of the changes effected by Archbishop Laud in the 1630s intended to elevate the dignity of the clergy and emphasize its separation from the congregation. They also wanted some guarantee from the king of what they considered the traditional liberties of English subjects from arbitrary government. In the opening stages of the war, parliamentary leaders such as the Earl of Manchester and the Duke of Bedford merely hoped for a compromise that would preserve but also check the king's authority. Manchester reflected the early attitude of the parliamentary high command in his famous statement that Parliament could 'beat the king nine-and-ninety times, he is king still, and his posterity after him; but if he beat us once we shall all be hanged, and our posterity made slaves'.

Once Parliament took up arms against the king, its leaders needed to find a theoretical justification for armed rebellion against a legitimate monarch. The Puritan John Goodwin's 1642 tract, *Anti-Cavalierisme* provided an early justification for the rebellion based on Protestant resistance theory, which had originated in the sixteenth century. As one might expect given the religious nature of Charles's Puritan opposition, Goodwin sought biblical parallels, particularly those with the oppression of the Israelites by Egypt vividly described in the Book of Exodus. The Irish Rebellion of 1641 also fit neatly with the religious context of the justification for Parliament to raise an army; it allowed Parliament to place the English Civil War in the larger context of the continuing conflict with Catholicism and the papal Antichrist.[1] Parliamentarian theorists advanced political arguments as well. Henry Parker asserted the primacy of the House of Commons as the true representatives of the people in his 1642 treatise *Observations upon Some of His Majesties Late Answers and Expresses*. Philip Hunton's 1643 *Treatise of Monarchy* put forth a view of the state as a joint enterprise among the king and both houses of Parliament.

Charles began the war with an army of about 14,000 men, putting him roughly at equal strength with his adversary. As the war escalated the size of both armies increased, but not exponentially; about 45,000 men participated in the Battle of Marston Moor in 1644, the largest battle of the entire war. In September the Scots agreed to enter the war on the side of Parliament in a treaty known as the Solemn League and Covenant. The alliance with the Scots turned many people against Parliament, especially those who had no desire to see England become a Presbyterian nation. The Scots invaded England with 21,500 troops, but the Royalists compensated for this somewhat by attracting additional mercenary troops from the European continent. It was not uncommon for people to switch sides during the war, while both sides relied upon conscription to fill their armies, even after the formation of the New Model Army under Oliver Cromwell in 1645. Soldiers changed sides for a variety of reasons ranging from anti-Irish prejudice after Charles made an alliance with Ireland in 1646 to techniques of persuasion used on captured prisoners. Charles Carlton suggests, however, that 'the most persuasive explanation for the ease with which most soldiers changed sides was that they had little ideological commitment to either side in the first place'.[2]

The first turning point in the English Civil War came when the Scots invaded England in January 1644. At this point, a Royalist victory was entirely conceivable; even to refer to Charles's opponent as 'Parliament' is somewhat misleading, since Charles had his own 'Parliament' at Oxford, which first met in January 1644 and adjourned for good only in March 1645. Shortly after the Scots invaded, they placed York under siege, which lasted until lifted under pressure from Charles's nephew, Prince Rupert, the German son of the Elector of the Palatinate, at the beginning of July. After that, the war quickly became a struggle for position, in which Parliament's army defended London while attempting to occupy the territory controlled by the king, while Royalist forces tried to solidify the lands under their control until they became strong enough to take London or force Parliament to surrender. The Scots secured the North, especially after the Battle of Marston Moor in July 1644, which forced Charles's army under Prince Rupert to regroup in the West, relying to a large degree on the Welsh, who tended to favour the Royalist cause, for reinforcements. Charles could never have continued his war effort as long as he did if it were not for the support of the Welsh. The king's son, Charles, the Prince of Wales, had personally visited Wales in 1642 to promote the Royalist cause. The Welsh had given Prince Charles an enthusiastic reception, telling the royal heir that 'it is the glory of the Britaines, that we are the two remaining and only one people of this Land'.[3] With Charles I in control of the West, the main goal of the Scots was to retain control of the North, allowing their parliamentary allies to win the war by defeating the Royalist army in the Midlands.

The civil wars of the 1640s brought disorder throughout the British Isles and opened the door to increased brigandage, theft, and piracy. Plunder of Royalist households and towns by supporters of Parliament and vice versa became justified as a legitimate act of war. However, one could not always readily identify who supported whom, or on which side residents of a town or household fought because these were often divided among themselves. This situation provided an opportunity for criminals to steal at will by simply declaring an allegiance at variance with that of their intended victims. The political divisions within the Midlands made the war there particularly destructive as armies of occupation could not necessarily depend on the support of the people in the areas that they controlled.

During the English Civil War, the Midlands were aptly named for they lay right in the middle of those lands controlled by the two competing sides. The Midlands became the location of the most frequent and significant battles between the two sides and a patchwork of local regions controlled by one side or the other. As the Royalist and parliamentary armies traversed the Midlands throughout the war they appropriated supplies and sequestered houses from the local populations as needed, regardless of which side they were on. In fact, it was during the lengthy intervals between battles that private citizens tended to suffer the most. Many people, in fact, would have preferred to remain neutral, especially after witnessing the despicable behaviour of and damage inflicted by soldiers of both armies. But those who did not actively cooperate were subjected to even higher rates of taxation and greater mistreatment. In an attempt to curb the excesses of drunken Royalist soldiers at Oxford, Charles I ordered 'that neither vintner nor any other victualer in Oxford should afford any wyne or drinke to be sold in his house to any body after nine of the clocke at night &c. upon payne of forfeiting 10s'.[4] This might be contrasted with the policy of the commander in charge of the siege of Gloucester in 1643, who according to one captured Parliamentarian gave his soldiers 'as much wine and strong waters as they desired' before a raid.[5]

Meanwhile, in Ireland, the Catholic rebels, after consolidating their position in Ulster, had begun to expand their military activity to the west and south in order to force the king to negotiate. Both Protestants and Catholics committed atrocities in Ireland, but Catholic atrocities not only received the most attention in Britain, but were greatly exaggerated in the retelling. Ireland complicates the story of the English Civil War because, at least temporarily, there the Scots and Royalists were fighting on the same side to put down the Catholic rebellion even as the Scots were sending aid to Parliament to assist in its struggle against the king. James Butler, the Earl of Ormond, led a Royalist army against the Catholic rebels in Ulster at the same time that the Scots' forces were fighting them. This situation did not last long, however. In September 1643, Ormond opened negotiations with the Irish Catholics on behalf of the king, who needed all of the troops he could get for the war back in England.

As the war progressed, the stakes became higher for both sides as they sought to justify the mounting losses, to punish the enemy, and – especially in the case of the adherents of the parliamentary cause – to achieve a greater degree of constitutional and religious reform than they originally intended. To a large degree, the shift in the war aims of Parliament coincided with the rise of Oliver Cromwell (1599–1658) to a position of military and political leadership. Oliver was the only one of three sons born to Robert Cromwell and his wife Elizabeth to survive infancy, a fact that may have contributed to Cromwell's belief that all events were part of God's plan and to his own personal trust in God, or, in other words, to his Puritan ethic. Cromwell had little chance to make his mark in national politics before the English Revolution because he had only just been elected an MP from Huntingdon in 1628, the year before Charles I disbanded Parliament and began his eleven years of Personal Rule. Deprived of the opportunity to become a national figure by Charles's determination to rule without Parliament, Cromwell did become involved in local politics in that period, moving in 1636 to nearby Ely where he had inherited a house and property. In 1640 he was elected MP for Cambridge and became a key parliamentary figure, leading the attack on the church hierarchy and religious reform. When the Civil War broke out, he joined the army and fought at the opening Battle of Edgehill, before gaining a reputation as a brilliant organizer and leader that was confirmed by the decisive role that his cavalry forces played in the victory over the Royalists at Marston Moor. In 1644, Cromwell received a promotion to lieutenant general and set about the organization of the New Model Army, which achieved a major victory at the Battle of Naseby in June 1645. Cromwell did not yet envision overthrowing the king, much less abolishing the monarchy, but he was much more in a mood to dictate terms to the king rather than to negotiate a compromise, as had been the policy of Manchester and Bedford at the beginning of the war, and to augment the power of Parliament at the king's expense.

In 1646, Charles exploited the growing gap between the New Model Army and the Presbyterian Scots by seeking an alliance with the latter. The New Model Army had become divided internally as well between Presbyterians and Congregationalists, now known as Independents because they favoured the autonomy of independent congregations without the centralized church structure of the Presbyterians. The Presbyterians in England and Scotland had not fought the king only to witness the triumph of the Independents, but the Scots now realized that if they wanted to challenge the New Model Army their only recourse lay in preserving the authority of the same king who had attempted to eradicate Presbyterianism in the late 1630s. The growing power of the New Model Army now allowed Charles to pose as the defender of the liberties of the people and 'the true religion', a remarkable and entirely unforeseen about face.

Just as the hostility of Anglicans towards Presbyterianism had worked to the Royalists' advantage earlier in the war, Charles's alliance with the Scots now provoked renewed determination among his opponents, especially those religious radicals who had benefited from the freedom they had gained during the civil wars. Liberty of conscience emerged as the main theme of the army debates that took place at Whitehall in 1648. Cromwell himself had proved receptive and drawn to this principle by the end of the decade. Meanwhile, within the army a group advocating political and social reform called the Levellers began to advocate for popular sovereignty, universal manhood suffrage, and religious liberty. In May 1647, they presented to the House of Commons the *Petition of Many Thousands*, also known as the 'Large Petition'. Those writers such as John Lilburne and William Walwyn who have been identified as Levellers (those accused of being Levellers actually rejected the term) presented their demands for the rights of the people and popular sovereignty in terms of secular politics, but they came out of the same Puritan background as Cromwell and the Independents. Although the Levellers remained a small minority and their ideas had a limited appeal at the time, they did present a positive approach to political change and for a time attracted significant support within the army, including among the highest ranked officers.

The period from 1646 to 1648 in England is known as the Second Civil War. At the beginning of this next stage in the conflict, in which Charles and the Scots were now aligned against the New Model Army, Cromwell and Parliament still hoped to negotiate a settlement with the king. The main problem in achieving a settlement was that Parliament and the army increasingly represented different viewpoints, a divide that Charles believed he could exploit. His promise to suppress all religions in England except Presbyterianism was not only meant to appease the Scots but to further divide his enemies in England as well. Many people in England had tired of military rule and not only wanted peace but sought a return to pre-Civil War religious customs and festivities that had been banned by the Puritans. As Royalist sentiment began to revive throughout England, the army proved unwilling to face the prospect that all of its victories and the shedding of so much English blood might have served no constructive purpose. Seeking revenge for the man whom they blamed for the conflict, in April 1648 the Army's Council of War met at Windsor and swore revenge against 'Charles Stuart, that man of blood'.

The fall of the monarchy and the Interregnum

In January 1649, Parliament placed Charles on trial for his life, in the words of Lucy Hutchinson, whose husband John was among the regicides, 'for leavying warre against the parliament and people of England, for betraying their publick trust reposed in him, and for being an implacable enemie to the commonwealth'. Charles refused to acknowledge the authority of the court or to enter a plea to the charges against him. It bothered Hutchinson, and no doubt others, that Charles seemed to express no great remorse for all of the blood that had been shed defending his throne. His biggest regret, it seemed, was his role in permitting the death of Strafford, Charles feeling personally responsible for having abandoned him. To Hutchinson it appeared that Charles was so unrepentant that his judges feared God would punish them if they did not sacrifice the king to atone for the sanguinary conflict, which, in their eyes, he had precipitated over the previous six years:

> The gentlemen that were appointed his judges, and divers others, saw in him a disposition so bent on the ruine of all that oppos'd him, for it was upon the conscience of many of them that if they did not execute justice upon him, God would require at their hands all the blood and desolation which should ensue by their suffering him to escape, when God had brought him into their hands.

It later became politically expedient for some to claim that they had voted for Charles's execution under pressure from the army, but Hutchinson disputes this:

> Some of them after, to excuse, belied themselves, and sayd they were under the awe of the armie, and overperswaded by Cromwell, and the like; but it is certeine that all men herein were left to their free liberty of acting, neither perswaded nor compelled; and as there were some nominated in the commission who never sate, and others who sate at first, but durst not hold on, so all the rest might have declin'd it if they would, when it is apparent they should have suffer'd nothing by so doing. For those who then dclin'd were afterwards, when they offer'd themselves, receiv'd in againe, and had places of more trust and benefit than those who run the utmost hazard; which they deserv'd not, for I know upon

certain knowledge that many, yea most of them, retreated not for conscience, but for feare and worldly prudence, foreseeing that the insolency of the armie might grow to that height as to ruine the cause, and reduce the kingdome into the hands of the enemie; and then those who had bene most courageous in their country's cause should be given up as victims. These poore men did privately animate those who appear'd most publiquely, and I knew severall of them in whom I liv'd to see that saying of Christ fulfill'd, 'He that will save his life shall loose it, and he that for my sake will loose his life shall save it'; when it fell out that all their prudent declensions sav'd not the lives of some nor the estates of others.[6]

The trial had been carried out as if by normal constitutional means with the formal apparatus of the state, even if Charles regarded its proceedings as illegal. Charles had a case, if one accepted the proposition that all law derives ultimately from the authority of the king. The regicides justified the execution of the king as necessary for the benefit of the nation, further asserting that it was an act that reflected the will of the English people. The latter was a dubious claim; Cromwell and the regicides acted so quickly precisely because they feared that support for the king would mount or even that the army might intervene on his behalf if they delayed.

Kevin Sharpe suggests that the execution of the king had the opposite of the intended effect by deifying the monarchy, making the long-term prospects of its continued abolition highly unlikely.[7] Almost immediately there appeared a publication purporting to be Charles's pre-death confession called the *Eikon Basilike*, which cast the king and his behaviour in a positive light.

John Milton responded to the *Eikon Basilike* in his *Eikonoklastes*, which he followed up with his *Tenure of Kings and Magistrates*, in both of which he defended the decision to execute the king. In *Eikonoklastes* Milton argued that if Charles had acted on the sympathetic sentiments sincerely expressed in *Eikon Basilike* while he had been king he would never have lost his throne or his life; even so, he acknowledged that since Charles's execution too many people were 'ready to fall flat and give adoration to the Image and memory of this Man, who hath offered at more cunning fetches to undermine our Liberties and put Tyranny into an Art, than any British King before him'.[8]

The execution of Charles I and the abolition of the monarchy reverberated throughout the British Isles, nowhere more so than in Scotland; Charles was also the king of the Scots and they had been deprived of a say in his fate or the choice of his successor. The Scottish Covenanters had started the Bishops' Wars with Charles to preserve their religious autonomy and were just as determined to defend their independence in the face of a new threat from Cromwell's army. On 3 September 1650 Cromwell engaged and defeated a Scots army at Dunbar, despite being outnumbered, by his estimate, by 6,000 to 3,000 in cavalry and 11,000 to 7,500 in infantry troops. This, however, did not stop the Scots from crowning Prince Charles as King Charles II on 1 January 1651. The last battle in Britain during the civil wars took place at Worcester that September, in which Cromwell won a final victory over the Scots, after which Scotland and England became temporarily, for all intents and purposes, a single nation with Cromwell at the head. Cromwell ruled in Scotland not by popular consent, but by the sword and became greatly resented by the Scots, who believed he had betrayed the Solemn League and Covenant.

In Ireland, Cromwell hoped to undermine Catholic opposition by promoting freedom of religion as he had in Scotland, where he treated the Catholics well and granted them liberty of conscience. The Irish Catholic leadership feared the people's acquiescence with Cromwell's rule and determined to fight from its fortified base at Drogheda. The Marquis of Ormond ordered his Catholic followers to resist Cromwell's army 'upon any terms save in the language of the sword, but upon all occasions to fight it out to the last man'.[9] The slaughter of the defenders of Drogheda on 11 September 1649 fulfilled Ormond's wishes, yet Cromwell has borne the brunt of the blame for the massacre ever since. Drogheda was just the beginning of a protracted war that embittered Cromwell towards his opponents in Ireland as much as it enflamed the hatred of Irish Catholics towards Cromwell. Cromwell's decisive victory in Ireland led to a new wave of migration and land grants to people who joined the 'New English' who had settled there during the reigns of James and Charles. The prior inhabitants resented the new arrivals, particularly the Baptists and Quakers who came to Ireland with Cromwell's army. The Quaker Edward Burrough complained that the Baptists

> are seated in darkness and takes their ease in the flesh upon their lofty mountain and have turned their victory into their own exalting and now are waxed fat and kicks against the Lord, but open war I proclaim against them in every town and city and sounds a defiance against the idols Gods which they have set up in their hearts to bow down unto, and a fire is kindled in this nation and in every town burns about me, and yet I am not consumed and in lies and slanders the Dragon and His servants abounds even to the taking away my life if they have power.[10]

Meanwhile, in England, ironically, the protests against Charles's economic policies and taxes such as ship money had not only contributed to a revolution and civil war that caused great disruption to the economy, but also had culminated in a government that taxed people at a higher rate than they had ever known before. The presence of a standing army made it much more difficult to avoid paying taxes than had been the case under Charles. The army imprisoned John Lilburne and other Levellers for daring to suggest that England had simply exchanged one tyranny for another. Lilburne's acquittal provided not only a challenge to the political power of the army but also to the legitimacy of its legal position.[11] Unfortunately, as Peter Laslett has observed, we cannot know the extent of support for the Levellers or how many people would have supported them if exposed to their ideas.[12] Cromwell's regime also provoked opposition because of its elimination of religious festivals such as Christmas and other holidays deemed too close to paganism. As a result, Charles's Personal Rule acquired a reputation for being 'merry old England' and people began to long for a return of the monarchy and the established church.

Cromwell sought to find a permanent political solution for England's constitution, but he depended so much on the army for his legitimacy that there was little to no chance that whatever he came up with would long survive his death. The Putney Debates in the army in 1647 had brought no consensus, nor had the deliberations of the diminished 'Rump Parliament', which after December 1648 sat only by the authority of the army and consisted of only about 200 representatives. (The House of Lords was abolished altogether following the king's execution.) When the Rump failed to live up to its responsibilities to 'the people' and its members began to pursue their own economic self-interests and to perpetuate their own power, Cromwell had the army in 1653 dissolve the Rump and replace it with the 'Nominated' or 'Little' Parliament.

Cromwell refused to accept the title of 'king', but accepted that of 'Lord Protector', a merely semantic difference that mainly served the purpose of assuaging Cromwell's conscience as he did not want to think he had overthrown the king to usurp the throne. As Lord Protector, Cromwell tried to use his position to establish the godly Commonwealth that he envisioned England could become. A loosely organized system of independent churches was created and Puritan clergy installed in churches throughout England in place of ministers deemed objectionable. Cromwell attempted twice more to have a Parliament elected that he would find satisfactory, but dissolved both when faced with opposition from Presbyterians, Republicans, and Monarchists. After he died in 1658, the political situation in England rapidly deteriorated with only the army, again, preventing the outbreak of total chaos. After Richard Cromwell succeeded his father, Charles Fleetwood, at the time the highest ranking officer in the army, presented him with a petition signed by other leading officers requesting higher pay for the army and soliciting his commitment to only promote 'Men of known Godliness and sober Principles'. When Parliament met on 27 January 1659 no unity of purpose prevailed over the divisions emerging among various factions comprising Royalists, Presbyterians, and defenders of the Commonwealth. General George Monck, a former Royalist who had switched his allegiance to the Commonwealth, fearing anarchy, with his Army of Scotland behind him, decided to explore the option of restoring Charles II to the throne to provide a modicum of political stability.

The Interregnum had been a critical time for Puritanism, given the high hopes attached by Cromwell, Milton, and others to a government by the godly that had the power not only to reform the church but society as well. When Cromwell spoke at the opening of his new 'Little' Parliament on 4 July 1653 he, perhaps unsurprisingly, attributed the revolution that had placed the army in control of civil affairs to the will of God. In 1654, however, the Puritan minister John Cotton reminded his readers in *The New Covenant* that, whereas the old covenant was one of works, the new covenant was one of grace. Few Puritans shared Cromwell's belief in religious toleration, or at least thought it should not extend as far as the Lord Protector was willing to take it. The Quakers turned away from the Protestant emphasis on the authority of scripture and focused more on the inner light possessed by each individual that they sought to reawaken with their preaching. They preached a doctrine of total equality that manifested itself in their refusal to lift their hats and they became something of a disruptive force in Interregnum society. The Ranters were even more disruptive, engaging in blasphemy, parodies of the Eucharist, and general moral dissolution (at least according to their enemies); these and a plethora of new dissenting sects that emerged during the Interregnum only reinforced the desire for a return to order that increasingly coalesced around a yearning for the restoration of the Stuart monarchy.

The Restoration in the British Isles

In preparation for his return to England from exile on the Continent, Charles II (r. 1660–85) issued the Declaration of Breda calling for a general amnesty and a broad measure of religious toleration, a principle to which he closely adhered as opposed to the perfunctory commitment of Parliament, with whom, furthermore, Charles had to work in the first years of his reign. In this respect, Charles found himself at odds with his most loyal supporters, the Anglican Royalists, without winning over the Puritan Dissenters, whose activities were now severely restricted by a series of acts collectively known as the Clarendon Code. Charles left in power many of the Justices of the Peace and other officials who had obtained their positions during the Interregnum, his desire for stability trumping his desire for revenge.

For Scotland, the Restoration meant a return to its political independence from England, even if it once again shared a king with its southern neighbour. The Scottish Parliament was restored, a single-chamber body where clergy, nobility, and representatives of the towns sat together, unlike the English bicameral legislature with its Houses of Lords and Commons. The Restoration in Scotland also meant, however, a religious settlement along English lines that had some fearing another Presbyterian rebellion as early as 1663. The Scots had rallied to the support of Charles II after the execution of his father, just as they had sought an alliance with Charles I in the Second Civil War, but their support had been contingent upon the preservation of their Presbyterian church. Now the Scots had to accept an episcopal hierarchy, the abolition of their church's general assembly, and the reordination of all their ministers.

These measures struck deeply at a people whose national identity at the time was so much tied up with their independent national church. On the one hand, they rejoiced to be rid of Cromwell and the forced union achieved only through their military defeat, but on the other they did not wish Charles II to return to the pre-1640 policies of his father. Many ministers who lost their positions formed a vocal opposition against the regime, though these were mostly confined to the region south of Glasgow.[13] They often resorted to holding illegal religious meetings known as conventicles, which had been proscribed by the Conventicle Act of 1662. The church played an extremely important role in the lives of its parishioners, many of whom were reluctant to abandon ministers who had performed their wedding ceremonies, baptized their children, or presided at their family members' funerals. One of the most serious threats to the new regime occurred in the Pentland Rising of 1666, which originated in southwest Scotland when Covenanters used force to protest the mistreatment of an older man by members of the army.

Some of the dismissed ministers were allowed to return to their parishes starting in 1669, as long as they were willing to receive their ordination from a bishop. They had little choice but to acquiesce because the landowning aristocrats held the upper hand in Scottish political culture at the time of the Restoration and they understood that their best interests lay in supporting the restored king. On a local level, royal authority was restored to Scotland through the appointment of justices of the peace acceptable to the local populations but loyal to the monarchy. As in England, where Charles left local militias under the control of the most prominent families in the area, whether they had supported the king or Parliament in the Civil War, in Scotland the

JP positions were dominated by the heads of the leading clans, such as the Campbells and Macleans in Argyll and the Frasers and the Mackintoshes in Invernesshire.

Military force was necessary at times, however, to deal with the unruly elements of Highland society during the 1660s and 1670s. Meanwhile, the central government continued to be dominated by Lowlanders, especially Charles's commissioner for Scotland, John Maitland, the Duke of Lauderdale. Lauderdale appointed Archibald Campbell, the Earl of Argyll, to keep order in the Highlands, while he focused on managing Parliament and enforcing the Restoration religious settlement in the Lowlands. Lauderdale's religious policies fluctuated, as did those of Charles II in England, which merely added to the confusion and instability of the period. For example, a Declaration of Indulgence in 1672 called for a greater level of toleration, but Lauderdale abandoned that policy two years later and dismissed those charged with implementing it. By the time Lauderdale died in 1680, Scottish opposition was increasing and the government was in jeopardy of losing control of the situation.

Charles II had a fair amount of support in Ireland. Catholic landowners, in particular, regained a portion (though not nearly all) of the lands they had lost under Cromwell. Charles wanted to support the Catholics in Ireland, but could not afford to alienate loyal Protestants there who backed the monarchy. He therefore made conflicting promises to Protestant landowners who had gained land for supporting the Royalist cause and to Catholic landowners who had been deprived of some of those same lands. Parliament passed three separate land acts for Ireland during the 1660s, but none of them could achieve Charles's contradictory goals for the land settlement there. In 1682 Irish Protestant peers outnumbered Catholics by 80–39 according to one source and 67–37 according to another. If one takes into account the number of Protestant peers who actually lived in England, the balance looks very different; Toby Barnard calculated that only nineteen Irish Protestant peers resided in Ireland during the reign of James II (r. 1685–88) and that only two Catholic peers lived in England.[14] Protestants also dominated in administration and trade, but a significant minority of Catholics participated in commerce and the law as well. Presbyterians in Ireland fared even worse under the Restoration and had no more legal rights than the Catholics. Like Catholics, Presbyterians were nonconformists who refused to accept the authority of the established Church of Ireland.

Some sentiment for bringing Ireland into political union with England and Wales existed during the period; the economic theorist William Petty was one advocate of a union on the grounds that it would facilitate trade between Britain and Ireland. Such proposals foundered on English attitudes towards Ireland that regarded the island as an English colony that should be treated accordingly. In 1663, for example, Parliament passed an act restricting the importation of Irish cattle in support of English cattle owners during an agricultural recession. Anti-Irish prejudice further fuelled support for the bill, especially in the House of Lords where it was heatedly debated. The bill passed the House of Lords by sixteen votes after the word 'nuisance' was eliminated; the Commons voted by sixteen votes to retain the word in order to restrict Charles's right to grant exceptions.[15] In 1667, Arthur Annesley, Earl of Anglesey, responded by cautioning that 'Ireland is a conquered nation' but 'it must not be so treated, for the conquerors inhabit there'.[16] With union seemingly out of the question, William Molyneaux's *The Case for Ireland Stated* (1698) argued for autonomy for the Irish Parliament. Molyneaux excluded demands for Catholic rights in order to make his proposal more palatable to the English. But this proposal was also rejected, as was an Irish request for annual parliaments as an alternative to a union.

The Welsh had the easiest time adapting to the shift from Commonwealth back to monarchy, given their adherence to Anglicanism and their support for the Royalist cause in the civil wars. Although the Welsh gentry and aristocracy most vocally supported the monarchy, the Welsh as a whole had never exhibited much sympathy for the religious and political radicalism that had emerged in England in the 1640s and 1650s, though ninety-three Welsh ministers did lose their positions shortly after the Restoration. Philip Jenkins goes so far as to suggest that 'there was no such thing as Welsh politics in the seventeenth century, at least in the sense of a culture or movement distinct from that of England'.[17] Not that England had a single political tradition to which everyone adhered, but Wales does not stand out in such a way as to make it distinct from those divisions extant in England. As in Ireland, interest in history and antiquarianism trumped political activism for most of the late seventeenth and eighteenth centuries. Unlike Ireland such work did not tend towards establishing a separate political identity for Wales. In fact, Jenkins regards sympathy for the monarchy and the union with England as the defining characteristics of the political culture of Wales for most of the seventeenth century. This only began to change during the Exclusion Crisis of 1679–81. At that time, two political parties began to emerge in English politics: the Tories, supporters of the right of Charles's Catholic brother, James, the Duke of York, to inherit the English throne, and the Whigs, who wanted to exclude James from the succession based on his Catholic religion. Welsh MPs divided over the issue as well, yet another way in which Welsh politics was largely an extension of English politics during the Restoration period.

In England, the licentious moral tone of Restoration society received an early challenge from the Great Plague that struck London in 1665 and the Great Fire that destroyed much of the city the following year. Neither, however, produced a revival of political opposition from the largely discredited Puritans. John Bunyan perhaps best exemplified the political quiescence of Restoration Puritans. In his most famous work, *The Pilgrim's Progress* (1678), Bunyan reminded his readers of the central tenet of Protestantism: no righteousness exists outside that which is bestowed by Jesus Christ. Bunyan's novel treats in allegorical fashion the sinner's journey from the depths of despair – resulting from his own unworthiness, the challenges of human nature, and the temptations to which we are all susceptible – to his acceptance of God's grace and assurance of his salvation. Bunyan downplayed traditional doctrinal disputes and niceties to focus on his central message and a simplified, moral vision. Bunyan decried hypocrisy and promoted an internal version of Christianity that did not depend on enforcement from the church or the state: 'I have heard many cry out against sin in the pulpit, who yet can abide it well enough in the heart, and house, and conversation.'[18]

Despite the general level of support that he enjoyed when he returned to England, Charles II still faced difficulties in his efforts to re-establish the power of the monarchy. He still lacked a standing army, apart from the one regiment that served as his guard under General Monck, whom Charles made the Duke of Albemarle. He did possess a navy, however, which he put to use in two wars with the Dutch in 1667 and 1672. The Second Anglo-Dutch War of 1667 (the first had occurred under Cromwell in the 1650s) had occurred while Charles was still somewhat in the honeymoon phase of his rule amid an upsurge in English nationalism. However, by the time of the Third Anglo-Dutch War, the Duke of York had converted to Catholicism and Charles had negotiated a secret treaty with King Louis XIV of France, leading many of Charles's subjects to sympathize with the Protestant Dutch; when Charles issued a Declaration of Indulgence granting toleration to Catholics and Protestant Dissenters in 1672, Parliament became even more suspicious of his intentions and soon began demanding an end to the war.

The political culture of the 1670s and 1680s

The key to understanding the political culture of the British Isles in the 1670s and 1680s is to realize that the political categories of the period do not break down along neat lines with democracy and support for religious toleration on one end of the spectrum and absolute monarchy and oppression on the other. Both Charles II and James II, for example, continued to support religious toleration far more than did Parliament, which insisted on enforcing the discriminatory and exclusionary Clarendon Code. Charles II renewed the royal charters of Connecticut and Rhode Island, both of which allowed for religious pluralism. Under Charles, Pennsylvania also emerged as a highly tolerant colony led by Quakers, as did New Jersey and New York, both previously part of the Dutch colony of New Netherlands prior to their acquisition by England in the Second Anglo-Dutch War.

What worried Charles's parliamentary critics even more than his support of toleration for Protestant Dissenters, however, was his pro-Catholic foreign policy and suspicions that the king himself was a crypto-Catholic. There is no question that the alliance that first Charles and then James forged with King Louis XIV of France damaged them both politically, especially because of Louis's ambitions for European dominance, the absolute power that he wielded in France, and – after 1685 – his persecution of the Protestant Huguenots. Anti-Catholicism represented a prevalent theme in English political culture throughout the Restoration period; in his poem 'Advice to a Painter', written in the 1660s, Andrew Marvell already voiced the growing fear that Charles would attempt to return England to Rome:

> I'll raise my Papists, and my Irish bands;
> And by a noble well-contrivéd plot,
> Managed by wise Fitz-Gerald, and by Scot,
> Prove to the world I'll make old England know,
> That Common Sense is my eternal foe. (ll. 16–20)

Marvell's *Account of the Growth of Popery, and Arbitrary Government in England* was just one of a number of anti-Catholic works to appear in England during the 1670s. In August 1676, John Aubrey noted in his diary that 'feeling against Roman Catholics is rising again in England'.[19]

In 1678 a disgraced Anglican clergyman and recent convert to Catholicism named Titus Oates returned to England from the Continent claiming to possess inside knowledge of a Jesuit conspiracy to burn the city of London, execute Charles II, and place James on the throne. Oates alleged that this coup was to be accompanied by a foreign invasion that would force England to return to the Catholic Church. Furthermore, Oates accused hundreds of Roman Catholic nobles and priests in England of complicity in this 'Popish Plot', as it became known. Those he accused included high-ranking members of the household of the Duke of York, including his wife, Mary of Modena, and James's former secretary, Edward Coleman. The plot caused something close to a mass hysteria in England and ultimately led to the arrest and execution of about thirty-five prominent English Catholics.

The Popish Plot cannot be understood without the context of the growing hostility towards France that led to actual fears of a foreign invasion and the accompanying insecurity that motivated the search for internal traitors. Contemporary sources reflect the extent to which people took Oates's conspiracy theory seriously, despite gross inconsistencies in his testimony and the fantastic nature of his accusations. The plot seemed more credible, at least to the general public, with the discovery of the murdered body of Justice Edmund Berry Godfrey and the discovery of letters that Coleman had sent to Louis XIV and the pope requesting funds for the purposes of bribing members of Parliament.

In 1679, even as the frenzy caused by the Popish Plot began to die down, some members of Parliament began to express concern over how to confront the possibility that England could soon have a Catholic king, with James, having survived the plot, still poised to inherit the throne after Charles's death. With opposition to James mounting, his supporters based their defence of the monarchy on the political writings of Sir Robert Filmer, whose book *Patriarcha* (1680) challenged emerging ideas of popular sovereignty. Filmer reserved sovereignty for kings alone and did not believe that they owed their crowns to the consent of the people – thereby making any attempts to exclude James from the throne illegitimate.

As for James, the Duke of York had come to his Catholic religion honestly, having little to gain politically by his conversion and much to lose. Despite popular belief to the contrary, James had no intention of forcing his Protestant subjects to convert to Catholicism, just as he would not be coerced to abandon his faith by a bigoted and intolerant Parliament. He developed a close friendship with William Penn, who had done much in the Restoration period to moderate the radical influences of Quakerism, and the two shared similar views on religious toleration. Penn consistently advocated for freedom of worship and the inviolability of conscience in matters of religion. He made an economic argument for religious toleration as well, a point driven home by the deleterious effects on the French economy of Louis XIV's persecution of the Huguenots. James fits Penn's definition of an ideal ruler as one best positioned to arbitrate among competing religious interests in his kingdom. As a Catholic, he could be expected to defend the interests of Catholics; as a member of a religious minority, he would understand the importance of liberty of conscience to Protestant Dissenters; as king, he was sworn to defend the interests of the Church of England.

James did succeed his elder brother as King James II and VII upon Charles's death in 1685. His accession to the throne was met with opposition in both England and Scotland. In England, Charles II's illegitimate son, James, the Duke of Monmouth, launched a rebellion in the southwest that James II's army easily crushed. In Scotland, a rebellion headed by the ninth Earl of Argyll reflected the pent-up frustrations of the

Covenanters over the religious policies of Charles II. Argyll's rebellion also proved short-lived, but it revealed the determination of the Scots to return Scotland to its Presbyterian system of church government. James's accession was naturally greeted more warmly by Catholics in Ireland who hoped that the new king would sympathize with his coreligionists across the Irish Sea. But Irish Protestants shuddered at the prospect, with some deciding to leave the island. Catholics began to regain their influence in the towns and cities, as James's Lord Lieutenant, Richard Talbot, the Earl of Tyrconnel, set about to redress the power imbalance between Protestants and Catholics.

In England, once the initial crisis had passed even prominent Whigs settled in and decided to reach an accommodation with James's rule by acceding to his determination to grant religious toleration for Dissenters. Even John Locke, a critic of James who had written his *First Treatise on Government* to challenge Filmer's defence of absolute monarchy, had penned an important *Letter on Toleration* in 1685. Locke had also helped his patron, the Earl of Shaftesbury, draft the religiously liberal constitution of Carolina, the colony founded in 1663 that was named after Charles II. Scott Sowerby has shown that opposition to anti-popery and defence of toleration for Catholics crossed party lines and did not represent either a Whig or a Tory stance per se.[20] If some Whigs supported religious toleration and were even prepared to support James's plans in that direction, most Tories, committed as they were to the established church, did not. This does not mean, however, that they opposed James's right to rule or that they shared the hostility of many Whigs towards popery.

There is no question that people feared James's intentions and disliked his pro-Catholic policies, which cast some of his other actions in a more adverse light than they would otherwise have been seen. For example, James tried to manipulate the parliamentary election of March 1685 to engineer the election of a supportive majority with which he could work. He did so by issuing new charters and having his agents both intervene in borough elections and pressure aristocrats who had the ability to influence the nomination of pro-royal candidates. According to complaints made at the time, he went further than his predecessors had in this regard, his agents even resorting to violence and intimidation; initially, these tactics had their desired effect, James allegedly saying that there were no more than forty members whose election did not please him. However, James suspended Parliament in November 1685 after losing a crucial vote in the House of Commons (by one vote) on his proposal to suspend the Test Acts, which prevented Catholics from holding public office. Nothing that James had done was strictly illegal, but these measures, along with his desire to maintain the army that had crushed Monmouth's rebellion, as well as its Catholic officers, created a serious level of mistrust among his leading subjects.

However, it was the birth of a son and heir by his wife, Mary of Modena that precipitated the immediate crisis that led to his downfall. Before the birth of his son, his Protestant daughter Mary stood to inherit the throne. Before 1688, Mary's husband, the Dutch stadtholder William of Orange had good reason to hope that his wife would succeed her father and bring England and its resources to bear on his struggle to defend Holland from the predations of Louis XIV. Now he either had to act decisively or see the English throne pass to a new line of Catholic kings. Fortunately for William, James's support within England had waned to the point where his opponents, as much as they wanted to avoid a repeat of the 1640s, had begun contemplating action to challenge or even overthrow their king.

The Revolution of 1688

The contemporary Gilbert Burnet, who chronicled these developments in his *History of My Own Time*, wrote that the revolution was almost totally unexpected and he called the fall of James 'one of the strangest catastrophes that is in our history'. Burnet believed that the causes of the revolution needed closer examination instead of merely attributing it to the Dutch invasion. Recent historians have focused more on the popular uprisings that accompanied William's invasion and the support that it had among the general public; popular disturbances occurred in northern England as well as in the Midlands at the time of the invasion. In fact, riots in London by anti-Catholic mobs, not fear of William's army, had led James to flee the capital in the company of Sir Edward Hales and Ralph Sheldon, both loyal officers in James's army.

Bishop Burnet described James's downfall thusly:

> A great king, with strong armies and mighty fleets, a vast treasure and powerful allies, fell all at once; and his whole strength, like a spider's web, was so irrecoverably broken with a touch, that he was never able to retrieve what, for want of both judgment and heart, he threw up in a day.[21]

The point here is not to downplay the significance of William's invasion – he did have 21,000 soldiers with him – but to emphasize that James certainly could have stayed and fought if he had the support of his own people and his army. Instead, James failed to command the fealty of his own people and the soldiers left James's army to join William's. In fact, William would never have embarked from the Netherlands if he had not received assurances of popular support for his cause in England.

William's invasion complicated the political situation, not only because it provided military support for a revolution that would not have succeeded without it, but also because he and his wife provided viable candidates to replace James once he had fled London. The entire state of affairs made the political theorizing of John Locke and Robert Filmer relevant in an immediate and practical way. In his *Second Treatise on Civil Government*, written at the time of the Exclusion Crisis, not, as used to be thought, after the revolution of 1688, John Locke went so far as to affirm that 'it is evident that absolute monarchy, which by some men is counted the only government in the world, is indeed inconsistent with civil society, and so can be no form of civil government at all'. Even the defender of absolute monarchy, Robert Filmer, acknowledged in his *Patriarcha* (1680) that there were times when God might find it necessary to remove a ruler from power:

> If it please God, for the Correction of the Prince, or punishment of the People, to suffer Princes to be removed, and others to be placed in their rooms, either by the Factions of the Nobility, or Rebellion of the People; in all such cases, the

Judgment of God, who hath Power to give and to take away Kingdoms, is most just: Yet the Ministry of Men who Execute Gods Judgments without Commission, is sinful and damnable.

Filmer's thought is as directly relevant to the political culture of the 1680s that produced the Revolution of 1688 as Locke's. Indeed, many of those who participated in the revolution were Tories who retained their belief in absolute monarchy, even as they found it expedient to remove this particular absolute monarch. Locke's central argument against absolute monarchy was that the people needed some recourse should a monarch act in such a way as to violate not only the laws of his own kingdom but people's fundamental or natural rights as human beings. Filmer, on the other hand, compared the authority of a king to that of a father, the only difference being that whereas the father had responsibility for defending and providing for his family, the king had this responsibility for the entire Commonwealth. According to Locke, once a king began to act in such a way as to threaten rather than defend the safety and well-being of his people he had already thrown them back into a kind of natural state in which they had no choice but to defend themselves and reconstitute civil society under a different government or ruler. To Filmer, the stability provided by an absolute monarchy outweighed the instability that would result from allowing subjects the right to change rulers or that attended any other form of government.

A key to understanding the triumph of the Lockean perspective in 1688 was the temporary abandonment of the ideas of Filmer by the Tories. During the Exclusion Crisis, Tories sympathized more with the ideas of Filmer and defended James's right to rule. They changed their position not based on theoretical considerations or because they had become convinced by Locke's arguments, but because they disliked James's policies so much, particularly his religious policies, which they saw as undermining the established church. But would they have continued with their resistance – or even had the capacity to resist – if James had fought back and imprisoned his opponents or, as his father had done, merely bided his time until he had the ability to fight back? Would James have attracted the support of Tories who might have ultimately defended the monarchy in the face of popular uprisings that threatened the same kind of anarchy as had accompanied the civil wars? Would James, faced with an almost unified opposition to his policies among Whigs and Tories, have negotiated to keep his crown and avoid the fate of his father if given more time without the pressure of William's invading force pressing upon London?

When James chose not to fight back with extreme measures, he enhanced the chances that the Dutch invasion would, in fact, succeed. Instead of negotiating with his political opponents and/or William, he fled. On 11 December 1688 James left London with the intention of going to France to seek military support for a counterattack that would allow him to regain a throne that was not yet lost. In doing so, however, James gave his opponents the opportunity to claim that James had abdicated his throne (something that he never actually did).

One of the most bizarre incidents of the events that accompanied the Revolution of 1688 occurred that same night when a group of sailors captured the king at sea and returned him to England. The sailors who captured James did not come on him entirely by accident – they were patrolling the coast in case he might try to flee the country. From 11 December to the 14, James received rough treatment at the hands of his captors at Favesham. He suffered a series of indignities that included a close inspection of his own person, down to his private parts, at the hands of his subjects, which must have been deeply humiliating to a reigning monarch.[22] But James's presence on English soil, to which he had returned by being forced to wade to shore, provided a problem for both William and those who wished to crown the Dutch stadtholder as James's replacement, who now would find it more difficult to justify their actions if they could not claim that James had willingly abdicated; therefore, when James escaped from his purposefully neglectful guards while under house arrest in Rochester, he faced no impediments to his leaving the country.

When James returned to the British Isles with an army less than three months later, it was not to England but to Ireland, where the majority of the population still regarded him as king. From 16 April until 12 August, James's forces besieged the city of Derry, while the Protestants gathered there awaited deliverance from William, now crowned King William III of England, with his wife Mary II as co-ruler. William brought his army to Ireland in June, landing in Ulster and heading in the direction of Dublin for a military confrontation with James's troops. William III defeated the army of James II at the Battle of the Boyne in July 1690, and again at the Battle of Antrim a few months later, resulting in the confirmation of the dominance of the Protestant landowning class in Ireland, as well as William's control over the entire British Isles. The dramatic events that saw the overthrow of two British monarchs within a span of four decades occurred against a backdrop of equally significant changes in thought and society that transformed the history of the British Isles as much as – or more than – the political developments detailed in this chapter thus far.

Changes in thought and society

In his *Leviathan* (1651), Thomas Hobbes (1588–1679) moved away from the emphasis on divine-right monarchy and provided a predominantly secular justification for the power of established governments. Locke had Hobbes very much in mind when he developed his own political ideas in the 1660s and 1670s, as well as the natural law tradition associated in the seventeenth century primarily with the Dutch thinker, Hugo Grotius (1583–1645). Whereas Hobbes had characterized the state of nature as total anarchy, a 'war of all against all' in which life was 'solitary, nasty, brutish, and short', Locke based his contract theory of government on the natural rights that individuals enjoyed prior to their entrance into civilized society, which existed only to preserve those rights. Yet Locke believed that natural right derived from God and that civilized society did not exist merely to protect people's rights to pursue their own agendas independent of that of society as a whole. Of course, Hobbes wrote in the immediate aftermath of the civil wars during the early years of the Interregnum; it is no coincidence that Locke, who began his career as a conservative political thinker, only shifted his political views the further removed he became from the 1650s. Yet if Locke's ideas were revolutionary, they were only moderately so; he found a way to defend private property despite the communitarian emphasis of natural law theory. Locke's political works, like those of Hobbes and others, need to be read in the context of their times; Locke wanted to prevent English subjects from arbitrary taxation by the English monarch – not to set down a theory that would apply in universal circumstances. He also was writing in response to the French absolutism of Louis XIV, whose influence on English politics during the reigns of Charles II and James II we have already witnessed. Locke became more politically progressive for his times as he moved away from Hobbes, but both based their ideas on a secular view of the foundations of government that did not depend upon scriptural support.

FIGURE 16 *Title page of* Leviathan, *by English philosopher and author Thomas Hobbes (1588–1679).*
Time Life Pictures/The LIFE Picture Collection/Getty.

Locke is also famous for his *Essay Concerning Human Understanding* (1689), in which he argued that all of our ideas derive from experience, either sensation or reflection, the mind being a *tabula rasa* or 'blank slate' at birth with no innate ideas or preconceived notions of reality. If Locke was correct, then individual minds could be improved through the right education. In fact, Locke worked out some of these implications himself in another treatise, *Some Thoughts Concerning Education* (1693). In the seventeenth century, most childhood and even university-level education were based on rote learning reinforced by strict discipline. Moral education relied heavily on the Christian doctrine of original sin, in which the child was born with evil impulses that needed to be controlled through strict rules and, if necessary, corporal punishment. Based on his concept of the mind as a blank slate, Locke believed that children would respond as well to positive encouragement, in fact respond better, than to discipline and threats. He believed children to be capable of rational thought and understanding and that they would respond better to reasoned explanations and kindness than to parental or educational authorities who used their physical power to intimidate them into obedience.

In science, the invention of the microscope opened up whole new worlds previously invisible to humankind, while the scientific rivalry between the Dutch and the English led to corresponding research that produced innovations in timekeeping such as the 'pendulum clock (1658), the longitude pendulum timekeeper (1665), and balance-spring regulator (1674)', as well as disputes between the English and the Dutch over who had priority of discovery.[23] A similar dispute erupted later in the century over whether the English scientific thinker Isaac Newton or the German mathematician-philosopher Gottfried Lebiniz first discovered the infinitesimal calculus (Newton discovered it first, but Leibniz discovered it independently). Newton was a mathematical and scientific genius, whose 1687 work *Principia* explained that the same gravitational forces that operate on earth exert an influence on bodies in space as well, but he was a product of a society that valued natural philosophy and the expansion of knowledge best exemplified by the founding of the Royal Society in 1660 at the beginning of Charles's reign.

Newton changed how people viewed the laws of motion and the movements of the heavenly bodies, just as the Englishman William Harvey (1578–1657) had changed the common understanding of human anatomy and Robert Boyle (1627–91), born in County Waterford, Ireland, had made significant contributions to both chemistry and physics. Harvey is credited with the discovery of the circulation of the blood, which he explained in *On the Motion of the Heart and Blood* (1628). In this work, Harvey explained that the heart moves when it contracts (systole) and rests when it expands (diastole), in the process causing blood to circulate through the arteries, which carry blood away from the heart, while blood returns to its coronary centre via the veins. Boyle challenged preexisting ideas about the nature of matter and reduced the study of chemistry to one involving chemical elements. He is perhaps best known for the discovery that the pressure of gas is inversely proportional to its volume, a principle which became known as Boyle's Law (1662). The main difference between Newton and the scientific tradition emanating from the Royal Society was that his work was largely mathematical and theoretical as opposed to experimental and observational. Together, however, the empirical studies of a new microscopic world previously unseen and Newton's seeming ability to unlock the mysteries of the cosmos fostered a new appreciation for and confidence in humanity's ability to pursue and attain true knowledge about the world and universe we inhabit.

In some circles, contemporary science and philosophy seemed to lead in the direction of atheism. In *Pilgrim's Progress*, Bunyan's Christian encounters an atheist who is 'blinded by the light of this world'. Perhaps an even more serious threat to orthodox Christianity during this period, however, came from anti-Trinitarianism, otherwise known as 'Unitarianism'. Brent Sirota calls the Trinitarian controversy 'the defining event in church politics in the postrevolutionary era'.[24] Unitarianism was one of the strains of thought that led to the emergence of Deism, which was based on a monotheistic belief in a Creator-God, but denied that God either intervened in human history or earthly events following the creation or that men and women would have to answer for their sins in the afterlife. In fact, contemporaries drew little distinction between Deism and atheism because of the corrosive influence that even the former was believed to have. The Church of England taught not only religious doctrine but also ideas about authority and political obedience, leading people to wonder what would happen to the political order should its main doctrines be called into question. One of the first works to elicit such a concern was the poem 'A Satyre against Reason and Mankind', written in 1674 by the second Earl of Rochester, John Wilmot. Rochester particularly upset the Anglican establishment by conflating atheism with religious fanaticism, as reflected in his remark to Burnet that 'he was sure Religion was either a meer Contrivance, or the most important thing that could be' since either position challenged the existence of a state church.[25]

Yet Anglicanism depended on taking a more rational approach to Christianity than did Catholicism, which was criticized by mainstream Protestants as too mysterious and superstitious, as evidenced by their equating the doctrine of transubstantiation with magic. Even some thinkers who defended Christianity emphasized the importance of reason; Locke wrote his *Reasonableness of Christianity* in 1695, while John Toland came out with his *Christianity Not Mysterious* in 1696. Unlike Toland, however, Locke recognized that there was a difference between reason and faith, which depended on revelation from God; in other words, you could not entirely remove revelation from Christianity without removing the essence of the Christian faith.

Yet Locke stated in *An Essay Concerning Human Understanding* that 'No man inspired by God can by any revelation communicate to others any new simple ideas which they had not before from sensation or reflection'.[26] That is, ideas have to have some foundation in what we already know or a previous conception that has been introduced to us in order for it to be at all comprehensible. Privately, Locke may have become a Unitarian and his *Letter on Toleration* took a comprehensive view of those beliefs that should not be proscribed by the state, but he never went as far as Toland in his published views on Christianity.

John Webster contributed to this rationalizing tendency by taking on what he regarded as contemporary superstitions related to witchcraft and sorcery in his descriptive but lengthily titled treatise, *The displaying of supposed witchcraft wherein is affirmed that there are many sorts of deceivers and impostors and divers persons under a passive delusion of melancholy and fancy, but that there is a corporeal league*

made betwixt the Devil and the witch ... is utterly denied and disproved ... (1677).
Webster made a distinction between

> Imposters, Cheaters, and Active Deceivers, and those that are but under a mere
> passive delusion through mere ignorant and Superstitious education, a melancholy
> temper and constitution, or led by the vain credulity of inefficatious Charms,
> Pictures, Ceremonies and the like traditionally taught them.

As the witch trials in Salem, Massachusetts would demonstrate in 1692, belief
in witchcraft continued in the English world, but Webster and others had raised
significant objections that would make such events more the exception than the rule,
at least in England, in the second half of the seventeenth century.

The Great Plague which afflicted London in 1665, although it might have killed
as many as 100,000, did not produce anything like the religious hysteria that
might have been expected from an earlier age. In his famous diary written at the
time, Samuel Pepys worried that people from other infected villages would come
to London and make matters worse, but otherwise he recorded information about
those affected by the plague in the same matter-of-fact tone used to describe daily
events and various other aspects of his life and times. In his entry for 9 August, for
example, he wrote that he 'met also with Mr. Evelyn in the streete, who tells me the
sad condition at this very day at Deptford for the plague, and more at Deale..., that
the towne is almost quite depopulated'. Society still lacked the means to understand
the cause of the plague and so attributed it to God; Andrew Marvell wrote, for
example, in his 'Third Advice to a Painter':

> War, fire, and plague against us all conspire;
> We the war, God the plague, who raised the fire? (ll. 417–18)

But, as Marvell's lines indicate, he did not consider the Great Fire of London of 1666
as God's responsibility, but rather the result of human agency.

Socially, the seventeenth century saw the beginning of what historians have called
a 'consumer revolution', in which a greater quantity and variety of goods became
available to people up and down the social ladder. The economy grew after 1650
and with it so did credit and income. The growth of the English navy, as well as of
maritime trade in the second half of the century contributed to this change, not only
because of increased imports but also because of the many needs of ships and sailors,
ranging from guns to everyday necessities, such as food, candles, and ale. British
merchants imported increasing quantities of tobacco from North America and sugar
from the Caribbean, as well as tea and silk or cotton textiles from India.

There were other signs of the growth of a market society that catered more to
consumer demand than necessity. A growing variety of objects d'art and other
items valued for their beauty, interest, or symbolic meaning rather than pure utility,
many also coming from overseas, entered the market as well. Advertising, both in
newspapers and shop displays, started to become central to commercial enterprise;
if people were going to buy items that they did not need they first needed to be
convinced that they wanted them and to be made aware of their availability.

Food also became more widely available, leaving people free of the cycle of bad harvests that could lead to severe malnutrition and greater susceptibility to disease if not starvation, even if older generations could still remember times of real hardship from earlier in the century. The late seventeenth century was a time of marked growth in agricultural productivity on the eve of what historians would later term an 'agricultural revolution' that took place in the first half of the eighteenth century. Most people, even those who lived in the countryside, increasingly bought their food and other household items from the market rather than depending on what they could grow or manufacture at home. This left them somewhat more susceptible to market forces, such as the demands of war, which could still leave individuals destitute or even homeless. The local distribution of aid to the poor provided for in the Elizabethan Poor Laws supplemented the market as a means of ensuring that even disadvantaged people did not starve in bad times. However, authorities responsible for such distribution still made a distinction between the 'deserving' and 'undeserving' poor, the latter of which were often forced into a life of crime or prostitution in order to keep the body and soul together, social problems that would increase in the eighteenth century.

The experience of the civil wars had caused a disruption in social relations that created even greater social mobility and lessened the differences between gentlemen and those who used to be regarded as their social inferiors. Population decline following the turmoil of the middle decades of the century also provided more economic opportunities for the labouring classes compared to the preceding period when inflation and a surplus of people in regard to resources and opportunities had provided economic challenges to many. But, as Peter Laslett has noted, nothing like the social rebellions based on rising expectations that accompanied the late fourteenth century, another period of population decline, reoccurred during the mid- to late seventeenth century.[27] Fears about the erosion of social and political order engendered by changes in scientific, political, and religious thought did not prove warranted; tenants and workers had plenty of economic motivations for remaining subservient to their landlords and masters.

Women made little notable progress during the second half of the seventeenth century, outside of the increased role that they played in Quaker congregations, which valued equality of the sexes as much as it did equality among individuals of different social classes. Social convention prevailed in other Protestant denominations in discouraging female education, still regarding it as threatening to the general order of things. Such attitudes were part of the socially conservative reaction in Britain after the civil wars, in which women exercised a great deal of independence, either at home in the absence of their soldier husbands or by participating in the war itself as soldiers, spies, and nurses.

Of course, women found a place in the new market economy, participating alongside men in the manufacture of textiles and the making and purveying of other goods in ports and market towns. Elite women in the countryside supervised work around their farms, particularly over activities such as dairying conducted primarily by female labourers. The number of women who professionally brewed beer and ale declined in the seventeenth century, but this did not stop upper-class women from setting up their own domestic breweries.

Economic and social changes in the second half of the seventeenth century did create new employment opportunities for women that culminated in the more dramatic shifts that occurred with industrialization in the eighteenth century, but they did not substantially alter women's subordinate position with respect to male authority. This did not stop clergymen from affirming this position; for example, in 1673 Richard Allestree first published the popular work, *The Ladies Calling*, affirming their religious duty to restrict their activities to household pursuits. Similar works included *The Queen-Like Closet, or Rich Cabinet* (1681) and *The Compleat Servant Maid* (1683) by Hannah Wooley, who also emphasized the personal traits, such as a quiet and pleasant demeanour, that she associated with femininity. It is notable that women authors like Wooley not only supported contemporary male expectations of women, but that others, such as Mary Astell and Aphra Behn, were politically conservative as well.

Conclusion

The Bill of Rights that Parliament passed in the wake of the Revolution of 1688 did not radically alter the political culture of England in the direction of anything like real democracy or preclude William from ruling as a divine-right monarch, albeit a Protestant one. The early-twentieth-century historian George Macaulay Trevelyan believed that the primary reason why a second revolution had to occur in seventeenth-century England was because the first one did not succeed and had failed to resolve important constitutional and religious issues. Civil War had resulted in religiously motivated Puritans led by Cromwell using military power not only to execute the king, but to abolish the monarchy, bring Parliament under the control of Cromwell and the army, and overturn the rule of English law. The separate kingdoms of Scotland and Ireland fell under Cromwell's control as well, essentially as a result of military conquest, although Cromwell did have allies in both places. But William III's overthrow of James II raised similar questions of legitimacy in Scotland and Ireland, even as Parliament attempted to address the unresolved issues of the English constitution. William was acceptable in England and Wales in a way that Cromwell was not because he supported the Church of England, was married to James's daughter, and had the backing of both Whigs and Tories, at least at first. For the search for political stability was not over, nor did the Scots or the Irish prove as willing to accept William as the English or the Welsh were.

FIGURE 17 *Glencoe, Scotland.*
Mathew Roberts Photography – www.matroberts.co.uk/Moment/Getty.

9

The British Isles in the first half of the eighteenth century:

From the Bill of Rights to the Battle of Culloden

If Marlborough had cut himself adrift from the Tory Party and become a mere adherent of the Court he would soon have lost all influence upon events. His own power would have been reduced to his own personal ability, while at the same time his usefulness to the king would have vanished. William knew England almost as well as he knew Europe, but he despised the ignoble strife of its parties, and underrated the factor of party as an element in his vast problem. In his embarrassments he would turn from Whig Ministers who could not manage and would not face the House of Commons, to the turbulent Tories, only to find them ignorant of world facts and with a view of national interests which was at that time wrongheaded and utterly at variance with his own purposes.

WINSTON CHURCHILL, *Marlborough: His Life and Times* (1933)

The English Bill of Rights, the Treaty of Limerick, and the Revolution Settlement

The Bill of Rights that followed the Revolution of 1688 provided the basis for the modern relationship between Parliament and the British monarchy. The final version of the Bill of Rights approved by Parliament did not go as far as some had originally intended, as can be seen by a comparison with a previous document called the 'Heads of Grievances'. This earlier document asserted demands that would have required new legislation, such as a law prohibiting the interruption of Parliament in the middle of a session. The House of Commons was reluctant to approve any measure that would leave the revolution open to being interpreted as a *coup d'etat,* instead of as a change necessitated by James's alleged abdication. The Bill of Rights was based instead on a modification of a different document, the Declaration of Rights. It began by asserting that the king did not have the right to suspend any laws without the consent of Parliament. It then confirmed the illegality of the monarch maintaining a standing army. In addition, the Bill of Rights abolished the court of commissioners for ecclesiastical causes; declared illegal the levying of taxes without parliamentary consent; asserted the right of Protestants to bear arms; and guaranteed the free election of members of Parliament, parliamentary freedom of speech, and the prohibition of cruel and unusual punishment.

Parliament also attempted to deal with the religious divisions within the kingdom by passing in 1689 'An Act for exempting Their Majesties Protestant Subjects, dissenting from the Church of England, from the Penalties of certain Laws'. Popularly known as the 'Toleration Act', it granted religious liberty (but not political privileges, such as the right to vote or hold office) to Protestant Dissenters, provided they take an oath of loyalty to William and Mary and swore to their belief in the doctrine of the Trinity. The refusal to extend the same opportunity to Catholics was Parliament's attempt to win back the loyalty of the Dissenters after James II had sought their support in his effort to gain toleration for English Catholics.

High Church Tories such as Henry Sacheverell (c. 1674–1724) heavily criticized those Whigs and moderate Tories who wanted to grant toleration to the Dissenters. In his *Shortest Way with the Dissenters or, Proposals for the Establishment of the Church*, Daniel Defoe, imitating the arguments of Sacheverell so well that contemporaries missed the satirical elements, noted the irony of Dissenters appealing for toleration when they had harboured the desire to destroy the church for much of the seventeenth century and used their power to bring it down under Cromwell. But how far did this 'Toleration Act' actually extend toleration to the Dissenters? Not much. Religious meetings still needed to be certified by the local bishop, archdeacon, or justice of the peace. Those without such a certificate were still required by law to attend Anglican services on Sunday. Religious Dissenters could still even be thrown in prison if they could not produce four Protestant witnesses to testify to their exemption under the act.

Following the passage of the Toleration Act, Parliament passed a number of new laws culminating in the 1701 Act of Settlement that have collectively become known as the Revolution Settlement. The Act of Settlement stipulated that the right to the English throne would pass to the Protestant electress Sophia of Hanover and her heirs should Mary's sister Anne die without heirs. In North America, British colonists celebrated the limits that the Settlement placed upon absolute monarchy, but did not necessarily accept its replacement by the absolute power of Parliament. In fact, one possible interpretation of the Settlement was that the monarchy retained its authority as long as the ruler worked within the confines of Parliament as the main legislative body for the kingdom. Seen in this light, the Revolution Settlement helped to shift the thought of the American colonists in a direction that led to their stand against both George III and Parliament after Parliament began to assert its rights to tax the colonists and legislate for them without their consent in 1763.

Both Scotland and Ireland still had their own parliaments and remained separate kingdoms, but how free they were to set their own course under this new Settlement was an open question. The Revolution Settlement in Scotland, for example, abolished the parliamentary committee known as the Lords of the Articles, through which Scottish kings since the late fifteenth century had influenced legislation. This rendered the Scottish Parliament more independent and impaired the power of the monarchy. William III, therefore, had to rely on more personal connections to influence the Scottish Parliament, but this became a catch-22 because anyone supportive of the king had trouble influencing a parliament determined to protect its new-found autonomy.

The Revolution Settlement had perhaps the greatest impact on Ireland. The Treaty of Limerick of 1691 essentially redefined the relationship between Ireland and England, once again to the disadvantage of Irish Catholics. Ireland retained its parliament, but it now became an essentially Protestant body that was nonetheless still completely subservient to the English Parliament. In fact, the English Parliament had asserted its right to legislate for Ireland by depriving the king of his independent authority, a principle that Parliament extended to Ireland. Making matters worse, even the Whigs did not extend their principles of popular sovereignty and religious toleration to Ireland. Though aimed primarily at the Irish Catholics, the passage of a new set of penal laws that also discriminated against religious nonconformists is just as much a part of the Revolution Settlement as the Toleration Act. There is reason to think that the new penal laws were not enacted as a permanent system of anti-Catholic repression but rather as an immediate response to England's wars with Catholic France, as the Sun King was still threatening to place Europe under his Catholic sceptre.

In England, interpretations of the Settlement and its meaning varied widely as well. For the Tories, the revolution had prudently preserved the delicate balance of the ancient constitution and prevented the monarchy from usurping powers that did not belong to it; in other words, it was a conservative revolution. Tories continued to support divine right of kings, a concept William III fully embraced. In 1693, Robert Spencer, the Earl of Sunderland, could still get away with advising William to ignore Parliament, even if he could not legally rule without it. For the Whigs, the revolution represented a more progressive development that pointed more to the future than to the past. Tim Harris cites its amorphous character and susceptibility to conflicting viewpoints as one of the main reasons for the success of the Revolution Settlement.[1] But a case could be made that this success was neither guaranteed nor prolonged, the flexibility of the Settlement's principles both an advantage and a disadvantage. Either way, by 1710 the War of the Spanish Succession not only represented a continuation of the ongoing struggle against Catholic France, but also threatened to undo the Revolution Settlement within a few years of its consummation.

Marlborough's war: The War of the Spanish Succession

The War of the Spanish Succession was fought to a large degree over who would inherit the Spanish throne following the death of childless Carlos II; the principal candidates were Philip, the Duke of Anjou and grandson of Louis XIV, and Archduke Charles, the younger son of the Austrian emperor Leopold I by his third marriage. Both the English and the Dutch became involved, not only because they wished to further temper the influence and territorial ambitions of Louis XIV, but also because they saw an opportunity to weaken Spain's hold over its empire and expand their own power in the Americas. Apropos, the British enlisted the support of the Yamassee and Creek Indians, helping the English to invade Florida.[2] Both the English and the Dutch had hoped to gain access to Spain's empire peacefully, but Louis XIV's intransigence precluded this. Indeed, the Sun King asserted the right of his grandson to the throne, flouting previous treaties. Thereupon, England and the Netherlands went to war because they did not wish to see Spain and its empire fall under the control of France, preferring the Habsburg candidate put forward by Leopold. Louis exacerbated the situation by invading the Spanish Netherlands, once again posing a threat to the Dutch border. Louis further provoked the Dutch and the English by raising French tariffs, a serious economic blow to the Dutch and English merchants. The idea of the French extending economic protection to the entire Spanish empire was too much for either the English or the Dutch to take. Finally, when James II died in 1701, Louis recognized James's son, James Francis Edward, as king of England and Scotland, a serious violation of his previous treaty with William III. The English and Dutch received backing from a number of smaller German states, including Hanover, where the Elector, George Louis, had just been designated the heir to the English throne by Parliament in the Act of Settlement.

John Churchill, the Duke of Marlborough, Queen Anne's (r. 1702–14) leading military commander during the war, and Sidney Godolphin, a political ally of Marlborough who served as Anne's Lord Treasurer, pioneered the patronage system, in which government ministers used the resources of the Crown to establish 'connections' in the House of Commons. These connections were miniature political parties that consisted of members who would support the policies of their patrons. In addition, the Duke's wife, Sarah Churchill, was a close confidante of Anne's. Marlborough relied heavily on his wife's friend, Elizabeth Burnet, the wife of the bishop of Salisbury, Gilbert Burnet, for inside information on the Tories. During this period, factional strife between Whigs and Tories led to a frequently divided Parliament. Godolphin and Marlborough were both Tories, but their main concern was the prosecution of the war, not the pursuit of a domestic political agenda. This led them into conflict with less moderate members of their party who wished to use Parliament to crack down on their Whig rivals by passing legislation that would punish occasional conformity among Whig Dissenters, who attended Church of England services just often enough to avoid being labelled as such. Some Dissenters took communion often enough in the Anglican church to avoid being removed from political office, but retained their private nonconformist beliefs. The Tories deeply resented this, not only because of their loyalty to the Church of England but also because they thought it made the Whigs more susceptible to Dutch influence. Nor had they forgotten the political turmoil caused by the Puritans during the previous century. Therefore, the Tories determinedly pushed for passage of a bill against occasional conformity, once trying to sneak it through at the end of a tax bill. Marlborough and Godolphin sought to stifle the measure as they needed the support of the Whigs so that they might pursue their expensive war and foreign policy.[3] Godolphin managed to defeat the proposed bills, thanks partly to his informers, such as Elizabeth Burnet, his use of patronage, and, of course, the votes of the Whigs.

In 1704, Marlborough hearing that French troops were headed for Vienna realized that he needed to insert his army in their path, lest they deal the Austrians a crushing blow and effectively end the war in France's favour. After a 250-mile march through Flanders and Germany, Marlborough's army reached the Danube, where he coordinated with Prince Eugene of Savoy to achieve a tremendous victory over the French at the Battle of Blenheim in early August. In May 1706, Marlborough followed up that victory with another at Brabant, before moving into Flanders. Marlborough's occupation of Flanders led Louis XIV to seek peace with the Dutch. With Austria safe and the Low Countries secure, the English turned their attention to the Mediterranean, where the navy needed to play a larger role. In 1707, the successful siege and bombardment of Toulon, the main naval base of the French situated 30 miles southeast of Marseilles, left the English navy in control of the Mediterranean Sea.

Even though Marlborough and his campaigns received most of the attention in the English press, the war extended beyond Europe. Known in North America as Queen Anne's War, the French and their Indian allies frequently attacked English frontier settlements, while the British attacked Spanish Florida at St Augustine and attempted to take Nova Scotia and Quebec from the French. Unable to commit any significant number of troops because of the fighting in Europe, the colonists largely had to rely on their own resources. The lack of protection they were afforded led to episodes such as the Deerfield Massacre, the result of a French and Indian raid on Deerfield in the Connecticut Valley in 1704 in which forty-seven colonists were killed and 112 captured and held for ransom.

As the war progressed, Marlborough continued to exert his influence on, or one might even say power over, the queen, forcing her to appoint his son-in-law, the Earl of Sunderland as one of her secretaries of state in 1706. In 1708, against her better judgement, Anne removed Robert Harley from his position as secretary of state at Marlborough's insistence. That same year, Anne's husband, Prince George, died and Anne gradually started to drift away from her support for Marlborough and the war. That winter, which proved harsh and bitter, Anne grew more concerned about the welfare of her subjects, who were wearying of the sacrifices necessitated by war. In March 1711 Anne brought Harley back into government as Lord Treasurer, a further indication that the tide had turned against Marlborough and the war. The polemicist Jonathan Swift denounced the decision to continue the war in his important pamphlet, *The Conduct of the Allies; and of the Late Ministry, in Bringing and Carrying on the War*. Swift wondered why, after ten years of continuous success, the war could not be brought to a close on reasonably favourable terms. Despite several military victories in the campaign of 1710, Marlborough was still not in a position to deliver the coup de grace because he lacked the funds and the soldiers to break through the insuperable French defences protecting Paris.

At the end of the war in 1713 the British gained Gibraltar and the island of Minorca at the expense of the Spanish, as well as the right to control the slave trade between Africa and the Americas, known as the *asiento*; they also gained additional territories in North America, including Newfoundland and Nova Scotia, from the French. In addition, Louis XIV agreed to recognize the legitimacy of the Hanoverian succession and to promise that neither he nor his successors would

> give at any time any aid, succour, favour, counsel, directly or indirectly by Land or by sea, in money, arms, ammunition, warlike instruments, ships, soldiers, seamen, or in any other manner whatever, to any person or persons, whosoever they be, who on any cause or pretext should hereafter endeavour to oppose the said succession.

By this time, England had been at war almost continuously for almost twenty-five years, during which time the size of the English army had increased enormously, the apparatus of the state had grown commensurately, and Parliament felt more empowered because of the constant need for additional fiscal grants required by the monarchy to fight the war. At the end of the War of Spanish Succession, the English army stood at 92,708 men, compared with 76,404 in 1697, and only 8,865 in 1685.[4] The cost of the war, the increased taxation necessary to fund it, and the growth of the army had their critics, especially among those concerned about the preservation of English liberties and those who thought England's national interests did not coincide with fighting land wars in Europe.

The Act of Union, the Hanoverian succession, and the Jacobite rebellion of 1715

The War of the Spanish Succession also provided the context for one of the most momentous shifts in British history: the union between England and Scotland in 1707. Ever since the overthrow of James VII and II, relations between the two kingdoms had grown increasingly unstable. Not all Scots had been keen to accept William as king after the English Parliament had done so, while others actively supported the fallen James. Those who since 1689 supported and fought for the restoration of James became known as Jacobites, from the Latin name for James, 'Jacobus'. Jacobite sentiment remained so strong in Scotland that William III demanded an oath of loyalty be taken by all clan chiefs by 1 January 1692. When the chief of the Macdonald clan was a day late in taking the oath, the head of the Campbell clan led his soldiers under stealth of night to Glencoe, a narrow valley in the southern Highlands, where they massacred thirty-eight members of the Macdonald clan, sending an additional forty men and women fleeing from their homes only to die later from exposure to the elements. An incriminating letter from the Earl of Stair dated 3 December 1691 indicates that the massacre had been planned prior to Macdonald's delay in taking the oath.

The Glencoe Massacre was followed by the fiasco known as the Darien Disaster, which further alienated the opinion of many Scots towards William III and the English. The scheme involved plans to establish a Scottish colony in Panama, thereby attracting Scottish investments upwards of £200,000, perhaps the total currency circulating in Scotland at the time. It failed miserably because of William's perfunctory support and implacable English opposition.

William had his allies and supporters in Scotland, including his court chaplain, William Carstares, and George, the Earl of Melville, his secretary of state for Scotland, but he had little inclination to negotiate Scottish politics. The Scottish Parliament was already proving extremely quarrelsome; the Darien Disaster only exacerbated measures. Parliament, which formed an antagonistic faction against William, became even more obstinate at the beginning of Queen Anne's reign. In 1703, the Scottish Parliament passed three acts that threatened to separate Scotland completely from England. The Wine Act asserted Scotland's right to make its own trade agreements and was clearly directed at increasing trade between Scotland and France. The Act of Peace and War declared that England could not declare war on behalf of Scotland without the approval of the Scottish Parliament. Finally, the Security Act demanded assurances from England that it would not interfere with Scottish trade or the Presbyterian church.

In response to this anti-English legislation in the Scottish Parliament, Godolphin impetuously threatened to declare war on Scotland on sundry occasions. England responded in kind, passing the Alien Act in 1705, mandating that Scots in England be treated as aliens. The English also threatened economic sanctions. The combined effect of the positions adopted in each kingdom, paradoxically, was to push them closer towards actual union: the English had more economic clout, but they could also not afford to see Scotland alienated from England, especially in the midst of a war with France.

From Marlborough's perspective, if the union failed the possibility existed that his entire anti-French foreign policy might be doomed. In October 1706, Marlborough's Scottish ally, John Campbell, the second Duke of Argyll, returned from Flanders to Scotland just in case he needed to pacify an uprising in the city of Edinburgh, Godolphin having received word of the possibility of violent protests against the union. However, the greater opposition to the union from among the Scots came from the Highlands rather than the Lowlands. Merchants and members of the landed gentry in the Lowlands saw themselves as having more to gain from the union than did residents of the Highlands; Lowlanders at this time tended to think they had more in common with the English than with the Highlanders. Union would presumably give Scottish merchants access to the huge trading network provided by the British Empire, as well as protection from the British navy. Scottish opponents of the union believed that their independence had been bought with English bribes and considered those who voted in favour of the treaty in the Scottish Parliament as traitors to their country.

Venality played its role, to be sure, but there were important principles in the offing. Perhaps most importantly, leading members of the Protestant gentry saw protection from foreign invasion as emanating from the British army; the prospects of reviving the 'auld alliance' with France seemed unappealing. Still, without the right blend of political adroitness and diplomatic skills to bolster the Scottish Parliament's approval of the Treaty the negotiations would have fallen apart. In the end the Treaty of Union succeeded in Scotland because of a combination of English pressure and bribery and the disorganization and ineffectiveness of the anti-Union faction in Scotland, compared to the political acumen and ideological commitment of the pro-Union party.

In England, opponents of the union saw Scotland as a barbarous, undeveloped country, which would benefit far more from unification than would England, though they exhibited no such qualms about the union that already existed between England and Wales. Linda Colley has argued that both the Welsh and the Scots had more in common with the English than they did with each other, or at least that they both would have seen it that way.[5] The main difference between Wales and Scotland at the time was that the Welsh belonged to the Church of England, whereas Presbyterianism continued to predominate in Scotland. For whatever reason, the London press reacted with alarm that the border between England and the barbaric and uncivilized Scots was about to be obliterated.

The English writer Daniel Defoe, a great polemicist like Swift, pointed out what he saw as the obvious advantages of the union between England and Scotland:

> It would be worth their while who opposed this UNION, and still refuse to own the advantage of it, to look back upon the years of blood, and the terrible devastations these two sister nations suffered in the years of their separation; let them examine the history of the past ages; let them enquire there of the particulars of three hundred and fourteen battles, and calculate the blood of a million of the bravest men in Europe, lost in the senseless feuds of these two nations.[6]

Defoe suggested to Scottish opponents of the union that what they gained in political and religious liberty would make up for any short-term economic losses. He also pointed out that the hopes for the preservation of their Presbyterian church, whose continued existence was guaranteed by the terms of the treaty, actually depended on union with England. Indeed, the Scots retained not only their national church, but also their own legal and educational systems under the proposed treaty. The Scottish army, however, would officially cease to exist and become fully integrated into the army of Great Britain.

In time most Scots came round to conceding the advantages of union. In its immediate aftermath, however, the union revived the commitment of the Jacobites to preventing the succession of George, the Elector of Hanover, scheduled to take place following the death of Queen Anne. Within a year the Jacobites had already planned an uprising, with support supposedly coming from France in the form of 5,000 troops assembled at Dunkirk under the command of Admiral Forbin. The fleet left Dunkirk on 6 March 1708. Forbin eluded a British blockade and arrived at the coast of Scotland on 12 March. He returned to France as soon as he encountered an English fleet blocking the entrance to the Firth of Forth. The revolution never materialized, but Jacobite opposition to the union was strong enough in Scotland that if a more determined leader than Forbin had actually landed the troops, the rebellion would have had a reasonable chance of success. A second planned invasion of 1709 never got off the ground. Louis XIV's recognition of the Hanoverian succession in the Treaty of Utrecht dampened the prospects of a rising in 1714 when George of

Hanover succeeded Queen Anne as king of Great Britain, but that did not prevent Scottish Jacobites from mounting a serious challenge to the new regime a year later.

With the benefit of hindsight, it is easy to dismiss the Jacobites as an anachronism, but this would be historically spurious, because their blend of nationalism and religious conservatism would prove a potent combination in the eighteenth century and beyond. Furthermore, such a view minimizes the possibility that a Jacobite rebellion in 1715 could have succeeded and does not take into account the effort in planning and marshalling of men and resources necessary to carry out such a rebellion. Those who, knowing the punishment for treason, willingly risked their lives by supporting the rebellion tended to believe they had the higher moral ground. This was even more the case for those who participated in the 1715 uprising because, unlike the participants in each of the other Jacobite rebellions, those who fought in the '15 had not pinned their hopes on foreign intervention.

The 1715 rebellion did not have widespread support among Presbyterians in the Scottish Lowlands, but the Jacobite army outnumbered the British army in Scotland under the Duke of Argyll by 4 to 1. The rebellion failed mainly because of the abysmal military leadership exhibited by the Scottish Jacobite commander, John Erskine, the Earl of Mar. Scottish historian Bruce Lenman explains:

> There was no need for tactical skill on Mar's part. All he had to do was attack and keep on attacking. ... Once Argyll had been brushed aside, the prospects facing the Jacobite army would have been spectacular. ... The British political system in 1715 was so corrupt and so obnoxious that it was ripe for a fall, but it was saved by the fact that the challenge was led by one of its own. The many gallant gentlemen who rallied to Mar's standard rallied, in the last analysis to a self-centered, monstrously incompetent poltroon.[7]

A brief abortive uprising supported by Spanish troops followed in 1719, but it collapsed when a fleet led by James Butler, the second Duke of Ormonde failed to make it through a storm in the Atlantic. Jacobitism did not die, but it would be another twenty-six years before the next rebellion, long after most people in England and Scotland stopped believing the movement represented a credible threat to the Hanoverian regime.

The political culture of the British Isles in the first half of the eighteenth century

The largest changes in the political culture of the British Isles in the eighteenth century as compared to that of the seventeenth was the emergence of public opinion as a political force and the incipient growth of a popular press that increasingly shaped or influenced popular opinion. It is certainly not the case that public opinion was entirely new in the eighteenth century, as can be readily seen in the sermons, broadsides, and pamphlets that proliferated in the seventeenth century, especially around the time of the civil wars, but the weekly, bi-weekly, or thrice-weekly newspaper was a relatively new development that made contemporary news both more available and more immediate. A key moment in this development came with the end of censorship in 1695, abolishing the monopoly on publishing held by the Stationers Company and allowing for a wider range of views to be openly expressed than at any time since the conclusion of the civil wars (when a lack of censorship resulted from the political chaos of the period rather than from government policy). In fact, three new thrice-weekly newspapers emerged in the year following the official end of censorship: the *Flying Post*, the *Post Boy*, and the *Post Man*. The first daily newspaper, the *Daily Courant*, began publication in 1702.

In his 'Life of Milton,' who in 1644 had made a strong case for the free exchange of ideas in his *Areopagitica*, Dr Samuel Johnson argues that

> if every dreamer of innovations may propagate his projects, there can be no settlement; if every murmurer at government may diffuse discontent, there can be no peace; and if every skeptick [*sic*] in theology may teach his follies, there can be no religion.[8]

Johnson argued for the need for limits on a free press, some of which actually still existed in England in the forms of laws against blasphemy and libel. But Johnson still thought it better to punish people who abused the freedom of the press after the fact instead of restricting what could be published beforehand. Earlier in the century, in his 1704 *Essay on the Regulation of the Press*, Daniel Defoe argued that to put an end to free licence for the press 'would be a check to Learning, a Prohibition of Knowledge, and make Instruction Contraband'. He denounced works promoting atheism or attacking the doctrine of the Trinity, saying such works could be published anywhere but in England, but he questioned how to deal with such works. He pointed out that even laws against theft and murder are helpless to prevent the crimes, but instead punish those who commit them after the fact.

Anthony Ashley-Cooper, the third Earl of Shaftesbury, thought that censure and ridicule went hand-in-hand with British freedom, writing in 1711 that

> 'Tis only in a free nation, such as ours, that imposture has no privilege; and that neither the credit of a court, nor the power of a nobility, nor the awfulness of a Church can give her protection, or hinder her from being arraigned in every shape and appearance.[9]

Shaftesbury, one of the leading philosophers of his age, was not known for his egalitarian tendencies, but here he recognizes the necessity of freedom of thought in order to allow ideas to contend with one another. A Deist, he rejected the monopoly of the church on truth and was generally opposed to censorship of any kind. Shaftesbury saw in the War of the Spanish Succession a struggle for English liberty against French absolutism and oppression, as well as against the religious tyranny and superstition of the Catholic Church.

Freedom of the press and public opinion changed the extent and nature of political discourse, but political power still remained overwhelmingly the locus of the aristocracy and the gentry. In 1754, fifty-nine merchants sat in Parliament, only a slight increase from the fifty-four included in the Parliament of 1641.[10] The landed classes remained determined to dominate the political life of the nation in large part because they had a huge economic stake in the security of the nation from both foreign invasion and domestic unrest, as England had witnessed during the 1640s. They also knew that election to Parliament provided opportunities to pursue their own personal interests. These included acts of enclosure that allowed them to make more efficient, and profitable, use of their lands.

The aristocracy took a special interest in agriculture during this period, which helped produce a series of cumulative developments, including crop rotation, the expansion of the use of crops like turnips that helped revitalize the soil, and Jethro Tull's invention of the seed drill, all of which helped to increase yield per acre and that historians have collectively dubbed the 'agricultural revolution'. Although this transformation occurred over a longer period of time, some of the key developments associated with it took place during the first half of the eighteenth century. For example, by mid-century Robert Bakewell (1725–95) had begun his experiments with sheep breeding and perhaps played an even larger role in publicizing the advantages of selective breeding of livestock among the farming community that would show dramatic results by century's end.

This does not mean that Parliament ignored the interests of the commercial classes in its deliberations and legislation. England's economy grew rapidly during the eighteenth century and many merchants, industrialists, and entrepreneurs took advantage of the conditions conducive to economic growth, against which Parliament placed few obstacles. It is tempting to see this favouritism towards commercial interests as a result of the Whig Party's reign, since the Tories eventually became associated more with a conservative defence of the interests of the landed aristocracy. In the eighteenth century, however, the divide between Whigs and Tories was a split within the landed class itself. Furthermore, most members of the landed elite belonged to the Whig Party after 1714, as war gave way to peace and political stability seemed to go hand-in-hand with commercial prosperity. At this point, the Tories had little reason to oppose the Whigs on ideological grounds, unless they became Jacobites out of conviction or obstinacy. Otherwise, Tory candidates appeared as if they were challenging the Whigs merely because they wanted their share of power and the financial rewards that accompanied it.

Prior to 1714, Whigs and Tories differed significantly, clashing over foreign policy, religious issues, and the legacy of the Revolution Settlement. Even though the Tories had supported the Revolution of 1688, they quickly had become dissatisfied with William's rule; their opposition to the monarchy, a reversal of their pre-1688 ideology, carried over into the reigns of Anne and George I. With the threat of a potential Jacobite restoration still a possibility, dynastic issues did not appear as settled to contemporaries as they do to later historians. Ironically, then, in the first half of the eighteenth century, the Whigs became more closely aligned with the monarchy than the Tories, who became the main critics of the Hanoverians. If the Whigs disagreed with the king, they challenged his ministers or his policy, not his power or role in the constitution. Toryism, on the other hand, had become more of a world view and an abstract political philosophy than a practical political programme for regaining power and implementing policy. An exception might be found in the work of Henry St John, Viscount Bolingbroke, whose *Idea of a Patriot King* (1738) has been seen as an attempt to gain the approbation of Frederick, the Prince of Wales and heir to King George II. In his writings, Bolingbroke lauded love of country and devotion to a divinely appointed monarch who stood above the factionalism and pursuit of self-interest that he argued was characteristic of the Whig ascendancy.

The contemporary desire to understand the world and the universe associated with the Scientific Revolution, which had led to the belief that the natural world operated according to a set of natural and discoverable laws, and the Enlightenment, which emphasized that reason could allow thinkers to apply the principles of science to the study of society, was adapted to the political thought of philosophers who in turn sought to make a science out of politics. Samuel Johnson referred to 'the science of government, which human understanding seems, hitherto, unable to solve'. The French philosophe Voltaire was among those thinkers who mistakenly equated the triumph of Parliament in the English revolutions of the seventeenth century with the triumph of liberty. In one of his famous English letters, Voltaire offered this optimistic assessment of the post-1688 English political system:

> The English are the only people on earth who have been able to prescribe limits to the power of kings by resisting them, and who, by a series of struggles, have at length established the wise and happy form of government where the prince is all-powerful to do good, and at the same time is restrained without insolence or lordly power, and the people share in the government without confusion.[11]

Parliament certainly had become a permanent fixture that deprived the monarchy of absolute power, but how far this meant that the people shared 'in the government without confusion' is certainly open to debate. Voltaire also praised England for equality before the law, in contrast to France. He especially liked the fact that noblemen paid their share of taxes, unlike in France where they were tax-exempt.

Nonetheless, Parliament was not immune to public opinion, whether it was expressed in newspapers, coffeehouses, or churches. Though the opportunities for office were becoming more restricted to the wealthiest landowners, voters took an active interest in national affairs, which frequently affected their local areas. James Rosenheim has calculated that Parliament passed some 14,000 acts between 1688 and 1801, most of which touched on local interests and had input from constituents, compared to only 2,700 passed between 1485 and 1688,[12] Precisely because political office was becoming so lucrative, candidates were more willing to make promises to local voters in return for their votes, which were not secret. (Secret ballots were not used in British elections until the passage of the Ballot Act in 1872.) Parliament was also, of course, responsible for funding the wars that the country fought, making foreign policy a major issue of concern as well. War sold newspapers, making it one of the most important topics in the political discourse among the electorate. Parliamentary influence over foreign policy remained limited, however, partly because Whigs had put themselves in a position where they felt they had no choice but to support the monarchy, yet another reversal from the politics of the seventeenth century.

From 1721 to 1742, under the steady leadership of Sir Robert Walpole, it was more common, however, for Parliament to work with the Crown in matters of war and peace. Walpole learnt how to assuage first George I, then George II, largely by keeping them fully informed about his domestic policies and political developments within Parliament. Walpole also perfected the use of patronage to keep the House of Lords and the House of Commons united behind his general policies and supportive of his administration. Walpole also succeeded politically, however, because he governed in a way that did not conflict with the economic interests of the landed aristocracy. Mostly, Walpole stood for a policy of peace, pursuing a policy of neutrality in the War of the Polish Succession from 1733 to 1738, despite the interventionist inclinations of George II. Walpole, regarded as Britain's first prime minister, enjoyed a long run in power, but the period was not without its controversies; rioters burnt Walpole in effigy in a crisis over the imposition of a new excise tax in 1733, for example. His pacific policy finally collapsed when Spanish aggression provoked the War of Jenkins Ear in 1739, a revival of the wars against France and Spain that morphed into the War of the Austrian Succession when Frederick the Great of Prussia invaded Silesia a year later.

There is a tendency among historians to portray the press as a progressive element in eighteenth-century society, but the reality was that there were as many newspapers that took a traditional point of view as there were of those that advocated change or reform. Different newspapers expressing a variety of opinions became available in London coffeehouses; it was not long before newspapers emerged outside of London as well. By 1723, twenty-four provincial newspapers were already in circulation, most of them in relatively close proximity to London.[13] Other periodicals also played a role in shaping public opinion, most famously Joseph Addison and Richard Steele's *Spectator*, which had its heyday in the closing years of the War of the Spanish Succession. In Walpole's age, Edward Cave's *Gentleman's Magazine; or Monthly Intelligencer*, founded in 1731, did much to shape public opinion, while appealing to both the aristocracy and the merchant class. As for newspapers during Walpole's time, these continued to follow party lines, with some actually patronized by the government, and others representing what Hannah Barker has called 'a lively opposition press ... which was generally not Jacobite, but which challenged his rule as one of corruption and undue influence'.[14]

In addition to the press, philosophers also made their contribution to eighteenth-century British political culture, both reflecting and shaping some of its underlying assumptions. For example, David Hume, though hardly a Whig, picked up on the theme of the relationship between economic and political liberty. But Hume developed a philosophy that stressed that people were endowed with positive passions and moral impulses that would temper unrestrained greed and selfishness in their economic endeavours. Bernard Mandeville's *Fable of the Bees* (1714) put forward the theory that 'private vices were conducive to "public benefits"'. To Mandeville, the pursuit of luxury led to a level of industriousness that in the end produced greater wealth for society as a whole, a philosophy well suited to an expanding commercial society such as that of Great Britain in the first half of the eighteenth century.

By mid-century, it was clear that a more stable political system had resulted from the Revolution of 1688 and that the economy was growing, but throughout the period from 1690 to 1746 people still feared a revival of the civil wars, revolutions, and political instability that had characterized the seventeenth century. The experience of military rule under Cromwell allowed eighteenth-century Tories to represent themselves as the true opponents of tyranny. The Anglican clergy remained particularly wary on the subject, fearing that another revolution might finish the job that Cromwell started and permanently destroy the established church. The seventeenth century had, in fact, left a deep and lasting impression that continued to affect the political culture of the British Isles well into the eighteenth century and beyond, nowhere more so than in Ireland.

Ireland in the first half of the eighteenth century

The dominant political force in Ireland in the first half of the eighteenth century was the Irish Parliament, even though it remained subordinate to the English Parliament. However, a thriving political culture centred on Dublin and influenced by the availability of newspapers and other printed material in the city's coffeehouses played an increasingly important role, as it did in England. Dublin was in the process of becoming a more viable commercial centre, increasing the demand for news by an increasingly literate and politically aware public that would soon take an interest in re-examining Ireland's relationship with England. Ireland shared in the market for ideas created by the European Enlightenment. The demand for printed material inspired the expansion of Dublin's merchants into the publishing and the importing of foreign books.[15]

At the centre of Dublin's political culture loomed the literary titan, Jonathan Swift, a cleric in the Church of Ireland, who sought to defend Ireland's interests without compromising with those Catholics and Dissenters whose extreme views clashed with his own moderate ones. In 1677, Sir William Petty had objected to the practices of Church of Ireland clergy who prevailed upon Catholic justices of the peace to impose harsh sentences on those who challenged the established church. According to Petty, an alliance had been forged in the seventeenth century between the Catholics and the 'Old Protestants' in the face of a common enemy, the Puritans, or 'New Protestants' associated with Oliver Cromwell. But the eighteenth century saw this alliance crumble under the weight of the new penal laws that formed part of the Restoration Settlement in Ireland.

Anglicans owned a staggering 90 per cent of the land of Ireland but only constituted 10 per cent of the population,[16] making it seem even more that the majority of the Irish population suffered under the weight of a foreign occupation. Even if the penal laws were not rigorously or consistently enforced in the eighteenth century, Catholics still operated at a disadvantage and made up a disproportionate number of Ireland's poor. Meanwhile, the Anglo-Irish expanded their economic interests in trade and commerce and enacted legislation in the Irish Parliament beneficial to their interests. Therefore, even the controversy about whether the Irish Parliament should have greater autonomy was driven by a ruling class that would likely use additional control to further its own interests, not to benefit the predominantly Catholic population of the island.

In Joseph Addison's 1712 tragedy, *Cato*, he includes an exchange between Syphax and Juba in which Syphax criticizes Juba's defence of the civilizing mission of Rome towards the barbarians. Contemporaries could easily have drawn the connection between Syphax's argument and a critique of England's attitude towards Ireland in the early eighteenth century. Here Addison attacks the hypocritical and self-aggrandizing attitude of British colonialism in Ireland. Syphax exclaims:

> Patience, kind heavens! – excuse an old man's warmth!
> What are these wondrous civilizing arts:
> This Roman polish, and this smooth behaviour,
> That render man thus tractable and tame?
> Are they not only to disguise our passions,
> To set our looks at variance with our thoughts,
> To check the starts and sallies of the soul:
> And break off all its commerce with the tongue;
> In short, to change us into other creatures,
> Than what our nature and the gods designed us? (Act 1, Scene 4, ll. 39–48)

In his novel *Gulliver's Travels* (1726), Swift addresses the issue with regard to the fictional celestial kingdom of Laputa, which demands taxes from and exercises dominance over the lands on earth directly below it. Gulliver wonders why they think they have the right to do this, but then remembers that 'they have been troubled with the same Disease to which the Whole Race of Mankind is subject; the Nobility often contending for Power, the People for Liberty, and the King for absolute Dominion'.[17] In the *Conduct of the Allies* (1712), Defoe had argued that the only just causes for war involved cases when a neighbouring country had grown too powerful, had inflicted a previous injury that needed to be avenged, or actually invaded one's own; clearly none of these cases could be used to justify the English conquest or continued domination of Ireland. Swift's mordant satire, which he put to use in *Gulliver's Travels*, is even more ostentatiously on display in his famous *Modest Proposal* (1729), in which he offered a radical, tongue-in-cheek solution to Ireland's twin problems of hunger and overpopulation, already a concern at a time when famine led to an early wave of Irish emigration. His proposed solution of feeding infants to the poor, he offers, would reduce the number of children who grow up to be thieves for lack of employment.

Daniel Defoe, eighteenth-century literature, and the rise of the individual

Unlike the Anglican Swift, his contemporary Daniel Defoe came out of a background of religious nonconformity that led him to recognize the continued importance of religion as a guarantee of private and public morality, even as he acknowledged that the world in which he lived had become more secular, commercial, and individualistic. Unlike Christian, the protagonist in John Bunyan's *Pilgrim's Progress*, the title characters in Defoe's two most important novels, *Robinson Crusoe* and *Moll Flanders* are not only highly individualized characters but also ordinary people to whom readers might relate, however extraordinary their circumstances. The literary critic Ian Watt wrote that Defoe 'expressed the diverse elements of individualism more completely than any previous writer, and his work offers a unique demonstration of the connection between individualism in its many forms and the rise of the novel'.[18] Robinson Crusoe, marooned alone on an island as the only survivor of a shipwreck, takes responsibility for his plight; he carries out his activities according to the same rational calculus that a merchant might use to account for his stores and provisions. He also keeps track of his activities and makes notes to learn from his experience. He engages those with whom he comes into contact on what can best be described as a code of business ethics in which both parties are bound to honour the terms of the contract to which they agree. The title character in *Moll Flanders* also exists as an individual rather than as a member of a group, and negotiates her way through life in a series of exchanges, which bring a combination of beneficial and adverse outcomes. The bulk of the first half of the novel sees Moll navigating a series of marriages and relationships, exhibiting, in her own words 'a readiness of being ruined without the least concern'; the second half of the novel shows the effects of that ruin, which led Moll into a life of crime and vice, before her moral, social, and financial redemption at the end.

For all of its emphasis on individualism and self-reliance, *Robinson Crusoe* is full of references to Providence and the existence of what Crusoe infers is an 'invisible intelligence' that guides him:

> A secret hint shall direct us this way, when we intended to go that way; nay, when sense, our own inclination, and perhaps business has call'd to go the other way, yet a strange impression upon the mind, from we know not what springs, and by we know not what power, shall over-rule us to go this way; and it shall afterwards appear, that had we gone that way, which we should have gone, and even to our imagination ought to have gone, we should have been ruin'd and lost.[19]

In the course of the novel, Crusoe comes to accept that, rather than blame God for his shipwreck and abandonment, he needed to accept the grace of Providence that had allowed him to survive for some unknown reason. It was only through reconciling himself with the fact of his survival that he could muster the strength and courage to take the actions needed to salvage his situation. The moral lesson would have been obvious to eighteenth-century readers confronted with the rise of Deism and the declining influence of the established church in everyday life: work brings salvation, morality brings its own rewards, and trust in God or Providence is still needed even if God now seemed somehow more remote in the commercialized and individualized society of the times. This is one of the reasons why in the early twentieth century the German sociologist Max Weber saw a connection between Protestantism and secularism.[20]

Moll Flanders, similarly, is buffeted throughout her life by forces seemingly beyond her control, that all work to her final advantage, but only after she commits to a life of moral reform. Not for nothing did Defoe once remark that the 'preaching of sermons is speaking to a few of mankind: printing of books is talking to the whole world'. No one capitalized more on the ability to reach a broad audience through novels in the eighteenth century than Samuel Richardson, whose controversial novels, particularly *Pamela* (1740) and *Clarissa* (1748), appealed to a large middle-class readership by critically portraying members of the aristocracy and the troubles that would befall young, vulnerable, girls of a lower station who allowed themselves to be seduced by them. In the case of *Pamela*, Richardson uses an epistolary style to have the serving-girl Pamela convey her feelings as her situation unfolds. Pamela emerges as a heroine who preserves both her own morality and that of her would-be seducer by resisting the advances of her aristocratic master until he actually proposes to marry her as an equal. If Pamela has its nineteenth-century equivalent in Charlotte Bronte's *Jane Eyre*, *Clarissa* more closely resembles Thomas Hardy's *Tess of the D'Urbervilles*, in which a virtuous young woman finds herself trapped and abused by an immoral and unscrupulous cur.

The theatre became another media through which contemporary anxieties about religion and morality could be addressed and presented to the public in a didactic way. In 1698 Jeremy Collier had written that

> The business of *Plays* is to recommend Virtue, and discountenance Vice; To shew the Uncertainty of Humane Greatness, the suddain Turns of Fate, and the Unhappy Conclusions of Violence and Injustice; 'Tis to expose the Singularities of Pride and Fancy, to make Folly and Falsehood contemptible, and to bring every Thing that is Ill Under Infamy and Neglect.[21]

Of course, no less than the novels of Defoe, theatre blurred the lines between fiction and reality; on the stage, men could play women, as they did in Shakespeare's time, or women could play men, as the popular actress Peg Woffington frequently did in the middle decades of the eighteenth century. Collier was aware of this and was especially wary of the ways in which art could deceive and as easily incite people to destructive passions as it could inspire them to virtue. Collier is especially critical of obscenity, especially when uttered by women, an offence that he found 'faulty to a Scandalous degree of Nauseousness and Aggravation'. Though the eighteenth century continued to produce its share of licentious plays, playwrights adapted to these concerns by looking for the same opportunities available to novelists to produce plays that conveyed serious moral lessons. The tendency of eighteenth-century drama to focus on didactic moral concerns has led to much criticism and neglect by literary critics and historians, but it clearly helps to illuminate an important aspect of the literature and culture of the period.

Women played an active role in writing and publishing beginning in the seventeenth century and continuing throughout the eighteenth. For example, Mary Astell had complained about the inadequacy of female education in *A Serious Proposal to the Ladies* (1694). Yet even Astell thought that women needed to be submissive to their husbands in order to make their marriages work, writing in *Some Reflections upon Marriage* (1700): 'She ... who marries ought to lay it down for an indisputable maxim, that her husband must govern absolutely and entirely, and that she has nothing else to do but to pleas and obey.'[22] In addition to religious and moral concerns, Defoe addressed gender relations as well in *Moll Flanders*, above all challenging the notion that women serve themselves best by being submissive towards their partners: 'Nothing is more certain than that the Ladies always gain of the Men by keeping their Ground, and letting their pretended Lovers see they can Resent being slighted, and that they are not afraid of saying No.'[23] Defoe writes that women are so often cheated by men that they have a thousand more reasons than men do to be careful and not rush into matrimony, a point strongly reinforced by

Richardson's novels. In Defoe's *Religious Courtship: Being Historical Discourses on the Necessity of Marrying Religious Husbands and Wives Only*, written in 1729, Defoe advises that there are two injunctions that a woman considering marriage should follow: that her husband be a religious man (not an atheist) and that he be of the same religion as she. When one young woman, in a fictional dialogue in the work, expresses indifference about marrying a non-Christian, her sister responds with shock: 'What, to marry an Atheist! a Man of no Principles! that knows neither God nor Devil?'[24] Previously, in *The Family Instructor* (1715), Defoe had attributed the deterioration of family relationships, as well as what he saw as an increase in public immorality, to a decline in religious worship:

> And as Sin entered in this Breach, so it made way for every other Breach; which made them more and more peevish, waspish, apt to quarrel and snarle at the least Occasion; removed all the sweetness of Conversation and Harmony of Affection that was between them before, and the house became destitute, not of religion only, but of every other pleasant thing.[25]

The Catholic poet Alexander Pope expressed much the same sentiment when he wrote in 'The Dunciad' (1728):

> Religion blushing veils her sacred fires,
> And unawares Morality expires.

Pope's greatest work was his 'Essay on Man' (1733–4), in which he puts forth a world view that stresses the divinely inspired order that underlies the apparent chaos of the natural world and discordant nature of human relationships. Pope was not naïve about the social problems or need for reform in his era, much less the lack of perfection in nature, himself suffering from asthma, tuberculosis, and a curvature of the spine that reduced his height to a mere 4' 6". But Pope overcame any tendency towards despair in a kind of cosmic optimism:

> in spite of erring pride, in erring reason's spite
> One truth is clear, Whatever is, is right.

In his 1697 *Essay Upon Projects*, Defoe also lambasted an economic system that gave every advantage to the creditor and none to the debtor, who, though honest, might never get the chance to get out of debt because he was so likely to be clamped in prison for his troubles. In the early eighteenth century, fear of debt drove many people who might otherwise have avoided it into a life of crime. In Defoe's novel *Moll Flanders*, the eponymous Moll makes the following remarks:

> If such a prospect of Work had presented itself at first, when I began to feel the approach of my miserable Circumstances, I say, had such a prospect of getting my Bread by working presented it self then, I had never fallen into this wicked Trade, or into such a wicked Gang as I was now embark'd with; but practice had hardened me, and I grew audacious to the last degree; and the more so, because I had carried it on so long, and had never been taken; for in a word, my

new Partner in Wickedness *and* I went on together so long, without ever being detected, that we not only grew Bold, but we grew Rich, and we had at one time One and Twenty Gold Watches in our Hands.[26]

Moll winds up in Newgate Prison, which was for a long time notorious for its unsanitary and deplorable conditions, as well as a breeding ground for brutality and vice. Even the conditions at Newgate and the threat of confinement in such a dreadful place did not prevent a growing underworld of crime, particularly prostitution, theft, and blackmail, but not excluding murder and other violent crimes. But if prison often begets more crime, for Moll it had the opposite effect. She says of Newgate that

> I liv'd many Days here under the utmost horror of Soul; I had Death as it were in view, and thought of nothing Night and Day, but of Gibbets and Halters, evil Spirits and Devils; it is not to be express'd by Words how I was harras'd, between the dreadful Apprehensions of Death and the Terror of my Conscience reproaching me with my past horrible Life.[27]

In 1728, John Gay followed up on Defoe's *Moll Flanders* with a theatrical work on the London underworld called *The Beggar's Opera*. Gay exposes some of the same corruption and injustices as Defoe did, but advocates for reform, not revolution. He does not treat thieves as romantic heroes bucking a corrupt system and society, giving the authorities what they deserve. Gay modelled his character Peachum after the notorious and powerful thief, Jonathan Wild. Wild, who made a living recovering stolen goods for the wealthy that his own agents had taken, became a famous outlaw and has been the subject of many other works besides that of Gay. Defoe, in fact, had just published a *True and Genuine Account of the Life and Actions of the Late Jonathan Wild* in 1725; Henry Fielding came out with *The Life and Death of Jonathan Wild* in 1743.[28] In Gay's play, Peachum compares himself to a lawyer, who 'acts in a double capacity, both against rogues and for 'em; for 'tis but fitting that we should protect and encourage cheats, since we live by them' (Act 1, Scene 2, ll. 9–12).

Eighteenth-century cities: London, Edinburgh, and Dublin

The population of London roughly doubled in the course of the eighteenth century from about 500,000 to a million people. London grew rapidly after 1713, with the West End in particular benefiting from the building boom that followed the end of the War of the Spanish Succession. Hanover Square, named after the new dynasty, was one of the projects that arose at this time. Many of the wealthiest aristocrats and leaders of London society resided there after 1720. With space at a premium, tall, narrow houses became characteristic of urban life in the eighteenth century. In 1720 the London stock market collapsed as a result of inflated shares in the bogus South Sea Company, which had attracted numerous wealthy and prominent investors and

whose ostensible purpose was to foster increased trade with Latin America. The
South Sea Company was formed in 1711 as an alternative to the Bank of England, the
latter established in 1694 to extend credit to the government that it needed in order
to finance the wars against Louis XIV. Government agents promoted investment in
the South Sea Company as a means towards encouraging private investors to share
in the country's debt. Even the collapse of the South Sea Bubble could not slow the
rising tide of investment, so enticing were the prospects of gaining greater returns
than those offered by the Bank of England.

Edinburgh did not enjoy a great reputation in the first half of the eighteenth
century, but it did show signs by mid-century that it was moving in the direction of
becoming a modern capital. The first newspapers in Edinburgh began publication
between 1710 and 1720, the Edinburgh Medical Society was founded in 1731, and
its Lord Provost George Drummond began to lay plans for the expansion and a new
building programme. These plans came to fruition in the second half of the century,
when the prestige of Edinburgh, not only within Scotland or even Britain but in
Europe as a whole, was enhanced by the Scottish Enlightenment and its reputation
as the 'Athens of the North'. The Scottish architect Robert Adam (1728–92) helped
inspire a neoclassical revival in Edinburgh and, indeed, throughout Britain, after
training in Rome. His brother John designed the neoclassical Royal Exchange, which
opened on Edinburgh's High Street in 1760. The city became more prosperous as
well, leading to the construction beginning in 1767 of Edinburgh's 'New Town',
which is regarded as an outstanding and beautiful model of municipal design,
though it did not really become popular among the Scottish middle classes until the
nineteenth century. However, it still remained a relatively small and manageable city,
especially compared to London, with a population of only about 80,000 at the end
of the eighteenth century.

London was the only city in the British Isles that had a larger population than Dublin.
Like London, Dublin was attracting migration from the surrounding countryside
of individuals looking to take advantage of the broad range of employment and
commercial opportunities available there. It even became increasingly common for
landlords with estates in the country to own townhouses in Dublin and to spend
part of the year there, just as their fellow aristocrats in England had started to do
in London. Dublin had its own viable commercial sector, one in which Catholics
and Dissenters, particularly Presbyterians and Quakers, increasingly participated,
as restrictions eased in the course of the eighteenth century. With land ownership
opportunities dwindling and legal prohibitions against Catholics and Dissenters
holding office, it was only natural that they might look to avail themselves of
careers in trade and commerce in an expanding economy, though not as many as
mainstream Protestants feared.[29] However, a small but important and discernible
Catholic merchant class began to emerge at this time. Like Edinburgh, financial
prosperity led to new buildings, most notably the construction of a new parliament
building on College Green, though eighteenth-century Dublin also became known
for its beautiful gardens and Georgian townhouses. In the second half of the
eighteenth century, the Dublin Parliament would become assertive enough to begin
making demands for greater independence. By contrast, Scotland would become
further integrated into the kingdom of Great Britain following the last great Jacobite
uprising of 1745–6.

Bonnie Prince Charlie, the Jacobite rebellion of 1745, and the Battle of Culloden

Political stability combined with economic prosperity seemed to ensure that the second Hanoverian king, George II (r. 1727–60) was secure on the British throne. His father, George I did not have much to recommend him as British monarch except his Protestant religion; to the English he was a foreigner who had little understanding of their politics, language, or culture. George I remained interested in his German lands, even though he more or less permanently resided in Britain after 1714. Furthermore, his accession had exacerbated relations with France, despite Louis XIV's pledge to honour the Hanoverian succession as part of the peace settlement that ended the War of the Spanish Succession, giving further encouragement to the Jacobites. However, the new Hanoverian regime survived the Scottish Jacobite rebellions of 1715 and 1719, as well as an English Jacobite plot proposed by Francis Atterbury, the bishop of Rochester, in 1720. George II's accession to the throne in 1727, a likely occasion for another Jacobite uprising, passed without incident. George II proved a much more active and deft manager of English politics, playing a large role in Walpole's government and exercising his authority to promote and dismiss ministers to prop up Walpole's administration during the excise crisis. But George II also retained an allegiance to Hanoverian interests and even led an army during the War of the Austrian Succession. He certainly would not have done so if he had any inkling that his British throne were in jeopardy. Yet when Prince Charles Edward Stuart defeated a British army led by Sir John Cope at the Battle of Prestonpans, which took place

FIGURE 18   *Leinster House, designed in 1745 as residence for Duke of Leinster; it has been the seat of the Irish Parliament and Senate since 1924.*
S. B. Nace/Lonely Planet Images/Getty

outside Edinburgh on 21 September 1745, a hostile army led by a rival claimant to the throne had gained control of Scotland.

'Bonnie Prince Charlie', as Prince Charles was known, believed that it was his divinely ordained destiny to regain the British throne for his exiled father, vowing when he sailed for Scotland on 5 July 1745 to 'conquer or die'. He raised his standard at Glenfinnan in northern Scotland on 19 August, where about 1,000 Highlanders joined him, though the first instinct of the Highland chiefs was to advise Charles to go home. The enforcement of the Disarming Act of 1725 had successfully deprived the Highlanders of many, though not all, of their weapons. Charles, however, contrary to his reputation as a simple-minded fool, knew that this was probably the last chance to attract French support for the Jacobite cause and that if he waited for a more auspicious time, chances were that time would never come. Furthermore, the Hanoverian regime was not especially beloved and he still hoped that English support might be forthcoming from Tories and disgruntled Whigs. Critics had long suspected that England's foreign policy was guided too much by the interests of Hanover in Germany. In fact, at the time of the Jacobite rebellion, George II's son, the Duke of Cumberland, was in Europe with 34,000 British troops.

Once ensconced in Edinburgh, Charles and his army leaders conferred through the month of October on what to do next; his generals advised staying put and fighting the English on their own turf, but Charles insisted on an invasion of England. On 30 October, Charles gathered his war council, consisting of his leading officers, the clan chiefs who had joined his army, and his personal advisers. Even Lord George Murray, widely considered the most brilliant military strategist and tactician on Charles's staff, urged caution, but the prince remained undeterred, despite the fact that English Jacobites had not, in fact, rallied in support. His decision to invade England turned out to be fateful, despite some initial success that allowed the Jacobite army to penetrate all the way to Derby – just 150 miles from London – by 4 December.

What went wrong? France, once again, disappointed. Louis XV did not believe the rebellion had much chance of success, when in fact his delay in providing support greatly hindered Charles's efforts, which might have succeeded with French assistance. Instead, George II recalled his army from Europe and ordered it to march towards Derby to destroy the Jacobites. The Jacobite invasion had come much too close for comfort and George was forced to take the threat seriously, placing his son, the Duke of Cumberland, at the head of his army. The Jacobite leadership once again deliberated on the best course of action, deciding at that point to retreat rather than risk becoming trapped in England cut off from their base of support. Charles and Murray led a brilliant retreat and managed to avoid a confrontation with English troops until 17 January at Falkirk, not far from Linlithgow, in the Scottish Lowlands. The Jacobites had managed to avoid defeat, but neither had moved any closer to victory and had now placed themselves in a defensive position. The Battle of Falkirk ended in a draw, forcing Charles to take his army even farther northward. He clung to the hope that his best chance of defeating the English army lay in fighting them on the terrain familiar to so many of the Highland chiefs who had supported him. Cumberland and his British army – comprising Highland and Lowland Scots, as well as English troops – decimated those hopes in a particularly brutal and utterly devastating manner on Culloden Moor.

The Battle of Culloden, which took place on 16 April 1646, brought the '45 Rebellion and indeed the entire Jacobite movement to a terrible and bloody end. The tragedy of Culloden was that Charles ignored the advice of his generals and determined to fight and sacrifice the lives of those who had supported him with virtually no chance of success. Outnumbered and lacking comparable and sufficient weaponry, Charles's cold, exhausted, and starving army marched into battle with little going for them beyond their own courage. At that point, very few of the Jacobite soldiers probably would have been able to articulate why they were still fighting or what they were fighting for, except that they were soldiers and these were their orders. The results were devastating. Perhaps as many as 2,000 Jacobite troops died that day, compared to fewer than 300 of Cumberland's men; Bonnie Prince Charlie fled the battlefield and hid until he managed to escape on a ship that returned him to France.

Writing in the early nineteenth century, Sir Walter Scott wrote that an 'attachment to the House of Stuart' had 'now almost entirely vanished from the land, and with it, doubtless, much absurd political prejudice – but also many living examples of singular and disinterested attachment to the principles of loyalty which they received from their fathers, and of old Scottish faith, hospitality, worth, and honour'.[30] At the time, the Hanoverian government pursued a ruthless policy to destroy Jacobitism once and for all that included executions, forced exile, and imprisonment. In Scotland Cumberland earned the sobriquet 'the Butcher', not only for the slaughter at the Battle of Culloden but for the extirpation of Jacobite soldiers and sympathizers in its aftermath. Bruce Lenman has written that 'it is very dubious whether these horrors served any useful purpose, apart from creating a fund of resentment in the Highlands from which the last Jacobite rebellion was to draw much of its retrospective justification'.[31] The Hanoverian dynasty had survived what turned out to be the most serious threat against it; however, the challenges that would face the next Hanoverian king, George III would include an armed rebellion against his authority that would end with an entirely different result than that which met its demise on Culloden Moor.

FIGURE 19 *Culloden Moor (aka Drummossie Moor) in Inverness looking towards the Moray Firth, with British soldiers firing on fleeing and dying soldiers who are being tended by their women, April 1746. The battle was the last one in the second Jacobite Rising when the supporters of Bonnie Prince Charlie were routed. Published 1836. Artist – Thomas Allom (1804–72). Engraving – Henry Griffiths.*
Rischgitz/Hulton Archive/Getty.

10

Reform, war, and rebellion:

Political culture in Britain and Ireland, 1746–1789

The colonists may not always know which laws are best for them, or which of their countrymen are the fittest for conducting their affairs; but, at least, they have a greater interest to coming to a right judgment on these points, and will take greater pains to do so than those whose welfare is very remotely and slightly affected by the good or bad legislation of these portions of the Empire. If the colonists make bad laws, and select improper persons to conduct their affairs, they will generally be the only, always the greatest sufferers; and like the people of other countries, they must bear the ills which they bring on themselves, until they choose to apply the remedy. But it surely cannot be the duty or interest of Great Britain to keep a most expensive military possession of these Colonies, in order that a Governor or Secretary of State may be able to confer colonial appointments on one rather than another set of persons in the Colonies.

The Report on the Affairs of British North America Presented to
Her Majesty by the Earl of Durham, 1839

Threats to the Whig oligarchy

At the midway point of the eighteenth century, the Hanoverians' final victory over the Jacobites at Culloden Moor promised a continuation of politics as usual in the British Isles. However, before long several challenges to the Whig oligarchy threatened to upset the political stability that had seemed the hallmark of post-1688 Britain.

In 1754 a 27-year-old gentleman named John Wilkes failed in his first attempt to gain election to Parliament as MP for Berwick-upon-Tweed. In 1757 he managed to get himself elected as MP for Aylesbury, but he did so largely through bribery and ended up in deep financial difficulty. This could have derailed and discredited a vacillating character, but Wilkes wanted to make his mark on politics. He began to attract the attention and patronage of prominent men within the Whig Party, including the secretary of state, William Pitt. However, the Whigs received a sudden jolt in 1760 when King George II died and was succeeded by his son, George III, who, at the age of twenty-two, determined to take an even more active role in politics than his father had. George III did not wish to be dictated to by Parliament and he came to rely heavily on his tutor, Lord Bute. Wilkes now had an issue that gave him an opportunity to play a leading role in the first major threat to the Whig oligarchy and the political unity of the British ruling class. Politicians resented the undue influence Bute had over the king and the power Bute had gained as a result of that influence. Bute actually had good intentions; he simply wanted the king to serve as a mediator between rival factions within Parliament in order to help steer the country in what they considered the right direction.

In 1760–1, this meant steering the nation towards peace in the conflict with France and Spain known as the Seven Years War. Pitt resigned from the government in October 1761 when his cabinet refused to approve his proposal for a preemptive strike on Spain, which had yet to join the fray. Wilkes remained loyal to his patron and joined the opposition when Pitt's ministry fell. At this point in British political history, MPs did not so much vote along party lines as they voted in favour or in opposition to the current government. In the preceding decades this had largely depended upon patronage and personal connections, but now substantive issues, often relating to foreign policy, increasingly influenced the way that MPs voted. Wilkes's propensity for stirring up trouble and his determined defence of his position in Parliament in the face of opposition from the king contested that political unity and began to revive political divisions dating back to the seventeenth century.

In 1763, George III became subject to rumours that his mother had asked him to appoint Bute, her suspected lover, as the next prime minister. It did not matter that the rumours were not true, for they gave Bute's opponents an opportunity to discredit him. Wilkes anonymously published an editorial repeating the rumour in issue 45 of the journal *The North Briton*, published 23 April 1763. Wilkes also went directly after Bute in the journal, referring to him as 'insolent', 'incapable', and 'despotic'. Harkening back to the Revolution of 1688, Wilkes praised the English people for not tolerating despotism then and urging them to stand up for their 'ancient liberties' in the present.[1] A main bone of contention for Wilkes was the nature of the peace negotiations to end the war with France. The journal suggested that Britain was on the verge of returning all of its conquests in the war back to France and that, in addition, British concessions in the proposed peace would ruin the East India Company.

Bute tried to shut down *The North Briton*, but the courts ruled in Wilkes's favour. In response, the government prosecuted Wilkes on a charge of seditious libel instead. Wilkes had made the constitutional argument that the king possessed all of the power of the executive, but that he remained 'responsible to his people for the due execution of the royal functions, in the choice of ministers, &c. equal with the meanest of his subjects in his particular duty'. Whatever the merits of this argument, Wilkes went too far in his attack on the king, a fact he himself acknowledged; he fled to France, where he spent four years in the mid-1760s rather than risk conviction on a charge of libel. However, he audaciously returned to England in 1768, stood for election to Parliament again and won again, only to have his election voided by the king. Wilkes became a martyr to the freedom of the press, personal liberty, and the rights of MPs when the government threw him in the Tower of London on the old libel charge.

Wilkes, who did not come from a privileged background, represented a broader trend towards greater demands for political participation that were emerging at this time; for example, women, too, began demanding a greater role in the political sphere in the second half of the eighteenth century. Indeed, historians now recognize that aristocratic women played a larger role in eighteenth-century politics than had previously been recognized. The world of politics already filtered out of Parliament into the world of high society where men and women freely mingled and discussed current issues. Whereas French women participated in the intellectual life of the salons, English and Scottish women participated in debating societies that addressed such issues as women's right to vote or female education. Women of the upper caste actively participated in elections by campaigning for their favoured candidates, using their position in society to bring MPs together who might have similar interests, and even by influencing the patronage system. As Parliament gained more influence at the expense of the Crown, so did those social circles in which MPs travelled play a greater role in the political life of the nation. A good example is Georgiana Cavendish, the Duchess of Devonshire, one of the most effective campaigners for the Whig Party, who was rumoured to have exchanged kisses for votes in the election of 1784. Some women also influenced public opinion through roles in the newspaper and printing industry; in London Mary Say published the *Gazetteer* in the last three decades of the eighteenth century, while Sarah Hodgson and her husband printed the *Newcastle Chronicle* from 1785 to 1800, after which Sarah continued to run the publication following her husband's death.[2] Many women found a way to be active without directly challenging male dominance; Hannah More (1745–1833), for example, moved from writing plays to writing religious and moral tracts and poems, while working for the amelioration of the poor in the Bristol area. In fact, the contemporary debate about whether women should remain entirely in the domestic realm itself can be seen as a reflection of the fact that many women were starting to do just the opposite.

Another threat to the Whig oligarchy came from a parliamentary reform movement that targeted corruption, patronage, and financial malfeasance within the government. MPs actually exercised their own judgement and did not, as it turns out, sell their votes to the highest bidder,[3] but public perceptions are often more important than reality. Curiously, demands for reform during this period did not generally emanate from the manufacturing towns with little political clout that had begun to emerge in northern England because the government remained sympathetic to commercial interests. Instead, demands for reform came from within the Whig Party itself, leading to a division between moderate and radical Whigs.

Much political debate in the second half of the eighteenth century centred on the position of the monarchy, causing yet another rift within the ruling class and precipitating a revival of the meaningful distinction between Whigs and Tories as opposed to the more meretricious party division of, say, the modern United States. The Whigs looked back to the Revolution of 1688 and became determined to remain in power in order to defend the principle of parliamentary supremacy. Some Whig representatives, such as Edmund Burke, sought to avoid a return to factionalism; others, however, saw in the increasing power of the monarchy under George III a threat to the very principles over which the Revolution of 1688 had been fought.

George did not see himself as a tyrant; his most recent biographer, Janice Hadlow, describes him as 'essentially a good-hearted man, who tried to observe the decencies of gentlemanly behavior even in the darkest and most trying times of his reign'.[4] In fact, Hadlow argues that George wanted to expand the active role of the monarchy in order to improve the moral milieu of British politics. George believed that as king he possessed certain prerogatives, including the right to select his own ministers, whereas his critics believed that he should at least restrict his choices to prominent leaders of the majority party in Parliament. Reducing royal patronage was one of the major goals of the economic reform movement. The issue evidently had major political implications; George consistently managed to exclude his Whig opponents from power and secure governments loyal to the monarchy. His success in doing so only further convinced him of his political omnipotence. Yet so long as his ministers pursued policies with which he concurred, he was content to remain in the background of affairs and allow them to conduct the business of the nation. His relations with his ministers were not always harmonious and he could at times insert himself into politics, as he did in the Wilkes case, but he always had to remain wary of those who would seek to trammel his power.

Another target of the opposition in the House of Commons was the House of Lords, which still preserved the hereditary principle regarding political power. The fact that lack of intelligence, illness, or even insanity could not prevent a member of the House of Lords or the monarchy from inheriting their position became an acute exigency towards the end of the century as a result of George III's bouts of insanity, proving Thomas Paine's dictum that hereditary monarchy frequently provides humanity with 'an ass for a lion'.

The question of monarchical power was raised in 1775 when petitioners started addressing their grievances to the king instead of Parliament.[5] Popular petitions had become the favoured means for a disgruntled public, including women, to put forward their grievances to the government. The fact that petitions could be presented either to the king or Parliament led to confusion among the people regarding where power reposed, as well as who best represented and served the interests of the people.

Meanwhile, a crisis was brewing in Britain's American colonies over a series of regulations and policy changes that followed the end of the Seven Years War, Britain's latest war with France in what was increasingly becoming a battle for world hegemony. The American crisis divided British political opinion so sharply and acrimoniously that it produced the greatest threat to the Whig oligarchy in the second half of the eighteenth century.

The Seven Years War and the American crisis

In 1756, the British once more found themselves in a war with France, one that would be fought in Europe, North America, the West Indies, and India. In this war, as a result of the 'diplomatic revolution', Britain would side with Prussia in Europe against Austria and France. This shifting of alliances had largely resulted from the work of Austria's foreign minister, Prince Kaunitz, who decided that Austria needed French assistance against the growing power of Prussia and was willing to forego Austria's claims on the southern half of the Netherlands in order to get it. At least in the early stages of the war, William Pitt left most of the fighting in Europe to Frederick the Great of Prussia, and used his naval forces to attack the French where they were most vulnerable. For example, the British lost interest in the Mediterranean theatre, focusing instead on attacking French shipping in the Atlantic and blockading France's Atlantic coast. British strategy also became concentrated on defeating the French in the West Indies and North America, viewed as a vital national interest. Pitt regarded the West Indies as critical to Britain's economic and strategic interests; 20 per cent of all British imports came from the West Indies in 1755.[6]

In North America, the French had long encouraged Indian raids upon colonial settlements as part of their effort to chip away at British expansion. In 1755, on the eve of what was known in the colonies as the French and Indian War, in the words of its historian, D. A. Sherrard:

> Dumas, the new commander at Fort Duquesne, had organized a series of Indian attacks along the western borders of Pennsylvania, Maryland and Virginia. The sufferings of the colonists were indescribable: their homes were burnt, their wives and daughters ravished, their children murdered, their young scalped and tormented. There seemed no escape from the horror, and in despair they entreated the Assemblies for protection. But the Assemblies were too far away to be frightened and too engrossed in politics to be interested.[7]

Once the war started in earnest, Pitt treated the Americans more as allies than subjects, knowing that he needed their cooperation in order to win the war in North America. The French had won some initial victories in 1756 and 1757, including a victory over General Braddock at Fort Duquesne. Pitt pledged that he would reimburse colonial legislatures for their expenses if they would raise armies to fight the French and their Indian allies. The colonial militias thus played an important role in fighting and winning the war, operating autonomously under British auspices.

In 1759, the British launched a major invasion of Canada. General Wolfe won one of the decisive battles of the war, the Battle of the Plains of Abraham on 13 September 1759, when he defeated the French commander, General Montcalm, on the plateau above Quebec City, at the cost of the lives of both generals. Before he died, Wolfe made his famous assertion that the Highland Scots under his command should be among the first sent into battle because 'they are hardy, intrepid, accustomed to a rough country, and no great mischief if they fall'.[8] Meanwhile, a force led by General James Forbes, who was accompanied by George Washington, retook Fort Duquesne in 1759 and renamed it after Pitt. The war changed the way George Washington and other colonial leaders thought of their position in the British Empire and the world.

As late as 1772 he still viewed himself as a loyal servant of the Crown, proud of the role he had played in the British victory, but he was also apprehensive about what the increase in British power meant for the long-term future of the colonies.

The war ended when both France and Spain sought peace terms in 1763. The British emerged from the war the clear victor, gaining Florida from the Spanish, acquiring all French possessions east of the Mississippi River and in Canada, along with a few additional islands in the West Indies. The military victories of Robert Clive on behalf of the British East India Company also made Britain the leading power in India.

The Britain never intended to provoke a war with any of its colonies in North America. American complaints about British rule seem to have increased in the years leading up to the revolution, but they were actually quite common by the mid-eighteenth century so it seems that we only think that American grievances against the expansion of British power led to the revolution because we know with hindsight that a revolution began in 1775. In fact, the submission of grievances was not only normal but also one of the main ways in which colonists communicated with the mother country. It was common for colonists to present their grievances to Parliament, although sometimes they appealed directly to the king. Of course, the Crown also had its representatives in the colonies to whom Americans could appeal, royal officials ranging from customs officers to royal governors.

American colonists actually enjoyed a relative degree of freedom and a low rate of taxation compared to people in other countries, even after a series of financial impositions by Parliament after 1763. Of course, the Americans did not so much object to being taxed, but rather to their lack of say over those taxes as embodied in the slogan 'no taxation without representation'. The first new tax to receive significant attention was the Stamp Act of 1765, which was deeply unpopular because it required a stamped paper for the purchase of common and necessary printed materials such as newspapers and legal documents. Then, in another effort to maximize revenue, Britain introduced a new American Customs Board, consisting of five commissioners located in Boston who were charged with ensuring that what was owed in customs duties was paid and collected.

Increased taxation, however, cannot account for the American Revolution. Instead, the decision of the British to station regular troops of the army in the colonies may have been a tipping point in the direction of revolt, if not revolution. The Seven Years War had increased Britain's strategic interest in its North American colonies. Pitt had deployed some 20,000 regular British troops in North America during that conflict. Once they were secure from the French, American colonists naturally reassessed their relationship with Britain, one consequence of which was that they shifted their focus to the British army as a threat to their autonomy. Together Lord Halifax, the secretary of state for the Southern Department, which included responsibility for the American colonies, and the prime minister George Grenville essentially reversed the policy of William Pitt, treating the Americans not as allies but as part of a larger empire whose interests took precedence over their own. In 1768 the British sent regular troops to Boston in response to a riot that had broken out when royal officials seized John Hancock's ship, appropriately named the *Liberty*. Boston merchants responded with an economic embargo that significantly reduced British exports to America. Workers displayed open hostility to British soldiers; they were especially resentful because of the soldiers' willingness to hire themselves out at lower wages. One demonstration of that hostility in March 1770 resulted in an ice-throwing incident that led British soldiers to fire into a crowd, killing five and wounding six civilians – an event known as the Boston Massacre. The war began in 1775 when the British general Gage sent about 800 troops to confiscate weapons and ammunition stored by rebels at the Massachusetts town of Concord.

The Seven Years War had produced what may be called the first truly British army because of the inclusion of numerous troops from the Scottish Highlands, its soldiers, including those held in contempt by Wolfe, now willing to fight for the regime that many Highlanders had opposed in the Jacobite rebellions. As early as 1747, the government offered amnesty to those Jacobite soldiers willing to enlist in the British army. As time went on, they became the most trusted and respected troops in the British army. The British also recruited troops from Ireland, in addition to the regulars from England, Wales, and the rest of Scotland. Most of the men who joined the British army came from the plebeian caste of society and those stationed in the colonies frequently presented themselves as undisciplined and unruly. In addition, the British contracted for the service of almost 30,000 troops from various German principalities in the course of the war; because the largest contingent (12,500) came from Hesse Cassel, they are all frequently referred to as Hessian mercenaries. Finally, many loyalists from the colonies themselves, including a significant number of African American troops (see below) fought with, alongside, or in addition to the British army.

Significant numbers of women travelled with the British armies that fought in the Seven Years War and the American War for Independence. The army needed women to cook their food, mend their clothes, and heal their wounds. Prostitutes also accompanied the troops, but even they provided ancillary services. Many of the women were soldier's wives who came to the new world as a way to remain close to their husbands. Some even brought their children with them, or took care of other children who had decided to tag along. Although these women did not generally participate in combat, they frequently shared the same risks of illness, capture, and death that accompanied the army in its travels. These included the wife of a Hessian general, Madame de Riedesel, who was captured, along with her three young daughters, and had to endure insults, rude treatment, hunger, and deprivation on a forced march from New York to Virginia.

France entered the war in 1778 after the Americans demonstrated that they had a chance to win the war by achieving victory at the Battle of Saratoga in 1777. Once the French intervened, the British found themselves trying to balance their efforts to defeat the colonists against their desire to support their interests in Europe and the West Indies. The West Indies took precedence given the quantity of the West Indian trade and the importance of sugar to the economy of the British Isles. Juxtaposed with the comparatively smaller volume of trade in North American products such as tobacco, one can easily understand why.

In North America, the British found themselves involved in a guerrilla war in which the colonial militias supplemented the efforts of the Continental Army under George Washington by harassing the British Army. After General Cornwallis had surrendered to Washington at Yorktown, Virginia in August 1781, George III would have had the British fight on, but by then his prime minister, Lord North, had lost support in the House of Commons and George had to agree to a peace ministry or face calls for his own abdication.

The British public had divided on the American crisis, throughout which the government received petitions supporting a hard line against the colonies in addition to those that advocated appeasement. In contrast to his effusive denunciation of the Jacobites, Edmund Burke viewed the American Revolution as in the same tradition as the Revolution of 1688, a conservative movement that sought to defend the traditional rights of Englishmen from the arbitrary tyranny of George III and North, as opposed to the sanguinary élan of the French Jacobins during the later French Revolution. Wilkes re-emerged as a critic of the government, once again posing as the defender of personal liberty on the side of the American colonists. Wilkes, who endured arrest and imprisonment for his defence of free speech and his right to sit in Parliament as a critic of the government, gained great respect in America and helped to inspire a whole line of libertarian political theory.[9] In gratitude, colonists named the Pennsylvania town of Wilkes-Barre after him and another advocate of the American cause, the Irish politician, Isaac Barré. Another critic of the government was William Pitt the Younger, who in 1782 at the age of twenty-two gave a ninety-minute speech in the House of Commons attacking government corruption and the perverse influence of the Crown on the workings of the British political system. However, George III apparently decided he would rather have Pitt as an ally than an enemy and made him prime minister in 1783, from which position Pitt continued his programme of economic reform without focusing as much on the position of the monarch. Pitt remained in power until 1801, providing an important measure of stability at a time when the king was becoming increasingly unstable as a result of his mental illness.

The success of the American Revolution did nothing to slow Britain's rise as a dominant economic and military power in the world. The importance of the Revolutionary War for Britain resided more in the political and social rifts that it caused at home. Violent clashes erupted in Bristol in 1776, 1777, and 1779 between supporters and opponents of the war. An arson campaign conducted by one 'John the Painter' in that city created an atmosphere of fear and terror. Because the war brought economic hardships, it can be difficult to discern the role that political as opposed to economic concerns played in the minds of those demonstrating or rioting against the government and its war policies.

Moreover, religion may have divided the supporters and opponents of the American Revolution, in both Britain and the colonies, even more than political ideology or economic concerns. Some habits lingered from the past; for example, the anti-Catholic Gordon Riots in London in 1780 recalled the anti-Catholic hysteria that accompanied the Popish Plot a century earlier. Furthermore, as Kevin Phillips has shown, loyalties among the colonists during the American Revolution tended to split along religious lines. The two main hotbeds of the revolution were Puritan Massachusetts and Virginia, where 'Low-Church' Anglicans, who favoured a less ritualistic ceremony and less hierarchical church structure, generally opposed the twin emphases of the Tories on High-Church Anglicanism and the prerogatives of the Crown. They would have been joined in this opposition by Baptists, Methodists, Quakers, and other Protestant dissenters. British loyalists during the revolution tended to side with the Tories religiously as well as politically.[10]

Race also played an important role in the revolution, with many black soldiers fighting on the side of Britain. Those African Americans who did so were attracted by promises of freedom and the hopes that a British victory would sooner bring an end to slavery in the colonies than an American one. The British were so anxious to achieve black assistance that they also offered land in exchange for service. Both the subsequent growth of slavery in the United States and its territories following American independence and the British decisions to outlaw the slave trade in 1807 and to abolish slavery in the British Empire in 1833 raise questions about who really fought on the side of liberty in the American War for Independence. Slavery expanded significantly beyond the Appalachian Mountains for the first time after the war. The British historian Simon Schama has argued that African Americans would have benefited more from a British victory in the war. Those African Americans who fought for the British may very well have believed this at the time, even though they were well aware of Britain's previous heavy participation in the slave trade. Schama states emphatically that 'during the Revolutionary War there is no question that tens of thousands of Africans, enslaved in the American South, did look to Britain as their deliverer, to the point where they were ready to risk life and limb to reach the lines of the royal army'.[11] It is important to remember, however, that prior to the revolution the colonies themselves had been British and that slavery had significantly expanded under British rule, as it had in the French and Spanish Empires in the Americas as well. Furthermore, free blacks sometimes fought against the British, such as the eighty African Americans who participated in the invasion of Baton Rouge in September 1779. Even Schama acknowledges the presence of African American soldiers on the American side in virtually every battle from Bunker Hill to Yorktown.

Britain's defeat in America's War for Independence was deeply humiliating to the government, all the more so because it represented a major victory for France as well. Popular concern about the growth of French power probably helped salvage some support for the government, even in the aftermath of such an ignominious defeat. But the loss of its American colonies taught the British some valuable lessons that had a significant impact on its colonial policies in the nineteenth century. First, British trade with its former colonies actually increased after American independence, helping to support the arguments of the free trade movement in Britain. Furthermore, Britain was determined not to repeat the mistakes it made during the American crisis and loosened its reins over colonies such as Canada and Australia. In 1838, when Lord Durham was asked to report on recommendations for Canada in the wake of recent rebellions there, he wrote:

> It is said that it is necessary that the administration of a colony should be carried on by persons nominated without any reference to the wishes of its people; that they have to carry into effect the policy, not of the people, but of the authorities at home; and that a colony which should name all its administrative functionaries, would, in fact, cease to be dependent. I admit that the system which I propose would, in fact, place the internal government of the colony into the hands of the colonists themselves; and that we should thus leave to them the execution of the laws, of which we have long entrusted the sole making to them. Perfectly aware of the value of our colonial possessions, and strongly impressed with the necessity of maintaining our connexion with them, I know not in what respect it

can be desirable that we should interfere with their internal legislation in matters which do not affect their relations with the mother country. The matters, which so concern us, are very few. The constitution of the form of government, – the regulation of foreign relations, and of trade with the mother country, the other British colonies, and foreign nations, – and the disposal of the public lands, are the only points on which the mother country requires a control. This control is now sufficiently secured by the authority of the Imperial Legislature; and by the protection which the Colony derives from us against foreign enemies; by the beneficial terms which our laws secure to its trade; and by its share of the reciprocal benefits which would be secured by a wise system of colonization. A perfect subordination, on the part of the Colony, on these points is secured by the advantages which it finds in the continuance of its connexion with the Empire. It certainly is not strengthened, but greatly weakened, by a vexatious interference on the part of the Home Government, with the enactment of laws for regulating the internal concerns of the Colony, or in the selection of the persons entrusted with their execution.[12]

The British, however, did not apply these principles to Ireland, whose relationship to Great Britain was also greatly altered by the American Revolution.

Ireland and the American Revolution

Eighteenth-century Ireland had strong economic connections to Britain's American colonies, particularly involving the heavy import of sugar from the West Indies to the refining plants that made up Dublin's largest process industry. Family and personal bonds connected Ireland to America as well. Between 1700 and 1750 an increasing number of Irish migrants left for North America instead of going to Europe or the Caribbean, the most frequent destination of Irish immigrants in the seventeenth century. Among them were numerous Presbyterian Scots-Irish who still had relatives in Ulster with whom they remained in contact. In fact, other than the English themselves and African Americans, the Scotch-Irish made up the single largest group of immigrants in the American colonies at the time of the revolution.[13] Although estimates vary and precise statistical information is hard to come by, Fitzgerald and Lambkin estimate that perhaps 40,000 to 80,000 people left Ulster for North America between 1750 and 1775, out of a total from Ireland somewhere between 100,000 and 250,000 for the entire first three-quarters of the eighteenth century.[14] When the American Revolution came, many Presbyterians in Ireland frequently sympathized with the colonists, all the more so when they saw the British recruiting Catholic soldiers in Ireland to fight in the American War. This generally supports Phillip's thesis about the role of religion in the American conflict, although support for the revolution was by no means unanimous among the Scotch-Irish, some of whom remained loyalist, largely depending on where they settled in America.

Moreover, people in Ireland paid keen attention to the ways the British started to impose their authority on the Americans following the Seven Years War. The principles being contested between the American colonists and the British Parliament regarding its right to tax the colonists without their permission resonated with Irish Protestant politicians. In addition, rebel Protestant organizations such as the Whiteboys had already begun their own tax revolt, mirroring that being conducted in America in the 1760s. But the Whiteboys were a vigilante organization that was as hostile to Irish Catholics as it was to the English government.

The American Revolution interfered with Ireland's trade and had an adverse effect on the Irish economy. The English put their own interests ahead of those of the Irish and refused to lift any of the constraints on Irish trade with England. The Irish responded by forming volunteer militias that the British viewed as a palpable menace, especially with so many British troops away fighting in America. In addition, a group of Irish politicians led by Sir Henry Grattan, an accomplished and passionate orator who argued eloquently on Ireland's behalf, formed a Patriot Party in the Irish Parliament to advocate for greater legislative autonomy for Ireland. While Catholics mainly wanted a repeal of the discriminatory Penal Laws, Irish Protestants such as Grattan believed that Ireland could not prosper unless it attained a degree of autonomy. At first, Grattan's proposals were thwarted by a pro-government coalition within the Irish Parliament held together largely by royal patronage, but higher taxes and the economic distress caused by the war ensured that his popularity would increase as the war continued.

However, France's entry into the American War motivated the British Parliament to pass legislation favourable towards Catholics throughout the British Isles in an effort to ensure their loyalty. The Catholic Relief Act of 1778 did much to gain the support of Irish Catholics for the British war effort in America. Unfortunately, these measures did not meet with popular support in Britain. However, in Ireland both Protestants and Catholics sought to capitalize on Britain's wish to avoid an Irish revolution there in the wake of the American imbroglio by demanding greater legislative autonomy, which they achieved in 1782. It did not take long, however, for the Irish to realize that their newly granted autonomy was illusory, as the island was still governed by a royally appointed lord lieutenant who controlled not only the executive branch of the government but also had enough patronage to influence the legislative branch. The Irish were not content merely with the concession of legislative independence, especially after seeing America successfully defeat the British and establish the fledgling republic. American independence raised hopes that the Irish might achieve a similar settlement, especially if the British did not deal with them fairly. Grattan's influence now began to wane as he remained committed to continued ties with Britain, while popular opinion moved in advance of his ideas, which now seemed moderately conservative. In particular, the new Parliament of 1782 was entirely dominated by Protestants, meaning that the majority of the Irish population still lacked political representation. The noted politician and philosopher Edmund Burke was among those who thought that free citizenship and equal rights should be granted to the Irish people, including Catholics, in the aftermath of the American Revolution. In fact, Burke's experience in Ireland had informed his political position on the American War, which he very much opposed, believing the Americans were within their rights to want control over their affairs. Burke's advocacy for Catholic rights in Ireland in 1776 was thus directly related to his support for the rights of the American colonists.

Meanwhile, Arthur Young's account of his travels in Ireland, published in 1780, called attention to the horrible conditions of the poor in both urban and rural Ireland. Young acknowledged that the conditions of the poor varied, writing at one point that they

> have, generally speaking, such plenty of potatoes as always to command a bellyful; they have flax enough for all their linen, most of them have a cow, and some two, and spin wool enough for their clothes; all a pig, and numbers of poultry, and in general the complete family of cows, calves, hogs, poultry, and children pig together in the cabin; fuel they have in the utmost plenty.[15]

But he describes the poor of the county of Kerry as 'exceedingly miserable', blaming their extreme poverty on the abuses of Anglo-Irish Protestant landlords who conspire to charge the highest rents feasible, which gave the peasants no recourse to seek more favourable terms.

In 1785 William Pitt the Younger responded to calls for changes in Ireland's status by proposing the incorporation of Britain and Ireland into a single free-trading zone. Such a proposal could have worked from an Irish perspective, since this had been the objective of Irish advocates going back to William Molyneaux's *Case of Ireland Stated* at the end of the seventeenth century. The failure of Pitt's proposal and increased Irish agitation in the 1790s eventually led Pitt to propose an Act of Union that would incorporate Ireland and Britain into a single United Kingdom.

The Industrial Revolution in England, Wales, and Scotland

Meanwhile, the social and economic changes brought about by the Industrial Revolution increased the amplitude of political agitation in Britain during this period. The loss of the American colonies was offset for Britain to a large degree by the growth of industry at home, which made Britain a wealthy nation poised for a rise to global dominance. Recent historians have de-emphasized the role of inventors and inventions in the Industrial Revolution that used to be celebrated as uplifting tales of creativity and ingenuity that drove the transition to the factory system and, by extension, the modern world. Yet no account of the Industrial Revolution would be complete without some mention of innovations like James Watt's invention of a more efficient version of the steam engine, which was first invented by Thomas Newcomen earlier in the century. Watt said that the point of his invention was to 'save both fuel and steam'. Watt's steam engine did not catch on right away, but when it did it revolutionized the cotton industry and had a profound impact on the metal industries, stimulating increased demand for machines used in textile manufacturing that could no longer be made of wood, which was no longer compatible with the new invention.

Britain's early industrialization occurred in part because of a combination of population growth, the ready availability of natural resources, and technological innovation, but also because it possessed both a financial system that made it easy

Bank of England

to mobilize capital for investment and the existence of colonial and global markets that provided incentives to do so. This surplus capital not only came from overseas trade but also from the profits accruing to landowners over their more profitable estates owing to enclosure and advances leading to higher crop yields. Once the shift to factory work had occurred, the payment of cash wages also increased the number of consumers, making the domestic market more attractive as well. In addition, England had a system of navigable rivers, enhanced by the construction of numerous canals in the eighteenth century that facilitated the transport of goods and coal, which is heavy and difficult to transport over land. The 1707 Act of Union also played a role, as it facilitated movement of Scottish labourers across the border to areas that needed workers; between England, Scotland, and Wales Britain had perhaps the largest single territory in Europe without any trading barriers or borders restricting the movement of people. Towards the end of the nineteenth century, John Sinclair noted in his *Statistical Account of Scotland* that the borderlands between Scotland and England had lost population and that the movement of people would naturally be in the direction of England, the wealthier of the two. Britain had begun to exploit its natural resources to a much greater degree, with a corresponding shift in population to northern England where much of the coal and iron so critical to industry, especially after the invention of Watt's steam engine, could be found. But the most dramatic changes in this period occurred in the cotton textile industry, which achieved growth so unprecedented that the twentieth-century economist W. W. Rostow thought it significant to ignite a 'take-off' phase for the entire industrial economy.

It is true that the technological innovations that heavily affected the economy took the form of a series of rather modest but important innovations, starting with John Kay's 1733 invention of the flying shuttle, which significantly increased the rate of production in the textile industry. In addition, Maxine Berg and Pat Hudson have argued that the rapid growth in the cotton textile industry could not have occurred without other supporting technological changes in other areas of the economy, like the metal trades.[16] The ability to manufacture a much higher volume of cotton goods created a greater demand for the raw material, part of which was met by the seizure of Guadeloupe in the West Indies from the French in 1759. At the time, Pitt remarked that he regarded Guadeloupe as worth more to Britain than all of Canada; in the previous three years, Britain imported an average of 1,588,813 pounds of cotton per year from the West Indies; in the following four years, that number grew to 2,375,156 pounds yearly.[17]

The expansion and increased mechanization of the cotton industry had profound effects not only on the British economy but on British society as a whole. By the end of the eighteenth century, a new class system had begun to emerge in England as a result of the transition to a more industrial economy, even though a majority of people still lived and worked in the countryside. The rise in population meant that there were substantially more people living in cities and factory towns in the second half of the eighteenth century, even as the population in rural areas continued to rise as well. It also meant that an increasing number of workers could be shifted to factory settings, even though domestic industry still flourished and many traditional craftsmen and textile workers continued to produce goods manufactured in a more traditional manner. Furthermore, changes in the textile industry continued to inspire further technological change, which in turn had additional social consequences. Contemporaries were certainly aware of the dramatic social and economic changes that were occurring around them. If industrial growth in the second half of the eighteenth century seems modest by comparison with later growth rates, from the vantage point of those living at the time the appropriate comparative base is not what came after but what came before. As Professor Christine Eisenberg has said: 'One of the outstanding characteristics of English market society around 1800, and one that requires no further discussion, was its modernity.'[18] Eisenberg suggests that people at that time would not have understood what modern historians define as 'capitalism', but that the modern capitalist system of a market society was in place by the end of the eighteenth century. These changes led the poet William Wordsworth at the end of the century, in a poem first published in 1807, to write:

> The world is too much with us; late and soon,
> Getting and spending, we lay waste our powers:
> Little we see in Nature that is ours;
> We have given our hearts away, a sordid boom!

Part of the conundrum for the historians who argue about the significance of economic growth in the latter decades of the eighteenth century is the difficulty of measuring and defining growth, since the kind of statistical data available for all sectors of the economy in more recent times is not available for this earlier period. Statistics can be used to argue that no Industrial Revolution occurred, or that, if it did, it paled in comparison to later measures of economic growth, but the Industrial Revolution, much like any such historical concept, is a linguistic contrivance that in this case is well suited to understanding that a relatively rapid and significant transformation of British society had occurred in the second half of the eighteenth century. As early as 1969, Harold Perkin cited statistics that are still jarring, especially because they stop around 1800 and show how much had changed already by that date:

> Between 1780 and 1800 British foreign trade, whether measured in shipping tonnage cleared from the ports or in export and import values, nearly trebled. Between 1750 and 1800 coal production doubled, from under five to ten million tons. Between 1788 and 1806 pig iron production, already four times that of 1740, almost quadrupled again, from 68,000 to 250,000 tons. Most spectacular of all was the growth of the pioneer machine industry, cotton: between 1781 and 1800 raw cotton imports quintupled, from 10.9 to 51.6 million pounds.[19]

No amount of statistical manipulation in the past forty-five years has been able to make these numbers go away.

But it also remains true of the fin-de-siècle eighteenth century that agriculture still played a larger role in the economy than it did once industrial capitalism became more advanced and that British financial institutions had not changed significantly since early in the century. The major factor influencing changes in the countryside in the second half of the eighteenth century was the dramatic increase in the number of enclosure acts passed by Parliament from a total of 75 in the two decades before 1750 to 137 from 1750 to 1760, 385 in the following decade, and 660 between 1770 and 1780. Tensions between landowners and dispossessed peasants were already high, owing to the passage of the Black Act in 1723 aimed at poachers who disguised themselves by painting their faces black. Peasants and small farmers did not entirely disappear, as used to be thought, but many agricultural labourers were forced to relocate. Changes in land ownership also increased significantly, alongside higher rates of enclosure. These changes mainly involved the sale of land by small farmers, defined by Overton as owning between 5 and 25 acres, rather than the owners of large estates.[20] There is some truth, therefore, in Oliver Goldsmith's poem *The Deserted Village* (1770), in which he bemoaned the disappearance of many small villages throughout England.

The main purpose of the enclosure acts was to give landowners more control over their land so that they could practice agricultural innovations that would lead to higher productivity without outside interference. But they also used their control to enhance the aesthetic qualities of their landscapes, as evidenced by the popularity of Lancelot or 'Capability' Brown (1715–83), who designed gardens at over 200 estates, including such prominent locations as Blenheim, Kew, Stowe, and Warwick Castle. Brown capitalized on the affinity that his contemporaries had for nature, which he tried to reproduce using simple landscaping techniques involving water, trees, and grass, such that he practically created the image in most people's mind of what the English countryside is supposed to look like.

Furthermore, the trends that led to factory growth also led to the growth and prosperity of domestic industry and wares made by hand by skilled artisans – just because factory work was expanding does not mean that agricultural or domestic industry was contracting, especially in this transitional period. Still, a dynamic and powerful new emphasis on manufacturing had transformed Britain into what historian Peter Mathias called 'the first industrial nation'. The accumulation of capital from this initial outburst would sustain industrial growth well into the nineteenth century and finance the rise of a capital goods industry in connection with the construction of the first railway in the next stage of the Industrial Revolution.

The relationship between philosophy and society

Adam Smith, the author of *The Wealth of Nations* (1776), is the thinker most often associated with the intellectual rationale for the rise of free-market capitalism associated with the Industrial Revolution. In his book, Smith praised division of labour as 'the greatest improvement in the productive powers of labour, and the greater part of the skill, dexterity, and judgment with which it is any where directed, or applied'. To illustrate his point, Smith used the famous example of the manufacture of pins, stating that without machinery and the division of labour a single craftsman would at most manage to produce a pin a day, and definitely no more than twenty. Smith also opposed legislation that would restrict imports, preferring open competition that would encourage domestic manufacturers to produce quality goods at reasonable prices. Smith did not deny that these manufacturers would benefit from protection or from monopolies, but he believed that this would have deleterious effects on the rest of society.

FIGURE 20 *David Hume, Scottish philosopher, historian, and economist, 1837. Portrait made in the nineteenth century after an eighteenth-century original of Hume (1711–76), whose most important work was* A Treatise on Human Nature *(Edinburgh, 1739–40). From* The Gallery of Portraits *by Charles Knight (London, 1837).*
Print Collector/Hulton Archive/Getty.

Smith was one of the leading figures in a loose intellectual movement that has come to be known as the Scottish Enlightenment. His contemporary and fellow Scot, David Hume, expanded on the work of John Locke and George Berkeley in attempting to provide an epistemological foundation for human understanding, which Hume suggested came in the only three forms that allowed us to connect one idea to another: 'resemblance, *contiguity* in time of place, and *cause* or *effect'*. For Hume, however, cause and effect was an experiential relationship rather than an actual one that we could be certain had a firm foundation in reality. Past experience can only be a guide to what has happened, not to what will happen; just because the sun has risen every morning in the past does not necessarily mean that it will do so in the future. Hume did not wish people to succumb to 'philosophical melancholy' by dwelling too much on questions inaccessible to human understanding, advising that the best cure for such a problem was re-engagement with human society. For Hume, scepticism did not lead to pessimism, but rather taught him even to be sceptical about scepticism itself. He did not reject religion out of hand, but only challenged those of his contemporaries who attempted to claim a rational basis for religious belief instead of considering it a matter of faith alone. If Hume's philosophy had a major weakness, one might say that he adhered too closely to Locke's view of the mind as a *tabula rasa*, which totally relied on sense experience, and that Hume did not do enough to account for the creative and introspective aspects of human thought.

Hume's fellow Scot, Adam Ferguson, wrote in his *Essay on the History of Civil Society* that art was not to be distinguished from nature, but rather was a part of man's nature, whose first instinct is 'to invent and contrive'. Ferguson agreed with Smith on the extent to which the division of labour had become characteristic of modern society. However, he expressed concern that it would have detrimental effects on the unity of the nation and the connection that human beings felt towards one another. Responding to a trend in political writing that ran through Hobbes, Locke, and Rousseau that emphasized the distinction between the 'state of nature' and organized society, Ferguson made no such distinction, arguing that

> if we admit that man is susceptible of improvement, and has in himself a principle of progression, and a desire of perfection, it appears improper to say, that he has quitted the state of his nature, when he has begun to proceed; or that he finds a station for which he was not intended, while, like other animals, he only follows the disposition, and employs the powers that nature has given.

Ferguson believed in natural rights that preceded the establishment of property and carried over into society, so that any person had a right to rationally conclude whether they were being treated justly or unjustly by another person and to act on the basis of that conclusion. But he did not ignore the fact that in civil society the needs of the community overshadowed those of the individual; he sided with the British government in the conflict with the American colonies. Ferguson believed that modernity and commercialization contained disadvantages as well as advantages; he was one of the first Scottish intellectuals to display a sympathy for Highland society in the aftermath of the Jacobite rebellions. Ferguson basically tried to strike a balance between excessive individualism and passive acquiescence to authority; for him government required political participation and engagement from its citizens.

While working-class women were becoming absorbed in the factory system, educated women were striving to become more politically active and productive members of society, despite the severe legal and social restrictions placed upon them. Most girls in Britain did not go to school, generally receiving only an informal education at home. In 1798 Maria Edgeworth suggested that the education of girls should eliminate 'sentimental stories' and 'books of mere entertainment'. Edgeworth, herself a significant novelist whose works such as *Castle Rackrent* and *Ennui* provide important perspectives on land reform and social issues in Ireland, believed that romance novels dulled the mind, prematurely stimulated the emotions of young girls, and vitiated the ordinary pleasures of daily life that represent the true path to happiness. Novels set people up for unrealistic expectations, such as believing that virtue and grace always make their appearance in the same person. Edgeworth's contemporary, Mary Wollstonecraft, shared the belief that the more women focused on love and sentimentality the less prepared they were for playing a public role of which they were perfectly capable, disparaging those 'women who are amused by the reveries of the stupid novelists, who, knowing little of human nature, work up stale tales, and describe meretricious scenes, all retailed in sentimental jargon, which equally tend to corrupt the taste and draw the heart aside from its daily duties'.[21]

Catharine Macaulay wrote a history of England, the first woman writer to do so, suggesting that women had a role in interpreting history as well as shaping it.

Macaulay argued for the ways in which greater education for women would help them and society as a whole even within the domestic sphere to which they were traditionally confined. She suggested that women would become better daughters, wives, and mothers as a result of acquiring a higher and more intellectual education than most of them were allotted. Macaulay was also concerned for the well-being of women themselves, however, arguing that their current lack of education had debilitating effects on both their minds and their bodies.

Concerns about women's education overlapped with discontent with women's legal status, which had not improved in the course of the eighteenth century. The author of *The Laws Respecting Women, As They Regard their Natural Rights* (1777) thought that 'a nation of men characterized by bravery, generosity, and a love superior to mean suspicions, must consider the happiness of women as inseparably blended with their own'.[22] At least women could obtain the equivalent of a modern restraining order, if their husbands threatened to beat them 'outrageously', as husbands could against their wives. In contrast to this, *Laws Respecting Women* also discusses the accepted practice among the common people of wife selling:

> Among the common people, a method is sometimes practiced of dissolving a marriage, no less singular than compendious. When a husband and wife find themselves heartedly tired of each other, and agree to part; if the man has a mind to authenticate the intended separation by making it a matter of public notoriety, thinking with Petruchio, that his wife is his goods and chattel, he puts a halter about her neck, and thereby leads her to the next market place, and there puts her up to auction to be sold to the best bidder, as though she were a brood-maid or a milch-cow.[23]

A century later Thomas Hardy centred the plot of his novel *The Mayor of Casterbridge* on an example of just such a wife-sale. This is perhaps an extreme example of the subordination of women to their husbands, but this is only a difference of degree rather than of kind in comparing this to the general legal position of married women in eighteenth-century society.

The renowned English jurist Sir William Blackstone held that marriage laws served the essential purpose of protecting women, even though they deprived them of the same rights accorded to their husbands. For example, Blackstone noted in his famous and influential *Commentaries on the Laws of England* that husbands are legally required to provide for their wives and to pay their debts, even those that were contracted without the husband's permission. Blackstone wrote that for legal purposes a husband and a wife should be considered a single person. However, he highlighted the ways in which they were nonetheless not equal, placing women in a subordinate position within the marriage.

Among the more important changes in the eighteenth century was the passage of Hardwicke's Marriage Act of 1753, officially titled 'An Act for the Better Preventing of Clandestine Marriage', which required an official wedding ceremony for all valid marriages. This law had the primary effect of extending parents' control over their children. Social commentary in the early eighteenth century lamented the ability of adolescents in their early teens to contract binding marriages without their parents' permission.

Observers of society in the second half of the eighteenth century also continued to concern themselves a great deal with moral issues, starting with the rising crime rate that afflicted England at mid-century. In addition to crime, luxury and vice came under frequent attack, as did the theatre and even the proliferation of pleasure gardens among the upper classes. The novelist Henry Fielding produced *An Enquiry into the Causes of the late Increase of Robbers* in 1751. Fielding concluded that the poor needed greater assistance from society and that the criminal law needed overhauling, but also believed that the poor often cultivated bad habits that contributed to their plight because of the proliferation of opportunities for vice during the eighteenth century:

> The gentlest method which I know, and at the same time perhaps one of the most effectual, of stopping the progress of Vice, is by removing the Temptation. ... Voluptuousness or the Love of Pleasure is that alone which leads them into Luxury. ... Now what greater Temptation can there be to Voluptuousness then a Place where every Sense and Appetite of which it is compounded, are fed and delighted, where the Eyes are feasted with Show, and the Ears with Music, where Gluttony and Drunkenness are allured by every Kind of Dainty; nay where the finest Women are exposed to View, and where the meanest person who can dress himself clean, may in some degree mix with his Betters, and thus perhaps satisfy his Vanity as well as his Love of Pleasure?[24]

To Fielding's credit he did not treat the problem of poverty as exclusively the fault of the poor or as arising from social causation beyond their control. But Fielding's distinction between the able-bodied poor and those too ill or disabled to work as a means test for poor relief was a precursor to the nineteenth-century attitudes that found consummation in the New Poor Law of 1834.

Adam Smith's work has received a re-evaluation by Emma Rothschild, who argues that Smith did not present his theory of the 'invisible hand' in a generally positive way, precisely because of the moral implications that seemed to deny personal accountability for one's own actions. In proposing the existence of an 'invisible hand', Smith built on the tradition of Mandeville and the idea that public vices sometimes had public benefits by increasing demand for goods that boosted the economy and enhanced trade. However, Rothschild points out that Smith's limited use of the term 'invisible hand' occurs only in respect to disreputable characters, including hypocritical and self-interested merchants.[25] Smith remained an optimist who believed that people were essentially rational and had the ability to act in the long-term interests of themselves and society instead of merely living for this day and the next. Many of his contemporaries would not necessarily have agreed and saw scant evidence that this was the case, which further accounts for the eighteenth-century preoccupation with moral issues.

Religion, morality, and the Enlightenment

Concerns about the lack of morality in eighteenth-century Britain coincided with concerns about a decline in religious belief. David Hume used his philosophical scepticism to criticize revealed Christianity, which he did in his treatment of miracles in his *Enquiry Concerning Human Understanding*, but he also challenged the beliefs of the Deists in his *Natural History of Religion* (1757). Hume confined his studies of religion to the history of religion, which he saw as progressing from polytheism to monotheism as human beings grew less fearful of the natural world. But, according to Hume, our limited capacities simply do not allow us access to truths beyond what our senses can ascertain, and even these he considered to be unreliable in any kind of an absolute way regarding the true nature of the universe. In his *Dialogues Concerning Natural Religion*, Hume did not deny the existence of a deity, but stated that

> when we look beyond human affairs and the properties of the surrounding bodies: when we carry our speculations into the two eternities, before and after the present state of things; into the creation and formation of the universe, the existence and properties of spirits; the powers and operations of one universal spirit, existing without beginning and without end; omnipotent, omniscient, immutable, infinite, and incomprehensible: we must be far removed from the smallest tendency to skepticism not to be apprehensive, that we have got quite beyond the reach of our faculties.[26]

Lacking proof for the claims of religion, either Christianity or Deism, Hume believed that doubt or agnosticism was the only rational position on the matter. His challenge to the belief in miracles was so important because he used experience to undermine phenomena that by definition run counter to normal human observation. He notes that claims of miracles have diminished with the rise of education and points out that they generally occur among people prone to superstition because of a lack of knowledge of the natural world.

What contemporary moralists tried to do was to devise a new basis for a moral code rooted in the shared beliefs and judgements of society, which in turn could lead to introspection as something that each individual could measure himself against.[27] Oliver Goldsmith condemned pride and luxury in his 1766 novel, *The Vicar of Wakefield*, in favour of a life of 'temperance, simplicity, and contentment'. In his 1779 novel *Columella* Richard Graves argued that withdrawal from society, which might be so appealing to some, would do neither the individual nor society any good; work and making a positive contribution in the world, Graves suggests, is the real road to happiness, not retirement and leisure. These both followed the heavily moralistic and sentimental novels of Samuel Richardson (1689–1761), whose influence pervaded middle-class thinking on sex, marriage, and probity in the second half of the eighteenth century.[28] In best-selling novels such as *Pamela* (1740), *Clarissa* (1748), and *Sir Charles Grandison* (1754), Richardson especially warned young women of the importance of preserving their virtue and their reputation, especially against the depredations of young aristocrats. Richardson's novel *Pamela* was adapted for the theatre, a further illustration that literature and drama both focused on concerns about morality in an age of reason.

The Seven Years War and the War of American Independence only inflamed concerns about the moral tone of society and the need for further reform. The American Declaration of Independence appealed both to 'the Laws ... of Nature's God' and 'the opinions of mankind' in essentially making a moral argument for the separation of the American colonies from Great Britain. Men had 'certain unalienable rights', such as 'life, liberty, and the pursuit of happiness' because a Creator had endowed them with such, according to Thomas Jefferson, the author of the Declaration. J. C. D. Clark has argued that the Americans could never have asserted their independence if they did not challenge the theological premises of the monarchy.[29] Many of the colonists had originally immigrated to North America in order to freely practice their religious beliefs, thus perhaps predisposing them to the cause of liberty, whereas, the thought goes, Anglicans and Catholics were more likely to remain loyal and obedient to established authority. But if echoes of the religious warfare of the seventeenth century survived into the American War for Independence, so did the secular political thought of the earlier period, especially the social contract theory initiated by Hobbes and Locke and continued in the eighteenth century by Rousseau. Thomas Paine based his defence of American independence on reason and 'common sense', the title of the famous pamphlet he issued in 1776 that is widely credited with playing a decisive role in swinging the support of a majority of colonists towards independence. Jefferson referred to the importance of the consent of the governed in the Declaration of Independence and the right of the people to withdraw their allegiance and form a new government if they believed that their rights were being violated. Furthermore, religious reform movements had already begun to emerge in the first half of the century in the First Great Awakening in America, the emergence of Pietism in Germany, and the formation of the Society for the Propagation of Christian Knowledge and the rise of Methodism in England and Wales.

Religion did not exist apart from or in opposition to the Enlightenment, however; many Enlightenment figures, such as Samuel Johnson, held sincere religious beliefs; Johnson said that he first began to think seriously about religion after reading at Oxford a book by William Law called *A Serious Guide to a Holy Life*, which Johnson admits he took up expecting to find it dull and perhaps even laughable. Moreover, religious thinkers of the period shared with the Enlightenment an emphasis on the importance of reason. The American Calvinist preacher Jonathan Edwards (1703–58) was best known for fiery and passionate sermons such as 'Sinners in the Hands of an Angry God', but he warned against the dangers of an entirely emotional approach to religion and frequently employed appeals to reason in his writings and sermons. The Anglican theologian Joseph Butler (1692–1752) argued in his *Analogy of Religion* (1736) that God worked through what we understand as natural causative processes to move us towards Him; Butler used reason instead of a defence of miracles in responding to the Deists and sceptics. George Whitefield (1714–70) contributed both to the Great Awakening in America and the religious revival in England and Wales after undergoing a conversion experience in 1735, while John Wesley introduced a more practical set of guidelines or rules for his followers that led to his designation as a 'Methodist'. Calvinists attacked Wesley for making salvation too much the product of a rational free choice, thus contradicting their belief that salvation came only through God's grace, which could not be swayed by human actions.

Wesley has been associated with the rise of democracy and with establishing a conservative creed that played a major role in preventing revolution in Britain in the nineteenth century (the thesis of the French historian Elie Halevy), but he would have seen his own mission in terms of the salvation of the souls and the preaching of the Gospel to thousands of British labourers who otherwise would not have heard its teachings or understood its central doctrines. Wesley wished not only to bring a more emotional, evangelical brand of Christianity to the people, but also to transform them into a readily identifiable religious following who would socialize and intermarry among themselves to avoid exposure to excessive worldliness. Perhaps for this

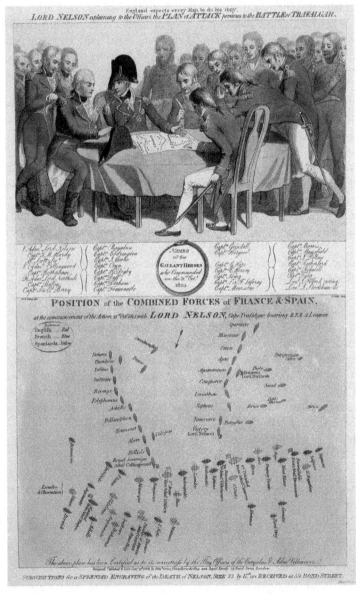

FIGURE 21 *Nelson discussing the battle plan for Trafalgar. Napoleonic Wars, England, nineteenth century.*
DEA/G. NIMATALLAH/De Agostini/Getty.

reason, Wesley's message seems to have appealed mainly to people in areas that already had a long association with religious nonconformity, especially in the north and west, rather than in the more conservative southeast. The Church of England in the eighteenth century had become to many people a formalistic, coldly rational, and emotionally devoid brand of Christianity that did not appeal to the common people. Anglicanism seemed to straddle Wesley's emphasis on revealed religion and the formal worship of the God of Nature favoured by the more devout Deists. Wesley admonished his followers to be respectful of the Anglican clergy, despite his own criticisms of them. Wesley shared with other Enlightenment moralists a desire to reform the habits and behaviour of the lower classes, but he also shared with them a belief in the importance of reason, which he did not regard as mutually exclusive with his teachings or his faith.

Thomas Paine took up the subject of religion in his *The Age of Reason*, published in 1794. Paine did not wish to challenge people's right to believe or worship as they chose, but he instead attacked the church hierarchy and its political influence, something for which he could find no more justification than he could for the hereditary rights of the monarchy and aristocracy. What separates a Wesley from a Paine, however, or an Edwards from a Hume, is that Wesley and Edwards combined the rational approach of the Enlightenment with a continued belief in the supernatural aspects of revealed religion with which Paine and Hume felt uncomfortable. Paine had familiarity with the variety of faiths that proliferated in eighteenth-century England, perhaps one of the reasons why he did not adhere to any one exclusively and chose to develop his own personal creed. Just as Wesley knew and understood the positions of the Deists and Anglican theologians like Joseph Butler, not to mention Enlightenment philosophers such as Bernard de Mandeville, John Locke, and Francis Hutcheson, Paine knew and understood the positions of the Quakers and the Methodists, as well as that of the Church of England.

Finally, eighteenth-century concerns about contemporary morality and the period's emphasis on moral self-evaluation also helped produce a significant political and social movement to abolish the slave trade. In 1779, William Wilberforce made an impassioned plea for the abolition of the slave trade in the House of Commons; his main point was that the merchants involved in the slave trade were not solely to blame for the practice of it but rather everyone who ignored, tolerated, or benefited from the wealth that it produced also shared in the blame. Wilberforce sought to turn the arguments for or against the slave trade away from general principles and towards the effects that the slave trade actually had on real human beings, all of whom should be treated as individuals rather than as members of a group – an important challenge to traditional ways of thinking that would grow stronger over the course of the nineteenth century.

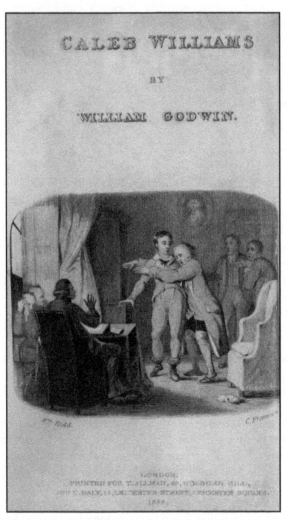

FIGURE 22   The Adventures of Caleb Williams, *a novel by William Godwin (3 March 1756–7 April 1836). Frontispiece to 1838 edition, published by T. Allman (London). First published 1794.*
Culture Club/Hulton Archive/Getty.

11

The French Revolution, the Napoleonic Wars, and their aftermath, 1789–1832

*Little did I dream when she added titles of veneration to those of
enthusiastic, distant, respectful love, that she should ever be obliged
to carry the sharp antidote of disgrace concealed in that bosom; little
did I dream that I should live to see such disasters fallen upon her in a
nation of gallant men, in a nation of men of honour and of cavaliers.
I thought ten thousand swords must have leaped from their scabbards
to avenge even a look that threatened her with insult. – But the age
of chivalry is gone. – That of sophisters, oeconomists, and calculators,
has succeeded; and the glory of Europe is extinguished for ever. Never,
never more, shall we behold that generous loyalty to rank and sex,
that proud submission, that dignified obedience, that subordination
of the heart, which kept alive, even in servitude itself, the spirit
of an exalted freedom.*

EDMUND BURKE, on MARIE ANTOINETTE,
Reflections on the Revolution in France, 1790

*That which I glory in, in the French Revolution, is this: That it has been
upheld and propagated as a principle of that Revolution, that ancient
abuses are not by their antiquity converted into virtues ... that man
has rights which no statutes or usages can take away ... that thought
ought to be free ... that intellectual beings are entitled to the use of their
intellects ... that one order of society has no right, how many years*

soever they have been guilty of the pillage, to plunder and oppress the
other parts of the community. ... These are the principles that I admire,
and that cause me, notwithstanding all its excesses, to exult in the
French Revolution.

JOSEPH THELWALL, 1795

The impact of the French Revolution
on the British Isles

The French Revolution of 1789 caused an even greater rift within British political culture than had the American Revolution. At first George III and William Pitt were by no means displeased to hear of the internal troubles affecting France, their long-time rival. It did not take long, however, for Edmund Burke to think that the French revolutionaries had gone too far in the direction of the assertion of rights for which he believed they had no political justification. He was particularly appalled by the decision to abolish the French aristocracy; Burke correctly feared that the monarchy would be next. Burke tried to make it clear that he was no enemy of liberty, but argued that forming a government had to take into account experience and tradition as opposed to theoretical justifications for government. He believed that it was incumbent upon political leaders to chart the direction a country should take rather than follow the wishes of an irrational and capricious populace. Burke feared that if democracy replaced a hereditary government rooted in long-standing traditions the most sensible politicians would soon be excluded from power in favour of those willing to support the crowd and its short-term interests. In contrast to Burke, writers such as Thomas Paine and Mary Wollstonecraft thought that the French Revolution had not gone far enough, particularly, according to Wollstonecraft, with regard to the rights of women. Paine directly responded to Burke in his *Rights of Man*, stating that the French people did not presume to tell the British Parliament how to run its affairs and that Burke should accord them the same respect. Wollstonecraft saw a clear connection between a hierarchical political and social system and the subjugation of women.

The ideas of the French Revolution and the rights of man swept through British society, even carrying over into the British military, where rebellions such as the famous 1789 mutiny on the HMS *Bounty* had political overtones; the British military was sometimes willing to negotiate with deserters in order to keep them in the army, but never with mutineers.[1] By 1791, organizations devoted to the principles of the French Revolution had arisen in Britain and these would continue to flourish throughout the decade. The Constitutional Society of London and the London Corresponding Society were two prominent societies; Pitt had the leaders of both societies arrested in May 1794 as part of a more general attack by the government on associations that it started to see as subversive. These organizations, like that of the United Irishmen across the Irish Sea, were strongly influenced both by the ideas of Paine and the French Jacobins, the most prominent political club to emerge out of the revolution.

The political divisions that occurred in Britain over the French Revolution were much more likely to break down along class lines than the schisms that had occurred during the American crisis. Most members of Parliament were alarmed by the radical actions in England of organizations like the Sheffield Society, which celebrated France's military victory at Valmy in September 1792 with a bull roast to feed the poor, including those languishing in debtors' prisons.[2] In the course of the next several years, public assemblies, petitions, and radical publications that the government regarded as seditious flourished throughout the British Isles, creating a panic among the British ruling classes.

By 1791 King George had started to sympathize with the French king, who unsuccessfully tried to flee France with his family in September of that year. The conservative monarchies of Austria and Prussia were just as alarmed at the developments in France as George III, if not more so. At first the British government tried to stay neutral when Austria declared war on France in April 1792, but Prussia declared war a month later. At that point, the French diplomat Talleyrand explored the possibility of an alliance with Britain, but the British were not interested in an alliance that might lend credibility among their own soldiers and populace to French Revolutionary ideas. Furthermore, the political situation in France had become tumultuous and the British could not have been certain that the same government with whom they negotiated would remain in power. Failing to secure their support, the French declared war on the British instead.

The outbreak of war in 1793 hardened political attitudes and made the British government and military even less willing to tolerate political dissent. Perhaps it was natural that some politicians would see the French Revolution through the lens of British history and reflect back on the English revolution of the seventeenth century in which subjects had executed one king and driven another into exile. Thomas Paine looked for a precedent for what was happening in France in the Revolution of 1688. Paine believed that the Revolution of 1688 was appropriate *for its time*, but argued that the British people were not bound by the ensuing Revolutionary Settlement for eternity. Paine considered any clause that attempted to bind a people to a form of government for eternity inherently a nullity because no people should possess a right to legislate for people who live at a later time.

Like Paine, the venerable Whig political leader Charles James Fox supported the right of the French to change their government and became an opponent of Pitt and the war with France. In his *History of the Early Part of the Reign of James II* (1808), Fox provided a reconsideration of the first English Revolution in order to provide context for the second one in 1688, but it is hard to read his account without discerning a connection to the French Revolution. This must have been even more difficult to do for his contemporaries, who had lived through the French Revolution and were still at war with France at the time that his book was published. Although Fox had supported the French Revolution, when he carefully examined the 1641 execution of the Earl of Strafford he found that the failure to adhere to normal principles of jurisprudence made the verdict illegal, irrespective of Strafford's crimes. Nor could Fox find any justification, with hindsight, for the execution of Charles I, since the king at that time did not pose any immediate danger and his death was unlikely to deter any future monarchs from tyranny. Fox could buttress his point by noting the extent to which European rulers, including George III, had only learnt from the downfall and execution of Louis XIV in January 1793 to increase repression rather than to consider the factors that had gotten him into trouble in the first place. For these reasons, Fox opposed the execution of the French king.

Meanwhile, the war gave a huge boost to British industries, especially to the construction of ships and the manufacture of armaments, but also to various industries that provided materials and supplies to a larger army and navy over an extended period of time. The initial stimulus to the economy, combined with the outburst of nationalism that usually accompanies the beginning of any war, contributed to the war's popularity. As the war dragged on, the French Revolution saw increasing violence, leading public sentiment in Britain to become ever more conservative. Even the Sheffield radical Henry 'Redhead' Yorke had changed his views in a conservative direction by the early nineteenth century, beginning with his trial for seditious activities in 1795 at which he claimed to have opposed the teachings of Thomas Paine. The British government responded to the Reign of Terror in France by suspending the right of habeas corpus and passing the Treasonable Practices and Seditious Meetings Acts in 1795.

In Britain, the coinciding of the French Revolution with the acceleration of the Industrial Revolution exacerbated the conditions of the working classes because political repression now operated alongside economic exploitation. The French Revolution also had a particularly profound effect upon Ireland, which had cultivated a number of important ties with France in the course of the eighteenth century largely as a result of the Jacobite movement and as a result of the number of Irish people who lived in France, which included many Irish soldiers who fought in the French

FIGURE 23   *Industrial Revolution, England: mining. Nineteenth-century engraving.*
Universal Images Group/Getty.

army. War with France once again made Ireland's allegiance suspect, leading to a further crackdown on political dissent that mirrored that being conducted in Britain.

The Irish Rebellion of 1798 and the Act of Union

The Irish had shown signs that they might rebel against British rule throughout the second half of the eighteenth century, but the French Revolution provided both an ideology to justify a rebellion and the possibility of French assistance to support one. The ideals of Paine and the French revolutionaries provided hope that Irish Catholics and Protestants might unite in the secular cause of Irish unity and nationhood. Wolfe Tone, one of the Protestant leaders of the United Irishmen, in particular, not only called for toleration of Catholics but also went to France to solicit French aid in the hopes that a French invasion could oust the British and minimize the need for mass casualties among the Irish. When Irish radicals took up arms against the government in 1798, the rebellion turned out to be the bloodiest episode in Irish history since 1641. Yet Elizabeth Malcolm has argued that the violence would have been much worse except for the attempts of those Irish inspired by republican ideals to minimize the amount of bloodshed. They hoped to prevent the rebellion from deteriorating into the kind of sectarian atrocities that had characterized the 1641 rebellion.[3]

Religious differences helped prevent the kind of unified strategy between the largely Protestant United Irishmen and the Catholic Defenders that might have given the rebellion a greater chance of success. Just as many Americans supported the British government during their revolution, many of the Irish opposed the 1798 rebellion and large numbers of them fought in the British army, making the rebellion something of a civil war.

The catalyst for the rebellion occurred in March 1798, when, as part of a campaign against the United Irishmen that had started the previous year, the government struck at the heart of the movement by arresting a number of their leaders, threatening to peremptorily crush any hope of a rebellion before it even started. The campaign had the opposite effect, precipitating uprisings in the counties around Dublin, followed by a more successful assault on government forces in Wexford farther south, along with additional uprisings in Mayo and Wicklow. After the rebels defeated the British at Oulart Hill in Wexford on 27 May and captured Wexford town three days later, the British pacified the rebellion. On the same day (5 June) that the rebels drove government troops out of northern Wexford, the British crushed a rebel army at New Ross, followed by a rebel defeat at Arklow on 9 June, and the capitulation of the Wexford rebels on 21 June after a devastating defeat at the Battle of Vinegar Hill. Following the defeat at the Battle of New Ross, rebel troops, as they retreated from the battlefield, massacred over 100 mostly Protestant loyalists, including women and children, being held in a barn at Scullabouge in County Wexford. The pogrom was a sign that the rebels were becoming desperate and that their commanders had lost control.

The rebellion in the north met with no more success than its southern counterpart. On 7 June, after a few minor victories, loyalist forces won a crucial victory at Antrim town that prevented the Antrim rebels from coordinating with those who rose at

Down and had defeated loyalist forces at Saintfield on 9 June. Only four days later, loyalists reversed the outcome in another skirmish at Saintfield, a week before the Battle of Vinegar Hill. Not only had rebels in the North and South failed to forge a cohesive movement, but the Catholic Defenders and United Irishmen too had failed to effectively coordinate their efforts in the North. In addition, British intelligence and their successful infiltration of the United Irishmen played a role in the failure of the rebellion. By the end of June the rebellion was, for all intents and purposes, over. The anticipated intervention by the French had failed to materialize and the Catholic Church had withheld its support for the rebellion, limiting its support among the population at large. When the French did arrive in County Mayo on 22 August, they were too late to save the rebellion, and the invading force was probably too small to have made a difference anyway. At Lough Swilly in County Donegal, the British captured Wolfe Tone, who, ignominiously or heroically, depending on one's perspective, committed suicide in prison.

The consequences of the 1798 rebellion were both immediate and long lasting. In the subsequent period, the rebellion had seemed an abject failure that had doomed the nationalist cause to oblivion. The government carried out some reprisals, though it was limited by its failure to locate any lists of United Irishmen in Wexford, the centre of the most serious resistance. The rebellion had failed, but Wolfe Tone and the 1798 rebellion would eventually come to play an important role in Irish nationalist mythology during the nineteenth and twentieth centuries. The rebellion had also exposed deep schisms within Irish society that were to last for generations. The defeat of the rebellion had created martyrs to the nationalist cause, even if the immediate effects were to bring Ireland and England closer together. For the rebellion had scared the British and Pitt was now ready to negotiate with his mind made up to unify Britain and Ireland as the only way to ensure control over the island.

Ireland, however, retained its Parliament and the failure of the rebellion did not mean that an Act of Union was a fait accompli. A contemporary Irish historian, Jonah Barrington, wrote of the feeling that it was 'impossible that England should judiciously govern a people with whose feelings she was wont to trifle and with whose national and political character she was so imperfectly acquainted'.[4] The United Irishmen tried to rally their forces in 1799 to oppose any move towards union, but their chance to attain Irish independence was lost. The rebellion had upset the Anglo-Irish ruling class enough for some of them to look favourably upon Pitt's overtures for an Act of Union. Achieving a majority vote in the Irish Parliament, in the face of opposition from old Patriots, led once again by Henry Grattan, was another matter.

How did Pitt achieve this approbation by 1801? Since Pitt did not know how many votes he could count on, his representatives in Ireland spent profligately in the negotiations leading up to the parliamentary vote. Second, Pitt promised forthcoming concessions to Irish Catholics, while his new Lord Lieutenant in Ireland, General Cornwallis downplayed such concessions in dealing with Protestant leaders. Third, the Union did have genuine support – from both Catholics and Protestants. The Catholic Church had opposed the rebellion and now looked to a union as a means of gaining concessions for the church that its leaders, such as John Troy, the archbishop of Dublin, believed they had no chance of gaining otherwise. Finally, the government launched a campaign to put forth the advantages of a union for Ireland, led by a pamphlet called 'Arguments for and against an Union between Great Britain and Ireland Considered', written by Edward Cooke, the undersecretary for Ireland.

In the Act of Union, which passed in both the Irish and British parliaments in 1800 and took effect on 1 January 1801, the Irish, just as the Scots had done in 1707, gained representation in the English Parliament at Westminster, 100 seats for Ireland in the House of Commons and twenty-six in the House of Lords. The critical difference accounting for the failure of the Irish Act of Union relative to that between England and Scotland, however, was predicated upon the exclusion of a majority of the Irish people from Parliament based on the stipulation that denied Catholics the right to be elected, something that ran counter to Pitt's original intentions. The Anglo-Irish Protestants had little to complain about, but the British failed to deliver on Pitt's promises of Catholic emancipation when King George III refused to go along with the plan. Those promises had gained him the support of the Catholic hierarchy in Ireland for the Act of Union, support for which they gained nothing in return. Catholic Ireland remained under the control of its Protestant minority and the British, who had officially engineered Ireland's incorporation within the UK.

The Napoleonic Wars

The rebellion in Ireland had caused such grave concern in Britain because of the very real fears associated with the French Revolution and the rise of Napoleon, who became Consul and de facto head of the latest French executive body, the Consulate, in 1799. When other members of the First Coalition against France made peace in 1798, Britain alone remained at war with the French until a Second Coalition formed in 1799 that added Russia, Sweden, and the Ottoman Empire, among other countries. In March 1802 the two sides agreed to the Peace of Amiens, but no one on either side thought of this as anything other than a provisional agreement. Napoleon was too ambitious to settle for the gains that he had achieved at that juncture, and everyone knew it. This was not pure hubris on Napoleon's part; he and many of his followers sincerely believed that they had a historic, if not a divine, mission to conquer and spread French Revolutionary ideas to the rest of Europe. It seemed that all that Britain could do was prepare to defend itself until it could put together another coalition to stop Napoleon from achieving this objective.

The British admiral, Horatio Nelson, wrote in 1802 that 'under the providence of God The Safety Honor and Wealth of this Country chiefly depends on the Navy, therefore when either of these are attacked, the quickest possible should be adopted to call forth this defence'.[5] But the British quickly conceived a plan to trammel French clout by sending a fleet into the Mediterranean to make a preemptive blow against French naval power. Britain needed its navy to defend it shores, its colonial possessions, and its trade, but Nelson could now be used to fight an offensive war against the French. When Spain declared war on Britain in December 1804, the French had 102 ships of the line battle ready, compared to only eighty-three of the British.[6] On 28 March 1805 Nelson wrote in a letter that he hoped the French navy would soon embark from its safe haven in Toulon so that he might engage with it. In autumn, Napoleon finally sent Admiral Villeneuve and the French fleet to the

Spanish port of Cadiz to blockade the British fleet. On 21 October the British won the ensuing Battle of Trafalgar, despite being outmanned.

Nelson's victory only went so far; it preserved British naval power but did little to impede Napoleon's domination of the European continent. While Napoleon sought to implement his 'Continental System', a blockade designed to impede British trade, the British decided to fight a rearguard action against France by invading the Iberian Peninsula. In 1808, the British under Arthur Wellesley (who went on to become the Duke of Wellington) began the Peninsular War with a rout of the French at Vimeiro, driving them from Portugal. Wellington's army tied a significant portion of Napoleon's forces down in Spain for the next six years; Spanish resistance fighters further antagonized the French as well, depriving Napoleon of troops that he could have used to fight elsewhere in Europe. Wellington's victories at Orthez and Toulouse in 1814 ended the French presence in Spain and, following Napoleon's failed invasion of Russia in 1812, marked the beginning of the end for the French dictator.

The Napoleonic Wars corresponded with onerous economic times in the British Isles and the government had little difficulty recruiting sailors for its navy or soldiers to fight in its army. But popular sentiment was divided and the war provoked opposition within the British Isles. On the one hand, invasion fears were eminently tangible, as were Napoleon's intentions to launch one. Consequently, support for the war tended to climb in proportion to the threat posed by Napoleon, particularly after war resumed following the Peace of Amiens. The French invasion never came to pass, partly because of Britain's ability to form yet another coalition against Napoleon and partly because of Nelson's offensive in the Mediterranean. On the other hand, as the wars dragged out and invasion fears lessened after Nelson's victory at Trafalgar in 1805, popular discontent grew stronger. In general, Quakers and Unitarians tended to oppose the war, while Methodists and Anglicans, consistent with their respect for established authority, more often supported it.

The response to the Napoleonic Wars pervaded every aspect of British political culture, including the call for a nationalistic British art. Not only did British commercial galleries flourish during this period, but they mainly exhibited British artists, who now focused on scenes from British history or from the works of British writers, such as Shakespeare and Milton. British collectors now had a chance to display their patriotism through their collections, though they defined the word nebulously enough to fit a variety of genres and artistic tastes.[7] Patriotism was, of course, encouraged by the political authorities through mediums with a greater chance to reach the common people. Linda Colley includes in her important book *Britons: Forging the Nation 1707–1837* several published prints that convey the attempt to house nationalistic feeling at various dates during the French Revolutionary Wars. One from 1803 contains an image of Napoleon's head on a pitchfork, with the caption 'Buonaparte 48 hours after Landing!' Another image from 1803 titled 'The Freeman's Oath' shows a group of men brandishing swords with a cannon to the right, a woman and two children to the left, and the female figure of Britannia with a trident rising above them.[8]

Napoleon abdicated in 1814 after his army was defeated at the Battle of Leipzig. He accepted his exile to the island of Elba in the Mediterranean, as the allies began to discuss a peace settlement with Talleyrand, who temporarily became the head of the French government. In the First Treaty of Paris, signed on 30 May 1814, France had its monarchy and its 1792 boundaries restored and Britain agreed to return most of the French colonies it had seized, while retaining several Caribbean islands and the island of Malta in the Mediterranean.

The British quickly reprised their coalition after Napoleon escaped from Elba in March 1815, at first planning to launch an invasion of Paris itself. However, Napoleon once again went on the offensive with an invasion of Belgium that drew Wellington there to try to stop him. Wellington had an army of 68,000 troops, compared to Napoleon's hastily assembled army of 72,000, but the British general hoped that the 45,000 troops commanded by the Prussian general Blücher would arrive in time to tip the balance in his favour. Napoleon had forced Blücher to retreat after their forces met at the Battle of Ligny, about 19 miles from Waterloo, on 16 June.

The Battle of Waterloo, which took place two days later, deserves special attention because of the prominent place that it, like Nelson's victory at Trafalgar, would play in the collective historical memory and national mythology of the British, even though only about 36 per cent of Wellington's force had come from the British Isles (the remainder comprised mainly German, Dutch, and Belgian troops).[9] Wellington's plan to hold off the French and lull them into a false sense of victory until the Prussians under General Blücher could arrive with Prussian troops worked almost to perfection. The Battle of Waterloo took place in an incredibly confined space, 200,000 men and 60,000 horses fighting in an area of about 5 square miles.[10] The carnage was so great that wounded soldiers lay untended on the battlefield for several days; by the end of the month, all of the wounded had finally been removed. The battle became famous almost instantly. Authors and publishers rushed accounts of the battle into print in its immediate aftermath. Two of the earliest works to appear were Captain Arthur Gore's *An Historical Account of the Battle of Waterloo* and Christopher Kelly's *Full and Circumstantial Account of the Memorable Battle of Waterloo*. Sir Walter Scott came out with a poem, 'The Field of Waterloo'. Tourists flocked to the battlefield to collect curios. Meanwhile, Wellington and his army pursued Napoleon into France, where he was captured by the British Admiral Hotham on 22 June.

The French Revolutionary and Napoleonic Wars had lasted over twenty years, resulting in the deaths of about 200,000 military personnel from the British Isles and costing the British government an estimated £1,600 million per year (compared to £160 million a year during the Seven Years War just a half-century earlier).[11]

The Prussian Carl von Clausewitz, in his famous book on military strategy inspired by the Napoleonic Wars, *On War*, divided war aims into intermediate aims, focused on what it takes to win a war, and aims related to the final cause or the ultimate purpose of the war – what the victor hoped to achieve when it went to war in the first place. In the case of Britain's aims in the Napoleonic Wars, these had been mainly defensive, but the British had also opposed Napoleon's domination of Europe, leading the British to adopt the larger war aim of restoring the balance of power in Europe. Aside from its own relatively modest territorial gains, Britain had contributed significantly to the defeat of Napoleon, thereby helping to achieve its larger aim, though at a cost that went well beyond the sums expended on the war effort.

The Highland Clearances and Scotland
in the early nineteenth century

When absentee landlords started to take over the Highland estates from the clan
chiefs who had been dispossessed after the Battle of Culloden, tenants in the
Highlands slowly started to migrate from the area, especially after 1770. After the
French Revolution, those tenants who remained began to organize into political
associations similar to those that were springing up in other parts of the British Isles.
Between the economic interests of the landlords, who wished to force peasants off
the land so that they could use them for grazing sheep, and the political authorities
who were concerned with the rebellious ethos of the peasantry, the motivation for
the forced removal of Highland tenants was well in place by the beginning of the
nineteenth century.

During this epoch, rural society in Scotland underwent a dramatic transformation
that included a massive exodus of people from the Highlands and a shift in the
status of many Lowland farmers from tenants to agricultural labourers. As in
Ireland, and to some extent in England, Scottish political agitation increased during
the 1790s. The Society of United Scotsmen was the Scottish equivalent of the United
Irishmen. A riot in the small southeastern town of Tranent in 1797, which resulted
in at least a dozen deaths at the hands of the authorities, was partially provoked by
rumours that Scotland was about to be subjected to compulsory military service.
These concerns need to be understood against a backdrop that included political
agitation associated with the revolutionary decade, continued Scottish disaffection
with the union, and the depopulation of the country, which needed its people for
other jobs.

Sir Walter Scott was among those who romanticized the Highlands to such a
degree that they soon became a part of Scottish identity as a whole. Tartans and
kilts became ubiquitous symbols of Scotland, as they still are, despite the fact that
it was an Englishman who invented the kilt in the 1720s. Scott has been criticized
for his romantic treatment of Scottish history instead of calling attention to the
contemporary plight of Highland society. Scott provided a revisionist account of the
1745 rebellion in his prototypical historical novel, *Waverley* (1814). Scott would
not have been likely to have supported the Jacobite rebellions, committed as he was
to the union and the Hanoverian dynasty, but he could romanticize the '45 from
the safe distance of the early nineteenth century precisely because he knew that the
Jacobite threat had ceased to exist. In doing so, he helped to forge a single Scottish
identity, even if it was not one with which every Scot would have acquiesced. But
Scott also truly believed that something was lost with the defeat of the Jacobites
and the subsequent obliteration of Highland society; he wrote in his postscript to
Waverley that 'the most romantic parts of this narrative are precisely those which
have a foundation in fact'.

A few years later, in *The Heart of Midlothian* (1818), Scott included some urban
riot scenes that made rural or Highland life look appealing by comparison. The
Lowlands, in fact, had their own issues, including a reaction against strict Scottish
Calvinism that had begun in the eighteenth century. One of the most successful
indictments of Calvinist hypocrisy came from the pen of the famous Scottish poet

Robert Burns in the form his satirical poem, 'Holy Willie's Prayer' (1785). The narrator of the poem is a hypocritical Presbyterian elder who condemns the sins of others while finding excuses for his own. The judgemental and self-righteous Willie refuses to see – or is incapable of seeing – the inconsistency in his petition because he believes himself one of God's chosen elect, who therefore can do no wrong in the eyes of God, or at least nothing that would alter the divine decree of predestination that Willie believes has ensured his salvation. The Calvinist Presbyterian aspect of Scottish identity came under further attack with the publication in 1824 of James Hogg's *The Private Memoirs and Confessions of a Justified Sinner*. In this novel, Hogg takes the Calvinist doctrine of predestination and its bastard child, antinomianism, to an extreme conclusion but with great psychological insight. The main character, Robert Wringham, is convinced that he, as a justified sinner, can do no wrong in the eyes of God. He commits a series of crimes and moral offences that appear different from his first-person perspective than they do in the account of a third-person narrator, these two perspectives each taking up one-half of the book. From the perspective of the narrator Wringham 'weens every one of his actions justified before God, and instead of having stings of conscience for these, he takes great merit to himself in having effected them'.[12] Presbyterianism remained an important part of Scottish identity in the nineteenth century, making it a prime target in the culture wars that would emerge from the legacy of Burns, Scott, and Hogg during the reign of Queen Victoria (r. 1837–1901).

British and Irish political culture, 1815–1832

At the end of the Napoleonic Wars the Tory government of Lord Liverpool continued in power, meaning that many of the conservative measures intended to repress dissent and keep Britain politically stable remained in place. Liverpool's foreign minister, Lord Castlereagh represented Britain at the Congress of Vienna, where he and the other representatives of the great powers agreed to collaborate to prevent further revolution in Europe as a whole while also negotiating a territorial settlement in the wake of French conquests under Napoleon.

Meanwhile, Parliament approved regulations known as the Corn Laws to artificially keep the price of wheat from falling, since, now that the war had ended, foreign grain was going to be cheaper and provide competition to the grain grown by British landowners. Landowners had been expanding their lands under cultivation, both in association with enclosure and to take advantage of inflation caused by the war. After the war, inexpensive foreign grain would have driven the price of English grain (and bread) downward if not for this legislation. It became illegal to sell imported wheat in the UK unless the price exceeded 80 shillings per quarter. This measure annoyed the manufacturing bourgeoisie, not only because it ran afoul of their deeply held belief in the doctrine of free trade, but because it seemed that the politically hegemonic landed class was now using its power to prop itself up economically. In response, they would eventually organize an Anti-Corn Law League to advocate not only for the repeal of the Corn Laws but for free trade and the economic interests of their class in general. Liverpool made some attempt to assuage merchants and manufacturers by lifting some of the remaining restrictions on trade and commerce when he relaxed the enforcement of the Navigation Acts after 1823, but the Corn Laws remained in place until 1846.

The end of the Napoleonic Wars led to a period of economic depression in Britain; between 1816 and 1819 demobilized soldiers looked for work in years characterized by bad harvests, an industrial slump, and the artificially high price of bread. Amid this economic crisis, radical movements began to sprout up in Britain, as they did throughout Europe during this period. One particular demonstration that took place outside of London at Spa Fields in 1816 led Parliament to adopt what were known as the Coercion Acts, which suspended the right of habeas corpus once again and kept other laws in place that banned potentially subversive political assemblies. Political reform societies, proscribed under a wave of anti-sedition legislation that accompanied the Napoleonic Wars, began to spring up again. Women participated actively in these associations and activities, when they were not forming their own. E. P. Thompson identified Female Reform Societies in Blackburn, Preston, Bolton, Ashton-under-Lyne, and Manchester, all founded in 1818 or 1819.[13] It was in Manchester that a large demonstration took place at St Peter's Field in August 1819 which provoked an even stronger reaction than that following Spa Fields in the form of the so-called Six Acts, which imposed additional censorship on political writing and placed further restrictions on the right to assemble and bear arms. These acts represented the height of political repression against the working classes and helped sow the seeds of the reform movements that flourished for the rest of the century.

Castlereagh presented the Six Acts to Parliament on 29 November 1819 as an omnibus bill. Castlereagh refused to acknowledge the economic provenance of popular discontent, seeing any demands for change as inspired by the kind of political radicalism that had led to the blind zeal of the French Revolution. He would be proved wrong by the decline of political discontent amid the improvement in economic circumstances that generally characterized the 1820s. Meanwhile, however, Castlereagh's adamant refusal to acknowledge economic difficulties as a real problem and a source of discontent led key members of the Whig Party to rethink their own political priorities and allegiances.

Out of power for three decades, in the 1820s the Whig Party faced a dilemma that has confronted numerous political parties in the course of history – whether to change or face the possibility of remaining out of power indefinitely. The Whigs benefited from the fact that Britain itself was changing in ways that would inevitably challenge the Tory consensus, just as changes in the second half of the eighteenth century had led to the break-up of the Whig consensus.

One indication of political change in the 1820s was the growing literacy of the working classes and the political pressure they applied, despite the restrictions of the Six Acts, which had simply forced protest groups underground. An increasing number of members of the working classes became more generally aware of rural labourers who were driven off their lands as a result of enclosure, the artificially high price of bread thanks to the unpopular Corn Laws, and the abuses of the factory system. The popular radicalism of the lower classes manifested itself both in the industrial protests of the machine-smashing Luddites and the agrarian violence carried out in the name of the mythical figures of Captain Swing in England and Captain Rock in Ireland, both of which allowed the real leaders of rebellion to retain their anonymity.

Britain was also changing religiously, with the growth of nonconformity the most obvious trend, one that included much more than the rise of Methodism. For example, in Wiltshire alone the number of Baptist churches doubled from sixteen to thirty-two between 1798 and 1830, a number that would eventually reach eighty.[14] Another undercurrent of religious change was the Sunday school movement, which focused on education for workers; this movement originated in the eighteenth century and was at its height by the beginning of the 1830s. Fortunately for the British ruling classes, the Baptists and the Sunday school movement were both politically conservative, as the Methodists had been. Both the Methodists and the Baptists focused on the transformation of the individual as the road to transforming society.

Still, political rights for Dissenters remained one of the most contentious political issues of the 1820s. Even the majority of Tories were becoming convinced in the 1820s, not only that religious discrimination needed to end with a repeal of the seventeenth-century Test and Corporation Acts aimed at Protestant Dissenters, but also that Catholic emancipation was both inevitable and politically expedient. In 1823, the House of Commons voted to approve a measure that would have given Catholics the right to vote, though not to hold political office. This would have been a halfway measure on the way to emancipation, but the House of Lords rejected it by a narrow margin. Parliament repealed the Test and Corporation Acts in 1827, making the repeal of the anti-Catholic Penal Laws the next obvious item on the reform agenda that the Tories under Wellington and his home secretary, Robert Peel, had reluctantly started to embrace. They did so, however, only with the intention of controlling reform, keeping the Whigs out of power, and preventing more radical change, if not revolution.

Repealing the Penal Laws was going to be more of a hassle than repealing the Test and Corporation Acts, for a number of reasons. After the end of the Napoleonic Wars, Irish immigration began to evoke a great deal of prejudice and hostility in the industrial North of Britain. In 1829, most of the petitions against Catholic emancipation came from industrial towns located there. Glasgow alone sent twenty-one petitions with a combined 24,000 signatures against the bill.[15] The main grievance against the Irish was their willingness to perform unskilled labour at low wages. But the Irish also made a ready target because of their Catholic faith, which still did not mesh with Protestant England. Furthermore, authorities in London increasingly viewed the Irish poor as a drain on the state and a potential danger to public order. Concomitantly, writers on crime started to portray the Irish in stereotypical terms as generally violent and lawless.

With anti-Irish prejudice a major factor, Wellington did not have the full support of his party for the repeal of the Penal Laws, which he steered through Parliament in 1829. In doing so, he split his party and paved the way for the first Whig government in four decades. In 1830, King William IV succeeded his deceased brother George IV. The Whigs took advantage of the election called in conjunction with the beginning of a new reign to oust the divided Tories from power. The Whig Party that assumed control of the government under the aristocrat Lord Grey in 1830 now had a much broader agenda and mandate than it had even a decade earlier, one that included social and economic reform in addition to the long overdue political reforms needed to give more property owners the right to vote and redress the inequities in parliamentary representation caused by population shifts associated with the growth of the manufacturing sector. Once in power, the Whig government would go on to pass Britain's first Factory Act limiting children's working hours in 1833, a controversial New Poor Law in 1834 establishing a system of workhouses for the unemployed and indigent, and a Municipal Corporations Act in 1835 standardizing a more democratic form of government for all municipalities. By far, however, the most well-known legislative act of the Whigs was the Great Reform Act of 1832, which expanded the size of the electorate, redistributed some parliamentary seats in accordance with population trends, and eliminated many unpopulated 'rotten' boroughs that had continued to send representatives – usually handpicked by a local magnate – to Parliament.

The passage of the Great Reform Bill appears a relatively moderate and conservative measure in retrospect, but contemporaries certainly did not see it that way. The outbreak of a cholera epidemic in 1831 had pointed to a greater need for social reform and created an atmosphere of fear and hysteria that seeped into the political realm. The established church for the most part opposed the bill; twenty-two of twenty-four bishops in the House of Lords voted against the measure. Clerical opposition to the Reform Bill provoked a strong reaction against the established church in what was increasingly becoming a culture war that had strong religious as well as political overtones.[16] For those committed to the Church of England, the Great Reform Bill has to be seen in the context of the repeal of the Test and Corporation Acts and the Penal Laws, in which it became another stage in the erosion of the ordered hierarchy of altar and throne. As important as these political changes were, however, they were largely overshadowed by the social and economic changes associated with the next stage of the Industrial Revolution.

The coming of the railway and the next stage of the Industrial Revolution

Already in the seventeenth century coal had begun to replace timber as the main fuel used for cooking and heat in Britain (the Irish relied heavily on peat). The demand for coal had increased during the eighteenth century with greater urbanization, the growth of iron manufacturing, and the improvement of transportation networks, particularly the building of canals, which made it easier to transport heavy material. Lower taxes on coal in London and other cities also helped to increase demand.[17] The first railways used tracks that allowed miners to transport heavy loads of coal more efficiently to waterways where they could be more efficiently transported than over land. In the eighteenth century, the first steam engines to power the movement of heavy wagons of coal were stationary. Then in the early nineteenth century Richard Trevithick built a steam locomotive that he designed to move along rails. Trevithick's locomotive was first put into practice in 1804, moving ten tonnes of iron about 12.5 miles from Merthyr Tydfil to Pontypridd in South Wales. Still, the rails were not robustly built until wrought iron was used in their manufacture, starting in 1808. By the end of the decade collieries throughout Britain had started to use steam locomotives instead of horses to haul coal. Eventually the railways began to replace water transport as the main means of transporting coal from one part of Britain to another. By 1830, a railway boom was underway that would see the construction of most of the main rail lines that connected the country by mid-century.

Even though the demand for coal and iron antedated the railway's transportation of the material, the coming of the railway called forth an incredible demand for both iron and coal, as did the manufacture of machinery, ships, and war material. Fortunately, Britain possessed vast quantities of both natural resources, iron being abundant in South Wales and the Mendip Hills in southwestern England. The Dowlais iron works, located near the Welsh village of Merthyr Tydfil, was founded in 1759 and the Blaenavon iron works in 1789, inter alia. By 1845 Dowlais had 7,300 workers and was producing 88,400 tonnes of iron annually.

The railway appealed to investors' imaginations as much as it did to their pocketbooks; at the initial phase of the railway age, companies such as the famous Stockton and Darlington paid a return in the neighbourhood of 10 per cent, an attractive number compared to the 3.4 per cent return that Eric Hobsbawm estimated public stocks brought in the 1830s.[18] But the combination of over investment and the costs of construction had reduced the rate of return by the 1850s to perhaps 5 per cent or less, and many people lost money in a mania for railway stocks in the 1840s that resembled the South Sea Bubble of 1720. Clark and Jacks propose that the main growth area of the economy continued to be cotton textiles and that, since textile manufacturing did not rely excessively on coal, the abundance of coal supplies in Britain was actually incidental to the occurrence of the Industrial Revolution there, and that too much emphasis has been placed upon coal and iron as the driving impetuses of the economy.[19]

Industry in the British Isles in fact encompassed much more than cotton textiles and the railway; the linen textile industry was also robust, particularly in Ireland and Scotland, while copper and tin mining supplemented that of iron and coal. Manufacturing encompassed everything from children's toys to weapons. Shipbuilding remained strong throughout the nineteenth century; the most famous ship works included the Thompson and Kirwan Company and Harland and Wolf in Belfast, the Neptune Works in Waterford, and Austin and Son in Sunderland. Josiah Wedgwood's Etruria pottery works in Staffordshire and the Waterford Crystal Factory in Ireland were prototypes for industrial organizations using highly skilled labour. Everyday household items started to become popular, increasing demand in a number of trades and industries. The increase in population necessitated more housing and industries associated with construction, and not solely for the workers who crowded into the factory towns. The wealth accumulated by early industrial entrepreneurs stimulated the construction of lavish and expensive mansions, while middle-class managers and other professionals such as lawyers, physicians, teachers, and civil servants who benefited from the wealth created by industry needed or desired new residences as well.

Responses to industrialization and social change in the late eighteenth and early nineteenth centuries

The Industrial Revolution had made Britain the leading economic power in the world and provided employment for a rising population, but it had come at a tremendous social cost. In the preface to his 1794 novel, *Caleb Williams*, the British political theorist William Godwin wrote that 'the question now afloat in the world respecting THINGS AS THEY ARE is the most interesting that can be presented to the human mind'.[20] One of the main characters, Mr Falkland, attempts to persuade the vile landlord Tyrell that the need for some kind of hierarchy in society does not justify the oppression of the lower orders. 'It makes one's heart ache to think', Falkland tells Tyrell, 'that one man is born to the inheritance of every superfluity, while the whole share of another, without any demerit of his, is drudgery and starving; and that all this is indispensable.' Falkland continues:

> We that are rich, Mr. Tyrell, must do everything in our power to lighten the yoke of these unfortunate people. We must not use the advantage that accident has given us with an unmerciful hand. Poor Wretches! They are pressed almost beyond bearing as it is; and, if we unfeelingly give another turn to the machine, they will be crushed to atoms.[21]

This speech is consistent with the following passage from Godwin's *Enquiry Concerning Political Justice*:

> Few things have contributed more to undermine the energy and virtue of the human species, than the supposition that we have a right, as it has been phrased, to do what we will with our own. It is thus that the miser, who accumulates to no end that which diffused would have conduced to the welfare of thousands, that the luxurious man, who wallows in indulgence and sees numerous families around him pining in beggary, never fail to tell us of their rights, and to silence animadversion and quiet the censure of their own minds, by observing, 'that they came fairly into possession of their wealth, that they owe no debts, and that of consequence no man has authority to enquire into their private manner of disposing of that which appertains to them'.[22]

In *Caleb Williams*, Falkland is so outraged by Tyrell's insensitivity to the plight of other human beings that he ends up committing murder, perhaps a warning from Godwin not only to the Tyrells of the world but also to those sympathetic to Godwin's point of view not to let the inhumanity of the oppressors lead them to inhuman acts themselves.

In 1822 the Scottish writer John Galt published a novel called *The Entail*, which provides a bucolic version of rural life. In this novel, Galt contrasts the simplicity of life in rural Ayrshire with the busyness and materialistic concerns of Glasgow and Edinburgh. Glasgow and Edinburgh were both old cities, with Glasgow becoming more of an industrial centre in the early nineteenth century, but the growth of cities with industrialization had only served, in Galt's view, to highlight the fundamental differences between rural and urban life. He wrote at a time when industrial work had brought about a greater degree of psychological separation between workers from employers and furthered the trend in the direction of a more competitive, individualized society. Hogg's *Private Memoirs and Confessions of a Justified Sinner* has also been taken to exemplify the disillusionment of an author who moved from the countryside to find a world of inverted and perverted values.[23]

In Percy Bysshe Shelley's poem 'Helas', published the same year as Galt's novel, he predicts the rise of another Athens as Britain prepared to take up its role on the world's stage as its next great empire. Yet just when one thinks that this is a development of which the poet approves, we read the lines:

> O cease! must hate and death return?
> Cease! must men kill and die?
> Cease! drain not its dregs the urn
>   Of bitter prophesy!
> The world is weary of the past –
> O might it die or rest at last! (ll. 37–42)

After surveying ancient history, Shelley was left doubting whether the glories of Athens had justified the suffering that its rise to power had entailed and wondering whether Britain was going down the right path. The romantic poet Lord Byron also turned to the past for the subjects of much of his poetry as a means towards commenting on the present. In 'The Corsair', which sold 10,000 copies the day it was published in 1814, Byron presents a story about a beneficent prince, in which he incorporates much of his romantic appreciation of life in the past, as well as the need to appreciate nature and the present moment. For example, he describes the majestic beauty of a Greek sunset:

> Slow sinks, more lovely ere his race be run,
> Along Morea's hills the Setting Sun;
> Not, as in Northern climes, obscurely bright,
> But one unclouded blaze of living light! (ll. 1169–72)

Byron's romantic nature was attracted to the southern European appreciation of nature for its own sake contrasted with the analytical and utilitarian approach towards nature that seemed to characterize British culture and society at the time.

William Blake addressed the age's veneration of science and its relegation of Christianity to the realm of superstition in his poem 'The Everlasting Gospel':

> Like Dr. Priestly and Bacon and Newton –
> Poor spiritual knowledge is not worth a button
> For thus the Gospel Sir Isaac confutes:
> 'God can only be known by his attributes;
> And as for the indwelling of the Holy Ghost,
> Or of Christ and His Father, it's all a boast
> And pride, and vanity of the imagination,
> That disdains to follow this world's fashion.' (ll. 112–19)

For Blake, the age's emphasis on science and experimentation had rendered the central teachings of Jesus moot:

> To teach doubt and experiment
> Certainly was not what Christ meant. (ll. 120–1)

Perhaps the most successful, and certainly the most famous, cautionary tale regarding science and experimentation from the early nineteenth century came in the form of Mary Shelley's novel, *Frankenstein or The Modern Prometheus* (1818). When Dr Frankenstein, the narrator of the novel and creator of the monster who has come to bear his name in popular culture, arrives in Ingolstadt to study, he says that he encounters two different views of science: one sympathetic to an older more medieval and mystical approach characterized by the works of Albertus Magnus, Paracelsus, and Agrippa, the second hostile to learning from the past. Frankenstein becomes enamoured of the second view and becomes obsessed with his desire to create life by artificial means – passing an electrical current through a human being that he has fashioned from the body parts of different corpses. Shelley's novel takes a dramatic turn when Frankenstein rejects the being he has brought to life, creating an existential crisis in the creature himself, who rejected and abandoned by his creator and finding no place in or warmth from human society, lusts for revenge against Frankenstein and human beings in general. Shelley, the daughter of William Godwin and Mary Wollstonecraft and wife of Percy Bysshe Shelley, wrote *Frankenstein* at the age of twenty-one as a 'ghost story' that was part of a friendly competition. However, the novel, whether Shelley intended to or not, raises profound questions about what it means to be human, the morality of science and technology that fails to consider human costs, and the responsibility of society to its constituent parts.

Mary Shelley and the romantic poets lived in an age in which those who could not afford to pay their debts were still sent to prison for their failure to do so. In 1802 James Neild offered an account of the conditions in debtors' prisons throughout England and Wales. Conditions varied, but the worst of them he described were quite dreadful:

> The debtors have only one square courtyard, about 19 square feet. The women lodge in the common day-room. No bedding, or even straw to lie upon. No mops, brooms or pails, to keep the prison clean. No fire in the winter; the casements rotting off their hinges, and scarce a whole pane of glass in the windows. Out of the nine poor wretches who were confined, seven of them were half-cloathed, three very ill, and without any medical assistance whatever.[24]

Many of the early responses to industrialization among the workers came not from the factory hands, who in the period from 1789 to 1832 remained a minority of the working class, but from workers outside the factory system who felt threatened by it. Thomas Hardy, the founder of the London Corresponding Society (1792), a workers' association, was a shoemaker. The Luddites, almost by definition, consisted of traditional workers such as handloom weavers threatened by the invention of the power loom by Edmund Cartwright in 1785. In industrial Glasgow, as late as 1831 it was thought that perhaps more than 24,000 of the 36,000 textile workers in the city worked outside of the factory system.[25] In Britain as a whole in 1833 most male weavers remained handloom weavers, with women working almost all of the power looms and constituting over half of the workforce employed in textile factories. Furthermore, factories varied in size from small mills employing perhaps two or three dozen workers to large-scale operations with hundreds on the payroll, so factory workers did not yet conceive that they had solidarity with one another, let alone the wherewithal to organize effectively at this time.

Among those who defended modern society and industrialization, Jeremy Bentham (1748–1832) stands out as the founder of the philosophy of utilitarianism, which exerted a strong influence on the thinking of the middle classes in the nineteenth century. Bentham based his philosophy on the assumption that pain and pleasure were the two guiding principles of human behaviour. The virtue of utilitarianism was supposed to be that it provided a rational basis for decision making for individuals and society as a whole based on an arithmetical calculation of the likely consequences with regard to pain and pleasure of a particular decision. In Bentham's own words:

> By the principle of utility is meant that principle which approves or disapproves of every action whatsoever, according to the tendency which it appears to have to augment or diminish the happiness of the party whose interest is in question: or, what is the same thing in other words, to promote or to oppose that happiness. I say of every action whatsoever and therefore not only of every action of a private individual, but of every measure of government.[26]

David Ricardo extended many of the principles of Adam Smith in his work on economic theory, *The Principles of Political Economy* (1817). Ricardo stated his ideas as if they were scientific principles, but in reality they provided a justification for a capitalistic society in which it was considered irrational to raise workers' wages beyond the minimum that they would accept because it would cut into the profits of business. He treated labour as an abstract phenomenon in a mathematical equation without considering the individual human beings who fell into that category. Ricardo thought that employers had an obligation only to provide workers with subsistence wages that would allow them to 'propagate their race', consistent with his tendency to view workers as a collectivity rather than as individuals. And subsistence wages were only necessary in order to ensure a future supply of workers for their employers; in other words, workers existed to service an economy that benefited their employers instead of themselves. But wages have to be tied to the prices of the commodities necessary to keep the workers alive and healthy enough to work and have children. According to Ricardo's 'iron law of wages', wages would rise when the price of those items necessary for their subsistence rose and fall when the prices of those items declined.

William Cobbett offered an alternative perspective, providing a radical critique of the new industrial society. Unlike Ricardo, he treated the working classes as individuals with their own minds and appealed to them on that basis. However, Cobbett represented a backward-looking strain of radicalism that gave into nostalgia instead of providing a practical solution to the problems of the lower classes. His *Rural Rides* (1830) was based on a journey that he took on horseback through southern England to observe what he believed, sadly, was a social world on the verge of extinction. If there was any solution for the members of the working classes in Cobbett's philosophy it had to be an individualistic one based on self-help and a return to traditional values in the face of an oppressively modernizing society.

Finally, William Hazlitt (1778–1830), whose lifetime spanned almost exactly the period covered by this chapter, attempted to combine the best ideals of the Enlightenment and the French Revolution with his critique of contemporary industrial society. In *The Spirit of the Age* (1824), Hazlitt criticized the pessimistic demographic calculations of Thomas Malthus, from which the thought of the 'dismal scientists' like Ricardo had been derived. Hazlitt was a witty essayist, who delighted in pointing out the contradictions in people's beliefs and the hypocrisy that accompanied the disjunction between most people's words and actions; he once wrote that 'it is essential to the triumph of reform that it shall never succeed'. In this statement, he could have been predicting the fate of the Whig Party after its apparent triumph in the Great Reform Act of 1832 or the ongoing efforts at reform that would characterize British political culture during the Victorian period, which would last for the remainder of the nineteenth century.

FIGURE 24 *Irish politician and activist Daniel O'Connell (1775–1847, centre) arrives to take his seat in Parliament after the passing of the Catholic Emancipation Act in April 1829. The act made Catholics eligible for a wide range of public offices including that of Member of Parliament. Looking on from the middle distance are the British prime minister, the Duke of Wellington (1769–1852), and home secretary and leader of the House of Commons, Sir Robert Peel (1788–1850).*

Hulton Archive/Getty.

12

The Victorian period:

Politics, society, and culture in the nineteenth century

There is, I speak humbly, in common with Natural Evidence, in the study of Living History, a gradual approximation to a consciousness that we are growing into a perception of the workings of the Almighty Ruler of the World; that we are growing able to justify the Eternal Wisdom, and by that justification to approve ourselves His children; that we are coming to see, not only in His ruling of His Church in her spiritual character, but in His overruling of the world, to which His act of redemption has given a new and all-interesting character to His own people, a hand of justice and mercy, a hand of progress and order, a kind and wise disposition, ever leading the world on to do better, but never forcing, and out of the evil of man's working bringing continually that which is good.

WILLIAM STUBBS, *Lectures on Medieval and Modern History* (1887)

Political change from the First Great Reform Act to the repeal of the Corn Laws: 1832–1850

The passage of the Great Reform Bill in 1832 had caused a great deal of consternation among Britain's ruling classes, had provoked a constitutional crisis, and was accompanied by the threat of revolution from the lower orders if it failed to pass. However, Patrick Joyce has recently argued that the First Great Reform Act represented a '*closing down* not an opening up of real democracy', in other words, a missed opportunity to provide a heightened degree of greater political participation.[1]

[handwritten top margin: 4 Started a trend of legislation that didn't help]

[handwritten top right: It did in fact change, but not enough for a difference]

The Act had expanded the electorate, but only by about 300,000 voters so that the vote was still restricted to less than 6 per cent of the total population, with women still totally excluded. Indeed, to the increasingly thoughtful and articulate skilled labourers, the law had simply bolstered those who held capital and clout with increased political leverage, while the continued absence of secret ballots meant that bribery would remain commonplace, giving the wealthiest manufacturers ample opportunity to throw around their financial weight. Prior to its passage, workers and employers both had at least one thing in common – their opposition to the vested interests of the aristocracy – which they no longer shared.

[handwritten left margin: Was suppose to help the lower class, but really didn't]

In addition, the social legislation of the 1830s that was intended to benefit the workers failed to do so. The Factory Act of 1833 applied only to child labour and was virtually unenforceable at the time, while the New Poor Law of 1834 generally proved detrimental to the well-being of the working classes. The workhouses that it mandated for poor and sick men, women, and children were intentionally designed to be unpleasant places that separated families and imposed a strict regime of manual labour and moral discipline. The whole objective of the workhouses was to make them so unattractive an option that people would only resort to the shelter they offered if absolutely necessary. In this the law succeeded, and some refused to go there even as a last resort, risking or choosing death as a preferable alternative. The intellectual milieu for the passage of the New Poor Law was the seriousness with which the authorities took the apocalyptic predictions on population issued by Thomas Malthus. This was a small consolation, of course, to the individuals who endured that misery.

[handwritten left margin: they wanted people in the workhouses ended with death]

In 1834 Lord Melbourne (1779–1848) replaced Lord Grey as prime minister; his home secretary, John Russell, was determined to carry out further reforms, such as ending state support for the Protestant Church of Ireland. Russell's pro-Catholic sympathies enabled him to reach a modus vivendi with Daniel O'Connell, the charismatic leader of the Catholic Association who wanted to see the Act of Union repealed and Home Rule granted to Ireland. In advocating such reforms as the disestablishment of the Church of Ireland, Russell had gone beyond the ken of his own party and in May 1834 Melbourne faced an internal party revolt that included the resignation of four cabinet members and the overt displeasure of some forty Whig MPs. King William IV asked for Melbourne's resignation, but was left with no choice but to call for him after the Whigs won a large majority in the subsequent parliamentary election.

[handwritten left margin: two big extremes actually gave upper class more power]

Henceforth, Melbourne became more interested in administration than in legislation; the reform agenda of the Whigs largely broke down under his leadership. Then, in 1837, in the middle of Melbourne's second administration, King William IV died of a heart attack; the death of a monarch necessitated a general election according to custom. His successor, Queen Victoria, reigned until 1901 and provided a backdrop for the political stability and economic dominance to which the UK could lay claim for the rest of the century. In the 1837 election, the Conservatives gained forty seats in the House of Commons and had an outright majority of the English seats, meaning that Melbourne and the Whigs could continue to hold power only as long as they received support from O'Connell and his Irish supporters.

[handwritten left margin: Also legislation intended to help workers didn't help]

While these political developments were unfolding, three men – Francis Place, William Lovett, and Henry Hetherington – founded the London Working Men's

Association in 1836. Two years later they issued a *People's Charter*, containing a reform programme that included universal male suffrage, annually elected parliaments, secret ballots, the abolition of property qualifications and payment for MPs, as well as proportional electoral districts. Chartism, as the movement became known after 1838, emerged from a decade that had seen a radical transformation in British society that reinforced the importance of politics. This can also be seen in the formation of the Anti-Corn Law League in 1839, which allowed for women's membership, and in the formation of approximately 150 women's political associations and societies that formed around the same time. Chartist women were left to form their own organizations, leading one to conclude that the middle classes were a bit less chauvinistic at the time than the leaders of working-class activism. Still, this did not stop Chartist women from participating equally in demonstrations or making speeches in support of the movement, even to the point of encouraging violence and risking arrest.[2] The Chartist movement stemmed from a wing of working-class radicalism that looked to the future and collectivist solutions in the political realm as opposed to the backward-looking individualistic approach of someone like William Cobbett. The difficulty of organizing the fractious working classes provided one obstacle to the success of the Chartist movement. In addition, most workers were more interested in economic issues as opposed to politics.

Melbourne did not respond well to the Chartists, primarily because he had come to fear political radicalism and was committed to upholding the status quo rather than to introducing further political reform. Melbourne's scandalous personal life did not help his reputation; he was known to engage in unusual sexual activity with a number of aristocratic ladies and also seemed to delight in whipping the orphan girls he 'rescued'. Politically, however, Melbourne may have helped to save Britain from revolution by agreeing to enough reform measures to prevent revolution while resisting change strongly enough to satisfy the ruling classes. Melbourne not only opposed the introduction of the secret ballot, but referred to the Reform Act as 'the foolishest thing ever done'.

The most immediate effect of the passage of the Reform Act was the constitutional precedent established when Grey persuaded King William IV to threaten the appointment of enough peers to ensure the bill's passage if the House of Lords proved choleric. Perhaps largely for this reason, Wellington, despite his own participation in the repeal of the Test and Corporation Acts and Penal Laws, saw the 1832 measure as being of immense significance: 'Power is transferred from one class of society, the gentlemen of England, professing the faith of the Church of England, to another class, the shopkeepers, being Dissenters from the Church.'[3] Such fears help to explain why Melbourne also opposed allowing nonconformists to attend Oxford or Cambridge. The Whig politician and historian Thomas Babington Macaulay defended the Reform Act, which had brought the wealthier members of the middle class into the political system but excluded everyone else, including the workers, on the grounds that the middle class was best positioned to steer Britain into a prosperous future. The Chartists, by stark contrast, laid out a political programme to which future workers could aspire despite enormous limitations; with the exception of annually elected parliaments, all of the demands of the Chartists came to pass eventually.

For a brief period in 1834–5, Robert Peel, Wellington's home secretary and the man responsible for reorganizing London's police force, members of which are still referred to as 'bobbies' in his honour, served as prime minister, a position he would take up again in 1834. In 1834, lacking the support of a majority in the House of Commons, Peel attempted to unite the country through his Tamworth Manifesto, issued at the beginning of his administration. He began by acknowledging the Tory Party's acceptance of the Great Reform Act. Peel stated emphatically that he considered the Reform Bill to be 'a final and irrevocable settlement of a great constitutional question – a settlement which no friend to the peace and welfare of this country would attempt to disturb, either by direct or by insidious means'. Peel thus began to steer his party in a moderately conservative direction away from its marked reactionary spirit and ethos.

Undoubtedly, the greatest exigency that Peel faced upon returning to his post as prime minister in 1841 was the growing controversy over the Corn Laws. The Anti-Corn Law League sought to overturn legislation that, to the middle classes, had caused wages to rise by artificially inflating the price of bread. This protectionist legislation violated their quasi-religious devotion to the economic doctrine of free trade and the laissez-faire economics of Adam Smith; the league's leaders, Richard Cobden and John Bright, believed that the repeal of the Corn Laws would usher in a utopian age of free trade that would finally see the vision of the industrialists for a prosperous and beneficent future eclipse the superannuated dominance of the aristocracy over the nation's political life.

Robert Peel knew that the Corn Laws needed to be repealed and he assumed that the rest of his party would come to realize this too. He waited, however, for the expedient moment to propose repeal; he finally informed his cabinet on 2 December 1845, with famine threatening in Ireland, that he supported the repeal of the Corn Laws. In doing so, Peel created as large a rift not only in the Tory Party but also in the aristocracy than any which had occurred since the English Civil War. Many members of the party, including Lord George Bentinck, who had been a quiet and anonymous backbencher until Peel announced his decision to repeal, and Benjamin Disraeli, a maverick politician who had begun his career as a Radical, felt blind-sided when Peel announced his decision. Disraeli argued that the Corn Laws helped to preserve the balance between the landed agricultural interests and the growing economic strength of the manufacturers, something he believed necessary for a holistic society.

Disraeli had been a member of a group calling itself Young England that called for a reinvigoration of the country through the rise of heroes who would lead and serve as exemplars for the rest of the population. In his novel *Coningsby* (1844), he defended the interests of the aristocracy and made the case for their continued leadership of the country. In his 1846 novel, *Sybil*, Disraeli put forward his conception of Tory Democracy in which the aristocracy, not the bourgeoisie, had the true interests of the people in mind. The aristocracy, he argued, ruled out of a sense of stewardship as opposed to the self-interested rule of the middle class. Disraeli's opinion of the 1832 Reform Act was complex and helps to illuminate his political philosophy. On the one hand, he did not believe it had brought about any amelioration in the conditions of the working classes and had instead enshrined class interests as the defining reality of mid-nineteenth-century British politics. On the other hand, he saw the potential in the Reform Act for encouraging the members of the lower classes to believe that they might someday participate in the political process. As this exigency had not yet occurred, he regarded the power of the aristocracy as the main check on middle-class self-interest, a principle that he sought to uphold in his defence of the Corn Laws.

On 28 May 1846 the House of Lords voted by a majority of forty-six to approve the bill repealing the Corn Laws. Peel had won the battle, but at great cost to his career; in June Queen Victoria asked John Russell to once again form a government. Meanwhile, Disraeli's political strategy failed to pay off at the polls, leaving the Whig Party regnant for most of the next four decades. Furthermore, defence of the Corn Laws seemed a particularly quixotic cause on which to take a stand. The rest of the British economy operated according to the principle of free trade and Peel had already begun steering the party in that direction before he came out against the Corn Laws. The Tories' best chance of remaining in power was to acknowledge defeat on this issue and adjust their philosophy accordingly, just as Peel had done in response to the Great Reform Act. The Tories who opposed repeal largely did so on symbolic, not economic, grounds, which actually made their opposition more implacable. Their continued support for the Corn Laws in the face of events unfolding in Ireland, however, reveals a political obstinacy that almost defies rational explanation.

Ireland: Famine, migration, and Irish nationalism

Towards the end of the summer of 1845 a deadly killer fungus named *phythopthora infestans* travelled from the United States to Ireland; it was a fungus that was fond of potatoes and rendered them completely inedible. Unfortunately, potatoes happened to be the main subsistence crop on which much of the Irish peasantry depended for their livelihood, their health, and their survival.

Contrary to what some might think, the Catholic peasantry had become, at least in some parts of Ireland, more sophisticated in their agricultural techniques so that in the 1830s some of the most prosperous lands on the island were in regions dominated by Catholics, not Protestants. Protestant settlers often preferred less populated lands to those that might have been more fertile but contained too many native Catholics.[4] But prosperity was not spread over the entire island, which experienced food shortages in 1839 and again in 1842. Parliament had passed an Irish Poor Law in 1838 creating a system of workhouses for Ireland, but these did not provide adequate relief during periods of scarcity. In 1845, as autumn approached, Peel immediately responded by making secret arrangements to purchase 100,000 tonnes of American corn from the United States to try to alleviate the pending crisis. Although the grain did not arrive until late January, the Irish had enough resources to avoid a catastrophic number of deaths during the winter.

A second year of the potato blight, however, was an unmitigated disaster. Local relief agencies were supposed to supplement the efforts of the national government; they helped but were quickly overwhelmed by the enormity of the crisis. In November 1845 Peel had created a relief commission to administer food distribution. He placed Sir Randolph Rough, who had experience providing food for the British army in Canada, in charge of this commission. The head of the Treasury, Charles Trevelyan, has taken most of the abuse from historians for the government's failure to do more to stop the famine from getting worse and to assist those who were already starving;

deservedly so, for in the first year of the famine he refused a request from Rough to buy additional corn from America. Still, by August 1846 the British had imported into Ireland from America 20,000 tonnes of corn and oats, costing a total of £185,000.[5]

It did not prove to be enough. Nor did an attempt to organize a system of public works to allow the Irish poor to earn money prove an adequate response to the crisis. Work and jobs did not matter if there was no food to purchase with one's pay. Therefore, in January 1847 the government passed a Temporary Relief Act, also known as the Soup Kitchen Act. The key word, however, was 'temporary', as the government believed that the main solution was to allow the Irish Poor Law to do its work and make the Irish responsible for their own aid.

Committed as it was to free trade and laissez-faire economics, the Liberal government had a difficult time reconciling its economic philosophy with the kind of governmental response that would have been necessary to substantially alter the course of the Great Famine. Meanwhile, the second year of crop failure attracted greater levels of international attention to the calamity. American citizens responded to the famine with a significant amount of aid to Ireland, and they were joined by others around the world. Religious charities in Britain and Ireland also increased aid, with the Quakers in particular coming to the fore, though the Anglican and Catholic churches also made substantial charitable contributions. These contributions, however, still could not match the aid of the state, which in and of itself did not prevent the greatest demographic crisis in Ireland's history. By the end of the winter of 1847, death and starvation seemed to be everywhere. The Great Famine resulted in about a million Irish deaths and the migration of another million from the island in the years immediately following; the after-effects led to a steady pace of migration from the island for the rest of the nineteenth century. Ireland simply did not have enough industry to absorb those forced off the land by economic circumstances.

Irish migrants who had worked only on the land in Ireland had to find new jobs in factories and in the streets or docks in the cities of Britain and America. When the social reformer Henry Mayhew wrote his classic sociological survey *London Labour and the London Poor* in 1861 he found that the English peddlers and costermongers of London showed an obvious prejudice to the Irish among their ranks; Mayhew estimated that there were 10,000 Irish street sellers in London at that time.[6] The lack of opportunities and discrimination that the Irish faced abroad, especially in the United States, contributed to growing support for the Irish nationalist cause, which had already begun to attract backing from Irish-Americans because of the strong belief among many of the Irish that the British were to blame for the famine. It did not help that some in England believed that the Irish were responsible for their own problems, regarding them as generally more slothful and less industrious than the English.

A rise in literacy since the 1820s had already changed the crucible of Irish political protest from sporadic agrarian violence to the more ambitious and organized programme of the nationalist movement known as Young Ireland. Young Ireland failed to attract much support in the 1840s, largely because people do not care about political causes when they are trying to survive, but it left a legacy, along with the famine, that would greatly increase the appeal of Irish political and cultural nationalism as the century went on. It was just that the tactics of Young Ireland were too tame for a younger brand of radicals affected by the famine and desperate to do something about the plight of their homeland. Among the leaders of the newly founded Irish Republican Brotherhood, also known as the Fenians, were James Stephens and John O'Mahony, who had learnt from French radicals who had participated in the Revolution of 1848 in Paris. In the end, however, the Fenians could come up with no more viable strategy than the failed stratagem of Young Ireland. The movement stalled until 1867, when they made an ill-fated attempt at revolution, which also failed, but did create martyrs for their movement and elicited further sympathy for the Irish nationalist cause.

Ireland suffered most during the 1840s, but the decade was also a period of dearth for Britain. Scotland's poor law was passed in 1845 amid its own economic crisis that saw a quarter of its population on poor relief. The Scots organized an extensive system of foster care in order to prevent orphaned children from having to enter the Scottish workhouses. In England, the decade known as the 'hungry forties' was characterized by poor harvests, escalating food prices, rising unemployment rates, and declining wages. A report issued in 1842 by Edwin Chadwick, the secretary of the Poor Law Commission, drew a strong correlation between diseases such as typhus, dysentery, and tuberculosis and the overcrowded and unsanitary districts in Britain's growing cities. A growing sense of discontent brought about by similar conditions contributed to the wave of revolutions that rolled over Europe in 1848; England avoided revolution, but the works of popular novelists – especially those of Charles Dickens – reflected a growing awareness of and dissatisfaction with the problems afflicting the new industrial society and the free-market economy that supported it.

Charles Dickens and mid-nineteenth-century literary responses to industrial society

No writer has done more to influence our perceptions of Victorian society in the middle of the nineteenth century than Charles Dickens. Dickens was not intrinsically opposed to industrialization or the amenities of modern life that it brought to the middle and upper classes, but he took issue with the philosophies of Malthus, Bentham, and Ricardo that considered the welfare of the population as opposed to the good of the poor, economic laws rather than moral imperatives, facts rather than feelings, the head with no consideration for the heart.

In Dickens's *A Christmas Carol* (1843), when Ebenezer Scrooge asks his nephew Fred derisively what good Christmas had ever done him, Fred responds that 'there are many things from which I might have derived good, by which I have not profited, I dare say, ... Christmas among the rest'. The speech that follows reflects why Dickens put so much stock in Christmas as the holiday that most thoroughly embraced the virtues that he thought were missing in the prevailing philosophy of his age. To Dickens, Christmas was

a kind, forgiving, charitable, pleasant time: the only time I know of, in the long calendar of the year, when men and women seem by one consent to open their shut-up hearts freely, and to think of people below them as if they really were fellow-passengers to the grave, and not another race of creatures bound on other journeys.

This passage accords with an observation made by the German socialist Friedrich Engels in his study of the *Condition of the Working-Class in England in 1844* that, under the new industrial system, 'population becomes centralised just as capital does; and, very naturally, since the human being, the worker, is regarded in manufacture simply as a piece of capital for the use of which the manufacturer pays interest under the name of wages'. Engels recognized the necessary items that industry produced for people and the jobs that it provided, but he hated that people trained to work in the mills had acquired the skills necessary to manufacture goods for the benefit of society and the profits of the factory owners, only to have those same factory owners reduce their wages, cut their hours, or lay them off if the economy slowed and then fire any workers who dared to protest or strike in order to obtain higher wages, better working conditions, or greater job security. Dickens was probably unaware of Engel's work, which was not translated into English until 1885, but he shared the same sentiments and described the capitalist class in similar terms. When Scrooge is asked for a charitable donation for the poor who, he is told, would rather die than submit to the horrors of contemporary prisons and workhouses, the miser responds that they should die then and 'decrease the surplus population'.

Dickens further explored the attitudes of the middle class towards the workers in *Hard Times* (1854):

For the first time in her life Louisa had come into one of the dwellings of the Coketown Hands: for the first time in her life she was face to face with anything like individuality in connection with them. She knew of their existence by hundreds and by thousands. She knew what results in work a given number of them would produce in a given space of time. She knew them in crowds passing to and from their nests, like ants or beetles. But she knew from her reading infinitely more of the ways of toiling insets than of these toiling men and women.

Something to be worked so much and paid so much and there ended; something to be infallibly settled by laws of supply and demand; something that blundered against those laws and floundered into difficulty; something that was a little pinched when wheat was dear and overate itself when wheat was cheap; something that increased at such a rate of percentage, and yielded such another percentage of crime, and such another percentage of pauperism; something wholesale, of which vast fortunes were made; something that occasionally rose like a sea, and did some harm and waste (chiefly to itself), and fell again; this she knew the Coketown Hands to be. But she had scarcely thought more of separating them into units than of separating the sea itself into its component drops.[7]

A mill owner in Elizabeth Gaskell's novel *Mary Barton* (1848) compares his factory workers to 'cruel brutes', saying 'they are more like wild beasts than human beings'. In her 1861 novel, *Silas Marner*, George Eliot captured inimitably the connection between worker and machine that led them to become dehumanized, sometimes even in their own minds. Eliot compares work of the weaver, Marner, to that of an insect:

> He seemed to weave, like the spider, from pure impulse, without reflection ... Silas, in his solitude, had to provide his own breakfast, dinner, and supper, to fetch his own water from the well, and put his own kettle on the fire; and all these immediate promptings helped, along with the weaving, to reduce his life to the unquestioning activity of a spinning insect.[8]

Dickens's populist sympathies were also exemplified in his distrust of the government, along with businessmen, seeing politicians, and public officials as allies of the manufacturers, mutually benefiting at the expense of the people. In *Hard Times*, Coketown's representative in the House of Commons is a man named Gradgrind, who also oversees a school whose curriculum is dominated by useful 'facts' and shuns any impulse towards creativity or imagination. Gradgrind's daughter, Louisa, is married to the mayor of Coketown, a wealthy mill owner named Josiah Bounderby. Bounderby frequently avers that if he were to give his workers a raise they would soon be expecting to eat turtle soup with a golden spoon; similarly, in Gaskell's *Mary Barton*, the mill owners take a hard line against the workers, fearing that any pay raise will only embolden the workers to ask for more and strike if they do not get their way.

Dickens himself lived a comfortable middle-class lifestyle at his home on Doughty Street in London. He believed in progress and celebrated with the rest of London the marvels of the 1851 Great Exhibition, which might be regarded as the first World's Fair. In *Barnaby Rudge* (1841), set in 1775, Dickens tells his readers 'it would be difficult for the beholder to recognize his most familiar walks in the altered aspect of little more than half a century ago'. He describes the streets in the earlier period as 'very dark', relating that

> it was no wonder that with these favouring circumstances in full and constant operation, street robberies, often accompanied by cruel wounds, and not unfrequently by loss of life, should have been of nightly occurrence in the very heart of London, or that quiet folks should have had great dread of traversing its streets after the shops were closed.[9]

But Dickens never succumbed to the complacency of his contemporary Harriet Martineau, who excused factory conditions in mid-nineteenth-century England on the basis of their efficiency and the improvement that had taken place in them over the worst conditions of the past.[10] In one of his last novels, *Our Mutual Friend* (1865), Dickens continued to satirize the middle classes who thought that the poor law and the workhouses were adequate: '"There is not", said Mr Podsnap, flushing angrily, "there is not a country in the world, sir, where so noble a provision is made for the poor as in this country"'. Just to make sure that no one would quote this passage out of context or confuse Podsnap's sentiments with his own, Dickens added a postscript to the novel in which he cited a recent study by *The Lancet* (Report by the Lancet Sanitary Commission for Investigating the State of the Infirmaries of Workhouses) that was harshly critical of workhouse conditions. Dickens stated bluntly: 'That my view of the Poor Law may not be mistaken or represented ... I believe that there has been in England, since the days of the STUARTS, no law so often infamously administered, no law so openly violated, no law habitually so ill-supervised.'[11] In this novel, Dickens continued to attack the utilitarian philosophy of the middle class and its emphasis on money as the unifying force in society as inimical to sociability, a motif that appears as well in his earlier novels such as *Oliver Twist*, *Little Dorrit*, and *Dombey and Son*.

Dickens always allowed his readers to see the members of the working classes as individuals, including women and children. So, too, did contemporary reports such as those issued by the Children's Employment Commission (CEC) and the parliamentary reports of 'blue books' based on investigations carried out about the same time. For example, forty-year-old Jane Peacock Watson, who worked at the Ormiston colliery in Scotland, told the CEC that she had started in the mines at seven, married at seventeen, bore nine children, six of whom had survived, with two others dead at birth. Twenty-three-year-old Elizabeth Bentley of Leeds told a Parliamentary Commission that she had started in a flax-mill at the age of six, generally worked from seven in the morning till nine at night (longer when demand was high), and that she and other workers had been severely beaten for slacking off their work. But the stories of these actual people did not reach nearly as many hands as did the fictional ones penned by Dickens. Readers identified with Dickens's characters, even though most of those characters came from a lower socio-economic status than did the majority of his readers.

A fellow-novelist and business associate of Dickens, William Harrison Ainsworth (1805–82), responded to the effects of industrialization in a somewhat different vein. Ainsworth looked to the past to romanticize a history based on venerated architectural sites in novels such as *The Tower of London* (1840), *Old St. Paul's* (1841), and *Windsor Castle* (1843). Historical sites also featured prominently in weekly publications such as the *Penny Magazine* and the *Saturday Magazine*, which flourished in the 1830s and 1840s; at the apogee of its popularity the *Penny Magazine* sold 200,000 copies an issue.[12] Contemporary organizations such as the City Church and Churchyard Protection Society sought to preserve ancient churches from their demolition. In Dickens's time, while cities were expanding geographically away from their centre, older buildings were being demolished to make room for the new. Urban renovation took a particularly heavy toll on older city churches.[13] Medieval and Tudor structures were demolished to make room for the great train stations built in London in the Victorian period, including King's Cross (1852), Victoria (1860), and St Pancras (1868). In *The Condition of the Working-Class in England*, Engels commented on the great growth of the manufacturing towns and on how economies of scale and competition among builders made it easy and inexpensive to put up new constructions to meet the housing needs of cities swelled by the demand for factory labour. Ainsworth, Engels, and the founders of the CCCPS, together with Dickens and contemporary novelists such as Gaskell and Eliot, all recognized that something had been lost on the way to modern industrial society and each hoped to preserve what they thought was best from an earlier time.

In short, the Victorians were well aware that their society was changing, and with it their physical surroundings. They tended to conflate the two, leading to a desire to preserve as much as they could of the English countryside, for example, even if land was now needed more for cities, industries, and railways than for agriculture.

FIGURE 25 *Snowdon Valley railway, Wales.*
Jasonmgabriel/RooM/Getty.

Yet, the enclosure movement had largely come to an end, so that those lands that remained dedicated to agriculture relatively unchanged in the course of the Victorian period. At least something could be counted on as remaining the same, as reflected in the traditional scenes of rural life in Dorsetshire that form the basis of Thomas Hardy's novels.

The Crimean War: Britain and Europe

In 1854 the UK became engaged in a European war for the first time since 1815, this time on the side of France in opposition to Russia, whose territorial ambitions at the expense of the Ottoman Empire they perceived as threatening the delicate balance of power that had been enshrined at the Congress of Vienna. Incipient popular enthusiasm was encouraged by the press, which played both on the growing fear of the Russian bear, which by seeking to expand its influence southward was perceived as encroaching on the trade routes to India, and on the contemporary value attached to martial valour and heroism.

The Crimean War may have been the first modern war in the sense that people at home were able to follow the war on an almost daily basis for the first time in history. Not only did newspapers cover the events of the war, but they also printed first-hand accounts of experiences of participants in the war itself.[14] The government was also more forthcoming with information about the war, even the strategic plans of the military, than would have been possible in earlier conflicts or would be considered prudent in later struggles.

The Crimean War has become immortalized in literature through Alfred Lord Tennyson's 'Charge of the Light Brigade'. Although Tennyson capitalized on the public hunger for tales of excitement, adventure, and heroism, his tale of a doomed expedition of 600 men going straight into enemy fire in the valley at Balaklava offered a contrary take, emphasizing the generally unheroic nature of a war in which many more thousands died from sickness than from wounds suffered in combat.

The hopeless Charge of the Light Brigade was just one example of the maladroitness, inefficiency, dearth of planning, and poor communication that characterized the British war effort as a whole. In August 1854 the British army moved from Varna on the western shores of the Black Sea, despite being weakened by an outbreak of cholera among the troops, to the Crimean Peninsula where the Russian army awaited them. There they began an eleven-month siege of the Russian fortress at Sevastopol, during which the British army suffered grievously. Tsar Nicholas I died in early March 1855, followed by the fall of Sevastopol six months later, leading the new tsar, Alexander II, to negotiate the Treaty of Paris that ended the war in 1856. The Russians conceded lands to Moldavia and Wallachia in the Balkans and agreed to permit all neutral commercial ships access to the Black Sea, while Britain and France guaranteed the sovereignty of the Ottoman Empire in exchange for its agreement to recognize the rights of its Christians. The British managed to emerge from the war victorious, and with the loss of only 17,500 men (compared to 100,000 Russians, 90,000 French, and 35,000 Turks), but the war had still shaken the people's confidence in their political and military leaders and whetted the appetite for further reforms in the army and at home.

Victorian values and social change

The term 'Victorianism' has certain cultural connotations that help to deepen an understanding of this period in the history of the British Isles. Perhaps the most important aspect of Victorianism is a concern with a rather strict code of morality. This concern represented a continuation of a trend that dated back to the beginning of time and was not exactly a new point of emphasis, but the Victorian middle class adopted a code of morality that was specifically designed to support the utilitarian values that they cherished: hard work, sobriety, thrift, and chastity.

Education, which the Victorians saw as essential to other ideas that many of them cherished, such as a belief in progress and the evolution of representative government, also ranks high on any list of nineteenth-century values. There was a direct connection between the passage of the Second Great Reform Bill in 1867 (see below) and the Education Act of 1870, which made primary education compulsory for the first time in the history of the British Isles. The passage of the Education Act no doubt contributed to the confidence displayed by Parliament when it passed an additional Reform Act in 1884 extending the right to vote to agricultural labourers.

By introducing compulsory primary education, reformers optimistically hoped that educating the working classes would reduce the crime rate and generally contribute to a more stable social order. They also promoted education as essential to the efflorescence of the British economy. Even prior to the passage of the Education Act, members of the middle class began to establish what were called Mechanics' Institutes for the purposes of educating the working classes and introducing them to practical knowledge.

Democracy was not a value shared by all Victorians; in fact it was still a rather controversial notion in the nineteenth century. But even the Conservatives, led by Benjamin Disraeli, came around to support the expansion of democracy in the second half of the nineteenth century. Disraeli had the opportunity to put his concept of Tory Democracy, which emphasized the harmony of the interests of the upper and lower classes, into practice when he entered government as Chancellor of the Exchequer under the new prime minister, Edward Stanley, the Earl of Derby, in 1866. It is remarkable that within a generation of the issuing of the *People's Charter* that Disraeli could write in 1867, the year of the Second Great Reform Bill, that 'none are so interested in maintaining the institutions of the country as the working classes'. Disraeli personally cultivated relationships with workers' associations because he believed that workers would be willing to vote for and support a Conservative government, as he continued to make the argument that the aristocracy cared more about the interests of the workers than did the middle classes.

The emphasis on the heroic and an aristocratic code of honour is one area of Victorian culture where religion and morality were relegated to secondary status. Alfred Lord Tennyson's poem 'Ulysses', written in 1833 (shortly before the beginning of the accession of Victoria but published in 1842), reflects the age's continuing obsession with aristocratic heroism; it is a call to action:

How dull it is to pause, to make an end,
To rust unburnish'd, not to shine in use!

A year before the publication of Tennyson's poem, Thomas Carlyle emphasized the importance of the heroic in his book of collected lectures *On Heroes, Hero-Worship, and the Heroic in History*, in which he portrayed the hero or man of action as essential to advances in the society based on a noble vision of the future.

The British public schools were expected to play a major role in preparing these heroes, as well as disciplined public servants, to defend and manage a vast empire. Strict discipline, sportsmanship, deference to authority, and austere living conditions were all part of the culture that permeated these institutions. Deference to authority included the power that older boys, who commonly abused the privilege, had over younger ones. Homosexuality was common, as was bullying; in his autobiography, *Something of Myself*, Rudyard Kipling describes being bullied until the age of fourteen at the United Services College of Westward HO! in North Devon, after which, he writes, 'either my natural sloth or past experience did not tempt me to bully in my turn'. Lewis Carroll's experiences at Rugby, in the words of a recent biographer, 'confirmed his sense that innocence was a special preserve of childhood that was constantly in danger of being breached'.[15] Thomas Arnold (1795–1842), the headmaster at Rugby school was the leader of a reform movement in the public schools that was designed primarily to instil greater discipline among the students that gained in popularity after his death. The result was a sense of pride that was inculcated among graduates, including Thomas Hughes, a political radical whose popular novel, *Tom Brown's Schooldays* (1857) was based on his own experiences at Rugby and did much to shape common perceptions of public school life in the nineteenth century.

The mature members of the aristocracy continued to operate in their own social world in many respects, spending half the year in London during 'the season', organizing frequent social gatherings partly for the purposes of strengthening their political and social connections and partly to allow for their marriageable children to meet in the hopes of attracting a financially advantageous or socially prestigious match. For the aristocracy, with its closed network of social relationships and political alliances, the choice of a marriage partner carried added weight and significance beyond one's prospect for personal happiness. In the country, aristocrats continued to oversee their huge estates, the successful financial management of which was key to their continuing political and social influence.

The middle class latched on so strongly to the philosophies of utilitarianism and laissez-faire capitalism partly because they provided a rationale for their own position in society and their authority over the workers and partly because they helped them to justify their attack on the aristocracy as parasitical members of society, something they measured in strictly economic terms. The middle classes, with the value they placed on work and discipline, found both the aristocracy and the working classes corrupt. The middle class believed that the triumph of British industry, for which they gave themselves credit, had contributed not only to the prosperity of the nation but also to the general cause of humanitarian progress that included the relative absence of war in a period sometimes known as the *Pax Britannica*.

The expansion of government, industry, and commerce required a much larger number of civil servants, managers, and bureaucrats, contributing to a burgeoning middle class. Even if these members of the bourgeoisie ranked below the factory and business owners socially and economically and did not have quite the cachet as those in more traditional professions such as medicine or the law, they nonetheless shared many of the same values of the wealthier or more prestigious members of their class. By the late nineteenth century, more women also started to move into white- or pink-collar jobs as teachers, nurses, secretaries, and telephone operators, positions that were either much fewer in number or completely unknown when the century began.

At the same time, skilled workers developed a sense of superiority over unskilled workers, a divide that hindered the unity of the working classes and any attempt they might have made to challenge the prevailing economic system. After 1875 the leading trade unions maintained a relatively conservative political stance that fell far short of embracing Marxist socialism. These unions tended to be based on older, more traditional skills and crafts and did not represent the unskilled or poorer members of the working classes. The Trades Union Congress was founded in 1868 as an organization dedicated to supporting the combined interests of trade unions throughout the country. Its Parliamentary Committee, established in 1871, lobbied on its behalf; only at the end of the century did it begin to evolve in a more radical direction.

In addition to morality, education, democracy, and work, the Victorians also professed to value family, and they enforced a rather strict separation between home life centred on women and children and the professional world dominated by men. The prevalence of domestic servants in middle-class households where the men generally went to work left mothers and children with a great deal of leisure time, which they might use to create an idyllic and imaginary utopia. Of course, many nursery rhymes and fairy tales antedated the Victorian period, but now serious adult authors began to address themselves to children. In the 1850s, Dickens wrote a *Child's History of England*. Lewis Carroll's view of childhood as an entirely distinct phase of life was thus one that was shared by the Victorian middle class as a whole, contributing to the growth in the genre of children's literature and the popularity of Carroll's own works, *Alice's Adventures in Wonderland* (1865) and *Through the Looking Glass and What Alice Found There* (1872). Carroll's books were an absolute sensation, their influence extending well beyond the nineteenth century and retaining their interest to the present day. Because of Carroll's ongoing fascination with preadolescent girls and his close personal relationship with the young Alice Liddell, the inspiration for her fictional namesake, modern writers have viewed him as at least a kind of latent pederast, although his most recent biographer cautions against imposing contemporary categories of sexuality on our Victorian predecessors.[16]

The Victorians wrestled with prostitution and sex in general, which they very much tried to obscure; they may have been obsessed with de-emphasizing sex precisely because they feared the strength of sexual impulses and their ability to unravel their carefully crafted cultural ideals. In 1857 Dr William Acton first published his *Prostitution Considered in its Moral, Social, and Sanitary Aspects in London and other Large Cities*, in which he argued that demand created prostitution rather than the other way around. But it was clear to others that the Industrial Revolution had created circumstances that led larger numbers of single women into prostitution who otherwise could not support themselves as well those who preferred it to the drudgery and unpleasantness of factory work. Poverty, or the threat of it, obviously contributed to a rise in the numbers of women resorting to prostitution; for example, in Dublin the number of women arrested for prostitution reached a peak of 4,784 in 1856, when Ireland was still suffering from the after-effects of the famine, compared to 2,849 in 1838 (another difficult year economically) and 1,672 in 1877.[17] While many Victorians feared or pretended to disdain sex, they recognized how widespread prostitution had become; for example, the Parliament passed a Contagious Diseases Act in 1864 requiring medical examinations for prostitutes in military towns and the detention of those found to be infected with venereal disease until cured. Seven years earlier, in 1857, the Parliament had passed a Divorce and Matrimonial Causes Act, which shifted divorce litigation from the House of Lords to a civil court that also replaced church courts in overseeing marital separations. The new law not only allowed men to divorce their wives on grounds of adultery, but also allowed women to divorce their husbands on grounds of adultery, cruelty, or desertion.

Another important cultural trend in the Victorian period was a general fascination with science and technology inspired by Britain's industrial success, further evinced in the huge crowds attracted to London's Great Exhibition of 1851. But the success of Charles Darwin's 1859 book, *The Origin of Species*, is perhaps the best example of the confidence and fascination with science that was characteristic of the Victorians. The majority of naturalists and biologists accepted the theory of natural selection by 1870, but Darwin's ideas did encounter some resistance from clerics such as Bishop Samuel Wilberforce, who, in a famous debate at Oxford, challenged Darwinism on the grounds that it contradicted the Bible, as well as from some in the scientific community, such as St George Mivart, a fellow of the Zoological Society and the Linnean Society, a member of the Royal Institute, and a lecturer at St Mary's Medical School in London. Like most biologists, Mivart accepted the theory of evolution at first, but came to have his doubts as time went on, mainly because he did not believe that natural selection was an adequate explanation for human beings and because he believed that only teleological forces could explain the existence of new types of species that were so diverse from previous ones. Significantly, Mivart, although a Catholic, did not object to Darwin's ideas on religious grounds, believing that the theory of evolution was not incompatible with the Bible, a position that most Christians and scientists came to adopt by the end of the nineteenth century.

Victorian belief and confidence in science helped to support common assumptions about the difference between the sexes based on the perceived biological inferiority of women. Women were still regarded as more intuitive and emotional, men as more rational, women more charitable and men more practical. Contemporary physicians reinforced the notion of the biological difference between the sexes. They used feminine disorders to explain any variety of psychological or physical disorders that women might experience, thus contributing to a belief in women's biological inferiority. Middle-class and upper-class women who wanted to work outside the home generally did so in charity organizations; they did not receive remuneration but they did have a chance to operate in a public sphere that gave them a platform for political activity, which included in the later decades of the century advocating for women's rights.

So great was the Victorians' confidence in science that they believed that it could explain and solve the problems of human society and not just those of the natural world. The historian Henry Thomas Buckle believed in the scientific regularity of history, which followed patterns that could be clearly discerned if historians had access to the statistics that would reveal its tendencies. Buckle went even further than his famous German contemporary, Leopold von Ranke, in his devotion to scientific history, which he thought demonstrated that history advanced through intellectual rather than moral progress. Of course, the Industrial Revolution and the rapid rate of technological advancement provided much of the basis for the belief in progress. By the second half of the nineteenth century, however, the Victorians' confidence in history as the story of progress included a belief that even the end of the war was imminent.

Of course, both religion and superstition continued to coexist alongside the Victorians' emphasis on reason, science, and progress, just as they had during the preceding century. For example, David Barrie has demonstrated how Scottish Presbyterians used modern print culture to perpetuate premodern shaming rituals: 'The construction of shaming in trial reports ... helped to mirror and even define middle-class parameters of acceptable feminine and masculine conduct and understandings of childhood while also reflecting changing conceptions of what was perceived to constitute shameful behavior per se.'[18]

In addition, the importance of religion and the Presbyterian church can be seen in two contradictory movements that emerged during the 1830s. The first was a highly successful church extension campaign that united Scots Presbyterians of all classes in the financing and constructing of new parish churches throughout Scotland. This move towards unity, however, was completely undermined by the passage in May 1834 of a controversial Veto Act, which allowed a congregation to veto a minister appointed to its church if a majority of male family heads voted against accepting the proposed candidate. Four years later, in response to an appeal by a rejected minister named Robert Young, the Court of Session ruled that the Veto Act itself was unconstitutional, having violated Young's civil rights, a decision upheld by the House of Lords. This decision infuriated those Presbyterians, including a man named Thomas Chalmers who emerged as the leader of the disaffected party, who resented the undue influence that aristocratic patrons had within the Scottish church and bristled at the implication that a spiritual institution must bow to a ruling by civil authorities. Moderates within the church, however, defended the old system and were glad to see the Veto Act overturned. The controversy inexorably led to rancour and a division within the Church of Scotland known as the great Disruption of 1843, in which about a third of its ministers and approximately half of its members left the established church and founded a separate Free Church of Scotland. The Disruption caused a serious rift within Scottish society, with both sides passionately believing in the righteousness of their cause in ways that were reminiscent of both the Protestant Reformation and the church–state conflicts of the Middle Ages.

Religion also remained extremely important in Wales, which saw a significant growth in the number of churches and church attendance during the Victorian period, thanks largely to the appeal of dissenting congregations. The encroachment of nonconformist denominations on membership in the established church was one of the most important trends in nineteenth-century Welsh history. Wales had church seating for more than 75 per cent of its population, whereas by contrast England only had seats for about 50 per cent of its people.[19]

William Gladstone was among those who felt the need to defend religion against the inroads of science and modernity; in December 1875, he wrote to Bishop Stubbs:

> I believe that it is the truly historical treatment of Christianity, and of all the religious experience of mankind, which, in conjunction with a rational philosophical method such as that of [Joseph] Butler, will supply under God effectual bulwarks against the rash and violent unbelief, under the honourable titles of physical and metaphysical science, rushing in upon us.[20]

The Oxford Movement, also known as Tractarianism, represented a powerful quest for a new religious identity among conservatives within the Church of England in the mid-nineteenth century. John Henry Newman, Dr Edward Bouverie Pusey, and James Anthony Froude mounted a serious spiritual and intellectual defence of traditional religion against the forces of modernism and the belief in progress that eventually led Newman to join the Catholic Church in 1845, where he eventually was made a cardinal in 1879.

As for superstition, there is an episode in Thomas Hardy's *The Return of the Native* (1878), where the character Susan Nunsuch plots revenge on the female protagonist Eustacia Vye, whom she believed caused the illness of her child through the use of malign powers. Susan attempts to counteract the perceived evil influence of Eustacia by fashioning an image of her intended victim out of beeswax, sticking it with pins, and consigning it to the fire, a practice, says Hardy, not unknown in his own day. Hardy takes an ambiguous attitude towards the effects of this practice, which he seems to dismiss as superstition but which also seems to have its intended effect in the novel. Dickens, of course, included numerous ghosts and supernatural elements in his stories, but he made it easy for his readers to dismiss them as figments of his characters' imaginations if they chose. The appearance of the ghost of Jacob Marley and the three spirits of Christmas in *A Christmas Carol* could just as easily be taken as occurring in a dream of Scrooge's as actual spiritual manifestations in the material world.

The onset of a major economic depression in 1873 provided a major challenge to the Victorian belief in progress and unbounded confidence in the future. Furthermore, by 1875, both a United States recovering from the devastation of its Civil War and a recently unified Germany were emerging as economic competitors to Britain, leading to some questioning of the country's free trade policies. In the last decades of the nineteenth century, British thinkers also continued to wrestle with the effects of industrialization on British society. In 1894, at the beginning of yet another economic depression, the British economist J. A. Hobson addressed the issue in *The Evolution of Modern Capitalism: A Study of Machine Production*. In Hobson's view, the excessive reliance of the economy on machinery led to overproduction and created the very slumps that the proponents of the idea of progress thought industrialization had eradicated.

Parnell, Gladstone, and 'Home Rule' for Ireland

British politics in the period from the mid-1860s to the mid-1880s had once again become a relatively equal contest between the Liberal and Conservative parties. Reunited under the skilful and charismatic leadership of Disraeli, the Conservatives held power from 1866 to 1868, and 1874 to 1880, while the Liberals, under the sincere but sometimes sanctimonious Gladstone, held the reins of government from 1868 to 1874 and again from 1880 to 1885. The Conservative Party regained power in 1866 after Disraeli engineered the defeat of a proposed measure by Gladstone to expand the British electorate. In 1867, on Disraeli's initiative, Parliament passed the Second Great Reform Bill, which gave all householders and all tenants who paid at least £10 a year in rent the right to vote, more than doubling the electorate to over 2 million voters. Disraeli convinced his party to support this 'leap in the dark', only to have the newly expanded electorate vote in a Liberal majority under Gladstone, who became prime minister in 1868. The Second Great Reform Act still enfranchised only a minority of men; its failure to include any women was one of the catalysts for the women's suffrage movement that emerged in the later decades of the century. Political reform continued under Gladstone, including the passage of the Ballot Act in 1872, the 1883 Corrupt and Illegal Practices Act, the Third Great Reform Act of 1884, and the 1885 Redistribution of Seats Act. Yet, when in power, the Conservatives passed their own share of significant reform legislation, validating to a degree Disraeli's claim that theirs was the party that best represented the interests of the working classes, including a Public Health Act (1875), the Artisans' and Labourers' Dwelling Improvement Act (1875), the Sale of Food and Drugs Act (1875), the Rivers Pollution Prevention Act (1876), two Factory Acts in 1874 and 1875 magnanimously raising the age limit for children who worked in mines to ages nine and ten, respectively, and a Factory and Workshop Act in 1878.

In 1885, the Liberal Party returned to power with a large majority and this time Gladstone was determined to solve the 'Irish problem' by introducing a Home

Rule Bill that would grant Ireland the right to self-government in all matters except economic and foreign policy. Liberal MPs now outnumbered Conservative MPs by 333 to 251; the additional eighty-six MPs from the Irish Party meant that he should have been able to get a Home Rule Bill through relatively easily as long as he had the support of his own party. Gladstone had come to his convictions about Ireland relatively late in his career; Ireland was not among the major issues on the Liberal Party agenda in the election of 1868, but after he had assumed the position of prime minister Gladstone announced that it was his mission to 'pacify Ireland'. Ireland had remained economically underdeveloped, despite the growth of industries in Belfast and a few other areas. Therefore, 'pacifying Ireland' would mean addressing economic issues such as land reform in addition to the political cause of Home Rule.

Gladstone had an imperious personality, lent credence by the extent to which he relied on his own conscience in politics, which in turn added conviction to his positions. The American showman William Cody – better known as 'Buffalo Bill' – met Gladstone while touring England and described his encounter with the Liberal leader:

> The fine old statesman [Gladstone], looking like intellect personified, glanced around him with an amused expression as the savage Indians came flocking out with their characteristic cries of 'ugh/ugh' and engaged at once in conversation with Red Shirt. ...
>
> A luncheon followed in the exhibition building at which I sat beside Mrs Gladstone. The Grand Old man spoke in warm and affecting terms of the instrumental good work we had come to do. He proposed 'success to the Wild West Show' in a brilliant little speech which aroused the enthusiasm of all present. He was highly complimentary to America and dwelt upon the great deeds of its westward pioneers in a glowing peroration, and on subsequent occasions, when we met, his demeanour was such that I could quite understand the fascination he exercised over the masses of his countrymen. His is a singularly attractive personality and his voice is either a balm to comfort or a living sword, two-edged and fire tipped, for the oratorical combat as occasion may demand.[21]

By1885, Ireland was in the middle of a 'Land War' that had previously led Gladstone to introduce a bill that became known as the Coercion Act, which passed in February 1881, and to suspend habeas corpus, giving authorities the right to imprison suspected troublemakers indefinitely without charge. The Land League declared a rent strike in response, which resulted in the imprisonment of a number of its members under the terms of the new Act. More violence ensued, including the murder of the chief secretary for Ireland, Lord Frederick Cavendish. A rent strike in County Mayo aimed at Lord Erne and his land agent, Captain Boycott, led to the introduction of a new word in the English language. The Coercion Act violated many of Gladstone's Liberal principles, but he needed to reassure the Parliament that he was willing to use force if necessary to bring the Irish tempest under control before he could get the support needed to carry out his desired land reforms. Two months later he introduced a land bill that promised to meet all of the demands of the Land League, specifically, the fixed right of tenants to remain on their land if rent was not in arrears, fair rents, and the freedom of tenants to sell their share in the land; collectively these demands were known as the '3 F's'.

Meanwhile, the Irish Party had come under the leadership of Charles Stewart Parnell, a debonair and sophisticated Protestant Irish landowner who first entered the Parliament at the age of twenty-nine in 1875. Three years later he became president of the Land League, a position that gave him added leverage as a spokesperson for the Irish tenants. In the Parliament Parnell was able to use the threat of violence to prod Gladstone and the Liberals to hasten legislation favourable to the demands of the League. With eighty-six Home Rulers in the House of Commons in 1885, Parnell knew that he had the votes to block any and all legislation if he chose, forcing the Parliament to deal with his demand for Home Rule. The Conservative Party, led by Lord Salisbury, could have regained power if they trumped the Liberals by supporting Home Rule, but Salisbury rejected this idea after briefly considering it.

The election of 1885 had been dominated not only by Gladstone, but also by a radically Liberal politician named Joseph Chamberlain (1836–1914), whose 'unauthorized program' included land reform, the disestablishment of the Anglican church, free education, inheritance taxes, a graduated tax rate, universal manhood suffrage, elections for county government, and payment for members of the Parliament. This was the first election in which agricultural labourers could vote, giving Chamberlain's programme an appeal in areas such as East Anglia not previously known for support of such radical ideas.[22] Gladstone found himself in a position of not only having to satisfy the more conservative Whigs in his party but also the substantial number of radicals who followed Chamberlain and were extremely angry about the Coercion Act, as well as the attention that the Irish situation was taking away from social issues in Britain.

Meanwhile, Salisbury and the Conservatives wanted to see the Land League crushed altogether. In June 1885, Gladstone had to resign, having lost the confidence of the Irish Party, which swung its support temporarily to the Conservatives. This enabled the Conservative Party to make an effort to appease Ireland with the most sweeping Land Act to date; the measure, known as the Ashbourne Act (after Lord Ashbourne, the Chancellor of Ireland), offered tenant farmers the opportunity to purchase their lands with long-term government loans with a low interest rate. Although this seemed to address the demands of the Land League, when agitation for Home Rule continued after the passage of the Ashbourne Act, Salisbury concluded that coercion was the only possible solution for handling the Irish situation.

Gladstone was committed to Home Rule for Ireland partly because he believed it to be the right thing to do on principle, and also because of the deleterious effect that he believed the Irish situation was having on the British political system. Nonetheless, Matthew Arnold thought it had 'every fault which a project of state can have'.[23] History has perhaps vindicated Gladstone at the expense of Arnold, but at the time Gladstone's Home Rule Bill had enormous consequences for British political culture. The divide in the Liberal Party over the bill allowed the Conservatives to regain power in 1886 under Salisbury, who tried to undo some of what Gladstone had achieved for Ireland, including a proposal to repeal the provision of his Land Act that fixed tenants' right to stay on the land or to be compensated for their eviction. Gladstone had shattered the unity of his party, ruining at least its short-term chances for electoral success, without even the consolation of the passage of a

Home Rule Bill; the Liberal Party split into wings led by Gladstone and Chamberlain, whose commitment to the empire led to his designation as a Liberal imperialist. Irish Protestants forged a unionist movement centred in the North that was determined to resist Home Rule in the future. Meanwhile, the entry of another 2 million workers to the electorate in 1884 marked another significant shift in British politics, with unintended and unforeseen consequences. If the Liberal Party could find a way to reunite, the expanded electorate would work to its advantage, but only if it could keep a nascent Labour Party from siphoning off too many working-class voters.

As for the Irish Party of Parnell, it suffered a devastating blow when Parnell was named a co-respondent in a divorce case in 1890. Gladstone, who still hoped to regain power and introduce another Home Rule Bill, broke with Parnell, who refused to relinquish his position at the head of his party. Parnell, disgusted by the moral hypocrisy of his critics, turned on Gladstone and accused him of first using and then betraying the Irish cause. Parnell married his former mistress, Kitty O'Shea, in June 1891, but died later that year with both the Irish and Liberal parties in disarray and Home Rule pushed far down the British political agenda. The UK – to the delight of the vast majority of Conservatives, most of the Liberals, and all of the Irish Unionists – remained temporarily intact. Home Rule was not dead yet, but it would take some radical changes in the British political system, a world war, and an Irish civil war in order to finally make it a reality.

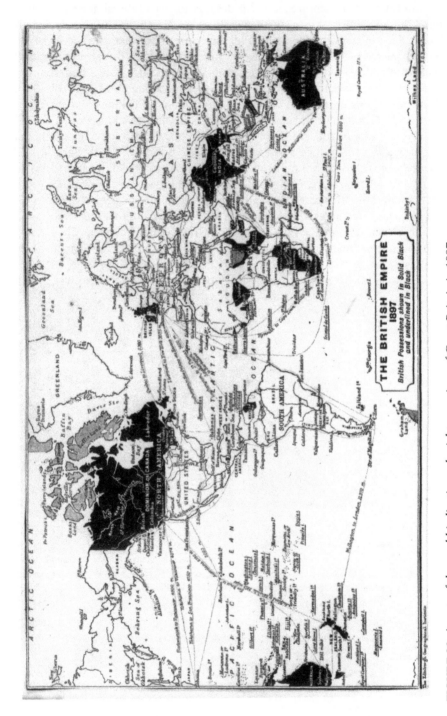

FIGURE 26 *A map of the world indicating colonial possessions of Great Britain in 1897.*
Hulton Archive/Getty.

13

Britain's moment as a world power:

The British Empire in the nineteenth century

England, it is true, in causing a social revolution in Hindostan, was actuated only by the vilest interests, and was stupid in her manner of enforcing them. But that is not the question. The question is, can mankind fulfill its destiny without a fundamental revolution in the social state of Asia? If not, whatever may have been the crimes of England she was the unconscious tool of history in bringing about that revolution.

KARL MARX, 'British Rule in India', June 1853

We seem, as it were, to have conquered and peopled half the world in a fit of absence of mind.

SIR JOHN SEELEY, *The Expansion of England*, 1883

The Liberal Party should not dissociate themselves, even indirectly or unconsciously or by any careless words, from the new sentiment of Empire which occupies the nation ... for the statesman, however great he may be, who dissociates himself from that feeling must not be surprised if the nation dissociates itself from him.

LORD ROSEBERY, December 1901

The imperial idea: Attitudes towards empire

In the course of the nineteenth century, the British developed a view of themselves as an imperial nation responsible for bringing the benefits of civilization to the farthest provinces of the globe. The progress of the territories over which the British gained control also became a template for measuring the course and direction of English society. The colonies in the British Empire helped to define not merely the empire but Britain itself by encouraging its people to become geographically aware of their place in the world and more culturally cognizant of the differences between themselves and their imperial subjects. This had not been the case in the eighteenth century. Although British involvement in India intensified after the collapse of the Mughal dynasty and Robert Clive's victories at the time of the Seven Years War, the controlling power at the end of the eighteenth century in India was still the East India Company, not the British government. Furthermore, the British defeat in the American War for Independence seemed to suggest that the British Empire was contracting, not expanding.

As the empire increasingly became a prominent part of British identity, the British viewed empire building not only as indicative of domestic greatness, but essential to their cachet on the world stage. In our own age, power and imperialism have acquired almost entirely negative connotations among many contemporary historians, but nineteenth-century attitudes towards empire were much more favourable.

At the beginning of the nineteenth century, the British government had inherited a diverse and widely dispersed collection of colonies and global interests hardly deserving of the epithet 'empire', at least if that term means anything beyond the accumulation of individual territories, because no collective unity or connection among them existed. By the end of the Seven Years War in 1756, Britain had already acquired colonies in the Caribbean and the Mediterranean, while its North American colonies extended from Quebec to Florida. What did the Spanish settlers in Spain have in common with the French settlers in Quebec, or either of them have with the inhabitants of British possessions elsewhere? At this juncture the British thought of the members of their empire as 'subjects' who were fundamentally different from them.[1] The British only began to think of the empire as a unity towards the middle of the nineteenth century as a result of an imperial project that included a proliferation of maps, globes, and atlases that familiarized the public with the location and extent of Britain's overseas possessions.

Britain emerged from the Napoleonic Wars in 1815 as the dominant naval power in the world. The British also emerged with more than a dozen new colonies, including Malta in the Mediterranean, the Cape Colony in South Africa, Ceylon (Sri Lanka), off the coast of India, and Guiana, Trinidad, and Tobago off the coast of South America. Attitudes towards empire at this time, however, were unenthusiastic at best; the increase in trade with Britain's former colonies following the independence of the United States seemed to argue against the necessity of political dominance in territories where British merchants wished to trade. Great Britain, meanwhile, had its hands full with domestic unrest at home and only reluctantly intervened in India, which was still officially under the authority of the East India Company. Free trade, the very opposite of colonialism, was the dominant ideology of the Liberal Party, so it tended to oppose any expansion of the empire. Even the Conservative Party restricted its protectionist legislation to agricultural products and, under Peel, moved in the direction of supporting free trade, culminating in the repeal of the Corn Laws in 1846 (see Chapter 12).

In the second half of the nineteenth century, certain events began to arouse debate among the British and its colonial elites about the rights of their subjects and the indigenous people with whom they intermittently came into conflict. For example, Herman Merivale, the author of the 1861 book, *Lectures on Colonization and Colonies*, argued that the British had a moral imperative to interfere with the practices of their subjects that offended their ethical sensibilities of right and wrong, as well as those that they simply considered uncivilized. This position was in accord with the Victorian emphasis on morality and the belief that the nineteenth century was an age of progress. Of the practice of Indian women throwing themselves on the funeral pyres of their husbands known as 'sati', the British governor general for India, William Bentinck, wrote in 1827:

> I do not believe that among all the most anxious advocates of that measure any one of them could feel more deeply than I do, the dreadful responsibility hanging over my happiness in this world and the next, if as the governor-general of India I was to consent to the continuance of this practice for one moment longer, not than our security, but that the real happiness and permanent welfare of the Indian population rendered indispensable.[2]

As Catherine Hall has put it:

> The idea that the British were saving Indian women from the barbarities of their archaic world, and that this was a necessary precondition for modernizing India, became a critical tool in the legitimation, whether amongst colonial officials, missionaries, or social reformers, whether utilitarian or evangelical, of their country's right to rule.[3]

The British saw themselves not only as less despotic than other regimes around the world or previous regimes, such as that of the Mughal dynasty, but as positively enlightened by Christian values and holistic advances in European civilization. They

FIGURE 27 *Attack of the mutineers on the Redan Battery at Lucknow, 30 July 1857. From* The History of the Indian Mutiny, *published 1858.*
Universal Images Group/Getty.

quixotically and perhaps naively believed that self-interest was not in opposition to the best interest of their subjects. This belief manifested itself in the era of social engineering that characterized British policy in India from about 1830 until the Great Indian Mutiny of 1857 (see below).

In addition, the British, having abolished slavery throughout the empire in 1833, now sought to eradicate the slave trade in Africa. The African slave trade was a leading concern of the Scottish missionary David Livingstone, who frequently encountered it during his travels in Africa from the 1850s to the early 1870s. Livingstone's travels and mission were of great interest to a British public who saw him as the cynosure of a policy designed to open up Africa to civilization, trade, and Christianity. It is not clear that Livingstone saw himself wholly in this light and there were moments when missionaries found themselves at odds with other aspects of the imperialist agenda. In his view, the British had a mission to ameliorate the conditions of the people they conquered even as they consolidated and augmented their power. Livingstone's desire to abolish slavery in Africa had nothing to do with the commercial advantages slavery supposedly brought to Britain. Although slavery had been abolished in the British Empire, there was nothing to stop British merchants from participating in the slave trade in those territories outside the empire in which the trade still flourished.

Other British imperialists believed that the primary responsibility owed by the British to native people was to defend them from unjust deprivation of their lands, rights, and cultural traditions; Kenton Scott Story has shown how both sides in the debate over British conduct in the Taranaki War that took place in New Zealand in the early 1860s drew on Christian moral precepts to defend their positions. Critics of the war with the Maori people appealed to the British responsibility to treat them fairly in accordance with British principles of justice. Supporters of the war, including the governor of New Zealand, Thomas Gore Browne and his wife, Harriet Louisa, also posed as defenders of Maori rights, arguing that the Maori natives had the right to sell their land to the British.[4] In the end, despite their protestations, it became difficult to justify a war in which the local inhabitants put up such implacable resistance and had so much of their land destroyed and which concluded with no real resolution for either party in the conflict.

What characterizes both sides of this debate is an attitude of paternalism, in which the British, as did other Europeans during the nineteenth century, saw themselves as superior to non-Europeans, who would benefit from the protection, education, social reforms, technology, and culture that the West had to offer, as if non-European peoples could not take care of themselves or manage on their own. For example, the Evangelicals hoped to eventually convert the Indian people to Christianity, but they carried with them other assumptions about the benefits of modernizing India through European education and technology. The Victorians also regarded themselves as more politically progressive than other European nations, and sought to spread British ideas of constitutionalism and representative government abroad. These ideas did not invariably take effect in the colonies, but they did provide British imperialists with an additional measure of self-justification for the empire. British paternalism could be said to have reached its apogee in Rudyard Kipling's famous poem, 'The White Man's Burden', even though Kipling composed the poem at the end of the nineteenth century in response to American occupation of the Philippines.

These ideas helped to provide an imprimatur that legitimized the empire at a time when only about a quarter of Britain's trade involved its colonies.

By the late nineteenth century, two schools of thought about imperialism were postulated, each side arguing for the validity of their position. The first, exemplified by the historian John Seeley and supported by Joseph Chamberlain and the Liberal imperialists, continued to regard the empire as crucial to Britain's position as a world power, especially in the face of the incipient strength of Germany, Russia, and the United States. This perspective also drew support from 'social imperialists', who believed that the perpetuation of the empire was in the best interests of the British working class. The second case, most eloquently stated by Charles Pearson in his 1893 book, *National Life and Character: A Forecast*, argued that Britain had a responsibility to foster the independence and equality of the peoples of Africa and Asia, who were destined to grow into a role as independent nations in the twentieth century. Pearson's book, although popular, seemed unrealistic to most people, especially given the imperial fervour that gripped not only Britain but most European nations in the last decade of the nineteenth century. Pearson's ideas also ran counter to the notions that settlers in the so-called white dominions (Canada, South Africa, Australia, and New Zealand) held about their superiority over indigenous populations and their determination to maintain power over them.

There is no doubt that nineteenth-century racialist thinking reinforced these feelings of superiority and affected interactions between colonial regimes and their non-European subjects. Nonetheless, Pearson provided a powerful challenge to the notion of white supremacy; according to one early-twentieth-century publication, 'it shook the self-confidence of the white races and deprived them of the absolute sense of assured superiority which had hitherto helped them to dominate'.[5] Of the two opposing principles about imperialism discussed above, the second, best represented by Pearson, would come to dominate intellectual circles in the middle of the twentieth century as the British people readjusted their priorities following two world wars and the Great Depression, but at the end of the nineteenth century, the views of Chamberlain still represented the most popular views on the empire in Britain.

In 1902 John Hobson summarized the arguments of the garden variety imperialist in the following:

> We must have markets for our growing manufactures, we must have new outlets for the investment of our surplus capital and for the energies of the adventurous surplus of our population: such expansion is a necessity of life to a nation with our great and growing powers of production. An ever larger share of our population is devoted to the manufactures and commerce of towns, and is thus dependent for life and work upon food and raw materials from foreign lands. In order to buy and pay for these things we must sell our goods abroad.[6]

Hobson's emphasis on the financial motivations for imperialism has frequently found support among historians of the British Empire; this was still the main thesis of the 2002 book *British Imperialism 1688–2000* by Peter Cain and A. G. Hopkins. Hobson noted that so long as Britain had a commercial advantage it could maintain its hegemonic economic position by trading with other countries and the colonies it already possessed without having to add new possessions to its empire. To Hobson, imperialism became necessary solely when Britain lost its monopoly on the world's markets as a result of the rising competition from Germany, the United States, and Belgium. Hobson acknowledged that British trade had not decreased as a result of this competition, but argued that competition had cut into British profits and deprived its merchants of lucrative markets.

In 1967, Ronald Robinson and John Gallagher in their important book, *Africa and the Victorians*, described the course of late-nineteenth-century British expansion in Africa primarily in strategic terms related to the opening of the Suez Canal in 1869. The Suez Canal shortened the trade routes to India and gave northeastern Africa added significance in the calculations of those defending Britain's imperial interests, especially India. Robinson's and Gallagher's book focuses to a large degree on India's central place within the British Empire, a point with which the Victorians would have concurred.

Britain and India

British interest in India began with the charter Elizabeth I granted to the East India Company at the beginning of the seventeenth century. As of 1836, British soldiers still numbered only 17,000, of whom, according to Lawrence James, a leading historian of the Raj, 'over a thousand were utterly unfit for duty and another 1,400 were invalids, most of them victims of venereal diseases or chronic alcoholism'.[7] The British East India Company had little difficulty attracting Indians to serve in its army, drawing heavily from the poorer classes who were attracted by steady pay, regular meals, and the promise of a pension. Philippa Levine estimates the total number of British residents in India in the 1830s at about 45,000 and sets the total Indian population at that time at about 150 million.[8] These numbers made the British position in India more precarious than it appeared on the surface.

During this juncture, the potential impact of British rule in India became a great exigency to both Indians and the British. In 1823, the Indian intellectual Ram Mohan Roy criticized a British proposal to establish a new Sanskrit school in Calcutta, even though he applauded the good intentions of the British in desiring to improve the education of Indians. Roy thought the learning of Sanskrit was a time-consuming and arduous task, which, though intrinsically worthwhile, would not prepare Indians for the modern world nor offer a pragmatic benefit. Instead, he wished to see the British introduce a system of education in India that emphasized 'mathematics, natural philosophy, chemistry and anatomy, with other useful sciences'. The doyens of Indian policy largely agreed with Roy and began to turn from the goal of preserving India's past to one of shaping India's future along Western lines. Liberals such as James Mill and his grandson John Stuart Mill both spent time working for the East India Company, where they attempted to apply their liberal principles in shaping a philosophy for the governance of India. Both of them adopted a paternalistic approach to the government of India that favoured a benevolent but absolute rule that would benefit the Indians but brook no opposition from them. The younger Mill's attitude towards empire was ambiguous; as a Liberal he favoured freedom and thought colonialism was fundamentally wrong. Therefore, he thought that colonial rule could not exist for the sake of augmenting power alone. Although the Mills had some respect for Indian tradition, they helped legitimate the social engineering in India that was initiated by the Liberal government in the 1830s.

Such a policy was wholly consistent with the reform movement taking place in Britain in the 1830s that produced the First Great Reform Act and other reforms. Lord Macaulay was responsible for the reform of the Indian Civil Service in the 1830s, which was considered so successful that it later became a model for civil service reform in Britain in the 1850s. An important turning point came with Macaulay's *Minute on Indian Education* in 1835. Macaulay believed that all education in India should be conducted in English to familiarize Indians with the basic precepts of British values and civilization. Although this seemed consistent with Roy's goal for the modernization of India, it evinced a lack of respect for Indian culture; however, it introduced Indians to liberal ideas regarding representative government and individual rights.

Simultaneous with this policy of social engineering, merchants of the East India Company, seeking to bolster its financial viability, had turned to the sale of opium, the one commodity for which there was a large enough demand to provide access to the huge China market. The Chinese government, however, did not welcome either the British merchants or their opium, since addiction to the drug had become a social epidemic with deleterious effects on the Chinese economy. By the time of the Opium War in 1839, it was obvious that the East India Company had lost its *raison d'être* and was now illicitly trading opium in China to finance its governance of India, which was costing far more than the profits Britain generated from legitimate trade.

In July 1853, Karl Marx provided an indictment of British rule in India, suggesting that the British were only carrying out improvements in India, such as railway building, in order to expedite the export of cotton and other raw materials for their own benefit. Marx predicted that the British would lay the foundations for Indian independence because they would have to establish a solid economic and industrial base in India in order to support a technological enterprise as large as building a network of railways across the huge sub-continent. Marx believed that industrialization and the accompanying division of labour would have the effect of dissolving the Indian caste system and would prepare India for entering the modern world and, eventually, the triumph of socialism.

Meanwhile, there were growing numbers of Indians, increasingly dissatisfied with British efforts to uproot their social and cultural traditions. The situation reached a critical juncture when a mutiny broke out in the Indian army in 1857. The mutiny began when the nineteenth regiment at Berhampore refused to use new cartridges issued to them that were rumoured to be greased with either beef or pork fat, the first a serious affront to Hindu soldiers, the second a profound indignity to inflict upon Muslims. The British decided to disband the regiment, the impetus for a rebellion and a far broader insurrection that revealed a profound dissatisfaction with British rule.

The British press vilified prominent British administrators, particularly the governor-general, Lord Canning, for not providing centralized leadership during the crisis, but army leaders responded to the mutiny with great force. They hung rebels in public, burnt villages suspected of disloyalty, and pacified the resistance.

The British tried to downplay the mutiny as the work of a few fanatical agitators, but the immediate cause of the mutiny – the rumours regarding the lubricant used on cartridges – would not have provoked such widespread resistance without deep underlying sources of discontent within the Indian army and Indian society at large.

The Great Mutiny was as much a turning point in the history of British rule in India as the Great Famine was for British rule in Ireland. First, it provided the primary incentive for the significant increase in British troops in the Indian army. Twenty years earlier, Lord Auckland had warned that the British might need a larger military presence in India if they faced opposition from even a fraction of their Indian subjects or if the Russian threat to India, the result of Russian expansion that had already led the British to fight a war in Afghanistan, became more serious. Perhaps more importantly, the mutiny officially ended the rule of the East India Company, which completely relinquished its authority to the British government, which in turn instituted an efficacious and bureaucratic regime. The British government immediately began to expand its administrative reach, partly through the establishment of more than eighty hill stations reaching the foothills of the Himalayas. One of them, the prominent administrative centre of Simla in northwestern India, became the summer capital of the British government. Ashley Jackson describes the Viceregal Lodge at Simla as 'specifically designed to emphasize the authority of the Raj and its leading representative, one of the most powerful men in the world'.[9] Another example of the attempt to impose a bureaucratic regime over the entire Raj was the Press and Registration of Books Act, passed in 1867, which required the Indian Civil Service to keep track of all books published in British-controlled India. Members of the public were never given access to this bibliography, prompting the historian Robert Darnton to ask, 'If they did not intend to repress any "native" literature, why did they follow its production in such exhaustive detail?'[10] In addition, once the British government took control of India from the East India Company, it established an India Office in London, which communicated through paper memoranda sent to the administrative offices of the Indian Civil Service, communications designed to make British rule more efficient but of occasional ambiguity.

Once the British government assumed total responsibility for India, it took the threat of Russian encroachment upon India more seriously, precipitating a national rivalry known as the 'Great Game'. The Russians never proved a real threat to British domination of India, but the British failed to recognize this at the time. Furthermore, the Russians were happy to engage in activities that made the British think that they had designs on India. As the Anglo-Afghan Wars of 1839–42 and 1878–80 demonstrate, the British were determined to remove any regime they determined hostile in Afghanistan, which separated India from Russia.

The effect of all these changes spelt the demise of Britain's social engineering, auguring an age in which the British no longer justified their position in India by their ability to reform Indian society but rather justified dominion based on India's place in their overall global strategy and its importance for Britain's position as a great power.

British colonialism in India had important implications related to race, sex, and gender, as can be seen by the number of native women who became the sexual partners of British men. Durba Ghosh has found almost one-tenth (26 of 278) of the births of baptized infants recorded by the East India Company in Bengal in 1810 were illegitimate children born to native women. These women, even when married to British men, were not accorded the same rights as European wives and frequently had trouble claiming their inheritances when their husbands died.[11] The Raj also reinforced notions of women's inferiority at home and for that reason supporters of women's rights in Britain sought to change the position of British women in India. Because they played no official role in the Raj, British women remained relatively isolated from the native population. But their very willingness to go to India gave women's rights advocates in Britain the opportunity to use them as examples of women's willingness to play an active role in public affairs and support the interests of the state.[12]

Some women served in India, as elsewhere, as missionaries, teachers, doctors, and nurses. For example, Dr Mary Scharlieb (1845–1940) studied in India at the Madras Medical College, after which she became a strong advocate of the need for women doctors to tend to the medical needs of Indian women. Others accompanied their missionary husbands, a practice favoured by missionary societies in order to minimize the temptation that males might face to engage in sexual liaisons with native women. However, most British women in India lived in a controlled social milieu in which they had little outlet for their creative or productive capacities, an environment more stultifying than the one found in Britain. This does not mean that women did not wish to share in the general mission of 'civilizing' India, a concept central to the Victorian ethos and a project to which they no doubt saw themselves as contributing.

The desire to improve the position of native women in India became one of the main arguments used later in the century by suffragettes. They affirmed their own feminism, according to Antoinette Burton, by associating themselves with the cause of Indian women, which they tended to lump together in a single group.[13] Furthermore, the British women who did go to India did not do so reluctantly or without some interest in Indian culture. As Joan Gaughan put it, 'Far from withdrawing from India, many women reached out to India as far as their sex and race allowed, and embraced her with exuberant enthusiasm.'[14]

In 1880, the Indian political advocate, Dadabhai Naoroji, composed an important work titled *Poverty and Un-British Rule in India*, in which he elaborated on Marx's criticism that the British had established the Raj for the sole intention of self-aggrandizement and had done so at the cost of wrecking the native economy and pauperizing the Indian people. But Naoroji was also concerned about the moral effects of British rule. He particularly objected to the British arrogation of all the most important administrative positions in the country, depriving Indians of the chance to gain the experience necessary to effectively govern themselves. Naoroji provided a powerful and persuasive critique of British rule in India, but failed to do holistic justice to the actual state of affairs engendered by the Raj.

British government in India included many well-meaning civil servants who did their utmost to keep India safe from famine, internal disorder, and foreign invasion. Many British administrators came to view India as their home and developed a deep fondness for the land and its people. The British army mercilessly repressed the Great Mutiny, but could not have done so if the majority of sepoys (Indian soldiers) proved pernicious; the army otherwise conducted itself as a disciplined, professional force that was generally in concordance with the native population. According to the

Indian census of 1881, the first ever taken for all of India, 145,000 Europeans resided alongside 250 million Indians.[15] Nonetheless, Englishmen in positions of authority carefully cultivated a social distance between themselves and their Indian subjects, so as to avoid losing any degree of respect as a result of increased familiarity; by isolating themselves in this way, they fell back on a social life that revolved around other members of the small British administrative elite that could easily fall out of touch with the people that they governed.

British–American relations in the nineteenth century

While Britain's position in India was changing dramatically in the course of the nineteenth century, so too was its relationship with the newly founded United States of America. After the end of the Napoleonic Wars, during the course of which Britain had found itself fighting the United States in the War of 1812, British diplomacy softened towards the nation that comprised some of its former colonies. In 1823 President James Monroe of the United States pronounced the Americas free from future colonization by European nations, threatening American military intervention should any nation embark on such an enterprise in the future. The Monroe Doctrine drew support from Britain, which had no interest in acquiring additional colonies in the Americas but nor did they wish to see other European nations acquire any either. In fact, the British navy was largely responsible for enforcing the Monroe Doctrine militarily and stood as the biggest obstacle to any further pretensions that Spain or France might have had in the Americas.

However, one potential source of conflict between Britain and the United States persisted; Canada remained part of the British Empire. The US government and army showed little respect for existing boundaries elsewhere in North America, whether with regard to the tribal lands of American Indians or lands belonging to Spain or Mexico in California and the southwest. The United States had actually invaded Canada in 1812 with an army of 12,000 men. Therefore, whenever tensions did arise along the US–Canadian border, the British would have been well advised to take them seriously; indeed, some of the more bellicose among the British leadership were led to consider a pre-emptive strike against the United States. Furthermore, as of 1818 the border between the Rocky Mountains and the Pacific Ocean had not yet become firmly established or agreed upon by Britain and the United States. In practice, this left the vast region open to both British and American fur traders, but as Americans began migrating west in larger numbers Britain was either going to have to negotiate a settlement with the United States, as it did with Russia over Alaska in 1826, or face the possibility of war. In 1844 the US president James Polk threatened war on behalf of American settlers demanding that the US border extend to the 54° 40' parallel that would push the boundary north of Vancouver Island. In 1846, the British foreign secretary Lord Aberdeen successfully negotiated an agreement with Polk that set the Canada–US boundary at the forty-ninth parallel, a major victory for Britain but one that still left the United States with a vast tract of land that was subsequently named the Oregon Territory.

The next major crisis in British–American relations occurred with the outbreak of the American Civil War in 1861. The British officially took a position of neutrality, siding neither with the Union nor the Confederacy, torn between the growth of domestic opposition to slavery and the economic dependency that many of their merchants had developed on trade with the American South. Throughout 1861, the Confederacy had tried to get Britain to use its navy to lift the blockade that the Union navy had imposed on the South and that was choking off trade between Britain and the Confederate states. Britain's neutral position meant British merchants were allowed to trade with the Confederacy. But as long as Britain remained neutral, its merchants could trade openly with the Union while surreptitiously evading the Union blockade to continue trading with the Confederacy. However, neither the Union nor the Confederacy were satisfied with this state of affairs and both pressed Britain to choose a side.

On 29 January 1862 a three-man delegation from the Confederate States of America headed by William L. Yancey landed in England with the goal of persuading the British to end their neutrality in the American Civil War. In addition to hoping that they could convince the British to take action against the Union blockade, the delegation also hoped that Britain would grant the Confederacy diplomatic recognition as a sovereign nation. The British might have supported the Confederacy for three reasons. First, the British had economic incentives to support the Confederacy, given how heavily the mills of Lancashire relied upon cotton supplied by the American South. Secondly, in 1862, the North was not yet fighting to end slavery, much less did the Confederacy openly acknowledge that the defence of slavery was the main reason for their rebellion. Thirdly, Irish nationalists had found a receptive audience to their message among those who had recently migrated to the United States. The fact that the United States harboured Irish nationalists who openly advocated rebellion against Britain was yet another sore spot between the two countries that might have turned the British towards support for the Confederacy.

Irish anti-British propaganda, however, was inimical to the hopes of the Confederacy for British support because, by provocatively suggesting that Britain supported slavery in the United States while ignoring the interests of the Irish tenant farmers who had starved to death or been driven from their lands, Irish nationalists made the British disdain the social order of the Confederacy. Furthermore, the British realized that they had more to lose from a war with the United States than they did from the temporary loss of American cotton; British textile manufacturers could at least make up for this inconvenience by importing cotton from other global nodes such as India or Egypt. The Union used British-manufactured textiles, particularly blankets and uniforms, partially compensating for the decrease in trade with the American South. Finally, British neutrality in the American Civil War had revived fears of American attacks on Canada, which would become a very real possibility if Britain ever declared for the Confederacy or even intervened to end the Union blockade.

The British prime minister, Lord Palmerston and John Russell, Palmerston's foreign secretary did not wish to suggest that they were considering ending the blockade by entertaining the Confederate delegation. Palmerston and Russell knew that, if the issue did come before Parliament, then the subject of slavery could not be kept out of any discussion of the relative merits of supporting either side. They were right and the slavery issue factored heavily in Britain's ultimate refusal to grant the

Confederacy recognition. In Parliament, the supporters of the Confederacy clearly lost the debate and British intervention on its behalf became a fantasy. As the war progressed, had the Confederacy enjoyed more military success it might have forced Britain to reconsider its position, but the failure of the South to achieve significant victories at Antietam in western Maryland in September 1862 and Gettysburg in southern Pennsylvania in 1863, combined with Lincoln's Emancipation Proclamation freeing the southern slaves, doomed the Confederacy to fight on without support or recognition from the most powerful country in the world.

Following the American Civil War, some British thinkers, including Sir Charles Dilke and the Earl of Rosebery, actually began to envision some kind of political union between two English-speaking nations that might approximate something like the relationship that Britain already had with Canada, which had achieved dominion status in 1867. In his 1868 book *Greater Britain*, Dilke referred to the United States as one of Britain's 'true colonies'. Rosebery, who twice served as foreign secretary under Gladstone, argued that the United States should be included as part of any trade union protected by future tariffs.[16] Such proposals failed to reach fruition, but the fact that they were considered reflects both British imperial anxieties and the easing of tensions between Britain and America by the end of the nineteenth century.

Tensions occasionally still arose between the United States and Britain; Britain took offence when the United States attempted to interfere in a boundary dispute with Venezuela during the presidency of Grover Cleveland in 1895. But by that time, the British now faced the growing economic power of Germany, while a British–French colonial rivalry had emerged in northern Africa. Furthermore, once the American Civil War ended in 1865, relations between the two countries normalized and fears about Russian intervention in India began to take precedence over any remaining anxiety regarding the US–Canada border. More importantly, the construction of the Suez Canal by a French company in 1869 had shortened the trade route to India and given Africa and the Eastern Mediterranean a new significance in British strategic thinking. Finally, difficulties in Ireland created tacit concerns for politicians worried about the future of the British Empire.

The impact of imperialism on Ireland

In the nineteenth century, Britain continued to treat Ireland more as a colony than as an equal part of the UK, despite the Act of Union. Daniel O'Connell's demands for Irish Home Rule may have been premature, but O'Connell did speak to the fundamental reality that Ireland had still not become fully integrated into the prevailing political culture of Britain. The Young Irelander, Thomas Davis, wrote in 1846 that 'this island has been for centuries either in part or altogether a province'.[17] The British, for their part, regarded Irish membership in the UK as important, but mainly as an extension of British power and imperialism. The Great Famine drove this point home to the Irish, who had already been disappointed by the Act of Union and had begun to dream of autonomy (or at least home rule) even before the famine struck, which many Irish blamed, at least in part, on British neglect (see Chapter 12).

Making matters worse, nineteenth-century racial theories reinforced the idea among many people in Britain that the Irish belonged to an entirely separate, and inferior, race. Among advocates for Irish Home Rule in the late nineteenth century, E. L. Godkin in particular stressed British racial prejudice against the Irish as a primary reason to justify the demand for Irish autonomy, presenting his arguments lucidly in an 1882 article published in Britain titled 'An American View of Ireland'. Religion also continued to set Ireland apart. Even though the British tried to show more respect for the position of the Catholic Church in Ireland in the nineteenth century, first by allowing the church to retain control over education and then by disestablishing the Protestant Church of Ireland in 1869, the Catholicism of the majority of the population still made the Irish distinct from the predominantly Protestant populations of England, Wales, and Scotland.

There were, of course, those in Ireland who benefited from and supported the union, including most of the landed aristocrats. Dublin merchants also benefited, growing prosperous from the importation of tea, coffee, and alcohol. In addition, the British army continued to rely heavily on Irish recruits, who joined in significant numbers. One estimate places the percentage of Irish non-commissioned officers in the British army at over 42 per cent in 1830; in 1850 about half of the troops serving in the army of the East India Company were Irish.[18] Furthermore, after the famine and the failure of the non-denominationalist Young Ireland, Protestants grew staunch in their commitment to the Union. The rise of Protestant unionism was an indication that religious differences were becoming more important in the second half of the nineteenth century, since the leaders of both the 1798 and 1848 uprisings had not viewed Irish nationalism in sectarian terms. Neither Davis nor any of his fellow Protestants in Young Ireland wished to see British rule replaced by Catholic dominance, however, and Irish nationalism was increasingly becoming a Catholic phenomenon, even though it failed to gain the official sanction of the Catholic Church. Daniel O'Connell, an Irish Catholic lawyer who founded the Catholic Association in 1823, had been the first important Irish nationalist to view the Irish nation in primarily Catholic terms. His vision provided the main inspiration for the home rule movement in the second half of the century, even though his two successors, Isaac Butt and Charles Parnell, were both Protestant.

The industrial growth and economic prosperity of Belfast though, relative to the rest of Ireland, further deepened the schism between the largely Protestant North and the Catholic South. The industrialization of Belfast also brought about closer economic ties with Britain and furthered the Unionist commitment among the city's leading Protestants. Irish Protestants became concerned, if not alarmed, by the extent to which the Catholic Church exercised control over the educational system in the south. The rise of the Fenians and Catholic violence against Protestant landlords embittered and amplified tensions.

In 1874, Butt, the leader of the Home Rule League, made a speech in the House of Commons in which he demanded 'a constitutional government, and the benefit of those free institutions which make England great'. Butt argued that the presence of 103 Irish representatives in the House of Commons out of over 600 total members did not guarantee Ireland any say over its own affairs. In fact, Butt pointed out in his speech that 'the whole record of the legislations for Ireland since the Union is made up of successive Arms Acts, suspensions of the Habeas Corpus Act, two Party Procession Prevention Acts, and Coercion Acts, each one more severe than its predecessor'. Most of these acts, he lamented, had been passed by a Liberal government supposedly well disposed to Ireland! Significantly, however, Butt argued for home rule, not independence, and thought it important to note that Home Rule for Ireland would in no way imperil the state of the British Empire.

In fact, one of the main reasons many British politicians opposed and even feared Home Rule for Ireland was the fear that other subalterns might make similar demands if even a measure of self-rule were granted to Ireland. Nor did it help that the local judiciary and law enforcement proved incapable of stemming the agrarian unrest and violence afflicting the countryside. Gladstone had basically been forced to suspend Habeas Corpus to assuage the fears of his own party that order could not be restored in Ireland without recourse to extraordinary measures. The Land War increasingly took on the dimensions of a colonial uprising rather than a domestic disturbance and the British government treated it as such.

The ostensible mission of the Land League was land reform, but the pandemonium it fostered, including murder, the killing of livestock, and arson, seemed designed to achieve more, namely to get the British out of Ireland. The Irish rebels' view of the British as foreign occupiers and the British view of the Irish as a foreign subject people mutually reinforced one another, making the Irish conflict seem like a colonial uprising, even if, strictly speaking, Ireland was not a colony but part of the UK. It did not help that the Conservative leader, Lord Salisbury, in 1886 compared the Irish to the Hottentots of South Africa. Herein lies the importance of the failure of Gladstone's home rule legislation, because once proposed and rejected, the seeds had been planted for a movement advocating total independence for Ireland. In addition, the British had alienated Irish Protestants by attempting to appease the Catholics with land reform, without satisfying the Catholics by vesting Ireland with home rule. In response, the Protestants clung to political union as the only means of preventing Catholics from taking power. At the same time, the failure of repeated attempts to legislate Home Rule for Ireland radicalized a minority of Irish nationalists who would emerge to lead the fight for independence in the early twentieth century.

Scotland, Wales, and the empire

Like the Irish, the Scots also made up a significant portion of the British army and participated heavily in the conquest and maintenance of the British Empire. Scottish troops helped crush slave rebellions in the West Indies. Although their participation in the wars of conquest in India was perfunctory, a Scottish battalion did fight in the Third Mahratta War of 1817–18. Furthermore, the East India Company benefited significantly from the technical expertise and educational backgrounds of many Scots in the late eighteenth and early nineteenth centuries. Such Scotsmen benefited from Warren Hastings' reform of the Indian Civil Service, in which he established meritocratic benchmarks between 1773 and 1785. Hastings promoted the study of native languages and Indian culture within the company, a project that appealed to educated Scots influenced by the Scottish Enlightenment. Thomas Munro was among those Scots who in the late eighteenth century played a prominent role in India, for which he prepared himself by learning Persian, the language used by the Indian soldiers.

Scots did not emigrate at the rate of the Irish after the famine, but many did leave for other parts of the globe in the course of the nineteenth century. They brought with them a strong Scottish identity, but Scottish migrants differed from many of their Irish counterparts, as their decision to leave was not accompanied by a desire to see Scotland freed from British rule. By the nineteenth century, most Scots genuinely believed that Scotland had benefited from union with England, a belief that was reinforced by their participation in the British Empire. I. G. C. Hutchison goes so far as to say that 'the prominent part played by Scots in acquiring and running the Empire cemented wholehearted identification with Britain'.[19]

In 1819, Thomas Pringle left Scotland for South Africa. Inspired by the poetry of Robert Burns, Pringle, like many of his fellow countrymen, found the beauty of the land where he settled reminiscent of his Scottish homeland. In fact, it has frequently been suggested that the Scots were drawn to frontier regions precisely because they resembled the rugged landscapes of Scotland. Pringle's poetry, such as his 1822 poem 'Afar in the Desert', captured the willingness of the Scots to endure harsh conditions from which others might have shied away.[20]

Canada, Australia, and New Zealand were also popular destinations for rural Scots who decided to migrate within the British Empire. They made important contributions in these places to the economy, particularly through sheep raising, although they also built railways, worked in mines, and fulfilled the broad range of jobs required of any frontier community, including farming, blacksmithing, and brewing, inter alia. Of the Scots' contributions to Canadian history, Ken McGoogan writes:

> Thanks to the deals cut by a few Scots, suddenly the CPR [Canadian Pacific Railway] covered twenty-four million acres of prime prairie land. Because these same Scots were canny businessmen, they hired agents in Europe and began offering potential immigrants package deals that included a voyage to Canada, a train ride across the country, and good farmland waiting at the other end. Tens of thousands of people took them up on their offer, and the CPR became the driving force in the development of western Canada. ... In the nineteenth century, Scottish Canadians pulled this far-flung country together by building a railway and inventing the telephone and universal standard time.[21]

Nineteenth-century Wales was more thoroughly integrated with England than either Ireland or Scotland. Nonetheless, when the British and Foreign School Society was established in 1814, Wales came under its auspices and fell under the category of a 'foreign mission' until the establishment of Her Majesty's Inspectorate of Schools in England and Wales in 1839. Furthermore, the British government consistently tried to prevent Welsh children from learning or speaking Welsh in school, although many Welsh parents wished their children to learn English and the dispute over the use of the Welsh language was as much an internal debate in Wales as it was between England and Wales.[22] The religious revival of the late 1850s in particular put a focus on preaching in the Welsh language. The Welsh revival movement of the early twentieth century must also be seen in this context as representing a conservative reaction to the growing influence of modern and secular ideas conveyed through an English education.

The Scots had no analogous cause for complaint, as they had retained their own church and their legal and educational institutions. The Scots, therefore, were not as inclined as either the Irish or the Welsh to regard the English as their colonial overlords. The Napoleonic Wars had further reinforced the common defence interests of Scotland and England and helped to consolidate support for the union. By contrast, although the Welsh did not experience any single motivating factor such as the Irish Famine, religious differences, economic hardship, and feelings of cultural discrimination did lead many Welsh to leave their homeland in the mid-nineteenth century, along with the Irish.

When the Welsh began to leave Britain in the mid-nineteenth century, most emigrants left for the United States or South America rather than territories within the vast British Empire. In 1852 Thomas Benbow Phillips of Tregaron established a small Welsh community of about 100 people in southern Brazil. In 1865, 163 Welsh people left England aboard a ship out of Liverpool for southern Argentina, but two years later their community had declined to under 100, despite subsidy from both the British navy and the Argentine government.[23] Those Welsh settlers who settled in the United States, unlike the Irish by whom they were greatly outnumbered, preferred rural farming or mining communities similar to those they had left in Wales over large cities such as New York and Chicago.

Later in the century, when the British were expanding their influence in Africa, it was again the Scots who responded with elán. Enlistment in the British army among Scots rose after the call for volunteers because of the consternation aroused by the death of General Charles Gordon during a Muslim revolt in the Sudan in 1884–5. Scots were attracted to the army because of the opportunity to serve with other Scots, taking great pride in their regimental colours, while enjoying the esprit de corps, discipline, possibility for adventure, steady income, and other common attractions of military life. In early December 1884, the Welsh-American journalist and explorer Henry Stanley addressed the Edinburgh Chamber of Commerce on the topic of 'The Congo: Its past history, present development, and future commercial prospects'. Stanley spoke to the Edinburgh business community about the recently awakened desire for European goods throughout the interior of the African continent. He went on to play up the possibilities that European investment had for transforming Africa, telling his audience that

> in the wake of every forward step into the interior of Africa rises a greater demand for the products of Europe. ... Who knows but that in some distant future the memories of the founders of the International Association will also be revered as the principal factors in the civilization of regenerated Africa?[24]

Britain and the New Imperialism:
The race for colonies in Africa

Stanley had been attracted to Africa initially when he went to search for the Scottish missionary and explorer David Livingstone (1813–73). He spoke for many initial visitors to the continent when he wrote that 'one day's life at Zanzibar made me thoroughly conscious of my ignorance respecting African people and things in general'. But British knowledge and understanding of Africa was growing in the nineteenth century, thanks to the fascinating adventures of men like Livingstone and the explorers Richard Burton (1821–90) and John Hanning Speke (1827–64), who were most famous for their 1858 discovery of Lake Tanganyika, the largest freshwater lake in the world. Through his published journals and accounts of his travels, Livingstone probably did the most to make the idea of Africa seem more accessible to people at home, while simultaneously shaping their views of the land and its people. When he arrived in Africa he brought with him his own Western conceptions of morality and he based his description of the natives on a comparison between the poor of Africa and the poor of England and Scotland, whom he judged morally superior.

The British government suddenly became more interested in Africa when Benjamin Disraeli took a special interest in the Suez Canal, which may have had something to do with his own rather sudden support for imperial expansion in the early 1870s. In 1874, Gladstone and the Liberal Party lost an election to Disraeli and the Conservatives at least in part because of Disraeli's commitment to the British Empire and the perceived lack of commitment to the empire among Liberals. Political leaders in Britain were not unified in their desire to further expand the empire; Gladstone campaigned against Disraeli, now the Earl of Beaconsfield, in 1880 on an anti-imperialist platform criticizing his rival's penchant for embroiling Britain in foreign adventures. Even Gladstone, however, realized in 1882 that he could not allow Egypt to fall into the hands of a nationalist government that would be hostile to British and European interests. At the time Egypt had become a virtually independent country under the leadership of a pro-European ruler known as the Khedive. The Khedive's close ties with European governments, especially the French, alienated both Islamic fundamentalists in the Egyptian-controlled Sudan and Egyptian nationalists.

In the Sudan, Mohammed Ahmed ibn Abdullah proclaimed himself the 'Mahdi', a Muslim holy man prophesied to emerge to defend Islam against hostile forces and reign in the true interests of the faith. The rebellion he inspired there in 1881 was followed by a revolution in Egypt led by Arabi Pasha, who sought to overthrow the Khedive and promised to oust foreigners from the country. When the British intervened by sending a small cavalry force supported by a thousand infantry under the command of General Garnet Wolseley, Wolseley's badly outnumbered army quickly dispatched Arabi Pasha's forces in under 30 minutes. Gladstone attempted to mitigate the view of Britain as a hostile force by proclaiming Britain's presence in Egypt as an ephemeral state of affairs; he turned out to be right, but no one in the late nineteenth century would have taken this to signify that Britain would remain the dominant power in Egypt until 1948.

The British asked the same questions about Egypt that the writer of an 1877 editorial did about South Africa: 'What kind of combination of circumstances and systematic arrangement of means, what development of resources and of motive power is to press South Africa forward in civilization and prosperity?'[25] The Cape Colony of South Africa had received home rule in 1871, shortly after the discovery of diamond fields brought new interest among British imperialists in the region, including the newly annexed area of West Griqualand, north of the Orange River. A contemporary participant in the diamond rush captured the initial enthusiasm associated with the discovery:

> This now celebrated field was first 'rushed' in August 1871. It is situated on the farm 'Vooruitzicht,' commonly called 'De Beers' – the name of the owners at the time diamonds were discovered here – and is about one mile westward of the field known as 'De Beers (Old) Rush', and about three miles northwestward of Dutoitspan, and Bultfontein, and eighteen miles from the Vaal River diggings. This field has proved itself to be the richest known diamond-field in the world. Thousands of gems have been found here. Most claims yield something, and the richness of some is almost beyond belief.

Cecil Rhodes was among the British investors who derived enormous profits from the extensive diamond mines at De Beers. For the remainder of the century, Rhodes set about to establish his own political power in conjunction with the expansion of the British Empire in Africa. He even named one colony – Rhodesia – after himself; his will indicates that he thought of the land as his own personal property where he wished to be buried and which, in the meantime, he could dispose of as befitted his interests. The British government tended to back individual traders rather than officially intervening in South Africa, sometimes with calamitous and expensive consequences. Attracted by the rich diamond mines of South Africa, Lord Kimberley also began to assume authority in the region, despite the knowledge that this would bring him into conflict with the Dutch Afrikaner settlers there. But British claims to diamond mines in disputed territories brought them into direct conflict with the Orange Free State, which also asserted its possession of the diamonds. Without their consent, the Boers became incorporated into the new British dominion controlled by Theophilus Shepstone.

The British went even further when they invaded Zululand in 1878. Under their tribal leader, Cetshwayo, the Zulus fought back, amassing an army of 20,000 warriors to resist the British army. At Isandlwana, Cetshwayo and the Zulus dealt the British a humiliating defeat in which the British commander Chelmsford left many of his men to be slaughtered on the battlefield. The British defeated Cetshwayo the following year and incorporated the land of the Zulus within the British Empire in 1887. Meanwhile, the Boers in the state of the Transvaal were ominously organizing to defend their territory against British encroachments.

To some British imperialists, Africa appeared as the inescapable next step in the search for markets for British goods; in 1893, F. D. Lugard wrote in *The Rise of Our East African Empire: Early Efforts in Nyasaland and Uganda* that 'as long as our policy is one of free trade, we are compelled to seek new markets; for old ones are being closed to us by hostile tariffs, and our great dependencies, which formerly were the consumers of our goods, are now becoming our commercial rivals'. Yet Lugard also argued that native populations would benefit from British rule. He regarded the introduction of Western medicine and technology as the most important contributions the British had to offer. Lugard believed that some African tribes had greater aptitude for working with machinery, but thought all Africans could benefit 'if not only mechanical and artisan work, such as the carpenter's and blacksmith's craft, but also the simpler expedients of agriculture are taught'. He continued:

> The sinking of wells, the system of irrigation, the introduction and planting of useful trees, the use of manure, and of domestic animals for agricultural purposes, the improvement of his implements by the introduction of the primitive Indian plough, etc. – all of these, while improving the status of the native, will render his land more productive, and hence, by increasing his surplus products, will enable him to purchase from the trader the cloth which shall add to his decency, and the implements and household utensils which shall produce greater results for his labor and greater comforts in his social life.[26]

For devout Christians in Britain, the expansion of the British Empire in Africa still had a moral and religious significance. By the end of the century, the Church of England took pride not only in the numerous missions founded across Africa but also in the church's role in the changes to the legal status of slavery in areas controlled by the British. However, an 1890 editorial in *The Guardian* saw fit to point out that 'the millions in men and money consecrated by the nation to the suppression of the slave trade in Africa, while leaving it triumphant in Europe, may have been like pouring water into a vessel with a leak'.

Although individual merchants such as Cecil Rhodes accumulated huge fortunes in Africa, direct colonial rule was unlikely to be profitable because of the undeveloped nature of the economy in Africa. Africa had simply become the next continent on which the European powers projected their rivalries; once one power – the British – began to expand their influence there, others followed, motivated by a desire to maintain the balance of power. France balked at the British presence in Egypt, fearing that they might encroach upon its interests in Algeria. By the end of the century, the British and the French almost went to war over control of the Sudan, while the Germans had staked their claim to a number of colonies in an attempt to find their 'place in the sun', as Bismarck put it, before alienating the British by siding with the Dutch in South Africa prior to the outbreak of the Boer War in 1899.

The literature of empire

The British Empire inspired literary responses that both reflected and helped to shape the realities and perceptions associated with the acquisition and defence of empire, ranging from H. Rider Haggard's *King Solomon's Mines* (1885), an adventure novel set in Africa, to Rudyard Kipling's *Kim* (1901), a coming-of-age story of an Irish boy raised as a native Indian who simultaneously accompanies an Indian holy man on a spiritual quest for a sacred river and is recruited for an espionage mission that was part of the 'Great Game' to keep the Russians out of India. Set in an age in which white hunters were slaughtering buffalo to the point of near extinction in the American West, Haggard's book reflects the values of a bygone age in which his characters dine on giraffe meat and kill elephants for their ivory without thinking twice. Haggard could certainly be patronizing, if not racist towards African peoples, though he does pay the Zulus the compliment of being 'by no means devoid of poetic instinct and of intellectual power'. In Kipling's *Kim* the treatment of the natives is quite different. The title character Kim experiences something of an identity crisis, moving back and forth between the role of a European and an Indian in the novel. He is taken from the lama, his holy man, to attend a school for Europeans, but when he rejoins the lama, he slips back to living, eating, speaking, thinking, and even dreaming like an Indian. The blurring of identities in an imperialistic setting was not an uncommon literary theme; G. A. Henty's 1896 novel *The Tiger of Mysore* deals with the son and daughter of an Englishwoman and an Indian prince. When their mother dies young, the daughter, Margaret is sent back to England for her education, while the boy, Dick, remains, where he says he tried 'my hardest to show that in riding, or the chase, or in exercises of any kind, I was as worthy to be the son of an Indian rajah as if I had no white blood in my veins'. Yet, whereas Kim learns through the lama to accept both parts of his identity and discovers that he is simply who he is, Kim, without needing to label himself Indian or European, in Henty's novel Dick comes to a different realization, telling Margaret: 'As I grew up I became wiser. I saw how great the English were, how steadily they extended their dominions, and how vastly better off were our people under their sway than they were in the days when every rajah made war against his neighbor, and the land never had rest.'

Writers such as Henty thought themselves capable of distinguishing between good wars and bad wars in the name of the empire. Perhaps he was contrasting the war against the Sikhs with the baneful Opium War when he made the following remarks in his Preface to *Through the Sikh War: A Tale of the Conquest of the Punjab* (1894):

> It is satisfactory to know that the conquest of the Sikhs – a brave and independent race – was not brought about by any of the intrigues which marred the brilliancy of some of our early conquests, or by greed for additional territory, but was the result of a wanton invasion of the states under our protection by the turbulent soldiery of the Punjaub, who believed themselves invincible, and embarked upon the conflict with a confident belief that they would make themselves masters of Delhi, if not drive us completely out of India.[27]

Henty admitted that he did not like to write about British defeats. He emphasized the importance of the Sikh Wars of the 1840s because, if the Punjab had not become attached to Britain and remained loyal during the Mutiny then the future of the British Empire could have been in even greater danger. Kipling's Kim speaks of the Great Game with a kind of reverence as he learns what is at stake; for Kipling and his readers the choice for India was not British rule or Indian self-rule but British rule or Russian rule, which they believed would have been infinitely worse for India. *Kim* was first published in 1901, and, while it looked more to the past than to the future, it did reflect the reality of the dearth of support in England for an India outside the British Empire's aegis.

Kipling's novels were extraordinarily popular among young readers, but so were simple adventure tales told in stories published in magazines aimed at teenage boys who might themselves soon be expected to serve in the empire. During the Boer War, the magazine *Young England* published a cover that included items such as tennis racquets, cricket bats, and rowing oars alongside a British soldier to emphasize that he was fighting for British values.[28] Henty himself published adventure stories in *Young England* on a regular basis. In *Through the Sikh War*, Henty wrote:

> It is pluck and endurance, and a downright love of adventure and danger, that
> have made us the masters of the greater part of India, and will ere long make us
> rulers of the whole of it; and it is of no use anyone coming out here, especially to
> take service with one of the native princes, unless he is disposed to love danger for
> its own sake, and to feel that he is willing and ready to meet it whatever quarter
> it may come.[29]

The impact of Henty's ideas seemed to romanticize the British Empire, particularly in the minds of young boys, many of whom would grow up to witness – and frequently lament – its decline and fall.

Another romantic perspective came from Alfred Lord Tennyson, whose 1879 poem, 'The Defense of Lucknow' celebrated the heroic defence of Delhi during the mutiny that kept the British flag 'flying over the residency'. The mutiny inspired other literary works, most notably Flora Annie Steel's *On the Face of the Waters: A Tale of the Mutiny* (1896), one of a number of works authored by Steel on British India. In *On the Face of the Waters*, Steel focuses on the experiences of several women at the time of the mutiny, including her central character, Kate Erlton, who finding herself in need of protection from some Indian mutineers, adapts herself to Indian cultural practices, which ends up setting her apart from other British women in India who remained subservient to British men.

The novel that did the most to change perceptions of European imperialism in the mind of British readers was Joseph Conrad's *Heart of Darkness*, written in 1899. The main character of Conrad's short novel, a man named Kurtz, is a ship captain sent to Africa to replace his predecessor who had been killed in a quarrel with some natives. The murder had occurred over a dispute about chickens. In Conrad's description of the incident, the murdered captain, a Dane named Fresleven, peremptorily attacked an African man with a stick until another man intervened by thrusting a spear between the aggressor's shoulder blades. The main effect of the novel was to call attention to the brutalization of African natives by European merchants, particularly in the Congo where Conrad had spent some time and where many of the worst abuses of the native population had occurred. For Conrad, literature provided a means of attempting to understand his own experiences while at the same time speaking to the larger issues related to imperialism with which the twentieth century would be continue to grapple.

In addition to literature about the empire, English novels such as Charlotte Brontë's *Jane Eyre* (1847) became so popular throughout the English-speaking world that Charlotte MacDonald has called it 'one of the archetypal spines of the British empire'. What made the popularity of this book so significant, as MacDonald points out, was its strong feminist bent and the extent to which it challenged a patriarchal political and legal system that treated women as 'chattels, decorative dependents, dutiful companions, or conduits for family reputations, names, and fortunes'.[30] MacDonald notes the fortuitous literary explosion of the mid-nineteenth century that supplied this demand – in 1847 and 1848 alone, in addition to Jane Eyre, William Thackeray's *Vanity Fair*, Elizabeth Gaskell's *Mary Barton*, Charles Dickens's

Dombey and Son, Emily Brontë's *Wuthering Heights*, Anne Brontë's *Tenant of Wildfell Hall*, and Thomas Babington Macaulay's *History of England* all became available. This outpouring of British literature played a strong role in affirming ties of settlers throughout the empire to their homeland, while also providing a cultural unity to the larger British world as a whole.[31] Macaulay's history of England provided the British Empire with a historical mythology of the birth and rise of a great nation committed to individual rights and representative government, while at the same time justifying British imperial expansion and providing inspiration for self-government in places like Canada and Australia.[32]

If literature and history kept British settlers abroad in tune with cultural and intellectual currents from the homeland, then nonfiction travel literature, much of it written by women, also played an important role in providing information about the empire – and the wider world – and promoted interests in them to the reading public at home in the British Isles. Constance Gordon Cummings (1837–1924) and Marianne North (1830–90) both wrote extensively of their travels in North America in the nineteenth century. Isabella Bird (1831–1904), the first woman elected to the British Geographical Society, published extensively on her travels in Asia, Australia, and North America. In addition to the popular works by Livingstone, Burton, and Speke, those of Mary Kingsley (1862–1900), based on her travels and experiences in west Africa, contributed significantly to British views of the empire and the people living therein.

The empire continued to exert a strong influence on British literature in the twentieth century, much of it critical of the imperial enterprise and reflective of declining levels of confidence in Britain's place in the world. E. M. Forster's 1924 novel, *A Passage to India* is perhaps the best known of this genre. George Orwell's *Burmese Days* (1934), based on the years he spent in Burma from 1922 to 1928, is hypercritical and speaks explicitly of the Englishman's loathing of the imperial system of which he is a part. Paul Scott's *The Jewel in the Crown* (1966) and Forster's *Passage to India* both highlight the problems with Indians receiving justice from a British judge, while also revealing issues revolving around racial prejudice and a sexual double-standard regarding interracial sex, given the many opportunities that British men had for sex with Indian women. The Australian-born British writer James Clavell took on the subject of the Opium War in his historical novel, *Tai-Pan* (1966). More recently, the left-wing English novelist Julian Rathbone (1935–2008) revisited the subject of the mutiny in his 2007 novel, *The Mutiny*, which evoked parallels with the revival of religious fundamentalism in the contemporary world.

The foundations of the British Commonwealth

Finally, the British Empire of the nineteenth century helped to lay the groundwork for the British Commonwealth of Nations that emerged in the twentieth century. The ties between Britain and the colonies of Canada, Australia, New Zealand, and South Africa were strengthened by the large number of people from the British Isles who settled there, drawn by better economic opportunities in the course of the nineteenth century. In the difficult years between 1819 and 1925, the British began to allocate funds (a total of £95,000 for these years) to assist poor people desiring emigration.[33] While many of those who left the British Isles in this period went to the United States, other regions attracted considerable interest as well. Australia and New Zealand began to attract more immigrants during the Australian gold rush of 1851 and a similar flood of people to New Zealand during the 1880s after another gold strike. As we have seen, South Africa attracted heightened interest in the 1870s and 1880s as well, thanks to the economic opportunities opened by the discovery of diamonds and gold there. Canada had gradually gained more attention in Britain and in the early twentieth century became a much more popular destination than it had been for much of the nineteenth century. Canada, like the United States, was obviously much closer than Australia or New Zealand, but, unlike the United States, had the advantage of feeling more like home as it retained more of its British identity. In 1905, for the first time, Canada received more British immigrants than did the United States.[34]

Not all of these colonies achieved dominion status at the same time, but the principle elaborated in the Durham Report for Canada in 1839 that led to its virtual independence in 1867 set an important precedent. Around the same time Canada, Australia, New Zealand, and South Africa all acquired their own constitutions and legislatures, as well as control of the physical territory under their jurisdictions.

The ideas of a common bond among these dominions took a variety of forms prior to the establishment of the Commonwealth; in 1903, for example, the historian James Bryce spoke at the first Allied Colonial Universities Conference of the desire to foster a closer relationship among 'the universities of the British world'.[35] There was undoubtedly a certain racial element to the desire to unite these white dominions and predominantly white institutions such as universities to the exclusion of the native inhabitants of those same regions. The colonizers assumed a certain level of superiority that allowed them to dominate and legislate for the non-European populations of their dominions while asserting their own right to independence from Britain.

The support provided by these dominions to the British war effort during the First World War further solidified the common feeling among these nations of strong historical and cultural ties that needed to be preserved in some way. Britain could not expect to continue to exercise any direct control over these former colonies, but it welcomed the continuation of a voluntary association based on a nominal allegiance to the British monarch and British traditions. At the end of the First World War, Canada, Australia, New Zealand, and South Africa all joined the League of Nations as independent countries, as did India, even though it would not achieve its independence until 1947. Yet this was also the same time during which the term 'British Commonwealth' gained habitual use. The Irish Free State became a member of the Commonwealth upon its ultimate achievement of home rule in 1922 and remained so until Ireland achieved full independence in 1948. But the membership of the Irish Free State in the British Commonwealth points to the tenuous nature of the concept since not even all white settlers would feel the same level of connection with Britain, other examples besides the Irish being the French in Quebec and the Dutch Afrikaners in South Africa.

The Commonwealth was, in a sense, an attempt to preserve some vestiges of the British Empire after Britain had lost its ability to legislate for its former colonies or to intervene in their internal affairs. Rhodesia and Kenya also became dominated by white settlers by the time of the emergence of the Commonwealth, of which Rhodesia became a member in 1923 even though it, like India, did not have full independence. Its existence was acknowledged by an Imperial Conference in London in 1926 and became official with the passage of the Statute of Westminster in 1931. After the Second World War, with the independence and participation in the Commonwealth of India, Pakistan, and Burma, the Commonwealth lost its primarily white identity and was renamed the Commonwealth of Nations, although Burma would withdraw its membership almost immediately in 1948.

The principle had been established by a judicial ruling by Lord Mansfield as early as 1765 that those who left Britain retained the rights of British subjects wherever they went. Unfortunately, these rights did not extend to the indigenous peoples of the lands where they settled.

FIGURE 28 *Workers at Hampton's Munitions Works, Lambeth, London, 1914–18. This scene shows workers in a factory making buckets. Note how the men and women are working in separate areas; they are probably performing different tasks. 'Come along and Join the Army: Duty Calls', the poster says, which suggests that this picture was taken before conscription was introduced in early 1916.*

Heritage Images/Hulton Archive/Getty.

14

In the shadow of the Great War,
c. 1890–1918

If in some smothering dreams, you too could pace
Behind the wagon that we flung him in,
And watch the white eyes writhing in his face,
His hanging face, like a devil's sick of sin,
If you could hear, at every jolt, the blood
Come gargling from the froth-corrupted lungs
Bitter as the curd
Of vile, incurable sores on innocent tongues, –
My friend, you would not tell with such high zest
To children ardent for some desperate glory,
That old lie: Dulce et decorum est
Pro patria mori.[1]

WILFRED OWEN (1893–1918), 'Dulce et Decorum Est'

Political culture and the threat to stability in the late nineteenth and early twentieth century

In the late 1880s William Gladstone had split the Liberal Party over Home Rule for Ireland, providing an opportunity for the Conservative Party to dominate British politics for the foreseeable future. A few years later the demise of Charles Stewart Parnell weakened the Irish Party, another boon for the Conservatives. Furthermore, a group of politicians known as the Liberal imperialists, led by Joseph Chamberlain, shared with the Conservatives pro-Empire principles, which led to an alliance that contributed to the Conservative majority. This alliance should have been conducive to a prolonged period of political stability, but by 1914 the British Isles faced one of the gravest political crises in their history, one that threatened to unravel the entire political and social fabric of the UK. Many people would look back to the years before the First World War, which started in 1914, as a kind of golden age before the war ravaged the national psyche and led to radical changes in social customs and mores. However, in retrospect, signs of the threat to political and social stability throughout the Isles were tangible at the turn of the century.

First, labour unrest throughout the British Isles spanned the years on both sides of 1900. Parliament passed a new Factory Act in 1895, which drew widespread support, except for some employers and advocates of women's suffrage who objected to the bill on the grounds that it denied women their economic freedom and discouraged them from taking personal responsibility for their lives. However principled the supporters of the Act were in their attempt to diminish the exploitation of female factory workers, the Act did not assuage labour discontent elsewhere. A miner's strike in South Wales in 1898 led to a showdown between owners and miners regarding whether or not the colliers had the right to receive poor relief while they were on strike. Welsh coal miners had good reason to strike for higher wages and safer conditions; they suffered from a disproportionate number of accidental deaths. The Welsh coal miners faced especially difficult workplace exigencies, even when compared to the hazards of the profession in other parts of Britain. In 1900, the *Merthyr Tydfil* ruling of the High Court went against the miners, stating that they had no legal right to poor relief during a strike. This decision reversed a ruling from the previous year that had affirmed the right of striking miners to public assistance, a position that did not provoke any kind of a public outcry because of public support for the colliers. The subsequent decision was an augur of the political direction in which the court was headed in its thinking on business–labour relations, as can be seen in the Taff–Vale judgement of 1901. In that famous case, the Law Lords ruled that the National Union of Railway workers could be held liable for civil damages caused by their strike. This decision in effect deprived unions of the right to strike, leading labour leaders to turn to politics as their sole means of redress.

Contemporary with labour unrest, the conflict in South Africa known as the Second Boer War (1899–1902) made a profound impression on those living at the time and would no doubt receive more attention from historians today if it were not eclipsed by the First World War. In fact, the process of memorializing the war dead that became so ubiquitous throughout the British Isles after the Great War had already begun in earnest in the decade following the Boer War. The Queen Victoria School, founded in Perthshire, Scotland in 1908, provided one such example. The practice of erecting war memorials to commemorate the dead indicates a growing ambivalence towards war that would only be reinforced by the devastating ordeal of the First World War. Furthermore, the Boer War was largely the product of growing imperial tensions endemic to Britain at the nadir of the nineteenth century. The British, who had been engaged in a struggle in South Africa with the Dutch-descended Boers for decades, sought in the 1890s to augment and consolidate their control over the region in the face of the European-wide 'scramble for Africa'.

The Boer War was particularly brutal, with civilian atrocities, concentration camps, and guerrilla warfare, all, of course, foreshadowing characteristics of modern warfare that would become so familiar over the course of the twentieth century. Analogous to the First World War, the British failed to gain the quick and easy victory that the public expected. Unlike in the Great War, more than three times as many British soldiers died from sickness than from combat: 22,000 compared to 6,000.[2] The *London Times* did much to cover up the atrocities and ineptness that were part of British conduct during the war, focusing on military incompetence in its criticisms, rather than issuing an indictment of the war itself. The generation that had grown up since the Education Act of 1870 was more literate; what television did to bring the war in Vietnam into people's homes in the 1960s, cheap newspapers did for the Boer War. The Boer War also presaged the situation in the First World War when so many educated members of the ruling class would be called upon to do their supposed duty to God and country.

Following the Boer War, the Liberals regained power in 1906 determined to make progress in social and political reform. They committed themselves to preserving free trade, but now supported collective bargaining for labour. The Liberal Party also drew strong support from Scotland and Wales, in addition to its continued alliance with the Irish Party, whose best hopes for Home Rule for Ireland were still thought to repose with the Liberals. Support from these other parties helped the Liberals overcome the determined opposition of the Conservative and Unionist parties and remain in power for the next decade.

The decisive triumph of the Liberal Party sent a wave of panic through Conservative circles, which did not regard the election as merely another turn in the cycle of alternating Liberal and Conservative governments. More seemed at stake because of the variety of issues emanating from the political culture of the Edwardian period. Labour unrest, constitutional change, the role of government, the future of the Empire, Britain's relative economic decline (especially vis-à-vis Germany), the future of Ireland, and women's suffrage were all issues that potentially affected millions of people. Deep ideological differences divided the parties on most of these issues. Many people still clung strongly to the free trade tradition and distrusted government intervention in the economy, even though the Conservative Party had been responsible for seminal social legislation in the nineteenth century.

In short, the new Liberal government had to overcome significant opposition to its reform agenda, including within the victorious party itself, despite its apparent possession of a mandate to carry out popularly supported ameliorative legislation. The Liberal imperialists still constituted something of an antagonistic wing within the government of the Liberal prime minister, Henry Campbell-Bannerman. Yet the main barriers came from a new obstructionist attitude on the part of Conservatives within the House of Lords, who still possessed the constitutional power to veto legislation passed in the House of Commons. Since the members of the House of Lords held their position by appointment or hereditary right, they historically had exercised discretion in rejecting too much legislation based on political ideology, irrespective of the party that happened to hold power, but not at this juncture. The Lords abandoned their circumspectness and began actually vetoing legislation in response to the Liberal Party's reform agenda.

In addition, new Conservative organizations, such as the Women's Unionist and Tariff Reform Association (WUTRA), arose in response to the Liberal victory. The WUTRA was headed by Mary Maxse, a passionate opponent of women's suffrage as well as an adherent of Chamberlain's ideas on tariff reform. As it turned out, women's suffrage was a cause that the Liberal Party was not yet ready to propagate and support through feminist legislation. Despite growing support and a deep conviction among the British populace that women deserved the same political rights as male citizens, the Liberal Party dragged its heels. The Chancellor of the Exchequer, Herbert Henry Asquith, who became prime minister in 1908 upon the death of Campbell-Bannerman, was implacably opposed to the idea. A bill that would have granted the right to vote to unmarried women had failed in 1892, with Gladstone urging members of the Liberal Party to reject the measure. Advocates for women's suffrage were more sanguine after 1906; their continued disappointment only motivated them to take more extreme measures and to state the proto-feminist case even more forcefully. Christabel Pankhurst, the daughter of Emmeline Pankhurst, the first lady of the suffragettes, wrote in 1913 that men would never think of women as equals until women had the right to vote; instead they would continue to regard women as a 'sub-human species ... to be bought and soiled and degraded and then cast away'. For Christabel Pankhurst, as for other suffragettes, the future of humanity in general depended upon the liberation of women, an objective that would possess later generations with even greater ardour. While the militant suffragettes received most of the attention from the press and society at large, an increasing number of suffragists who also supported women's right to vote were represented by the National Union of Women's Suffrage Societies headed by Millicent Garrett Fawcett.

Although no immediate progress on women's suffrage was forthcoming, the Liberal Party did manage to secure approval for some reform measures from the House of Lords. For example, the Old Age Pensions Act of 1908 provided some measure of relief for those over the age of seventy, although few members of the working class were likely to live long enough to benefit from this legislation. In fact, many workers resented the deductions from their wages intended to help finance the unpopular measure. The passage of such measures only temporarily forestalled the brewing political crisis, however, which came to a head when David Lloyd George introduced the 'People's Budget' in 1909, which attacked the Lords where they were most vulnerable: their pocketbooks. The budget introduced land duties, which the financially straitened aristocracy could not afford, but Lloyd George saw an opportunity to attack their sense of privilege and went on a speaking tour to make his case for trammelling the power of the aristocracy. An election in January 1910 saw the Conservatives gain a majority of the votes, but they failed to gain a majority of the seats because of continued support for the Liberals from Scotland, Wales, and Ireland. A second election in December 1910 again produced a deadlock between the Conservatives and the Liberals, but the Irish Parliamentary Party triumphed decisively in Ireland, again swinging the plurality of seats in the House of Commons towards support for a Liberal government.

With the passage of the Parliamentary Act in 1911, Home Rule once again took centre stage in the political arena. As a result of the Act, the House of Lords now possessed a merely suspensory veto that could only postpone legislation passed by the House of Commons. Any law passed in three consecutive sessions would now become law regardless of how the House of Lords voted on the matter. The Act thus put Home Rule for Ireland on a schedule to become law as soon as 1914. In September 1911, 50,000 people turned out at a protest against Home Rule in Craigavon in Northern Ireland. It would be a mistake to think that unionist sentiment at that time was confined to Northern Ireland, however. Indeed, the union with Ireland still had popular support throughout England, Scotland, and Wales. Even in Ireland, the Irish Unionist Party drew support from both north and south and generally sent about twenty representatives to the House of Commons. The existence of two antagonistic Irish parties raised the growing possibility of conflict over Ireland and made celebrities of their two leaders, the Unionist Edward Carson and Parnell's successor, John Redmond.

Many historians, following George Dangerfield, believe that if not for the outbreak of war in 1914, the Liberal government and perhaps the entire political system would have crashed as a result of the dearth of support from women and workers in the face of a civil war led by Irish Unionists in alliance with the Conservative Party. Such a view is far from universally accepted among historians, however. The Liberals still had a fairly strong consensus on many issues in 1914 and may still have found a compromise on Home Rule that would have preserved the peace in England, if not in Ireland. The large voter turnout in 1906 and 1914 reflects a high level of political engagement, as well as an equally strong vote of confidence in the existing political system. By 1914, that enthusiasm may have diminished, but the government was solvent, the economy still strong, and whether or not the British upper classes would have condoned a civil war certainly contentious. The Conservatives had no love for the Liberal government, but ipso facto, due to their political ideology, we must think it likely that they would have drawn back from the precipice if the entire governmental structure started to crumble. Even if the outbreak of war did temporarily save the Liberal government in 1914, the First World War proved disastrous for the Liberal Party, which the war eventually shattered, along with much else in British political culture.

Cultural revivals and survivals

The political crisis in Ireland had its advent in the continuing demand for Home Rule from a segment of the Irish population and the commitment of the Irish Party and one of the two main political parties in Britain to that cause. In the meantime, however, some Irish men and women had become more concerned with a different kind of national movement: the revival and preservation of Irish culture. The beginnings of the Irish cultural renascence can be traced to an 1888 book called *Glimpses of Erin*, coauthored by a father and daughter, Seaton and Alice Milligan. They believed that Ireland could carve out its own cultural identity within the confines of the British Empire; they regarded Ireland's long history as so inextricably intertwined with England's that attempts to completely escape English influence was futile and fruitless. They emphasized the importance of Irish poetry – Alice Milligan included some of her own in the book – and Irish history based on authentic Irish sources and archaeological discoveries. They personally began their own collection of Irish books, manuscripts, and historical photographs. Being members of the Belfast Naturalist Field Club, they stressed the importance of the study of Irish geography as well.[3] The Milligans, like other cultural nationalists, were concerned with the question of national identity, whose locus they sought to situate in Irish literature and culture rather than in a national political movement.

The same view was shared by the most important figure in the Irish cultural revival of the late nineteenth and early twentieth century: W. B. Yeats. Yeats shared the Milligans' special emphasis on poetry and, indeed, became one of Ireland's greatest poets. He based his lengthy 1889 poem *The Wanderings of Oisin* on the famous Fionn cycle of stories from early Irish history. Yeats also took a particular interest in Irish drama. Not only did he write plays based on Irish history and literature, including a series on the mythological Irish hero, Cuchulainn, but as president of the National Theatre Society, Yeats also collaborated with Lady Augusta Gregory and the playwright J. M. Synge (who had belonged to the same Field Club as the Milligans) to arbitrate on the plays performed at the Abbey Theatre in Dublin. The decision to stage Synge's own controversial play, *The Playboy of the Western World*, in 1907 precipitated riots and demands to shut the play down, which Yeats refused to do.

Other threads contributed to the sense of a rebirth of Irish culture as well. The writing of autobiographies became central to the Irish cultural revival because of their ability to tell an authentic story rooted in one's own personal and historical experience. Lady Gregory, for example, wrote a half-dozen works that were autobiographical in nature, in addition to a number of plays. The Gaelic League, to which Lady Gregory belonged, sought to foster a revival of the Irish language. Lady Gregory also helped to promote an interest in Irish folklore, which she helped to popularize through such works as *Cuchulain of Muirthemne* (1902), *A Book of Saints and Wonders* (1906), and *The Kiltartan Wonder Book* (1910).

Wales experienced a cultural revival similar to that of the Irish in the early twentieth century, but one that stood in direct opposition to many of the secular forces dominating the modern world, including socialism, contemporary science, and psychology. Welsh identity, like that of the Presbyterian Scots, came from having their own nonconformist religious tradition rooted mainly in Methodism that set them apart from the Church of England. Therefore, the Welsh revival manifested a greater religious character than that of the Irish, which was more associated with the forces of modernism and thus drew serious opposition from the Catholic Church. Welsh culture remained embedded within its nonconformist churches; instead of political societies or literary associations, the Welsh joined prayer meetings. Beginning in southern Wales and spreading to the north, the religious revival even attracted both men and women of a younger Welsh generation. Evan Roberts (1878–1951), a young and charismatic Methodist minister and former coal miner and blacksmith's apprentice, was a key figure in this religious revival, drawing huge crowds to hear him speak and attracting a strong following in Wales until he collapsed from exhaustion in 1906, forcing him to curtail his activities.

On the other hand, cultural nationalists in Wales and Ireland, more so than in Scotland, became preoccupied with the survival of their native languages. John Davies has calculated that more people spoke Welsh in 1914 than in 1850, but that the percentage of residents of Wales who spoke in their native tongue had dropped from about 67 per cent to about 40 per cent, with those who spoke Welsh exclusively constituting an even smaller minority at the later date.[4] Most people in Ireland and Wales spoke English, with native languages falling into disuse largely as a result of the Education Act of 1870. In Ireland, the decline in the number of Gaelic speakers also resulted from the deaths and emigration of many rural residents in the more remote parts of the island hardest hit by the Great Famine. The Gaelic League sought to reverse this trend and in the process restore to the Irish a greater sense of their identity vis-à-vis the English. Upon becoming president of the Gaelic League, Douglas Hyde titled his inaugural address *On the Necessity for De-Anglicising Ireland*.

Even those individuals who would have considered themselves Scottish nationalists had as little desire for political independence in the early twentieth century as the Welsh and far less than their counterparts in Ireland. This, despite the fact that Scotland remained underrepresented in Parliament in proportion to its population, though the government had made some effort to redress this imbalance among the political reforms of the 1860s and 1880s. Nor did Scottish issues receive the undivided attention from the larger assembly of the House of Commons. Yet because the Scottish retained a penchant for autonomy (rooted perhaps in the democratic tendencies of the Presbyterian church), they seemed to feel more confident in their separate identity even within the confines of the UK. The Scots also possessed an excellent education system even before 1870, which made them one of the most literate and best educated people in Europe. To the degree that Scotland experienced any kind of cultural revival at the end of the nineteenth century, it remained linked with interest in the novels of Sir Walter Scott and images of tartans, kilts, and bagpipes that pervaded the diverse cultures of the Lowlands and Highlands into a stereotypical, homogeneous Scottish culture. This trend also manifested itself in the sentimental 'Kailyard' school of literature, which included the works of Ian McClaren, J. M. Barrie, and George MacDonald.

Yeats famously dated the beginnings of modern Irish literature to the fall of Parnell in 1891. This may have been self-aggrandizing, since Yeats himself founded the National Literary Society in Dublin in 1892. Yeats continued to flirt with the revolutionary society, the Irish Republican Brotherhood (IRB), in the 1890s, not resigning his membership until 1900. Furthermore, Yeats spoke in defence of Irish nationalism during the centenary of the 1798 rebellion and during royal visits to Dublin by Queen Victoria and King Edward VIII in 1900 and 1903, respectively.[5] When forced to choose, however, Yeats would opt for cultural over political nationalism.

The other well-known Irish writer from the period, James Joyce, rejected political nationalism in even stronger terms. Although Joyce will always be considered an Irish writer and drew inspiration from his personal life experiences in his native land, he belonged to a larger modernist tradition and focused more on universal literary themes that transcended the Irish revival. Yeats dealt with universal themes as well, especially in his poetry, but he remained quintessentially Irish and stands out as the main representative, if not the leader, of the Irish cultural revival. Yeats was less interested in the revival of Gaelic than he was in the translation of Gaelic literature into English; in the 1880s he had become personally acquainted with individuals such as Standish O'Grady, Samuel Ferguson, and James Clarence Mangan who had done just that. Ferguson was among the poets quoted by the Milligans in *Glimpses of Erin*, along with others whose work they attempted to revive such as the eighteenth-century writer Oliver Goldsmith and the nineteenth-century poets, Thomas Moore and John Savage. To the extent that they were successful, however, interest remained confined to a minority of the population; most people in Ireland, as in the rest of the British Isles, had enough to deal with from the demands of everyday life.

The world of yesterday: Life in the British Isles at the beginning of the twentieth century

Any economic decline on the part of the UK at the turn of the twentieth century was only a relative decline; the standard of living was rising for a majority of the population and would continue to do so in the first dozen years after 1900. In 1910, Britain was importing and exporting six times that which it had in 1850.[6] In 1913, the United Kingdom still produced 19 per cent of the world's cotton goods, a number surpassed only by the United States at that time; the cotton industry was still growing, not contracting. At the turn of the century, 656,000 women worked in the manufacture of textiles;[7] men, of course, worked in the mills of northern England as well.

Even though the UK was still a leading industrial nation, only a minority of the population actually worked in factories. Since the cotton textile industry remained largely centred in Lancashire, mill work should not be regarded as typical of working-class life in all parts of the United Kingdom. In other trades associated with the textile industry, such as dressmaking and tailoring, women frequently laboured in unregulated sweatshops for low wages in abysmal conditions, but conditions tended to be better in factories that turned out more expensive clothing for reputable stores such as Harrods and Selfridge's. These trades, whatever their drawbacks, also provided an alternative to those women who wanted to avoid domestic service or prostitution. By the turn of the century, new opportunities existed for women in relatively new clerical professions in banks and offices, as teachers or librarians, nurses or secretaries, all of which were generally considered feminine professions.

Large numbers of male labourers still worked in agriculture, despite the decrease in the amount of farmland under cultivation that had occurred towards the end of the nineteenth century. (Peter Clarke estimates that one-sixth the amount of arable land under cultivation in 1880 was no longer so in 1900.[8]) Others found employment in construction or maintenance as carpenters or metalworkers. Among the working classes, the miners had arguably the toughest and most dangerous jobs. In the last two decades of the nineteenth century, 2,238 British miners died in major disasters (defined as taking the lives of more than twenty-five people). A disproportionate number (48 per cent) of these deaths occurred in Wales, which accounted for only 18 per cent of the more than one million British miners. In 1913, an estimated 232,000 workers hauled 57 million tonnes out of Wales's 620 coal mines.[9] Altogether, Britain possessed more than 2,500 mines, producing 290 tonnes of coal annually at that time.[10] Yet miners remained far more likely to die in an individual accident than in a collective disaster. Dockworkers in port cities such as Liverpool, Bristol, Cardiff, and Swansea, as well as London, also comprised a significant portion of the workforce, essential to the transport of coal and other heavy materials.

Not all working-class women worked; in fact, they tended to work until they were married, but to allow their husbands to support them afterward if he made a living wage. Works such as Florence Stacpoole's *Handbook of Housekeeping for Small Incomes* (1898) and Mrs Henry Reeve's *Cookery and Housekeeping: A Manual of Domestic Economy for Large and Small Families* (1882) provided advice to working-class wives and mothers. Such works contributed to a political and social campaign to extend concerns about cleanliness, safety, and order from the public to the private sphere. Of course, not all working-class women had husbands and not all working mothers had the time or income to avail themselves of such works.

Britain, of course, remained a class-ridden society to the extent that the life of the aristocracy differed radically from that of the classes below them. The landed aristocracy showed some signs of retrenchment by the end of the nineteenth century. Large landowners had never quite recovered from the agricultural depression of the 1870s, as evidenced by the relatively few houses built by them in the ensuing decades. They compensated for any threats to their social position, however, by preserving a conservative attitude towards social mores and values, which the upper-middle class very much attempted to emulate. E. M. Forster's 1910 novel, *Howard's End*, illuminates the social gap between the family of a wealthy businessman who aspires to the manners and lifestyle of the aristocracy and a petit bourgeois couple struggling to make a better life for themselves, while providing a glimpse into the quotidian world of both. Members of the upper and upper-middle classes still very much frowned on any of their children marrying beneath their social class, a theme developed by John Galsworthy in his popular trilogy, *The Forsyte Saga* (1906–21). George Bernard Shaw took up the same theme in his play, *Pygmalion*, which first appeared on the stage in 1910. Unlike its incarnation later in the century as the musical *My Fair Lady*, in *Pygmalion* the class divide proves too large to bridge for the two main characters, Professor Henry Higgins and the working-class street vendor, Eliza Doolittle.

At the bottom of society, poverty remained a societal problem of immense proportions, despite social legislation that dated back to the first Factory Act of 1833. Laws restricting the number of hours that women could work did not necessarily benefit the working classes economically and provoked some resistance from women's advocates, even though women were 'limited' to working 54 hours a week. Even among the lower classes there remained strong suspicion against government intervention. Still, the working classes had other advocates, such as the Fabian Maud Pember Reeves, whose 1913 publication, *Round About a Pound a Week*, called attention to the nutritional deficiencies of working-class infants. The price of food had decreased, in recent years, but this was not yet enough to significantly impact the health of the working classes, largely due to a paucity of fruits and vegetables in the British diet. Most British farmlands remained devoted to staple grains such as wheat, barley, and oats.

For the most part, however, the decades at the start of the new century witnessed a series of improvements that changed people's lives and boosted their confidence in the future. The telephone, electricity, the gramophone, and the bicycle, not to mention the internal combustion engine that led to the automobile, all contributed to a dramatic change in everyday life within the period of a generation. The increase in the number of commuter trains and the regularity of their routes made it possible for more and more people to live in safer and more sanitary environs outside of the manufacturing districts where they worked; for example, by 1890 forty trains a day entered Manchester's Central Station, a new train arriving every 10 minutes during the morning and evening rush-hours.[11]

For entertainment, urban residents increasingly turned to sports, especially Association Football (known to Americans as soccer), which had first become popular especially in the industrial towns of northern England and Scotland. However, the sport expanded to almost every major British city by the end of the first decade of the twentieth century. In addition, London hosted the Summer Olympics in 1908, the host nation ending with a haul of fifty-six Gold Medals and 146 total medals, by far the most of any of the twenty-one competing countries. Cricket was a sport considered the preserve of gentlemen, learnt at public schools and universities, though village competitions took place that attracted broader participation by the twentieth century. By the end of the nineteenth century, women's cricket teams had emerged as well. Lawn tennis was another leisurely sport of the refined class, but one that members of all classes could enjoy as spectators. The Wimbledon tournament had commenced at the All England tennis club in a London suburb in 1877. Sports became more important in Ireland with the formation of the Gaelic Athletic Association in 1884, which promoted a sport called Gaelic football and hurling at the expense of English sports such as cricket and rugby, which owed its name to the public school where it is said to have originated in 1823.

Despite the rise of industrial cities such as Manchester, more people resided in London than in any other city in the British Isles, or the world for that matter. Its population of approximately six and a half million people almost equalled that of New York and Paris combined. London possessed the first underground electric railway in the world, the City and South London Railway, which had opened in 1890, though horse-drawn trams remained in use by aristocrats until 1915. In 1896 work began on the Central London Railway, which opened in 1900 and later became known as the 'Twopenny Tube'; its tunnels still form the basis for the underground transport system in central London. London, an immense city, certainly had its dark side, sensationalized in the tales of Jack the Ripper's murder spree and as the backdrop for Arthur Conan Doyle's popular fictional detective stories featuring his eccentric investigator, Sherlock Holmes. Smoke, rain, and the famous London fog often gave the city a dismal, dreary feel. Yet the impression that London gave to most visitors was that of an orderly and safe city in which friendly 'Bobbies' patrolled the streets without needing to carry firearms.

Vera Brittain later referred to the years until 1912 as an 'age of rich materialism and tranquil comfort, which ... appeared to us to have gone on from time immemorial, and to be securely destined to continue forever'.[12] At the time, however, there were some signs of ambivalence towards technological progress and social change. On example would be the preservationist movement, which began in the late nineteenth century and valued buildings and historical sites on the sole basis of their antiquity. If anything shook the public's confidence in progress prior to the Great War, it was the sinking of the RMS *Titanic* on 15 April 1912. The British government launched an official inquiry almost immediately, the United States a short time after. Those who still wished to emphasize the positive could point to the numbers rescued and the value of the wireless in helping to avoid a much higher death toll. Others, however, emphasized the social and economic inequality reflected in the selection of passengers whose lives were to be spared. More commonly, the disaster seemed to affirm the dangers of too much technological progress, shattering the confidence of a middle class far removed from the glories of the Great Exhibition of 1851. Still others found depressing the morbid and sensationalistic approach to the disaster in the press. Newspaper and magazine articles, books, and pamphlets devoted to the shipwreck quickly flooded the market. Writing in June 1912, the novelist Joseph Conrad confessed that it was 'with a certain bitterness that one must admit to oneself that the late S. S. *Titanic* had a "good press"' and that 'the white spaces and the big lettering of the headlines have an incongruously festive air to my eyes, a disagreeable effect of a feverish exploitation of a sensational God-send'. In other words, people lamented the tragedy, but became fascinated by the details of it, presaging the modern gutter press. It almost seemed as if people took some pleasure in the sinking as a sign of the nemesis of the technological hubris that led to the notion of an 'unsinkable' ship. Little did they know that this disaster foreshadowed a much larger catastrophe and rebuke to the unmitigated value of technological progress with the onset of the First World War in August 1914.

The UK, Europe, and the origins of the First World War

George Tomkyns Chesney's *The Battle of Dorking: Reminiscences of a Volunteer* appeared in 1871; it described a fictional invasion of Britain by a thinly disguised Germany. This was the beginning of a vast literature speculating on the nature of the next war or capitalizing on the public's thirst for international intrigue, perhaps best exemplified by Erskine Childers' 1903 spy novel, *The Riddle of the Sands*. As of the 1890s, however, the UK remained more at odds with France and Russia than with Germany, despite the growing economic power of a united Germany and the volatility of its new emperor, Kaiser Wilhelm II (r. 1890–1918). German imperial expansion caused some concern, especially after Wilhelm condemned the raid on Boer territory by 60,000 British troops led by Leander Starr Jameson in late December 1895 that aimed at overthrowing the Boer government. He did so in a telegram to President Kruger of the Transvaal, prompting a reaction in Britain that Miranda Carter describes as a 'violent and sudden outpouring of hysterical anger, a confused combination of defensiveness, entitlement and aggression'.[13]

By the time the Liberal Party returned to power in 1906, the foreign secretary Sir Edward Grey had started to think that perhaps Britain had more to worry about from Germany than from France. Much of the growing distrust of Germany resulted from that country's recent efforts to expand its navy, ostensibly to challenge Britain's dominance of the seas. Kaiser Wilhelm had a special fondness for the navy and insisted that Germany have a strong one, but he desired one more to imitate Britain than he did to threaten it. This did not matter to the British, who already felt anxious about Germany's growing economy and industrial capacity, not to mention its recent acquisition of a colonial empire. Wilhelm's bellicose rhetoric certainly exacerbated matters, giving the impression that he did intend to expand Germany's overseas empire. In 1900, Wilhelm plainly stated:

And as My grandfather [did] for the Army, so I will, for My Navy, carry on unerringly and in similar manner the work of reorganization so that it may also stand on an equal footing with My armed forces on land and so that through it the German Empire may also be in a position abroad to attain that place which it has not yet reached.[14]

In 1907, Germany commissioned the construction of nine of the age's new super-battleships known as dreadnoughts.

The potential threat from the German navy did not attract much attention, however, until about 1908, when Lloyd George said that he first became aware of the issue. In December of that year, the First Lord of the Admiralty, Reginald McKenna, informed the Cabinet that the navy would request six new dreadnoughts in order to meet the growing threat from Germany instead of the four the Cabinet had expected. McKenna also told his audience that the navy would require twelve more of the behemoths by 1911. Furthermore, McKenna and Admiral John Fisher, the man most responsible for modernizing the navy and bringing it into the twentieth century, threatened to resign if these demands were not met. This surprised Lloyd George and Winston Churchill, then president of the Board of Trade, both of whom did not believe that more than four were required at that time. However, the Liberal Party in general still regarded the navy as an essential guarantor of British safety and free trade. As a result, the navy received enough money to carry out its construction programme and by 1912 was prepared to blockade Germany in the event of war between the two countries.

In addition, the Liberal secretary of state for war Richard Haldane instituted a number of reforms in the British army between 1906 and 1911, including the creation of an Expeditionary Force that would train in preparedness for supporting the army abroad in case of war, a Territorial Force whose focus would be on home defence, and the introduction of an Officer Training Corps in public schools and universities. The other principal manifestation of military preparedness came in the form of the expanding manufacture of armaments. Opposition to the arms industry came mainly from British intellectuals, such as George Bernard Shaw, whose 1905 play *Major Barbara* deals partly with the attempts of an arms manufacturer named Andrew Undershaft to justify his profession to his daughter, an officer in the Salvation Army. Even the Labour Party was unlikely to take up opposition against an industry that provided employment for so many workers. Only once war had broken out, did the peace movement become more pronounced. The Cooperative Women's Guild, which was founded in 1883 and before the war mostly focused on women's issues such as health, social welfare, and suffrage, became a leading advocate for peace and opponent of the arms industry after the war.

Prior to 1914, however, fear of Germany did not exactly grip the public; it seemed vague and obscure at best and for the majority of the British populace not worthy of direct concern. Nor did everyone share the hostility to Germany that many scholars have emphasized as a factor in the war between the two great powers. Many people in Britain respected, even admired, Germany and its achievements since its unification in 1871, while still regarding the Germans as more natural allies than the French based on the similarities between cultures and languages. A recent study has found a combination of positive and negative images of Germany in the press and popular literature during the period leading up to the war, as opposed to a monolithic besmirchment of 'the Hun'.[15] For example, Germany attracted a significant tourist trade from Britain, providing the Baedeker travel guides used by most English-speaking travellers to that country. On the other hand, a negative campaign focusing on the contents of German sausages, according to a recent article, did reflect some anxiety about Germany's rising position in the world and the potential threat that it posed to Britain.[16]

Even after the formation of the Triple Entente with France and Russia in 1907, Sir Edward Grey continued to maintain the country's latitude in deciding whether to actually take part in a war if one should break out on the European continent. The formation of the Triple Entente itself had more to do with anxiety over the security of the British Empire than it did with increased fear of or hostility towards Germany. In 1911, Grey wrote a private memorandum to Asquith that a time might come when the French would request British support, though he did not speculate in what form, nor if the aid would include military support. The successful resolution of the 1898 Fashoda Incident, in which the French and the British averted a clash over the Sudan by reaching a territorial agreement in Africa, had foreshadowed the 1904 Entente Cordiale between the two countries. As long as the British were willing to concede French control over Morocco, the French were content to give Britain a free hand in the Sudan. Feeling that improved relations with France had secured Britain's position in Egypt and control of the Suez Canal, Grey decided to secure the north Indian border by negotiating with Russia. Russia's humiliating defeat in the Russo-Japanese War and the political upheaval that followed in St Petersburg in 1905 considerably assuaged British fear that the Russians would risk launching an invasion of northern India. The negotiations concluded with an Anglo-Russian colonial agreement in 1907, thus paving the way for the Triple Entente between Britain, France, and Russia, as France and Russia were already allies.

The Russian-Anglo entente created apprehension in Germany, though many Germans continued to believe that Britain would remain neutral if a European conflict broke out. As late as June 1914, Grey disavowed plans for an Anglo-Russian naval convention and provided assurances of friendship and cooperation between Germany and Britain to the German ambassador, Prince Lichnowsky. Lichnowsky reported as much to Berlin on 24 June. Four days later, however, a Serbian nationalist named Gavrilo Princip ominously assassinated the Archduke Franz Ferdinand, the heir to the Austrian throne, in the Bosnian capital of Sarajevo, setting a chain of events in motion that would lead to war.

For much of the month that followed the assassination, most politicians in the UK still seemed more concerned with domestic affairs than the growing international crisis. The Cabinet ignored the topic altogether until the Austrians issued an ultimatum to Serbia on 23 July. The press did not ignore the international situation, but also seemed to regard domestic affairs as having greater import. The Irish situation was of more immediate concern; civil war still seemed a palpable possibility.

So what ignited the earth-shattering conflict, from whose seeds the Second World War was sown? Scores of books have been written on this period of European history; what follows is a brief attempt to summarize how the events unfolded from the British perspective. On 6 July, Lichnowsky cautioned Grey that Germany planned to support Austria in its efforts to deal harshly with the Serbians in retaliation for the assassination of Franz Ferdinand. German leaders would sometimes keep Lichnowsky in the dark during the next month, but he must have known of the infamous 'blank check' or promise of unconditional support by Germany to Austria should the Austrians decide to launch a war against Serbia. Shortly after Austria presented Serbia with its ten-point ultimatum on 23 July, Grey received word from the British ambassador in Vienna that Austria intended to go to war with Serbia and had written its ultimatum to achieve exactly that end. Churchill read the ultimatum and concluded that 'it seemed absolutely impossible that any State in the world could accept it, or that any acceptance, however abject, would satisfy the aggressor'.[17]

Any expectation that King George V might intervene with his royal cousin, Wilhelm, would have been ill-formed for two reasons. First, at the time of the crisis Wilhelm was not in charge of German foreign policy; in fact, his ministers deliberately misled him and kept him in the dark at crucial moments as they plotted to move the country towards war. Second, George, who had spent some time in the British navy, had a much stronger allegiance to his own country than he did to his German relative. During the war, on 17 July 1917, George would demonstrate this by officially changing the name of the ruling dynasty to the House of Windsor, replacing the Germanic name of Saxe-Coburg-Gotha.

On 26 July, Prime Minister Asquith intimated to Venetia Stanley, an aristocratic socialite with whom he had fallen in love and frequently corresponded in the years leading up to the war, that he thought Russia intended to force Britain to declare war on Germany.[18] As events moved Britain closer to war, Asquith hoped to keep the Liberal Party unified. Despite Lichnowsky's earlier warning, Grey still remained unconvinced of Germany's bellicose intentions. Still, on 27 July, in the first meeting exclusively devoted to the European crisis, he asked the Cabinet to decide if Britain would support France and Russia in the event of a war with Germany. He still hoped to maintain peace, and the following day expressed the hope that an open dialogue between Russia and Austria could avert a general war. By 29 July, he had personally come to the conclusion that it was necessary to support Russia and France, even threatening to resign if the government failed to do so. Asquith also began leaning towards war, as evinced by a mordant comment in a letter to Stanley on 30 July that Germany was shamelessly attempting to buy British neutrality. Winston Churchill, now First Lord of the Admiralty, also favoured war if necessary to support Britain's allies.

Three years earlier, on 21 June 1911, David Lloyd George had made the following remarks in what became known as the Mansion House Speech:

> I would make great sacrifices to preserve peace. But if a situation were to be forced upon us in which peace could only be preserved by the surrender of the great and beneficent position Britain has won by centuries of heroism and achievement, by allowing Britain to be treated where her interests were vitally affected as if she were of no account in the Cabinet of nations, then I say emphatically that peace at that price would be a humiliation intolerable for a great country like ours to endure.[19]

It now seemed that such a situation might have arisen. Britain had signed on as a guarantor of Belgian independence in an 1839 treaty that the Cabinet now felt honour-bound to uphold. On 1 August the Cabinet authorized Grey to inform Lichnowsky that any flouting of Belgian neutrality could lead Britain to declare war. This authorization came too late, for the same day Germany declared war on Russia. German war strategy called for a quick victory over France in the event of war with Russia and, therefore, a quick strike through Belgium as a shorter route to Paris. Nevertheless, Grey had breakfast with Lichnowsky the next morning and warned him that Germany should think twice before marching its army into Belgium. Later that evening the Germans informed the British that they intended to march through Belgium, regardless of British intentions. On 3 August, the Germans declared war on France and did just that.

In the hour of decision, on the night of 3–4 August, the British Parliament voted to declare war on Germany. It did so reluctantly after much hesitation and deliberation, a mark of a still conservative society reluctant to challenge a bellicose Germany seeking to preserve its own power and independence vis-à-vis the power bloc of Russia and France. Most historians regard German violation of Belgian neutrality as the determining factor in Britain's ultimate decision to go to war. No treaty imposed the same obligation to go to war in defence of France or Russia. Even after Germany declared war on Russia on 1 August, three left-leaning newspapers – the *Daily Chronicle*, *Daily News*, and *Manchester Guardian* – came out in favour of peace. The war was not of Britain's making. Most of the events that led to it were beyond its control. Grey did what little he could to try to prevent it. Unable to stop it, in the end, he felt that Britain had no choice but to become involved. He told a friend that 'the lamps are going out all over Europe; we shall not see them lit again in our lifetime'.

Britain's entry into the First World War and the response throughout the Isles

The declaration of war on 4 August caused an immediate wave of emotion to wash over the British Isles, a mixture of excitement, anticipation, anxiety, fear, joy, and profound sadness. Historians have had a tendency to simplify the story of the relationship of the First World War and British society through a narrative arc moving from heroic anticipation, national pride, and widespread enthusiasm for the war at the beginning to a universal recognition of the tragedy and futility of the war in its aftermath. Such a picture does not do justice to the range of viewpoints expressed at the beginning and end of the war, as well as during the conflict. However, the traditional narrative still contains elements of truth. Germany had declared war on Russia, France, and Belgium within the space of three days; at first some mistakenly thought that Germany had declared war on Britain as well.[20] It would be incorrect to think that the British press simply whipped the British people into a jingoistic frenzy; writers took the war seriously and recognized that a great principle – the sovereignty of smaller nations like Serbia and Belgium – was at stake. A month into the war, Vera Brittain wrote to a friend that 'it seems to me that to refrain from fighting in a cause like this because you do not approve of warfare would be about as sensible as refusing to defend yourself against the attacks of a madman because you did not consider lunacy an enlightened or desirable condition'.[21]

The president of the British National Union of Women's Suffrage Societies, Millicent Garrett Fawcett, waited all of one day before speaking to her membership about the need to suspend their political campaign and support the war. She asked her members to 'bind ... together for the purpose of rendering the greatest possible aid to our country at this momentous epoch'.[22] Many women, including Vera Brittain, began taking nursing classes in preparation for doing their part to assist the war effort and the men who would be called to fight it. Many more women joined the workforce and became ubiquitous on the commuter trams of major cities like Glasgow. Women's suffrage suddenly seemed less important than the war.

The Scots enlisted at a higher rate than those from any other part of the British Isles, perhaps because the war seemed to provide a way out of the lethargy that afflicted Scottish society and opened opportunities for many young men who had viewed their prospects in life as dreary and limited. Offices of political parties quickly became recruiting stations and so many soldiers enlisted that the army decided in September to increase its physical requirements in order to keep more men out of the army. Members of the working classes responded quickly to the call to arms; more than a quarter of Scottish miners and industrial labourers enlisted within a year of the beginning of the war.[23] While enlistment rates in Wales and Ireland did not approach those in Scotland (by the end of the war, more than half a million Scots had enlisted in the British army), 272,924 joined the army from Wales by 1918, while another 134,202 enlisted from Ireland. From the empire, Canada sent 628,964 to serve in the British armed forces during the war, while 52,561 Australians enlisted by the end of 1914 out of a total of about 416,000 in the armed services during the entire war; other dominions and colonies were also well represented.[24]

People enlisted for a variety of reasons, including employment opportunity, a desire to serve with one's friends and not be thought cowardly, lassitude, or fear of missing out on the action and adventure associated with war. Therefore, enlistment does not provide an accurate measure of support for the war. Still, with some notable exceptions – the pacifist leader of the Labour Party, Keir Hardie, spoke up immediately against the war, while the leaders of the South Wales Miners Federation refused to send their members back to work early from their yearly vacation when the government requested that they do so on 3 August – it almost seemed as if the war had immediately transformed the political culture of the British Isles in ways that smoothed out the differences that had agitated so many in the years leading up to it.

Life changed on the Home Front almost immediately. On 21 August Vera Brittain wrote from Lowestoft to her friend Roland Leighton that she could not go for a walk after dark without likely encountering one of the sentries placed in charge of guarding the bridges and the harbour. To Brittain, the war had come 'not as a superlative tragedy, but as an interruption of the most exasperating kind to my personal plans'.[25] If Vera Brittain found the war at first inconvenient, the situation was much worse for German immigrants, some of whom had their shops attacked in the early weeks of the war. The construction of new housing came to an abrupt halt, leading to a rise in rents as demand quickly outpaced supply. In Ireland the cost of living rose by 10 per cent before the end of the year and by another 22 per cent for 1915; the price of coal rose from 22 shillings per ton in July 1914 to 40 shillings six months later.[26]

The Great War

The war itself had broken down into a tedious stalemate by the end of 1914, with any 'victories' costly, short-lived, and well-nigh meaningless. Military leaders had not prepared for this eventuality, entering the war with the belief that the railway and modern technology would place a premium on speed and turn the war into one of rapid movement. Instead, technological advances in the firepower of artillery and the invention of barbwire gave an overwhelming advantage to troops who dug into heavily fortified positions in trenches along a line that became known as the Western Front. The Schlieffen Plan utilized by the German High Command called for a quick six-week victory over France based on the belief that the Germans could send 800,000 men through Belgium, overwhelm the French defences, and capture Paris by the middle of September. The plan failed, partly as a result of logistical problems with transporting so many men through Belgium in time to achieve the desired result and partly because of stronger French resistance than anticipated. Once the German offensive stalled, the Germans had to commit themselves to a defensive war of attrition in France while they engaged the Russians on the Eastern Front. By the end of November, the Germans had already suffered 241,000 casualties on the Western Front, the French and British 306,000, leading to the first of many lulls in all-out assaults due to the exhaustion of the combatants.

By 1915, voices of dissent against the war became more frequent. Helena M. Stanwick wrote a pamphlet titled 'Women and War', published by the Union of Democratic Control. Stanwick argued the government did not factor the interests of women into its decision making, although it was perfectly willing to enlist their support. Yet for the most part enthusiasm for the war remained high. Parents dressed their children in miniature field or sailor uniforms, apparently to encourage them to vicariously identify with those doing the fighting. Peace demonstrations drew little support and sometimes faced active opposition from the general public.

As the war dragged on, certain moments stand out as deeply affecting the confidence of the general public. A misguided and ill-fated attempt to break the stalemate through an invasion of Turkey at Gallipoli turned into an unmitigated disaster at the cost of almost 188,000 Allied casualties, 120,000 of which were suffered by troops from the UK. Gallipoli met all of the qualifications for a strategic disaster: a far-flung foreign adventure poorly led with little hope of success to begin with that received perfunctory support to achieve its objective because the British had underestimated the implacable strength and resolve of its opponent. Worse still, even if the campaign had succeeded, the stalemate on the Western Front would have remained intractable. The Battle of Jutland, the only significant naval battle of the war that occurred on 31 May to 1 June 1916, later regarded as a victory, was at first reported as a shocking British defeat. The wreck of the armoured battleship the HMS *Hampshire* on its way to Russia a few days later came as an additional heavy blow. The ship probably ran into a German mine, causing the death of most of its crew. The fact that the secretary of war, Lord Kitchener, happened to be aboard made it seem like even more of a national tragedy. The Battle of the Somme that summer quickly eclipsed any previous bad news. An all-out assault on German lines near the Somme River immediately resulted in 60,000 British casualties, including 20,000 deaths, on 1 July, the first day of the battle, the bloodiest day in British history. The battle dragged on until November, with an additional 360,000 casualties on the British side without any significant alteration in the Allied position.

To this point, the main technological innovation since the beginning of the war had been the use of poison gas, introduced by the Germans at the second Battle of Ypres in the spring of 1915. This did not do much to change the tide of the war, however, or to alter the basic tactics used by both sides partly because the Allies quickly adapted means of protection for their soldiers and partly because the Germans never learnt how to employ it effectively in conjunction with their frontal assaults. In fact, major offensives by both sides continued to fail and became less frequent as the war dragged on into 1918. The British did attempt one more desperate attempt to drive the German lines back in the third Battle of Ypres, better known as Passchendaele, which lasted from July to November 1917 and again involved enormous numbers of casualties on both sides. The withdrawal of the Russians from the war following the Bolshevik Revolution of October 1917 was counterbalanced by the entry of the United States in the war earlier that year. The deployment of 1.3 million fresh American troops helped to convince the Germans that they could not win the war, although they hung on until November 1918, by which their domestic economy was in a state of nearly total collapse.

Meanwhile, Asquith's ministry had fallen in December 1916, replaced by a coalition government of Liberals and Conservatives headed by Lloyd George that attracted the backing of the Labour Party by including in the war cabinet one of its members, Arthur Henderson, who had already served in a first coalition government under Asquith. After this, Lloyd George became a true war leader who shook up British government and expanded the role of the state by creating a number of new ministries to oversee vital areas of the economy essential to the war effort and appointing practical men with business experience to head them instead of career politicians. These included Ministries for Food, Labour, Shipping, Food Production, and National Service, to complement the already-established Ministry of Munitions.

British involvement in the First World War affected other regions of the world, including Africa, the Middle East, and Asia, because of the global reach of the British Empire. In 1915 Turkey launched an attack on the Suez Canal from its position in Palestine. The British, in response decided that their best opportunity to defeat Turkey and protect their interests in Africa and the Middle East without committing huge numbers of their own troops was to foster Arab nationalism in the region to weaken the hegemony of the Turks in the region. The Allied victory in the First World War left Britain as the leading power in the Middle East, in addition to the vast amount of territory that it still controlled in India and around the world. India's participation in the war, however, led to accelerated expectations of Indian independence. Finally, both Japan and China had allied with Britain and France during the war, with victory contributing to Japan's expectations of gaining territory at war's end; when the territory they gained came at the expense of China, it set the stage for a radicalization of Chinese politics exemplified by the May Fourth Movement there that protested the terms of the peace settlement in Asia, and the rise of the Chinese Communist Party led by Mao Zedong and the right-wing nationalist Guomindang led by Jiang Jieshi (known in the West as Chiang Kai-Shek).

The Easter Rising, 1916

The First World War also had a lasting impact on the history of the relationship between Britain and Ireland, especially after the Easter Rising of 1916. The Easter

Rising was the work of the IRB, hitherto a minority organization dedicated to the establishment of an independent Irish republic that lacked the broad appeal of the Irish Party led by Parnell and his replacement, John Redmond. A new generation of rebels inspired by the Fenian tradition and the cultural revival led by the Gaelic League and the Gaelic Athletic Association was prepared to terminate the compromises and half-measures that had seemed to characterize the actions of the parliamentary party. By 1916, the leaders of the Military Council of the IRB, Tom Clarke and Sean MacDermott, had become restless and anxious to make at least a symbolic gesture attacking British rule in Ireland. They had support from the paramilitary organization called the Irish Volunteers, led by Patrick Pearse, Joseph Plunkett, and Thomas MacDonagh. They took action on Easter Monday (24 April) 1916 when they occupied the Dublin General Post Office (GPO) and a number of important buildings. From the steps of the GPO, beginning with the words, 'in the name of God and of the dead generations from which she receives her old tradition of nationhood, Ireland, through us, summons her children to her flag and strikes for her freedom', they announced the formation of a Provisional Government for an independent Irish republic with Pearse as president. In renouncing Home Rule and going straight for independence, they temporarily ignored the problem of the North and the likelihood of partition if they succeeded, but for now that was a problem of the future. The news of the rising came as a complete shock to the Irish people, as well as to Eoin MacNeill and Bulmer Hobson, the official leaders of the IRB. This was largely by design, as the leaders of the rising attempted to keep their plans secret and counted on the element of surprise.

Prior to the war, the British had faced more potential opposition from the Northern Unionists who threatened rebellion to preserve their membership in the UK.

FIGURE 29 *Smoking ruins in Earl Street, Dublin, during the Easter Rising, 1916.*
Photo by Topical Press Agency/Getty Images.

The Volunteers in the south had little chance of attracting widespread support as long as Home Rule was virtually guaranteed to take hold in 1914. The war temporarily mitigated the stress caused by the situation in Northern Ireland, but in the South it resurrected fears that Irish interests would suffer from subordination to those of Britain, as had occurred during the Great Famine. The leaders of the rising knew their history and saw themselves as part of an ongoing resistance movement against British rule. There had always been a minority of nationalists who favoured outright independence and rejected the moderate approach of the Home Rule movement. However, the rising and its aftermath can only be understood within the context of the war. No general elections were held for the duration of the war, but the results of Irish by-elections, including one for Dublin Harbour in October 1915, indicated that support for the Irish Party was slowly eroding. Membership in the Volunteers grew in 1915 and 1916. They represented the military wing of the republican political party Sinn Féin ('We Ourselves') that advocated complete independence for Ireland.

Even if the leaders of the rising did not plan for the rebellion to fail all along, they certainly acted like it. They had not chosen positions in the city that were easily defensible. They did not have enough victuals and had made no provision for receiving additional supplies. If they thought that the British would concede Irish independence without a fight in the middle of a war, they had badly miscalculated. Within a week, Pearse had surrendered and the rising came to an end, having resulted in 450 deaths and injuries to over 2,600 people. Civilians accounted for the vast majority of the casualties. The Easter Rising, like the holy day for which it is named, has come to symbolize the resurrection of a lost cause, with the rebels cast in the role of Christ as martyrs whose deaths would bring salvation to the Irish people.

The execution of fifteen leaders of the rebellion did bring about an abrupt shift in Irish sentiment towards the Volunteers, which attracted a new wave of recruits eager to avenge the deaths of the rebels, now exemplified as patriots. This resulted mainly from the British response to the revolt than from the act of rebellion itself, which at first attracted little sympathy from the Irish people and was condemned by the Catholic Church. Some Irish historians now think that more of the Irish public had greater sympathy for the rising than traditional accounts have acknowledged, but public opinion was mixed at best before the British reprisals. Many years later, Michael Finucane, a resident of Kerry, reflected that 'the mood of the Kerry people at the time was that they didn't want any Rising, they were quite happy with the way life was, and there was no mention of the word "republicanism"'.[27]

Despite his bad reputation among the Irish, Lloyd George was troubled by the need to take action against the Irish Volunteers, especially because the government had failed to take action against the Ulster Volunteers. The difference seemed to be that the war had left him little choice. In Scariff, police arrested three members of the Volunteers for attempting to dissuade the owners of sawmills to shut down rather than send timber to support the British war effort. Once repression began, Lloyd George lost control of forces on the ground in Ireland. British authorities in Dublin overstepped their bounds in cracking down on critics or opponents of the government who had nothing to do with the rising. This led Ireland to become an even bigger problem after the war; rising levels of violence and attacks on British targets led the government to intervene by sending special forces dubbed by the Irish the Black n' Tans after the colours of their uniforms. A war for independence followed the end of the First World War, quickly succeeded by a civil war between those republicans willing to accept partition, led by Michael Collins, who successfully negotiated a treaty with London, and those who held out for complete independence of the entire island, led by Eamon de Valera.

In one of his most famous poems, 'Easter 1916', William Butler Yeats recognized the lasting effect that the rising was likely to have on Ireland.

I write it out in a verse –
MacDonagh and MacBride
And Connolly and Pearse
Now and in time to be,
Wherever green is worn,
Are changed, changed utterly:
A terrible beauty is born.

Meanwhile, poets and other writers attempted to come to grips with the meaning and significance of the larger conflict in which the Easter Rising had been set. They found little beauty in it, however, terrible or otherwise.

The literary response to the First World War

In his diary entry for 25 January 1916 the British poet and officer Siegfried Sassoon compared the attitude of the British towards their French allies with those of the English army that invaded France 500 years earlier during the Hundred Years War. 'Their arrogance is overweening, they move with an air of conquest,' he wrote.[28] This quote represents just one of the myriad ways in which those who wrote about their war experience did so in multivariate ways and challenged the official patriotic and anti-German stance of the government for which they fought.

Of course, the war memoirs and poetry that emerged from the war are replete with the horrors that men suffered on the front. Robert Graves wrote in his 1929 autobiography, *Goodbye to All That*, that 'even a miner can't make a joke that sounds like a joke over a man who takes 3 hours to die, after the top part of his head has been taken off by a bullet fired at twenty yards' range'.[29] In R. C. Sheriff's 1929 play, *Journey's End*, an officer tells his commander that he simply cannot return to the trenches, that he can no longer stand the sights and the smells any longer, and that he would rather die than continue to live in such conditions. Stanhope, the commanding officer, replies:

If you went – and left Osborne and Trotter and Raleigh and all those men up there to do your work – could you ever look a man straight in the face again – in all your life! You may be wounded. Then you can go home and feel proud – and if you're killed now – you won't have to stand this hell any more. (Act 2, Scene 2)[30]

Many men cultivated such a death wish, or took unnecessary risks in the hopes of being wounded. Fear of death was replaced by the fear of the *kind of death* one might experience if they stayed at the front too long.

Religion was a common theme among those who wrote about the war; a number or works testify to the questioning of the Christian faith that occurred in wartime. In his poem, 'Prince of Wounds', written on 27 December 1915, Sassoon asked:

Have we the strength to strive alone
Who can no longer worship Christ?
Is He a God of wood and stone,
While those who served him writhe and moan,
On warfare's altar sacrificed?[31]

Graves observed that hardly any men at the front retained any religious feeling and told of one episode in which even the most ardent Christians fired upon a crucifix for target practice. Yet the disappearance of religion, he noted did not mean the end of superstition, for which he noted a marked increase during the war; he confessed that he found himself believing in 'signs of the most trivial nature'. However, Michael Snape, in his important book *God and the British Soldier*, challenges the notions that religion was unimportant to those who fought in the British army during the First World War and that religion fundamentally declined in society at large as a result of it. He uses the term 'diffusive Christianity' to refer to the widespread influence of religion even among those who did not attend church services and challenges the simple dichotomy of Christian/atheist by including in his study the large numbers of soldiers who were unclear about the exact nature of their beliefs and their significance.[32]

The literary output associated with the First World War compared to previous wars was no accident. Not only did the war provoke a response because of its length, futility, dreadful conditions, and high risk of death, but it also affected a more literate population of soldiers than ever before because of the continuing effects of the Education Act of 1870. For all that the soldiers realized the inadequacy of language to express the actual nature of their experience, the fact that so many tried and that so many others were interested in reading their attempts speaks volumes, as if the only thing worse than writing about the war would have been not writing about it. In a poem like 'Enemies', written in early January 1917, Sassoon implies that only witnessing the face of a dead comrade could truly convey the reasons why so many of the enemy also had to die, but only by writing about it was he able to adequately express this feeling and come to a better understanding of himself.

The war has continued to provide material for novelists, perhaps most successfully in the the First World War trilogy written by Pat Barker in the 1990s. In *Regeneration*, *The Eye in the Door*, and *The Ghost Road*, Barker juxtaposes the experiences of a fictional officer named Billy Prior with those of historical figures, particularly Siegfried Sassoon, Wilfrid Owen, and Dr William Rivers, who was involved in counselling men who suffered from 'shell-shock' and a range of psychological disorders caused by the war. Barker's novels brought to a new generation an understanding of the hopelessness and despair, as well as the horror and tragedy, of the war. Her novels reveal the deep divisions within British society with regard to the war; in one exchange between officers in *The Ghost Road*, a man named Potts insists that the war had 'absolutely *nothing*, to do with Belgian neutrality, the rights of small nations or anything like that' and had more to do with the interests of war profiteers and British interest in the oil fields of Iraq. His opponent, Hallett, counters that the war *is* about Belgian neutrality and French independence and remains a just war because German troops occupied France, not the other way around. Although Barker represents both sides of this debate fairly, she lets Wilfrid Owen have the last word: 'I say we fight because men lost their bearings in the night.'[33]

Despite some recent attempts to downplay the significance of war literature as unrepresentative of the feelings of the larger population, it had an important role in voicing the emotional, physical, and psychological scars that the Great War inflicted not only on soldiers but also on British society as a whole. While it is true that both men and women sometimes found life at the front exciting and exhilarating – Mary Sinclair, who served in a Belgian ambulance unit said that she 'wouldn't have missed this run for the world'[34] – this does little to mitigate the horrors and bloodshed that occurred there. In his memoirs, Lloyd George sought to convey the feelings of his experience of the war by recourse to the analogy of a nightmare, in the same way that poets and memoirists used the language at their disposal to convey their experience of war. It does not matter if their descriptions are technically accurate or that not everyone experienced the war in exactly the same way. It matters that they tried to convey something of what they had experienced and that in doing so they helped to shape the political and cultural response to the war in the larger society to which they spoke.

Social change and the psychological legacy of the First World War

The First World War had blurred the lines between civilian and military life, both because the government put the entire economy on a war footing and as a result of the threat to the civilian population through aerial bombardment for the first time. The government did what it could to keep morale high throughout the war, mostly as an aid in continuing to recruit the necessary volunteers in order to keep the war effort going.

The war left behind a large number of ex-soldiers whose physical wounds could frequently be seen, as in the case of amputees, to serve as a visual reminder of the legacy of the war. People could not always see the emotional and psychological wounds, but these did not lie far below the surface in many instances. It was even worse for former POWs, who frequently suffered physical abuse, deprivation, and public humiliation in captivity, which for some prisoners outlasted the war itself. Some British POWs were even forced to fight for the Germans on the eastern front! In fact, so many former soldiers suffered from psychological neuroses that 'shell-shock' became emblematic of the war experience as a whole. The war created a psychological gap between former combatants and civilians, somehow made worse when civilians attempted to empathize or understand, probably because of the frustration of soldiers who knew that they never could. Yet avoiding talk about the war could prove equally disastrous for interpersonal relationships since many soldiers had little tolerance for the niceties and trivialities of everyday life.

Another casualty of the war that had a great impact on British society was the Victorian code of sexual morality that seemed largely irrelevant to young people to whom 'waiting for marriage' might appear as nothing but a cruel joke. The increase in cases of venereal disease to near-epidemic proportions by 1917 was one result of the change in sexual mores. The government not only mounted a campaign against sexual promiscuity by publicizing the dangers of venereal disease, but also made an effort to convince soldiers that sex would somehow sap their military prowess that was still regarded as vital to their survival on the battlefield – in effect a combination of two myths. (Women who transmitted venereal disease to men in the military were actually open to prosecution under the Contagious Diseases Acts, which dated back to 1864.) Homosexuality increased among soldiers during and immediately after the war, as men formed stronger emotional bonds with others who shared and understood their experience of war. However, societal pressures and prejudices made such relationships difficult to sustain at home, one reason why soldiers on leave at times preferred life at the front, a point illustrated by Barker in *The Ghost Road*.

After the war, even the most vocal critics of the women's suffrage movement dropped their opposition, leading to the inclusion of the right to vote for all women over the age of thirty in the Representation of the People Act of 1918 (although this would have happened at some point without the war), while granting all men over the age of twenty-one the right to vote. (Ten years later, all women over the age of twenty-one received the right to vote.) Leading up to the vote on the Act, one MP acknowledged that Britain could not have waged and won the war without the support of its women. Lloyd George, who had supported women's suffrage before the war, thought it 'inconceivable' that they now be denied the vote, given the sacrifices they had shared during the war. Even Asquith had come around and supported this measure, something that would have seemed inconceivable to all who knew him before the war. Of course, women helped their cause by refraining during the war from some of the more extreme measures employed to pressure Parliament before the war, including hunger strikes, vandalism, and physical attacks directed at political opponents.

Of course, the war had brought other changes for women as well. They became accustomed to drinking and smoking in public, where they now had more freedom to roam without male accompaniment. This trend represented a continuation of the ideal of the 'new woman' that had emerged in the United States and Europe in the two decades before the war, referring to the desire of women to gain more independence to assert themselves socially and politically while freeing themselves from the expectations of male patriarchy. In 1915 Sylvia Pankhurst encouraged women's participation in the trade union movement to help protect the rights of women workers, while at the same time insisting that women's suffrage not wait until the end of the war. In 1916, the early feminist, Helena Stanwick also expressed the concern that the rights of women workers be protected after the war, rather than see them lose their jobs – or to keep them only because they could be paid less than their male counterparts. In the meantime, women began to insist on having a say in negotiating their wages, hours, and working conditions.

The war did not eliminate the barriers between social classes, but it did puncture them to a degree. The trenches had a way of making everyone seem equal. Furthermore, officers from the aristocracy died at a higher rate than in any previous war because of the conditions in warfare in which they led their men 'over the top' of the trenches into the deadly line of fire streaming from the enemy across no-man's land. At home, the aristocracy faced a shortage of domestic servants, with an estimated 400,000 male servants joining the military and large numbers of women preferring factory work to domestic service. Most did not return to domestic service after the war and those who did commanded higher wages because of the labour shortage.

The war finally ground to a halt with Germany's unconditional surrender and the signing of an armistice on 11 November 1918. Soldiers returned home to join with civilians in making an effort to resume the normal business of living. Some recovery was inevitable, even after the incredible trauma of the war. However, the effects of the war on the political culture of the British Isles did not end with the armistice. The people of the British Isles would continue to live in the shadow of the Great War for some time to come.

FIGURE 30 *A typical row of two-bedroom hovels in Ebbw Vale, South Wales. A family of seven was found living in one of these rooms, and many such houses have subsequently been condemned as unsanitary. This photograph was taken on 17 December 1934.*
Richards/Hulton Archive/Getty.

Political culture
Ireland
Scotland
Wales
Social changes
thought + literature
background to WWII

15

The interwar years

*When my uncle, who was a friend of Asquith and Grey, talked about
Lloyd George, I began to wonder whether this statesman was not a
demonic spirit nurtured within the soul of the Liberals, like the frightful
nightmare of some maiden aunt.*

STEPHEN SPENDER, 1951[1]

*Few statesmen are likely to succeed who are either startlingly original or
startlingly sensitive.*

HAROLD LASKI, 1927[2]

British political culture in the interwar years

The man who emerged seemingly out of nowhere to guide Britain in the calm seas
that followed the tempestuous years of the First World War was a Conservative
pragmatist named Stanley Baldwin (1867–1947). Popular English sentiment favoured
a leader who could act as a stabilizing force and a bulwark against change and found
one in Baldwin. Baldwin became Chancellor of the Exchequer when Andrew Bonar
Law formed his Conservative government in 1922, but was still largely unknown to
the British public when he succeeded Bonar Law as prime minister in 1923. Baldwin
derived his political principles from the nineteenth century and borrowed Disraeli's
principles of Tory Democracy in an attempt to appeal to the working classes. He
also glorified rural England and celebrated the traditional English village as most
in keeping with the English zeitgeist. Yet Baldwin could not merely sit back and
preserve the status quo, although the British public desperately wanted to believe
that he could do just that.

The most important political change was the rise of the Labour Party, which
replaced the Liberal Party in the two-party system of British electoral politics. David
Lloyd George hoped to salvage the remnants of the Liberal Party into a cohesive
mainstream party that excluded both the far right and the far left wings of the

Liberal and Conservative Parties. However, the Liberal Party did not recover from the split between the more dynamic and political activist Lloyd George and the more conservative Asquith, whose government had the dubious distinction of having led Britain into the First World War. After the disaster of the introduction of the Black n' Tans into Ireland, Lloyd George had lost political capital as well, having badly mishandled the situation following the Easter Rising. He then only further alienated some of his supporters by negotiating the Anglo-Irish Treaty with the rebels. Finally, he made the ill-fated decision to send British troops to Russia to interfere in its civil war, which followed the Bolshevik takeover of 1917.

The emergence of the Labour Party as a viable rival insured that Britain would not slip back into one-party government, as it had following the War of the Spanish Succession in the eighteenth century. The conflation of the Labour Party with socialism frightened Baldwin and the Conservatives, but Labour chose as its leader Ramsay MacDonald, who was committed to working within the existing political system and was trying to make his party electable by downplaying its socialist principles.

Meanwhile, Baldwin had to cope with the perplexing challenges arising from the aftermath of the Treaty of Versailles and the decision of the Allies to impose heavy reparations on the Germans. It soon became clear that Germany had no way to fulfil its scheduled payments, as the great economist John Maynard Keynes had predicted in *The Economic Consequences of the Peace* (1919). Keynes believed Germany would eventually seek revenge through war if reparation payments drained its economy of money it could not afford to lose. He believed an economically powerful Germany would be the best guarantor not only of the future peace of Europe but also of a strong European economy. He therefore wanted to see the reparations payments greatly reduced and used only for the rebuilding of Belgium and France, which had suffered extensive physical destruction during the war. But Keynes's advice was unavailing for Baldwin did not dare to take such a proposal to the British electorate, and when the Great Inflation of 1922–3 almost wrecked Germany, the United States stepped in to renegotiate the payment schedule and float Germany a loan, instead of abolishing payments altogether. Sympathy for Germany increased in the former Allied nations as they questioned, along with Keynes, the initial wisdom of the Carthaginian peace, a development that later played into Hitler's hands when he began to unilaterally defy its conditions.

Another challenge for the Conservatives involved adjusting to the introduction of universal male suffrage in 1918 and universal female suffrage in 1928. With the expanded electorate the Conservatives did not dare reverse the benevolent social legislation already passed by the Liberals, including policy inimical to the financial interests of the aristocracy. The Conservatives now had to balance the need for support among members of all social classes to remain in power and keep the Labour Party at bay.

A third challenge to the Conservative Party came from demands for independence from within the British Empire, which was particularly galling for Baldwin because commitment to the empire was a leading tenet in the traditionalist vision that he tried to bring to the British public.

Finally, Baldwin could not wholly restore the faith that the younger generation had in an older generation that had just put them through the pitilessly sanguinary Great War. As Noel Annan put it:

> Every generation turns on its fathers; but the Great War, which most of Our Age considered was a war that could have been avoided and should have been stopped, made Our Age preternaturally critical of what one of their number Henry Fairlie, called the Establishment – the network of people and institutions with power and influence who rule the country.[3]

The problem was that many of the same men of the generation who had been in power before and during the war either retained a role in the leadership of the country or a strong voice in British politics during the interwar years. These statesmen included Winston Churchill (b. 1874), David Lloyd George (b. 1863), and Neville Chamberlain (b. 1869). Stanley Baldwin himself was born in 1867. British politicians were so anxious to mollify fears of a future conflict and were confident that the nations of the world would do anything to avert a repeat of the Great War that the Baldwin government decided to base its military budget on the assumption that another war would not occur for at least ten years.

Furthermore, it was an especially difficult challenge for the country as a whole to integrate the men who had fought at the front into civilian life. These ex-soldiers provided the main audience for Oswald Mosley and the British Fascists in the 1930s; Mussolini and Hitler had appealed to the same group of men in Italy and Germany in the interwar years. The British were not immune from the fascist temptation and the annihilatory power it brought to rational thought. In Britain, as elsewhere, fear of socialism led some people to see fascism as the most reliable antidote.

Despite these challenges, Britain weathered the early post-war years without any significant upheaval, after the Anglo-Irish Treaty ended the rebellion in Ireland. The most noteworthy development between 1921 and 1926 was the formation of the first Labour government under Ramsay MacDonald in January 1924. MacDonald's government only lasted until October of that year, but in the meantime it had managed to pass the much-needed Wheatley Housing Act (after John Wheatley, who introduced the bill) providing funds to build affordable housing for low-paid workers, and, more importantly, to demonstrate that it could govern the country in accordance with the political traditions of the country.

The first major tempest to disturb the relatively peaceful political milieu regnant in 1920s' Britain was the declaration of a general strike by the Trades Union Congress (TUC) on 3 May 1926. The primary reason for the strike was a proposed pay cut for coal miners. In the 1920s, unemployment skyrocketed in traditional export businesses, particularly cotton textiles, heavy machinery, shipbuilding, and coal. Even the newspapers were shut down by the strike and the only publications available were those published by the government and the Trades Union Congress, each of which completely slanted their version of the news in opposite directions. The government publication, *The British Gazette*, accused the striking workers of betraying the nation and of embracing Bolshevism. The coal miners had actually hoped to force the government to take over management of the mines, a socialist solution reflecting the anti-capitalist stance of the TUC publication, the *British Worker*.

Baldwin hoped to prevent the country from adopting a radical political solution on either the right or the left by preserving the unwritten traditions that made up the British constitution as a solid measure of stability. But in June 1929, Baldwin resigned rather than form an alliance with Liberals, resulting in Ramsay MacDonald returning to power as prime minister. MacDonald's government was greeted by the Great Depression, which hit Britain following the collapse of the New York stock market in the autumn of 1929. H. G. Wells later summed up the basic cause of the Depression in terms that indicted the capitalist system, a sentiment that had widespread popular support:

> The expansion of productive energy was being accompanied by a positive contraction of the distributive arrangements which determined consumption. The more efficient the output, the fewer were the wages-earners. The more stuff there was, the fewer consumers there were. The fewer the consumers, the smaller the trading profits, and the less the gross spending power of the shareholders and individual entrepreneurs. So buying dwindled at both ends of the process and the common investor suffered with the wages-earner. This was the 'Paradox of Overproduction' which so troubled the writers and journalists of the third decade of the twentieth century.[4]

MacDonald was somewhat hamstrung by his reluctance to employ too radical measures to salvage the economy for fear of scaring the public away from supporting a Labour government. Following the advice of the leading economists on whom he had called for advice, MacDonald in fact pursued a conservative agenda that involved cutting government expenditure similar to that pursued by the Republican president of the United States, Herbert Hoover. The ensuing division within his own party caused the failure of this second Labour government, although MacDonald stayed on as the head of a coalition government dominated by the Conservative Party and its leaders, Baldwin and Neville Chamberlain.

In 1931 panic precipitated a run on the banks similar to the run that had occurred in the United States in the autumn of 1930. Unemployment rates in Britain soared past 20 per cent by 1933. In these dire economic circumstances, the socialists seemed to have a better case for applying their collectivist ideas than the Conservatives did for continuing to implement ordinary governmental policy. The prominence of the bourgeoisie at a time of penurious circumstances for the masses came under attack. The continued existence of wealth and privilege seemed even less justifiable in an age of such extreme economic hardship. However, the government managed to keep social unrest at a minimum because unemployment benefits were deemed satisfactory enough to the jobless to minimize the chance that they would rebel against a government on which it depended. Furthermore, Baldwin deliberately played down class divisions and continued to argue that a Conservative government could meet the needs of the people better than a Socialist one.

This may have actually been more than simple political pragmatism on Baldwin's part; Jonathan Rose has cited Baldwin's reading of nineteenth-century critics of capitalism such as Charles Dickens, Thomas Carlyle, and John Ruskin in support of the likelihood that Baldwin was sincere in his support for a programme of social legislation.[5] Baldwin's soporific speaking style and traditionalist personae therefore appear at odds with his commitment to social activism. Surprisingly, the Conservatives were much more open to working with Labour than they had been to working with the Liberals in the past, while the Labour leadership welcomed the opportunity to share power with the Conservatives and sought, if anything, to prove their loyalty to the British state, and diminish their socialist bona fides. In the words of David Marquand, a historian of interwar Britain, 'Labor's private respect for the Conservatives went hand in hand with public respect for tradition.'[6] From the perspective of the Conservatives, after the demise of the Liberal Party they needed a worthy adversary and Labour had emerged as the only viable party to help preserve British democracy.

These factors all help to explain why – while Germany turned to Hitler and the American electorate dismissed the conservative Republican Herbert Hoover in favour of the Democrat Franklin Roosevelt – the British allowed Baldwin to continue in office. The generation that had been disillusioned by the war became somewhat less so as a result of the response of the government to the Depression, which reflected Baldwin's own belief that the government had a responsibility to promote social equity and fairness, whether through regulation of business and industry, providing unemployment and disability benefits, or ensuring that all children went to school. The case for government spending during the Depression also received a boost from Keynes, who argued in 1929 that government spending on public works could help stimulate the economy. Keynes de-emphasized the importance of a balanced budget at times of financial emergency. One of the ironies of the Depression was that those who did work had stronger purchasing power because of lower interest rates and the decline in the value of the pound. This situation led to something of a housing boom in the 1930s and an increased demand for consumer goods that allowed some businesses to profit even in the midst of an economic depression characterized by inordinately high unemployment rates.

No discussion of British political culture in the interwar years would be complete without some discussion of the role of the British monarchy and the crisis precipitated by the abdication of King Edward VIII in December 1936 after he had decided to marry Wallis Warfield Simpson, an American divorcee from Baltimore. Edward's relationship with Simpson led the British press to violate a long-standing tradition of not openly criticizing the monarchy or exposing its dirty laundry for public view, as hard as this may seem to believe given the feeding frenzy of the tabloid sharks constantly circling members of the royal family in recent decades. In November, an emergency meeting of the Cabinet was called in an effort to get ahead of the situation after news broke of the king's intentions to marry his American paramour. Baldwin had hoped to find a solution that would allow Edward to stay on as king, and made a proposal to permit the marriage as long as Simpson was not made queen and any children of the marriage would be barred from ever inheriting the throne. When the Cabinet winced at this solution as unconstitutional, Edward was given a choice between abdication and marriage; despite some popular support – including from the British Fascists – for Edward to defy the Cabinet and get married without abdicating, he relented on 10 December and the unwritten British constitution had survived another potential challenge to the political stability of the nation.

Ireland: Home rule and partition

In July 1921, the British agreed to a truce in the conflict with Ireland that had followed the Easter Rising and the end of the First World War and sat down to negotiate with the Irish nationalist party, Sinn Féin. Sinn Féin had increased greatly in popularity in the years between the 1916 Rising and the end of the war. Under the leadership of Eamon de Valera and Michael Collins, Sinn Féin swung in a radical direction and began to plan for the revolution that would finally oust the British from Ireland once and for all. In the parliamentary election that followed the end of the war in December 1918, seventy-three members of Sinn Féin were elected to the British Parliament, including Constance Markievicz, the first woman ever elected to the House of Commons. The election was considered a landslide victory for Sinn Féin in Ireland, but those elected from the party refused to take their seats on principle because they did not recognize the British Parliament as having any authority over Ireland.

The British government came under pressure in England from former suffragettes and other sympathizers of the Irish cause who wished to see no more blood spilled over the issue of Home Rule for Ireland, which, after all, had been promised by legislation and would have already taken effect had the Great War not intervened. Critics of British policy reacted particularly strongly to the harsh and brutal measures taken in Ireland by Field Marshal John French who failed to distinguish between the IRA and ordinary members of Redmond's Irish Party in his harsh and bloody reprisals. French's troops regarded civilian casualties and destruction of property as acceptable costs of repressing the rebellion, but not many in the British public were inclined to agree after four years of slaughter during the First World War. In order to prevent a prolonged conflict that might lead to Irish independence, the government finally acquiesced to Irish Home Rule, but not for the entire island. The British government refused to abandon the Unionist majority in Northern Ireland who wished to remain within the UK.

Northern Ireland received its own parliament in the Government of Ireland Act of December 1920. This act made the partition of Ireland a virtual fait accompli in advance of the British government's negotiations with Sinn Féin. The British decision to grant Irish Home Rule to the rest of Ireland put an end to the moderate Irish Parliamentary Party that traced its lineage from O'Connell to John Redmond, while Sinn Féin and the Irish Republican Army (IRA) divided between those willing to accept Home Rule and partition as an intermediate step towards eventual independence and those who wanted to continue to fight for immediate independence and to preserve the political unity of the island.

At first, de Valera supported discussions with the British and even helped to arrange them, but he rejected the compromise agreement negotiated by Collins. To Collins and his supporters, the Anglo-Irish Treaty of December 1921 gave Ireland exactly what they wanted – the right to govern themselves – but de Valera and his supporters were prepared to reject the treaty for falling short of granting Ireland complete independence. On 7 January 1922, the Irish Parliament, known as the Dáil, voted 64–57 in favour of the Treaty. In the June 1922 elections to the Dáil, the supporters of Eamon de Valera, who opposed the treaty, won only thirty-six seats, while supporters of the treaty, headed by Michael Collins garnered fifty-eight seats. Those who voted for the treaty were seen as traitors by those who followed de Valera as he left the Dáil following the vote, but they had pragmatic reasons for not supporting the prolongation of a war against the British that would cost more Irish lives and probably end in the same result. Britain had ceded a remarkable amount of control to the Irish Free State, but was not about to concede the ability of the Irish to align themselves with any potential foreign enemy and insisted on the continued use of Irish naval bases as part of the agreement.

With control of Dublin and the apparatus of the military, the new government defeated the rebels in a horrific civil war that ended in May 1923. Michael Collins was assassinated on 22 August 1922 while travelling on a road between Cork City and the town of Bandon, a prominent casualty of the civil war. While the Easter Rising became a celebrated part of Ireland's national mythology and history, the violence and sacrifices made in the civil war were elided and failed to gain the same degree of propitiation as the Easter Rising.

The Irish revolution and civil war created an anarchical and liberal atmosphere in Ireland, a milieu the new government of the Irish Free State sought to transcend. It did so largely by building on the religious legacy of Ireland as a Catholic nation and by adhering to a relatively conservative social and political agenda. The new government placed a marked emphasis on the family and defined women's roles in society primarily as those of wives and mothers. The government and the church agreed that the restoration of the nuclear family and stricter parental control were necessary to bring about the kind of society they wanted, one sanctified by the support of the church, which had long opposed the growth of secular national sentiment but now saw an opportunity to play a larger social role in the newly independent Ireland.

Therefore, while young adults in Britain were enjoying the 'Roaring Twenties' and the introduction of new dances such as the Charleston and Black Bottom, the Catholic Church discouraged dancing and drinking as leading to illicit sex. This conservative attitude permeated much of Irish society, particularly when contrasted with British society during the same period. When Virginia Woolf went to Dublin in 1934, she recorded in her diary that an 'air of inferiority sleeps or simpers or sneers or rages everywhere'. As she continued to reflect, however, her conclusion was that freedom, at least as of yet, had not brought to Ireland the hoped-for results:

> Yet what can happen when the best restaurant in the capital is Jammers, when there's only boiled potatoes in the biggest hotel in Dublin? ... At last I gather why, if I were Irish, I should wish to belong to the Empire: no luxury, no creation, no stir, only the dregs of London, rather wish-washy if suburbanised. Yet, I thought too at the Gate, they may have spirit in them somewhere, that could make something, if freed. But they are freed, I continue – & indeed the play said, sardonically, & only this provinciality is the result.[7]

Scotland in the interwar years

The economic downturn of the interwar years hit Scotland even harder than it did the rest of Britain, with unemployment rates consistently above 10 per cent, beginning well before the start of the Great Depression. The Scottish economy relied too heavily on those traditional industries associated with the Industrial Revolution – textiles, railways, shipbuilding, and iron and steel – that declined so rapidly during the interwar years. When the government passed a Special Areas Act in 1934 that provided for the relocation of workers from 'distressed areas' to those regions that had continued to flourish, a separate commissioner was appointed for Scotland, which was considered an economically distressed area in its entirety. To make matters worse, housing was more expensive in Scotland than in the rest of Britain. Scotland was unique in asking both owners and renters to pay property taxes, making it both less profitable to own and more expensive to rent. In Scotland new home construction per capita was only 2.1 per cent in 1931 compared to 7.2 per cent for the rest of the UK.[8] An estimated half a million Scots left Britain between the wars, continuing an exodus that had begun before the First World War.[9] The less economically developed Highlands continued to lose an even higher percentage of its population and, combined with the Western Islands, held only 293,000 people in 1931, which Charles Mowat estimated at about one-twentieth of the Scottish population.[10] The stagnant population figures for this region are in keeping with the profile of those most likely to leave – single, male agricultural workers.

Politically, Scotland's economic problems benefited the Labour Party, to which the majority of Scots switched their allegiance following the decline of the Liberal Party. Prior to 1918, a lower percentage of adult males could vote in Scotland than in either England or Wales, so the addition of so many working-class voters made the Labour Party the beneficiary of Scottish economic woes. The rise of Labour was not immediate; the Liberal Party still garnered 39 per cent of the vote in 1922 and 28 per cent in 1923. However, Michael Lynch notes the rapid ascent of the Labour Party in municipal elections during the interwar years, especially in Glasgow where Labour won a majority of seats on the town council in 1933.[11]

In addition, women's organizations in Scotland, including the Glasgow Society for Equal Citizenship and the Edinburgh Women Citizens Association, organized educational programmes for the benefits of new women voters. They were part of a larger Women's Institutes movement, which sought to educate women on everything from government to housekeeping, from childcare to arts and crafts and folk dancing. Their efforts paid off; by 1939 a quarter of the women MPs in the House of Commons had been elected in Scotland, even though Scotland only held one-eighth of the total seats in the House.[12] By contrast, the Women's Institute founded at Llanfairpwll, Wales in 1915 continued to focus more or less exclusively on homemaking, even as it expanded its membership throughout the 1920s.[13]

The British Fascist Party did not attract much support in Scotland, despite the extremely poor economic climate there. The largest chapter of the party was led by James Little in Dalbeattie and it numbered only a few hundred members in 1934. But the Scottish Nationalist Party (SNP) originated in 1928 and made some headway during this period. The Fascist Party and the SNP were among several attempts by disaffected people to form an alternative to the Labour–Conservative dichotomy that had resulted from the demise of the Liberals. The British Fascist Party found that it could not compete with the SNP in Scotland, however, and disbanded its entire Scottish staff in 1935 to save money.[14]

Wales in the interwar years

During the interwar years, the Welsh suffered economically even more than did the Scots, particularly those who lived in South Wales. The end of the First World War brought about a significant realignment of the world's economy, hurting the demand for and price of coal in comparison to oil and other commodities. Related heavy industries shut down or laid off workers, as they did in the industrial areas of northern England. When mine owners tried to cut wages, the miners went on strike, first in 1921, and then again in 1926 in conjunction with the general strike.

Government relief did little to help the miners and families most affected by lay-offs and unemployment. The deprivations that the Welsh mining villages in that region suffered beginning in the 1920s invite comparisons with those endured by the Irish during the Great Famine (though obviously the Irish Famine affected millions of more people). In 1928, a family of five was expected to survive on twenty-nine shillings a week from the dole if the head of the household was unemployed. It was not uncommon for a family's diet to consist of mainly tea, bread, and margarine, with only small amounts of meat available for a weekly stew and virtually nothing to eat on some days. In certain villages, churches closed because the congregation had no money to support a minister; those members of the clergy who chose to stay faced the same conditions of poverty and deprivation as the rest of the population. Even beer was beyond the means of the long-term unemployed. So was gas and electricity. The headline that accompanied an article filed on a visit by one reporter to Trealaw in the Rhondda Valley sums up the conditions found there: 'MINERS' SUFFERING IN WALES DEPICTED: Families of Five, Living on $7 a Week, Are Foodless One Day in Seven. NO NEW CLOTHES IN 2 YEARS Stores Are Closed, Furniture Is Sold, and Houses Dark for Lack of Candles. Valley Shivers and Hungers. Trip Reveals Suffering.'[15]

To make matters worse, in November 1931 the government introduced a means test that would be administered for anyone who had already received twenty-six weeks' worth of unemployment benefits. Opponents of the means test strongly argued that it would only make a bad situation worse, exacerbating the effects of a soul-numbing poverty that had already done so much to crush the spirits and maim the bodies of the poor. Men and women who had worked hard and were willing to work again saw the latest measure as an indignity further stigmatizing them for a poverty that was not their fault. During the Depression, many people chose to work rather than to go 'on the dole', even if their unemployment benefits were sometimes higher than their actual wages – sometimes they did not always have a choice, as a family might be denied unemployment benefits if it was deemed that the head of household had access to a job, however low paying.

Changes in society

Despite the economic hardships of the period, technology played an important role in social change during the interwar years, especially in the sources of people's entertainment, with the radio, cinema, and the gramophone all becoming widely accessible. Not everyone could afford a radio or a gramophone, of course, but even the poorest and remotest villages seemed to have picture houses, even if they were the only businesses that remained open during hard times. American films enjoyed a great popularity in the 1920s and 1930s, but Britain had its own film-making industry and box office stars. These included the musical–comedy team of George Formby and Gracie Fields, as well as individual stars such as Jessie Matthews and Jack Hulbert. Hulbert starred in over a dozen films in the 1930s, the most popular of which was *Alias Bulldog Drummond* (1935), based on a contemporaneous series of detective novels by H. C. McNeile, whose penname was 'Sapper'.

The English, despite their reputation for being technophobic, positively embraced technology in all its mediums, not only the radio and the cinema, but especially the aeroplane. David Edgerton, in his important book, *England and the Aeroplane*, successfully challenges 'the picture of the English elite as anti-scientific, anti-industrial, of English business as congenitally short-sighted, or of the English people trapped in an idiotic longing for all things rural'.[16] The aeroplane possessed a romantic appeal and provided dash and élan for the general public, in addition to the important military advantages that derived from its ability to compensate for Britain's undersized population in the event of another war with the Germans. Aviation clubs advertised for private lessons and developed their own subculture within British society, albeit one that constantly sought to share its enthusiasm with the rest of the general public. In the spring of 1928, the 24-year-old Amy Johnson, only two years before her famous solo flight to Australia, exclaimed, 'I am going to learn flying! I'm joining the London Aeroplane Club and then I can get tuition and always use their aeroplanes.'[17] In P. L. Travers' extraordinarily popular children's novel *Mary Poppins* (1934), when young Michael Banks tells his governess, Mary Poppins, that he is saving his money, she scoffs, 'Huh – for one of those aeryoplanes, I suppose!'

Auto racing also captured the public's imagination, reflecting the fascination that people had in the interwar years with the combination of technology and speed. Henry Segrave gained the public's adulation first by winning the Grand Prix de France in 1923 and then by exceeding 200 miles per hour at Daytona Beach, Florida in 1929. The radio began to bring sports into people's homes during the interwar years; cricket was especially popular on the radio, perhaps for the same reasons that baseball appealed to such a broad listening audience in the United States having to do with the leisurely pace of the game and the way in which the sports lend themselves to visualization based on a verbal description of the action. The Football Association continued to grow in popularity; the FA Cup Final played at Wembley stadium in 1923 attracted more than 200,000 spectators. Throughout England, supporters of their local teams made football matches part of their yearly and weekly routines, their allegiance determined as much by religious affiliations as the location of the team they followed. Other sports, especially lawn tennis and rugby remained popular, though another sport that gained tremendously in popularity in the 1920s and

1930s was swimming, thanks largely to the number of open-air swimming pools that opened during this period.

During the interwar years the service ministries increasingly began to employ men and women with scientific and technological expertise. These individuals helped to get the nation prepared for the next war; without them Britain very well may have gone down to defeat relatively quickly. Even that critic of industrialization, George Orwell, recognized that technology and the age of the machine was here to stay, though he objected to its status as an end in itself and opposed it as the sole means to the betterment of human life. Responses to technology included the spread to Britain from the United States of the idea of 'technocracy' – the notion that industrial technicians should oversee government and society to distribute goods based on work produced instead of a price and wage-based economy.

The intervention by the government in the economy, while far from meeting the needs of all of its citizens, represented another important step not only in the direction of the welfare state but towards a more equitable and fair society. The social intervention of the 1930s was part of a slow and incremental process of change rather than a sudden departure from the past. The government continued to build on the social reform movement that had featured so prominently in the Liberal agenda in the decade before the Great War – and in many respects dated back to the social legislation of the nineteenth century. As late as 1939, however, there was still no national health service, so even middle-class families often had to spend most of their discretionary income on medical care.

Meanwhile, women still had enormous distances to go to achieve equal status in society despite having the right to vote. In the 1920s, three successive annual conferences of the Labour Party saw the subject of available birth control information on the agenda, a major issue for women's rights advocates. In the 1920s, the Women's Defence League organized to protect working-class women from outside interference in how they ran their homes. The 'Six Point Group', which counted as its members Vera Brittain and her college friend, the writer Winifred Holtby, advocated on behalf of women through their six points: pensions for widows, equal rights for women to guardianship over their children, legal protection for unmarried mothers, stricter laws protecting children from abuse, equal pay for women and men in the teaching profession, and equal opportunities for women and men in the civil service.

New dances borrowed from America became another means for young women, especially those known as flappers who adopted both shorter skirts and shorter haircuts, to express themselves freely with public displays of energy and athleticism. Those remaining women who had not already abandoned their whalebone corsets during the war did so soon after. Cigarette smoking became not only fashionable among women in the twenties, but a symbol of their liberation from previous societal norms. A nineteen-year-old Amy Johnson was thrilled when her Swiss boyfriend taught her to smoke in 1922.

Even more importantly, greater economic opportunities were opening up for them, including the chance to rise into some of the white-collar professions. Many young women worked not out of desire but out of necessity. The number of men killed in the Great War left behind a much larger number of women in their twenties and thirties in the interwar years; simple demographic mathematics would determine, therefore, that many women would remain single. A number of middle-class women even turned to farming as an occupation. Farming brought with it a greater measure of independence, but the work of women farmers was hard and time-consuming, leaving them little time to enjoy the social freedoms that benefited middle-class women in the cities.[18]

Married middle-class and working-class women still had less freedom than their single counterparts and frequently were expected simply to stay at home to keep house and provide childcare. Trade unions, in fact, tried to encourage married women to leave their jobs and stay home to preserve the jobs of married men and single women who were presumed to need them more. In her 1927 novel *To the Lighthouse*, Virginia Woolf provided a glimpse into the dissatisfaction that women could feel in such a role, something that a majority of women would only began to express more openly in the 1960s: 'They came to her naturally, since she was a woman, all day long with this and that; one wanting this, another that; the children were growing up; she often felt she was nothing but a sponge sopped full of human emotions.'[19]

Children began to be treated differently during the interwar years. Some parents began to send their children to Montessori schools, especially those parents whose children had discipline problems or were troubled in some way. The Italian reformer Maria Montessori's educational philosophy, which closely resembles both those of Locke and Rousseau in many respects, focused on developing the natural abilities of the child, allowing the child greater freedom of expression, and encouraging learning through positive incentives rather than fear of discipline. (Montessori schools continue to flourish throughout the UK; there are at present a dozen in North London alone.) Childhood was also, in a sense, extended. In 1921 Parliament passed an act that raised the age at which one could leave school to fourteen and made suitable education for blind and deaf children mandatory for the first time; in 1936 the age until which one had to remain in school was raised again to fifteen.

In his famous book *The Road to Wigan Pier* about his travels through northern England during the Great Depression, George Orwell celebrated working-class culture and claimed that any self-respecting working-class youth would much prefer to go to work on his sixteenth birthday rather than to continue his lessons in history or geography. According to Graves and Hodge, however, an increasing number of working-class youths were winning scholarships to secondary schools and even gaining access to a university education. This democratization of education contributed further to the gradually eroding social distinctions occurring during the interwar years. Governmental activism and the raising of the age for mandatory schooling led to the construction of many new secondary schools, and thus gave more students the opportunity to prepare for higher education. From 1918, and increasingly in the interwar years, free places and scholarships became available to students who displayed marked intellectual abilities, regardless of their socio-economic background. In the nineteenth century, a public school education was available only to the privileged or wealthy elite, but the interwar years now featured hundreds of schools that had moved into that category, blurring one of the main signs of social distinction. The effect of all of these changes was to encourage social mobility and significantly dampen the spirit of caste, perhaps preparing the way for the shared spirit of sacrifice that would often be evoked during the coming world war.

As for the wealthier rural aristocracy, portrayed by the fictional Grantham family in the popular twenty-first-century television series *Downton Abbey*, the increase of the inheritance tax to 40 per cent in 1919 was particularly depressing and the clearest signal that their privileges were under attack and that they would have to make financial adjustments. The aristocracy mainly adjusted by selling off their land; it is worth repeating the estimates by F. M. L. Thompson that an estimated 6–8 million acres changed hands between 1918 and 1921 and 36 per cent of the farmers owned their own land by 1927 compared to 11 per cent in 1914.[20] Rural society was not helped by the continuing decline of British agriculture that had begun in the 1870s. The war had temporarily forced farmers to bring more land under cultivation in order to compensate for food shortages, but this proved economically feasible only as long as the war lasted. Britain had become an importer of food and by 1936 the agricultural sector was in such dire straits that the government was paying subsidies of £40 million annually to prevent them from raising their prices during the Depression.

Behind all of these changes and developments there still lurked a despondency from the Great War that the British people found ineluctable. Stephen Spender described the war as having 'knocked the ballroom floor from under middle-class English life', writing that 'people resembled dancers suspended in mid-air yet miraculously able to pretend that they were still dancing'.[21] It is axiomatic that this period involved a challenge to traditional moral values and discipline on the part of many young people shaken by the war and the damage that it had done to British society and the British psyche.

Interwar thought and literature: Troubled minds

Christopher Hilliard in his book *To Exercise Our Talents: The Democratization of Writing in Britain* (2006) challenged the position taken by historian Jonathan Rose that the British working classes in the interwar years rejected bourgeois modernism in favour of 'traditional values'.[22] Rose had studied the reading material available to members of the working classes in places like miners' libraries and found more popular Victorian novels than recent modernist literature. Hilliard suggested that conservative literary tastes could actually be more commonly found among those members of the middle and lower middle classes who did not have a university degree than among the working classes.

Both authors qualified their arguments and are not as much at odds as it might seem from the above description of their positions. Hilliard did not completely dispute Rose's finding, but rather argued for a catholic variety of literary tastes among the working-class readers, while Rose had actually acknowledged the popularity of adventure stories and American westerns among British workers, but simply noted that they were reading Brontë and Dickens as well. In fact, Rose explicitly states that the '"mass reading public" was not an undifferentiated mass' and that 'even within the circumscribed area of the Welsh coalfields, reading tastes could vary considerably over time and between communities'.[23]

Perhaps a more important point is that, even if it is true, to whatever degree, that the British working classes rejected modernist literature, in a sense they were rejecting literature that reflected not only the age in which they lived but to a large degree their own experience, especially those who had fought on the Western Front. In *To the Lighthouse*, her modern, experimental, stream-of-consciousness novel, Virginia Woolf captures the heightened emotions that lay just beneath the surface of everyday life, of the 'strife, divisions, difference of opinion, prejudices twisted into the very fibre of being'.[24] In one particularly illuminating passage, she describes the overreaction of a man scarred by the war to an innocuous comment upon the weather:

> The extraordinary irrationality of her remark, the folly of women's minds enraged him. He had ridden through the valley of death, been shattered and shivered; and now, she flew in the face of facts, made his children hope what was utterly out of the question, in effect, told lies. He stamped his foot on the stone step. 'Damn you', he said. But what had she said? Simply that it might be fine tomorrow. So it might.[25]

Evelyn Waugh's 1928 novel *Decline and Fall* has been compared to Voltaire's *Candide*, as it deals with a relatively innocent young man, in this case named Paul, who endures a series of calamities that land him 'in the soup', despite his best intentions. Paul, like everyone of his generation, was deeply affected by the war, but its main effect seems to be his inability to take British society or its conventions seriously. He defines a 'modern churchman' as one 'who draws the full salary of a beneficed clergyman and need not commit himself to any religious belief'. Like Candide, he tries to believe that all is for the best, that 'God's in his heaven, all's right with the world'. But it is clear that this is Paul's defence mechanism against a modern society in which, as Waugh writes, 'As individuals we simply do not exist. We are just potential home-builders, beavers, and ants.'

J. R. R. Tolkien provided a different kind of escape from memories of the war and the drabness of everyday life by creating a pseudo-medieval fantasy world in such novels as *The Hobbit* (1937) and, later, his *Lord of the Rings* trilogy (1954–5). Tolkien attracted a huge readership among the British public, beginning in the interwar period. Tolkien found in the atmosphere of war and barbarism he associated with the Middle Ages a parallel with his own time, although his works affirm the possibility of goodness in evil times and the necessity for the righteous to fight and struggle in the face of danger and darkness.[26] It is also worth noting that T. H. White wrote most of his popular retelling of the King Arthur tales, *The Once and Future King*, in the 1930s, although the work was not published until 1958, further illustrating the cultural resonance that the medieval period had for British writers during the interwar years and the continuing popularity of the Arthurian legends in British popular culture.

Scotland enjoyed something of a literary renaissance during the 1930s, best exemplified by Lewis Crassic Gibbon's trilogy, *A Scots Quair* (1932–4) and Neil M. Gunn's *Highland River* (1937). Gibbon's novels stand in opposition to the Kailyard tradition in Scottish literature because of his rejection of small-town values and his depiction of the emotional aridity of village life. In the first novel of the trilogy,

Sunset Song, his female protagonist, Chris Guthrie, sees her life and her homeland transformed by the Great War, which takes her husband, leaving her to struggle with its after-effects on her own. The subsequent novels, *Cloud Howe* and *Grey Granite*, see Chris marry a minister who symbolically dies in the pulpit before she reunites with her son, Ewan, from her first marriage as they jointly become involved in the socialist movement. Gunn's *Highland River* is rather more sympathetic to the rhythms of village life, which are contrasted with the trauma inflicted by the war on the main character, Kenn. The stream-of-consciousness nature of Kenn's childhood reflections, however, put this novel in the same modernist tradition as Gibbon's novels, despite their different views on politics and their native land.

The variety of literary experiences available to the reading public can be seen as well in the genre that Nicola Bishop has identified as 'rambling fiction', largely written by lower-middle-class urban and suburban clerks whose characters rediscover their masculinity through travel through the English countryside and direct contact with nature. This genre includes the novels of Victor Canning, which centre on the character of Edgar Finchley. Bishop suggests that these novels appealed to the entire lower middle class, even if they focused on a particular segment of it, especially those who lived and worked in an urban environment and did not have frequent access to the wide open spaces or diminishing woodlands of rural England.[27] By contrast, industrial magnates and British politicians frequently occupy the role of villain in those post-First World War novels examined by Christine Grandy. Grandy points to *If Winter Comes*, a 1921 novel by A. S. M. Hutchison, as a prime example of how the capitalist driven by profit differs from the common soldier inspired by patriotism.[28] She notes the same theme recurring in McNeile's Bulldog Drummond detective novels and Warwick Deeping's novel *Sorrel and Son* (1925), while citing Arnold Bennett's *Lord Raingo* as an exception about a rich business owner whose physical pain and fear of death endow him with pathos.

In a different way, John Maynard Keynes made the same point about the difference between the capitalist and the worker in his 1926 essay, 'The End of Laissez Faire', in which he pointed out that

> it is *not* true that individuals possess a prescriptive 'natural liberty' in their economic activities. There is *no* 'compact' conferring perpetual rights on those who Have or on those who Acquire. The world is *not* so governed from above that private and social interest always coincide.[29]

Keynes's proposed solution centred on the establishment of what he called 'semi-autonomous bodies within the state' whose focus would be the public good and from which private interest would be excluded from their deliberations. Keynes, despite his criticisms of unbridled capitalism, was no socialist, referring to socialism as 'little better than a dusty survival of a plan to meet the problems of fifty years ago, based on a misunderstanding of what some one [*sic*] said a hundred years ago'.[30]

Interest in the life experiences of members of the working classes found expression as well in both feature and documentary films. The 1927 film, *Hindle Wakes*, directed by Maurice Elvey, allows the audience to vicariously share the experience of two girls at the seaside resort of Blackpool, while on holiday from their jobs in a cotton mill. In *Sing as We Go* (1934), Gracie Fields plays a factory worker who journeys to Blackpool, but, reflecting the impact of the Depression, unlike her counterparts in *Hindle Wakes*, she is unemployed.[31] In the 1930s John Grierson made a series of documentary films to provide glimpses into the daily lives of workers. Grierson, who made his first documentary 'Drifters', about North Sea herring fishermen, in 1929, said that 'I took on cinema as a pulpit'.[32]

In his 1939 novel *Coming Up For Air*, George Orwell describes a scene that must have already played out in a million households on an almost daily basis throughout the Depression:

> Hilda was in her 'I don't know what we're going to DO!' mood, partly owing to the price of butter and partly because the Christmas holidays were nearly over and there was still five pounds owing on the school fees for last term. I ate my boiled egg and spread a piece of bread with Golden Crown marmalade. Hilda will persist in buying the stuff. It's fivepence-halfpenny a pound, and the label tells you, in the smallest print the law allows, that it contains 'a certain proportion of neutral fruit-juice'. This started me off, in the rather irritating way I have sometimes, talking about neutral fruit-trees, wondering what they looked like and what countries they grew in, until finally Hilda got angry. It's not that she minds me chipping her, it's only that in some obscure way she thinks it's wicked to make jokes about anything you save money on.[33]

The quintessential Depression novel would have to be Walter Greenwood's *Love on the Dole* (1933). Unlike Orwell, who came from a middle-class family and received a public school education, Greenwood had working-class roots, lost his father when he was nine, and left school at the age of thirteen to help supplement the income of his mother, who worked as a waitress. Greenwood's novel centres on a young woman who becomes the mistress of a wealthy bookmaker to help save her family from the utterly debilitating effects of an inexorable poverty.

Aldous Huxley in his dystopian novel *Brave New World* (1932) addressed issues such as thought control in reaction to the rise of fascism on the European continent:

> 'Till at last the child's mind is these suggestions, and the sum of the suggestions is the child's mind. And not the child's mind only. The adult's mind too – all his life long. The mind that judges and desires and decides – made up of these suggestions. But all these suggestions are our suggestions!' The Director almost shouted in his triumph. 'Suggestions from the State'.[34]

In Huxley's novel, the last thing that the Director, the sobriquet of the fictional dictator in the novel, wants is for people to study history; one of the 'suggestions' with which the people are imbued is Henry Ford's quote that 'history is bunk'. Huxley writes of the Director:

> He waved his hand; and it was as though, with an invisible feather wisk, he had brushed away a little dust, and the dust was Harappa, was Ur of the Chaldees; some spider-webs, and they were Thebes and Babylon and Cnossos and Mycenae. Whisk. Whisk – and where was Odysseus, where was Job, where were Jupiter and Gotama and Jesus? Whisk – and those specks of antique dirt called Athens and

Rome, Jerusalem and the Middle Kingdom – all were gone. Whisk – the place where Italy had been was empty. Whisk, the cathedrals; whisk, whisk, King Lear and the Thoughts of Pascal. Whisk, Passion; whisk, Requiem; whisk, Symphony; whisk.[35]

As George Orwell contemplated the coming of the next war in *Coming Up For Air*, it was the kind of society and government that were leading to war as much as the war itself that concerned and scared him:

But who's afraid of war? That's to say, who's afraid of the bombs and the machine-guns? 'You are,' you say. Yes, I am, and so's anybody who's ever seen them. But it isn't the war that matters, it's the after-war. The world we're going down into, the kind of hate-world, slogan-world. The coloured shirts, the barbed wire, the rubber truncheons. The secret cells where the electric light burns night and day, and the detectives watching you while you sleep. And the processions and the posters with enormous faces, and the crowds of a million people all cheering for the Leader till they deafen themselves into thinking that they really worship him, and all the time, underneath, they hate him so that they want to puke.[36]

In 1936, the German Nazis under Hitler openly defied the Treaty of Versailles by marching into the Rhineland, while Mussolini invaded Ethiopia in defiance of the League of Nations. The Spanish Civil War began the same year and seemed a possible precursor to a larger European conflict. News came in 1937 that Japan, which six years earlier had invaded the Chinese province of Manchuria, had now launched a full-scale invasion of China itself. Louis MacNeice's 1937 poem, 'Sunlight in the Garden' speaks wistfully of a light that is fading, of freedom advancing towards its end, of a time approaching when 'we shall have no time for dances', while expressing gratitude for the small amount of time spent in the 'sunlight in the garden'. In his 1938 poem 'The Newsreel', Cecil Day-Lewis suggests that while people might pretend that life is normal ('There is the mayor opening the oyster season: / A society wedding: the autumn hats look swell: / An old crocks' race, and a politician / In fishing-waders to prove that all is well'), people need to awaken to the threat before them:

Oh, look at the warplanes! Screaming hysteric treble
In the low power-dive, like gannets they fall steep
But what are they to trouble –
These silver shadows – to trouble your watery, womb-deep sleep?

See the big guns, rising, groping, erected
To plant death in your world's soft womb.
Fire-bud, smoke-blossom, iron seed projected –
Are these exotics? They will grow nearer home!

Grow nearer home – and out of the dream-house stumbling
One night into a strangling air and the flung
Rags of children and thunder of stone niagaras tumbling,
You'll know you slept too long.

International relations in the interwar years:
The background to the Second World War

On 30 September 1938 Prime Minister Neville Chamberlain returned from Munich and a meeting with Adolf Hitler proclaiming that he had achieved 'peace in our time' by negotiating an agreement whereby Chamberlain had granted Hitler recognition of the German annexation of the Sudetenland in exchange for the German dictator's promise to respect the national sovereignty of Czechoslovakia. Chamberlain is often characterized as a passive dupe who failed to stand up to Hitler in favour of a policy of 'appeasement'. In Volume I of his history of the Second World War, Churchill wrote, 'The Prime Minister has believed in addressing Herr Hitler through the language of sweet reasonableness. I have believed that he was more open to the language of the mailed fist.'[37] Francis Williams called Munich 'the peculiar and inevitable achievement of Chamberlain's inflexible talent for excluding from the range of his vision anything he did not wish to see'.[38]

In actuality, Chamberlain took a proactive stance in his foreign policy that had several advantages. First, by forestalling conflict with Hitler, he gave Britain more time to prepare for war technologically and militarily, regardless of whether or not this was his actual aim. Even Churchill acknowledged that the government was 'hideously unprepared for war', though to him this was obviously not to its credit. However, three years earlier, at the same time that the government had finally begun

FIGURE 31 *British statesman and prime minister Neville Chamberlain (1869–1940) at Heston Airport on his return from Munich after meeting with Hitler, making his 'peace in our time' address, 30 September 1938.*
Central Press/Hulton Archive/Getty.

the process of rearmament, the British physicist Sir Robert Watson-Watt began work as head of the radio section of the National Physical Laboratory on a means of using radio waves to locate the position of flying aircraft. Radar, as the new system became known (it was an acronym for 'Radio Detection and Ranging'), ended up playing a decisive role in the Royal Air Force's ability to defend the country during the Battle of Britain in 1940. So too did the development of effective fighter planes such as the Spitfire and the Hurricane, despite the Air Command's general emphasis on long-range bombers whose objective was to attack the enemy directly.

Secondly, Chamberlain did not drag Britain into a war at a time in which it would have had very little public support, despite the paroxysms of Churchill, who fumed that he found 'unendurable the sense of our country falling into the power, into the orbit and influence of Nazi Germany, and of our existence becoming dependent upon their goodwill or pleasure'. The House of Commons, in fact, voted 366 to 144 in support of the prime minister's agreement with Hitler. Chamberlain did not yet know if he could count on French support either, or how effective the French military would be at that point, and he certainly knew that he could not count on the deeply isolationist United States.

Thirdly, if Chamberlain would have opposed Hitler at Munich over annexation of a land largely populated by Germans, he risked challenges to Britain's own imperial policies during the interwar years. The background to the Second World War did not begin in 1938, but went back much earlier to the end of the First World War when Germany received exceptionally harsh terms, which the Germans naturally resented. The British risked appearing as hypocrites because, after depriving Germany of its colonies and accepting for much of Europe US president Woodrow Wilson's principle of national self-determination, they not only held on to their empire but actually expanded their influence, particularly in the Middle East. While the defeated Austro-Hungarian and Turkish empires were dismantled with a number of smaller, independent nations left in their wake, the British and French empires remained virtually intact, if not larger. Former German colonies became mandates of the League of Nations, largely administered, however, by Britain and France. Some colonies became the mandate of members of the British Commonwealth, as was the case for New Guinea (Australia), Samoa (New Zealand), and German South-West Africa (South Africa). One of Britain's new mandates was Palestine, turned over to the British by the League of Nations with the expectation that Britain would prepare the way for a Jewish state there based on the Balfour Declaration of 1917. The problem for Britain in the Middle East resided in the conflicting expectations held by Jews and Arabs, both of whom had been led to believe that Britain would support their nationalist aspirations in the region. The British were not necessarily being duplicitous towards either; their policy was to attempt to find a way to satisfy both. Not that all within the British government were of a single mind when it came to Middle Eastern policy; both the Jews and the Arabs had their defenders and their detractors.

The British also faced growing opposition to imperial rule in India; Churchill, who favoured standing up to Hitler, also favoured standing up to Nehru and Gandhi and defending British rule there, going so far as to form an Indian Empire Society dedicated to that aim. The movement for Indian independence might have been more effective in the 1930s had it been more unified, but the Hindu–Muslim divide that would later lead to the partition of India into the separate countries of India and Pakistan had already started to manifest itself in Indian politics. But by then the nationalist movement had already gained significant momentum, fuelled largely the passage of the Rowlett Act of 1919 and the Amritsar massacre of the same year. The Rowlatt Act (officially the Anarchical and Revolutionary Crimes Act) gave law enforcement the right to detain suspects for up to a year without trial without having to produce evidence to support the detention and denied jury trials and the right of appeal to those prisoners accused of political crimes. Protests erupted in Amritsar in April when the British arrested and threatened deportation to two local leaders of the Indian National Congress. As the protesters marched towards the part of the city where most of the British residents lived, British soldiers, badly outnumbered and not knowing the intentions of the crowd, opened fire, killing hundreds and wounding well over one thousand.

In January 1931 a Round Table Conference proposed a new constitution for India. Gandhi temporarily withdrew from politics to focus on the cause of the 'Untouchables', who were even refused admission into Hindu temples. Indian nationalist feeling was running high and India was set on a course for independence, so Chamberlain needed to take the moral high ground with Hitler instead of appearing as the aggressor, not only to gain more popular support for war at home but to help ensure that India would remain loyal to the British should war develop.

Still, how had the world come to the brink of war by 1938 in the first place? International relations after the First World War were supposed to be governed by the League of Nations, but this organization, the brainchild of Woodrow Wilson approved at the Paris Peace Conference, was hindered from the start by the failure of the United States to join and its effectiveness mocked when Germany withdrew on 14 October 1933. H. G. Wells later wrote the following about the League:

> This premature and ineffectual League was a hindrance rather than a help to the achievement of world peace. ... It prevented people from thinking freely about the essentials of the problem. Organizations of well-meaning folk, the British League of Nations Union, for example, came into existence to support it, and resisted rather than helped any effectual criticism of its constitution and working. They would say that it was 'better than nothing,' whereas a false start is very much worse than nothing.[39]

This is not the place to detail the causes of the rise of extremely nationalistic and militarily aggressive governments in Germany, Italy, and Japan, but suffice it to say that none of them were hindered by the toothless League of Nations and that they took advantage of the inevitable reluctance of other countries to relive another world war soon after the first had ended.

Chamberlain shared with much of the rest of those who had lived through the First World War the conviction that such a catastrophe should not be repeated under any circumstances. The other two leading politicians of the interwar years, Stanley Baldwin and Ramsay MacDonald, shared this view and each pursued a pacifist foreign policy during their terms as prime minister as well. Churchill, as we have seen and as is well known, vehemently opposed Hitler from the start, but his stance was at odds with the prevailing view throughout the country; furthermore, his uncompromising stance towards the Labour Party had contributed to a rift with his own party leadership, which believed that national solidarity was more important than partisan politics during the crisis of the Great Depression. The Labour Party disliked Hitler intensely for his virulent opposition to communism, as well as for his treatment of the Jews, but they, like Chamberlain, did not necessarily think that war was the best means to oppose him. Neville Henderson, the British ambassador to Germany, believed that Hitler could be appealed to on a rational basis. The American ambassador, Charles Dodd, only very gradually came to the realization that Hitler's policies needed to be more stringently opposed and condemned, a position that earned him nothing but rebukes from his superiors in Washington.[40] Chamberlain may have known that he alone could not prevent another world war from occurring, but he was determined to do everything he could to try. He may have been prone to underestimating or misreading Hitler – if so, he was certainly not the only one – but Michael Howard has shown that Chamberlain went to Munich armed with advice and knowledge provided by the Committee of Imperial Defence that war with Hitler would mean a world war that would include Japan and for which Britain was not prepared. Nor did Chamberlain sit idly by after Munich and wait for Hitler's next move; maximum aircraft production without budgetary restraints began in February 1939.

On 14 March 1939 the German army marched into Czechoslovakia; the British did not respond militarily; it is a fair criticism of Chamberlain that he had made the Munich Agreement without any intention of enforcing the pact if Hitler violated it. At first, Chamberlain reacted to the German invasion of Czechoslovakia with his customary caution, but a month later the British introduced military conscription and began talks with France about allying for a potential war with Germany. They settled on Poland as the line they would not permit Hitler to cross without risking war with Britain and France. They did so despite the certainty that they lacked the military capacity to save Poland from a likely German invasion and occupation. The mood of the British public, which had overwhelmingly supported the Munich Agreement, began to shift to acceptance of the idea that war might be inevitable, even necessary. Even Chamberlain had come to the view that Hitler could not be trusted, though he may not have entirely given up hopes of avoiding war just yet. He did not actually approve mobilization for war until 24 August. Ten days later, the Second World War began.

FIGURE 32 *The British prime minister Winston Churchill giving a speech (on the BBC) he had just delivered at the House of Commons, 13 May 1940: 'I have nothing to offer but blood, toil, tears and sweat. ... What is our aim? ... Victory, Victory at all costs – Victory in spite of all terrors ... for without victory there is no survival. ... No survival ... for the impulse of the ages, that mankind shall move forward toward his goal. I feel entitled at this juncture, at this time, to claim the aid of all and to say, "Come then, let us go forward together with our united strength".' The following summer the Battle of Britain started, causing extensive destruction in London; the Royal Air Force nevertheless succeeded in pushing back the German air attacks.* Keystone-France/Gamma-Keystone/Getty.

16

The Second World War

If we can stand up to [Hitler], all Europe may be free and the life of the world may move forward into broad, sunlit uplands. But if we fail, then the whole world, including the United States, including all that we have known and cared for, will sink into the abyss of a new Dark Age made more sinister, and perhaps more protracted, by the lights of perverted science. Let us therefore brace ourselves to our duties, and so bear ourselves that, if the British Empire and its Commonwealth last for a thousand years, men will still say, 'This was their finest hour.'

WINSTON CHURCHILL, 18 June 1940

The outbreak of the Second World War

Hitler may have been surprised when the British declared war on Germany after his invasion of Poland on 3 September 1939, but Chamberlain had finally penned himself into a corner from which he could not escape without acknowledging the complete failure of his decision to intervene diplomatically in Eastern European affairs. In fact, Chamberlain had guaranteed the territorial sovereignty not only of Poland, but also of Romania, based on a rumour purveyed by Romania's ambassador to Britain that Hitler planned to invade there as well. Britain had no strategic interests in either Poland or Romania any more than they had in Czechoslovakia or the Sudetenland. But Hitler had made it increasingly difficult for the British government to ignore the warnings of critics like Churchill who saw in Hitler a menace to Christendom. It would certainly have behoved Chamberlain to have forged some kind of alliance with the Soviet Union, however, if the British had any hope of preventing Hitler from continuing Germany's eastward expansion. It was difficult, however, for Chamberlain to contemplate an alliance with the Soviet bear, the bête noire for the English bourgeoisie.

Behind Chamberlain's failure to seek such an alliance lay not only British hostility to Communism but also the continued hope that war might be avoided. This, of course, was based on the deep-rooted determination to avoid at all costs a repeat of the First World War. Had Chamberlain accepted the fact that another war was inevitable, he may have overcome his reluctance to deal with the Soviets; instead Hitler convinced Stalin, or rather Ribbentrop convinced Molotov, to sign a Nazi–Soviet non-aggression pact that gave Germany a free hand in western Poland. The Nazi–Soviet Non-Aggression Pact also provided the Soviets an opportunity to annex the Baltic states of Estonia, Latvia, and Lithuania, as well as part of eastern Poland. The Nazi–Soviet alliance certainly made the task ahead more formidable for Britain.

In the course of the 1930s, Britain had sat idly by while Japan invaded Manchuria, Italy assaulted Ethiopia, and Hitler annexed the Rhineland, Austria, and Czechoslovakia. Why, therefore, would it choose such an inauspicious time as September 1939 to declare war in what seemed to be such a futile gesture since it had no actual means of defending Poland from German aggression?

One explanation has mainly to do with a change in popular attitudes that made it permissible for Britain to declare war on Hitler in September 1939 than it was even six months earlier. Parliament, far from putting up resistance, almost unanimously endorsed the decision of the government to declare war that month, after it had overwhelmingly, supported Chamberlain's pact with Hitler at Munich the previous year. A second explanation is that even Chamberlain now recognized that Hitler was not a man who could be dealt with rationally or through normal diplomatic means. Even Hitler's alliance with the Soviet Union did not dissuade the prime minister from honouring his commitment to Poland, as meaningless as it was when it came to actually helping the Poles.

The Phony War

In response to those whom Churchill labelled 'thoughtless dilettanti or purblind worldlings who sometimes ask us: "What is it that Britain and France are fighting for?"', he responded, 'If we left off fighting you would soon find out.'[1] When Churchill said this he did not know of France's perfunctory approach to the war, or that France would soon be occupied and subjected to the odious apparatus of Nazi rule. Nonetheless, once the British had declared war, they knew that they had no choice but to fight to the end or submit to German control, as would eventually happen in France, the Netherlands, and most of the rest of Europe.

The first nine months of the war, however, involved very little fighting on the part of either the British or the French. This period has thus been dubbed the 'Phony War'. The French relied on a defensive strategy that centred on the Maginot Line, a string of heavily fortified positions and psychological boundary intended to prevent a repeat of the German invasion through Belgium that had accompanied the start of the First World War. The British planned to eventually fight the Germans in North Africa and Italy, where they were considered weaker, but seemed in no hurry to do so.

In the meantime, the British planned to use the navy to blockade Scandinavia, a major source of iron ore for the Germans. Blockades aimed at Germany and Austria had helped the Allies immensely in the First World War, with Germany running perilously low on food and critical supplies by the time the Kaiser surrendered in November 1918. The British hoped the Royal Navy could play a similarly vital role this time around. But Norway remained neutral, allowing the German ships to safely travel back and forth between the two countries lest Britain violate Norwegian waters and neutrality. Even if they had, this would not have stopped the megalomaniacal Hitler. The British considered but decided against placing mines in international waters as one means to trammel German shipping.

Chamberlain also vetoed a French proposal to attack Russia by bombing its oil fields, having no desire to fight Russia too at a time when Britain lacked the wherewithal to effectively fight Germany – at least on land. The British navy, on the other hand, was perfectly capable of engaging the Germans at sea, and did so in the Atlantic from the beginning of the war. They did not have much of a choice; a German U-boat torpedoed a British ship on the first evening of the war. 1,418 passengers, including 311 Americans, were aboard the SS *Athena*, which was travelling from Glasgow, via Liverpool and Belfast, to Montreal.[2] Thus, even at sea the British were mostly thrown onto the defensive. But the British could not afford to deploy its entire fleet to protect British shipping in the Atlantic because of the exigencies of home defence. British ships were also necessary to block the entrance to the North Sea to close those waters to merchant ships bound for Germany, but the Royal Navy dispersed, also charged with protecting the shipping lanes that brought oil from the Middle East via the Mediterranean.

Then there was the empire to consider, given the looming threat of a Japanese invasion of British colonies. The British thus had to contend with the German, Italian, and Japanese navies, a daunting task that proved one of the greatest challenges of the war. Britain had increased its naval strength significantly in the previous decade, but it was not sufficient in battling the navies of the fascist and imperialist Axis powers. In the face of all of these challenges, it is not surprising that the British would opt for concentrating first and foremost on their home defences, meaning that war against Germany had to take priority over the defeat of the Italians or the Japanese.

The Phony War ended on 9 April 1940 when Germany launched an air and sea invasion of Norway. The British responded with a counterattack that had some success sinking German ships and destroying German aircraft, but it could not prevent the German army from advancing on land. The paucity of British troops who did land in Norway soon retreated and it became evident that the government and military had been unprepared and ill-equipped for Hitler's adroit coup de main. Churchill was largely to blame for the failure of the campaign, but the lion's share of responsibility for the fiasco fell on Chamberlain, as he was still prime minister. In fact, Churchill had been the one to order the placement of mines in Norwegian waters, where he hoped to bait the Germans into a naval battle, a decision which had inspired Hitler to launch his invasion in the first place.

The fall of Chamberlain and the ascent of Churchill

After the Norway disaster, Chamberlain, realizing he needed support and solidarity from the entire British populace, asked Labour to join him in a coalition government. However, Labour leaders no longer believed in the viability of a Chamberlain-led

government. Chamberlain had also lost the support of much of his own party, 100
members of which voted with Labour in a vote of no-confidence in the House of
Commons. Then, when Germany launched a simultaneous invasion of France,
Belgium, and the Netherlands on 10 May, the fate, not just of Chamberlain, but of all
of Europe, seemed to hang in the balance. King George VI preferred the Conservative
leader Lord Halifax, one of the other priests of appeasement, to Churchill as prime
minister, but Conservative leaders, including Halifax had concluded that Churchill
was the man to lead the government and the country at this critical juncture. Both
men realized realistically that Britain may have to come to terms with Germany at
some point, but to surrender when Britain was at its weakest would subject them to
whatever harsh terms Hitler may have been inclined to impose.

On 10 May Churchill took over as prime minister. He formed a coalition
government, with the tacit understanding that he would oversee the war efforts while
the minister of Labour and National Service, Ernest Bevin, would direct domestic
policy. Bevin had previously served as the head of the Transport and General Workers'
Union, so his appointment represented a major coup for the Labour Party, given his
strong union ties and relative lack of political experience. Churchill was joined in
the War Cabinet by Chamberlain and Halifax, along with Clement Atlee and Arthur
Greenwood from the Labour Party. As First Lord of the Admiralty, Churchill had
overseen the disastrous Norwegian operation, but this did not hurt him politically
once he became prime minister. At first, however, even members of his own party
were wary of him and reluctant to give him their unreserved support. Churchill's
bellicosity was legendary; he was like the boy who cried wolf, except, this time, the
wolf was really knocking at the door. Other Conservative leaders had been at odds
with Churchill over appeasement in the 1930s and even now many of them were
not so sure that it was such a good idea to fight on instead of making some kind of
a deal with Hitler. This sentiment was shared among some members of the British
aristocracy. No one yet took quite seriously the pro-Nazi propaganda broadcasts
from Berlin by the Englishman William Joyce, who appeared on the air under the
pseudonym 'Lord Haw-Haw'. At this juncture, it was not at all certain that Britain
would remain at war with Germany at any cost.

In the House and in the nation at large attitudes changed quickly. Churchill
believed that his entire life had prepared him for that moment when he became
prime minister. He had rehearsed for the moment when he would take power, telling,
first his minsters and then the House of Commons, on 13 May that 'I have nothing to
offer but blood, toil, tears and sweat'.[3] Churchill's wartime rhetoric benefited from
a lifetime of making political speeches, his experience as a writer and a student of
the English language, and his nineteenth-century conviction in the almost complete
moral superiority and special virtues of what he called 'the British race'. Churchill
saw Hitler as the menace that he was and made Hitler's defeat a personal priority,
even if it meant sacrificing the long-range interests of his beloved British Empire or
making a deal with the detested Communist government of the Soviet Union headed
by the brutal dictator, Joseph Stalin.[4] Britain also very well might not have survived
as an independent country had he not made a wartime alliance with the Soviets – or
if Britain had made a deal with Hitler.

Throughout the war, Churchill would enjoy the confidence and support of the
overwhelming majority of the British public. Although the war involved tremendous

sacrifice and innumerable hardships among the British people, as well as the deaths of many British servicemen, the public never viewed the Second World War in the same way that they had viewed the First World War. The First World War had quickly deteriorated into slaughter and stalemate on the Western Front. People took the war seriously, but lacked a sense that the actual survival of the country's independence was at stake. During the Second World War, the knowledge of the possibility of German conquest actuated a greater sense of shared sacrifice that unified the nation in support of the war effort. Churchill's fighting spirit and personal resiliency that had not let him quit on his own political career now became the exact qualities that matched the needs of his time and the qualities necessary to keep Britain fighting the Germans despite the gloomy prognosis of their chances of success at the outset.

The war against Germany

Churchill would need all the resolve that he could muster to keep Britain in the war after the Germans surprised the French and circumvented their defence strategy by sending their panzer tanks through the dense Ardennes Forest to the west of Paris, where they smashed through the French forces stationed at Sedan. Then, instead of advancing on Paris, the Germans headed for the Channel, where the British Expeditionary Force appeared to lay at their mercy. British vessels, large and small, evacuated the BEF, along with 100,000 French and Allied troops, from Dunkirk in late May and early June in a glorious or ignominious retreat, depending on the view of history one takes. The government, at least, tried to spin this as an Allied victory at the time. France surrendered on 17 June, with Marshal Pétain, a famous French general from the First World War known as the 'hero of Verdun', heading a puppet regime under Nazi auspices. Churchill had approved RAF support for the French army in an attempt to prop it up, but nothing that the British could have done would have saved the French at that point.

With France out of the war, Britain stood virtually alone against Hitler, who was talked out of an immediate amphibious invasion of Britain by Herman Goering, an art collector and huntsman who also served as the head of the Luftwaffe. Goering wanted to use his planes to bomb the British into submission. Halifax was among those questioning whether Britain should sue for peace with Germany after the French surrender. Churchill refused to contemplate negotiations, which he thought must inevitably lead to surrender on whatever terms Hitler proposed – at least at that point in the war when Britain would have been negotiating from a position of weakness.

Britain did not know that Hitler had postponed an armed invasion of the island by sea and immediately began the virtually impossible attempt to provide defences for its many beaches. These included efforts to protect 113 Scottish beaches, in case the Germans – who now controlled both Norway and Denmark – decided to invade from the north. For that same reason, 181,000 British troops were stationed in Scotland in 1941, when they clearly might have been needed in the south had Hitler not listened to Goering and launched his invasion across the English Channel instead of by air.[5] During the ensuing Battle of Britain, which lasted from July to October, the Royal Air Force proved able to the task and saved Britain from the humiliating defeat that Churchill had warned against. On 20 August Churchill paid tribute to the heroic pilots of the RAF in another of his famous speeches:

> The gratitude of every home in our island, in our Empire, and indeed throughout the world, except in the abodes of the guilty goes out to the British airmen who, undaunted by odds, unwearied in their constant challenge and mortal danger, are turning the tide of the World War by their prowess and by their devotion. Never in the field of human conflict was so much owed by so many to so few. All hearts go out to the fighter pilots, whose brilliant actions we see with our own eyes day after day. But we must never forget that all the time, night after night, month after month, our bomber squadrons travel far into Germany, find their targets in the darkness by the highest navigational skill, aim their attacks, often under the heaviest fire, often with serious loss, with deliberate careful discrimination, and inflict shattering blows upon the whole of the technical and war-making structures of the Nazi power.

Surviving the Battle of Britain kept Britain in the war but still a long way from actually winning it. The British High Command had always known that the ultimate defeat of Germany could not be accomplished unless either the Soviet Union or the United States entered the war against Hitler. In 1941, both were brought into the war, the Soviet Union in June when the German army invaded, and the United States in December when the Japanese bombed Pearl Harbor and Germany declared war against the United States immediately thereafter.

Four months prior to the Japanese attack on the American naval base, however, on 14 August Churchill had met President Roosevelt in Newfoundland, where they had agreed to a common set of war aims in a document known as the Atlantic Charter. Most importantly, Churchill and Roosevelt agreed that neither Britain nor the United States would seek to profit from the war by seeking territorial gains at its end, they committed to the principle of national self-determination in the territorial changes that would inevitably result from the war, and they set forth a vision of an idealistic post-war world that would recognize the right of every country to peace and freedom from invasion, as well as 'improved labor standards, economic advancement and social security'. More unrealistically, the Charter expressed the hope of lightening 'for peace-loving peoples the crushing burden of armaments'.

It was important to Roosevelt that, should the United States enter the war, its war aims not include the preservation of the British Empire, while Churchill, again, put the defeat of the Nazis and the end of tyranny in Europe ahead of his imperial ideals. At the same time, Roosevelt never considered not supporting Britain in its struggle against Hitler, considering the Nazi regime as fundamentally different from the British Empire. With the United States just coming out of the Depression, Roosevelt had economic reasons as well for preserving British independence and preventing a Nazi-dominated Europe.

Then, in December 1941, the British foreign secretary Anthony Eden flew to Moscow in an attempt to reach a similar agreement with the Soviets. What was most striking about his visit was that the Soviets and the British were already jockeying for position in the post-war world, long before their victory could have been assured.

Once again, as at the beginning of the war, the British, who found it difficult to honour their commitments to Poland in the face of Stalin's demands, kept mum about this at the time. Stalin was concerned about anti-Soviet feeling in Poland – with good reason, as it turned out, because of the atrocities committed by Soviet troops, including the infamous Katyn massacre at the beginning of the war, which Stalin blamed on the Nazis – and the British had to resist making Poland cipher traffic available to the Soviets. The British–Soviet alliance was tenuous and marked with acrimony throughout the war, a marriage of expediency and realpolitik. Although the British were aware of Stalin's atrocities in Poland, they had to temporarily ignore their moral qualms in the interest of winning the enormous struggle against the Nazis.

Meanwhile, the British continued their efforts to thwart the Nazis. The Royal Navy still operated in the North Sea waters off the coast of Scotland trying to prevent German surface raiders from reaching the Atlantic where they could threaten the convoys bringing supplies from the United States under the Lend-lease programme. Churchill would later write in his memoirs that by mid-1943

> The strain on our destroyers was more than we could bear. The March convoy had to be postponed, and in April the Admiralty proposed, and I agreed, that supplies to Russia by this route should be suspended till the autumn darkness.[6]

This decision placed the Soviets at a severe handicap and Churchill acknowledged the difficulty of the decision given the ferocity of the fighting occurring on the Eastern Front at that time. In September Molotov officially protested to the British ambassador in Moscow and requested that the British resume shipments. Furthermore, while the Russians were sacrificing millions of men at the battles of Kursk, Orel, and Kharkov, the Allies had yet to open up the second front in France that Stalin desperately needed to take the pressure off his armies and people. But Vichy France remained under Nazi control, and therefore the entire French Empire as well, placing the British at a huge disadvantage and unwilling to commit to the kind of sacrifice that Stalin seemed to be demanding, even though the Russians were undergoing sacrifices on a much larger scale than their British or American allies.

The British did have some advantages against the Germans, including the secret codebreakers at Bletchley Park who, benefiting from the work of Polish mathematicians who had previously reconfigured their own replicas of the German Enigma machine, were able to figure out how to decipher coded messages used by all branches of the German military. The Enigma machine used electrical wiring to randomly substitute one letter for another – unlike traditional codes where the same letter might be repeatedly represented by a single different letter or symbol – so the only way to break the German code was through the construction of a similar machine, which the Poles had successfully accomplished by September 1938. The British used their own machines under the codename of 'Ultra' to read German radio traffic in a project so secret that it was not revealed to the public until 1974.

The British also supported and benefited from the existence of the French government-in-exile headed by General Charles de Gaulle, whose 'Free French' forces provided valuable support and ensured France a place among the victorious Allied powers at the end of the war. Perhaps of equal importance, Churchill and Roosevelt were able to recognize de Gaulle as the true head of the French government, denying the Vichy regime even the illusion of legitimacy. De Gaulle initially made London his headquarters before forming a provisional government in Algiers later in the war. He remained committed to preserving the French Empire, particularly control over Algeria, which he considered a part of France, making the alliance somewhat problematic for Churchill and Roosevelt, given their commitments in the Atlantic Charter. The Free French Army grew throughout the war and helped play a role in the Allied campaigns in North Africa, Italy, and the eventual liberation of Paris itself on 25 August 1944 following the Allied landing at Normandy on 6 June (D-Day).

The war against Japan

British resources were stretched extremely thin during the war, with both its dominions and its colonies expected to provide material and human resources that put a heavy strain on them and put pressure on their relationship with Britain. The British military could hardly be expected to defend Britain and contribute to the defeat of the Germans in Africa and Europe, while at the same time defending its colonies and interests in the Middle East, Asia, and the Pacific. Still, they thought that they had enough sea power to defend Singapore against a Japanese naval attack – or to evacuate that strategic port city if necessary. In doing so, they failed to account for the aggressive, highly skilled, and strategically innovative Japanese military that was sweeping its way through China and the Pacific.

Meanwhile, the leaders of the Indian independence movement, Subhas Chandra Bose and Jawaharlal Nehru, sought to take advantage of the war, Bose by aligning with the Nazis and the Japanese to proclaim the formation of a Provisional Government of Free India, and Nehru, who supported Britain at the beginning of the war, by forming the Quit India movement, a civil disobedience campaign aimed at ending British rule. The political activist Mohandas Gandhi and the prominent industrialist Ghanshyam Das Birla were more accommodating towards the British, favouring collaboration to defeat the Japanese without the threat of resistance. Another group, the Congress Socialist Party, a faction that formed within the Indian National Congress in 1934, sought to pressure the British through strikes, boycotts, and rebellions aimed at putting an end to British repression. For the more radical of the Indian revolutionaries, the alliance between the Nazis and the Soviets had put Britain in exactly the weakened position that they thought they could finally exploit. The British Viceroy in India responded by threatening to suspend Indian self-rule for the duration of the war if necessary. Bose argued against supporting the British in another war, but Nehru stopped short of supporting the fascist regimes of Germany and Italy, towards which he had been openly hostile. In the end, India still made a significant contribution to the British war effort, with the Indian army expanding from 200,000 to 2 million men, 25,000 of whom died in the war, and a financial contribution estimated at £286 million, including raw materials, although the Indian army understandably lost enthusiasm for sustaining its efforts with each Japanese victory in Asia.[7]

Shortly after the Japanese attacked Pearl Harbor, they captured Hong Kong, followed by an invasion of the Malay Peninsula. The Japanese then greatly damaged

British naval strength in the region when they sunk the HMS *Repulse* and the HMS *Prince of Wales* in the Indian Ocean. The British army was unable to prevent Japanese troops from gaining control of the Isthmus of Kra that forms the narrowest part of the Malay Peninsula, which provided a base for the successful – and unexpected – land attack on the British colony of Singapore.

The fall of Singapore on 15 February 1942, which involved the surrender of about 60,000 British, Australian, and Indian troops marked a low point for British fortunes in the Pacific war. Winston Churchill called it 'the worst disaster and largest capitulation in British history'. This catastrophe included the capture of some 85,000 British and Australian troops, and seemed to leave Australia and New Zealand vulnerable and unable to rely on British protection. Instead, the United States would play the role of defender of Australia and New Zealand and lead the efforts to turn back the Japanese in Asia and the Pacific. The entire British imperial enterprise seemed to be crumbling; Bayly and Harper write of the loss of Singapore that 'the entire legitimacy of the Asian empire had been shaken'.[8] The Japanese next launched a major invasion of Burma, another territory that the British were ill-positioned to defend. The loss of Singapore was replayed once again in Rangoon, which the Japanese started to bomb on 13 December 1941, leading to a mass exodus in which an estimated 80,000 Indians, Anglo-Indians, and Anglo-Burmese refugees died from a combination of malnourishment, illness, and exhaustion.[9] Meanwhile, those subject to German bombs in Britain and Northern Ireland had no place to which to flee.

The home front

German aerial bombing attacks on Britain throughout the war gave new meaning to the words 'home front', bringing the war directly to the British people where they lived and worked. On 'Black Sunday' – 7 September 1940 – the first day of the Blitz, German bombs killed or seriously wounded 1,800 Londoners in aerial raids that lasted throughout the day and night. London historian Jerry White estimates that these raids destroyed 50,000 homes in the inner city and another 66,000 homes in the outer city, seriously damaged another 288,000 houses, and slightly damaged about 2 million homes throughout the city in the course of the almost nightly raids that followed for the next three months.[10] As a result of the raids on London, the British began to move vital industries outside of the city and spread production facilities around the country. As the capital and most populated city, London and the suffering of its people always carried a more symbolic importance than other targets of devastating raids by the Germans, including Belfast, Coventry, Hull, Liverpool, and Manchester.[11] Belfast, for example, sustained more than £200 damage to an estimated 271,925 houses, or about 84 per cent of the total.[12]

Espionage became an important part of the war effort on the home front, where the British government launched an extensive campaign to warn the British public not to talk about anything that could compromise the war effort with slogans such as 'Careless Talk Costs Lives' and posters of Hitler and Goering eavesdropping on women shoppers.[13] The task of British propaganda agencies was certainly made easier by the thuggish and murderous regimes against which the British were fighting, all the more so as the stories of mass exterminations and death camps filtered in to the West as the war went on. Wendy Webster has shown that the British press focused much more on resistance efforts against the Nazi and fascist regimes throughout Europe than on the wartime efforts of Britain's Soviet or American allies. She cites *Night Train to Munich* and *Pimpernel Smith* as examples of early war films that portrayed resistance efforts aimed at the Nazis in Germany and Austria.[14] The British press throughout the war played an important role in keeping morale high among the general public, something made easier because journalists were frequently kept in the dark about divisions and the darker ruminations within the War Cabinet.[15]

It was important at the time, for both foreign and domestic purposes, to represent the British people as entirely unified behind the war effort. Between June 1940 and June 1941, after the fall of France, while the United States and the Soviet Union refused to enter the war, the British fought on alone against Hitler, its government and people knowing that if London fell to the Nazis Hitler would be in control of all of Europe. The 1942 film *Mrs Miniver* adapted the likeable character from Jan Struther's 1939 novel for the purposes of boosting morale and solidifying unity behind the war effort. It portrays an England under attack from a Germany intent upon destroying the English way of life and the determined resistance put up by ordinary people such as the Miniver family. Mrs Miniver's husband Clem assists in the rescue of the British Expeditionary Force from Dunkirk, her son Vin joins the RAF and trains as a fighter pilot, while Mrs Miniver herself confronts a downed German pilot and turns him over to the police, in addition to her role as a comforting mother of two younger children, supportive wife, and embodiment of all that was

FIGURE 33 *London during the Blitz. A new road is being built across the pavement of a London street to bypass a bomb crater.*
Planet News Archive/SSPL.

good in the English people. The film ends with an exhortation to viewers that this war was a 'people's war' in which everyone must do their part in order to defend the country and defeat the nefarious Nazis.

But the image of the British people putting up a brave front and keeping a stiff upper lip, embodied in the famous and resurgently popular slogan 'Keep Calm and Carry On', can too easily ignore the very real fear and terror experienced by people in their daily lives, which Amy Bell has found reflected in wartime diaries, as well as in contemporary literature such as Elizabeth Bowen's 1941 short story, 'The Demon Lover' and Graham Greene's 1943 novel *The Ministry of Fear*.[16] The British government was not only aware of such anxieties at the time, but itself fearful that civilians would suffer the same debilitating effects of 'shell-shock' as had the First World War soldiers and took active steps to counteract this; for example, to keep morale up, Dunkirk was celebrated as a tremendous victory thanks to the heroic efforts of Britain's skilled seamen rather than as a humiliating retreat.

Radio played a critical role in providing the British public with a common frame of reference that did more to unite them than was possible in any previous war. Radio also provided a means of communicating directly with troops stationed overseas, allies, and the empire. Special Christmas broadcasts heard throughout the empire represented one such effort to provide a sense of imperial unity behind the war. The BBC expanded its personnel from 4,889 to 11,663 between the start of the war and March 1943 and worked closely with other branches of the government throughout the war. In addition, the number of programming hours tripled and the BBC increased its transmitter power availability by 500 per cent.[17]

But fear and panic were not all the British government had to contend with or that belies the image of a united resolute British public; crime rates soared as some people took advantage of the chaos and destruction wrought by German bombers, while British workers still went out on strike (though legally prohibited from doing so during wartime) and had higher rates of absenteeism than would be expected on the basis of both wartime propaganda and the nationalistic portrayal of the British war effort in popular histories and films. Crime rates in Britain rose by 54 per cent during the war years, compared to a 22 per cent rise during the last five years of the Depression before the war, while convictions for juvenile delinquency increased by 39 per cent.[18] Italian communities in Scottish cities found themselves under attack when Mussolini declared war on Britain in 1940. Interestingly, the British people did not tend to blame the German people as a whole for the war to the extent that they had during the First World War, mainly seeing them as victims of Nazi tyranny as well – therefore, anti-German sentiment was not as high in wartime Britain as one might think.

Another aspect of life on the home front during the war was the large number of Allied troops stationed there during the war and the large numbers of foreign refugees who made Britain their home. The Poles were particularly prominent, and not particularly welcomed, especially in Scotland. The British were ambivalent at best about the sizeable number of American troops who overran the country, especially southern England. Canadians, Norwegians, and Free French also had a noticeable presence, along with refugees from varied places, all at a time when the British were experiencing rationing and shortages, indicating that there was barely enough to go around for them.

Finally, the Second World War, unlike the First, seemed to reinforce rather than break down gender stereotypes. In 1939, women's unemployment initially rose as workforces in consumer industries such as textiles, pottery, and shoes were dismissed because of reduced demand for their products. Women were rejected from service in the Home Guard and employers actually proved more reluctant to hire women for jobs they regarded as men's jobs than during the First World War.[19] However, in the course of the war the percentage of women in the labour force did increase from 26 per cent in 1939 to a high of 33 per cent in 1943, while by war's end about 470,000 women had 'served in the Auxiliary Territorial Service (ATS), the Women's Auxiliary Air Force (WAAF), and the Women's Royal Naval Service (WRNS)'.[20] Another change involved the amount of compulsory service required of women and the extent to which they had their fates controlled by the government instead of choosing where to work or in what service to volunteer. In the end, however, the war seems to have contributed to a growing sense of self-confidence and satisfaction among many women in Britain because of the contributions that they made to the war effort and because they had again proven capable of doing 'men's jobs' when given the opportunity or called upon to do so.

Ireland

The Irish Free State under the leadership of Eamon de Valera remained officially neutral throughout the Second World War. De Valera was for all intents and purposes asserting Irish independence and removing Ireland from the British Commonwealth of nations. For the most part, the Irish people supported this decision, even though the country endured some economic hardships as a result. De Valera and his many supporters were still upset by the partition of the island and unwilling to join military forces with the nation that they held responsible for it.

The dubious morality of de Valera's decision in the face of the German bombing of Britain and Northern Ireland and the possibility of a Nazi conquest of the British Isles makes his commitment to neutrality all the more striking. Furthermore, Ireland itself faced a threat to its independence should the Germans have defeated the British, a consideration that lessened after the RAF emerged victorious in the Battle of Britain. In fact, however, although most of the Irish people did support the policy of neutrality, this did not equate to sympathy for the Nazis; many citizens of the Irish Free State even voluntarily joined the British armed forces during the war.

As the war went on, de Valera found himself under pressure, from President Roosevelt among others, to enter the war on the side of the Allies. The British put sanctions on trade with Ireland in retaliation for Ireland's continued refusal to join the Allies after the Battle of Britain. Ireland objected when the British proposed introducing conscription into Northern Ireland in May 1941, as the Irish government still considered the residents of Northern Ireland rightful citizens of Ireland, not the UK. In this way, the government in the south sought to encourage people in the North to think the same way and they took positive action to further such an identification when they sent fire brigades to Belfast after it had been hit by German fire bombs on 15–16 April 1941. In the end, however, even the Irish Free State gave assistance to Britain and its allies in various ways, even though it remained officially neutral until the end of the war.

The social consequences of the war

Britain ended the war ostensibly with its global position intact, enjoying its status as one of the major victorious powers occupying Germany, as seemingly the dominant power in the Mediterranean and the Middle East, and, for the time being, still in possession of its empire. But both Britain and its world position had in actuality been fundamentally altered by the experience of the Second World War.

The British people had shared the threats, dangers, and hardships of war to a degree unprecedented in history and in a way that lessened the importance of social distinctions and class and promoted a more egalitarian society. This was not merely a matter of popular perception; the raising of taxes on the wealthy to as high as 90 per cent significantly reduced the degree of economic inequality that existed in post-war society. (Twenty years later George Harrison of the Beatles would strenuously object to these absurdly high tax rates in his song 'Taxman'.) High society no longer functioned as it had before the war, with its elaborate social rituals and dinner parties; ostentatious displays of wealth during and immediately after the war appeared unseemly at best. A very large proportion of the population had to be mobilized to fight or support the war effort, much more so than the United States, for example, though not so large as Russia, which bore the brunt of the fighting and faced invasion by massive numbers of German troops. Individuals from different social classes found themselves sharing shelter from aerial raids, fighting together in the army or sharing the same risks in the navy or RAF, or working in volunteer organizations or expanding industry necessitated by the war. Paul Addison alludes to the fact that by the end of 1940 both Home Guard and the Civil Defence services employed about a million and a half people, while in the course of the war 5 (out of 38) million men and women served in the various branches of the armed services.[21]

Then there was the sheer cost of the war: Harold Perkin placed the total at £28 billion, more than twice the cost of the First World War.[22] The UK suffered a tremendous amount of physical destruction as a result of German bombs, which involved an immense loss of wealth in the form of property, real estate, and material assets. Addison notes that during the war years out of the population of 38 million there occurred 60 million changes of address.

Yet perhaps the most important social consequence of the war had to do with the activist role that the government had played in domestic policy during the war, preparing the way for the victory of the Labour Party and the emergence of the welfare state in 1945. By doing away with the means test for governmental health services, for example, Labour had benefited the middle class financially just as much as the working class. The Labour victory in 1945 might have been anticipated by the party's success in the by-elections held during the war years.

The blueprint for the welfare state had come largely in the form of the Beveridge Report, which was introduced in December 1942. The Beveridge Report enjoined the state to provide financial support for all retired, disabled, and unemployed citizens, assistance to families where earned income did not meet their basic needs, and healthcare, along with contributions from workers and employers. The state, of course, would administer the entire apparatus and guarantee fairness in how the benefits were doled out. This meant the welfare state was coloured by paternalism, which both critics and beneficiaries could find annoyingly patronizing. The Beveridge Report produced its share of sceptics who did not see how enough money could possibly be raised for the Treasury to pay for this, but the eminent economist John Maynard Keynes was among those who defended it.

Furthermore, the economic recovery of the Soviet Union under Stalin in the 1930s and the Soviet contribution to the war effort had softened many people's views towards state-run socialism at a time when few people in the West knew the full extent of Stalin's crimes against his own people. The Conservative Party had not only underestimated the Soviet Union, but its failure to cultivate an alliance with the Soviets had dearly cost Britain in the early years of the war. Such sympathies soon faded, however, as Britain found itself embroiled in a new Cold War with the Soviet Union and the challenges of economic recovery, the loss of its empire, and the need to redefine its position in a world dominated by two large and ideologically hostile superpowers in the United States and the Soviet Union.

FIGURE 34 *British troops searching a war-damaged building in Egypt during the Suez Crisis, November 1956.*
Express/Hulton Archive/Getty.

17

The post-war period, 1945 to 1973:

Social change and the end of empire

The fact is that these measures of ours are not theoretical trimmings. They are an essential part of a planned economy that we are introducing into this country. They are designed to help in promoting full employment, economic prosperity and justice for all. They are vital to the efficient working of the industrial and political machine of this country. They are the embodiment of our Socialist principle of placing the welfare of the nation before that of any section and of dealing with every problem in a practical and business-like way.[1]

Prime Minister CLEMENT ATLEE, 1946

The Labour Party and the rise of the welfare state

In 1938 the British government, at a time when it was starting to realize that a new war with Germany might be unavoidable, founded two new agencies called the Emergency Medical Service and the National Blood Transfusion Service. After the war, these agencies became subsidiary to the National Health Service, one of the several new initiatives – including policies that were aimed at guaranteeing adequate wages, housing, employment, and social insurance – to provide a better life and more security for the people of the UK. These admirable goals of Prime Minister Clement Attlee and his Labour government resonated strongly with the voting public after years of sacrifice in two world wars and the woes produced by the Great Depression. But they did not bring immediate relief to a severely damaged nation facing a prolonged period of austerity before the nation began to share in the prosperity that began almost immediately after the war in the United States.

The goal of the National Health Service, created in November 1946, was universal healthcare, wholly subsidized by the government. This system was administered on a national level, although local authorities still remained in charge of home healthcare, immunization, and emergency transport. It was based on the idealistic philosophy defining healthcare as a right, open to all irrespective of caste or economic status. Attlee had cut his teeth on these principles during the interwar years and had accrued valuable experience as a member of coalition governments during the Depression and the war. The planned economies of the First World War, the 1930s, and the Second World War seemed to demonstrate, at a time when free-market economics no longer seemed viable, the state's power to intervene in the economy and society efficaciously without succumbing to totalitarian communism or fascism. By 1948, however, Beveridge himself began to complain that the high rate of inflation had rendered his proposed benefits inadequate for the purposes they were meant to serve. Inevitably, certain citizens fell through the cracks, while others, like some grown children of middle-class parents, took advantage of a system that was not designed especially for their needs. Other complaints had to do with the excessive bureaucratization of the hospital system. The system had other foibles, which would come to be exposed, such as the inadequacy of funds available for retiring pensioners. But in the late 1940s the welfare legislation of the Labour government was generally seen as a significant and liberal ameliorative measure.

The creation of the welfare state was merely one indication of the generally positive outlook regnant in the post-war period. Britain began to look towards a roseate future after the war instead of wallowing in the mire of the past. This was the first time in British history when the government attempted to manage the economy when the country was not in the midst of war or in the throes of a serious economic depression, as the programme was designed to engender social engineering as opposed to measures promulgated to avert a crisis. The movement also featured what would later be known in the United States as 'urban renewal', which involved the clearing of slums, the building of new housing projects, and the creation of open areas around these developments known as 'green belts'. The Town and Country Planning Act of 1947 placed all land development under government oversight and required an onerous tax of 100 per cent on the increased valued of land for which development permits were granted.

Another component of the welfare state was the move made by the Labour government to nationalize major industries and administer them like the National Health Service. The first industries to be nationalized were coal (January 1947), electricity (April 1948), gas (May 1948), and steel (February 1951), while nationalization extended as well to the Bank of England (May 1946) and the railways (May 1948). In addition, the Agriculture Act of 1947 aimed at providing governmental support for farmers to increase the food supply and make the UK less dependent on foreign imports. Agriculture became more mechanized and less labour-intensive during the post-war period, making it more profitable for farmers to bring additional lands under cultivation. The Scottish Highlands in particular underwent something of an economic revival during this period.

At any other time in the twentieth century, these measures might have been denounced as socialist, but, like Franklin Roosevelt's New Deal in the United Stated during the 1930s, the introduction of the welfare state in Britain did not mean the end of capitalism and may just have saved it. Many people bristled at the changes imposed by the Labour government and still wished to preserve the past, but even the Conservatives seemed to recognize a need for change by giving their implicit assent to the nationalization programme.

Attlee's government remained in power from 1945 to 1951, propelling a social transformation in the country that had begun in the interwar period. One salient change included an increase in the number of women in the workforce. The number of married women in the workforce at first declined from a high of 7.2 million during the war to 5.8 million in September 1946.[2] After the war, women generally continued to work after they got married, but left the workforce once they became pregnant with their first child. Childbirth was encouraged for women because of concerns about population decline, while women's magazines such as *Good Housekeeping*, *My Home*, and *Woman's Weekly* generally reinforced the stereotypical image of women as wives, mothers, and homemakers. Most women who did work still laboured in lower-paying clerical or teaching jobs and did not earn the same pay as men when they practised similar vocations. Atavistic prejudices persisted, especially on the types of jobs defined as 'women's work', even though thousands of women had shown themselves capable of performing the same jobs as men in both world wars when a dearth of men necessitated an increased amount of female participation in the workforce.

Many women regarded their experience in the Second World War similarly to the way in which their counterparts had recalled their experience in the Great War – as a time of relative freedom, independence, and satisfaction, even though, beginning in 1941, the government required them to register if they were available for work. After the war, women right's advocates continued to push for equal pay, building on demands made during the war that resulted in equal compensation for civilian men and women for injuries sustained from the Nazi bombing campaigns. The Labour Party and even the Trades Union Congress spurned women's demands for equal pay, mainly because neither thought its political base would be sympathetic to policies fostering equity between the sexes. British unions negotiated men's wages separately from those of their women members, giving the former top priority.

Even though the British government did not legislate equality for women in the private workplace, it at least removed the ban on married women working in the Civil Service in 1946. Women were admitted to the Foreign Service in the same year. In 1955, the Conservative government surprisingly took the civil service legislation one step further by introducing equal pay for non-manual civil servants, teachers, and nurses. Many businesses, however, including most banks and insurance companies, kept a ban on hiring married women in place until the end of the 1950s.[3] By continuing to define certain jobs as women's work, they could lower the pay associated with those jobs, in confirmation of the gender bias of what was still a male-dominated society.

As prime minister, in addition to overseeing the transition to the welfare state, Attlee also had to address issues related to the downfall of the British Empire and the emerging US-led Cold War with the Soviet Union. Therefore, post-war governments in the UK sometimes had difficulty following through on a progressive domestic agenda, which even the Conservative Party had largely come to accept by 1951 when it returned to power. The British had shifted their priorities to a large degree and become more insular after the war, but they still saw themselves as a great nation with a proud history and did not wish to see the UK relegated to the status of a third- or fourth-rate power. The novels of Ian Fleming elucidate this; in them the CIA agent, Felix Leiter is maladroit and bumbling, constantly requiring salvation from the deft British secret agent, James Bond. Such concerns led to a proactive foreign policy designed to preserve Britain's place among the leading nations of a divided world threatened by the expansion of Communism and the possibility of nuclear annihilation.

The Cold War

The attitudes of the Labour and the Conservative parties towards the Soviet Union did not differ markedly; Labour was not as sympathetic as might be expected, the Conservatives not as antagonistic. Nonetheless, Britain's former ally was transformed into its mortal enemy almost overnight. It is perhaps hard to understand in the twenty-first century how real the Soviet threat seemed after the Soviet Union had exploded its first atomic bomb in 1949. Military bases and weapons were installed throughout Britain as a defensive measure against the Soviets. Concerns about Soviet power became aggravated with each new European country that adopted Communism under the bayonets of the Red Army and fell under Soviet influence – East Germany, Poland, Bulgaria, Romania, Hungary, Czechoslovakia; Yugoslavia was Communist but charted an independent course, while Communist parties formed part of the political landscape in France and Italy. 1949 also saw the triumph of the Communist Party in China in its civil war with the Guomindang and the founding of the People's Republic under Mao Zedong. In 1949 the UK joined the North Atlantic Treaty Organization (NATO), a military alliance of the United States, Canada, and a number of Western European nations forged to maintain a balance of power with the Soviet Union and its Communist bloc allies. The fears of the Cold War period were heightened by suspicions, which proved to be well founded, that there were traitors and Soviet agents working for British intelligence. While some former Soviet sympathizers had become completely disillusioned with Communism by the late 1940s, others, such as the double-agent Kim Philby, secretly retained their allegiance to a nation that still symbolized their youthful ideals.

When Churchill returned to power at the head of a Conservative government in 1951, he sought to augment Britain's international position in an effort to diminish the level of the Soviet threat by gaining the respect of its former ally and making it possible for them to peacefully coexist. Perhaps his wartime collaboration with Stalin and the debt Churchill knew Britain owed to the Soviets for their major role in the defeat of his mortal enemy, Hitler, had softened his attitudes to the point where he no longer wished to annihilate the Soviets, as some hard liners within the Conservative Party still wished to do. Churchill also recognized that the Soviet desire to annex the Baltic states of Estonia, Latvia, and Lithuania and to install sympathetic governments across Eastern Europe was largely the result of insecurity and a somewhat justified paranoia, given the horrors endured and sacrifice of 10 million

Russian people during the just-past Nazi invasion and occupation. Furthermore, Cold War tensions eased slightly in 1953 with the death of Stalin and his replacement by Nikita Khrushchev and with the end of the Korean War, the first armed conflict of the Cold War which had begun in 1950. But in 1955 NATO welcomed an officially rehabilitated West Germany into its embrace, further hardening the dividing line between East and West.

To George Orwell, who parodied Soviet rule in his 1946 novelistic parable, *Animal Farm*, the Soviets had sacrificed liberty in order to elevate the principles of equality and fraternity, but had even failed at those, giving rise to his famous aphorism that 'all animals are created equal – but some are more equal than others'. Orwell had come to view all Soviet claims for equality and the identification of the state with the people as propaganda and outright lies. When viewed from an ideological perspective, the 1948 Soviet blockade of the roads and rails leading from East to West Berlin that eventually led to the construction of the Berlin Wall seemed a particularly ominous development. In addition to recent converts to the anti-Soviet cause like Orwell, there were those who had always viewed the Soviet Union as the real enemy, many of whom would have even liked to see Hitler triumph in the East if it meant the end of Soviet rule. Many in both the British and the American governments willingly employed or worked with former Nazis, despite or even perhaps because of their past, given the extent of the hostility that existed towards communism.

Those who did continue to sympathize with the Soviets, in the political context of the Cold War, generally kept it a secret, particularly those involved in actual espionage, such as Philby, who shocked the country when he defected to the Soviet Union in 1963. Philby had completely fooled and bamboozled his colleagues in MI6, Britain's foreign intelligence service; the extent of his deception contributed to his ability to escape to Russia. Philby had resigned from the Foreign Service in 1951 and Edward Heath, the future prime minister who at the time held the position of Lord Privy Seal, quickly tried to reassure the British public that Philby had done no significant damage to national security, but this was small consolation to a paranoid public. The Philby case was the most spectacular failure of British intelligence during the Cold War, but the Profumo Affair, which broke in the same year, was not far behind. This scandal centred on the revelation of an affair eighteen months earlier between Prime Minister Harold Macmillan's secretary of state for war, John Profumo, and a prostitute named Christine Keeler, who was simultaneously having an affair with a man named Yevgeny Ivanov, a Russian naval officer engaged in espionage for the Soviets. Both episodes cast British intelligence in a bad light, but the Profumo scandal had greater political repercussions, helping to bring about the downfall of Macmillan's Conservative government (see below).

If the Philby defection and the Profumo Affair combined to raise alarm, a third landmark development related to the Cold War in Britain also occurred in 1963 with the publication of John Le Carré's novel, *The Spy Who Came in from the Cold*. Le Carré, a member of the Foreign Service who resigned his position in 1964 and has since written more than a score of additional novels, arrestingly captured the moral ambiguity of the Cold War. In *The Spy Who Came in from the Cold*, the head of

FIGURE 35 *Former model and showgirl Christine Keeler, 1985. Her affair with war secretary John Profumo in the early 1960s was instrumental in the fall of the Conservative government.* Reg Burkett/Hulton Archive/Getty.

Control, Le Carré's fictional agency based on MI6, responds to a question from the main character, the British agent Leamas:

> 'We do disagreeable things so that ordinary people here and elsewhere can sleep safely in their beds at night. ... Of course, we occasionally do very wicked things,' he grinned like a schoolboy. 'And in weighing up the moralities, we rather go in for dishonest comparisons; after all, you can't compare the ideals of one side with the methods of the other, can you now?'
>
> 'I mean you've got to compare method with method, and ideal with ideal. I would say that since the war, our methods – ours and those of the opposition – have become much the same. I mean you can't be less ruthless than the opposition simply because your government's *policy* is benevolent, can you now?'[4]

Le Carré had portrayed the Cold War in shades of grey and his later novels would continue to provide a much more realistic and nuanced treatment of the issues it raised than the black-and-white, good versus evil scenarios of Ian Fleming's James Bond novels; 1963 was also the year when the first two Bond films based on Fleming's novels, *Dr No* and *From Russia with Love*, were released. Fleming's novels, and the films on which they were based, generally had Bond fighting a Soviet Union or an evil villain intent on global domination or annihilation, leaving little room for the kind of moral ambiguity that could be characteristic of Le Carré's novels.

Ireland: The significance of 1949 and the continuation of partition

The creation of the Republic of Ireland in 1949 amounted to a de facto recognition of the semi-permanent partition of the island between the Republican South and the six counties of Northern Ireland that remained part of the UK. Ireland officially withdrew from membership in the British Commonwealth, but Britain made a significant decision that year not to classify Irish citizens as foreigners, a decision that facilitated travel, trade, and friendlier relations between the now-separate countries. The new Republic would prove amenable to better relations with the UK now that it was, free, in the words of its new Constitution, 'to develop its life, political, economic, and cultural, in accordance with its own genius and traditions'.

In the context of Irish history and the historical relations between England and Ireland, this generally meant in accordance with Catholic traditions and beliefs. These had already become enshrined in the Constitution of 1937 promulgated by De Valera's government, which referred to the 'Most Holy Trinity' as that 'from Whom is all authority and to Whom, as our final end, all actions both of men and States must be referred'. The religious differences no longer represented an insuperable barrier to relations with England, but they would make relations with Protestant Northern Ireland problematic. The religious overtones of the Irish Constitution manifested themselves primarily in an emphasis on the sanctity of the family and a conservative attitude towards women's role in society. In this respect, Ireland seemed to put itself beyond the mainstream of political developments in the rest of Western Europe.

Politics in the Republic of Ireland in the 1950s saw bitter faction develop between the rival parties of Fianna Fail and Fine Gael, although ideologically there was little difference between the respective parties. The generally conservative nature of the Republic is perhaps best exemplified by the controversy surrounding the 'mother and child' proposals by Dr Noel Brown, the minister of health from 1948 to 1951. These proposals, which essentially amounted to granting free medical care to mothers and children, alarmed conservatives who thought that they somehow violated the sanctity of family life. Such opposition might have been anticipated by the Irish Constitution, which stated that 'by her life within the home, woman gives to the State a support without which the common good cannot be achieved' and that women 'shall not be obliged by economic necessity to engage in labor to the neglect of duties in the home'.

Internationally, the main direction of Ireland's foreign policy in the 1950s and 1960s was towards integration with Europe, in an effort to improve the Irish economic outlook, which led to Ireland's entry into the United Nations in 1955, its application to join the European Common Market in 1961, and its eventual entry into the European Community in 1973.

The independence of the Irish Republic led British prime minister Clement Attlee to immediately issue a guarantee that Northern Ireland would remain in the UK until Northern Ireland voted otherwise. Attlee did not wish to abandon Northern Ireland and risk a civil war closer to home than those that had followed the end of British rule in India and Palestine (see below). As the Republic forged ahead with its own domestic and international agenda, the lacuna grew wider between Ireland and Northern Ireland, much to the disappointment of Irish nationalists on both sides of the border.

In 1957 the Irish nationalist Donal Barrington took other Irish nationalists to task for blaming their failure to unify the island on the British. He held the Irish, not the British, responsible for partition:

> It is quite misleading to say that Partition was forced on Ireland by the British Government against the wishes of North and South. It would be more correct to say that Partition was forced on the British Government by the conflicting demands of the two parties of Irishmen. It is true that both North and South were dissatisfied with Partition but that was because the North wanted all of Ireland for the Act of Union and the South wanted all Ireland for Home Rule.[5]

There is, of course, a great deal of truth in Barrington's assertions; the majority of people – including many Catholics – in Northern Ireland did not wish to unite with the less economically developed south and many people in the south were content to let the North remain part of the UK.

The Irish Republican Army made little headway in the 1950s and for most of the 1960s because it lacked support in both the North and the Republic, which the IRA, in echoes of De Valera's original stance that led to the Irish Civil War, denounced as an illegitimate government because it had acquiesced in partition. The peaceful status quo between Protestants and Catholics in Northern Ireland that had survived the formation of an independent Ireland in the south, and the activities by the IRA in the north in the 1950s, began to break down in the 1960s, particularly in the city known to Catholics as Derry and Protestants as Londonderry, where political marches and demonstrations increasingly yielded to violence. A more politically aware Catholic citizenry inspired by the American Civil Rights Movement led by Martin Luther King Jr began to demand its own rights and greater political equality for Catholics, only to be met with increasing hostility and repression from a Protestant-dominated police force and Protestant paramilitary organizations.

In Northern Ireland, the more politically aware the Catholic minority became, the more the Unionists sought to strengthen their connections with the UK and to identify themselves as British, not Irish. The Northern Ireland government at Stormont could not decide whether to use repression or to introduce reforms aimed at appeasing the Catholic minority. Any move towards the latter of these options stirred up tremendous opposition from Protestant loyalists, while the use of force to quell Catholic discontent only fanned the flames of rebellion and increased support for the IRA. The British, meanwhile, now sought, if anything, to extricate themselves from the situation. Finding it impossible to do so as a result of the inability of the Royal Ulster Constabulary to respond constructively to the mounting crisis, the British introduced an ill-advised policy of internment of suspected Provisional IRA members. This decision only served to further enhance the appeal of the PIRA among the Catholic population of Northern Ireland. Then, in Londonderry, in January 1972,

British soldiers fired into a crowd of Catholic demonstrators, killing fourteen civilians on what became known as 'Bloody Sunday'. This atrocity had the effect of escalating the violence in Northern Ireland. The 'Troubles' that followed claimed the lives of more than 3,000 people in Northern Ireland before a tentative peace was reached in 1997 (see Chapter 18).

Questions of identity: England, Scotland, and Wales

The dominant position of England within the UK was reinforced by the 1948 Summer Olympics, the first since 1936, which drew the attention of the country – and the world – to London. Three years later London hosted the Festival of Britain in commemoration of the hundred-year anniversary of the Great Exhibition of 1851; the Festival was also intended to show how much progress the country had made since the end of the war. A third event that served as a unifying force for the UK occurred on 2 June 1953 with the coronation of the 27-year-old Queen Elizabeth II, whose glamour has made her extremely popular to this day.

The UK, of course, still consisted of four separate universally recognized territorial entities – England, Scotland, Wales, and Northern Ireland – but all major decisions, especially on foreign policy and defence matters, were taken in London. Assertions of independent identity in these regions during the post-war period mainly took cultural forms rather than political ones such as the growth of nationalist or separatist political parties and calls for independence. One such cultural manifestation was the creation of the annual Edinburgh International Festival, which was first held in 1947. The 1948 festival featured the first performance since the sixteenth century of a Scottish play called *The Three Estates*, written by Sir David Lyndsay.[6]

But this was a fairly nominal gesture to Scottish nationalist sentiment; London remained the capital and epicentre of the UK and as such attracted Scottish, Welsh, and even Irish writers, artists, and actors whose identity tended to blend and merge into a single British one. Furthermore, the Scots did not necessarily feel the need to assert their cultural identity to the same degree as, say, the Welsh, because Scotland had always retained its own independent church and educational and legal systems. The Welsh, on the other hand, only had their language and culture to give them a separate identity from the English.

An exception to the lack of success of nationalist parties in this period occurred in July 1966 when Gwynfor Evans, the president of the Welsh nationalist party Plaid Cymru, won a by-election, but even here he did so without gaining a majority of the vote (39 per cent). Welsh nationalism had strong support from a vocal minority, particularly at the University of Aberystwyth, where Prince Charles took up residence to study the Welsh language in 1969. Charles's presence at the university was met with classroom sit-ins, badges that read 'No Englishman for Prince of Wales', and even some short hunger strikes.

If the election of Evans in 1966 had remained a singular event, it might not have seemed that significant, but in 1967 Winnie Ewing, a candidate of the Scottish National Party, won an important by-election in Hamilton. In both cases, candidates had taken away what were considered to be safe seats for the Labour Party. Labour was generally the dominant political party in Scotland and Wales because Labour represented the issues that bound England with both Scotland and Wales, mainly social welfare issues, such as providing adequate housing and the suppression of poverty. But both Plaid Cymru and the Scottish National Party continued to make gains at the expense of Labour in the late 1960s and early 1970s, even though Evans lost his seat in the 1970 election; neither came close at that time to becoming a majority party, but they did represent a significant and vocal minority.

Militating against their designs in this period was the fact that England was cohesively attached to Scotland, Wales, and Northern Ireland (before the Troubles); furthermore, these disparate regions did not necessarily share that much in common with each other, preventing a benign unity. Nonetheless one unifying pillar that the British could all share and take pride in had been removed by the mid-1960s with the end of the British Empire; in the eyes of some this development presaged the eventual end of Britain itself.

The end of empire and the Suez Crisis

The seeds of nationalism in India had been sown long before the end of the Second World War and the desire for independence among Indians only grew stronger by the end of the war. Strong opposition remained within the Conservative Party, but as early as 1943 Churchill had sent instructions to the Indian Viceroy, Lord Wavell, stating unequivocally that the official policy in India was to prepare the colony for self-government and admission into the British Commonwealth. In 1945, British officials in India immediately began the negotiations that would lead to independence, while the British electorate voted Churchill and the Conservatives out of power. The defenestration of Churchill reflected British sentiment regarding the government's commitment to domestic reforms and the rebuilding of the country after the war without much regard for the preservation of the British Empire. Lord Mountbatten, a member of the British royal family, was sworn in as the last Viceroy of India in 1947 with the expectation that he would oversee the last step to independence.

Meanwhile, agitation for a separate Muslim state of Pakistan had already begun by 1944. Even Churchill thought partition might be necessary to preserve the rights of Muslims from a Hindu majority.[7] Muhammad Ali Jinnah, having split from the Indian National Congress in 1930, seized upon the idea of a separate Muslim state and sold the idea to his many followers; his efforts were largely responsible for the creation of the Muslim-dominated state of Pakistan at the same time that India achieved its independence in 1947. This was not achieved, however, without a sanguinary civil war that caused the deracination of millions and the deaths of perhaps 800,000.

India was not the only place where Britain faced pressure from independence movements among its former colonial subjects. In Palestine, for example, Britain became caught between the conflicting demands of the Arabs and the pressure to admit 100,000 Jewish refugees, pressure that was magnified by the additional burden of the Balfour Declaration of 1917 promising support for a Jewish homeland and the moral imperative arising from the deaths of 6 million Jews during the Holocaust. Having finally acquiesced in the independence of India, Britain found it easier to yield power and control elsewhere. The Labour Party had a pro-Israeli position as part of its platform; it recognized that a Jewish homeland would be meaningless unless Jews represented a majority in the new state. Therefore, the Attlee government did not stand in the way of Israeli independence, but it did withdraw from the region prior to the first Arab–Israeli war in 1948, which resulted in the creation of the state of Israel. Burma (Myanmar) gained its independence from Britain in the same year, despite mild opposition from Churchill, who thought the people there had failed to appreciate the benefits of British rule. While India, Pakistan, and Ceylon (Sri Lanka, which gained its independence in 1948) remained within the British Commonwealth, Burma did not.

The next place where the British faced demands for independence was the Gold Coast, where the nationalist Convention People's Party quickly coalesced under the leadership of Kwame Nkrumah by 1951. In 1957 the Gold Coast became the independent state of Ghana and also chose to remain a member of the British Commonwealth. Membership in the Commonwealth, for those countries that remained did not necessarily mean that they would wholly support British foreign policy as they generally preferred a position of non-alignment in the Cold War power struggle between the United States and the Soviet Union. The membership of these states in the British Commonwealth may have encouraged the British to continue to think in imperialistic terms that had quickly become anachronistic.

There was no question that Britain had lost any claim to a position of dominance vis-à-vis the United States and the Soviet Union, but it still sought to maintain some measure of autonomy as an independent actor on the world stage. Old habits die hard, particularly reactionary imperialist ones, and there were still plenty of people in Britain who thought of their country as a great power and one that deserved to again take up the mantle of empire. When Egyptian president Nasser moved to nationalize the Suez Canal in July 1956, the British acted as if they still possessed their empire and as if their vital interests in preserving their control over the route to India had been compromised. The hopes of those who wished to see Nasser humbled or even overthrown rested with the new Conservative prime minister, Anthony Eden, who had replaced Churchill in 1955 – and who responded by collaborating with the French and the Israelis to devise a plan to invade Egypt and bring about Nasser's downfall.

Eden's plan failed, primarily because he did not consult the United States, where the Eisenhower administration – particularly the secretary of state, John Foster Dulles – was in no mood to support any action that would preserve Britain's status as a great power. Dulles did not wish to push Nasser into the arms of the Soviets and was unprepared to back Britain or France, which feared Nasser's influence in North Africa might stir up trouble in Algeria. After Israel launched a pre-emptive strike on 29 October 1956, Britain and France, as planned, sent ships in to the Canal Zone in the guise of peacemakers between Israel and Egypt, but they quickly withdrew when the United States began flooding the market with British pounds, leading to a collapse of sterling. The Suez Crisis exposed the extent to which Britain and the United States were still not quite on the same page when it came to global strategy at the height of the Cold War. The Eisenhower administration had not only failed to support Britain but had unequivocally opposed the invasion of Egypt.

In the aftermath of the crisis, the new Conservative prime minister Harold Macmillan was quick to readjust Britain's global priorities, while Eden suffered a breakdown and withdrew from public life. In 1960, Macmillan gave a speech before the Parliament of South Africa that became a historical landmark in its acknowledgement that the sun had set on the British Empire, averring:

> In the twentieth century, and especially since the end of the war, the processes which gave birth to the nation states of Europe have been repeated all over the world. We have seen the awakening of national consciousness in peoples who have for centuries lived in dependence upon some other power. ... The wind of change is blowing through this continent, and whether we like it or not, this growth of national consciousness is a political fact. We must all accept it as a fact, and our national policies must take account of it.

Taken in the larger context of British strategy in the twenty years following the end of the Second World War, British actions in Suez stand out more as an aberration than a component of a coherent or consistent foreign policy. Britain had withdrawn from India rather quickly, unable to prevent the civil war that killed hundreds of thousands of people and led to the partition between India and Pakistan. The British withdrew from Palestine under pressure from the Israelis and chose to allow the Arabs and Israelis to fight for the holy land among themselves rather than assert their power and influence. The Suez Crisis wound down quickly as well, with the British backing down once its American ally forthrightly opposed itself to the invasion of Egypt. The further demands for independence by the remaining territories within the British Empire were met without resistance from Macmillan or his colonial secretary, Iain MacLeod.

The impact that the end of the empire had on British society has been a matter of debate among historians, some of whom argue that it had relatively little effect as a result of the continuation of the British Commonwealth and the entry of the United Kingdom into NATO and its alliance with the United States. Others argue that it had a more significant impact on British society as a result of the thousands of migrants from different parts of the empire to Britain to create a more diverse and sometimes more divided society.[8] Jordana Bailkin has argued the British were not so much optimistic or pessimistic, but rather ambivalent about their declining role as a global power.[9] This ambivalence was exemplified in the debate over entry into the European Economic Community and, subsequently, over whether Britain should leave or remain within the European Union. But in the short term, when the significance of Suez began to sink in, it contributed to an identity crisis related to Britain's role in the world and even raised questions about what it meant to be British.

Post-war prosperity, angry young men, and disillusion with post-war society

Just as Suez seemed to bring the curtain down on the British Empire, the fog began to lift over London, thanks to the Clean Air Act of 1956. The confluence of these two events symbolically represented a golden dawn for Britain, which after a decade had begun to recover from the physical damage caused by the war and had started to benefit economically from American tourism. With the welfare state securely consolidated, the working classes were regarded as vital to the economy and the construction of a new society, and were courted by both the Labour and the Conservative parties. Unions had grown in strength, and one could make a strong case for the marked improvement of the quality of life of the working class. There were plenty of jobs to go around, unions had used their bargaining power to gain higher wages and more vacation days for their members, and workers began to enjoy life's amenities, including holidays at a number of seaside resorts that catered to a new breed of tourist. Nonetheless, a strong sense of disillusion and discontent with post-war society manifested itself beginning in the mid-1950s, especially among the young.

Among the causes of this disillusion, the fear of a nuclear holocaust was becoming more pronounced, reflected in the Campaign for Nuclear Disarmament (CND) founded in 1958, and in novels such as Aldous Huxley's *Ape and Essence* (1948), Nevil Shute's *On the Beach* (1957), and Peter George's *Red Alert* (1958, published under the pseudonym Peter Bryant). The main supporters of the anti-nuclear movement were the clergy, disaffected scientists, and left-wing intellectuals, such as the Marxist historian E. P. Thompson. The CND arose initially out of concerns about the long-term effects of nuclear testing on the environment and in protest against Britain's plans to develop a hydrogen bomb. Anti-American sentiment also played a role, given the extent to which Britain seemed to be dragged into American hostility towards the Soviets, which at times bordered on the irrational, if not hysterical, as in the period of the anti-communist witch hunts led by Senator Joseph McCarthy of Wisconsin in the early 1950s. The British, seeking an independent role in the Cold War, conducted their first successful test of a hydrogen bomb on Christmas Island in November 1957.

For the youth of the British working classes, as well as some members of the middle class, the opportunities offered by new educational institutions such as art colleges and design schools created a greater level of awareness that exposed some of the other perceived flaws in post-war society. The dissatisfaction of the young created something of a generation gap; the generation that had survived the Depression and fought the war could not understand the ingratitude of the young or countenance their disrespectful attitude towards authority, which ran counter to older, deeply ingrained habits of thought. John Osborne, one of the leading authors of a literary movement of 'angry young men', captured well this general feeling of dissatisfaction and the gap between the generations in his 1958 play, *The Entertainer*. As Jean, a young woman, tells her grandfather, Billy Rice, she had attended a rally in Trafalgar Square that 'really started over something I wanted to do, and then it all came out, lots of things. All kinds of bitterness – things I didn't even know existed.'

The collective message of the novels and plays of writers such as Kingsley Amis, John Wain, John Braine, and John Osborne was that there was something wrong not only with British society but with modernity in general. In his classic, *Look Back in Anger* (1957), from which the 'Angry Young Men' movement derived its name, Osborne referred to the period as the 'American Age', giving us the first glimpse of a sense that television as a new mechanism for spreading American culture was promoting superficial values and creating cultural desolation. But mostly these writers were not so much disillusioned because the world had changed but because it had not changed enough; as Allison, the girlfriend of Jimmy Porter, the main character in *Look Back in Anger*, tells her father, 'You're hurt because everything has changed. Jimmy is hurt because everything is the same. And neither of you can face it.'

The 1959 film *I'm All Right Jack*, directed by the brothers Roy and John Boulting, also mordantly parodied the new society. The film highlights the increased bargaining power of the unions by centring the plot on a strike in a factory where a well-educated gentleman is surreptitiously placed as a manual labourer among the other workers by his uncle, the owner of the factory. *I'm All Right Jack* is a great film that holds up well despite being so firmly rooted in its period, but it does not do justice to the achievements that the working classes and their role in the construction of the general consensus surrounding the new welfare state. It does, however, portray the extent to which Britain had remained a class-conscious society, with ownership and management coming out looking no better than the unions. It is sensitive to the cultural chasm that existed between traditional elites and those below them, a theme shared in common with the writers of the angry young men movement.

Among those writers, Alan Sillitoe, whose father worked in a tannery and who had started out himself working in a bicycle factory, had the strongest working-class credentials, which he put to good use in his classic 1958 novel, *Saturday Night and Sunday Morning*. Sillitoe's main character, Arthur, played by a young Albert Finney in the 1961 film version, is repulsed by his parents' boring life of work, television, and cigarettes, and lashes out against such a future for himself because, he says at the end of the film, fighting was all he could do to keep from submitting to the same inevitable fate. This same situation led innumerable young people in Britain to search for some means of escape, whether through football or other sports, crime, or music.

Cricket, football, and rugby remained the most popular sports in the UK, although cricket was declining in popularity relative to the other two. Horse racing, auto racing, and greyhound racing were all enormously popular as well, while tennis and golf also had their niches in the British sporting landscape. Tony Jacklin, who in 1969 became the first British golfer to win the British Open since 1951, did the most to attract a native following for his sport, while British tennis stars of the era such as Roger Taylor and Virginia Wade put British tennis on the map. Football remained king, however, attracting the largest crowds, the strongest following, and the most press attention. It received a significant boost in England's victory over West Germany in the 1966 World Cup but the number of football clubs in England had already increased from 18,000 in 1948 to 25,000 in 1966 and as early as 1948 – 9.41 million spectators attended Football League matches.[10] The early 1960s saw concerns expressed about crowd behaviour at football matches, something that would become a much greater problem in the 1970s (see Chapter 18). Still, there was mostly optimism about the role played by sport in British society by the mid-1960s, reflected in the creation of a Sports Council in 1965 by Harold Wilson who referred to sports as 'essential to Britain's social and economic development'.

One of the most sensational and highly publicized crimes in modern British history occurred on 8 August 1963 when a gang led by 32-year-old Bruce Reynolds held up a train travelling from Glasgow to London in Buckinghamshire in what became known as 'the Great Train Robbery'. The gang of fifteen robbers in ski masks and helmets hit the driver in the head, and made off with a haul worth about £2.6 million, or the equivalent of about £40 million in today's money.[11] Although the crime subsequently became legendary and the subject of books and films, the police had by January 1964 arrested and charged twelve of the perpetrators, eleven of whom received prison terms of between twenty and thirty years, with the twelfth man who had arranged the location of their hideout receiving a considerably lighter sentence of only three years. It remains one of the most sensationalized crimes in modern British history. It seemed in some ways to symbolize the malaise born of rising expectations that accompanied the late 1950s and early 1960s. However, it was a new wave of rock n' roll music spearheaded by the Beatles in 1963 that most satisfied the yearnings of young people for a sense of meaning, excitement, and escape from boredom. A plethora of cultural changes followed in their wake.

Liverpool, the Beatles, and the Swinging Sixties

The Beatles – John Lennon, Paul McCartney, George Harrison, and Richard Starkey (better known as Ringo Starr) – came from Liverpool from backgrounds that could probably best be described as lower middle class, although their roots were closer to the working classes than most other rock groups of the 1960s, including the Rolling Stones, who did more to cultivate a working-class image and following. The Liverpool in which the Beatles grew up was neither the thriving port city and manufacturing centre that had rapidly expanded and flourished in its nineteenth-century heyday nor the modern cosmopolitan city one can visit today. At the time, Liverpool was a rough town that had a number of seedy areas and gangs of 'Teddy Boys' who dressed in Edwardian clothing and spent most evenings looking for trouble.

But, in Liverpool, as elsewhere, the post-war baby boom had created by the late fifties a large number of teenagers, many of whom found their outlet not in violence but in the burgeoning music scene that had produced some 300 rock n' roll bands in the city by the early 1960s. For most of them, music was seen as a temporary diversion rather than as a way out of working-class life; at one point in the late fifties even the members of the Beatles went their separate ways and began looking for steady jobs. But the opportunity to perform on a regular basis in Hamburg, Germany and a new infusion of great rock n' roll music from the United States in the early 1960s that essentially saved the genre from dying at a young age allowed the Beatles to rise above the level of club performers and begin a cultural revolution.

The Beatles, borrowing from American rock n' roll, Motown, and country and western, as well as British skiffle and pop traditions, and on the strength of the brilliant and frequently poetic song writing of Lennon and McCartney, created a unique, vibrant, and contagious sound. They polished their musical acumen through hundreds of live performances in the clubs of Liverpool and Hamburg. The Beatles, under the influence of their urbane manager, Brian Epstein, and benefiting from the experience, professionalism, and open-mindedness of their producer, George Martin, forged a new identity for themselves that shaped a generation. The enormous popularity of their early hits such as 'I Want to Hold Your Hand' and 'She Loves You' created a tremendous following in Britain and the United States among young teenagers who grew up with and followed the Beatles through an evolution of their music and consciousness that lasted until the end of the decade.

Without taking anything away from their prodigious talents, years of hard work, or amazing creativity, the enormous commercial success of the Beatles – and of all of the other rock bands and individual pop artists of the sixties – hinged on the disposable income that teenagers had at their disposal and thus would not have been possible at any earlier time in British history. Radio and television also played an immense role in their success; although the BBC was slow to incorporate pop and rock music into its format, leaving fans to rely on trying to pick up pirate radio stations that sprung up offshore to avoid licensing regulations, or the popular Radio Luxembourg, BBC radio noticed as the Beatles started to produce hit records and frequently had them on for live interviews and performances. The Beatles also appeared on such hugely popular television variety programmes as *Val Parnell's Sunday Night at the London Palladium*, which brought them to the attention of a much broader audience and made them acceptable to the parents of their teenage fans, as well as to the British establishment.

As influential as the Beatles were, rock musicians made up only one category of the pop celebrities who gravitated to London and set the trends for popular culture during the Swinging Sixties. The disposable income of young people was used not only on music, but also on clothing and personal adornment, hairstyles, and decorations or art for one's room or apartment, all of which provided an outlet for personal expression, making designers like Mary Quant, hairstylists like Vidal Sassoon, pop artists like Peter Max, and models like Twiggy and Jean Shrimpton enormous celebrities as well.

Film and a new generation of actors and actresses also highlighted the appeal, culture, and milieu of the Swinging Sixties, even as they simultaneously exposed the superficiality of a culture that was perhaps too focused on sex, drugs, and rock n' roll. For example, in the 1966 film *Alfie*, directed by Lewis Gilbert, Michael Caine played a young chauffeur seemingly incapable of forming any personal attachment, abandoning his pregnant girlfriend to continue a life in which sexual promiscuity had become an end in itself. The Italian director Michelangelo Antonioni may have best captured the atmosphere of Swinging London in his 1966 film, *Blow-up*, in which a hip young photographer, played by David Hemmings, becomes absorbed in a quest to solve a murder he unwittingly seems to have captured shooting photos in a London park, temporarily giving his life a sense of purpose that was previously lacking, despite an apparently glamorous and successful lifestyle that has girls begging to photograph – and sleep with – him. Perhaps one of the most telling scenes in the film occurs, though, when Hemmings visits one of the posh clubs for which Swinging London was famous to find a crowd of young people willing to tear at each other's throats for the neck of a broken guitar destroyed by a member of the band performing there. This scene highlights not only the celebrity status of rock musicians but also the tension between creativity and destruction in a scene similar to that re-enacted regularly on stage by the London rock band the Who. It also provides an excellent illustration of the crowd mentality that could lead artists and celebrities to easily become contemptuous of their own fans and the consumer society that produced them, even though those same fans were at the same time responsible for the artists' success. A third film from 1966, *Georgy Girl*, directed by Silvio Narizzano, introduces a young Lynne Redgrave as the 22-year-old title character forced to confront the sexual revolution of the 1960s, a development for which she is singularly unprepared, leading her to confront her own personal values and identity and decide what is right for her, even if what she decides conflicts with the hedonistic values of the society that surrounds her.

Of course, it was also in the 1960s that the James Bond movies starring the Scottish actor Sean Connery became smash hits at the box office, films that further reflected the sexual revolution and allowed ordinary people – admittedly, mostly men – to identify with the sophisticated and debonair Bond and vicariously experience the most thrilling, affluent, and glamorous lifestyle imaginable. The Bond films, rooted as they were in an increasingly superannuated vision of British power and influence, also provide an important bridge between popular culture and the political culture of Cold War Britain.

The political culture of the 1960s and early 1970s

In 1961 the UK submitted its first application for membership in the European Common Market. The decision to apply represented something of a reversal of previous British policy on Europe, although some historians have seen it mainly as a ploy to provide the country with leverage in its relations with the United States. Macmillan recognized in regard to Europe, just as he had with regard to Africa and the British Empire, that the winds had shifted and that Britain could no longer afford to ignore the growing economic and political importance of the European Community. Macmillan made a strong effort to steer Britain's application through the admission process, so his failure to do so – British membership was rejected on the strength of a veto by France in January 1963 – marked a serious political defeat for the Conservative Party and for him personally. This made his administration all the more vulnerable when the Profumo Affair broke later that year.

The Profumo Affair further contributed to the downfall of the Macmillan government and the election of a Labour majority in 1964. In general, the new Labour prime minister Harold Wilson opposed Britain's entry into Europe based on his desire to pursue his own socialist agenda for the country. He inherited an economy in which management was inclined to work with the trade unions rather than against them based on the influence and political clout of the Trades Union Congress. But there was a danger in pushing the socialist agenda too far that Wilson perhaps failed to appreciate. Furthermore, not all members of his party shared his views on Europe, including Roy Jenkins, who served in Wilson's cabinet in several capacities before becoming deputy leader of the Labour Party in 1970. The vote rejecting Britain's application for membership in the Common Market, however, meant that Wilson would get his chance to implement the policies he thought could solve the problems Britain faced at that time.

These problems were to some degree psychological; Harold Wilson's first Labour government was confronted with the early alarmist rumblings that Britain was a nation in decline, which would shake the nation to its core in the 1970s. This crisis of confidence shadowed Wilson throughout his first term as prime minister, which lasted until 1970. Wilson began his term by introducing a National Plan, designed to keep economic growth on a steadier and more even keel. The historian Edward Dell has called it 'an exercise in make-believe, which fostered fantasies about the potential performance of the British economy'.[12] The plan included the renationalization of the steel industry, which had been denationalized by the Conservative government in 1952, and called for higher rates of state expenditure independent of the growth rate of the economy as a whole. The plan was short-lived; Labour had won the 1964 election by a relatively small majority and lacked the political mandate needed to carry it through. Therefore, Wilson sought to augment his majority by calling for another election in 1966, in which Labour won only 48 per cent of the popular vote but increased its lead over the Conservative Party in the House of Commons from 13 seats to 111 seats (364–253, with the Liberal Party taking the remaining 12 seats).

Wilson's government coincided with the Swinging Sixties and the growing political consciousness among British students, who demonstrated, along with others throughout the Western world in 1968, against the Vietnam War. British demonstrators were also protesting against the Wilson government's complicity in the war through its support for American foreign policy. Wilson had essentially followed the same foreign policy as his Conservative predecessors, such as maintaining Britain's status as a nuclear power. In short, Wilson was as reluctant to accept the decline of Britain or a diminished role for the UK in international affairs as any Conservative. If the British demonstrations were less violent than those that occurred in France or less confrontational than those in the United States (where students actually faced the prospect of being drafted and dying in a war in which they did not believe), they were not without their share of aggression, which the Rolling Stones captured in their 1968 release, 'Street Fighting Man'.

Wilson had scored important points with the youth culture early in his administration by bestowing several awards on the Beatles, including the prestigious Members of the British Empire (MBE). However, unemployment started to rise in the 1960s, which combined with Wilson's foreign policy to help undercut the popularity of his administration. Some establishment figures became disenchanted as well; Cecil King, publisher of the *Daily Mirror* Newspapers, went so far as to propose to a select group that included Lord Mountbatten a coup to overthrow the Wilson government in 1968. Popular discontent with Wilson contributed to the rise of increased popularity of the Scottish National Party and its success in by-elections in the late 1960s. Not to mention the fact that the Northern Ireland Civil Rights Association was formed in January 1967 under his watch, which highlighted the inequalities and discrimination in that part of the UK. The changing times and Wilson's difficulty negotiating them culminated in a Conservative electoral victory that brought Edward Heath to office as prime minister.

In the early 1970s, Heath began to take on the trade unions and to strike the first ideological blows against the welfare state that would culminate in the rise of Margaret Thatcher to the position of prime minister by the end of the decade. Heath responded to laments about Britain's decline by calling for a return to individual initiative, free-market economics, and a renewed commitment to patriotism. Heath proposed measures that would come into vogue in the 1980s that seemed to threaten the very foundations of the welfare state, including lower tax rates for the upper and middle classes, legal restrictions on trade union activity, and the privatization of some of the smaller nationalized companies, such as the travel agency, Thomas Cook. Heath failed to reverse the direction of the British economy, however, and had to continue to address laments over the decline of Britain. The crisis in Northern Ireland escalated under his leadership as well, including the introduction of the internment policy and the tragedy of Bloody Sunday. Heath responded by championing both devolution in the UK and another attempt to secure the entry of the UK into the European Community.

In many ways, the UK during the Heath Years, which lasted until 1974, was a country that seemed to have lost its way and did not have a clear path to recovery or a strong sense of its own political identity. Even the special relationship with the United States seemed to suffer, though this was perhaps a good thing given Nixon's escalation of the Vietnam War and the political corruption that led to his resignation over the Watergate scandal. Culturally, the values and ideals of the counterculture gave way to a culture of depression and a search for individual gratification that has earned the youth of the seventies the derogatory nickname of the 'me generation'. Even the Beatles broke up in 1970 to pursue individual solo careers. On their last released album, *Let It Be* (*Abbey Road* was their last recorded album, though released earlier), the Beatles included a song written by George Harrison called 'I Me Mine', which Harrison also used as the title of his autobiography. John Lennon moved to New York. Ringo Starr pursued an acting career in Hollywood while continuing to release songs as a solo artist. Paul McCartney formed a new group, Wings, with his American wife, the former Linda Eastman. McCartney continued to write catchy and popular songs, but he largely lost his relevance to the broader culture without Lennon to balance his tendency towards light-hearted pop. Heath and Thatcher had a different kind of individualism in mind as a solution for Britain's economic malaise, but Heath's commitment to Europe at least represented a recognition that the UK might no longer be able to afford going it alone.

Wilson, who had remained head of the Labour Party, tended to vacillate on the issue of Europe, but by now he had come around to supporting British membership. In 1971, however, Wilson could not get his own party, much less the country as a whole, to agree on whether or not to enter Europe. The trade unions in particular were intransigently opposed to integration. To appease them, and with Heath now supporting membership, Wilson found it necessary to reverse course once again and express his opposition to joining the European Community, which he now denounced as a 'rule-ridden bureaucracy'. Heath's government would not be remembered with any particular fondness, but he did achieve one notable success. In 1973 the UK, along with the Republic of Ireland, was approved for entry into the European Community. Wilson returned to 10 Downing Street in 1974, but he lost – or won, depending on how one divines his true intentions – the battle over Europe.

FIGURE 36 *A woman walks past a pavement piled high with rubbish due to a refuse collectors'*
strike, Shepherd Street, central London, during the 'Winter of Discontent', 1 February 1979.
Graham Turner/Hulton Archive/Getty Images.

18

Demands, disappointments, hopes, and promises, c. 1973–2004

The wisdom of hindsight so useful to historians and indeed to authors of memoirs, is sadly denied to practicing politicians.

MARGARET THATCHER, *The Downing Street Years*, 1993

We may as well be honest with ourselves as we approach the twenty-first century and recognize that there is no longer an ideological war to the death.

TONY BLAIR

The UK, the Republic of Ireland, and the European Common Market

The entry of the UK into the European Economic Community in 1973 was celebrated with enthusiasm across the political spectrum. However, the process had been extremely complex, the negotiations difficult, and the outcomes yet to be determined. Furthermore, despite the celebrations, residents of the UK remained divided on the subject. The Scots were more tentative towards the idea – if not hostile – of joining Europe than the English, while the Labour Party, though supportive, was more divided than the Conservatives on the issue. In the Republic of Ireland, by contrast, there was almost universal approval for entry into the European Economic Community (EEC). Still, in the UK it remained a tremendous victory for Ted Heath, who had made Britain's entry into Europe one of the central aims of his administration. Heath would later recall in his autobiography that he 'saw this as a wonderful new beginning and a tremendous opportunity for the British people'.[1]

However, the enthusiasm of Prime Minister Heath and the British people generated by entry into Europe was quickly undone by the Yom Kippur War launched by a coalition of Arab states against Israel in 1973. In response to US support for Israel, the Arabs reduced oil production, which led to shortages of that essential commodity in the UK. Heath saw the ensuing oil crisis as undermining the community's goal of finding 'common solutions to common problems'.[2] In the UK, a 'Get Britain Out' movement arose almost immediately, demonstrating, for observers, that opponents of the move into Europe would not just fade away or accept defeat graciously. When Wilson's new Labour government called for a referendum on continuing membership in the EEC in June 1975, only 67.2 percent of the British public voted in favour.[3] This indicated the potential for trouble down the road, but at the time even the subsequent Eurosceptic Margaret Thatcher saw Britain's membership in the EEC as a positive development and believed that Britain could have a salubrious influence in Europe.[4] Referring to the recent downturn in the British economy, the British commissioner in Brussels, Christopher Soames said, 'This is no time for Britain to be considering leaving a Christmas club, let alone the Common Market.'[5]

But the effects of the oil crisis cut deeper than its impact on the European Economic Community. In Britain, the crisis contributed further to economic and industrial stagnation that led many people to view the UK as a declining nation. Britain's membership in the European Community and the extent of integration were issues that continued to be debated on a regular basis, but in the meantime Britain had more serious issues to contend with. In the short term, however, the EEC contributed to the economic dissatisfaction of the British public as it imposed a Value Added Tax (VAT) on consumer goods, while agricultural prices rose as a result of the Community's Common Agricultural Policy. Of course, this helped farmers who relished their new-found prosperity, but it also hurt consumers in a declining economy. It also

FIGURE 37 *Map of Ireland.*
Omersukrugosku/E+.

did nothing to halt the continued decline of employment in agriculture and related sectors of the economy, which was especially marked in Scotland where employment in agriculture, fishing, and forestry had declined from 100,000 to 28,000 from 1951 to 1991.[6] Mark Clapson estimates that the rural workforce of Britain as a whole declined from 13 per cent in 1900 to 2 per cent in 2005.[7] Alun Howkins called his 2003 book *The Death of Rural England* to castigate changes in the landscape of the English countryside, which he partly blamed on European subsidies to English farmers that led to larger fields intended to grow cheaper food.

Meanwhile, unemployment and inflation threatened to spiral out of control. The ensuing recession resulted in the fall of Heath's Conservative government and the election of a Labour government in 1974, along with the return of Harold Wilson to 10 Downing Street. It took two elections that year to achieve that result, however, because the first in February had left the Labour Party thirty seats short of a majority even though they had four more seats than the Conservatives. Furthermore, the Conservative Party had won the popular vote, hardly a ringing endorsement for any kind of a Labour mandate. The second election, in October, did result in a 319–277 seat advantage for Labour and about a million more votes for Labour than the Conservatives, giving Wilson the support he needed moving forward. The recession abated somewhat in 1975, but the Labour government was no closer to solving its long-term economic problems.

Troubles in Britain: The energy crisis, economic decline, and the end of the 1970s

A new word was coined in the 1970s – 'stagflation', a combination of stagnation and inflation. Over the course of the decade Britain's annual economic growth averaged a meagre 2 per cent, while inflation rose by 12 per cent per year. Although the demand for coal was rising, the demand for British steel was in marked decline. Traditional industries like cotton and shipbuilding completely disappeared in many places. Manufacturers of items such as machine tools and semiconductors either went out of business or laid off swaths of their workforce. The British automobile industry suffered as well. London historian Jerry White calculates that manufacturing jobs in Britain as a whole declined by 25 per cent in the 1970s, with London suffering an even steeper loss of 36 per cent.[8]

The Labour government was divided on how to respond to the economic crisis. In 1974, Wilson agreed to a pay raise for striking miners of between 22 and 32 per cent, costing the government an additional £103 million.[9] The National Union of Mineworkers (NUM) sought to capitalize on the important position their industry now occupied in the British economy. Many workers who had left the coal mines in places like South Wales in the 1960s returned in the 1970s to take advantage of the higher wages and benefit from their improved bargaining position.[10] Other unions were just as robust. The National Union of Railwaymen, for example, could boast of a membership rate of 100 per cent, giving them a vocal interest in the management of their industry. But unions were perceived as holding down productivity and damaging Britain's position in the world, making Wilson's government look weak for caving into them from the outset. Critics of unions were not inclined to take into account the inherent dangers in professions such as mining or the continued need for improved working conditions in many of the mines. For the miners, strikes were never just about higher pay, although this was seen as important as validation for the risks they took and the hard labour they endured. Wilson's government went even further in its support of unions when it repealed the Industrial Relations Act in July 1974, a Conservative measure that had been passed in 1971 imposing restrictions on the unions' right to strike and setting up a National Industrial Relations Court to prevent harmful strikes and adjudicate labour disputes.

Wilson's government forged ahead with other progressive legislation as well, including the Sexual Discrimination Act of 1975, which built on the Equal Pay Act of 1970 and prohibited discrimination against married women in the work place while also promoting gender equality. Wilson increased spending on education and housing, while increasing the tax rate on the upper tier of income earners to 83 per cent.

In retrospect, there is probably little Wilson could have done to improve the economic climate. The youth who matured in the 1970s did so in an age when the government seemed to provide no answers to the country's current problems or much hope for posterity. The 1970s would have been a period of disillusionment anyway, after the failure of the idealistic youth of the Sixties to fulfil their utopian vision for a changed society. But symptoms of decline fomented a sense of outrage and rebellion, which manifested itself in quite different ways than the socially and politically conscious protest movements of the 1960s. Specifically, the rise of hooliganism and violence associated with football matches and the anarchistic tendencies of punk rock, beginning with Johnny Rotten and the Sex Pistols, helped define the vandal tendencies of the 1970s and 1980s.

In his 1990 exposé of British hooliganism, *Among the Thugs*, Bill Buford explains the subculture that existed among English football fans in the 1970s and 1980s:

> There is no sport in which the act of being a spectator is as *constantly* physical as watching a game of English football on the terraces. The physicalness is insistent; any observer not familiar with the game would say that it is outright brutal. In fact, those who do not find it brutal are so familiar with the traditions of attending an English football match, so certain in the knowledge of what is expected of them, that they are incapable of seeing how deviant their behavior is – even in the most ordinary things.[11]

Hooliganism and football-related violence escalated during the 1980s, culminating in a riot that left thirty-eight people dead at the hands of Liverpool fans at the site of the European Cup Final in Brussels on 29 May 1985. What was most disturbing about this incident, and hooliganism in general, especially among the millions of football fans who did not cross the line towards murder and mayhem, was that the violence seemed to be an end in itself with football fandom as a mere pretext for the crimes of drunken louts looking for trouble.

The music and cultural historian Greil Marcus observes, similarly, that Johnny Rotten did not seem to be protesting against anything in particular or seeking solutions to particular problems, but rather protesting for the sake of protesting.[12] Johnny Rotten thus became an extremely polarizing figure. He seemed to incite violence, which moved some outraged concert-goers to turn against him and the band. No one knew quite what to make of punk rock, but when people first heard it they knew it was different. Punk rockers had little respect for the traditions even of rock 'n' roll as represented by groups like the Beatles and the Rolling Stones, although it should be noted that punk is itself variegated and did not just consist of violent anarchism; the Clash, for example, could be considered the pacifist left wing of the punk movement.[13]

Wilson's government responded to the spread of hooliganism by passing the 1975 Safety at Sports Grounds Bill mandating and providing funds for architectural changes intended to minimize opportunities for violence. This measure, as Brett Bebber points out, contained economic motives as well, since the threat of violence and the economic recession had led to declining attendance at football matches.[14] This act had some effect, but there was little that he could do to stem the punk movement, which provided an outlet for the disaffection felt by so many of Britain's callow youngsters.

In another development symbolic of Britain's declining position in the world, the 1970s saw the sun completely set on the British Empire. In the Middle East, Qatar, Bahrain, and the United Arab Emirates gained their independence from the UK in 1971. Papua New Guinea gained its independence from Australia in 1975. The Solomon Islands became self-governing later that year and officially gained their independence in 1978. In the West Indies, Grenada became a nation in 1974, while Saint Vincent and the Grenadines became an independent nation in 1979, as did Saint Lucia. These developments might appear as mere historical footnotes to the end of the British Empire; they are not even mentioned in Timothy Parsons' recent book on the end of the Empire, *The Second British Empire: In the Crucible of the Twentieth Century*, which only takes the story up to 1970. However, in the context of Britain's paranoia about decline and its troubled economy of the 1970s they served as further reminders of Britain's fading past.

The British monarchy – that other symbol of past national greatness and Anglo-Saxon tradition – also came under closer scrutiny in this period, which was also extended to the royal family as a whole by the tabloid press. But, as Anthony Sampson pointed out in 1982, the more troubled and insecure Britain became, the more it found itself clinging to the one enduring institution that provided at least a symbolic sense of stability.[15] Furthermore, Queen Elizabeth II showed a strong interest in Britain's economic problems and possible solutions to them; she generally sought to validate her privileged position through a sincere regard for the people of the UK and the Commonwealth and in doing so helped to offset some of the dissatisfaction directed at the institution of monarchy.

By 1977, the work of novelists was beginning to reflect the pessimism and malaise of the times, perhaps captured best in the cynicism of Margaret Drabble's *The Ice Age*: 'Economically, the country was declared to be in acute decline, and yet, of course, record spending went on, accompanied by record moaning.' Drabble was right on two levels: first, public expenditure did increase throughout the 1970s, because the numbers of people out of work and the rising costs associated with healthcare and social services made it extremely difficult for the government to economize. Second, Drabble wryly observed that people's efforts to economize on their heating and electric bills was offset by their increased expenditure on alcohol and that people in the 1970s, despite their complaints, were still better off than their 1930s counterparts had been.

> Indeed, immeasurably better. Naturally enough, few people thought about this at all. People have short memories. There was an unusually high sale of electric blankets in the pre-Christmas period, which sales analysts interpreted in different ways: as a fear of unheated bedrooms and nonelectric power cuts; as a fear of a very cold winter (the snails in the valley of the Po had been reported to be behaving oddly again); as a relatively cheap substitute for the more elaborate presents that otherwise might have been given, such as second cars, outboard motors, diamonds and fur coats, dishwashers and so forth.
>
> In the nineteen thirties there were no electric blankets, and only the rich or the ill thought of sleeping in heated bedrooms.[16]

This passage from Drabble, however, does not account for the law of rising expectations or the importance of psychological malaise. People thought they were living through tough times and in difficult economic times; people tend to look for scapegoats. They frequently blame their troubles on those most recently arrived in the country, who are perceived as stealing jobs away from native residents. In the case of Britain, an influx of immigrants from various parts of the Empire that had entered the country in the 1950s and 1960s from Asia, particularly India and Pakistan, Africa, or the West Indies, now found themselves the targets of abuse or discrimination. They arrived at a time when Harold Macmillan could boast to the British public that they had 'never had it so good', and came to share in Britain's post-war boom. Many Britons found it difficult to adjust to the new, more ethnically diverse Britain, but when the recession hit a vague sense of uneasiness was transmuted into overt hostility, even though minorities were as badly affected by the recession as the rest of the population. Many immigrant workers laboured in factories or in jobs where they did not have the protection of union membership and suffered deplorable conditions and low wages reminiscent of the worst abuses of nineteenth-century industry. The Fidelity Radio factory in North Kensington was one of the most notorious examples of capitalist exploitation. In this instance, workers were paid extremely low wages, wages that were supposed to have been supplemented by potential bonuses that simply provided a mechanism to control and manipulate the workers.[17]

The economic crisis of the 1970s came to a head at the end of the decade with the so-called 'Winter of Discontent' of 1978–9. Many public service sector unions went on strike in response to the Labour government's efforts at limiting their wages to control spending, accompanied by continued high rates of inflation, and one of the coldest winters on record, which included three blizzards, one of which occurred on 14 February and left snow drifts of up to seven feet on the east coast of England.

The troubles in Northern Ireland

Meanwhile, in Northern Ireland economic distress and rising unemployment (along with doubt and despair) were added to the incendiary mix of religious sectarianism, social discrimination, and the politics of violence employed by both Unionists and the Provisional Irish Republican Army (PIRA). In December 1969, the PIRA split from the conciliatory members of the republican movement in Northern Ireland with the intention of putting greater pressure on getting the British out of Northern Ireland altogether. The major shift in the strategy of the PIRA after 'Bloody Sunday' was to gain sympathy for its cause through martyrdom rather than through military pressure, although it would continue to employ violence as well. The events of Bloody Sunday and the British policy of internment without trial had enhanced PIRA recruitment and brought about an escalation in the 'Troubles'. In response, the fanatical Protestant spokesperson and militant Unionist, Reverend Ian Paisley warned that additional PIRA activity would provoke retaliatory measures by Protestant organizations.

The problem for Britain was its guarantee that Northern Ireland would remain part of the UK for as long as it wished, a commitment that dated to 1949 when the Republic of Ireland came into existence. Unfortunately, a certain segment of the Protestant population thought this guarantee gave them carte blanche to perpetuate a political and social system that discriminated against Catholics, who had become an educated minority capable of analysing their situation and voicing their demands for social justice because of the educational reforms that took place in the UK after 1944. For the PIRA and its supporters, the issue was relatively simple – to drive the British out of Northern Ireland and allow the North to reunite with the Republic in the south, but the issue was never as facile as this demand makes it appear. Such a solution not only ignored the Protestant majority in Northern Ireland and their wishes, concerns, and interests, but also neglected the strained relationship between the PIRA and the republican government, which did not condone terrorism and had largely moved forward as an independent country without the North.

The Provisional Sinn Féin served or acted as the political representatives of the PIRA. The leaders of Provisional Sinn Féin were aware of the need to develop a practical solution that the authorities in Britain and Northern Ireland might actually agree to. Their idea was to convince the British to withdraw in stages while four regional assemblies convened across Ireland. Provisional Sinn Féin worked in tandem with the PIRA, the leaders of which realized that they also needed a political wing to carry out negotiations to move their agenda forward.

The campaign against the British in Northern Ireland gained support from Irish-Americans, as well as from Irish residents of Britain. However, according to Seán Sorohan, at least in London, this support and solidarity did not lead to active support or direct contributions to terrorist activity on the part of most members of the Irish community there. Demonstrations to protest the deteriorating state of affairs in Northern Ireland on 11 July 1971 drew 5,000 people to Trafalgar Square in London and 3,000 in Birmingham. However, Sorohan argues that protests dwindled throughout the 1970s after the Bloody Sunday massacre, with only one major protest in London for the rest of the decade, which occurred after the death of a PIRA hunger striker in 1974.[18] In fact, the PIRA got most of its monetary contributions from the United States and Eastern Europe, while importing weapons from places like Libya and Eastern Europe in the 1980s. In 1986, stashes that together totalled 100 guns and 18,000 rounds of ammunition manufactured in the Soviet Union and East Germany were found in County Sligo and Roscommon.

In an effort to deprive the PIRA of its support, the British government made the decision in 1976 to treat PIRA prisoners as criminals instead of awarding them special status as political prisoners. The government refused to recognize that politically motivated killing was anything but murder and did not wish to legitimize violent terrorist activity. The PIRA, of course, saw their actions as politically justified and necessary to help achieve their aims, given the overwhelming force possessed by its enemies, the British army and the Northern Irish police force, the Royal Ulster Constabulary. By the same token, however, the PIRA preferred to negotiate with the British directly and did agree to several cease-fires in exchange for concessions in the course of the 1970s.

Both the Labour governments of the 1970s and the Conservative governments of the 1980s preferred to allow the Northern Irish police force to combat terrorist activity and administer the region's prison system, but this strategy became increasingly problematic. In response to an initiative launched in 1977 to treat IRA prisoners as common criminals, prisoners attempted to call attention to their status and plight by smearing the walls of their cells with faeces, wrapping themselves in blankets and refusing to wear clothes rather than put on the mandated uniform issued by the prison, refraining from bathing, and engaging in hunger strikes. They mainly protested about such issues as the inability to congregate and their inability to send and receive mail, rather than the physical conditions of the prison or physically abusive treatment. The former issues were important to them because they needed the status of political prisoners to give legitimacy to their cause. But that is precisely what the British government did not want to do.

In 1979, the Conservative Margaret Thatcher succeeded the Labourite James Callaghan as prime minister. The early years of the Thatcher administration did not produce a coherent policy on resolving the problems in Northern Ireland or of dealing with the PIRA. Then the prisoners of Long Kesh prison began a hunger strike in 1980 that continued until 1981 and resulted in the death of Bobby Sands and three others, Francis Hughes, Raymond McCreesh, and Patsy O'Hara. Thatcher was slow to respond, not wanting, again, to give the PIRA the trappings of legitimacy as a political organization or to condone terrorism. The IRA escalated pressure on her government with an assassination attempt on Thatcher herself, exploding a bomb in her Brighton hotel room in October 1984. Her near escape did not alter her general policy towards the IRA in Northern Ireland, but Thatcher was hardly more sympathetic to the Protestant unionists, whom she blamed for exacerbating the situation. From this point forward, she decided she would have better luck resolving the situation in Northern Ireland by dealing with the Republic of Ireland and gaining its cooperation – instead of its opposition or insouciance – in her efforts to end the Troubles in the North.

In 1985 the Republic of Ireland and the UK reached an accord that led to the signing of the Anglo-Irish Agreement in which both parties pledged to back a process that would devolve authority to Northern Ireland. Both the Republic and the UK also agreed to find a solution that would be amenable to all major parties concerned in Northern Ireland.

The Troubles continued in the late 1980s and early 1990s, though a step in the right direction was the passage of the Northern Ireland Fair Employment Act of 1989 intended to provide more equal opportunities across the board. Meanwhile,

Thatcher tried to bring the Unionists into the negotiations by agreeing to meet with Paisley and James Molyneaux, the leader of the Ulster Unionist Party, in February 1986. She also sought to involve the United States in the peace process by sending her secretary of state for Northern Ireland, Tom King, to America to negotiate an economic aid package for Northern Ireland and to seek a joint policy on terrorism and extradition.

In the course of the 1990s, the Northern Ireland peace process was furthered by two major developments: the decision of US president Bill Clinton to get involved and the election of Tony Blair as Labour prime minister in 1997. In 1995, Clinton appointed George Mitchell as his special envoy to Northern Ireland and made a historic visit himself to Belfast later that year. Tony Blair had made a resolution of the problems in Northern Ireland one of the main issues of his campaign and followed through by negotiating the Good Friday Agreement of 1998, which was a major step forward in the peace process, calling for cross-border councils and getting all parties to recognize 'the right to equal opportunity in all social and economic activity, regardless of class, creed, disability, gender or ethnicity' while also acknowledging the right of Northern Ireland to 'pursue democratically national and political aspirations'. In May 1998 Sinn Féin officially endorsed the peace agreement, which was ratified that month in a popular referendum in which 71 per cent voted in support of it. When a splinter group calling itself the Real IRA set off a bomb in Omagh in August killing twenty-nine and wounding over 200 people, Sinn Féin leader Martin McGuiness condemned the act as harmful to the cause of peace in Northern Ireland. In the aftermath of the Good Friday Agreement, even Ian Paisley softened his vituperative tone. In his 1999 book, *For Such a Time as This*, he wrote that the time for peace had come.

The British government took another major step in January 2000, when it announced that it would change the name, reduce the size, and diversify the membership of the Royal Ulster Constabulary. The decision to change the title drew the most resistance from Protestant conservatives, but Northern Ireland secretary Peter Mandelson still managed to get the polarizing name changed to the Police Service of Northern Ireland. The proposal called for a force of 7,500, reduced from 13,500, comprising equal numbers of Protestants and Catholics. By 2008, Paisley and McGuiness would participate in a power-sharing arrangement that few would have thought possible twenty years earlier. Extremists on both sides still distrusted the arrangement, but it looked as if the Troubles, which had killed 3,600 people in a three-decade span, might finally be over. As Tony Blair put it, 'People who had wanted to kill each other were now wanting to work together.'[19]

Privatization and political culture under Margaret Thatcher

In the 1980s British political culture once again swung back in the direction of consumerism, capitalism, and conservatism, combined with a further increase in the Americanization of British popular culture and tastes and a revival of British patriotism. Margaret Thatcher's personal philosophy of individual responsibility, laissez-faire capitalism, and British nationalism may have seemed well timed to address the malaise and general level of dissatisfaction that afflicted the British society in 1979, but her political philosophy was decades in the making. It seemed that throughout the twentieth century the electorate returned regularly to the Conservative Party when it thought the nation had veered too far from its traditional values and roots that had once made Britain a great nation. Despite her hostility to the unions, Thatcher's desire to decrease government expenditure and lower taxes had a broad appeal to many members of the working classes hurt by unemployment, inflation, and high taxation rates that inhibited them from the ability to purchase their own homes. But at the same time that Thatcher wanted less state intervention in the economy, she also wanted to use the state to hold people accountable, whether it was the unions, the universities, or the National Health Service.

As prime minister, Thatcher prided herself on having as much knowledge and expertise as her advisers on every subject with which she had to deal. Nigel Lawson, a member of Thatcher's Cabinet from 1981 to 1989, wrote that she only needed 4 hours of sleep a night and studied each night for whatever was on her agenda for the next day as if she were preparing for an examination.[20] Her official biographer, Charles Moore, records that she took several books on Irish history ('none from a Unionist perspective') with her on holiday in the summer of 1980 so that she would better understand the situation in Northern Ireland.[21] She began her first term as prime minister without much experience or knowledge of Commonwealth Affairs, but she managed to cultivate strong relationships with the Commonwealth, which supported Britain in its management of the transition to the independence of Zimbabwe (formerly Rhodesia) in 1979, the independence of Belize in 1981, and the Falklands War with Argentina in 1983.[22] (It should be pointed out here, however, that Thatcher's refusal to issue sanctions against South Africa for its policy of apartheid did great damage to her reputation within the Commonwealth, as well as to her reputation at home.) Before the Falklands War of 1983, she had no military experience yet during the crisis emerged as a strong war leader who had helped to direct the overall strategy during the war, though she left specific tactical decisions in the hands of her admirals and chiefs of staff. She demonstrated a remarkable degree of flexibility when she responded to an assassination attempt by the IRA in 1984 with a renewed commitment to finding a solution for Catholic grievances, leading to the Anglo-Irish Agreement of 1985.

During her first term as prime minister, inflation declined to below 5 per cent by 1983, but unemployment rose during the first four years of her administration, hitting 3.3 million in August 1982.[23] At the same time, Thatcher cut the budget in the area of social services that were needed to cope with the growing number of unemployed. She wanted to hold all sectors of the economy accountable and to privatize the nationalized industries that she thought could be more efficiently run under private ownership. She went after the universities, demanding that they be held accountable for the results of the education they provided, much to the consternation of the dons who saw themselves as providing an education whose value could not be measured as just another commodity for sale.[24]

With Labour still reeling from its dismal performance in the 1970s and Thatcher's government alienating even some members of her own party, Shirley Williams, like Thatcher an Oxford-educated former education secretary, helped launch in 1981 a moderate Social Democratic Party as an alternative to Labour or the Conservatives. Williams especially disagreed with the anti-nuclear and anti-Europe stances of the Labour Party while opposing what she saw as the excessive privatization initiatives of the Thatcher government.

Then, on 2 April 1982, Argentina launched an invasion of the Falkland Islands in the South Atlantic, before proceeding to occupy South Georgia, South Shetland, South Orkneys, and South Thule as well. Unsurprisingly, the Falklands War that ensued between the UK and Argentina attracted enthusiastic public support, both within Parliament and among the British public. In fact, the war was exactly what Thatcher needed, not only to distract people from unemployment and domestic discontent, but to allow her to tap into the spirit of patriotism and her call for a defence of British values that was a major part of her appeal. It helped her cause that the aggressor against the British-held islands was a brutal dictatorship that had murdered 30,000 of its own people and hoped the invasion would restore its lustre in the eyes of the Argentinian people. The administration of Ronald Reagan was split on the Falklands War, but Thatcher's decisive leadership and lack of hesitation about using military force to bring a swift resolution to the matter and the support she received from US secretary of defense Caspar Weinberger forced Reagan' s hand.[25] In June 1983, a year after the successful conclusion of the Falklands War, Thatcher was re-elected to another term, during which she would translate her higher approval ratings into decisive action to tackle the problems that continued to plague the British economy, starting with the power of the unions.

For all of the concessions that Labour seemed to make to the unions in the 1970s, the era remained replete with strikes and industrial protests. In 1982, Arthur Scargill became president of the NUM, which did not augur well for future negotiations with the government to avoid a strike. Scargill took a revolutionary and antagonistic attitude into negotiations, determined not to make any concessions that would set the miners back in what he considered a key battle in a class war. In March 1984, Thatcher got her opportunity to deal with the miners head-on when they declared a strike that lasted until March of the following year. During the strike, miners who had taken jobs straight out of school and worked in the mines for twenty-five years lost their jobs, without any other skills or prospects to fall back on. As the strike dragged on, it became increasingly clear that those jobs were not coming back. Before it ended, the strike degenerated into violence directed by striking miners against those who went back to work, leading to police intervention. The strike damaged Thatcher's reputation because of the lack of sympathy she displayed towards the miners' families, but Scargill also emerged as an unsympathetic figure.

The Thatcher state also took some rather draconian measures to deal with crime, especially the epidemic of the use of heroine, crack cocaine, and designer drugs like Ecstasy. These measures further contributed to Thatcher's reputation as being cold-hearted, as she seemed insensitive to the true roots of drug abuse, homelessness, and crime, which the social policies of the government had arguably done much to cause or exacerbate. The Drug Trafficking Act of 1986 invested the police with additional power to confiscate any assets of an accused drug dealer that had been acquired within the past six years if the source of the funds to purchase them could not be accounted for. This might not sound so bad except that this law applied to anyone found with any illegal drugs at all, including those in possession of a single joint.

Despite being a polarizing figure, Thatcher and the Conservative Party retained power in the election held in May 1987. In calling this election when she did, Thatcher sought to take advantage of a boost in popularity that the Conservatives enjoyed as a result of the lowest unemployment rate since 1981 and the lowest inflation rate since before the energy crisis of 1973. Part of the problem for Neil Kinnock and the Labour Party was that Labour still carried an image of being out of step with the times and living in a past where workers were unduly oppressed and state intervention provided the answer to every problem. Behind the scenes, however, some leading members of Thatcher's own party were wearying of her imperious and brusque style, while the early appeal of her ideology was beginning to lose its cachet with the general public.

In foreign policy, Thatcher played a particularly important role in the important geopolitical changes associated with the end of the Cold War in the late 1980s, mainly through her cultivation of a close personal relationship with the leader of the Soviet Union, Mikhail Gorbachev. In fact, Archie Brown has discerned a strong shift in the relationship between the UK and the Soviet Union which he dates to a meeting at Chequers, the country estate of the prime minister, in September 1983, well before anyone had heard of 'Glasnost' or 'Perestroika'.[26] Thatcher publically supported the reform initiatives introduced by Gorbachev in the Soviet Union and expressed confidence that they would succeed in creating 'a much freer society with a proper rule of law and a genuine respect for human rights'.[27]

The year 1989 turned out to be Europe's *annus mirabilis*, with revolutions sweeping across Eastern Europe and bringing an end to Communist regimes in Poland, Hungary, Czechoslovakia, Romania, Bulgaria, and East Germany. To many observers and political pundits, these revolutions presaged the triumph of liberal democracy and the end of the Cold War. The fall of the Berlin Wall and the end of communism in Eastern Europe in 1989 had strong repercussions in the UK. The most immediate concern for Thatcher was the prospect of German unification. Thatcher was opposed to a united Germany and she told Gorbachev as much, believing that the status quo had actually helped to preserve peace in Europe for the past forty-four years. Though the public response to the revolutions and the fall of the Berlin Wall was euphoric, serious concerns about German unification seemed justified at the time. Still, as Richard Leiby puts it, 'Thatcher's guarded response seemed too restrained and historically inappropriate.'[28] She turned what could have been a triumphant moment into another occasion for criticism that she had gotten out of step with the British public. Her opposition to German unification also put her at odds with other NATO members. In addition, she had tried to convince Gorbachev in a private conversation in September 1989 to disregard any favourable comments made by NATO members about the unification of Germany, as if she spoke for the entire alliance.[29]

Margaret Thatcher's political career did not long survive the fall of the Berlin Wall – a year later she resigned as head of the Conservative Party when she failed to gain re-election on the first ballot because of a challenge from Michael Heseltine, a frequent critic of Thatcher who had resigned from her Cabinet in 1986. In the end, the Conservative Party abandoned Thatcher once her popularity had run its course, hastened by an unpopular poll tax she had introduced in Scotland in 1989 and England and Wales in 1990 that had provoked a wave of riots across

Britain. Thatcher's tenure had considerably changed the British political landscape and restored a measure of national pride, while most people would have said that Britain entered the 1990s in a much better position and more optimistic mood than it had the 1980s. However, Thatcher's policies had hit the more disadvantaged in society the hardest, and homelessness, drug abuse, crime, and the AIDS epidemic were problems that could not be ignored.

Tony Blair and the reinvention of the Labour Party: The political culture of the 1990s

The 1990s opened ominously in Britain with a riot among the prisoners at the extremely overcrowded HMP Strangeways in Manchester on 1 April. The riot at Strangeways resulted in 148 injuries and one death and caused £60 million worth of damage, but more importantly inspired prison riots at HMPs Bristol and Cardiff and numerous other prisons as well.[30] The riots called attention to the rising prison population under Thatcher and reinforced the notion associated with the poll tax that the Conservative agenda did not care who it left behind or the impact that it had on the lives of ordinary people. Rising crime rates, especially among juveniles, became a major public concern. To make matters worse, the economy had entered a recession as the next election approached in 1992. Nonetheless, John Major and the Conservative Party won yet another election on 9 April 1992 despite growing public dissatisfaction with many of the party's policies.

After Thatcher was replaced by John Major as prime minister, the Conservative Party made the mistake of thinking that Major could simply continue Thatcher's policies without making any significant changes in policy. The main reason for their confidence seemed to be the moribund state of the Labour Party, despite the efforts of Neil Kinnock in the late 1980s and early 1990s to gradually soften Labour's socialist agenda and revise his stance on issues ranging from unilateral nuclear disarmament to his previously unadulterated support of trade unions. John Smith, the Scottish politician who headed the Labour Party from 1992 to 1994 continued to provide an ideological counterpoint to the Conservative agenda. This made him popular with the left-wing within his party, but less so with the general public. Yet that public was wearying of fifteen years of Conservative government and was ready to embrace a Labour politician who would meet them halfway.

That politician turned out to be a charismatic 41-year-old lawyer and ex-hippie named Tony Blair, who was elected Smith's replacement as head of the Labour Party in 1994. Blair was a moderate who rejected Labour's previous socialist positions on nationalization and income redistribution. Blair advocated popular reform measures, such as granting more autonomy to regional assemblies in Scotland and Wales and purging the House of Lords of its hereditary peers. By the time the next election rolled around in 1997, Blair's election as prime minister was a given. He began his administration with a Labour majority in the House of Commons of 419. The election of 1997 was historically significant for other reasons as well; it featured the election of 101 female Labour MPs, up from thirty-seven in 1992, compared to thirteen female Conservative MPs, up from one in 1992.[31] The Liberal Democrats doubled their seats in the House of Commons to forty-six, making them more of a factor in British politics.

In the years between 1994 and 1997, Tony Blair helped create the political phenomenon known as New Labour, a hybrid between a continuing commitment to the welfare state and an emphasis on privatization, capitalism, and individual responsibility that were the hallmarks of Thatcher's conservative ideology. Blair had vowed to cut state spending and lower taxes. John Major derisively described New Labour as 'pretty much us'. In 1997, the new Conservative leader William Hague dismissed Labour's programme as 'mood music politics without values'. Such comments could, of course, be dismissed as the result of jealousy or envy; Blair had just won the largest electoral victory in the history of the Labour Party. But there is some truth in their comments; Margaret Thatcher, who predicted the Labour landslide, regarded the impact of her ideas upon the Labour Party as one of her greatest achievements.

Socially, the workforce was shifting in important ways in the 1990s, partly as a result of the deregulation of the labour market. First, companies were increasingly hiring specialists on temporary contracts instead of as permanent salaried employees. Secondly, workers could move about more freely to take advantage of mobile opportunities in a flexible job market, but they lost the advantages of benefits such as holiday pay and sick pay. A third major shift involved the growth of part-time employment, especially among women. The new economy had its advantages and disadvantages, but many workers were also left without security or political representation in a period in which it would have been political suicide for Blair to revert to the old Labour policies in support of unions, which the Conservatives accused him of wanting to do all along.

They also criticized Blair for his lack of foreign policy experience. In fact, although Blair was universally recognized as an extremely eloquent and articulate speaker with dash and élan, having never been a Cabinet member he did not have a great deal of experience in government in general. So even after his election there was some scepticism about how he would work out as prime minister. He had served as shadow home secretary during the Major administration, where he most notably took a tough stance on crime and called for increased power for the police, another position that moved him away from the traditional platform of the Labour Party. But Blair, a convert to Catholicism, had a political philosophy influenced by Christianity, which emphasized the importance of community and shared responsibility for the general welfare of others and would keep him from straying too close to the Conservative line.

The death of Princess Diana as a result of a tragic automobile accident on 31 August 1997 stunned Britain and the world and provided an early test of Tony Blair's political skills as prime minister. The public outpouring of grief and the massive crowds of mourners that turned out on the day of Diana's funeral were unlike anything Britain had ever seen. Winston Churchill's passing in 1965 had been a solemn occasion that had temporarily reunited the country in remembrance of his popular leadership during the Second World War, but Diana's premature death and her caring reputation as the 'people's princess' evoked a sadness surrounding someone who would be missed even more because she seemed to have so many years ahead of her. Lines of people waiting to sign condolence books stretched for blocks and thousands left bouquets of flowers outside of Kensington Palace. Diana's death was a bit of a crisis for the monarchy as well, as anger mounted at the initial lack of a response from Buckingham Palace; however, on 5 September, Queen Elizabeth II said, 'I for one believe that there are lessons to be drawn from her life and from the extraordinary and moving reaction to her death.' Just as Diana's death and the queen's eventual response to it softened her public image, Blair's demeanour and sympathy for Diana and the royal family in the aftermath of her death resonated strongly with the British public and furthered the feelings of unity and connection inspired by her death.

Blair's first term as prime minister was marked by his continuation of the special relationship with the United States and his advocacy for the deeper involvement of the UK in Europe. He developed a close relationship with US president Bill Clinton and called for an end of British isolationism and 'a policy of constructive engagement' with the European Union, although the UK under Blair still failed to adopt the new European-wide currency, the euro. Blair also made good his promise to do something about the hereditary peers, whom his foreign secretary Robin Cook once referred to as 'medieval lumber' from 'the cast of a Gilbert and Sullivan opera'.[32] The House of Lords Act of 1999 permitted ninety-two hereditary peers to remain in the upper chamber of Parliament, but removed 666 and reduced the overall membership in the House from 1,330 to 669.

In foreign policy, Blair's major achievement of the late 1990s was his cooperation with Clinton to stabilize the Balkans, which since the collapse of communism in 1989 had been embroiled in some nasty civil wars and ethnic conflicts, which had resulted in the first European instances of genocide since the Second World War. The Serbian nationalist leader Slobodan Milošević had fomented wars between Croatia and Bosnia to prevent them leaving a Serbian-dominated Yugoslavia, with Bosnia the site of the worst atrocities because of the large Serbian population there. The Clinton administration intervened to bring the Bosnian war to an end in 1995, followed by the presence of United Nations forces to keep the peace. After 1997, Blair proved that he was no puppet of the United States, as he and Cook acted independently in conjunction with the International Criminal Tribunal and in opposition to Milošević's dictatorship.[33] In 1999, Blair played a key role in NATO's intervention in Kosovo, where Milošević was responsible for a new round of murder and oppression that led 200,000 Kosovars to flee their country. NATO intervention brought about the downfall of Milošević, who agreed to withdraw from Kosovo before being indicted for war crimes, the first acting head of state to experience such an ignominy.

In another significant move, on 1 July 1997 Blair attended a ceremony, along with President Jiang Zemin of China, at which the UK officially turned over Hong Kong to Chinese rule. The yielding of its former colonial possessions was old hat by the end of the twentieth century, but this was the first British territory to be turned over to a Communist state and signalled the beginning of a new era in UK–Chinese relations.

The movement towards devolution in Scotland, Wales, and Northern Ireland

Blair also made good on his promise to grant devolution to Scotland, Wales, and Northern Ireland. In 1999, devolution came to Scotland as a result of a 1997 referendum in which 74 per cent of Scots voted in favour of a Scottish Parliament and the ensuing Scotland Act of 1998. The Welsh also voted in favour of devolution in a 1997 referendum, but by an extremely narrow margin of 50.3 to 49.7 per cent. The National Assembly of Wales was created in 1999, the result of the Government of Wales Act of 1998.

During the 1970s, the Labour Party, the dominant party in Scotland, had generally opposed devolution, seeing the Scottish National Party as a rival whose nationalist ideology contradicted the more international philosophy of Labour. Furthermore, at that time even those who advocated greater influence in Scotland wanted this process to occur within the context of the union rather than outside of it, their case bolstered by the discovery of oil in Scottish waters in the North Sea in 1969. In a Scottish referendum of 1979, a majority of Scots of almost 52 per cent did vote in favour, but that number represented only 32.9 per cent of the total electorate and the bill had stipulated 40 per cent as a minimum requirement.

Like Scottish nationalism, Welsh nationalism had been on the rise in the 1960s and early 1970s as a movement intent on preserving its cultural heritage. The movement in favour of devolution within Wales has been explained as related to the Welsh language as a manifestation of Welsh cultural and political identity.[34] That movement never translated into enough support for devolution or political independence. In the Welsh referendum on devolution in 1979 less than 60 per cent of the electorate turned out to vote and almost 80 per cent of those who did voted against the measure.

Among the reasons for the larger majority in favour of devolution in Scotland than Wales in the 1997 referendums was the Scots' growing dissatisfaction with the Conservative governments that had been in power from 1979 to 1997. The acrimonious feelings that resulted from the defeat of the miners' union during the strike of 1984–5 had helped to shift the Scottish Labour Party in the direction of devolution. In Scotland, 62 per cent of Catholics voted in favour of devolution in the 1997 referendum, contradicting the belief of observers that Catholics would not want to support a measure that would grant additional influence over Scottish affairs to its majority Protestant population. Steve Bruce also finds this reflected in the percentage of Catholics voting for the Scottish National Party in elections from 1970, when 4 per cent of Catholics voted for the SNP, to 1992, when the SNP drew 20 per cent of the Catholic vote, and 2011, when the percentage of Catholic SNP votes grew to 43 per cent.[35]

Interestingly, in the opening speech of the Scottish Parliament in 1999 Winnie Ewing referred to the 'reconvening' of the Scottish Parliament, suggesting that this was not a new institution but had some continuity with the Scottish past, dating back to before the Act of Union of 1707. The SNP regarded devolution as a temporary step in the right direction, similar to the way supporters of Michael Collins viewed the creation of the Irish Free State in 1922. This had important political implications because it was still unclear how much power London had actually yielded to the Scottish Parliament. For example, Blair had given the Scottish Parliament the authority to raise or lower the national income tax, but had restricted it to a margin of 3 per cent either way. Ewing's speech also opened a crack in the joint British identity that English and Scots had been crafting for the past 300 years.

The devolution of authority to the national assemblies of Scotland and Wales raised important questions about the future of Britain and what it meant to be British. Nationalist opponents of devolution believed that Blair had supported Scottish devolution only as a means of preserving the UK and forestalling Scottish independence. Others questioned whether the Welsh and the Scots deserved to continue to send as many representatives to the Parliament at Westminster once they had their own assemblies and more control in their own regions.

Northern Ireland was so obviously a case apart from either Scotland or Wales that, at times, it seemed more convenient for people and politicians in Britain to forget that it was still a part of the UK. Northern Ireland presented a different set of problems because of the Troubles, which had pushed Britain in the opposite direction of devolution there during the 1970s, including the suspension of the Northern Ireland Parliament at Stormont in 1972. The British could not consider granting devolution to Northern Ireland without an agreement between the Protestants and Catholics to enter a power-sharing arrangement. In the 1980s, Margaret Thatcher gradually shifted the UK position on Northern Ireland in the general direction of devolution, beginning with the Anglo-Irish Agreement of 1985 that called for a gradual process to bring about self-government.

While the Conservatives continued to insist that reunification with the South would only be possible with the consent of a majority of the population in Northern Ireland, the Labour Party saw devolution as an important step in the direction of Irish unification. Even though Protestants remained committed to remaining within the Union, they too began to chafe at their lack of autonomy by the 1990s. In 2007, with the power-sharing arrangement between Catholics and Protestants finally in place, Tony Blair negotiated the Belfast Agreement in which executive authority was returned to Northern Ireland for the first time since 1972 (see Chapter 19).

Life and politics in the Republic of Ireland

Ireland, like the UK, went through tough economic times in the 1970s and 1980s. But Ireland's economic troubles had started earlier, with rising unemployment and welfare enrolment leading to social protests in the late 1960s and early 1970s. At the same time, however, Dublin had become a modern city and economic centre, in which office space increased during the 1960s by 1,570,515 square feet.[36] Ireland, which had never had a particularly strong industrial base, was at least starting to develop a strong service industry and commercial economy. Sixty per cent of the people of the Republic lived in cities in 1979, compared to 45 per cent in 1961.[37] The percentage of people employed in salaried, professional, or managerial jobs had increased from 10 per cent in 1951 to 25 per cent by 1985.[38] Despite the rise in poverty and increase in social problems, the people of the Irish Republic did experience a cumulative increase in their standard of living from the 1960s to the 1980s.

By the 1980s, however, the economic situation seemed to be getting worse instead of better. Government expenditure increased from 54 per cent of GNP in 1980 to 62 per cent in 1986 and public debt grew from 87 per cent to 120 per cent of GNP during that same time.[39] Ireland experienced another wave of emigration, resulting in

200,000 people leaving the country in the course of the decade, mostly for Britain.[40] In retrospect, it seemed that the Irish economy was due for success, which it began to experience in the following decade.

In 1986, the government devalued the currency to rectify a situation in which the government had to borrow too much money to prop up its inflated value, which proved to be an important step in the right direction. One indication of Irish prosperity in the 1990s was the decline in welfare spending from 30 per cent in the late 1980s to about 20 per cent a decade later.[41] In the years from 1995 to 2007, Ireland earned the nickname the 'Celtic Tiger' for its strong economic performance. Unemployment declined and Ireland started to attract immigrants from Eastern Europe and elsewhere. An estimated 250,000 people migrated to Ireland in the second half of the 1990s.[42] Inflation and public debt also decreased, while in some years economic growth rates reached as high as 10 per cent. In a sense, this rapid expansion led to a shift in Irish attitudes towards the European Union; the Irish did not wish the EU to place restrictions on Ireland that might inhibit its economic growth. The Irish became more reluctant to help fund economic growth in other countries such as Greece, Spain, or Portugal, even though they had willingly accepted financial aid from the EU when they had needed it in the past.

During this period the Republic of Ireland also began to move further away from its Catholic identity and its vision of itself as a collective society, with both positive and negative repercussions. On the positive side, Ireland, which had decriminalized homosexuality in 1993, passed an Employment Equality Act in 1998 and an Equal Status Act in 2000 that collectively outlawed discrimination on the basis of sexual orientation. Ireland also became more ethnically and culturally diverse and became more sensitive to the Travellers, a self-identified Irish ethnic group who lived outside of the mainstream of Irish society. Women's rights had largely been addressed through legislation in the 1970s, but the 1990s saw further improvements in women's status, highlighted by the election of two women presidents during the decade, Mary Robinson in 1990 and Mary McAleese in 1997.

But with economic prosperity and the adoption of a more laissez-faire brand of capitalism came widening disparities of income distribution, an increase in organized crime, and corporate and political corruption that reached to the top of Irish society. The 1996 murder of investigative reporter Veronica Guerin occurred in the wake of a series of articles she had written on organized crime in Dublin and received attention as a national tragedy. Furthermore, increased ethnic diversity led to an increase in racial tensions, especially in poorer areas. Finally, the child sexual abuse scandal that struck at the heart of the Catholic Church created a further distrust of authority and seemed to reflect a society that was rapidly spinning out of control.

Cultural transitions and trends in music and literature in the UK and Ireland

Supplementing the novels of Margaret Drabble and the beginnings of punk rock in the late 1970s, a landmark book was published in 1979 by Peter Townsend titled *Poverty in the United Kingdom*, which showed the depth of poverty in the country and the extent to which it was not living up to its promise to deliver material and social benefits to large numbers of people. This book helped set the tone for the cultural transition to the Thatcher era, in which music, novels, and films responded to the social problems and inequalities that continued to haunt Britain.

It was symptomatic of the increased diversity of British culture that many of the most acclaimed and perceptive portrayals of Thatcher's Britain came from people of different ethnic backgrounds and focused on race and immigration as lenses through which to view the broader culture. In 1981, Salman Rushdie's novel, *Midnight's Children*, winner of the prestigious Booker Prize and hailed as an example of a new novelistic genre called magical realism, forced readers to confront the impact of Britain's colonial past on the people of India and Pakistan at a time when British neo-nationalism was on the rise. Stephen Frears' critically acclaimed 1986 film *My Beautiful Laundrette* deals poignantly with the struggles of a young gay Pakistani man in England trying to build a successful business in the face of racist hostility. *My Son the Fanatic*, a 1997 film directed by Udayan Prasad that was based on a short story by Hanif Kureishi, deals with a secular Pakistani taxi driver whose son converts to Islamic fundamentalism in eerie anticipation of tensions that have confronted the Muslim community and society as a whole in twenty-first-century Britain.

Mike Leigh's 1988 film *High Hopes* also reflects some of the social and cultural developments associated with Thatcher's Britain by contrasting the different effects that the period had on a variety of characters from both the working and middle classes. Cyril, a motorcycle courier played by Philip Davis, reflects the disillusionment of a working-class socialist. In one scene, he stands with his girlfriend in front of the grave of Karl Marx, telling her that without Marx there would have been 'no unions, no welfare state, no nationalized industries'. He goes on to lament how much things have changed, prophesying that 'by the year 2000, there will be 26 TV stations, 24 hours a day telling you what to think'.

In music, the cultural response to Thatcherism included two songs that practically bookended her years in power – 'Stand Down, Margaret!' released by the English Beat in 1980, and 1988's 'Margaret on the Guillotine' by the popular singer Morrissey, who had recently left his group, the Smiths, to begin a solo career. An indirect indictment of Thatcher's individualistic, pull-yourself-up-by-your bootstraps conservative philosophy was the massive rock concert 'Live Aid', organized by Bob Geldof and Midge Ure to raise money for Ethiopian famine relief and held at Wembley Stadium on 13 July 1985.

British pop music was changing in the 1980s, with punk no longer seeming as relevant to the historical moment. Significantly, one of Britain's most popular punk rock bands, the Clash, broke up in 1986. The fall of the Berlin Wall and end of the Cold War in 1989 produced a new kind of optimism in popular culture that was completely out of tune with punk's rebellious, anarchistic tendencies. 'Winds of Change', by the German rock band, the Scorpions, made it to no. 2 on the UK charts in September 1991 and 'Right Here Right Now', released in 1991 by the British alternative rock band Jesus Jones, speaks of 'watching the world wake up from history'.[43] For a generation that had come of age since the advent of punk rock and for whom the hopes and aspirations of the 1960s were part of the fading dreams of their parents' generation, it was exciting to think that they could be part of a generation that actually did change the world for the better.

The enthusiasm for the end of the Cold War and the hopes that it brought for a more peaceful and politically stable world were short-lived. In 1991, the very year the Soviet Union collapsed, John Le Carré would write the following in his novel *The Secret Pilgrim*:

> He [George Smiley] scoffed at the idea that spying was a dying profession now that the Cold War had ended: with each new nation that came out of the ice, he said, with each new alignment, each rediscovery of old identities and passions, with each erosion of the old status quo, the spies would be working round the clock.[44]

A few pages later, Smiley comes up with the following reflections:

> And perhaps we didn't win. Perhaps they just lost. Or perhaps, without the bonds of ideological conflict to restrain us any more, our troubles are just beginning.[45]

In the new geopolitical world described by Le Carré, Britain's role was less certain; the spies of MI5 or MI6 in his Cold War novels could at least feel that they had been on the right side of history, first in the Second World War and then in the Cold War, but after 1989 they not only had a less well-defined role, but Britain was frequently castigated for its imperial past and spy agencies themselves seemed inherently linked with the kind of totalitarian state that they were allegedly trying to combat. British intelligence had already started to lose some of its lustre with the controversial publication in 1987 of *Spycatcher*, written by a former assistant director of MI5, Peter Wright with co-author Paul Greengrass. The British government helped to call more attention to the book by attempting to ban it; the book featured a series of scandalous revelations, including an MI5 plot to bring down Harold Wilson's government and an assassination plot of MI6 directed at Nasser at the time of the Suez Crisis in 1956. In addition, the release of Michael Caton-Jones's film *Scandal* in 1989 brought the Profumo Affair back into the public consciousness and added to the doubts about how much trust should be accorded British intelligence agencies at a time when the end of the Cold War seemed to obviate them.

While the 1990s saw the ascendance of Grunge music in America, British musical groups responded to the apathetic lyrics and guitar distortions of Grunge with a style that became labelled 'Britpop', part of a larger cultural phenomenon dubbed 'Cool Britannia' that sought to revive the popularity of British music and fashion of the 1960s. The appeal of this movement contributed to the popularity of Tony Blair, who became head of the Labour Party in 1994, the same year that the Spice Girls formed and took Britain by storm, becoming one of the most popular female groups in history on a global scale. Band member Geri Halliwell's appearance at the BRIT Awards in 1997 in her now-famous Union Jack dress best encapsulated the Cool Britannia movement in the minds of many fans. To the extent that such symbolism became more important than the music, it helped to bring the Britpop movement to an end by the end of the decade. To the extent that Britpop did seek to appropriate the cultural symbolism of the 1960s, while jettisoning some of its more substantive ideals, it might help to prove Marx's famous statement that 'history repeats itself, the first as tragedy, then as farce'.

The 1990s also saw a kind of nostalgic nod towards the British past in films, which even inspired the appellation 'Britflicks', although this term has subsequently been applied to all British films in general. Here again 1994 featured prominently with the release of two films starring Hugh Grant: English director Mike Newell's *Four Weddings and a Funeral* and *Sirens* by the Australian director John Duigan. The former, which features Grant amid an all-star ensemble that includes iconic English comic Rowan Atkinson of *Mr Bean* fame and Diana Quick among others, is mainly notable for the extent to which it emphasizes the differences between the English Grant and his American love-interest, played by Andie MacDowell; the plot is based mainly on the ways in which the characters played by Grant and MacDowell are, well, English and American. In *Sirens*, which is set in 1930s Australia, Grant plays a young, moderate Anglican clergyman who travels with his wife, played by Tara Fitzgerald, to Australia to convince an eccentric artist, Norman Lindsay (based on a real artist by that name) to withdraw from an exhibition one of his paintings, a portrait of the crucifixion with a voluptuous woman in the place of Christ. Among the many other notable British films from the decade, Mike Leigh's 1997 *Secrets and Lies* deals as well with a clash of values in a story about a middle-class black woman who learns that her birth mother is a working-class white woman. Collectively, these three films deal with questions of British identity from their respective vantage points of nationality, religion, and race and class.

In the 1990s, the Irish cultural phenomenon *Riverdance* took the world by storm and signalled a renewed enthusiasm for Irish culture in general and Irish traditional dance in particular. The sense of pride that the Irish could feel in the popularity of *Riverdance* coincided with the early years of economic boom that produced the Celtic Tiger for Ireland. But the plot of *Riverdance* appealed more to the Irish diaspora than to the Irish themselves, providing yet another romanticized version of the holy ground of Ireland while pointing to hope in the revival and success of the Irish elsewhere.[46]

It was not only Irish dance that represented Irish culture to the world in the 1990s. The traditional Irish musical group the Chieftains, which first formed in 1962, continued to bring Irish music to the rest of the world, culminating in a fortieth anniversary album released in 2002, *The Chieftains: The Wide World Over*, in which they were accompanied on each of the nineteen tracks by a range of popular artists that included Joni Mitchell, Elvis Costello, and Ziggy Marley, as well as Van Morrison, the iconic Northern Irish folk–rock superstar, with whom they had made a well-received 1988 album called *Irish Heartbeat*. In addition, such diverse Irish artists and groups as Enya, Sinéad O'Connor, the Cranberries, the Corrs, Mary Black, and Christy Moore attracted huge international followings in addition to their popularity at home. The rock band U2 continued its success from the 1980s into the next decade, starting with their 1990 album *Achtung Baby*, recorded in Germany in the aftermath of the fall of the Berlin Wall. Many Irish films from the 1990s focused on the Troubles in Northern Ireland; among the most notable were Jim Sheridan's *In the Name of the Father* (1993) and *The Boxer* (1997), both starring Daniel Day-Lewis. Neil Jordan's *Michael Collins* (1997), starring Liam Neeson and Julia Roberts, also deserves mention for its dramatic portrayal of one of the heroes of Irish independence and its controversial treatment of Eamon de Valera's role in Collins's assassination.

Social and political criticism was just as relevant at the beginning of the twenty-first century as at any point in the past. Consider the following exchange that occurs early in John Le Carré's 2000 novel, *The Constant Gardener*:

'So when is a state not a state, in your opinion, Mr. Quayle?' Tessa inquired sweetly, one idle midday in Cambridge four years ago, in an ancient attic lecture room with dusty sunbeams sloping through the skylight. ...
     'Well – I suppose the answer to your question is –' Justin began – 'and you must please correct me if you think differently –' bridging the age gap and the gender gap and generally imparting an egalitarian air – 'that a state ceases to be a state when it ceases to deliver on its essential responsibilities. ...'
     'Essential responsibilities being what?' the angel-waif rapped back.
     'Well ... I would suggest to you that, these days, very roughly, the qualifications for being a civilized state amount to – electoral suffrage, ah – protection of life and property – um, justice, health and education for all, at least to a certain level – then the maintenance of a sound administrative infrastructure – and roads, transport, drains, et cetera – and – what else is there? – ah yes, the equitable collection of taxes ...'
     'So can you imagine a situation where you personally would feel obliged to undermine the state?'[47]

In 2005, the Australian director James McTeigue released the film *V for Vendetta*, based on the graphic novel written by Alan Moore and illustrated by David Lloyd in the 1980s. The main character in *V for Vendetta* is a rebel against a futuristic totalitarian British state who disguises himself as Guy Fawkes, the seventeenth-century Catholic terrorist arrested in connection with the Gunpowder Plot that aimed at blowing up the Parliament building and killing King James I in the process. The graphic novel took aim at the growing power of the state under Margaret Thatcher, but the film came out following eight years of the Labour government of Tony Blair.
     In between the start of Blair's administration and the release of the film, radical Islamic jihadists who belonged to Osama Bin Laden's terrorist organization, al-Qaeda, had brought down the twin towers of the World Trade Center in New York City on 11 September 2001. Most people in the British Isles would have sympathized with the United States in this tragedy and supported Blair's expression of support for the new American president, George W. Bush; sixty-seven citizens of the United Kingdom and six Irish citizens died in the attacks, which also included an attack on the Pentagon in Washington, DC, and the crash of another hijacked plane in central Pennsylvania. However, before long Blair had joined Bush by committing British troops to the US invasion of Iraq in 2003. That decision alienated many of Blair's former supporters and helped to contribute, along with several other factors to be considered in the concluding chapter that follows, to a new level of scepticism about the power of government.
     In conclusion, the period between 1973 and 2004 had changed the face of the British Isles in some dramatic and significant ways. The period started with the entry of both the UK and Ireland into the European Community, an energy crisis, an economic slump, and growing concerns about the decline of Britain. The Thatcher

Years had some of their own problems, but compared to the state of the nation in the Winter of Discontent of 1979, the UK seemed to have grown stronger, recovered economically, and asserted itself more forcefully on the world stage, even if with uneven results. The situation in Northern Ireland, which seemed intractable for much of the period, improved significantly after the Good Friday Agreement. In many other ways, Tony Blair's leadership seemed to reenergize the country by merging the best of both parties into a revitalized Labour Party and government. In addition, devolution had redefined the relationships among the constituent parts of the UK. Meanwhile, the Republic of Ireland was still enjoying its reputation as the Celtic Tiger because of the strength of its economy. Yet, when Tony Blair turned his back on Europe to support the United States in its war against Iraq, he initiated a new phase in the history of his country, and combined with an economic meltdown that shook the global economy, set it on an uncertain path. It is still not clear where that path will lead, as the concluding chapter in this book will show.

FIGURE 38 *London cityscape.*
Spaces Images/Blend Images/Getty.

19

Conclusion:

The British Isles in the twenty-first century

And the outriders of the City, those Orwellian cliffs of commerce.
St, Paul's Cathedral, Wren's domed fantasy, is blocked by the impertinent
brutalism of Baynard House and the Faraday Building, which were
constructed to remind us that the river is never more than a graph of
opportunism and mercantile self-interest.

IAN SINCLAIR

Every day I walk from my house in Stockwell a half mile to the southern
bank of the Thames by Lambeth Bridge. ... But mostly I head for a
small notch of beach in between the HQ of Britain's secret services and a
nondescript office block called Tintangel House. Here I can sense all the
strange circulations of the city's cerebrospinal fluid – the electronic chaff
yattered by the spooks in the block by the bridge that so encapsulates
London's woeful post-modernity that the steely trim and concrete cladding
might as well have been shaped into giant numerals: 1984.

WILL SELF (both the above quotes are from MATTHEW PERICOLI,
London Unfurled, 2011)

The Iraq war and the decline of Tony Blair

At a Labour Party Conference in October 2001, Prime Minister Tony Blair pledged
Britain's unqualified support for the United States in the impending war on terror.

The terrorist attacks of 11 September had led directly to a closer collaboration between Blair and the conservative US president George W. Bush. Blair's decision to support Bush's invasion of Iraq in 2003 alienated many of his supporters in Britain and the European Union. Twenty years earlier, most of the British public and press had supported Margaret Thatcher in her decision to stand up to the dictatorial Argentine government over its invasion of the Falkland Islands. But Blair's decision to stand up against a dictatorial regime in Iraq did not produce the same response, not the least reason of which was that the Iraqi dictator Saddam Hussein was mainly the enemy of the United States, not Britain. Nor was Hussein, however egregious his human rights abuses in Iraq, responsible for the terrorist attacks in 2001.

Blair's motives, which he has explained time and again, were well intentioned, based on the desire to end the reign of terror perpetuated by Hussein's brutal autocratic regime. Blair believed world leaders had an obligation to stand up to countries that threatened to destabilize world peace by developing weapons of mass destruction. But he, knowingly or unknowingly, greatly exaggerated Hussein's immediate military capacity and the stage of Iraq's weapons programme in a way that, in retrospect, would be seen as recklessly irresponsible. He was provided inaccurate information from British intelligence sources and sent British troops into harm's way based on fallacious information instead of asking for comprehensive verification. Blair's promise that the troops would be 'home by Christmas' was an unnerving and direct reminder of the start of the First World War, the length and catastrophic nature of which have mocked that same promise ever since it was first made in 1914 (though the body counts of the Iraq war would never compare to the sanguinary nature of the First World War).[1] The suspicion, which some critics voiced at the time, that Blair had already committed Britain to war prior to obtaining the falsified evidence used to support it has also cast a pall over the rhetoric employed by the prime minister to take Britain into war.

Then, in July 2003, David Kelly, a British scientist considered an expert on Iraq's military capacity, committed suicide after being identified as the author of a weapons report that contained the evidence on which Blair allegedly based his decision to go to war. The necessity of Blair's judicial exoneration on a charge of complicity in causing Kelly's suicide spoke volumes about the political quagmire into which Blair had sunk himself. Yet Blair responded to the allegations against him by insisting that the BBC retract its implied position that he had deceived the British public in leading it into war. The head of the BBC, Gavyn Davies, had to resign as a result of the implication that Blair was responsible for Kelly's death.

In 2005, a report by Brigadier Nigel Aylwin-Foster of the British army claimed that the US army in Iraq had trained its soldiers to kill as opposed to eliciting the support of the Iraqi people, further casting a pall on Blair's decision to support the United States, whose army, Foster also reported, was guilty of 'institutional racism'.[2] After the report about Iraq's nuclear capacity turned out to be wrong, they switched their justification to the overthrow of Hussein's regime. Critics regarded this as a dubious justification for war unless they planned to go after every brutal dictator – one that was unlikely to succeed unless they could win the hearts and minds of the Iraqi people, which the Aylwin-Foster report indicated was not happening. While the political situation in Iraq continued to deteriorate, the Afghanistan war became a protracted struggle. The Middle East imploded with civil war in Syria, leading to the rise of the radical Islamic State. With these developments, Blair's initial decision to support the Iraq war led to a further decline in his reputation in Britain. It looked more and more as if the United States and British had neither vision nor a plausible reason for waging war in Iraq. This consideration led to a military withdrawal that left the entire region more politically unstable than when they had gone to war, although the previous stability had been enforced by a dictator.

In 2003, Michael Howard replaced Iain Duncan Smith as head of the Conservative Party; Howard returned the Conservative Party to a programme consisting of tax cuts and diminished public spending. He also raised the issue of whether the UK should renegotiate its membership in the European Union, although the party was not yet ready for this step. Blair and Labour won re-election in 2005, causing Howard's resignation as leader of the Conservatives and his replacement by David Cameron.

In March 2007 Blair was briefly able to revel in one of his major accomplishments as prime minister with the signing of the power-sharing agreement in Northern Ireland. But by this time, in addition to the growing dissatisfaction over Iraq, Blair faced a challenge from fellow Labourite Gordon Brown over issues of ideology. Brown replaced Blair as prime minister in June 2007. Brown was a serious intellectual as well as a competent administrator, but he lacked Blair's charisma and took over a damaged and fractious party, making it uncertain how much longer he could keep Cameron and the Conservatives out of office.

Social trends

Rapid changes in technology continued to influence social trends in the early twenty-first century, mainly through the continued development of the internet and alterations in mobile phones and information devices. Changes in work patterns were a consequence, helping produce a shift away from older heavier industries to service industries, in particular tech support. Arthur McIvor writes in his book *Working Lives: Work in Britain since 1945*: 'In the early years of the twenty-first century it was perhaps the call centre that epitomized the almost apocalyptic vision of meaningless, degraded, monotonous and dehumanized work.'[3] McIvor points out that people have a tendency to romanticize the past and forget the vulnerability and alienation of workers that occurred in earlier times. Yet this is perhaps understandable, given the social inequalities that persist in the twenty-first century and the advantages retained by the wealthy, educated classes over the working classes. Race, ethnicity, and gender also remain an issue when it comes to employment opportunities, with women and minorities continuing to face disadvantages in the workplace.[4]

Yet the new economy has also created exciting opportunities and stoked the growth of multinational corporations doing business in Britain. These developments have engendered more diversity at the highest levels of business, especially those companies who place a premium on marketing and doing business with cultures around the world. In addition, with the ageing Baby Boomer generation living longer lives, healthcare has become one source of stable employment, with a corresponding expansion of job opportunities in the pharmaceutical industry.

In addition, Britain's involvement in the wars in Iraq and Afghanistan, despite their general unpopularity with the British public, has created employment opportunities, especially for groups such as women and ethnic minorities who might not have considered a military career in earlier periods. The British Army has an attractive website[5] designed solely to recruit women to enlist. According to the UK Armed Forces Annual Personnel Report in April 2014, the percentage of women in the regular armed forces was 9.9 per cent (up from 8.3 per cent in 2002), while the percentage of black and ethnic minority (BME) groups stood at 7.1 per cent.[6] In December 2015, David Cameron ordered the Ministry of Defence to open combat roles to women and to remove the remaining restrictions on the kinds of jobs permitted to women in the military. One significant difference between women and BME members of the armed services is that the RAF has attracted the highest numbers of women (14.3 per cent), whereas the BME groups are more represented in the army (10.3 per cent). In addition, women represent 15.3 per cent of the officer class, higher than the percentage in lower ranks, whereas the BME groups have a lower percentage of officers (2.4 per cent) than the percentage of members in lower ranks.[7]

Opportunities for higher education also expanded in the late twentieth and early twenty-first century, as growing numbers of young people from modest economic backgrounds sought education for an economy where factory jobs were in steep decline. As institutions of higher learning became open to a broad segment of the population, the jury is still out as to whether or not the universities have become too subject to market forces. There is some concern within academia that the need to prepare students for a competitive job market has come at the expense of the humanities.[8] These critics believe that the values of a liberal education might be more important for the well-being of the society in the long run than training for specific careers, though these are certainly not mutually exclusive.

Another notable social trend has seen a growing sense of disconnectedness from society despite, or perhaps because of, the ease with which people can communicate technologically with people from around the globe. Communication through texts, email, and social media sites such as Facebook, Twitter, Snapchat, and Instagram and the ubiquity of people looking at their phones was bound to have an effect on the social and interpersonal skills of the generation born after about 1990. Interestingly, a Rowntree Foundation Report in 2008 showed that young people turned to marijuana or cannabis primarily for the purposes of enhancing their own sociability.[9]

On the positive side, these social sites have allowed people to self-identify more and to choose their social associations from a broader spectrum. Social media has created the possibility of redefining one's identity, or even to create multiple identities, in a process that Nicole Ellison refers to as 'selective self-presentation'.[10] A poll conducted in 2007 by the Social Issues Research Centre revealed that 88 per cent of respondents surprisingly identified family as the group to which they felt they most belonged.[11] But this perception has been eclipsed by the reality of an extended network of friendships that form more of a basis for how people in the twenty-first century actually live their lives. Technology has become such a prominent part of the twenty-first-century milieu that it is easily taken for granted. Dating and marriage patterns have also been affected with more people meeting online or reconnecting with people that they knew and liked at school but in an earlier age might never have seen again.

Religion is one such way of choosing a group identity, especially for those left unfilled by the materialist values of a secular culture. Not all religious groups incline towards extremism; social media has brought together people with flexible and open-minded views on religion as well. Yet even these groups rely on science and technology to spread their message and communicate with one another.

The continuation of blatantly racist, anti-Semitic, and anti-Muslim sentiments into the twenty-first century after what Europe endured as a result of such attitudes in the twentieth century has definitely caused great concern and contributed to the radicalization of some British youth attracted by Islamic fundamentalism. This development is related to another social trend involving the growth of different ethnic groups who have entered the UK in increasing numbers in the twenty-first century. In 2014, the European Union approved full working rights for Romanians and Bulgarians, with a similar effect on immigration to that which occurred when Poles were granted the same status in 2004. In fact, as of 2014, Poles constituted the third largest minority ethnic group in Britain, behind only Indians and Pakistanis.[12] But the numbers of Romanians and Bulgarians are on the rise, totally 172,000 combined by the end of 2014.[13] This immigration actually represents a continuation of a trend of foreign immigration in the UK that dated to the end of the Second World War, another time at which a large number of Poles settled in the country. Nigel Farage's United Kingdom Independence Party (UKIP) has largely appealed to nativist sentiment and xenophobia. Farage himself expressed his discomfort at having Romanian neighbours, suggesting that Romanians are more likely to be criminals, a claim very similar to one made against Mexican immigrants by Donald Trump during the 2016 election campaign in the United States.

Young people are not immune to the appeal of parties like UKIP or to more extreme neofascist responses to immigration and multiculturalism, but for many of the youth in Britain and Ireland growing up in a more multicultural society has made them more tolerant and accepting of people different from themselves. One such indication of the level of interracial tolerance is the rise in the numbers of people who identify themselves as mixed race, which have doubled to 1.2 million people in the decade from 2001 to 2011. Indeed, the general approach towards religious and ethnic minorities in Britain since 2001, and especially after 2005, has been to promote assimilation and encourage them to think of themselves as British. But leaders have struggled to define what 'Britishness' exactly means. If it means, as the leader of the House of Commons, Jack Straw defined it in 2007, 'freedom, tolerance, plurality',[14] this would seem to associate 'Britishness' with 'multiculturalism', which could be taken to mitigate the sense of unity and assimilation that the government has sought to foster.

Finally, the twenty-first century has also seen two legal measures that together symbolize the continued decline of the British aristocracy, following the reconstitution of the House of Lords in the late twentieth century. In 2003, the Scottish Parliament passed a Land Reform Act that provided greater public access to lands on large private estates, while also enabling tenant farmers to purchase the lands on which

FIGURE 39 *Scottish Lion Rampant flag and girl at Dunotter Castle near Stonehaven, Scotland. 10 September 2014.*
Mark A. Leman/Moment Mobile/Getty Images.

they live, even if the landowner has no desire to sell the land. That was followed in 2004 by the Hunting Act of 2004 banning in England and Wales the hunting of wild mammals with dogs, (Scotland had already instituted such a ban two years earlier). This act was specifically aimed at the venerable tradition of the aristocratic fox hunt. The only place where fox hunting with hounds remains legal in the UK is in Northern Ireland, where progress, however, has been made on other fronts that seems at least equally significant.

The end of the Troubles in Northern Ireland?
Northern Ireland: British, Irish, or neither

The Good Friday Agreement of 1998 had been based on the principle of accepting religious differences and producing a power-sharing arrangement between Catholics and Protestants based on mutually agreed upon definitions of justice, equality, opportunity, and responsibility. The British government also reaffirmed its commitment to allowing Northern Ireland to leave the United Kingdom based on a popular vote. Catholics in Northern Ireland, however, have fewer incentives to want Northern Ireland to leave the UK, especially as conditions improve for them and discrimination evanesces.

The waning of the sectarian rivalry between Protestants and Catholics has opened the door to a more secularized society, which has had some surprising and interesting results. While rising secularism has helped to undermine religious differences, it has also tended to actually unite Protestant and Catholic leaders on the same side of a new moral divide. Gay marriage and more liberal abortion laws, for example, are two issues that have united the Catholic supporters of Sinn Féin and the Protestant members of the Democratic Unionist Party of Ian Paisley. Many Protestants in Northern Ireland have indicated that they would welcome a visit from Pope Francis to Belfast in 2018, an event that would still likely draw some Protestant protests but that would have been unthinkable until recently.

Northern Ireland has found it difficult to achieve its goal of moving beyond its past without ignoring it. In 2010, Northern Ireland prime minister Peter Robinson announced a strategy for ending segregation between Catholics and Protestants with the acronym of cohesion, sharing, and integration (CSI). But after it was derailed by the opposition on both sides, Robinson was forced to come up with a new proposal focusing on pedagogy. In addition, in 2013, a decision to convert the Maze, the prison where Bobby Sands had died during his hunger strike in 1981, into a centre for the study of peace and conflict resolution and a commercial area to house high-tech businesses caused controversy and brought the prison's controversial past into people's minds. The government commissioned Daniel Libeskind, who also worked on Ground Zero in Manhattan where the World Trade Center had stood and the Jewish Museum in Berlin, to design the centre in a way that reflects the complex story of the Troubles, but this has predictably created controversy over how that story would be told.[15]

In another controversial development, Sinn Féin leader Gerry Adams was arrested in 2014 based on testimony in an oral history project on the Troubles conducted at Boston College in the United States that linked him to IRA terrorist activity in the past. Adams's arrest threatened to derail the spirit of reconciliation that worked in South Africa by opening up the possibility of recriminations and accusations of past crimes on both sides. Adams denied his alleged involvement in IRA-ordered executions and accused the British of being involved in the effort to tarnish his reputation.

Despite these recurring issues, Protestants and Catholics have begun to reconstruct an identity based not on being British or Irish, but centred on their shared experiences in Northern Ireland. The history of Northern Ireland, though, has given it an identity at variance with how people in Britain or the Republic of Ireland identify with it and one that for the first time is an identity that all residents – Catholic, Protestant, and secular – have begun to embrace. In fact, even as migration from Northern Ireland has increased since the financial collapse of 2008, emigrants have taken with them their Northern Irish identity and expressed resentment at the negative stereotypes about their homeland, which has been reinforced by people who only associate it with the Troubles.

The latest census figures for Northern Ireland indicate the very real possibility that before long the Catholic population of the province will become a majority. In the 2011 census, the Protestant population declined to 48 per cent (down from 53 per cent ten years earlier), denoting the first time that Protestants had failed to constitute a majority of the population of Northern Ireland. Catholics have made up a majority of school-age children since 2001. But Catholics have also come to see themselves as having a Northern Irish identity separate from the Republic. Even if Catholics become a majority in Northern Ireland, its exodus from the UK is no longer guaranteed. One 2012 survey indicated that only one-third of Northern Irish Catholics supported uniting Northern Ireland with the Irish Republic, perhaps as a result of the economic problems afflicting the Republic since 2008.

The end of the Celtic Tiger and lessons from Ireland

The global financial crisis of 2008 hit Ireland particularly hard and brought the Celtic Tiger to a screeching halt. During the Celtic Tiger years, Ireland had attracted a great deal of foreign investment because of its low taxes and corporate-friendly environment. The governing Fíanna Fáil party rode the wave of this economic boom to political success, espousing a philosophy of individualism and laissez-faire capitalism reminiscent of Margaret Thatcher's philosophy in the UK in the 1980s. In 2004, when Poland and seven other countries from central and Eastern Europe joined the European Union, Ireland was one of only three countries, along with Sweden and the UK, to accept unrestricted numbers of immigrants from those new member-countries.

The economic achievements of the Celtic Tiger had helped Ireland to see itself as a proud, successful, modern country that was better off embracing the economic opportunities presented by modern capitalism than clinging to its past cultural heritage and retrograde traditions of nationalism. The economic failures of 2008 therefore hit Ireland particularly hard. In the winter of 2008, Fergus O'Donoghue expressed the sentiments of many Irish at the time when he wrote, 'We are ... bewildered by the swift change in our economic situation, angry with our government and unable to understand exactly what has gone wrong.'[16] But the warning signs were there years before; Ryan Thornton cautioned in the *Harvard International Review* in 2004 that 'the boom times are over', noting a drop in Ireland's annual economic growth rate from 8 per cent at the height of the Celtic Tiger to 2 per cent that year.[17]

The financial collapse in Ireland had a devastating impact on the housing industry in particular, leaving new housing developments unfinished and many houses abandoned while still under construction. Individuals who had put money down to buy or build these houses had little chance of recovering their investment or of seeing their houses completed. The problem was that businesses that had benefited from Ireland's low corporate tax rate invested large sums of money in housing or financial speculation, the two markets most affected by the economic downturn after 2008. The unemployment rate at the beginning of 2014 stood at 12.8 per cent and Ireland was beginning to relive the familiar story of watching people leaving the country for better economic opportunities elsewhere; between 2008 and 2014, almost 400,000 people had left Ireland, 90,000 between April 2012 and April 2013.[18]

As Ireland struggled to recover from the collapse of the Celtic Tiger, its people had learnt that they could not repose all its faith in the market or in unregulated financial institutions such as banks, investment companies, and stock markets. Ireland learnt that it could not ignore European Union stewardship when times are good and expect willing, unqualified assistance from the EU when hard times came. Ireland also learnt that one could not dispense with a system of financial checks and balances or expect one's political leaders to remain untainted by a society that operates on avarice and places so many opportunities and incentives for financial gain in their path. Fíanna Fáil leaders Bertie Ahern and his finance minister Charlie McCreevy had instituted policies intended to reduce the authority of central government and to further the strong record of economic prosperity during their administration, but some of these policies backfired and both were implicated in financial corruption scandals. Finally, Ireland learnt that its rate of investment in financial and housing markets could not be so far out of balance with the size of the rest of the Irish economy.[19]

Scotland and Wales in the twenty-first century

When Scots went to the polls in 1999 to elect their own Parliament for the first time since 1707, Labour won by a sizeable margin, taking fifty-six seats compared to thirty-five for the Scottish National Party, eighteen for the Conservatives, and seventeen for the Liberal Democrats. This was a moment of pride for Scots, some of whom viewed this as the next step towards independence and a victory for Scottish democracy. Scots gradually began to reaffirm their own distinct identity. In 2002, for example, Scottish journalist Neal Ascherson wrote that Scots tend to be 'communitarian rather than individualistic, democratic in their obsession with equality, patriarchal rather than spontaneous in their respect for authority, Spartan in their insistence that solidarity matters more than free self-expression'.[20] In elections to the Scottish Parliament in 2007, the Scottish National Party headed by Alex Salmond won forty-seven seats, one more than the Labour Party, and formed a minority government. In 2011, Scots again went to the polls and this time awarded the SNP sixty-nine seats, four more than were needed for an absolute majority in Parliament.

However, in September 2014, a referendum on Scottish independence resulted in 55 per cent of voters opting for Scotland remaining within the UK. The campaign leading up to the vote was bitter and vitriolic, with supporters of both sides heaping abuse on the other. On the economic side, pro-independence supporters argued that Scotland had enough resources to flourish as an independent country and deserved to be in charge of its own economic destiny. Those who supported a 'no' vote in the referendum expressed concern about the economic consequences of withdrawing

FIGURE 40 *UK supporters with flag.*
Image Source, DigitalVision.

from the UK. Those opposed to independence also stress that Scotland since joining the UK has never experienced the kind of oppression that has frequently justified independence movements in other places. As Christopher Whatley put it in a book published the year of the referendum:

> Has Scotland experienced anything like what has been observed in Estonia during the half-century of Soviet rule, where it was illegal to display the national flag or sing the nation's pre-war anthem (in Scotland's case, the challenge is to agree on a national anthem that is worth singing) or to talk or even dream of independence?[21]

However, the SNP, unlike say UKIP, has been careful not to present Scottish nationalism as an ethnic cause; for that reason it has even attracted a larger percentage of Pakistani support than from among the general population.[22] In other words, the SNP by claiming to represent the interests of all Scots may lead minority voters to support independence as a democratic initiative, not as a conservative nationalist cause tied to Scottish cultural identity.

More importantly, far from putting the matter to rest, the defeat seemed to galvanize the Scottish National Party and attract support to its cause. The month after the referendum failed to secure Scottish independence, new SNP leader and first minister Nicola Sturgeon declared that another referendum on Scottish independence was 'inevitable'. She singled out issues such as nuclear policy and the Cameron government's austerity policies as issues that would help keep the movement for Scottish independence alive. In January 2016, she followed up with a promise to renew the push for independence as part of her campaign for re-election. According to a YouGov poll conducted for the *Economist* the following spring, 48 per cent of British respondents believed that Scotland would be an independent country in 2035 compared to only 34 per cent who did not. According to that same poll, 49 per cent of English respondents thought that Scottish independence would be bad for the rest of the UK. But neither the English nor the Welsh cared that much about Scotland; 10 per cent or less were willing to pay anything to keep Scotland in or get Scotland out of the union.[23]

Predictions before the Scottish referendum focused on the potential effects of a yes or a no vote for Wales and the rest of the UK. It was widely assumed that Scottish independence would galvanize the Welsh independence movement and lead to the further break-up of the UK, whereas a no vote would put the matter to rest and strengthen the federation of the UK. The effects of the referendum's defeat, at least up to the point of this writing, have been far more ambiguous. One factor perhaps hindering a stronger independence movement for Wales is the division between North and South Wales, which the Welsh are much more sensitive to than the English. For example, in a posted comment on the *Guardian*'s website, Richard Kelly of Flintshire suggested that if the English are serious about devolution they might devolve power to a region comprising western England and northeastern Wales, which he argued have much more in common than North and South Wales.

When Scotland and Wales were granted their own parliaments, the federal government retained control over immigration policy, foreign policy and defence, broadcasting, and broad constitutional and economic matters. The Scottish Parliament also took over administration and legislation in the domestic areas of healthcare, education, transportation, housing, sports, and culture, inter alia. The complicated Government of Wales Act of 2006 created a separate Welsh executive branch and devolved additional authority to the Welsh legislature, but Wales still did not have the kind of political autonomy granted to Scotland. The Scottish Parliament obtained the power to tax, unlike the Welsh Parliament, for example. Yet calls for independence remain stronger in Scotland than in Wales, which continues to emphasize its unique cultural identity.

Then there is the concern that the kind of identity politics promoted by the devolution and independence movements provides a limited range of choices for political or cultural identity that are removed from the problems of quotidian existence for many ordinary people. Matthew McGuire cites the 2004 novel *You Have to be Careful in the Land of the Free* by James Kelman as an example of postmodern Scottish literature in which the main character finds the entire issue of his Scottish identity meaningless in the face of his own personal existential crisis in the midst of a globalizing society.[24]

Still, recent developments throughout the UK have led to a great deal of talk and angst about the decline of 'Britain'. Some individuals within the constituent parts of the UK have begun to redefine what it means to be British by reviving 'Celtic' as a term of identity, a trend that derives support from recent DNA studies that have confirmed how closely related the English, Welsh, Scots, and Irish are dating back to the first human settlements in the British Isles. Author Ian Bradley has gone so far as to redefine British identity in spiritual terms and noted that 'both Ireland and Wales have contributed disproportionately to what might be called the spiritual treasury of Britishness, especially in respect of religious writings, hymns, and church music'.[25] Such a spiritual identity, however, has been largely lacking in the scandal-ridden nature of British politics in the twenty-first century.

Scandals and what they reveal about politics and society in the twenty-first century

Political scandals are rife in the contemporary age, but there is something about recent scandals that reveals something deeper about British political culture in the first part of the twenty-first century. Financial and sex scandals are perhaps nothing new, but scandals involving technology, such as the phone-hacking scandal perpetrated by unscrupulous journalists and child sexual abuse scandals reaching to the highest levels of church and state in Ireland and the UK have created an even wider breach between the general public and those in positions of authority.

Financial scandals have hurt both political parties and seem to have become as much a feature of contemporary politics as patronage was in the eighteenth century. In 2009 charges claimed to the expense accounts of MPs were leaked to the *Daily Telegraph*, casting Parliament in a particularly bad light. The 2009 scandal led to widespread firings, retirements, and resignations, including that of the Speaker of the House of Commons, Michael Martin; five Labour MPs and two Conservative peers were convicted of crimes in the scandal and spent time in prison.

Even if both parties are implicated in a financial scandal, the public tends to blame the one in power more, so it is reasonable to assume that the financial irregularities of 2009 played a part in the Conservative victory of 2010. Yet things did not improve much under the new Conservative administration. Practically as soon as the Conservatives took over, David Laws, Cameron's chief secretary to the Treasury, resigned over irregularities in his expenses, making his career as a cabinet member one of the briefest in history. In April 2014 Iain Martin of the *Telegraph* published a column on 'the scandal that will not die', alluding specifically to the resignation of Cameron's culture secretary, Maria Miller, amid charges that she had used government expenses to make mortgage payments on her London house.

The 'reformed' House of Lords has continued to be a target of criticism and ridicule to the point that the only solution may be to eventually abolish the upper House altogether. One tabloid sting caught Lord Sewell, the chair in an ethics committee, on camera snorting cocaine from the breasts of a prostitute. Aside from this notorious example, the House of Lords continued to house scrofulous members, including some who had confessed to crimes, ranging from perjury and perverting the course of justice (Jeffrey Archer) to false accounting of parliamentary expenses claims (John Taylor and Paul White).

The state has failed British society in other ways as well. The phone-hacking scandal of 2006–11 not only cast the media – not necessarily a highly respected group to begin with – but also the government and the police in a bad light. A police investigation known as 'Operation Weeting' that was launched in 2011 uncovered over 4,000 victims of illegal phone hacking, that targeted not only celebrities and members of the royal family, but also families of crime victims in a horrific violation of individuals' rights to privacy. The most notorious instance involved the hacking of the phone of Milly Dowler, a schoolgirl later found to be murdered. In essence, journalists gained access to voice mails and text messages that were then used to further stories for the sole purpose of selling newspapers. One tabloid implicated in the scandal, the *News of the World*, was forced to shut down completely, with its editor, Andy Coulson, convicted for conspiracy to hack phones. Publishing and media mogul Rupert Murdoch and his younger son James, chief executive of News Corp's British newspaper group at the time when the phone hacking occurred, both had to testify before parliamentary committees, where they denied knowledge of or culpability in the phone-hacking scandal, but it furthered their already shady reputations nonetheless. The fact that Murdoch had close ties with political leaders in both main parties meant that the scandal implicated government leaders as well, especially since Coulson was a former press secretary for David Cameron. Another prominent figure indicted in the scandal, Rebekah Brooks, had also worked as a spokesperson for Cameron, was friendly with Tony Blair, and kept a horse owned by the Metropolitan Police on her farm.

Even more disturbing have been the revelations of widespread sexual abuse of children by Catholic priests, particularly in Ireland and by prominent figures in England, including figures in the media – popular entertainers like Jimmy Savile, Parliament, and even the Royal Family. The discrediting of the Catholic Church in Ireland resulted not only from the revelations of abuse, but also from the realization of the number of priests and church officials who knew of the abuse and kept priests in their positions or simply transferred them to positions elsewhere, not dismissing them or reporting them for fear that the scandal would become public. The Murphy Report on the Dublin archdiocese criticized the church for its failure even to apply its own standards of canon law in dealing with the offences of its clergy. Whatever apologies church officials made in the scandal sounded hollow, since it was clear that public exposure was the only reason that they were doing so or taking any action to prevent such occurrences in the future.

Some of the worst revelations of sexual abuse came from the report that Professor Alexis Jay made to the Rotherham Borough Council in August 2014, revealing that at least 1,400 girls had been the victims of sexual exploitation between 1997 and 2013, mostly by gangs of Pakistani men. This report followed an explosive report done by investigative journalist Andrew Norfolk of the *Times*. Norfolk's articles indicated that the practice went beyond Rotherham, and contained similar revelations about the towns of Oxford, Derby, Oldham, and Rochdale. Norfolk wrote of the widespread practice of mainly Pakistani and Bangladeshi men 'grooming' young, preteen white girls for sex work.[26] In one trial resulting from the investigation, six individuals (four men and two women) were charged with '51 counts of abuse including rape, indecent assault, false imprisonment, abduction and procurement of girls for prostitution or for sex with another'.[27]

One scandal seemed inevitably to follow another; when the Cameron government appointed individuals as head of two inquiries into systemic child sexual abuse in the media and government with family connections to some of the accused, it immediately raised suspicions of a government cover-up. Making matters worse, on 5 July 2015 the Home Office startlingly acknowledged that it had somehow misplaced 114 files from the 1980s that contained information about sexual abuse allegations in Westminster against at least ten politicians, some of whom were still in office at the time. On 6 July Sir Norman Tebbit, former chairman of the Conservative Party, made the stunning acknowledgement that a political cover-up of sexual abuse charges 'may well have' occurred during the 1980s. Tebbit said that 'people thought that the establishment was to be protected'.[28]

There is one unvarnished way to measure political engagement among the general public: voter participation rates in general elections. The UK Political Info website shows that voter participation rates peaked in 1950 at 83.9 per cent, but remained relatively high until 1992 in which 77.7 per cent of the electorate turned up at the

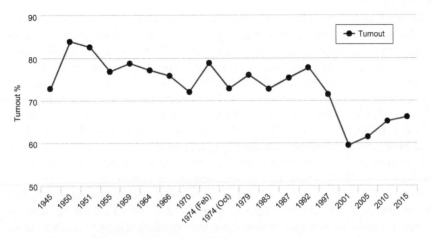

FIGURE 41 *General election turnout since 1945.*

polls. Apathy seemed to set in during the 1990s, with the biggest decline occurring between the 1997 and 2001 elections to a post-war low of 59.4 per cent in the latter. Voter turnout has increased in every election since 2001, with 66.1 per cent of the electorate voting in the 2015 election. One might have expected the cumulative effects of these scandals to be greater voter apathy, but instead they seem to have contributed to greater voter discontent, reflected in the rise of UKIP and the Liberal Democrats, both of whom provided more voter options to the traditional diarchy of Labour and Conservative.

The UK and the future of the European Union

David Cameron was forced by pressure from UKIP and within his own party to make a campaign pledge in the 2015 election that he would hold a referendum on Britain's EU membership by the end of 2017 if he were returned to office, which he was. Cameron was true to his word and a referendum was held on 23 June 2016. Cameron, who did not personally support leaving Europe and hoped that a vote would put the issue to rest once and for all, had badly miscalculated. By a margin of approximately 52 to 48 per cent, the British people voted to leave Europe. A majority of voters in England and Wales cast their ballots in favour of leaving the EU, while a significant majority in Scotland and Northern Ireland voted in favour of remaining part of Europe. Tony Blair wrote in his 2010 memoirs that for him, 'Europe was a simple issue. ... I supported the Europe ideal, but even if I hadn't, it was utterly straightforward: in a world of new emerging powers, Britain needed Europe in order to exert influence and advance its interests.'[29] Blair retained some of the idealism that sparked the creation of the European Community in the first place in the aftermath of two world wars that convinced European integrationists that they would be better off united than divided, not only from a security standpoint but economically as well. The rest of Britain did not necessarily agree and Blair was among those voicing his disappointment with the Brexit (short for 'Britain's exit' from the EU) vote.

The fact is that Britain has never fully embraced EU membership as much as some other European countries, as evidenced by its failure to adopt the euro as its standard currency and the requirement that its citizens still need to carry British passports instead of European identity cards to travel in Europe. It was partly the prospect of diminishing the special relationship between the UK and the United States if Britain were to invest itself fully in closer ties to Europe and partly pride in its own national traditions of independence as an island nation that have consistently worked against the British public embracing EU membership more fully. In 2009, Daniel Hannan, a Conservative representing southeast England in the European Parliament, called the 'unbroken decline in turnout since the first elections to the European Parliament were held in 1979 ... a serious embarrassment for Euro-integrationists'.[30] One of Hannan's main criticisms of the EU was its anti-democratic structure, in which the only legislation that could be proposed had to come from a board of twenty-seven appointed commissioners rather than from the popularly elected members of the EU parliament itself. Those who supported Brexit pointed to the fact that Britain did not join the Europe until 1973 and could simply return to a relationship with the EU that was not based on membership within it.

On the other side, some businesses feared job losses and a decline in foreign investment should Britain exit the EU. A 2015 report done by a group called Open Europe calculated that if the UK withdrew from the European Union that its GDP would drop by 2.2 per cent by 2030.[31] The need for concerted action on such issues affecting the future of the Continent as climate change was another argument offered by the 'Remain' campaign for staying within the EU. Roger Liddle, a life peer who had previously served as Blair's adviser on European policy, wrote a short book to correct the 'Euroskeptic perception of Brussels ... as an over-mighty agent of bureaucracy and regulation', which, he argued, 'flows from a complete misunderstanding of the difference between a free trade area and the much deeper economic integration that a single market requires'.[32] Writing in *Foreign Affairs* in 2015, Anan Menand argued that

> only the EU possesses structures to foster cooperation on everything from trade policy to sanctions to the defense industry. In a complex world, economic and security problems are intricately intertwined, and only a comprehensive approach to them has any chance of success.[33]

Cameron himself sought to use the leverage provided by a referendum and the threat of withdrawal to renegotiate British membership in the EU on more favourable terms. Cameron's agenda for negotiations with the EU mainly centred on additional deregulation and increased free trade opportunities. One of the problems with a renegotiated treaty, as Denis McShane has pointed out, is that it would require the approval of each of the governments of the twenty-seven member-countries of the EU.[34] This would also hinder any attempt by Britain to rejoin the EU, after its presumed exit. Populists viewed the EU as an anti-democratic, top-down organization and were not open to the kind of half-measures Cameron offered to negotiate.

Furthermore, the serious refugee crisis in Europe, first from North Africa and then from Syria, has caused much additional strain in the relationships among EU countries, including the UK. In 2014, the British erected security fencing at the entrance to the Channel Tunnel leading to France to keep potential refugees out of the country; Hungary adopted similar measures on its borders. Even Germany, which was one of the most receptive to accepting migrants to help with the humanitarian crisis caused by the displaced populations from the Syrian civil war, began to have second thoughts after a wave of physical assaults on women in Cologne on New Year's Eve in 2015 allegedly perpetrated by some of the recent arrivals. The growing divisions in Europe over the refugee crisis have shown cracks in EU unity, particularly between France and Germany, playing into the hands of Brexit advocates. Furthermore, the refugee crisis, along with the economic negotiations with troubled countries like Greece and Portugal, has preoccupied EU leaders on the Continent to such an extent that they took relatively little interest in threats from the UK to withdraw from the Union.

Then there was the issue of what Brexit might mean for the UK, specifically whether this would hasten support for Scottish independence since so many Scots clearly wanted to remain within the EU. Nicola Sturgeon, who replaced Alex Salmond as leader of the Scottish National Party after the defeat of independence in the 2014 referendum, said she would demand an immediate referendum on Scottish independence if Britain voted to leave the EU. Wales and Northern Ireland expressed concern, along with Scotland, over the use of the EU's development fund to channel financial assistance to wealthier countries instead of reserving it for those with the greatest need. While it seems clear at this writing that Wales will likely remain politically united with England, both Northern Ireland and Scotland may have already taken steps to leave the UK by the time that this book appears in print.

Furthermore, the possibility of Britain leaving the EU raised questions about whether it would mean an even closer relationship or dependence on the United States or whether it simply would be seen as, as Tony Blair feared, 'part of British eccentricity, something to be amused by, a "good old Brits" type of thing'.[35] In the end, perhaps the best argument for remaining within Europe came from John Peet, writing in the *Economist* in December 2015: 'Were Britain to walk out of Europe but find life outside uncomfortable, it would surely never be allowed to rejoin. If it decided to stay, however, it could always change its mind in a decade or two.'[36] This nuance was lost on a British public that had enough reasons to want to leave Europe that the last thing on their mind was potential obstacles to rejoining. It is a tricky thing to write history in the midst of significant changes unfolding, as is the case with the British Isles currently. But history is crucial to understanding those changes, and, since history is never finished, if one waited on events to write it, it would never get written at all.

Downton Abbey and the continuing importance of British and Irish culture

The political and social changes affecting twenty-first-century Britain have had a significant impact on British culture. Britain's involvement in the Iraq and Afghanistan wars and the war on terror; the rise of home-grown Islamic fundamentalism; political questions regarding devolution and the future of the UK; the financial collapse of 2008; and concerns about the long-term implications of technological change have all affected the ways in which contemporary writers and creative artists have engaged with their material.

In John Le Carré's 2013 novel, *A Delicate Truth*, for example, Islamic terrorists replaced his earlier villains: 'I would basically describe Punter as your jihadist Pimpernel par excellence, Paul, not to say your will-o'-the-wisp. He eschews all means of electronic communication, including cell phones and harmless-seeming emails'.[37] On the other hand, in his novel *Capital* (2012), John Lanchester illuminates the unwanted attention attracted to law-abiding Muslims by the jihadists, along with Britain's handling of the refugee crisis:

> Quentina's situation was this. In Harare in the summer of 2003 she had been arrested, interrogated, beaten, released by the police, snatched by goons on her way home, told that she had seventy-two hours to leave the country, then beaten and left by the roadside. After being treated in hospital she had been smuggled out

of the country by missionaries, and came to England on a student visa which she had always intended to overstay. To make a long story short, she had overstayed on purpose, applied for asylum, been rejected, been arrested and sentenced to deportation, but the judge at the final appeal had ruled that she could not be sent back to Zimbabwe because there were grounds for thinking that she would be killed. ... She had no right to work and could claim only subsistence-level benefits, but she couldn't be imprisoned and deported. She was not a citizen of the UK but she could not go anywhere else. She was a non-person.[38]

Contemporary British Muslim writers reject the term Islamic literature, not only because of the negative stereotypes that derive from the war on terror, but also because they reject Islam as a monolithic construction. Hanif Kureishi, the author of a provocative novel called *The Body* (2011), in which an ageing man takes advantage of changing technology to have his brain implanted in the body of a younger man, told Claire Chambers in an interview for her 2011 book on Muslim writers, 'People are always asking for comments on, say, the position of the Muslim in London today, and I think, "I don't know anything about it and no longer have anything new to say."'[39] Another writer, Tariq Ali, told Chambers, 'I don't accept this way of looking at Islam exclusively through the prism of the current need of the West to vilify Islam.'[40] Salman Rushdie, who explored issues related to Muslim identity more explicitly in his 1988 bestseller, *The Satanic Verses*, continues to use elements of fantasy and magical realism to address contemporary religious and philosophical issues in *Two Years Eight Months and Twenty-Eight Nights* (2015). Literature has been a means for each of these authors of Muslim background to address larger human concerns in which they have not allowed their religious identity to define them or their works.

Two of the most important British novels of the twenty-first century deal with the theme of the fallout from the 2008 financial crisis and the ethos that caused it. In Martin Amis's *Lionel Asbo: State of England* (2013), the title character carries the nickname 'Mean Mr. Mustard' (from a Beatles song) and has 'served five prison terms, two months for Receiving Stolen Property, two months for Extortion with Menaces, two months for Receiving Stolen Property, two months for Extortion with Menace, and two months for Receiving Stolen Property'.[41] But Asbo makes some good investments, instructing 'his young squad of free-market idealists to be as aggressive as possible', leading to a windfall that allows him to spend 'nine million pounds, nearly all of it on craps, blackjack, and roulette (there was also the unused Bentley "Aurora", and a seven-figure clothes bill)', within three weeks of getting released from prison.[42] Lanchester's *Capital* also reflects the cultural atmosphere and perverse values surrounding the financial crisis of 2008, describing the surreal economic climate that preceded the crash: 'It was like Texas during the oil rush, except that instead of sticking a hole in the ground to make fossil fuel shoot up from it, all people had to do was sit there and imagine the cash value of their homes rattling upwards so fast that they couldn't see the figures go round.'[43]

The pre-eminent Irish novelist of the twenty-first century would have to be Colm Tóibín, of whose novels Kathleen Costello-Sullivan has written that they tend 'to engage and contest the dominant political construction of the Irish citizen'.[44] Declan, the central character of his 1999 novel *The Blackwater Lightship* is a young man afflicted with AIDs, who attempts to bring his estranged family together; his sister and mother are divided by 'conflicts [that] were too sharp and too deeply embedded for him to fathom',[45] perhaps referring to the internecine divisions within Ireland itself. In Tóibín's critically acclaimed novel, *Brooklyn* (2009), the protagonist Eilis's life as an immigrant to 1950s New York is contrasted to her life in Ireland, with its restrictions on social life and her personal identity, in a way that does not oppress the reader or carry an overt political message independent of the story itself. Joseph O'Connor's *Ghost Light* (2011) traces the life of a young woman defying the social strictures of her time in early-twentieth-century Dublin to her later experiences in New York and London. The Troubles in Northern Ireland have provided the subject matter for many novels and films, but one of the most interesting and relevant works of contemporary fiction emanating from the North is a historical novel set in nineteenth-century Belfast by Glenn Patterson, *The Mill for Grinding Old People* (2012).

The enduring appeal of British culture can be seen in the continuing popularity of British films, perhaps most notably *The King's Speech*, which won the Academy Award for Best Picture in 2011. Although released shortly before the period covered by this concluding chapter, *The Lord of the Rings* trilogy has become a virtual cottage industry unto itself, as have films based on the novels of Jane Austen (*Pride and Prejudice*, 2005), about the life of Jane Austen (*Becoming Jane*, 2007), or the fictional lives of fans of Jane Austen, *The Jane Austen Book Club* (2007) and *Austenland* (2013), just to name a few. This is not to mention television films or miniseries made since 2004 based on the Austen novels *Sense and Sensibility*, *Mansfield Park*, *Emma*, *Northanger Abbey*, and *Persuasion*.

In television, probably the most significant cultural phenomenon was the surprise hit series, *Downton Abbey*, a melodramatic soap opera created and written by Julian Fellows, portraying the separate worlds but intertwined lives of a wealthy aristocratic family and their servants in early-twentieth-century England. As popular as *Downton Abbey* was for its six-season run from 2010 to 2015, it produced a backlash for its sentimental portrayal of a world that featured such stark class differences and the way in which the landed aristocratic Grantham family appeared in a generally sympathetic light. The show drew unfavourable comparisons among critics to the previous series on the English aristocracy such as *Brideshead Revisited*, based on the novel by Evelyn Waugh, and *Upstairs, Downstairs*. But the series did not ignore the social inequalities of the period and its portrayal of a rapidly changing time could account for much of its appeal in another new century which seemed to be experiencing changes just as far-reaching.

Other notable British series included *Hinterland* and *Broadchurch*, both of which premiered in 2013. *Hinterland* introduced viewers across Britain to life in rural Wales from the vantage point of a troubled English detective named Mathias, played by Richard Harrison, exiled to the region to escape his past and ostensibly to find meaning amid the hardy and unpretentious Welsh people. A similar lead character named Alec Hardy (David Tennant) dominates the series *Broadchurch*, which centres on a murder investigation into the death of a young boy and the impact that the murder and the investigation have on individual members of the community and the town as a whole.

If these two series have a dark side, they are nothing compared to the bleak plays of the Irish playwright Tom Murphy, a trilogy of which were performed at the London Festival in 2012: *Conversations on a Homecoming*, *A Whistle in the Dark*, and *Famine*. However, not all playwrights portray Irish life and history in such stark terms as Murphy does, as is illustrated in the plays of Brian Friel and Enda Walsh, for example.

In Scotland, culture was frequently put to nationalistic uses, following up on the success of 1995's biopic about William Wallace, *Braveheart*. In 2004, Edwin Morgan, appointed 'Poet for Scotland' by the newly devolved Scottish government, rewarded his benefactors with a translation of a fourteenth-century poem commemorating the Scottish victory at the Battle of Bannockburn in 1314. John Corbett finds in Morgan's translation a 'more nuanced revision of the clichés of the old enmity, and one that has uneasy contemporary relevance', based on its tragic depiction of the bloodshed and events that actually led to Scotland's independence at that time.[46]

This is perhaps a good example on which to end a book which has attempted to explore many of the complex ways in which culture has intertwined with political and social realities to form the multilayered fabric that defined life and politics in the history of the British Isles from the prehistoric period to the present. If the past is indeed prologue, the history of the British Isles in the twenty-first century will be just as complex, challenging, and fascinating as the people in these islands continue to define and redefine their cultural and political identity.

NOTES

Introduction

1 Dale Hoak, ed. (1995), *Tudor Political Culture*, Cambridge: Cambridge University Press, p. 1.

2 Ibid., p. xix.

3 Steven G. Ellis and Sarah Barber (eds) (1995), *Conquest and Union: Fashioning a British State, 1485–1725*, London: Longman, p. 3.

4 Tom Nairn (2011), *The Enchanted Glass: Britain and Its Monarchy*, rev. 2nd ed., London: Verso, p. xii.

5 Anthony Sampson (2004), *Who Runs This Place? The Anatomy of Britain in the 21st Century*, London: John Murray, p. 32.

6 Hugh Kearney (2006), *The British Isles: A History of Four Nations*, 2nd ed., Cambridge: Cambridge University Press, p. 1.

7 Raphael Samuel (1998), *Island Stories: Unravelling Britain: Theatres of Memory, Volume II*, edited by Alison Light, London: Verso, p. 61.

8 Andrew Sullivan (1999), 'There Will Always Be an England', *New York Times Magazine*, 21 February, p. 40.

9 John Ormond (1988), *The Divided Kingdom*, London: Constable, p. 11.

10 Selina Todd (2014), 'Class, Experience, and Britain's Twentieth Century', *Social History*, 39, 492–3.

11 Tom Nairn (2000), *After Britain: New Labour and the Return of Scotland*, London: Granta Books, p. 200.

Chapter 1

1 Julian Thomas (2013), *The Birth of Neolithic Britain: An Interpretive Account*, Oxford: Oxford University Press, p. 419.

2 Barry Cunliffe (2007), 'Continent Cut off by Fog: Just How Insular is Britain?', *Scottish Archaeological Journal*, 29, 99–112.

3 Chris Stevens, Dorian Fuller, and Martin Carver (2012), 'Did Neolithic farming fail? The case for a Bronze Age agricultural revolution in the British Isles', *Antiquity*, 86, 707–22.

4 Brian Dolan (2014), 'Beyond Elites: Reassessing Irish Iron Age Society', *Oxford Journal of Archaeology*, 33, 361–77.

5 Timothy Davill and Geoff Wainwright (2014), 'Beyond Stonehenge: Carn Menyn Quarry and the Origin and Date of Bluestone Extraction in the Preseli Hills of South-west Wales', *Antiquity*, 88, 1099.

6 Kate Ravilious (2015), 'Under Stonehenge', *Archaeology*, 68, 31.

7 Martin Borosan (2002), 'The Architecture of Enlightenment', *Building Material*, 8, 59–60.

8 See David Clarke (2003), 'Once Upon a Time Skara Brae was Unique,' in I. Armit, E. Murphy, E. Neilis, and D. Simpson (eds), *Neolithic Settlement in Ireland and Western Britain*, Belfast: Oxbow Books, pp. 84–92.

9 Fraser Hunter (2012), 'War in Prehistory and the Impact of Rome', in E. M. Spiers, J. A. Craig, and M. J. Strickland (eds), *A Military History of Scotland*, Edinburgh: Edinburgh Press, pp. 45–6.

10 Andrew P. Fitzpatrick (2007), 'The Amesbury Archer and the Boscombe Bowmen: Men of Stonehenge', in Brian M. Fagan (ed.), *Discovery! Unearthing the New Treasures of Archaeology*, London: Thames & Hudson, p. 42.

11 Ronald Hutton (2013), *Pagan Britain*, New Haven: Yale University Press, pp. 204–7.

12 Jarretta Lobell (2014), 'Oldest Bog Body', *Archaeology*, 67, 28.

13 Loretta Barnard, Monica Berton, Annette Carter, Dannielle Doggett, Judith Simpson, and Marie-Louise Taylor (2007), *The World Encyclopedia of Archaeology*, New York: Firefly Books, p. 139.

14 Quoted in 'Scottish prehistoric mummies made from jigsaw of body parts' (2011), http://www.bbc.com/news/science-environment-14575729.

15 Peter Rowley-Conwy (2007), *From Genesis to Prehistory: The Archaeological Three Age System and Its Contested Reception in Denmark, Britain, and Ireland*, Oxford: Oxford University Press, p. 3.

16 T. Douglas Price (2013), *Europe before Rome: A Site-by-Site Tour of the Stone, Bronze, and Iron Ages*, Oxford: Oxford University Press, p. 289.

17 J. P. Mallory (2013), *The Origins of the Irish*, London: Thames & Hudson, p. 270.

Chapter 2

1 Nennius (2008), *History of the Britons*, translated by J. A. Giles, London: Forgotten Books, p. 14.

2 Tacitus (1963), *Dialogus, Agricola, Germania*, translated by William Peterson, London: William Heinemann, p. 175.

3 Tacitus (1971), *The Annals of Imperial Rome*, translated by Michael Grant, rev. ed. London: Penguin, p. 329.

4 Quita Mould (2011), 'Domestic Life', in Lindsay Allason-Jones (ed.), *Artefacts in Roman Britain: Their Purpose and Use*, Cambridge: Cambridge University Press, p. 157.

5 John Wacher (2000), *A Portrait of Roman Britain*, London: Routledge, p. 50.

6 A. G. Brown, I. Meadows, S. D. Turner, and D. Mattingly (2001), 'Roman Vineyards in Britain: Strategic and Palynological Data from Wollaston in the Nene Valley, England', *Antiquity*, 75, 745–57.

7 J. P. Wild (2002), 'The Textile Industries of Roman Britain', *Brittania*, 33, 8.

8 Hella Eckardt, Gundula Muldner, and Mary Lewis (2014), 'People on the Move in Roman Britain', *World Archaeology*, 46, 537.

9 Adam Rogers (2013), *Water and Roman Urbanism: Towns, Waterscapes, Land Transformation and Experience in Roman Britain*, Leiden: Brill, p. 218.

10 Lindsay Allason-Jones (2011), 'Recreation', in Lindsay Allason-Jones (ed.), *Artefacts in Roman Britain: Their Purpose and Use,* Cambridge: Cambridge University Press, p. 240.

11 R. S. O. Tomlin (2011), 'Writing and Communication', in Lindsay Allason-Jones (ed.), *Artefacts in Roman Britain: Their Purpose and Use*, Cambridge: Cambridge University Press, p. 134.

12 Ronald Hutton (2013), *Pagan Britain*, New Haven: Yale University Press, p. 230.

13 Lucy J. E. Cramp, Richard P. Evershed, and Hella Ecklar (2011), 'What was a Mortarium used for? Organic Residues and Cultural Change in Iron Age and Roman Britain', *Antiquity*, 85, 1339.

14 Ibid., 1347.

15 Wendy A. Morrison (2013), 'A Fresh Eye on Familiar Objects: Rethinking Toiletry Sets in Roman Britain', *Oxford Journal of Archaeology*, 32, 221–30. Morrison argues that some of these cosmetic or toiletry items could have been used in the treatment of an eye disease known as trachoma that was particularly common in Roman Britain.

16 Lisa M. Bitel (1996), *Land of Women: Tales of Sex and Gender from Early Ireland*, Ithaca and London: Cornell University Press.

17 Gildas (1978), *The Ruin of Britain and Other Works*, edited by Michael Winterbottom, London: Phillimore, p. 17.

18 For example, Edward James (2001), *Britain in the First Millenium*, London: Hodder Education, pp. 66–7.

19 Peter Woodward and Ann Woodward (2004), 'Dedicating the Town: Urban Foundation Deposits in Roman Britain', *World Archaeology*, 36, 77–8.

20 Anthony King (2005), 'Animal Remains from Temples in Roman Britain', *Britannia*, 36, 334.

21 See, for example, 'The Crow on the Cradle', by the twentieth-century English songwriter Sidney Bertram Carter. The song has been covered by numerous artists.

22 Gildas, *The Ruin of Britain and Other Works*, p. 19.

23 Ben Croxford (2003), 'Iconoclasm in Roman Britain?', *Britannia*, 34, 81–95.

24 Lawrence Kepple (2004), 'A Roman Bath-House at Duntocher on the Antonine Wall', *Britannia*, 35, 205, 208.

25 Mike McCarthy (2005), 'Social Dynamics on the Northern Frontier of Roman Britain', *Oxford Journal of Archaeology*, 24, 56.

26 Bede (1968), *A History of the English Church and People*, translated by Leo Sherley Price; revised by R. E. Lathan, Harmondsworth, England: Penguin, p. 53.

27 Robin Fleming (2010), *Britain after Rome: The Fall and Rise 400 to 1070*, London: Penguin, p. 41.

28 Quoted in David Mattingly (2007), *An Imperial Possession: Britain in the Roman Empire, 54 BC–AD 409*, London: Penguin, p. 530.

29 John Moreland (2011), 'Land and Power from Roman Britain to Anglo-Saxon England?', *Historical Materialism*, 19, 181.

30 James Campbell (2011), 'The Romans to the Norman Conquest, 500 BC–AD 1066', in Jonathan Clark (ed.), *A World By Itself: A History of the British Isles,* London: Pimlico, p. 12.

31 Alan Lane (2014), 'Wroxter and the End of Roman Britain', *Antiquity*, 88, 501–15.

32 Martin Henig (2002), 'Review of *The Decline and Fall of Roman Britain*, by Neil Faulkner (Stroud: Tempus, 2001)', *English Historical Review*, 117, 442–3.

33 Michael E. Jones (1996), *The End of Roman Britain*, Ithaca: Cornell University Press, p. 111.

34 Ibid., pp. 128–9, 139.

35 Jane Webster (2001), 'Creolizing the Roman Provinces', *American Journal of Archaeology*, 105, 209.

36 Hugh Kearney (2006), *The British Isles: A History of Four Nations*, 2nd ed., Cambridge: Cambridge University Press, p. 32.

Chapter 3

1 *Beowulf: A Verse Translation* (2004), translated by Michael Alexander, rev. ed., London: Penguin Books, p. 51.

2 Nennius (2008), *History of the Britons*, translated by J. A. Giles, London: Forgotten Books, p. 38.

3 *The Annals of Ulster*, http://www.ucc.ie/celt/online/T100001A/.

4 Lisa M. Bitel (1996), *Land of Women: Tales of Sex and Gender from Early Ireland*, Ithaca and London: Cornell University Press, pp. 60–5.

5 Bede (1968), *A History of the English Church and People*, translated by Leo Sherley Price; revised by R. E. Lathan, Harmondsworth, England: Penguin, p. 56.

6 Robin Fleming (2010), *Britain After Rome: The Fall and Rise 400 to 1070*, London: Penguin, p. 32.

7 Andres Siegfried Dobat (2006), 'The King and his Cult: The Axe-hammer from Sutton Hoo and its Implications for the Concept of Sacral Leadership in Early Medieval Europe', *Antiquity*, 80, 883.

8 Carly Hilts (2014), 'Rethinking the Staffordshire Hoard: Piecing Together the Wealth of Anglo-Saxon Kings', *Current Archaeology*, http://www.archaeology.co.uk/articles/features/rethinking-the-staffordshire-hoard-piecing-together-the-wealth-of-anglo-saxLon-kings.htm.

9 James E. Fraser (2013), 'Warfare in Northern Britain, c. 500–1093', in E. M. Spiers, J. A. Craig, and M. J. Strickland (eds), *A Military History of Scotland*, Edinburgh: Edinburgh Press, pp. 75–6, 85.

10 Helena Hamerow (2012), *Rural Settlements and Society in Anglo-Saxon England*, Oxford: Oxford University Press, p. 6.

11 Ibid., p. 14.

12 Bede, *A History of the English Church and People*, p. 91.

13 Michael Swanton, ed. (1975), *Anglo-Saxon Prose*, London: J. M. Dent and Sons, p. 3.

14 Colin Symes (2009), 'Early Northumbrian Spirituality: The Fruit of Straitened Circumstances', *Journal of European Baptist Studies*, 10, 6–18.

15 Andrew Wawn (2000), *The Vikings and the Victorians: Inventing the Old North in Nineteenth-Century Britain*, Cambridge: D. S. Brewer, p. 3.

16 Janet L. Nelson (2003), 'England and the Continent in the Ninth Century II: The Vikings and Others', *Transactions of the Royal Historical Society*, 13, 1.

17 Angus A. Sommerville and R. Andrew McDonald (2013), *The Vikings and Their Age*, Toronto: University of Toronto Press, p. 16.

18 Nelson, 'England and the Continent in the Ninth Century II', p. 5.

19 Mary A. Valante (2008), *The Vikings in Ireland: Settlement, Trade and Urbanization*, Dublin: Four Courts Press, pp. 13–14.

20 http://www.archaeologyuk.org/ba/ba103/news.shtml#item1.

21 S. P. Ashby (2009), 'Combs, Contact and Chronology: Reconsidering Hair-Combs in Early-historic and Viking Age Atlantic Scotland', *Medieval Archaeology*, 53, 1–33.

22 Edward James (2001), *Britain in the First Millennium*, London: Hodder Education, p. 236.

23 Valante, *The Vikings in Ireland*, p. 46.

24 Michael D. C. Drout (2006), *How Tradition Works: A Meme-Based Cultural Poetics of the Anglo-Saxon Tenth Century*, Tempe: Arizona Center for Medieval and Renaissance Studies, p. 63.

25 David Clarke, Alice Blackwell, and Martin Goldberg (2012), *Early Medieval Scotland: Individuals, Communities and Ideas*, Edinburgh: National Museums Scotland, p. 6.

26 T. M. Charles-Edwards (2013), *Wales and the Britons, 350–1064*, Oxford: Oxford University Press, p. 603.

27 Bernard F. Huppé (1970), *The Web of Words: Structural Analyses of the Old English Poems Vainglory, the Wonder of Creation, the Dream of the Rood, and Judith*, Albany: State University of New York Press, p. 67.

28 Dorothy Whitelock, ed. (1955), *English Historical Documents, 500–1042*, Volume I, London: Eyre and Spottiswoode, p. 358.

29 Kathryn Powell (2008), 'Viking Invasions and Marginal Annotations in Cambridge, Corpus Christi College 162', *Anglo-Saxon England*, 37, 157.

30 *Beowulf and Other Old English Poems*, translated by Constance B. Hieatt with an introduction by A. Kent Hieatt, New York: The Odyssey Press, p. 89.

Chapter 4

1 David C. Douglas (1964), *William the Conqueror: The Norman Impact upon England*, Berkeley: University of California Press, p. 220.

2 James E. Fraser (2013), 'Warfare in Northern Britain, c. 500–1093', in E. M. Spiers, J. A. Craig, and M. J. Strickland (eds), *A Military History of Scotland*, Edinburgh: Edinburgh Press, p. 83.

3 Pierre de Langtoft (1866–8), *Chronicle*, edited and translated by T. Wright, 2 vols, London: Longmans, Green, Reader, and Dyer, p. 11.

4 Roger of Wendover (1849), *Roger of Wendover's Flowers of History*, translated by J. A. Giles, London: Henry G. Bohn, Volume I, pp. 173–4.

5 Ibid., p. 255.

6 Ibid., Volume II, pp. 432–3.

7 Robin Frame (1990), *The Political Development of the British Isles 1100–1400*, Oxford: Oxford University Press, p. 98.

8 Judith Green (2007), 'Henry I and Northern England', *Transactions of the Royal Historical Society*, Sixth Series, 17, 37.

9 John Guy (2012), *Thomas Becket: Warrior, Priest, Rebel: A Nine-Hundred-Year-Old Story Retold*, New York: Random House, p. 176.

10 Richard R. Heiser (2000), 'Castles, Constables, and Politics in Late Twelfth-Century English Governance', *Albion*, 32, 19–20.

11 W. L. Warren (1987), *The Governance of Norman and Angevin England, 1086–1272*, Stanford: Stanford University Press, p. 165.

12 Igor Djordjevic (2015), *King John (Mis)Remembered: The Dunmow Chronicle, the Lord Admiral's Men, and the Formation of Cultural Memory*, Farnham, England: Ashgate, p. 10.

13 Olivier de Laborderie, J. R. Maddicott, and D. A. Carpenter (2000), 'The Last Hours of Simon de Montfort: A New Account', *English Historical Review*, 115, 411–12, 461.

14 David Carpenter (2003), *The Struggle for Mastery: Britain 1066–1284*, Oxford: Oxford University Press, p. 510.

15 John Davies (1993), *A History of Wales*, London: Allen Lane, p. 161.

16 Ibid., p. 153.

17 David S. Bachrach (2006), 'Military Logistics during the Reign of Edward I of England, 1272–1307', *War in History*, 13, 428–9, 436.

18 David S. Bachrach (2004), 'The Ecclesia Anglicana Goes to War: Prayers, Propaganda, and Conquest during the Reign of Edward I of England, 1272–1307', *Albion*, 36, 396.

19 Kathryn Hurlock (2011), *Wales and the Crusades, c. 1095–1291*, Cardiff: University of Wales Press, p. 204.

20 Quoted in Michael Lynch (1992), *Scotland: A New History*, London: Pimlico, p. 116.

21 Bachrach, 'Ecclesia Anglicana', 397–8.

22 James E. Fraser (2002), '"A Swan from a Raven": William Wallace, Brucean Propaganda, and "Gesta Annalia" II', *Scottish Historical Review*, 81, 1–22.

23 Frank Barlow (1979), *The English Church, 1066–1154*, London: Longman, p. 219.

24 M. T. Clanchy (1979), *From Memory to Written Record: England 1066–1307*, Oxford: Blackwell, p. 193.

25 William of Malmesbury (1848), *William of Malmesbury's Chronicle of England*, edited by J. A. Giles, London: Henry G. Bohn, pp. 239–40.

26 Osborn Bergin (1970), *Irish Bardic Poetry*, Compiled and edited by David Greene and Fergus Kelly, Dublin: Dublin Institute for Advanced Studies, p. 259.

27 Judith Weiss (2009), *The Birth of Romance in England: Four Twelfth-Century Romances in the French of England*, Tempe: Arizona Center for Medieval and Renaissance Studies, pp. 1–2.

28 Ibid., p. 3.

29 William of Ockham (1993), *Whether a Ruler Can Accept the Property of Churches for His Own Needs, Namely in Case of War, Even Against the Wishes of the Pope*, in Cary J. Nederman and Kate Landon Forhan (eds), *Medieval Political Theory – A Reader: The Quest for the Body Politic, 1100–1400*, Routledge: London and New York, p. 213.

30 Christine Eisenberg (2013), *The Rise of Market Society in England, 1066–1800*, translated by Deborah Cohen, New York: Berghan, p. 22.

31 Paul Lattimer (2002), 'Estate Management and Inflation: The Honor of Gloucester, 1183–1263', *Albion*, 34, 193.

32 Sarah Rees Jones (2013), *York: The Making of a City 1068–1350*, Oxford: Oxford University Press, p. 238.

33 Sam Turner and Rob Wilson-North (2012), 'South-West England: Rural Settlements in the Middle Ages', in Neil Christie and Paul Stamper (eds), *Medieval Rural Settlement: Britain and Ireland, AD 800–1600*, Oxford: Windgather Press, p. 146.

34 Shulasmith Shahar (1983), *The Fourth Estate: A History of Women in the Middle Ages*, translated by Chaya Galai, London and New York: Methuen, p. 182.

35 Eileen Power (1975), *Medieval Women*, edited by M. M. Postan, Cambridge: Cambridge University Press, pp. 60–1.

36 Douglas, *William the Conqueror*, p. 314.

37 Jocelyn of Brakelond (1966), *The Chronicle of Jocelyn of Brakelond*, edited by L. C. Jane, New York: Cooper Square Publishers, pp. 7–8.

38 Kevin Down (1987), 'Colonial Society and Economy', in A. Cosgrove (ed.), *A New History of Ireland: Volume II: Medieval Ireland, 1169–1534*, Oxford: Oxford University Press, pp. 439–91.

39 Mark Gardiner (2012), 'South-East England: Forms and Diversity of Medieval Rural Settlement', in Neil Christie and Paul Stamper (eds), *Medieval Rural Settlement: Britain and Ireland, AD 800–1600*, Oxford: Windgather Press, p. 110.

Chapter 5

1 Sir John Froissart (1961), *The Chronicles of England, France, and Spain*, H. P. Dunster's condensation of the Thomas Johnes translation, New York: E. P. Dutton & Co, p. 207.

2 Charles T. Wood (1988), *Joan of Arc and Richard III: Sex, Saints, and Government in the Middle Ages*, New York: Oxford University Press, p. 88.

3 William Chester Jordan (1996), *The Great Famine: Northern Europe in the Early Fourteenth Century*, Princeton: Princeton University Press, pp. 31–2.

4 Samuel K. Cohn, Jr. (2013), *Popular Protest in Late Medieval English Towns*, Cambridge: Cambridge University Press, p. 115.

5 Ibid., pp. 116–17.

6 Some scholars have even questioned whether the bubonic plague was the disease responsible for the great mortality of the mid-fourteenth century, but given how detailed were the descriptions of the symptoms experienced by people at that time and how well they match those caused by the bubonic plague, the bacteria associated with it remains the most likely culprit, a scenario further confirmed by recent DNA analysis.

7 Assize Roll of Labor Offenders, 11 June 1352, Wiltshire, England in John Aberth, (2005), *The Black Death: The Great Mortality of 1348–1350: A Brief History with Documents*, Boston: Bedford/St Martin's, p. 92.

8 John Gillingham (2011), 'Conquests, Catastrophe and Recovery, 1066–c. 1485', in Jonathan Clark (ed.), *A World By Itself: A History of the British Isles*, London: Pimlico, p. 136.

9 A. J. Pollard (2004), *Imagining Robin Hood: The Late Medieval Stories in Historical Context*, London: Routledge, p. 100.

10 Caroline Dunn (2013), *Stolen Women in Medieval England: Rape, Abduction, and Adultery 1100–1500*, Cambridge: Cambridge University Press, pp. 54–5.

11 Christopher Ian Levy (2003), 'Texts for a Poor Church: John Wyclif and the Decretals', *Essays in Medieval Studies*, 20, no. 1 (2003): 94–107.

12 John Wycliffe (1993), 'The Duty of a King', in Cary J. Nederman and Kate Landon Forhan (eds), *Medieval Political Theory – A Reader: The Quest for the Body Politic, 1100–1400*, London and New York: Routledge, p. 223.

13 Froissart, *The Chronicles of England, France, and Spain*, p. 45.

14 See Gerald Morgan (2009), 'The Worthiness of Chaucer's Worthy Knight', *The Chaucer Review*, 44, 115–58.

15 Geoffrey Chaucer (1964), *The Canterbury Tales*, edited by A. Kent Hieatt and Constance Hieatt, Toronto: Bantam Books, p. 5.

16 Geoffrey Chaucer (1971), *Troilus and Criseyde*, translated by Nevill Coghill, Harmondsworth, England: Penguin Books, p. 67.

17 Pollard, *Imagining Robin Hood*, pp. 98–9.

18 Thomas Malory (2001), *Malory's Le Morte d'Arthur*, The Classic Rendition by Keith Baines, New York: Signet, p. 177.

19 J. A. Watt (1987), 'Gaelic Polity and Cultural Identity', in A. Cosgrove (ed.), *A New History of Ireland: Volume II: Medieval Ireland, 1169–1534*, Oxford: Oxford University Press, p. 347.

20 James Carney (1987), 'Literature in Irish, 1169–1534', in A. Cosgrove (ed.), *A New History of Ireland: Volume II: Medieval Ireland, 1169–1534*, Oxford: Oxford University Press, pp. 706–7.

21 Lynn Arner (2006), 'The Ends of Enchantment: Colonialism and Sir Gawain and the Green Knight', *Texas Studies in Literature and Language*, 48, 79–80.

22 Quoted in David R. Cook (1984), *Lancastrians and Yorkists: The Wars of the Roses*, London: Longman, p. 98.

Chapter 6

1 Eric Ives (2005), *The Life and Death of Anne Boleyn: 'The Most Happy'*, Malden, MA: Blackwell, p. 264.

2 Although fictional, Hilary Mantel's historical novel, *Wolf Hall* (New York: Henry Holt and Company, 2009) contrasts admirably with Bolt's hagiography of More, reflecting more recent trends in historical scholarship.

3 Anthony Fletcher and Diarmaid MacCulloch (2004), *Tudor Rebellions*, 5th ed., Harlow, England: Pearson Longman, p. 41.

4 Ethan Shagan (2003), *Popular Politics and the English Reformation*, Cambridge: Cambridge University Press, p. 137.

5 Laquita Higgs (1998), *Godliness and Governance in Tudor Colchester*, Ann Arbor: University of Michigan Press.

6 Eamon Duffy (2001), *The Voices of Morebath: Reformation and Rebellion in an English Village*, New Haven and London: Yale University Press, p. 111.

7 John Knox (1982), *The History of the Reformation of Religion within the Realm of Scotland*, edited by C. J. Guthrie, Edinburgh: Banner of Truth Trust, p. 107.

8 See http://www.visionofbritain.org.uk/census/SRC_P/6/GB1841ABS_1.

9 Robert O. Bucholz and Joseph P. Ward (2012), *London: A Social and Cultural History, 1550–1750*, Cambridge: Cambridge University Press, p. 64.

10 Ibid., p. 109.

11 Thomas Bartlett (2010), *Ireland: A History*, Cambridge: Cambridge University Press, p. 81.

12 Peter Cunich (2004), 'The Dissolutions and their Aftermath', in R. Tittler and N. Jones (eds), *A Companion to Tudor Britain*, Malden, MA: Blackwell, p. 228.

13 John Davies (1993), *A History of Wales*, London: Allen Lane, p. 227.

14 See G. W. Bernard (2011), 'The Dissolution of the Monasteries', *History*, 96, 390–409.

15 Jason A. Nice (2006), 'Being "British" at Rome: The Welsh at the English College, 1578–84', *Catholic Historical Review*, 92, 1–2.

16 Denis Hay, ed. and trans. (1950), *The Anglica Historia of Polydore Vergil A.D. 1485–1537*, Camden Series, Vol. LXXIV, London: Royal Historical Society, p. 327.

17 Margaret Aston (1993), *The King's Bedpost: Reformation and Iconography in a Tudor Group Portrait*, Cambridge: Cambridge University Press.

18 John Edwards (2014), *Archbishop Pole*, Farnham, England: Ashgate, p. 151.

19 Eamon Duffy (2009), *Fires of Faith: Catholic England under Mary Tudor*, New Haven and London: Yale University Press. See also Brad S. Gregory (1999), *Salvation at Stake: Christian Martyrdom in Early Modern Europe*, Cambridge, MA: Harvard University Press and Alexandra Walsham (2006), *Charitable Hatred: Tolerance and Intolerance in England, 1500–1700*, Manchester: Manchester University Press.

20 See especially Patrick Collinson (1979), *Archbishop Grindal, 1519–1583: The Struggle for a Reformed Church*, Berkeley: University of California Press.

21 Natalie Mears (2012), 'Public Worship and Political Participation in Elizabethan England', *Journal of British Studies*, 51, 4–7.

22 John Guy (1988), *Tudor England*, Oxford: Oxford University Press, p. 272.

23 John Guy (2013), *The Children of Henry VIII*, Oxford: Oxford University Press, p. 176.

24 'Queen Elizabeth's Speech to Bishops and Other Clergy at Somerset Place, February 27, 1585' in Elizabeth I (2000), *Collected Works*, edited by Leah S. Marcus, Janel Mueller, and Mary Beth Rose, Chicago and London: University of Chicago Press, p. 178.

25 Ibid., p. 179.

26 Evelyn Waugh (1935), *Edmund Campion*, London: Sheet and Ward.

27 Quoted in Anne Somerset (1991). *Elizabeth I*, New York: Alfred A. Knopf, p. 464.

Chapter 7

1 Andrew Gurr (2004), *Playgoing in Shakespeare's London*, 3rd ed., Cambridge: Cambridge University Press, p. 165.

2 Lisa Jardine (1996), *Reading Shakespeare Historically*, London and New York: Routledge, p. 9.

3 See the excellent book by James Shapiro (2015), *The Year of Lear: Shakespeare in 1606*, New York: Simon and Schuster.

4 See Garry Wills (1995), *Witches and Jesuits: Shakespeare's Macbeth*, New York: Oxford University Press, especially p. 29.

5 Amanda E. Herbert (2014), *Female Alliances: Gender, Identity, and Friendship in Early Modern Britain*, New Haven: Yale University Press.

6 Live Helene Willumsen (2013), *Witches of the North: Scotland and Finnmark*, Leiden: Brill, p. 45.

7 Thomas Dekker (1988), *The Wonderful Year* (1603), in *The Wonderful Year, The Gull's Horn Book, Penny Wise, Pound-Foolish, English Villainies Discovered by Lantern and Candlelight, and Selected Writings*, edited by E. D. Pendry, Cambridge, MA: Harvard University Press, p. 43.

8 Samuel Daniel (1963), *The Complete Works in Verse and Prose of Samuel Daniel*, edited by Alexander B. Grossart, New York: Russell & Russell, pp. 143–4.

9 See http://www.british-history.ac.uk/commons-jrnl/vol1/pp187-189#h3-0017.

10 David M. Bergeron (2002), 'King James's Civic Pageant and Parliamentary Speech in March 1604', *Albion*, 34, 222.

11 Arthur Wilson (1653), *The History of Great Britain, Being the Life and Reign of King James the First …* London, p. 151.

12 See Marvin A. Breslow (1970), *Mirror of England: English Puritan Views of Foreign Nations, 1618–1640*, Cambridge, MA: Harvard University Press, especially Ch. VI. Professor Breslow also discussed this point in a paper, 'Gustavus Adolphus in England', at the Western Conference of British Studies in October 1991.

13 Margo Todd (2000), 'Profane Pastimes and the Reformed Community: The Persistence of Popular Festivities in Early Modern Scotland', *Journal of British Studies*, 39, 137–8.

14 Quoted in Rosemary Goring (2007), *Scotland: The Autobiography: 2,000 Years of Scottish History by Those Who Saw It Happen*, Woodstock, NY: The Overlook Press, pp. 83–4.

15 'Where God commands, weake men must not dispute, Differing Worships, or. The Oddes, betweene some Knights Service and God's' (1640), in John Taylor (1891), *The Works of John Taylor Not Included in the Folio Volume of 1630*, Cornell: Cornell University Press.

16 Jane H. Ohlmeyer (1998), '"Civilizing of those Rude Partes": Colonization within Britain and Ireland, 1580s–1640s', in Nicholas Canny (ed.), *The Oxford History of the British Empire: Volume I: The Origins of Empire: British Overseas Enterprise to the Close of the Seventeenth Century*, Oxford: Oxford University Press, p. 139.

17 Sir Walter Raleigh (1971), *The History of the World*, edited by C. A. Patrides, Philadelphia: Temple University Press, pp. 216, 255.

18 Francis Bacon to James I, 1611, quoted in David Cressy, ed. (1975), *Education in Tudor and Stuart England*, New York: St. Martin's Press, p. 24.

19 Dekker, *The Wonderful Year*, p. 43.

20 Isaak Walton, *The Life of Dr. John Donne* (1639), http://anglicanhistory.org/walton/donne.html.

21 John Speed, *A Prospect of the Most Famous Parts of the World*, 2nd ed. (1662), p. 35.

22 See Anna Beer (2008), *Milton: Poet, Pamphleteer, and Patriot*, New York: Bloomsbury Press, pp. 45–51.

23 Kevin Sharpe (2010), *Image Wars: Promoting Kings and Commonwealths in England, 1603–1660*, New Haven: Yale University Press, p. 64.

24 Jessica Dyson (2013), *Staging Authority in Caroline England: Prerogative, Law and Order in Drama, 1625–1642*, Farnham, England: Ashgate, p. 16.

25 Nehemiah Wallington (1869), *Historical Notices of Events Occurring Chiefly in the Reign of Charles I*, London: Richard Bentley, Vol. I, p. 116.

26 Alexander S. Rosenthal (2008), *Crown under Law: Richard Hooker, John Locke, and the Ascent of Modern Constitutionalism*, Lanham, MD: Lexington Books.

Chapter 8

1 Ethan Shagan (1997), 'Constructing Discord: Ideology, Propaganda, and English Responses to the Irish Rebellion of 1641', *Journal of British Studies*, 36, 17.

2 Charles Carlton (1992), *Going to the Wars: The Experience of the British Civil Wars 1638–1651*, London and New York: Routledge, p. 255.

3 Clare McManus (2008), '"What ish my Nation?": The Cultures of the British Isles', in Jenny Wormald (ed.), *The Seventeenth Century*, Oxford: Oxford University Press, p. 205.

4 Roy Sherwood (1992), *The Civil War in the Midlands, 1642–1651*, Wolfeboro Falls, NH: Alan Sutton, p. 50.

5 Carlton, *Going to the Wars*, p. 82.

6 Lucy Hutchinson (1810), *Memoirs of the Life of Colonel Hutchinson ...*, 3rd ed., Vol. II, London: Longman, Hurst, Rees, and Orme, pp. 155–6.

7 Kevin Sharpe (2010), *Image Wars: Promoting Kings and Commonwealths in England, 1603–1660*, New Haven: Yale University Press, p. xv.

8 Jim Daims and Holly Faith Nelson (2006), *Eikon Basilike with Selections from Eikonoklastes [by] John Milton*, Peterborough, Ontario: Broadview, p. 225.

9 Quoted in Micheál Ó Siochrú (2008), *God's Executioner: Oliver Cromwell and the Conquest of Ireland*, London: Faber and Faber, p. 80.

10 Quoted in Craig W. Horle (1976), 'Quakers and Baptists, 1647–1660', *The Baptist Quarterly*, 26, 356.

11 James S. Hart Jr. (2003), *The Rule of Law, 1603-1660: Crowns, Courts and Judges*, Harlow, England: Pearson Longman, p. 250.

12 Peter Laslett (1984), *The World We Have Lost: Further Explored*, 3rd ed., New York: Charles Scribner's Sons, p. 220.

13 K. A. J. McLay (2013), 'The Restoration and the Glorious Revolution, 1660–1702', in E. M. Spiers, J. A. Craig, and M. J. Strickland (eds), *A Military History of Scotland*, Edinburgh: Edinburgh Press, p. 302.

14 Toby Barnard (2013), *A New Anatomy of Ireland: The Irish Protestants, 1649–1770*, New Haven: Yale University Press, p. 29.

15 Ronald Hutton (1985), *The Restoration: A Political and Religious History of England and Wales, 1658–1667*, Oxford: Oxford University Press, p. 255.

16 Quoted in Jim Smyth (1998), '"No remedy more proper": Anglo-Irish Unionism before 1707', in Brendan Bradshaw and Peter Roberts (eds), *British Consciousness and Identity: The Making of Britain, 1533–1707*, Cambridge: Cambridge University Press, p. 304.

17 Philip Jenkins (1998), 'Seventeenth-Century Wales: Definition and Identity', in Brendan Bradshaw and Peter Roberts (eds), *British Consciousness and Identity: The Making of Britain, 1533–1707*, Cambridge: Cambridge University Press, p. 215.

18 John Bunyan (1987), *The Pilgrim's Progress*, edited by Roger Sharrock, London: Penguin, p. 129.

19 Ruth Scurr (2015), *John Aubrey: My Own Life*, London: Chatto & Windus, p. 267.

20 Scott Sowerby (2012), 'Opposition to Anti-Popery in Restoration England', *Journal of British Studies*, 51, 26–49.

21 Gilbert Burnet (1840), *Bishop Burnet's History of His Own Time from the Restoration of Charles II to the Peace of Utrecht in the Reign of Queen Anne*, London: William Smith, Vol. IV, p. 397.

22 Ted Vallance (2009), 'The Captivity of James II: Gestures of Loyalty and Disloyalty in Seventeenth Century England', *Journal of British Studies*, 48, 853.

23 Lisa Jardine, (2008), *Going Dutch: How England Plundered Holland's Glory*, New York: Harper, p. 289.

24 Brent S. Sirota (2013), 'The Trinitarian Crisis in Church and State: Religious Controversy and the Making of the Postrevolutionary Church of England, 1687–1702', *Journal of British Studies*, 52, 26.

25 Sarah Ellenzweig (2005), 'The Faith of Unbelief: Rochester's "Satyre", Deism, and Religious Freethinking in Seventeenth-Century England', *Journal of British Studies*, 44, 45.

26 John Locke (1974), 'An Essay Concerning Human Understanding', abridged by Richard Taylor, in *The Empiricists*, Garden City, NY: Anchor Books, p. 119. Italics in original.

27 Laslett, *The World We Have Lost*, pp. 216–19.

Chapter 9

1 Tim Harris (2006), *Revolution: The Great Crisis of the British Monarchy, 1685–1720*, London: Allen Lane, p. 310.

2 The Indians, however, were more interested in capturing slaves than they were with ending Spanish rule in Florida. Anderson and Clayton estimate that their raids resulted in the enslavement of about 10,000 Indians or around 80 per cent of the Indian population of Florida, with another 3,000 killed. Fred Anderson and Andrew Clayton (2005), *The Dominion of War: Empire and Liberty in North America, 1500–2000*, New York: Viking, p. 87.

3 Melinda S. Zook (2013), *Protestantism, Politics, and Women in Britain, 1660–1714*, Houndmills, Basingstoke and Hampshire: Palgrave Macmillan, p. 185.

4 Hannah Smith (2011), 'Politics, Patriotism, and Gender: The Standing Army Debate on the English Stage, circa 1689–1720', *Journal of British Studies*, 50, 48.

5 Linda Colley (1992), *Britons: Forging the Nation 1707–1837*, New Haven and London: Yale University Press, pp. 13–14.

6 Daniel Defoe (1786), *The History of the Union Between England and Scotland, With a Collection of Original Papers Relating Thereto*, London: J. Stockdale, p. xxxvi.

7 Bruce Lenman (1980), *The Jacobite Risings in Britain, 1689–1746*, London: Eyre Methuen, pp. 153–4.

8 Samuel Johnson (1925), *Lives of the English Poets*, London: J. M. Dent and Sons, vol. I, p. 67

9 Anthony, Earl of Shaftesbury (1711; 1964), *Characteristics of Men, Manners, Opinions, Times*, edited by John M. Robertson, Indianapolis: Bobbs-Merrill, p. 9.

10 Jonathan Clark (2012), 'Restoration to Reform, 1660–1832', in Jonathan Clark (ed.), *A World By Itself: A History of the British Isles*, London: Pimlico, p. 345.

11 Voltaire (1949), 'Selections from the English Letters', in Ben Ray Redman (ed.), *The Portable Voltaire*, New York: Viking, p. 513.

12 James M. Rosenheim (1998), *The Emergence of a Ruling Order: English Landed Society 1650–1750*, London and New York: Longman, p. 132.

13 Bob Harris (2002), 'Print Culture', in H. T. Dickinson (ed.), *A Companion to Eighteenth-Century Britain*, Malden, MA: Blackwell, p. 286.

14 Hannah Barker (2000), *Newspapers, Politics and English Society, 1695–1855*, Harlow, England: Longman, p. 135.

15 See Hyder Abbas (2014), '"A Fund of Entertaining and Useful Information": Coffee Houses, Early Public Libraries, and the Print Trade in Eighteenth-Century Dublin', *Library and Information History*, 30, 41–61.

16 Paddy McNally (2002), 'Ireland: The Making of the "Protestant Ascendancy", 1690–1760', in H. T. Dickinson (ed.), *A Companion to Eighteenth-Century Britain*, Malden, MA: Blackwell, p. 407.

17 Jonathan Swift (1726; 2003), *Gulliver's Travels*, edited by Robert Demaria, Jr., London: Penguin, p. 128.

18 Ian Watt (1957), *The Rise of the Novel: Studies in Defoe, Richardson and Fielding*, Berkeley and Los Angeles: University of California Press, p. 62.

19 Daniel Defoe (1719; 2003), *Robinson Crusoe*, edited by John Richetti, London: Penguin, p. 139.

20 Max Weber (1904; 1930), *The Protestant Ethic and the Spirit of Capitalism*, translated by Talcott Parsons, London: George Allen & Unwin.

21 Jeremy Collier (1698; 1987), *A Short View of the Immorality of the English Stage: A Critical Edition*, edited by Benjamin Hellinger, New York: Garland, p. 8.

22 Quoted in Bridget Hill (1987), *Eighteenth-Century Women: An Anthology*, London: Allen & Unwin, p. 20.

23 Daniel Defoe (1722; 1989), *Moll Flanders*, edited by David Blewett, London: Penguin, p. 120.

24 Daniel Defoe (1729), *Religious Courtship: Being Historical Discourses on the Necessity of Marrying Religious Husbands and Wives Only*, London: Printed by J. Brotherton for E. Matthews, p. 8.

25 Daniel Defoe (1715; 2006), *The Family Instructor*, edited by P. N. Furbank, London: Pickering and Chatto, p. 11.

26 Defoe, *Moll Flanders*, p. 267.

27 Ibid., p. 353.

28 The lucrative business of reselling stolen goods to their previous owners and the London underworld presided over by Jonathan Wild is also one of the main subjects of David Liss's excellent 2001 historical novel, *A Conspiracy of Paper*, New York: Ballantine Books.

29 Toby Barnard (2013), *A New Anatomy of Ireland: The Irish Protestants, 1649–1770*, New Haven: Yale University Press, p. 270.

30 Walter Scott (1814; 1981), *Waverley: Or 'Tis Sixty Years Since*, 'A Postscript', Oxford: Clarendon Press, p. 492.

31 Lenman, *The Jacobite Risings in Britain, 1689–1746*, p. 264.

Chapter 10

1   *The North Briton. By John Wilkes, Esq., C. Church and others. Illustrated with Useful and Explanatory Notes, and a Collection of all the Proceedings in the House of Commons and Court of Westminster against Mr. Wilkes* ... (1772), London, vol. II, pp. 247–8. http://pages.uoregon.edu/dluebke/301ModernEurope/Wilkes%20North%20Briton%2045.pdf

2   Hannah Barker (2000), *Newspapers, Politics and English Society, 1695–1855*, Harlow, England: Longman, p. 100. Barker writes that these examples were 'in no way unusual'.

3   See Stephen M. Lee (2002), 'Parliaments, Parties and Elections (1760–1815)', in H. T. Dickinson (ed.), *A Companion to Eighteenth-Century Britain*, Malden, MA: Blackwell, pp. 69–80.

4   Janice Hadlow (2014), *A Royal Experiment: The Private Life of George III*, New York: Henry Holt and Company, p. 12.

5   James E. Bradley (2007), 'Parliament, Print Culture and Petitioning in Late Eighteenth-Century England', *Parliamentary History*, 26, 98.

6   Frank McLynn (2004), *1759: The Year Britain Became Master of the World*, New York: Atlantic Monthly Press, p. 92.

7   D. A. Sherrard (1955), *Lord Chatham: Pitt and the Seven Years War*, London: The Bodley Head, p. 120–1.

8   Wolfe to Rickson, 9 June 1751, Banff, quoted in Beckles Wilson (1909), *The Life and Letters of James Wolfe*, London: William Heineman, p. 139.

9   See Roger P. Mellen (2015), 'John Wilkes and the Constitutional Right to a Free Press in the United States', *Journalism History*, 41, 2–10.

10 See Kevin Phillips (1999), *The Cousins' Wars: Religion, Politics, and the Triumph of Anglo-America*, New York: Basic Books.

11 Simon Schama (2006), *Rough Crossings: Britain, the Slaves and the American Revolution*, New York: HarperCollins, p. 6.

12 *The Report on the Affairs of British North America Presented to Her Majesty by the Earl of Durham* (1839), London: J. W. Southgate, pp. 124–5.

13 Robert Middlekauff (2005), *The Glorious Cause: The American Revolution, 1763–1789*, rev. ed., Oxford: Oxford University Press, p. 33.

14 Patrick Fitzgerald and Brian Lambkin (2008), *Migration in Irish History, 1607–2007*, Houndmills, Basingstoke and Hampshire: Palgrave Macmillan, p. 123–4.

15 Arthur Young (1780), *A Tour in Ireland, with General Observations on the Present State of that Kingdom in 1776–78*, http://www.ucc.ie/celt/online/E780001-001.html, p. 25.

16 Maxine Berg and Pat Hudson (1992), 'Rehabilitating the Industrial Revolution', *Economic History Review*, 45, 24–50.

17 Trevor Griffiths, Philip Hunt, and Patrick O'Brien (2008), 'Scottish, Irish, and Imperial Connections: Parliament, the Three Kingdoms, and the Mechanization of Cotton Spinning in Eighteenth-Century Britain', *Economic History Review*, 61, 642.

18 Christine Eisenberg (2013), *The Rise of Market Society in England, 1066–1800*, translated by Deborah Cohen, New York: Berghan, p. 106.

19 Harold Perkins (1969), *The Origins of Modern English Society, 1780–1880*, London: Routledge and Kegan Paul, p. 2.

20 Mark Overton (1996), *Agricultural Revolution in England: The Transformation of the Agrarian Economy 1500–1850*, Cambridge: Cambridge University Press, p. 176.

21 Mary Wollstonecraft (1891), *Vindication of the Rights of Women*, New York: Humboldt, p. 272.

22 *The Laws Respecting Women, As They Regard their Natural Rights ...* (1777), London: Printed for J. Johnson, p. vi.

23 Ibid., p. 55.

24 Henry Fielding (1751), *An Enquiry into the Causes of the late Increase of Robbers*, 2nd ed., London: Printed for A. Millar, pp. 9–11.

25 Emma Rothschild (2002), *Economic Sentiments: Adam Smith, Condorcet, and the Enlightenment*, Cambridge, MA: Harvard University Press, p. 122.

26 David Hume (1779), 'Dialogues Concerning Natural Religion', in *The Empiricists: Locke, Berkeley, and Hume*, Garden City, NY: Anchor Books, p. 437.

27 See Dror Wahrman (2004), *The Making of the Modern Self: Identity and Culture in Eighteenth-Century England*, New Haven and London: Yale University Press, p. 200.

28 For contemporary reactions to Richardson's best-known novel, *Pamela*, see Thomas Keymer and Peter Sabor (2005), *Pamela in the Marketplace: Literary Controversy and Print Culture in Eighteenth-Century Britain and Ireland*, Cambridge: Cambridge University Press.

29 J. C. D. Clark (2000), *English Society 1660–1832: Religion, Ideology and Politics during the Ancient Regime*, 2nd ed., Cambridge: Cambridge University Press, p. 389.

Chapter 11

1 William D. Tatum III (2014), '"The Soldiers Murmured Much on Account of this Usage": Military Justice and Negotiated Authority in the Eighteenth-Century British Army', in Kevin Linch and Mattthew McCormack (eds), *Britain's Soldiers: Rethinking War and Society, 1715–1815*, Liverpool: Liverpool University Press, p. 111.

2 Amnon Yuval (2011), 'Between Heroism and Acquittal: Henry Redhead Yorke and the Inherent Instability of Political Trials in Britain during the 1790s', *Journal of British Studies*, 50, 618.

3 Elizabeth Malcolm (2013), 'A New Age or Just the Same Old Cycle of Extirpation? Massacre and the 1798 Irish Rebellion', *Journal of Genocide Research*, 15, 151–66.

4 Jonah Barrington (1835), *Historic Memoirs of Ireland Comprising Secret Records of the National Convention, the Rebellion, and the Union*, London: Henry Coburn, Volume I, p. 57.

5 'Horatio Nelson to Henry Addington, 25 October 1802' in Colin White (ed.) (2005), *Nelson: The New Letters*, Woodbridge, Suffolk: The Boydell Press, p. 310.

6 N. A. M. Rodger (2005), *The Command of the Ocean: A Naval History of Britain, 1649–1815*, New York: W. W. Norton and Company, p. 532.

7 Holger Hoock (2010), '"Struggling against a Vulgar Prejudice": Patriotism and the Collecting of British Art at the Turn of the Nineteenth Century', *Journal of British Studies*, 49, 566–91.

8 Linda Colley (1992), *Britons: Forging the Nation 1707–1837*, New Haven and London: Yale University Press, pp. 282, 311.

9 Brendan Simms (2015), *The Longest Afternoon: The 400 Men who Decided the Battle of Waterloo*, New York: Basic Books, p. 125.

10 Paul O'Keefe (2014), *Waterloo: The Aftermath*, London: Vintage Books, p. 50.

11 S. J. Stearns (2002), 'The Napoleonic Wars, 1789–1815', in F. W. Thackeray and J. E. Findling (eds), *Events That Changed Great Britain Since 1689*, Westport, CT: Greenwood Press, p. 47.

12 James Hogg (1824; 1983), *The Private Memoirs and Confessions of a Justified Sinner*, Harmondsworth, England: Penguin, p. 104.

13 E. P. Thompson (1966; 1963), *The Making of the English Working Class*, New York: Vintage, p. 415.

14 Alison Light (2014), *Common People: The History of an English Family*, London: Fig Tree, p. 87.

15 Colley, *Britons: Forging the Nation 1707–1837*, p. 329.

16 Robert Saunders (2014), 'God and the Great Reform Act: Preaching against Reform, 1831–32', *Journal of British Studies*, 53, 378–99.

17 Gregory Clark and David Jacks (2007), 'Coal and the Industrial Revolution, 1700–1869', *European Review of Economic History*, 11, 62–3.

18 Eric J. Hobsbawm (1999), *Industry and Empire: An Economic History of Britain since 1750*, rev. ed., New York: Free Press, p. 90.

19 Clark and Jacks, 'Coal and the Industrial Revolution, 1700-1869', 65.

20 William Godwin (1794; 1831), *Caleb Williams*, London: Colburn and Bentley, p. xix.

21 Ibid., pp. 104–5.

22 William Godwin (1971), *Enquiry Concerning Political Justice, with Selections from Godwin's Other Writings*, edited by K. Codell Carter, Oxford: Clarendon Press, p. 86.

23 Alan Riach (2007), 'The Literature of Industrialization', in Susan Manning (ed.), *The Edinburgh History of Scottish Literature: Volume II: Enlightenment, Britain and Empire (1707–1918)*, Edinburgh: Edinburgh University Press, pp. 236–7.

24 James Neild (1802), *An Account of Persons Confined for Debt in the Various Prisons of England and Wales ...*, London: Nichols and Son, pp. 63–4.

25 Michael Lynch (1992), *Scotland: A New History*, London: Pimlico, p. 385.

26 Jeremy Bentham (1789), *An Introduction to the Principles of Morals and Legislation*, http://caae.phil.cmu.edu/Cavalier/80130/part1/sect4/PofU.html.

Chapter 12

1 Patrick Joyce (2013), *The State of Freedom: A Social History of the British State since 1800*, Cambridge: Cambridge University Press, p. 189.

2 Krista Cowman (2010), *Women in British Politics, c. 1689–1979*, Houndmills, Basingstoke and Hampshire: Palgrave Macmillan, pp. 36–7.

3 Quoted in Stewart J. Brown (2008), *Providence and Empire: Religion, Politics and Society in the United Kingdom, 1815–1914*, Harlow, England: Pearson Longman, p. 76.

4 L. M. Cullen (2012), *Economy, Trade and Irish Merchants at Home and Abroad, 1600–1988*, Dublin: Full Courts Press, p. 31.

5 David Sim (2013), *A Union Forever: The Irish Question and U.S. Foreign Relations in the Victorian Age*, Ithaca and London: Cornell University Press, p. 41.

6 Henry Mayhew (1861; 1968), *London Labour and the London Poor*, New York: Dover Publications, Inc., I, p. 104.

7 Charles Dickens (1854; 2008), *Hard Times*, New York: Penguin, pp. 162–3.

8 George Eliot (1861; 1996), *Silas Marner: The Weaver of Raveloe*, Oxford: Oxford University Press, p. 15.

9 Charles Dickens (1840–1; 1944), *Barnaby Rudge*, New York: Dodd, Mead & Company, p. 109.

10 K. J. Fielding and Anne Smith (1970), 'Hard Times and the Factory Controversy: Dickens vs. Harriet Martineau', *Nineteenth-Century Fiction*, 24, especially 419–23.

11 Charles Dickens (1865; 2009), *Our Mutual Friend*, edited by Adrian Poole, London: Penguin, pp. 143, 840.

12 Simon Thurley (2013), *Men from the Ministry: How Britain Saved its Heritage*, New Haven: Yale University Press, pp. 8–9.

13 Ben Weinstein (2014), 'Questioning a Late Victorian "Dyad": Preservationism, Demolitionism, and the City of London Churches, 1860–1904', *Journal of British Studies*, 53, 400–25.

14 Stefanie Markovits (2008), 'Rushing into Print: "Participatory Journalism" During the Crimean War', *Victorian Studies*, 50, esp. 561.

15 Robert Douglas-Fairhurst (2015), *The Story of Alice: Lewis Carroll and the Secret History of Wonderland*, Cambridge, MA: The Belknap Press of Harvard University Press, p. 56.

16 Ibid.

17 Maria Luddy (2007), *Prostitution and Irish Society, 1800–1940*, Cambridge: Cambridge University Press, p. 18.

18 David G. Barrie (2015), 'Naming and Shaming: Trial by Media in Nineteenth-Century Scotland', *Journal of British Studies*, 54, 352.

19 Theodore K. Hoppen (1998), *The Mid-Victorian Generation 1846–1886*, Oxford: Clarendon Press, p. 531.

20 William Stubbs (1904), *Letters of William Stubbs*, edited by William Holden Hutton, London: A. Constable and Company, pp. 147–8.

21 William F. Cody (2012), *The Wild West in England*, edited by Frank Christianson, Lincoln: University of Nebraska Press, pp. 53–5.

22 See Luke Blaxill (2015), 'Joseph Chamberlain and the Third Reform Act: A Reassessment of the "Unauthorized Programme" of 1885', *Journal of British Studies*, 54, 88–117.

23 Matthew Arnold (1886), 'The Nadir of Liberalism', in Fraser Neiman (ed.) (1960), *Essays, Letters, and Reviews by Matthew Arnold*, Cambridge, MA: Harvard University Press, p. 271.

Chapter 13

1 Hannah Weiss Muller (2014), 'Bonds of Belonging: Subjecthood and the British Empire', *Journal of British Studies*, 53, 33–5.

2 Quoted in Niall Ferguson (2004), *Empire: The Rise and Demise of the British World Order and the Lessons for Global Power*, New York: Basic Books, p. 119.

3 Catherine Hall (2004), 'Of Gender and Empire: Reflections on the Nineteenth Century', in Philippa Levine (ed.), *Gender and Empire*, Oxford: Oxford University Press, p. 52.

4 Kenton Scott Storey (2014), 'Colonial Humanitarianism? Thomas Gore Browne and the Taranaki War, 1860–61', *Journal of British Studies*, 53, 111–35.

5 Quoted in Marilyn Lake (2014), '"The Day Will Come": Charles H. Pearson's *National Life and Character: A Forecast*', in Antoinette M. Burton and Isabel Hofmeyr (eds), *Ten Books That Shaped the British Empire: Creating an Imperial Commons*, Durham: Duke University Press, p. 91.

6 John A. Hobson (1902; 1948), *Imperialism*, London: Allen and Unwin, p. 76.

7 Lawrence James (1997), *Raj: The Making and Unmaking of British India*, New York: St. Martin's Griffin, p. 85.

8 Philippa Levine (2007), *The British Empire: Sunrise to Sunset*, Harlow, England: Pearson Longman, p. 69.

9 Ashley Jackson (2013), *Buildings of Empire*, Oxford: Oxford University Press, p. 139.

10 Robert Darnton (2014), *Censors at Work: How States Shaped Literature*, New York: W. W. Norton and Company, p. 104.

11 Durba Ghosh (2004), 'Decoding the Nameless: Gender, Subjectivity, and Historical Methodologies in Reading the Archives of Colonial India', in Kathleen Wilson (ed.), *The New Imperial History: Culture, Identity, and Modernity in Britain and the Empire, 1660–1840*, Cambridge: Cambridge University Press, pp. 302–4.

12 Antoinette Burton (1994), *Burdens of History: British Feminists, Indian Women, and Imperial Culture, 1865–1915*, Chapel Hill: University of North Carolina Press, p. 8.

13 Ibid., p. 105.

14 Joan Mickelson Gaughan (2013), *The 'Incumbrances': British Women in India, 1615–1856*, Oxford: Oxford University Press, p. 163.

15 Margaret Macmillan (1988), *Women of the Raj*, New York: Thames and Hudson, p. 42.

16 Andrew S. Thompson (2000), *Imperial Britain: The Empire in British Politics, c. 1880–1932*, Harlow, England: Longman, p. 35.

17 Thomas Davis (1846), *Literary and Historical Essays*, Dublin: J. Duffy, p. 169.

18 Bruce Nelson (2012), *Irish Nationalists and the Making of the Irish Race*, Princeton: Princeton University Press, p. 123.

19 I. G. C. Hutchison (2005), 'Worship of Empire: The Nineteenth Century', in J. Wormald (ed.), *Scotland: A History*, Oxford: Oxford University Press, p. 238.

20 John A. MacKenzie (2010), 'Scotland and Empire: Ethnicity, Environment and Identity', *Northern Scotland*, 1, 15.

21 Ken McGoogan (2010), *How the Scots Invented Canada*, Toronto: HarperCollins, pp. 166, 369.

22 I am thankful to an anonymous reviewer for this particular point and for helping to clarify my understanding of this subject.

23 John Davies (1993), *A History of Wales*, London: Allen Lane, p. 414.

24 *Edinburgh Courant*, 5 December 1884.

25 *Colonies And India*, 16 June 1877.

26 F. D. Lugard (1893; 1968), *The Rise of Our East African Empire: Early Efforts in Nyasaland and Uganda*, London: Cass, p. 70.

27 G. A. Henty (1896), *The Tiger of Mysore: A Story of the War with Tippoo Saib*, London: Blackie & Son, p. 51.

28 Lawrence James (1995), *The Rise and Fall of the British Empire*, New York: St. Martin's Griffin, p. 207.

29 G. A. Henty (1894), *Through the Sikh War: A Tale of the Conquest of the Punjab*, London: Blackie & Son Limited, p. 19.

30 Charlotte MacDonald (2014), '*Jane Eyre* at Home and Abroad', in Antoinette M. Burton and Isabel Hofmeyr (eds), *Ten Books That Shaped the British Empire: Creating an Imperial Commons*, Durham: Duke University Press, p. 60.

31 Ibid., p. 55.

32 Catherine Hall (2014), 'Macaulay's *History of England*: A Book That Shaped Nation and Empire', in Antoinette M. Burton and Isabel Hofmeyr (eds), *Ten Books That Shaped the British Empire: Creating an Imperial Commons*, Durham: Duke University Press, pp. 71–89.

33 James, *The Rise and Fall of the British Empire*, p. 307.

34 Gary B. Magee and Andrew S. Thompson (2010), *Empire and Globalisation: Networks of People, Goods and Capital in the British World, c. 1850–1914*, Cambridge: Cambridge University Press, p. 68.

35 Tamson Pietsch (2013), 'Rethinking the British World', *Journal of British Studies*, 52, 441.

Chapter 14

1 The last lines are a quotation from the Latin poet Horace, meaning, 'It is sweet and fitting to die for one's country.'

2 Peter Donaldson (2013), *Remembering the South African War: Britain and the Memory of the Anglo-Boer War from 1899 to the Present*, Liverpool: Liverpool University Press, p. 3.

3 Catherine Morris (2012), *Alice Milligan and the Irish Cultural Revival*, Dublin: Four Courts Press, pp. 86–8.

4 Ibid., p. 399.

5 Brian Arkins (2010), *The Thought of W.B. Yeats*, Oxford: Peter Lang, p. 72.

6 Peter Clark (1996), *Hope and Glory: Britain, 1900–1990*, London: Allen Lane, p. 16.

7 Gail Braybon and Penny Summerfield (1987), *Out of the Cage: Women's Experiences in Two World Wars*, London and New York: Pandora, p. 12.

8 Clarke, *Hope and Glory*, p. 7.

9 Davies, *A History of Wales*, p. 472.

10 Barry Supple (1989), 'The British Coal Mining Industry between the Wars', *Refresh*, 9, 1.

11 John Stevenson (1984), *British Society 1914–45*, Harmondsworth: Penguin, p. 25.

12 Vera Brittain (1933), *Testament of Youth: An Autobiographical Study of the Years 1900–1925*, New York: Macmillan, p. 50.

13 Miranda Carter (2011), *George, Nicholas and Wilhelm: Three Royal Cousins and the Road to World War I*, New York: Vintage Books, p. 164.

14 Samuel R. Williamson, Jr. and Russel Van Wyck (2003), *July 1914: Soldiers, Statesmen, and the Coming of the Great War: A Brief Documentary History*, Boston: Bedford/ St. Martin's, p. 77.

15 Richard Scully (2012), *British Images of Germany: Admiration, Antagonism and Ambivalence, 1860–1914*, New York: Palgrave Macmillan.

16 Keir Waddington (2013), '"We Don't Want Any German Sausages Here!" Food, Fear, and the German Nation in Victorian and Edwardian Britain', *Journal of British Studies*, 52, 4, 1017–42.

17 Quoted in Martin Gilbert (1991), *Churchill: A Life*, New York: Henry Holt and Company, p. 264.

18 H. H. Asquith (1985), *Letters to Venetia Stanley*, selected and edited by Michael and Eleanor Brock, Oxford: Oxford University Press, p. 125.

19 Annika Mombauer, ed. and trans. (2013), *The Origins of the First World War: Diplomatic and Military Documents*, Manchester and New York: Manchester University Press, pp. 45–6.

20 Vera Brittain (1982), *Chronicle of Youth: The War Diary 1913–1917*, edited by Alan Bishop with Terry Smart, New York: William Morrow and Company, pp. 87–8.

21 Alan Bishop and Mark Bostridge, eds (1998), *Letters from a Lost Generation: The First World War Letters of Vera Brittain and Four Friends: Roland Leighton, Edward Brittain, Victor Richardson, Geoffrey Thurlow*, Boston: Northeastern University Press, p. 29.

22 Quoted in Susan Bell and Karen M. Offen, eds (1983), *Women, the Family, and Freedom: The Debate in Documents: Volume II, 1880–1950*, Stanford: Stanford University Press, p. 260.

23 Michael Lynch (1992), *Scotland: A New History*, London: Pimlico, p. 422.

24 Additional statistics can be found at http://www.1914-1918.net/faq.htm.

25 Brittain, *Testament of Youth*, p. 17.

26 Christopher M. Kennedy (2010), *Genesis of the Rising, 1912–1916: A Transformation of Nationalist Opinion*, New York: Peter Lang, pp. 179–80.

27 Quoted in Jane O'Hea O'Keefe (2005), *Recollections of 1916 and Its Aftermath*, Trailee, Co. Kerry: Maurice O'Keefe and Jane O'Hea O'Keefe, p. 22.

28 Siegfried Sassoon (1983), *Siegfried Sassoon Diaries, 1915–1918*, edited by Rupert Hart-Davis, London: Faber and Faber, p. 36.

29 Robert Graves (1929; 1957), *Good-bye to All That*, Garden City, NY: Doubleday, p. 114.

30 R. C. Sheriff (1929; 2000), *Journey's End*, London: Penguin, p. 58.

31 Sassoon, *The War Poems of Siegfried Sassoon*, p. 19.

32 Michael Snape (2005), *God and the British Soldier: Religion and the British Army in the First and Second World Wars*, London and New York: Routledge.

33 Pat Barker (1996), *Ghost Road*, New York: Penguin, pp. 143–4.

34 Quoted in Niall Ferguson (1999), *The Pity of War*, New York: Basic Books, p. 362.

Chapter 15

1 Stephen Spender (1951), *World within World*, New York: Harcourt, Brace and Company, p. 72.

2   Quoted in Patrick Joyce (2013), *The State of Freedom: A Social History of the British State since 1800*, Cambridge: Cambridge University Press, p. 226.

3   Noel Annan (1990), *Our Age: Portrait of a Generation*, London: Weidenfeld and Nicolson, p. 12.

4   H. G. Wells (1945), *The Shape of Things to Come: The Ultimate Revolution*, New York: Macmillan, https://ebooks.adelaide.edu.au/w/wells/hg/w45th/chapter12.html.

5   Jonathan Rose (2014), *The Literary Churchill: Author, Reader, Actor*, New Haven and London: Yale University Press, p. 190.

6   David Marquand (2008), *Britain Since 1918: The Strange Career of British Democracy*, London: Weidenfeld & Nicolson, p. 84.

7   Virginia Woolf (1982), *The Diary of Virginia Woolf: Volume IV: 1931–1935*, edited by Anne Olivier Bell, London: The Hogarth Press, pp. 215–16.

8   Peter Scott (2013), *The Making of the Modern British Home: The Suburban Semi and Family Life between the Wars*, Oxford: Oxford University Press, p. 86.

9   Angela McCarthy (2004), 'Personal Accounts of Leaving Scotland, 1921–1954', *Scottish Historical Review*, 83, 196.

10 Charles Loch Mowat (1955), *Britain between the Wars, 1918–1940*, Cambridge: Methuen & Co. Ltd, p. 469.

11 Michael Lynch (1992), *Scotland: A New History*, London: Pimlico, pp. 428–9.

12 Kenneth Baxter (2013), 'The Advent of a Woman Candidate was seen ... as Outrageous': Women, Party Politics and Elections in Interwar Scotland and England', *Journal of Scottish Historical Studies*, 33, 264.

13 John Davies (1993), *A History of Wales*, London: Allen Lane, p. 561.

14 Stephen M. Cullen (2008), 'The Fasces and the Saltire: The Failure of the British Union of Fascists in Scotland, 1932–1940', *Scottish Historical Review*, 87, 313.

15 *The New York Times*, 27 December 1928.

16 David Edgerton (1991), *England and the Aeroplane*, Houndmills, Basingstoke and Hampshire: Macmillan, p. xv.

17 Quoted in Constance Babington Smith (1967; 2004), *Amy Johnson*, Phoenix Mill, Stroud, Gloucestershire: Sutton Publishing, p. 123.

18 Nicola Verdon (2012), 'Business and Pleasure: Middle-Class Women's Work and the Professionalization of Farming, 1890–1939', *Journal of British Studies*, 51, 409.

19 Virginia Woolf (1927), *To the Lighthouse*, New York: Harcourt, Brace & World, Inc., p. 51.

20 F. M. L. Thompson (1963), *English Landed Society in the Nineteenth Century*, London: Routledge and Kegan Paul, p. 332 .

21 Spender, *World within World*, p. 2.

22 Christopher Hilliard (2006), *To Exercise Our Talents: The Democratization of Writing in Britain*, Cambridge, MA: Harvard University Press, p. 8.

23 Jonathan Rose (2001), *The Intellectual Life of the British Working Classes*, New Haven and London: Yale University Press, p. 255.

24 Woolf, *To the Lighthouse*, p. 17.

25 Ibid., p. 50.

26 For a more detailed discussion of the relationship and works of these two authors, see Norman Cantor (1999), *Inventing the Middle Ages: The Lives, Works, and Ideas*

of the Great Medievalists of the Twentieth Century, New York: Harper Perennial, pp. 205–33.

27 Nicola Bishop (2015), 'Ruralism, Masculinity, and National Identity: The Rambling Clerk in Fiction, 1900–1940', *Journal of British Studies*, 54, 654–78.

28 Christine Grandy (2011), '"Avarice" and "Evil Doers": Profiteers, Politicians, and Popular Fiction in the 1920s', *Journal of British Studies*, 50, 669, 673.

29 John Maynard Keynes (1963), *Essays in Persuasion*, New York: W. W. Norton & Company, p. 312.

30 Ibid., p. 316. He was referring to the utilitarian ideas of Jeremy Bentham.

31 Lara Feigel (2010), *Literature, Cinema, and Politics 1930–1945: Reading between the Frames*, Edinburgh: Edinburgh University Press, pp. 36–7.

32 Quoted in Michael Deacon (2011), 'The British Documentary Movement: The Pioneering Documentary Film-makers who Fuelled Britain's Class War', *The Telegraph*, 26 July.

33 George Orwell (1939; 1950), *Coming Up For Air*, New York: Harcourt, Brace, p. 4.

34 Aldous Huxley (1932), *Brave New World: A Novel*, Garden City, NY: Doubleday, p. 30.

35 Ibid., pp. 36–7.

36 Orwell, *Coming Up For Air*, pp. 84–5.

37 Winston Churchill (1948), *The Second World War: Volume I: The Gathering Storm*, Boston: Houghton Mifflin Company, p. 292.

38 Francis Williams (1965), *A Pattern of Rulers*, London: Longmans, p. 182.

39 Wells, *The Shape of Things to Come*, https://ebooks.adelaide.edu.au/w/wells/hg/w45th/chapter11.html.

40 See Erik Larson (2011), *In the Garden of Beasts: Love, Terror, and an American Family in Hitler's Berlin*, New York: Crown.

Chapter 16

1 Quoted in William Manchester and Paul Reid (2012), *The Last Lion: Winston Spencer Churchill, Defender of the Realm, 1940–1965*, New York: Little, Brown and Company, p. 41.

2 Duncan Redford (2014), *A History of the Royal Navy: World War II*, London: I. B. Tauris, p. 7.

3 Jonathan Rose says that he had worked on the phrase, which he had largely appropriated from the nineteenth-century Italian revolutionary, Giuseppe Garibaldi, for forty years. Jonathan Rose (2014), *The Literary Churchill: Author, Reader, Actor*, New Haven and London: Yale University Press, p. 291.

4 An excellent book on this subject is John Lukacs (1990), *The Duel 10 May–31 July 1940: The Eighty Day Struggle between Churchill and Hitler*, New York: Ticknor and Fields.

5 Jeremy A. Crang (2013), 'The Second World War', in E. M. Spiers, J. A. Craig, and M. J. Strickland (eds), *A Military History of Scotland*, Edinburgh: Edinburgh Press, p. 562.

6 Winston Churchill (1953), *The Second World War: Volume V: Closing the Ring*, Boston: Houghton Mifflin Company, p. 228.

7 Timothy H. Parsons (2014), *The Second British Empire: In the Crucible of the Twentieth Century*, Lanham, MD: Rowman and Littlefield, pp. 110–11.

8 Christopher Bayly and Tim Harper (2004), *Forgotten Armies: The Fall of British Asia, 1941–1945*, London: Allen Lane, p. 154.

9 Ibid., p. 167.

10 Jerry White (2001), *London in the Twentieth Century: A City and Its People*, London: Vintage Books, p. 38.

11 Ibid., p. 158.

12 Diarmaid Ferriter (2004), *The Transformation of Ireland*, Woodstock and New York: The Overlook Press, 445.

13 Jo Fox (2012), 'Careless Talk: Tensions within British Domestic Propaganda during the Second World War', *Journal of British Studies*, 51, 936.

14 Wendy Webster (2009), '"Europe against the Germans": British Resistance Narrative, 1940–1950', *Journal of British Studies*, 48, 961, 965.

15 See, for example, John Lukacs (2001), *Five Days in London: May 1940*, New Haven: Yale University Press, pp. 162–3.

16 Amy Bell (2009), 'Landscapes of Fear: Wartime London, 1939–1945', *Journal of British Studies*, 48, 154.

17 Simon J. Potter (2012), *Broadcasting Empire: The BBC and the British World, 1922–1970*, Oxford: Oxford University Press, pp. 113–14.

18 Paul Addison (2005), 'The Impact of the Second World War', in Paul Addison and Harriet Jones (eds), *A Companion to Contemporary Britain, 1939–2000*, Malden, MA: Blackwell, p. 4.

19 Gail Braybon and Penny Summerfield (1987), *Out of the Cage: Women's Experiences in Two World Wars*, London and New York: Pandora, pp. 155–7.

20 Addison, 'The Impact of the Second World War', pp. 9–10.

21 Paul Addison (1975), *The Road to 1945: British Politics and the Second World War*, London: Jonathan Cape, p. 130.

22 Harold Perkin (1989), *The Rise of Professional Society: England since 1880*, London: Routledge, p. 408.

Chapter 17

1 Clement Attlee, 'Leader's speech, Bournemouth 1946', http://www.britishpoliticalspeech.org/speech-archive.htm?speech=156.

2 David Kynaston (2008), *Austerity Britain, 1945–51*, New York: Walker & Company, p. 99.

3 Dolly Smith Watson (2005), 'Gender, Change and Continuity', in Paul Addison and Harriet Jones (eds), *A Companion to Contemporary Britain, 1939–2000*, Malden, MA: Blackwell, p. 248.

4 John Le Carré (1963; 2013), *The Spy Who Came in from the Cold*, New York: Penguin, pp. 15–16.

5 Donald Barrington (1957; 2012), 'Uniting Ireland', in Bryan Fanning (ed.), *An Irish Century: Studies 1912–2012*, Dublin: University College Dublin Press, p. 164.

6 Rosemary Goring (2007), *Scotland: The Autobiography: 2,000 Years of Scottish History by Those Who Saw It Happen*, Woodstock, NY: The Overlook Press, p. 330.

7 Lawrence James (2014), *Churchill and Empire: A Portrait of an Imperialist*, New York: Pegasus Books, p. 344.

8 Jordanna Bailken (2015), 'Where Did the Empire Go? Archives and Decolonization in Britain', *American Historical Review*, 120, 889–90.

9 Jordanna Bailken (2012), *The Afterlife of Empire*, Berkeley: University of California Press, p. 98.

10 Richard Holt (2005), 'Sport and Recreation', in Paul Addison and Harriet Jones (eds), *A Companion to Contemporary Britain, 1939–2000*, Malden, MA: Blackwell, p. 112.

11 David Wilson (2014), *Pain and Retribution: A Short History of British Prisons, 1066 to the Present*, London: Reaktion Books, p. 126.

12 Edmund Dell (2000), *A Strange and Eventful History: Democratic Socialism in Britain*, London: HarperCollins, p. 322.

Chapter 18

1 Edward Heath (1998), *The Course of My Life: My Autobiography*, London: Hodder & Stoughton, p. 394.

2 Heath, *The Course of My Life*, p. 395.

3 Chris Cook and John Stevenson (2014), *A History of British Elections since 1689*, London: Routledge, p. 383.

4 Margaret Thatcher (1993), *The Downing Street Years*, New York: HarperCollins, pp. 536–7.

5 Quoted in Hugo Young (1998), *The Blessed Plot: Britain and Europe from Churchill to Blair*, Woodstock: The Overlook Press, p. 289.

6 Peter Leese (2006), *Britain since 1945: Aspects of Identity*, Houndmills, Basingstoke and Hampshire: Palgrave Macmillan, p. 127.

7 Mark Clapson (2005), 'Cities, Suburbs, Countryside', in Paul Addison and Harriet Jones (eds), *A Companion to Contemporary Britain, 1939–2000*, Malden, MA: Blackwell, p. 69.

8 Jerry White (2001), *London in the Twentieth Century: A City and Its People*, London: Vintage Books, p. 205–7.

9 David Marquand (2008), *Britain Since 1918: The Strange Career of British Democracy*, London: Weidenfeld & Nicolson, p. 257.

10 Ben Curtis (2013), *The South Wales Miners 1964–1985*, Cardiff: University of Wales Press, pp. 125–9.

11 Bill Buford (1991), *Among the Thugs*, New York: Vintage Books, p. 164.

12 Greil Marcus (1989), *Lipstick Traces: A Secret History of the Twentieth Century*, Cambridge, MA: Harvard University Press, p. 12.

13 I am thankful to Roger McCormick for pointing out this particular insight into the punk movement.

14 Brett Bebber (2012), '"The Misuse of Leisure": Football Violence, Politics and Family Values in 1970s Britain', in Brett Bebber (ed.), *Leisure and Cultural Conflict in Twentieth-Century Britain*, Manchester: Manchester University Press, p. 131.

15 Anthony Sampson (1982), *The Changing Anatomy of Britain*, New York: Random House, p. 3.

16 Margaret Drabble (1977), *The Ice Age*, New York: Alfred A. Knopf, pp. 183–4.

17 Arthur McIvor (2013), *Working Lives: Work in Britain since 1945*, Houndmills, Basingstoke and Hampshire: Palgrave Macmillan, p. 217.

18 Seán Sorohan (2012), *Irish London during the Troubles*, Dublin: Irish Academic Press, pp. 57–63.

19 Tony Blair (2010), *A Journey: My Political Life*, New York: Alfred A. Knopf, p. 199.

20 Nigel Lawson (1993), *The View from No. 11: Britain's Longest-Serving Cabinet Member Recalls the Triumphs and Disappointments of the Thatcher Era*, New York: Doubleday, p. 127.

21 Charles Moore (2013), *Margaret Thatcher: The Authorized Biography: From Grantham to the Falklands*, New York: Alfred A. Knopf, p. 597.

22 Philip Murphy (2013), *Monarchy and the End of Empire: The House of Windsor, the British Government, and the Post-War Commonwealth*, Oxford: Oxford University Press, p. 160.

23 Jonathan Aitkin (2013), *Margaret Thatcher: Power and Personality*, London: Bloomsbury, p. 376.

24 Noel Annan (1999), *The Dons: Mentors, Eccentrics and Geniuses*, Chicago: University of Chicago Press, pp. 291–2.

25 Richard Aldous (2012), *Reagan and Thatcher: The Difficult Relationship*, New York: W. W. Norton & Company, p. 95.

26 Archie Brown (2008), 'The Change to Engagement in Britain's Cold War Policy: The Origins of the Thatcher-Gorbachev Relationship', *Journal of Cold War Studies*, 10, 4.

27 Paul Johnson (1989), 'A Conversation with the Prime Minister', *New York Times*, 19 April.

28 Richard Leiby (2002), 'The Thatcher Era, 1979–1990', in Frank W. Thackeray and John E. Finding (eds), *Events That Changed Great Britain Since 1689*, Westport, CT: Greenwood Press, p. 188.

29 Mary Elise Sarotte (2009), *1989: The Struggle to Create Post-Cold War Europe*, Princeton: Princeton University Press, p. 27.

30 David Wilson (2014), *Pain and Retribution: A Short History of British Prisons, 1066 to the Present*, London: Reaktion Books, p. 158.

31 See http://www.ukpolitical.info/FemaleMPs.htm.

32 Sarah Lyall (1999), 'Black Rod and the Day Boys? No It's Not a Rock Group', *New York Times*, 14 November.

33 Jane M. Sharp (2003), 'Tony Blair, Iraq and the Special Relationship: Poodle or Partner?', *International Journal*, 59, 60.

34 Leese, *Britain since 1945*, p. 76.

35 Steve Bruce (2014), *Scottish Gods: Religion in Modern Scotland, 1900–2012*, Edinburgh: Edinburgh University Press, p. 63.

36 Erika Hanna (2013), *Modern Dublin: Urban Change and the Irish Past, 1957–1973*, Oxford: Oxford University Press, p. 13.

37 John Sweeney (1983; 2012), 'Upstairs, Downstairs: The Challenge of Social Inequality', in Bryan Fanning (ed.), *An Irish Century: Studies 1912–2012*, Dublin: University College Dublin Press, p. 227.

38 Richard Breen, Damian F. Hanna, David B. Rottman, and Christopher T. Whelan
    (1990), *Understanding Contemporary Ireland: State, Class, and Development in the
    Republic of Ireland*, New York: St. Martin's Press, p. 59.

39 Sean Dorgan (2006), 'How Ireland Became the Celtic Tiger', http://www.heritage.org/
    research/reports/2006/06/how-ireland-became-the-celtic-tiger.

40 Johanne Devlin Trew (2013), *Leaving the North: Migration and Memory, Northern
    Ireland 1921–2011*, Liverpool: Liverpool University Press, p. 52.

41 Eoin O'Sullivan (20014), 'Welfare Regimes, Housing and Homelessness in the Republic
    of Ireland', *European Journal of Housing Policy*, 3, 324.

42 Patrick Fitzgerald and Brian Lambkin (2008), *Migration in Irish History, 1607–2007*,
    Houndmills, Basingstoke and Hampshire: Palgrave Macmillan, p. 228.

43 Joshua Clover (1989), *1989: Bob Dylan Didn't Have This to Sing About*, Berkeley:
    University of California Press.

44 John Le Carré (1991), *The Secret Pilgrim*, New York: Alfred A. Knopf, p. 9.

45 Ibid., p. 12.

46 See Barbara O'Connor (2013), *The Irish Dancing: Cultural Politics and Identities
    1900–2000*, Cork: Cork University Press, especially pp. 124–31.

47 John Le Carré (2001), *The Constant Gardener*, New York: Scribner, pp. 135–7.

Chapter 19

1   Ross Wilson (2013), *Cultural Heritage of the Great War in Britain*, Farnham, England:
    Ashgate, p. 33.

2   Daisy Hernandez (2007), 'Racism in a time of War', *Color Lines Magazine*.

3   Arthur McIvor (2013), *Working Lives: Work in Britain since 1945*, Houndmills,
    Basingstoke and Hampshire: Palgrave Macmillan, p. 70.

4   Ibid., p. 74.

5   See http://www.army.mod.uk/join/Women-in-the-Army.aspx.

6   See https://www.gov.uk/government/uploads/system/uploads/attachment_data/
    file/312539/uk_af_annual_personnel_report_2014.pdf.

7   See http://researchbriefings.files.parliament.uk/documents/SN02183/SN02183.pdf.

8   See Peter Mandler (2015), 'The Humanities in British Universities since 1945', *American
    Historical Review*, 120, 1299–1310.

9   James H. Mills (2013), *Cannabis Nation: Control and Consumption in Britain, 1928–
    2008*, Oxford: Oxford University Press, p. 213.

10 Nicole Ellison (2013), 'Future Identities: Changing identities in the UK – the next 10
    years', https://www.gov.uk/government/uploads/system/uploads/attachment_data/
    file/275752/13-505-social-media-and-identity.pdf.

11 'Belonging', Social Issues Research Centre, http://www.sirc.org/publik/belonging.shtml
    (Accessed 1 December 2015).

12 Kimiko de Freytas-Tamura (2014), 'Britain's New Immigrants, From Romania and
    Bulgaria, Face Hostilities', *New York Times*, 31 May.

13 'Romanian and Bulgarian migration: Rise in workers in UK' (2015), BBC News,
    18 February, http://www.bbc.com/news/uk-31519319.

14 Sarah Lyall (2008), *The Anglo-Files: A Field Guide to the British*, New York: W. W. Norton & Company, p. 169.

15 Douglas Dalby (2013), 'A Prison Site's Future Stirs Up the Ghosts of Its Notorious Past', *New York Times*, 21 May.

16 Fergus O'Donoghue, S.J. (2008–9; 2012), 'The Doghouse No Longer Feels Lonely', in Bryan Fanning (ed.), *An Irish Century: Studies 1912–2012*, Dublin: University College Dublin Press, p. 303.

17 Ryan Thornton (2004), 'Caging the Tiger: Ireland's Economy Roars On', *Harvard International Review*, 26, 10–11.

18 Fintan O'Toole (2014), 'Ireland's Rebound is European Blarney', *New York Times*, 20 January.

19 Sean O Riain (2014), 'How to Avoid the Mistakes of the Celtic Tiger', *The Irish Times*, 29 May.

20 Neal Ascherson (2002), *Stone Voices: The Search for Scotland*, New York: Hill and Wang, p. 305.

21 Christopher Whatley (2014), *The Scots and the Union: Then and Now*, Edinburgh: Edinburgh University Press, p. 427.

22 Steve Bruce (2014), *Scottish Gods: Religion in Modern Scotland, 1900–2012*, Edinburgh: Edinburgh University Press, p. 201.

23 'Scotland is Another Country', *The Economist*, 2 May 2015.

24 Matthew McGuire (2007), 'Cultural Devolutions: Scotland, Northern Ireland and the Return of the Postmodern', in Berthold Schoene (ed.), *The Edinburgh Companion to Contemporary Scottish Literature*, Edinburgh: Edinburgh University Press, p. 315.

25 Ian Bradley (2007), *Believing in Britain: The Spiritual Identity of 'Britishness'*, London: I. B. Tauris, p. 73.

26 Jonathan Foreman (2014), 'Britain's Heart of Darkness: The Rot from Rotherham', *Commentary*, 138, 34–5.

27 Lisa O'Carroll (2015), 'Rotherham Grooming Victim was Abused Daily and used to Settle Debts, Jury Told', *The Guardian*, 20 December, http://www.theguardian.com/uk-news/2015/dec/10/rotherham-grooming-ring-targeted-teenagers-over-three-decades-court-told (Accessed 16 February 2016).

28 Tony Gosling (2014), 'Child Abuse Scandal Raises Disturbing Questions about UK Establishment', https://www.rt.com/op-edge/180616-british-home-secretary-child-abuse/ (Accessed 2 December 2015).

29 Tony Blair (2010), *A Journey: My Political Life*, New York: Alfred A. Knopf, p. 529.

30 Daniel Hannan (2009), 'Repatriating the Revolution: Democracy and Practice in the European Union', *Harvard International Review*, 31, 20.

31 'What if …? The Consequences, Challenges and Opportunities Facing Britain Outside the EU' (2015), Open Europe, http://openeurope.org.uk/intelligence/britain-and-the-eu/what-if-there-were-a-brexit/ (Accessed 2 December 2015).

32 Roger Liddle (2015), *The Risk of Brexit: Britain and Europe in 2015*, London: Rowman and Littlefield, p. 31.

33 Anan Menand (2015), 'Littler England: The United Kingdom's Retreat from Global Leadership', *Foreign Affairs*, 94, 97.

34 Denis MacShane (2015), *Brexit: How Britain Will Leave Europe*, London: I. B. Tauris, p. 6.

35 Blair, *A Journey*, p. 529.

36 John Peet (2015), 'Brexit or Bremain?', *The Economist*, December, 25.

37 John Le Carré (2013), *A Delicate Truth*, New York: Viking, p. 28.

38 John Lanchester (2012), *Capital*, New York: W. W. Norton & Company, p. 13.

39 Quoted in Claire Chambers (2011), *British Muslim Fictions: Interviews with Contemporary Writers*, London: Palgrave Macmillan, p. 234.

40 Ibid., p. 43.

41 Martin Amis (2013), *Lionel Asbo: State of England*, New York: Vintage International, p. 51.

42 Ibid., pp. 124–5.

43 Lanchester, *Capital*, p. 123.

44 Kathleen Costello-Sullivan (2012), *Mother/Country: Politics of the Personal in the Fiction of Colm Tóibín*, Oxford: Peter Lang, p. 14.

45 Colm Tóibín (1999), *The Blackwater Lightship*, New York: Scribner, p. 119.

46 John Corbett (2007), 'A Double Realm: Scottish Literary Translation in the Twenty-first Century', in Berthold Schoene (ed.), *The Edinburgh Companion to Contemporary Scottish Literature*, Edinburgh: Edinburgh University Press, p. 336.

INDEX